Car Camping with Zippy

A Guide to Public Campgrounds In Washington State

Black & White Version

Richard Goodhart
and
Alayne Goodhart

Legal Disclaimer

This book is designed to provide campers with adequate information to visit public campgrounds in Washington State. While we have made efforts, within limited resources, to make this book complete and accurate there may be mistakes; typographical, in mapping, and in content. Therefore the book should be used as a general guide, not the ultimate source of information.

The authors, publisher, local and governmental authorities, make no warranties and assume no liability for errors or omissions, or for any loss or damage of any kind incurred from using this information.

When following the suggested driving directions – if something does not seem right or if it seems you are driving too far into the *unknown*, turn around, retrace your steps to civilization, and get clarification. The included hand drawn maps are for reference purposes as only limited information is shown on each.

Regarding the recipes in this book and the safe temperatures of food – we want you to be safe and healthy. It is your responsibility to ensure foods are kept cool enough, when refrigerated, and heated enough, when cooked. The USDA is a possible source of information when determining acceptable temperatures.

TABLE OF CONTENTS

Acknowledgements

There were many folks who answered our questions: US Army Corps of Engineers – the kind folks at the Lower Granite Natural Resources Management Section, US Bureau of Land Management – Steve Smith, US Forest Service – Jasmine Lea Budrow, Pete Erbin, Molly Erickson, Ruth Forshere, SusanGraham, Anita Hall, Nancy Jones, Craig Newman, Pam Pnovitsky, Washington State Parks – Stacy Czebotar, Michael Thomas, Robert Wiggins, and Virginia Painter, and the myriad others who took time to share their insight. These are all people who do their job because they love it – and it shows.

A special thank you for the keen proofing eyes of Mike Phillips and his assistant Jean. Also, Peggy and Kurt, John and Roxie, Brian and Meaghan, and Mary for letting us write this book in their homes and especially their animals – Ricky, Shiloh, Charlie Banjo, Katie, Brody, Lexie, Annie Kitty, Gray–Boy, Jello, Jake, and Elwood – who got us away from our desks.

Sources

All information in this book was obtained by personal observation or through official government publications or through conversations with government entity representatives. Therefore, all source information (other than that personally observed by the authors) is available in the *Public Domain* or is data protected by *Fair Use*.

All photographs, including the cover design, are by Richard or Alayne Goodhart except as noted in a photograph's caption.

Introduction

It started with driving to a niece's June wedding and evolved into a 26,000 mile car–camping road trip in our 1999 mini–van, named *Zippy*. Circling the United States, we discovered a love for campgrounds on public lands – the relative remoteness, the wide variety of camping methods, seeing people of all ages, and being near streams, lakes, trails, and lots of trees.

Camping without a set itinerary appeals to us but this presented a problem. There are books about private campgrounds and back–packing trail guides, but we could not find a book that had good information about public campgrounds. Each government agency only has information about their own facilities. This means searching several federal, state, and local websites – an expensive and time consuming chore while traveling and looking for coffee shops offering Wi-Fi.

This is the reason for *Car Camping with Zippy - A Guide to Public Campgrounds in Washington State*. It is a book that combines information from four National Parks, six National Forests, the Bureau of Land Management, the Corps of Engineers, Washington State Parks, the Department of Natural Resources, Washington Fish and Wildlife, Public Power Utility Districts, cities, counties, and Port Authorities.

It was astonishing to find 580 public campgrounds that can be driven to in Washington State – a number requiring a book so big there would not be any room left in the car for camping supplies. So, we included only those campgrounds that had more than five sites, a toilet facility, a picnic table, and a fire ring. These criteria gave us a more manageable number. Unfortunately this eliminated all the Department of Fish and Wildlife campgrounds. (They provide many wonderful

locations but miss at least one of the above requirements.) As you will see, there are still many fishing holes at places administered by other agencies. It is also important to understand that we concentrated on campgrounds and their related activities. Many other parks offer day–use activities that are not necessarily covered.

There are several ways to use this guide. For the *Quick Starting* reader, we divided the state into five regions (Chapters 2 through 6). The first page of each regional chapter has a map showing campground locations with an associated number. This number represents the order each campground is listed in the book. (Campground 7 is found just after campground 6 but before campground 8.) As you thumb through the chapters, this number is shown next to the campground name and is followed by campground specifics – driving directions, facilities, activities, and other pertinent information.

For those who like to read a book from front to back or peruse randomly, Chapter 1 includes general information about car camping and the protocol for getting along with neighbors – both human and animal – as well as being good stewards of the campground. After all, you are part owner of the land you're camping on. In addition to specific campground information, Chapters 2 through 6 provide a smattering of historical background and some camping recipes – communing with nature doesn't mean you're only allowed to eat hot dogs and s'mores.

After the final regional chapter, the Appendices have general information about each controlling agency, camping regulations, procedures for reservations, and fee discounts. The Appendices are followed by an Index.

While we were diligent in our research, things may have been unintentionally omitted or recently changed. The final responsibility to verify information rests with the reader. You will find it helpful to obtain a Washington State driving map.

Zippy had a wonderful time visiting these locations and hopes your camping experiences create long–remembered fond family memories.

Let's go camping!

Sunset at Grayland State Park

Washington State with Overview of Campground Locations

Chapter 1   General Information

Shouldering a pack and walking into the wild for a week is an exhilarating experience. Driving a motorhome across the country, parking each night in the lot of a large box–store, is an economical way to travel. Both of these are done each year by very lovely people who are just doing their own thing. For millions of equally nice people, car camping in public campgrounds combines the closeness of nature with the convenience of driving to a campsite and is the answer for an economical vacation or weekend away.

Citizens and visitors to Washington State are fortunate. With so many publicly owned campgrounds available, we are never far from a spot to pitch a tent, park an RV, or unroll a sleeping bag. Amenities vary from paved pull–through motorhome sites with water, electricity, sewer, cable TV, and Wi–Fi to turnouts perched along a stream with a picnic table, fire ring, and just enough level ground to pitch a small tent. They also vary in price from over $50 a night to free. There is not one right–way or just one right–place to do it – just choices to be made.

Do you want to camp near an alpine meadow with snow–capped mountains as a backdrop? It is here. In Washington, you can choose ocean beaches, sunny lakes, rushing rivers, or camp next to a mighty river. There are campgrounds with trees so big your family's arms can barely enfold them, pine forests that stretch for hundreds of miles, and rolling grasslands that reach for the horizon.

Lake Creek Campsite

This rich diversity is partly caused by the Cascade Mountains. Running from Canada to Oregon, they divide the state into the sunny east and the wetter west. They wring moisture from Pacific winter storms causing perfect conditions for moss–hanging, fern–growing rain forests and let drier air flow east into Washington's central basin. The mountains are responsible for keeping western summer temperatures in the 70s while allowing the east to warm into the dry 90s – a choice for everyone.

Hoh River Valley Spruce Tree

Zippy

Zippy, a 1999 mini–van is our choice. Purchased for a cross–country road trip to a wedding, she evolved into our home for a 26,000 mile car–camping odyssey – an equivalent distance to a circumnavigation of the earth. As we traveled, minor changes helped us find our right way.

- Replaced *Zippy's* standard battery with a larger one so we wouldn't be worried about starting the car in the morning after watching a DVD the prior evening
- Made screens that attached to strips of magnetic rubber which clung to the outside of the van to keep out mosquitoes
- Kept the middle bench seat upright to use as a sofa until bedtime when we folded it forward to be part of the sleeping surface
- Built platforms to support our feet when sleeping and still allow storage below
- Made curtains that installed easily each evening

Two of our better discoveries were baby–wipes and make–up removing towelettes to use when there were no shower facilities or when water supplies were limited, and a long–handled fish grilling basket for cooking over a wood fire or charcoal – everything stayed easily contained on the clean grill.

Options

That is how we did it. Others prefer motorhomes, trailers, or campers. Still others pull tents out of car trunks while some just build shelters from plain blue plastic tarps. There are campers

Bumping Lake Campfire

who have every camping accessory available while others don't even bring a lawn chair. The one thing everyone does bring is excitement. Whether it's manifested through trail hikes, lake swimming, watching long sunsets, or pushing red campfire coals around with a stick, campers bring a sense of awe at being close to nature – and sometimes the makings for s'mores too.

As you go through the planning process, there are myriad places to look for the equipment that's right for you. A computer search on the web or looking through the phone directory at subjects like camping, camping supplies, tents, RV's, motorhomes, trailers, or truck campers will keep you busy for hours. If you want to try a motorhome before buying, think about renting. For potentially cheaper supply alternatives, look at newspaper or web ads for used equipment. Be sure to check thrift stores and pawn shops. If you want something still cheaper, look in your parent's or friend's basements. They may let you borrow everything you need. The point is – there is a way to be outfitted that fits almost every budget.

One special option for you to consider involves camp stove fuels. We enjoy cooking over a wood or charcoal fire but excessively dry conditions often makes this forbidden. Many people have a camp stove that uses 1 pound steel propane/butane bottles. Campers try to do the sensible thing and put the empty cylinders into a recycle bin but since they can't be processed with potentially explosive gas remaining, they are eventually tossed into the landfill. A possible replacement can be researched on the internet by searching "refillable 1 pound propane bottles."

Recipes

As children, our camping diets consisted mainly of hot dogs skewered by a stick and burned black over a campfire. These were served with baked–beans, heated in the can they came in. Dessert consisted of incinerated marshmallows that had been stabbed by the hot dog stick, set aflame by holding them too close to the fire, used as a torch for one running–pass through the campsite, blown out, and squeezed between two graham crackers with a piece of chocolate bar. That was dietary bliss then and still is now – just maybe not all the time.

Recipes are spread throughout this book – some of them even provide a nutritional counter–balance to traditional camp food. There is no reason why satisfying fresh foods can't accompany a camping trip. That is one of the benefits of car camping – you don't have to carry it in a backpack. With a little kitchen prep–time before departing home, almost any meal is possible. Often times, local fresh items can be purchased enroute – fruits, vegetables, or fish. While camping in Maine, *Zippy* bought live lobsters from a fisherman and had them ready to eat at the campsite in a couple of hours. That lobster was much more desirable than a can of beans, although a marshmallow torch is still a lot of fun.

Lobster Recipe

In case your local Washington seafood store has a live, Maine lobster swimming around in its tank, here is the simple recipe. The main precaution (no pun intended) is to be sure to have a cooking pot large enough. First, fill that deep container with enough salted water to cover the lobster – ½ cup of coarse salt per gallon of water. Bring the water to a boil. Insert the lobster head first. This kills it instantly and, more importantly, it can't stare at you. For a ¾ pound lobster, boil 12 minutes (a 1 pounder – 13 minutes, a 1 ½ pounder – 15 minutes, or a 2 pounder – 18 minutes). Do not overcook (the meat gets tough) but do not start timing until the water begins to re–boil. After cooking, break the claws and tail from the body, throw the body away, remove the shell from the rest, and eat the meat after dunking it into melted butter. Be careful not to burn yourself when retrieving the lobster from the pot and when removing the meat. You can crack the shell with a crab–cracker, a hammer, a pair of pliers, a pair of scissors, or in a pinch, a clean rock. Also, do not show your dinner to neighboring campers with burned hot dogs – they will be jealous.

Boiling Lobster

Etiquette

Speaking about camping neighbors, it is important to only make them jealous of your good cooking smells and not angry with your poor camping etiquette. While most places post required quiet–hours, there should be no need to run a noisy generator all day – no one wants to hear it. If you need a continuous power supply, go to a campground with electrical hook–ups.

Most people make noise when they play – certainly children do and that's expected. However, continuously running and yelling through someone else's campsite or having roaming off–leash pets is not appreciated.

While shinning a flashlight beam into your sister's eyes seems a lot of fun, blinding your neighbor is not much fun for them – don't do it.

You are part owner of these public lands but so is everyone else. Most campers are extremely courteous – continue the tradition. Treat others with respect and expect them to do the same.

Since we are now in a respectful mood toward others, let's continue by being respectful to ourselves. You are out camping to have a good time – it is important to return home in a condition at least as good as when you left.

Sanitation

Human waste contaminates water supplies. Use toilets where provided and do not put garbage into them – the next person wants the toilet to work also. Where no toilets exist, find an area more than 200 feet from water and away from camps. Dig a hole at least 6 inches deep and cover with dirt when done. Bury toilet paper, or better yet, carry it out in a trash bag. Also, dispose of soapy water away from fresh water supplies.

Potable water is available at most campgrounds. However if you are at all unsure, it should be considered unsafe. Drinking water taken from lakes or streams should be boiled for at least 5 minutes, chemically treated or pumped through appropriate filters. You could contract a serious waterborne illness called Giardia if you do not follow these recommendations.

A Very Sanitary Cow

Hypothermia

Your body usually does a good job of regulating its temperature but when it is unable to keep warm, a condition called hypothermia develops and it does not have to be arctic–cold to happen. It happens most frequently when the temperature is between 30°F and 50°F. You can help avoid it.

- Stay dry – wet clothes lose about 90 percent of their insulating quality. Wool and synthetic materials are generally better than cotton.
- Always check the latest weather forecast. Conditions can change quickly and you want to have the appropriate clothing and equipment.
- Put on rain gear before you get wet. Put on warm clothes before you start shivering. A breeze carries heat away from your body.
- Always let someone know your plans and time of return.

Hypothermia has the following symptoms: uncontrollable shivering, slow or slurred speech, memory lapses, fumbling hands, or frequent stumbling. If you notice any of these, get out of any wet clothes and into a sleeping bag or warm, dry clothes.

Fire

Always check the local fire danger level and observe any posted fire restrictions – open fires may be restricted during the fire season. If you spot a wildfire, report it to the nearest authority or dial 911 if a phone is available. Also, follow these guidelines.

- Most campgrounds do not allow gathering wood for fires – buy from a local vendor or bring your own. Do not bring wood from outside the area though. Many tree diseases are spread this way and we want to keep the forests healthy.
- Build fires only in designated areas.
- Consider using a camp stove to cook or boil water.
- Keep a bucket of water and shovel nearby.
- Never leave a fire unattended.
- Do not leave children unattended near a campfire.
- When leaving the area, extinguish the fire by drowning it, stirring it with dirt, then drowning it again. Ashes should be cool to the touch.
- Do not smoke while walking through the forest.

Thank you for your efforts – everyone will be happier if the campground and their car are not burned down.

Columbia Hills Petroglyph

Stewardship

Do not disturb, deface, or collect any plants, animals, rocks, and historic/archaeological objects. As part of our national heritage, these items belong to everyone – not just you. They should be left for all to enjoy. However, that does not mean you can't carry a bag and collect trail trash – bits of paper and discarded candy wrappers. Chances are, if it was brought into the woods and dropped by another hiker during the past few days, it is not an archaeological object and it may be collected.

Wildlife

We have discussed guidelines for keeping ourselves healthy and happy, and looked at ways to live in peace with other campers. Now we'll see how to get along with our wilderness neighbors. Almost everything relates to one major theme – do not feed the wild animals. Do not feed them your garbage, your food, your pets, your friends, your relatives, or yourselves.

Do Not Feed This Bird!
(Photo by Kathy Champoux)

A professional mountain guide friend breaks the animal kingdom into two groups – snaflies, who are small enough that they look cute and beg for food, and snarlies, who are large enough to take your food. It is important to not feed either. Little animals get used to it and forget how to feed themselves or they develop digestive problems – they die. Big animals get used to it and once they associate humans with food become a nuisance. Rangers generally try to relocate these animals but, if they come back to the area, they are killed. In many cases, feeding them is a death sentence.

When leaving the campsite or going to bed, put all food, garbage, beverages, and anything else that smells yummy into an animal resistant container. That container could be your car, RV, or a special box provided at the campground. If none of these is available, it could be a bag suspended from a rope high between two trees.

The one caution about wild–animal interaction not directly related to food usually involves photography. I used to live near Yellowstone National Park. Every year there were stories in the local paper about tourists who wanted a perfect picture of their wife, husband, son, or baby and the nice wooly buffalo or cute little teddy bear – just a little closer dear, oops. Do not let that happen to you. These animals are wild and can hurt or kill you. I saw an angry ground squirrel bite a woman's ankle at Zion National Park – it looked like it hurt a lot. I can't imagine what being bit by a bear would feel like. Do not get too close to wild animals.

Do Not Feed This Bear Either!

GPS

Latitude and Longitude positions listed in this book were obtained from the US Geological Survey website using their online topographical maps and coordinate system readout. We then converted all numbers into the traditional degrees, minutes, and seconds' format. This system uses the NAD 83 datum which may be important to readers who want to use GPS mapping systems when visiting the campgrounds to see how close we came. If you need more information on this, please see your GPS manufacturer's manual and the USGS website, http://store.usgs.gov and then select Map Locator – happy learning.

Maps

The maps used in this book are hand drawn using USGS topographical maps for source material. While they are based on very accurate data, they are no more precise than our hands could make them. The distances are as accurate as our mini-van's odometer. These maps, however, are much better than the ones my boss drew on the back of envelopes when I had a job delivering lumber in 1976 but just like his maps, only pertinent roads are drawn.

The suggested route directions are just one possible way of arriving at the campground. If you are coming from a different direction, you may want to modify your route.

Dispersed Camping

Many National Forests, Bureau of Land Management properties, and Corps of Engineers land allow dispersed camping. In those that do, camping is usually permitted anywhere in the forest outside of a designated campground and not specifically posted as closed. Chose a campsite on bare or compacted soil when possible, or areas that have already been established. Ideally, sites will be more than 100 feet (300 feet in Umatilla National Forest) from a lake or stream shoreline but in no case closer than 25 feet. Avoid alpine meadows. For the best information on dispersed camping opportunities, please contact the appropriate local agency office.

Campers are subject to the following restrictions.

- Do not blaze new roads to campsites or cut or harm vegetation, or construct a trail.
- Do not drive beyond constructed physical barriers, such as berms or gates.
- Do not drive through streams or wetlands to access a camp.
- Use proper precautions when building campfires.
- All food, beverages, and attractants must be stored in an animal resistant container.
- Pack out trash and dispose of human waste properly.

Driving on National Forest Service Roads

Getting around on National Forest roads is different from driving on a highway. Most are low-standard, one lane roads with turnouts for meeting oncoming traffic. Many on the east side of the Cascade Mountains are not graveled and not maintained or snow plowed during the winter. Food, gas, or lodging is seldom available. Encounters with logging trucks are likely – even on weekends.

The type of route marker displayed as you enter a road gives an indication of the type of conditions you may expect.

 This is a primary route marker and usually offers the better choice for passenger automobiles.

 This is a secondary route marker which may not be as smooth or well maintained as a primary. They are usually still suitable for passenger automobiles.

 This is a low-standard route marker indicating a road which may not be suitable for passenger automobiles. If used, you can expect the possibility of rocks on the roadway, washouts, or downed trees in the driving area. For safety, use a vehicle suitable for rough travel and carry necessary equipment.

When driving on one-lane roads, watch for turnouts and be prepared to stop and wait for oncoming traffic. Do not drive too fast for the conditions. If you are parking, be sure to do so well clear of the road and do not block turnouts.

Most of these recommendations are also appropriate for other agencies' back-country roads.

Host Programs

Most campgrounds listed in this book offer the opportunity to be a campground host. Some require a season's commitment while others allow for shorter periods of time. The usual compensation is a free campsite and only minimal tasks are required to be accomplished in return. Sometimes the campground is managed directly by the governing agency while other times it is through a concessionaire.

If you are interested in being a host, a good place to start is to contact the ultimate operating agency and ask them what procedures to use to volunteer. They will guide you to the contact person who will tell you what is available and any requirements.

During times of budget constraints, many recreation facilities remain open only because of volunteers. It is an excellent way to give back to your community and have a great time camping too.

Regulation Omission

When regulations are listed throughout this book, the omission of a regulation does not mean an activity is permitted. If there is any question, always check with the controlling agency before undertaking an activity.

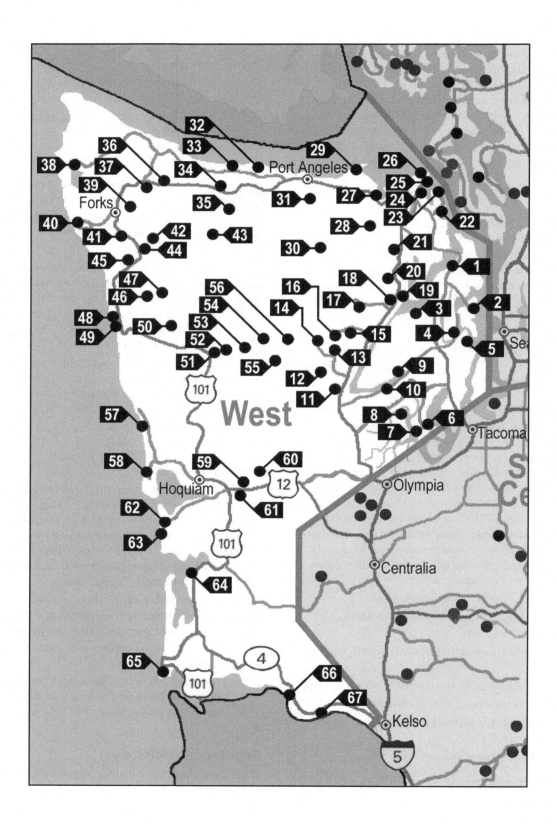

Chapter 2   West Region

1 Kitsap Memorial
Washington State Parks

Directions

Start at the intersection of WA–104 and WA–3 near Port Gamble. Travel south on WA–3 for 3.0 miles. Turn right onto Park Street NE and travel for 0.2 mile to park.

N47°48'59" – W122°39'03"   Elevation – 50 feet

Features

Kitsap Memorial is on the shoreline with sweeping views of Hood Canal. The saltwater beach has tide pools and opportunities for shellfish harvesting. Sites 1 through 18 are partial utility sites. The park has grassy playfields and children's play equipment in beautiful natural surroundings.

Reservations

Sites may be reserved on *www.parks.state.wa.us* or by telephone 1–888–CAMPOUT (1–888–226–7688). See Appendix B for details.

Season

Open all year

Activities

Beachcombing, Bird watching, Boating, Fishing or shellfish harvesting, Hiking, Metal detecting, Soccer fields, Volleyball court.

Cost

$12 primitive site
Peak season: mid May – mid September
$22 – $35 standard site
$30 – $40 partial utility site
$35 – $45 full utility site
Off–peak season
$20 – $30 standard site
$25 – $35 partial utility site
$30 – $40 full utility site
$10 extra vehicle (all year)
See Appendix C for available discounts.

Limitations

Maximum site length is 40 feet.
See Appendix A for camping regulations.

Contact

Phone: 360–779–3205
Web: *www.parks.state.wa.us*

Facilities

39 sites: 21 standard sites, 18 partial utility sites
Flush toilets
Potable water
Hot showers
Garbage service
Accessible toilet and shelter
Boat launch
Moorage buoys

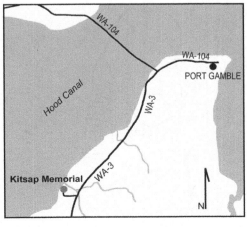

Driving Directions

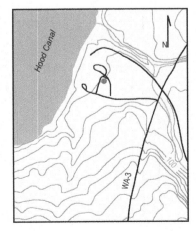

Location

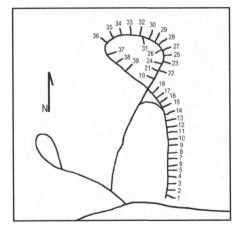

Campground

2 Fay Bainbridge
Bainbridge Island Metro Park & Recreation District

Directions

Start at the intersection of WA–3 and WA–305 near Poulsbo. Travel south on WA–305 for 10.5 miles. Turn left onto East Day Road and travel for 1.3 miles. Turn left onto Sunrise Drive NE and travel for 1.7 miles. Turn right into park.

N47°42'12" – W122°30'33"   Elevation – 40 feet

View of Puget Sound from Fay Bainbridge

Facilities

41 sites: 15 tent sites, 26 partial utility (W) sites
Flush toilet
Potable water
Hot showers
Garbage service
Mooring buoys

Features

Fay Bainbridge Park is located on the northeast corner of Bainbridge Island on the shoreline. The park offers sweeping views of Puget Sound and the Cascade Mountains and features a variety of water activities and sandy beaches.

Reservations

Reservations may be made online at *www.biparks.org* or by telephone at 206–842–2306 x 118.

Season

Open all year

Activities

Beachcombing, Bird watching, Boating, Fishing and shellfish harvesting, Hiking, Horseshoes, Scuba diving, Volleyball courts.

Cost

$25 – beach tent and RV sites
$35 – site 18 (host site when available)
$15 – standard site
$20 – premium tent site, partial utility site
$10 extra vehicle (all year)

Limitations

Some RV sites will accommodate vehicles up to 40' (limited availability).
See Appendix A for camping regulations.

Contact

Phone:206–842–3931
Web: *www.biparks.org*

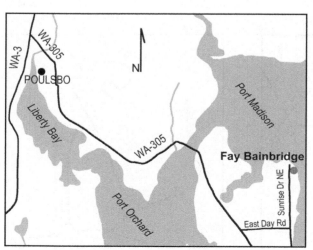

Driving Directions

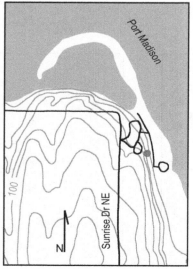

Location

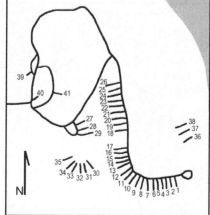

Campground

3 Scenic Beach
Washington State Parks

Directions

Start at the intersection of WA–3 and WA–310 near Bremerton. Travel north on WA–3 for 5.1 miles. Exit and turn left (west) onto Newberry Hill Road, and travel for 3.1 miles. Turn right onto Seabeck NW Hwy and travel for 5.1 miles. Turn right onto Miami Beach Road and travel for 0.9 mile. Turn left onto Scenic Beach Road NW and travel for 0.4 mile. Bear right at the 'Y' into park.

N47°38'51" – W122°50'56"   Elevation – 100 feet

Facilities

52 sites: 50 standard sites and 2 walk–in sites
Pull–through sites
Flush toilets
Potable water
Hot showers
Garbage service
RV dump station
Accessible toilet, water
Boat launch is 0.5 miles east of park (WDFW)

Features

Aptly named, Scenic Beach is located on Hood Canal and known for its stunning views of the water and the Olympic Mountains. Campsites are interspersed between native rhododendrons in a lovely wooded setting.

Reservations

Sites may be reserved online at *www.parks.state.wa.us* or by telephone 1–888–CAMPOUT (1–888–226–7688).
See Appendix B for details.

Season

Open all year

Activities

Beachcombing, Bird watching, Boating, Fishing and shellfish harvesting, Hiking, Horseshoes, Metal detecting, Scuba diving, and Volleyball.

Cost

$12 primitive site
Peak season: mid May – mid September
$22 – $35 standard site
$30 – $40 partial utility site
$35 – $45 full utility site
Off–peak season
$20 – $30 standard site
$25 – $35 partial utility site
$30 – $40 full utility site
$10 extra vehicle (all year)
See Appendix C for available discounts.

Limitations

Pull–through sites accommodate 60–foot camping units.
Some campsites are closed during the winter.
See Appendix A for camping regulations.

Contact

Phone: 360–830–5079
Web *www.parks.state.wa.us*

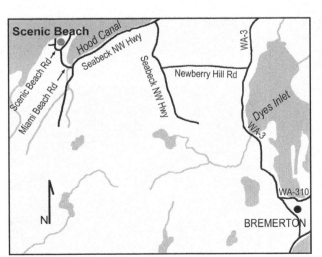

Driving Directions

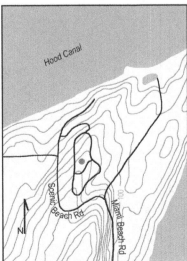

Location

Campground

4 Illahee
Washington State Parks

Directions

Start at the intersection of WA–303 and WA–304 in Bremerton. Travel north on WA–303 (also called Warren Avenue) for 2.1 miles. Turn right onto Sylvan Way and travel 1.6 miles. Turn left into park.

N47°35'50" – W122°35'46"   Elevation – 200 feet

Facilities

25 sites: 23 standard sites, 2 full utility sites
Flush toilets
Potable water
Hot showers
Garbage service
RV dump station
Accessible toilet, water, and campsite
Boat launch with 360 feet of dock

Features

Illahee State Park, located on Port Orchard Bay, has the last stand of old–growth timber in Kitsap County. The beach provides some sand and great views of Puget Sound. Offering access to a variety of water sports, as well as a kitchen shelter and interpretive displays, the park features a veterans' war memorial and one of the largest yew trees in the nation.

"Illahee" means earth or country in the local Native American language and the views of Puget Sound from the beach gives a sense of what that word meant to the native people.

Reservations

Sites may be reserved online at *www.parks.state.wa.us* or by telephone 1–888–CAMPOUT (1–888–226–7688). See Appendix B for more details.

Season

Open all year

Activities

Beachcombing, Bird watching, Ball fields, Boating, Fishing or shellfish harvesting, Hiking, Horseshoes, Metal detecting, Scuba diving, Swimming, Volleyball courts, Water skiing.

Cost

$12 primitive site
Peak season: mid May – mid September
$22 – $35 standard site
$30 – $40 partial utility site
$35 – $45 full utility site
Off–peak season
$20 – $30 standard site
$25 – $35 partial utility site
$30 – $40 full utility site
$10 extra vehicle (all year)
See Appendix C for available discounts.

Limitations

Maximum site length is 40 feet.
See Appendix A for camping regulations.

Contact

Phone: 360–478–6460
Web: *www.parks.state.wa.us*

Re–purposed Grill Basket

Originally sold for grilling fish, we discovered it is a good way to control many unruly meats and vegetables. Firepit rings, rocks, logs, or other found objects support the basket close to the fire.

Basket Supported by Firepit Ring

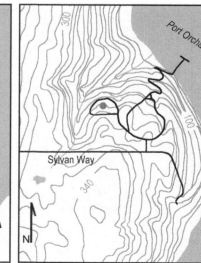

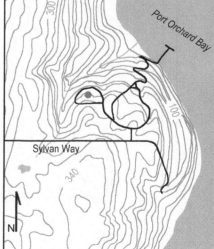

Driving Directions

Location

Found Objects Support Basket

5 Manchester
Washington State Parks

Directions

Start at the intersection of WA–16 and WA–166 near Port Orchard. Travel east on WA–166 (becomes Mile Hill Road) for 7.6 miles. Turn left onto Colchester Road and travel 1.7 miles. Turn left onto Main Street and travel 0.1 mile. Turn right onto Beach Road and travel for 1.9 miles. Turn right onto Hilldale Road and into park.

N47°34'27" — W122°33'11"   Elevation – 40 feet

Facilities

53 sites: 35 standard sites, 15 partial utility, 3 primitive
Pull–through sites
Flush toilets
Potable water
Hot showers
Garbage service
RV dump station
Accessible water

Features

Manchester State Park is along Rich Passage on Puget Sound. The park offers a view of Bainbridge Island and Seattle from the beach. An interpretive display is tucked inside the former torpedo warehouse. Fir and maple trees shade the campground. Sites number 3–10, 12, 14–17 and 20 are partial utility sites. The park is in a secluded forest with nearby lakes and wetlands.

In the late 1800s, the U.S. Coast Artillery built a defense installation on the property to protect Bremerton. A torpedo warehouse still stands in the park. Later it became an officer's club, a barracks, a mess hall, and is now a picnic shelter in the day–use area.

Reservations

The primitive sites are first come, first serve. Other sites may be reserved May 15 through September 15 online at *www.parks.state.wa.us* or by telephone 1–888–CAMPOUT (1–888–226–7688). See Appendix B for details.

Season

Open all year

Activities

Beachcombing, Bird watching, Boating, Fishing or shellfish harvesting, Hiking, Horseshoes, Mountain biking, Scuba diving, Swimming, Volleyball court.

Cost

$12 primitive site
Peak season: mid May – mid September
$22 – $35 standard site
$30 – $40 partial utility site
$35 – $45 full utility site
Off–peak season
$20 – $30 standard site
$25 – $35 partial utility site
$30 – $40 full utility site
$10 extra vehicle (all year)
See Appendix C for available discounts.

Limitations

Maximum site length is 60 feet.
See Appendix A for camping regulations.

Contact

Phone: 360–871–4065
Web: *www.parks.state.wa.us*

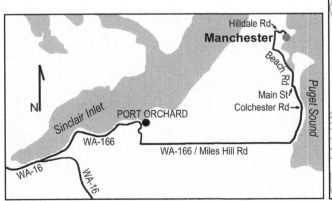

Driving Directions

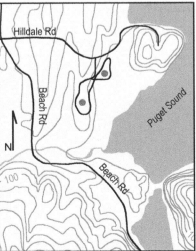

Location

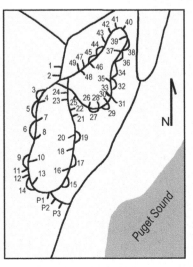

Campground

6 Penrose Point
Washington State Parks

Directions

Start at the intersection of WA–16 and WA–302 near Purdy. Travel west on WA–302 for 6.4 miles. Continue straight onto Key Peninsula Hwy N (WA–302 makes a right at this point – don't do it) and travel for 9.0 miles. Turn left onto Cornwall Road and travel for 0.5 mile. Turn right onto Delano Road and travel for 0.8 mile. Turn left onto 158th Avenue and travel for 0.3 mile to park.

N47°15'24" – W122°45'00"   Elevation – 60 feet

Facilities

83 sites: 82 standard sites,
1 primitive site
Pull–through sites
Flush toilets
Potable water
Hot showers, summer only
Garbage
RV dump station
Boat dock
Moorage buoys

Features

Penrose Point has saltwater beaches with a 1/2–mile long sand spit at low tide. Impressive stands of fir and cedar mixing with ferns and rhododendrons provide total or partial shade at campsites. Large stumps with springboard notches can be seen, evidence of early logging activity. There is a self–guided interpretive trail.

Reservations

Sites may be reserved from May 15 through September 15 online at *www.parks.state.wa.us* or by telephone 1–888–CAMPOUT (1–888–226–7688). See Appendix B for details.

Season

Park is open all year; however, only sites 1–21 are open October 15 – May 15

Activities

Beachcombing, Bird watching, Boating, Fishing or shellfish gathering, Hiking, Horseshoe, Interpretive center, Metal detecting, Mountain biking, Personal watercraft access, Scuba diving, Swimming, and Water skiing.

Cost

$12 primitive site
Peak season: mid May – mid September
$22 – $35 standard site
$30 – $40 partial utility site
$35 – $45 full utility site
Off–peak season
$20 – $30 standard site
$25 – $35 partial utility site
$30 – $40 full utility site
$10 extra vehicle (all year)
See Appendix C for available discounts.

Limitations

Maximum vehicle length is 35 feet. Some sites may allow a slightly longer RV but access turns are tight.
See Appendix A for camping regulations.

Contact

Phone: 253–884–2514
Web: *www.parks.state.wa.us*

Boat Dock at Penrose Point

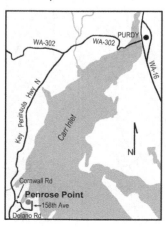

Driving Directions

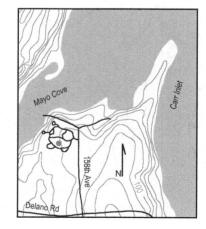

Location

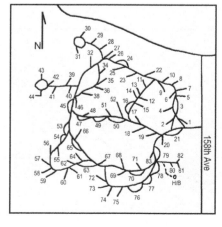

Campground

7 Joemma Beach
Washington State Parks

Directions

Start at the intersection of WA–16 and WA–302 near Purdy. Travel west on WA–302 for 6.4 miles. Continue straight onto Key Peninsula Hwy North (WA–302 turns right at this point – don't follow it) and travel for 9.6 miles. Turn right onto Whiteman Road and travel for 2.2 miles. Turn right onto Bay Road and travel for 0.8 mile to park.

N47°13'34" — W122°48'27"   Elevation – 60 feet

Facilities

21 sites: 19 standard sites, 2 walk–in sites
Vault toilets
Potable water
Garbage service
Accessible toilet and campsite
Boat launch and dock
Mooring buoys

Features

Joemma Beach is located on Puget Sound on the southwest shore of Key Peninsula. The forested park is an excellent place for fishing, boating, and crabbing. Some campsites overlook the saltwater beach.

Reservations

None, all campsites are first–come, first–serve.

Season

Open all year

Activities

Beachcombing, Bird watching, Fishing, Crabbing, and Shellfish harvesting, Hiking, Scuba diving.

Cost

$12 primitive site
Peak season: mid May – mid September
$22 – $35 standard site
$30 – $40 partial utility site
$35 – $45 full utility site

Off–peak season
$20 – $30 standard site
$25 – $35 partial utility site
$30 – $40 full utility site
$10 extra vehicle (all year)
See Appendix C for available discounts.

Dock at Joemma Beach

Limitations

Maximum site length is 40 feet.
See Appendix A for camping regulations.

Contact

Phone: 253–884–1944
Web: *www.parks.state.wa.us*

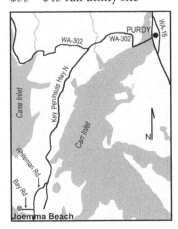

Driving Directions   *Location*

Joemma Beach Campsite

8 Jarrell Cove
Washington State Parks

Directions

Start at the intersection of WA–3 and WA–302 near Allyn. Travel south on WA–3 for 10.7 miles. Turn left onto Pickering Road and travel for 3.3 miles. Bear left onto Harstine Island Bridge Road and travel for 0.6 mile. Turn left onto North Island Drive and travel for 3.5 miles. Turn left onto Wingert Road and travel for 0.5 mile. Turn left into park.

N47°16'59" – W122°53'04"   Elevation – 60 feet

Facilities

22 standard sites
Flush toilets
Potable water
Hot showers
Kitchen shelters
Garbage service
Accessible campsite
Boat dock (260')
Mooring buoys

Features

Jarrell Cove is located on the northwest end of Harstine Island in south Puget Sound and is off the beaten path. Dense woods press to the water's edge at high tide. At low tide, the tidelands are mud flats. Some campsites are near the park's boat dock as well as on rolling, grassy areas.

Jarrell Cove State Park is named after Mrs. Philura Jarrel, the first pioneer woman to settle on the island. McMicken Island, Stretch Point, Eagle Island, and Hope Island are satellite parks accessible only by boat.

Reservations

Reservations can be made online at *www.parks.state.wa.us* or by calling 888–CAMPOUT (888–226–7688). See Appendix B for details.

Season

Open all year

Activities

Badminton and volleyball courts, Beachcombing, Bird watching, Boating, Canoe access, Fishing or shellfish harvesting, Hiking, Horseshoes, Scuba diving.

Cost

$12 primitive site
Peak season: mid May – mid September
$22 – $35 standard site
$30 – $40 partial utility site
$35 – $45 full utility site
Off–peak season
$20 – $30 standard site
$25 – $35 partial utility site
$30 – $40 full utility site
$10 extra vehicle (all year)
See Appendix C for available discounts.

Limitations

Maximum site length is 34 feet.
See Appendix A for camping regulations.

Contact

Phone: 360–426–9226
Web: *www.parks.state.wa.us*

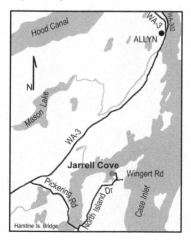

Driving Directions

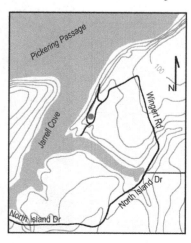

Location

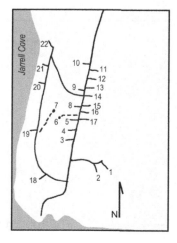

Campground

9 Belfair
Washington State Parks

Directions

Start at the intersection of WA–300 and WA–3 near Belfair. Travel west on WA–300 for 2.9 miles. Turn left into park.

N47°25'46" – W122°52'34"   Elevation – 20 feet

Facilities

153 sites: 116 standard sites, 37 utility sites
Pull–through sites
Flush toilets
Potable water
Garbage service
RV dump station
Accessible toilets, water, and campsite

Features

Belfair State Park is located at the southern end of Hood Canal and is noted for its saltwater tide flats and wetlands. In fall, salmon run up the creeks that flow through the park. Interpretive programs are held in summer. Generations of Native Americans used this area as a central meeting place. The Skokomish tribe camped here to gather shellfish.

Reservations

Sites may be reserved from May 13 through September 14 online at *www.parks.state.wa.us* or by telephone 1–888–CAMPOUT (1–888–226–7688). See Appendix B for details.

Season

Open all year however, Tree loop closes from mid September to mid May.

Activities

Badminton and volleyball courts, Beachcombing, Bird watching, Boating, Fishing and shellfish harvesting, Hiking, Scuba diving, Swimming.

Cost

$12 primitive site
Peak season: mid May – mid September
$22 – $35 standard site
$30 – $40 partial utility site
$35 – $45 full utility site
Off–peak season
$20 – $30 standard site
$25 – $35 partial utility site
$30 – $40 full utility site
$10 extra vehicle (all year)
See Appendix C for available discounts.

A Foggy Day at Belfair

Limitations

Main and Beach loops have a maximum site length of 60 feet (limited availability).
Tree loop has a maximum site length of 18 feet for trailers and 25 feet for RVs.
See Appendix A for camping regulations.

Contact

Phone: 360–275–0668
Web: *www.parks.state.wa.us*

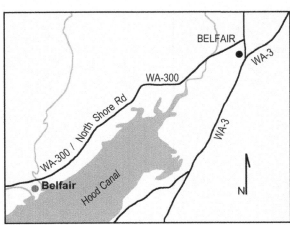

Driving Directions

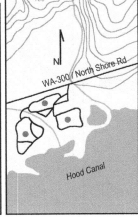

Location

Campground

10 Twanoh
Washington State Parks

Directions

Start at the intersection of US–101 and WA–106 south of Potlatch. Travel east on WA–106 for 12.4 miles. Turn right into park.

N47°22'38" – W122°58'18"   Elevation – 40 feet

Facilities

47 sites: 25 standard sites,
22 utility sites
Pull–through sites
Flush toilets
Potable water
Hot showers
Garbage service
RV dump station
Accessible water, utility campsite
Boat launch and 200 foot dock
Moorage buoys

Features

Located on the shores of Hood Canal, Twanoh has one of the warmest saltwater beaches in Washington state. WA–106 divides the park into two areas: the day–use picnic area is on the water side and the campground is along Twanoh Creek on the wooded side of the road. Historic park buildings were constructed in the 1930s by the Civilian Conservation Corps.

Twanoh's oyster beds are seeded annually and the clam season is usually open yearly from August 1 through September 30. In winter, there is a smelt run along the beach and, in late fall, a chum salmon run in Twanoh Creek (closed to fishing).

Reservations

Sites may be reserved online at *www.parks.state.wa.us* or by telephone 1–888–CAMPOUT (1–888–226–7688). Reservations are advised for the summer months. See Appendix B for details.

Season

Open all year

Activities

Badminton, Beachcombing, Bird watching, Boating, Fishing or shellfish harvesting, Hiking, Horseshoes, Metal detecting,

Personal watercraft access, Saltwater wading pool, Scuba diving, Swimming, Tennis, Volleyball, Water skiing.

Cost

$12 primitive site
Peak season: mid May – mid September
$22 – $35 standard site
$30 – $40 partial utility site
$35 – $45 full utility site
Off–peak season
$20 – $30 standard site
$25 – $35 partial utility site
$30 – $40 full utility site
$10 extra vehicle (all year)
See Appendix C for available discounts.

Limitations

Maximum site length is 35 feet.
Campground has limited winter water supply
See Appendix A for camping regulations.

Contact

Phone: 360–275–2222
Web: *www.parks.state.wa.us*

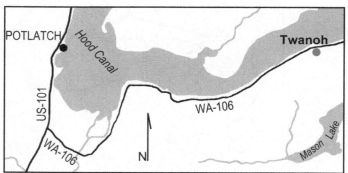

Driving Directions

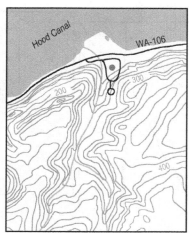

Location

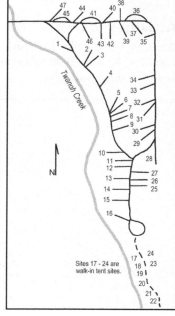

Sites 17 - 24 are walk-in tent sites.

Campground

11 Potlatch
Washington State Parks

Directions

Start at the intersection of US–101 and WA–106 near Potlatch. Travel north on US–101 for 1.9 miles and turn left into park.

N47°21'44" – W123°09'30"   Elevation – 20 feet

Facilities

75 sites: 38 standard sites, 35 utility sites, and 2 primitive sites
Pull–through sites
Flush toilets
Potable water
Hot showers
Garbage service
RV dump station
Accessible drinking water and utility campsite
Mooring buoys

Features

Located along the shoreline of Hood Canal, Potlatch State Park spans US–101. The day–use area is along the shoreline for those who want to harvest oysters, dig for clams, catch crab, or fish. The campsites are in the woods across the road. The park offers summer interpretive programs and Junior Ranger activities. Average annual rainfall is 64 inches.

The Skokomish Indian Tribe historically used this area as the site of their winter potlatches, or gift–giving ceremonies.

Reservations

Sites may be reserved from May 15 through September 15 online at *www.parks.state.wa.us* or by telephone 1–888–CAMPOUT (1–888–226–7688). See Appendix B for details.

Season

Open all year

Activities

Beachcombing, Bird watching, Boating, Crabbing, Fishing and shellfish gathering, Hiking, Sail boarding, and Scuba diving.

View of Hood Canal from Potlatch

Cost

$12 primitive site
Peak season: mid May – mid September
$22 – $35 standard site
$30 – $40 partial utility site
$35 – $45 full utility site
Off–peak season
$20 – $30 standard site
$25 – $35 partial utility site
$30 – $40 full utility site
$10 extra vehicle (all year)
See Appendix C for available discounts.

Limitations

Maximum site length is 60 feet.
See Appendix A for camping regulations.

Contact

Phone: 360–796–4415
Web: *www.parks.state.wa.us*

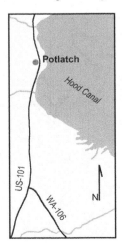

Driving Directions

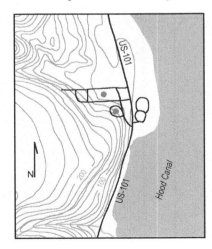

Location

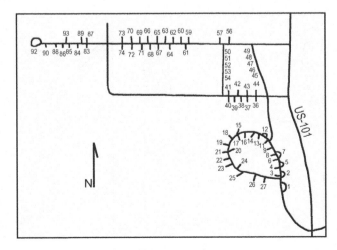

Campground

12 Brown Creek
Olympic National Forest

Directions

Start at the intersection of US–101 and WA–102 north of Shelton. Travel north on US–101 for 4.0 miles. Turn left on Skokomish Valley Road and travel for 5.6 miles. Turn right on Forest Service Road 23 and travel for 9.3 miles. Turn right onto Forest Service Road 2353 and travel for 0.6 mile to the South Fork Skokomish River Bridge. Cross bridge and immediately turn right onto Forest Service Road 2340 for 0.4 mile. Turn left into Brown Creek.

N47°24'42" – W123°19'19"   Elevation – 570 feet

Facilities

22 sites: 14 RV/trailer sites, 8 tent sites
Vault toilets
Potable water in summer
Pack out garbage
Accessible campsite

Features

Brown Creek campground lies at the confluence of the South Fork Skokomish River and Brown Creek. Campsites are wooded. Eight sites are suitable for tents, the remaining will accommodate trailers and RVs. Brown Creek Nature Pond Interpretive Trail is accessed from the campground.

Reservations

None, all campsites are first–come, first–serve.

Season

Generally open mid May through mid September however, six campsites along the river are open year around.

Activities

Fishing, Hiking, Interpretive trail.

Cost

$14
$5.00 extra vehicle
See Appendix C for available discounts.

Limitations

Maximum vehicle length is 21 feet.
See Appendix A for camping regulations.

Contact

Olympic National Forest – Hood Canal District
295142 Highway 101 S. – P.O. Box 280
Quilcene, WA 98376
Phone: 360–765–2200

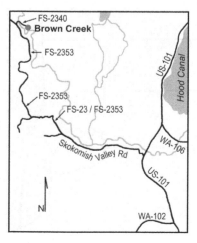

Driving Directions

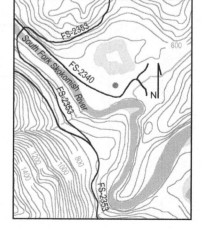

Location

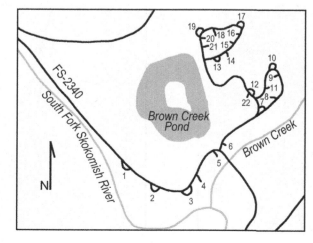

Campground

13 Big Creek
Olympic National Forest

Directions

Start at the intersection of US–101 and WA–119 in Hoodsport. Travel west on WA–119 for 9.4 miles. Turn left at "T" on WA–119 for 100 yards to Big Creek entrance on right.

N47°29'40" – W123°12'39"   Elevation – 980 feet

Facilities

23 standard sites
Vault toilets
Potable water
Pack out garbage
Shelter

Features

Big Creek campsites are in a second–growth forest, private, and with exceptional scenery. Big Creek, a small stream, is adjacent to the campground. The campground loop trail offers a view of Mt. Washington. The Upper Big Creek Loop Trail starts in the campground and Mt. Ellinor, Jefferson Pass, Mt. Rose, and Dry Creek trails are located within 8 miles of the campground.

Reservations

None, all campsites are first–come, first–serve.

Season

Open from May 15 to September 30

Waterfall Near Campground

Activities

Fishing, Hiking, Swimming at nearby Lake Cushman.

Cost

$14
$5.00 extra vehicle
See Appendix C for available discounts.

Limitations

Maximum vehicle length is 30 feet.
Maximum stay is 14 days.
See Appendix A for camping regulations.

Contact

Olympic National Forest
Hood Canal District
295142 Highway 101 S.
P.O. Box 280
Quilcene, WA 98376
Phone: 360–765–2200

*Mt. Washington
Behind Campground*

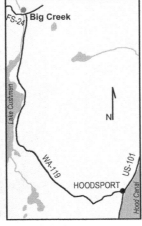

Driving Directions

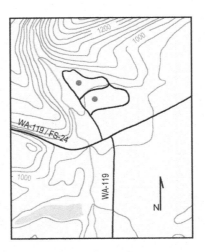

Location

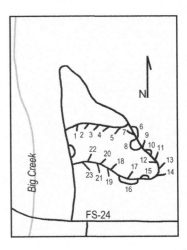

Campground

Looking Toward Staircase From Across Lake Cushman

14 Staircase
Olympic National Park

Directions

Start at the intersection of US–101 and WA–119 in Hoodsport. Travel west on WA–119 (becomes Forest Service Road 24) for 15.8 miles to Staircase.

N47°30'53" – W123°19'47"   Elevation – 765 feet

Facilities

49 standard sites, 5 walk–in only
Flush toilet and potable water available late May through late September
Pit toilet and no water in off–season
Garbage service
Animal–proof storage lockers
Accessible toilet (on loop A), water, and campsite

Features

Staircase campground is surrounded by old growth forest with some riverside sites along the Skokomish River. The campground offers access to several day hikes. Staircase Ranger Station opens intermittently in summer if staffing levels allow.

Reservations

None, all campsites are first–come, first–serve.

Season

Open from mid May through late October; sites are walk–in and primitive during winter months.

Activities

Hiking.

Cost

$20
See Appendix C for available discounts.

Limitations

If snowy, Forest Service Road 24, may be gated at park boundary(about 1 mile from the campground). Call 360–565–3131 for status.
Maximum recommended vehicle length is 21 feet, although some sites can handle up to 35 feet.
Pets and bicycles are not permitted on park trails.
See Appendix A for camping regulations.

Contact

Olympic National Park
600 East Park Avenue
Port Angeles, WA 98362–6798
Visitor Information: 360–565–3130, TTY: 800–833–6388
Road & Weather Hotline: 360–565–3131

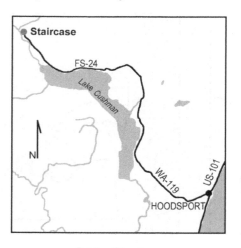

Driving Directions

Location

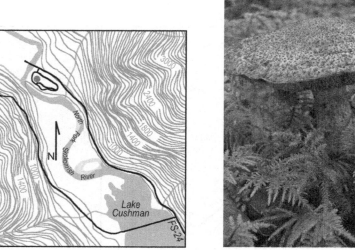

Forest Mushroom

15 Hamma Hamma
Olympic National Forest

Directions

Start at the intersection of US–101 and WA–119 in Hoodsport. Travel north on US–101 for 14.1 miles. Turn left onto Forest Service Road 25 (Hamma Hamma Road) to the Hamma Hamma Recreation Area and travel for 6.0 miles on a two–lane, paved road. Turn left into campground.

N47°35'42" – W123°07'20"   Elevation – 560 feet

Facilities

15 standard sites
Vault toilet
No water, potable water available 2 miles west at Lena Creek campground.
Pack out garbage
Accessible toilet and campsite

Features

Hamma Hamma campground is located along the shore of the Hamma Hamma River. The Living Legacy Trailhead is located in the campground. The first 1/4 mile 0f the trail is accessible and overlooks the river.

Reservations

None, all campsites are first–come, first–serve.

Season

Open May 1 through September 30

Activities

Fishing, Hiking.

Cost

$14
$5 extra vehicle
See Appendix C for available discounts.

Limitations

Maximum vehicle length is 21 feet.
See Appendix A for camping regulations.

Contact

Olympic National Forest – Hood Canal District
295142 Highway 101 S. – PO Box 280
Quilcene, WA 98376
Phone: 360–765–2200

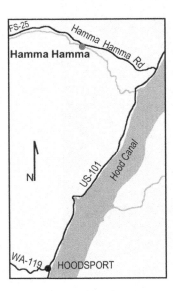

Driving Directions

Location

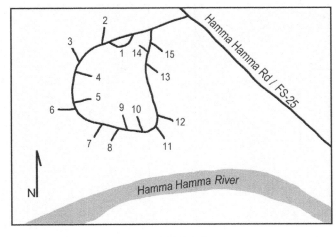

Campground

16 Lena Creek
Olympic National Forest

Directions

Start at the intersection of US–101 and WA–119 in Hoodsport. Travel north on US–101 for 14.1 miles. Turn left onto Hamma Hamma Road (Forest Service Road 25) to the Hamma Hamma Recreation Area and travel for 7.6 miles on a two–lane paved road. Turn left into Lena Creek.

N47°35'53" – W123°09'04"   Elevation – 720 feet

Facilities

13 standard sites
Vault toilet
Potable water
Pack out garbage

Features

Lena Creek campground is located along the shore of the Hamma Hamma River. The campground is adjacent to the Lena Lake trailhead which is also the trailhead for Upper Lena Lake and The Brothers trails.

Reservations

None, all campsites are first–come, first–serve.

Season

Open May 1 through September 30

Activities

Fishing, Hiking.

Cost

$14
$5 extra vehicle
See Appendix C for available discounts.

Limitations

Maximum vehicle length is 21 feet.
See Appendix A for camping regulations.

Contact

Olympic National Forest – Hood Canal District
295142 Highway 101 S. – PO Box 280
Quilcene, WA 98376
Phone: 360–765–2200

Coolers

A sheet of Mylar insulation in the cooler helps ice last much longer. If there is room, use block ice instead of cube ice. It will last even longer.

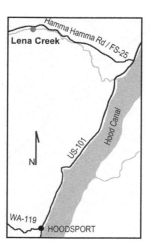

Driving Directions

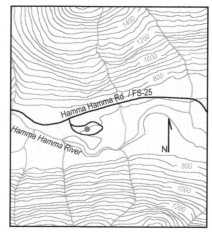

Location

17 Collins
Olympic National Forest

Directions

Start at the intersection of US–101 and WA–119 in Hoodsport. Travel north on US–101 for 22 miles. Turn left onto Duckabush Road (Forest Service Road 2510) and travel for 5.1 miles. Turn left into Collins.

N47°40'57" – W123°01'07"   Elevation – 360 feet

Road Along the Duckabush River

Reservations

None, all campsites are first–come, first–serve.

Season

Open mid May through mid September

Activities

Fishing, Hiking, Hunting.

Cost

$14
$5.00 extra vehicle
See Appendix C for available discounts.

Facilities

16 sites: 10 standard sites, 6 tent sites
Vault toilets
Bring your own water
Pack out garbage

Features

Collins is a quiet campground located along the shore of the Duckabush River. Several campsites are riverside. Potable water is available via a hand-pump well at the trailhead near *Interrorem Cabin* approximately 1.5 miles east of the campground.

Limitations

Maximum vehicle length is 21 feet.
The Duckabush River has swift water, rapids, waterfalls, and is not floatable. Use extreme caution in or near the water.
See Appendix A for camping regulations.

Contact

Olympic National Forest – Hood Canal District
295142 Highway 101 S. – PO Box 280
Quilcene, WA 98376
Phone: 360–765–2200

Moss Grows On All Sides of the Tree at Collins

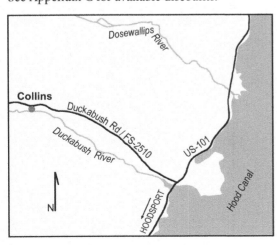

Driving Directions

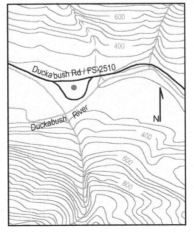

Location

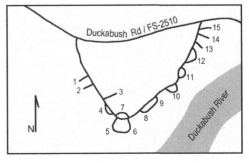

Campground

18 Dosewallips
Washington State Parks

Directions

Start at the intersection of US–101 and WA–119 in Hoodsport. Travel north on US–101 for 25.1 miles. Turn left into park.

N47°41'20" – W122°54'04"   Elevation – 40 feet

Facilities

123 total sites: 75 standard sites, 48 utility sites
Flush toilets
Potable water
Garbage service
Hot Showers
RV dump station
Accessible toilet and shower

Features

Dosewallips is located along the shores of Hood Canal and the Dosewallips River with breathtaking views of Hood Canal and the Olympic Mountains. Campsites are in grassy meadows and some sites are along the river. Campfire and Junior Ranger programs are conducted most weekends in summer.

Formerly called "Dose Meadows," the flat fields of the park were homesteads. Old rail beds remain where logs were hauled down the mountains and floated to waiting ships or to Puget Sound sawmills.

Reservations

Sites may be reserved on *www.parks.state.wa.us* or by telephone 1–888–CAMPOUT (1–888–226–7688). See Appendix B for more details.

Season

Open all year

Activities

Beachcombing, Bird watching, Boating, Fishing and shellfish harvesting, Hiking, Horseshoes.

Cost

$12 primitive site
Peak season: mid May – mid September
$22 – $35 standard site
$30 – $40 partial utility site
$35 – $45 full utility site
Off–peak season
$20 – $30 standard site
$25 – $35 partial utility site
$30 – $40 full utility site
$10 extra vehicle (all year)
See Appendix C for available discounts.

Limitations

The maximum site length is 60 feet.
See Appendix A for camping regulations.

Contact

Phone: 360–796–4415
Web: *www.parks.state.wa.us*

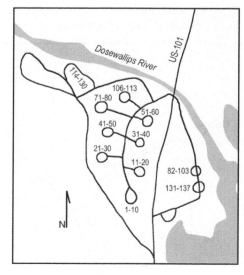

Driving Directions

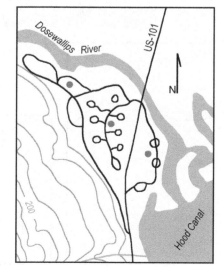

Location

Campground

19 Seal Rock
Olympic National Forest

Directions

Start at the intersection of US–101 and WA–119 in Hoodsport. Travel north on US–101 for 26.7 miles. Turn right into Seal Rock.

N47°42'35" – W122°53'22"   Elevation – 75 feet

Carry–in boats, such as canoes and kayaks, can be launched from the north landing.

Facilities

41 standard sites
Pull–through sites
Flush toilets
Potable water
Garbage service
Accessible toilet, water, and campsite

Features

Seal Rock campground, one of the few National Forest campgrounds located on salt water, has harvestable oysters. The campground offers beautiful views of Hood Canal and the mountains to the southeast and is located on Hood Canal. The lengths of sites vary, with those along Hood Canal capable of handling larger motor–homes and trailers. Sites are located among large trees.

Reservations

None, all campsites are first–come, first–serve.

Season

Open from May to September

Activities

Beach combing, Fishing and shellfish harvesting, Hiking, Scuba diving, Swimming.

Cost

$18
$5 extra vehicle
See Appendix C for available discounts.

Limitations

Maximum vehicle length is 21 feet.
Please obey all shellfish regulations. A shellfish license, required for oyster picking or clam digging, can be obtained at the Brinnon General Store, two miles south of the campground.
See Appendix A for camping regulations.

Contact

Olympic National Forest – Hood Canal District
295142 Highway 101 S. – PO Box 280
Quilcene, WA 98376
Phone: 360–765–2200

Driving Directions

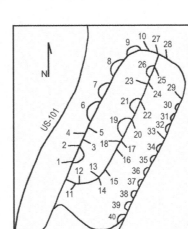

Location

Campground

Seal Rock Registration

20 Falls View
Olympic National Forest

Directions

Start at the intersection of US–101 and WA–119 in Hoodsport. Travel north on US–101 for 33.9 miles. Turn left to Falls View. (Campground is approximately 3.5 miles south of Quilcene on US–101.)

N47°47'23" – W122°55'40"   Elevation – 1070 feet

Facilities

30 standard sites: 14 RV/trailer sites, 16 camper/tent sites
Pull–through sites
Vault toilets
No water, bring your own
Garbage service
Accessible toilet and campsite

Features

Falls View campground, located in a forest with native rhododendrons high above the Big Quilcene River, has two separate camping loops to accommodate different types of camping vehicles. The right loop offers RV/trailer sites and the left loop offers camper/tent sites. Falls View Canyon Trail and Falls View Loop Trailhead are within the campground. One is a short scenic loop to a view point that overlooks a 100–foot waterfall into the Big Quilcene River and the second drops into the canyon to the river.

Reservations

None, all campsites are first–come, first–serve.

Season

Open May 15 through September 30

Activities

Fishing and shellfish harvesting, Hiking.

Cost

$10
$5 extra vehicle
See Appendix C for available discounts.

Limitations

Recommended maximum vehicle length is 21 feet but a few sites can handle up to 35 feet.
See Appendix A for camping regulations.

Contact

Olympic National Forest – Hood Canal District
295142 Highway 101 S. – PO Box 280
Quilcene, WA 98376
Phone: 360–765–2200

Falls View Campsite

Driving Directions

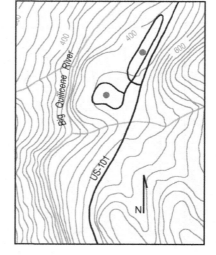

Location

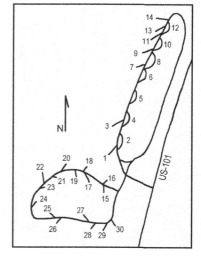

Campground

21 Lake Leland
Jefferson County

Directions

Start at intersection of US–101 and WA–20 southwest of Port Townsend. Travel south on US–101 for 6.3 miles. Turn right onto Leland Valley Road W. Travel 0.5 mile to campground.

N47°53'54" – W122°52'30"   Elevation – 220 feet

Facilities

22 total sites
Pull–through sites
Vault/pit toilet
No potable water – bring plenty to campground
No garbage service – pack it out
Boat launch
Fishing dock

Features

A beautiful park on a freshwater lake with a boat ramp and a fishing dock.

Reservations

None, all campsites are first–come, first–serve.

Season

Open April 1 through October 31

Activities

Bird watching, Fishing, Hiking, Kayaking.

Lake Leland Campsites

Cost

$18 – standard site
$10 – extra vehicle

Limitations

No alcohol allowed.
Maximum vehicle length is 30 feet.

Contact

Jefferson County
Phone: 360–385–9129
Website: *www.countyrec.com*

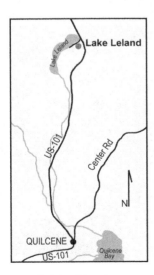

Driving Directions

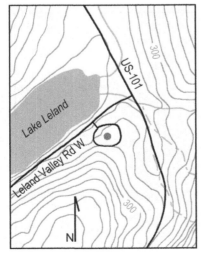

Location

Lake Leland Fishing Dock

22 Oak Bay
Jefferson County

Directions

Start at intersection of WA–19 and WA–116 in Hadlock. Travel east on WA–116 for 2.0 miles. Bear right onto Oak Bay Road and travel for 0.6 mile. Turn left onto Portage Road for Lower Oak Bay Campground or turn harder left onto Cleveland Street, travel for 0.1 mile and turn right into Upper Oak Bay Campground.

N48°01'26" – W122°43'58"   Elevation – 20 feet

Looking At Lower Campground From the Upper

Facilities

21 total sites: 5 partial utility (E), 16 standard
Vault/pit toilets
Potable water in Upper campground only
Garbage service

Features

Two beautiful parks in one: Upper Oak Bay campground features a large grassy area, a small playground, a salt water view, and a few sites with electricity. Lower Oak Bay campground is on a spit that forms an active estuary on Oak Bay.

Reservations

None, all campsites are first–come, first–serve.

Season

Open April 1 through October 31

Activities

Beachcombing, Bird watching, Fishing or shellfish harvesting, Hiking, Scuba diving.

Cost

$20 – standard site
$25 – partial utility site (E)
$12 – extra vehicle

Limitations

No alcohol allowed.
Avoid camping in Lower Oak Bay during very high tides.

Contact

Jefferson County
Phone: 360–385–9129
Web: *www.countyrec.com*

Lower Campground Campsite

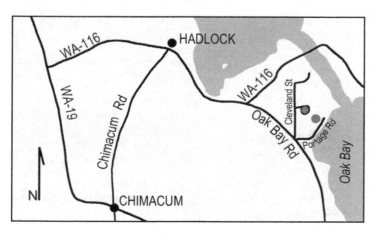

Driving Directions

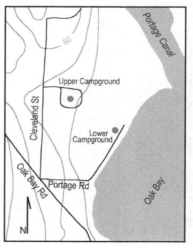

Location

Seagull on Oak Bay

23 Fort Flagler
Washington State Parks

Directions

Start at the intersection of WA–19 and WA–116 near Hadlock. Travel east on WA–116 for 10.5 miles. Turn left into park.

N48°05'37" – W122°42'50"   Elevation – 20 feet

Facilities

116 sites: 59 standard sites, 55 utility sites, 2 primitive sites
Pull–through sites
Flush toilets
Potable water
Hot showers
Garbage service
RV dump station
Accessible toilet, water, shower, and utility campsite
Boat launch
Interpretive center
Marina
Mooring buoys

Olympic Mountains Viewed From Fort Flagler

Features

Surrounded on three sides by water, Fort Flagler State Park rests on a high bluff overlooking Puget Sound with views of the Olympic and Cascade Mountains. There are two camping areas: the upper area has 49 sites and the lower area has 67 sites. The park offers a retreat center and food service.

Fort Flagler, along with the heavy batteries of Fort Worden and Fort Casey, once guarded the nautical entrance to Puget Sound. These posts became the first line of defense to prevent a hostile fleet from reaching such targets as the Bremerton Naval Yard and the cities of Seattle, Tacoma and Everett. Visitors may visit the military museum, which includes an interactive display, or arrange a guided tour of the historic buildings and features via the park office 360–385–3701.

(continued on next page)

Lower Campground

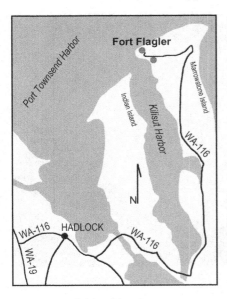

Driving Directions

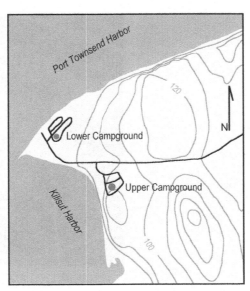

Location

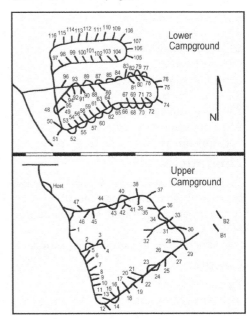

Campground

(Fort Flagler continued)

Reservations

Sites may be reserved from April 1 through October 31 online at *www.parks.state.wa.us* or by calling 1–888–CAMPOUT (1–888–226–7688). See Appendix B for details.

Season

Upper campground open May 1 – September 30
Lower campground open year round

Looking North Toward Whidbey Island

Activities

Beachcombing, Bird watching, Boating, Fishing or shellfish harvesting, Hiking, Metal detecting, Mountain biking, Scuba diving, Wind surfing.

Cost

$12 primitive site
Peak season: mid May – mid September
$22 – $35 standard site
$30 – $40 partial utility site
$35 – $45 full utility site
Off–peak season
$20 – $30 standard site
$25 – $35 partial utility site
$30 – $40 full utility site
$10 extra vehicle (all year)
See Appendix C for available discounts.

Limitations

Large RVs are not recommended in the upper campground because of the terrain and vegetation.
In the lower campground, the maximum recommended RV length is 50 feet.
See Appendix A for camping regulations.

Contact

Phone: 360–385–1259
Web *www.parks.state.wa.us*

Salmon Marinade

Kurt and Peggy are very good friends. Not only do they grill the best tasting salmon but they are also very giving – like when they gave us this recipe.

Ingredients

1 pound of wild salmon
½ cup olive oil
¼ cup soy sauce
¼ cup cider vinegar
1 teaspoon mustard powder
Juice of one lemon
1 clove garlic, minced

Preparation

Combine all ingredients and stir to mix. Put fish in a zip–top plastic bag, pour in marinade, seal bag, and put in cooler with ice. Marinate the fish at least one hour before grilling.

When grilling, do not over–cook the fish though the FDA recommendes a minimum internal temperature of 145°F.

Nothing Tastes Better Than Fresh Caught Wild Pacific Salmon

24 Fort Townsend
Washington State Parks

Directions

Start at the intersection of WA–19 and WA–20 near Port Townsend. Travel north on WA–20 for 0.5 mile. Turn right onto Old Fort Townsend Road and travel 1.0 mile to park.

N48°04'24" – W122°47'23"   Elevation – 160 feet

Facilities

44 sites: 40 standard sites,
4 primitive sites
Pull–through sites
Flush toilets
Potable water
Hot showers
Garbage service
RV dump station
Mooring buoys

Features

Fort Townsend State Park overlooks Port Townsend Bay and has a great reception building with fireplace and artwork. Designated a "Natural Forest Area," the park offers one of the best examples of a mature forest. It has large Douglas fir, western red cedar, and western hemlock trees with an understory of Pacific rhododendron, fairy slipper orchids and diverse parasitic plants. The park has 6.5 miles of hiking trails and offers a self–guided nature trail and a second trail highlighting historical information. Park rangers conduct nature and history interpretive events and provide an active Junior Ranger program.

The park has a rich military history dating from pioneer days. Today, it occupies a portion of the original Fort Townsend, which was built in 1856 to protect settlers and closed when

fire destroyed the barracks in 1895. During World War II, the property was used as an enemy munitions defusing station.

Reservations

Reservations can be made online at *www.parks.state.wa.us* or by calling 888–CAMPOUT (888–226–7688). See Appendix B for details.

Season

Campground closed October 15 – April 1

Activities

Beachcombing, Bird watching, Boating, Fishing and shellfish harvesting, Hiking, Mountain biking, Scuba diving.

Cost

$12 primitive site
Peak season: mid May – mid September
$22 – $35 standard site
$30 – $40 partial utility site
$35 – $45 full utility site
Off–peak season
$20 – $30 standard site
$25 – $35 partial utility site
$30 – $40 full utility site
$10 extra vehicle (all year)
See Appendix C for available discounts.

Limitations

Maximum site length is 40 feet.
See Appendix A for camping regulations.

Contact

Phone: 360–385–3595
Web: *www.parks.state.wa.us*

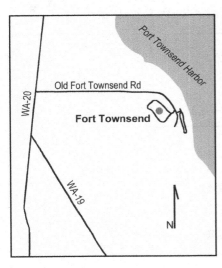

Driving Directions

Fort Townsend Campsite

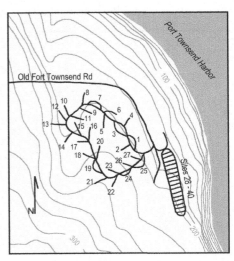

Location and Campground

25 Point Hudson RV Park
Port of Port Townsend

Directions

Start at intersection of WA–19 and WA–20, near Port Townsend. Travel north on WA–20 for 5.2 miles. Turn left onto Monroe Street and travel 0.1 mile. Turn right onto Jefferson Street and travel 0.1 mile to Point Hudson.

   N48°07'04" – W122°45'01"   Elevation – 20 feet

Facilities

48 total sites: 46 utility sites, 2 standard sites
Pull–through sites
Flush toilets
Potable water
Hot showers
Garbage service
Boat launch
Laundry

Features

The campground is located on Point Wilson overlooking Admiralty Inlet and the Strait of Juan de Fuca. The campground is within walking distance of the lighthouse at Point Wilson. Waterfront premium sites lie along the edge of the Strait. Except sites 360 and 361, which do not have utilities, all other sites have water, electricity, and sewer. Cable TV and Wi–Fi are available for a fee.

Reservations

Reserve sites on a rolling annual basis up to 12 months in

advance. Phone: 800–228–2803 or 360–385–2828 ($7 fee).

Season

Open all year

Activities

Beachcombing, Bird watching, Boating, Fishing, Hiking.

Cost

Summer (May through September)
$56 – Premium sites
$46 – Non–waterfront and front loop sites
Winter (October through May)
$45 – Premium sites
$40 – Non–waterfront and front loop sites
All year
$40 – Back row of loop sites
$30 – Sites with no utilities
$7 – Extra vehicle

Limitations

Beach fires and campfires are not allowed.

Contact

Port of Port Townsend
103 Hudson Street
Port Townsend, WA 98368
Phone: 800–228–2803 or 360–385–2828
Web: *www.portofpt.com*

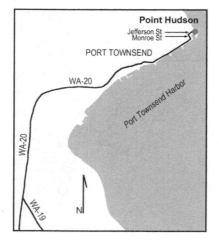

Driving Directions

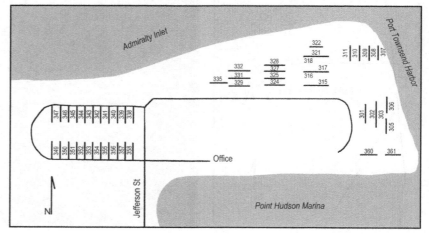

Campground

26 Fort Worden
Washington State Parks

Directions

Start at the intersection of WA–20 and WA–19 near Port Townsend. Travel north on WA–20 for 4.2 miles. Turn left onto Kearney Road and travel for 0.4 mile. Turn right onto Blaine Road and travel for 0.2 mile. Turn left onto Walker Road (becomes Cherry Road) and travel for 0.8 mile. Bear left onto Redwood Street and travel for 0.4 mile. Turn right onto "W" Street and travel for 0.1 mile to park entrance on left.

N48°08'09" – W122°45'51"   Elevation – 50 feet

Facilities

80 sites: 50 utility sites, 30 partial utility sites
Pull–through sites (Beach campground)
Flush toilets
Potable water
Hot showers
Garbage service
RV dump station (Upper campground)
Accessible toilet, water, utility campsite
Boat launch
Boat dock (235')
Interpretive centers

Fort Worden Office and Conference Center

Features

Fort Worden State Park and Conference Center rests on a high bluff overlooking Puget Sound. Many historic buildings remain at this 19th century military fort which offers a full–service conference center with a dining facility and meeting rooms. The park has two camping areas. The Beach campground has 50 utility sites tucked between the bluffs and the beaches of Point Wilson. The sites are level, spacious and open; most sites have an amazing view of the Strait of Juan de Fuca. The Upper

Beach Campground

campground has 30 partial utility sites that are mostly forested (some with privacy) and fairly level with long parking spurs.

Fort Worden, along with Fort Flagler and Fort Casey, once guarded the nautical entrance to Puget Sound. The fort closed in 1953 and the property was purchased as a state park in 1955. There are several notable historical, cultural, and environmental centers:

- The Coast Artillery Museum emphasizes Puget Sound harbor defenses from the late 1800s to the end of World War II. Open weekends in May and daily Memorial Day – Labor Day.

(continued on next page)

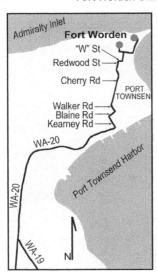

Dirving Directions

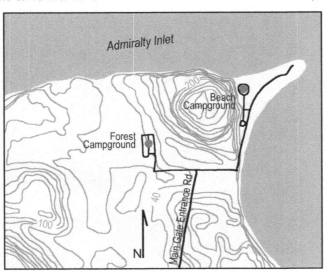

Location

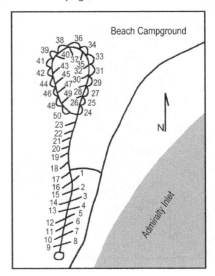

Beach Campground

(Fort Worden continued)

- Commanding Officer's Quarters, completed 1904, provides a glimpse into the life of an officer and his family. Special tours can be arranged. Hours vary.
- Rothschild House offers an accurate reflection of life 100 years ago. Open daily from May 1 – September 30.
- Port Townsend Marine Science Center promotes understanding and protection of the coastal and marine environment. Open April 1 – October 31. Hours vary.

Reservations

Reservations can be made online at *www.parks.state.wa.us* or by calling 888–CAMPOUT (888–226–7688).
See Appendix B for details.

Season

Open all year

Activities

Beachcombing, Bird watching, Ball fields and tennis courts, Bicycle rentals, Boating, Fishing or shellfish harvesting, Hiking, Kayak rentals, Lighthouse, Mountain biking, Scuba diving, Tennis courts.

Cost

$12 primitive site
Peak season: mid May – mid September

$22 – $35 standard site
$30 – $40 partial utility site
$35 – $45 full utility site
Off–peak season
$20 – $30 standard site
$25 – $35 partial utility site
$30 – $40 full utility sites
$10 extra vehicle (all year)
See Appendix C for available discounts.

Limitations

Maximum site length is 75 feet (with limited availability). Refer to Appendix A for camping regulations.

Contact

Phone: 360–344–4412
Web: *www.parks.state.wa.us*

Baked Apples
Ingredients

1 Granny Smith apple
1 teaspoon sugar
1 tablespoon butter
½ teaspoon cinnamon
1 teaspoon chopped walnuts
1 small handful of raisins

Preparation

Cut apple in half and core. Fill apple centers with sugar, cinnamon, and top with butter. Place nuts and raisins on top of butter. Wrap in foil and place, seam side up, in coals for 10 to 15 minutes. Remove foil packet from coals (being careful not to burn yourself), let cool, and enjoy.

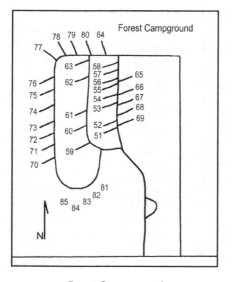

Forest Campground

Boat on Fort Worden Beach

27 Sequim Bay
Washington State Parks

Directions

Start at the intersection of US–101 and WA–20 south of Port Townsend. Travel north on US–101 for 13.6 miles. Turn right into park.

N48°02'21" – W123°01'40"   Elevation – 80 feet

Facilities

63 sites: 48 standard sites, 15 utility sites
Pull–through sites
Flush toilets
Potable water
Hot showers
Garbage service
RV dump station
Accessible toilet, water, utility campsite
Boat launch
Boat dock
Mooring buoys

Features

Sequim Bay State Park borders calm Sequim Bay on the Olympic Peninsula along the Strait of Juan de Fuca. This area is in the "rain–shadow" of the Olympics with an average annual rainfall of 17 inches. There are two loops of forested campsites, some very near the water.

The Olympic Discovery Trail runs through the park. It is a mostly paved trail that will ultimately go from Port Townsend to La Push on the Pacific Coast.

Reservations

Sites may be reserved online at *www.parks.state.wa.us* or by telephone 1–888–CAMPOUT (1–888–226–7688).
See Appendix B for details.

Season

Open all year

Activities

Ball fields, Basketball, Beachcombing, Bird watching, Fishing

or shellfish gathering, Hiking, Horseshoes, Metal detecting, Mountain biking, Personal watercraft access, Scuba diving, Swimming, and Tennis.

Cost

$12 primitive site
Peak season: mid May – mid September
$22 – $35 standard site
$30 – $40 partial utility site
$35 – $45 full utility site
Off–peak season
$20 – $30 standard site
$25 – $35 partial utility site
$30 – $40 full utility site
$10 extra vehicle (all year)
See Appendix C for available discounts.

Limitations

Standard sites can handle vehicles up to 30 feet.
Maximum vehicle length is 45 feet.
See Appendix A for camping regulations.

Contact

Phone: 360–683–4235
Web: *www.parks.state.wa.us*

Sequim Bay Campsite

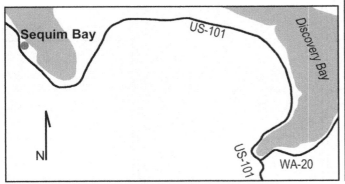

Driving Directions

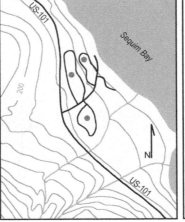

Location

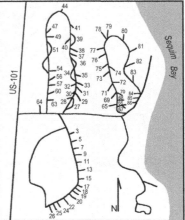

Campground

28 Dungeness Forks
Olympic National Forest

Directions

Start at the intersection of US–101 and WA–20, southwest of Port Townsend. Travel north on US–101 for 13.4 miles to Sequim Bay State Park. Turn left on Louella Road and travel for 0.9 mile. Turn left on Palo Alto Road and travel for 5.8 miles. Bear right at "Y" onto Forest Service Road 2880 and travel for 0.8 mile. Turn right into Dungeness Forks.

N47°58'19" – W123°06'42"   Elevation – 840 feet

Facilities

10 tent–only sites
Vault toilet
No water, bring your own
Pack out garbage
Accessible toilet

Features

Dungeness Fork campground is located at the fork of the Dungeness and Graywolf Rivers in a forested area.

Reservations

None, all campsites are first–come, first–serve.

Season

Open mid May through mid September

Activities

Fishing, Hiking, Hunting.

Cost

$14
$5 extra vehicle
See Appendix C for available discounts.

Limitations

Trailers and RVs are not recommended due to steep, one lane, unpaved road access.
See Appendix A for camping regulations.

Contact

Olympic National Forest – Hood Canal District
295142 Highway 101 S. – PO Box 280
Quilcene, WA 98376
Phone: 360–765–2200

A Fungus Among Us

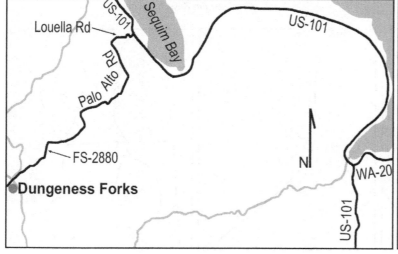

Driving Directions

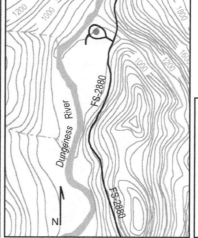

Location

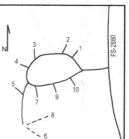

Campground

29 Dungeness Recreation Area
Clallam County

Directions

Start at the intersection of US–101 and WA–20 south of Port Townsend. Travel west on US–101 for 25.4 miles. Turn right on Kitchen–Dick Road and travel 3.2 miles. Turn right on Lotzgessell Road and travel 0.2 mile. Turn left on Voice of America Road to recreation area.

N48°08'17" – W123°11'22"   Elevation – 100 feet

High–Bank Shore View

Facilities

64 standard sites
Flush toilets
Potable water
Hot showers
Garbage service
RV dump station
Accessible toilet, campsites, and showers

Features

Dungeness campground is on a bluff overlooking the Strait of Juan de Fuca in a forested portion of the park adjacent to the Dungeness Spit National Wildlife Refuge. Sites 8, 10, 12, 13, 47, 49, 51, and 53 are nearest the bluff. Sites 17 and 60 are accessible sites.

Reservations

Reserve sites 34 – 66 (except the two host sites) online at *www.clallam.net/Parks/Dungeness.html* or via email at *ParksReservations@co.clallam.wa.us*. Sites 1 – 33 are first–come, first–serve. In November and December all sites are first–come, first–serve.
See Appendix B for details.

Season

Open all year

Activities

Beachcombing, Bird watching, Equestrian trail riding, Hiking.

Campsite

Cost

$25 – standard site
$5 – extra vehicle
Residents of Clallam County receive a $3 discount.

Limitations

No alcohol allowed.
See Appendix A for camping regulations.

Contact

Clallam County
554 Voice of America West
Sequim, WA 98382
Phone: 360–683–5847
Email: ccpdu@olypen.com
Web: *www.clallam.net/Parks/Dungeness.html*

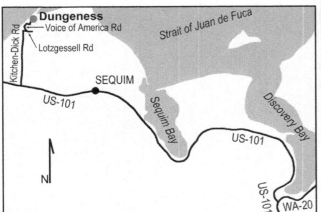

Driving Directions

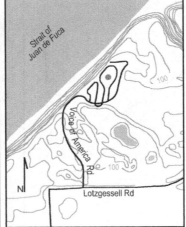

Location

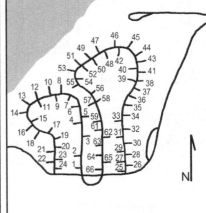

Campground

30 Deer Park
Olympic National Park

Directions

Start at the intersection of US–101 and WA–117 (also called Tumwater Truck Road) in Port Angeles. Travel east on US–101 for 6.9 miles. Turn right on Deer Park Road and travel for 16.5 miles to campground.

N47°56'54" – W123°15'33"   Elevation – 5,400 feet

Olympic Mountains Stretch Into the Distance

Facilities

14 primitive tent sites
Pit toilet
No water, bring your own
Pack out garbage
Animal–proof storage lockers
Accessible toilet

Features

Deer Creek campground is near the tree–line in groves of subalpine firs. The campground provides access to several hiking trails: Obstruction Point, Rain Shadow Loop, Three Forks and Deer Ridge. Dear Park Ranger Station is intermittently staffed during summer and fall.

Reservations

None; all sites are first–come, first–serve.

Season

Open mid June through mid autumn

Activities

Hiking.

Cost

$15
See Appendix C for available discounts.

Limitations

Not suitable for RVs or trailers. Deer Park Road is narrow and steep with occasional turn–offs. The last 9 miles are gravel. Use caution. From late fall until melt–out in late spring, the road is closed at the park boundary (about 9 miles from US–101). Open fires outside of campground fire pits are not permitted above 3,500 feet. When windy, watch for branches falling from trees that died in a 1988 fire.
See Appendix A for camping regulations.

Contact

Olympic National Park
600 East Park Avenue
Port Angeles, WA 98362–6798
Visitor Information: 360–565–3130, TTY: 800–833–6388
Road & Weather Hotline: 360–565–3131

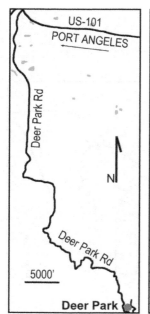

Driving Directions

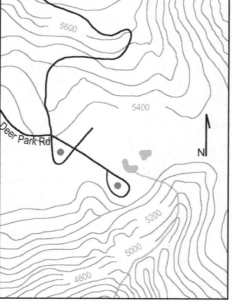

Location

Seed Clock

31 Heart O' the Hills
Olympic National Park

Directions

Start at the intersection of US–101 and Race Street in Port Angeles. Travel south on Race Street for 1.1 miles. Bear right on Hurricane Ridge Road, just after the Visitor Center, and travel for 5.4 miles. After entering the National Park, turn left to Heart O' the Hills.

N48°02'09" – W123°25'39"   Elevation –1807 feet

Facilities

102 standard sites
Pull–through sites
Flush toilets
Potable water
Garbage service
Animal–proof storage lockers
Accessible toilet, water, and campsites (loop A)

Heart O' the Hills Restroom Building

Features

Heart O' the Hills Campground is in old growth forest and the closest campground to Hurricane Ridge. Interpretive programs are given from late June to September. Heart O'the Forest trail, an easy 4 mile hike through pristine old growth forest, starts at loop E in the campground.

Reservations

None, all campsites are first–come, first–serve.

Season

Open all year, may be walk–in only if snowed in

Activities

Hiking.

Cost

$20
See Appendix C for available discounts.

Limitations

Maximum recommended vehicle length is 21 feet, although some sites can handle up to 35 feet.
See Appendix A for camping regulations.

Contact

Olympic National Park
600 East Park Avenue
Port Angeles, WA 98362–6798
Visitor Information: 360–565–3130, TTY: 800–833–6388
Road & Weather Hotline: 360–565–3131

Campsite

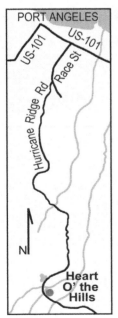

Driving Directions

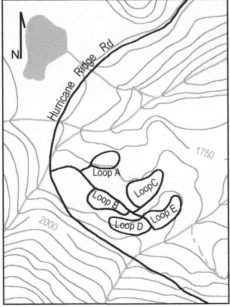

Location

32 Salt Creek Recreation Area
Clallam County

Directions

Start at intersection of US–101 and WA–112 west of Port Angeles. Travel west on WA–112 for 7.2 miles. Turn right onto Camp Hayden Road and travel 3.5 miles to recreation area.

N48°09'59" – W123°42'17"   Elevation – 20 feet

Facilities

90 total sites: 51 standard sites and 39 utility sites
(sites #40 – 49 are tent only)
Flush toilets
Potable water
Hot showers
Garbage service
RV dump station
Accessible toilets, campsites, (one with W/E hook–up)

Features

The campground is on a bluff with panoramic views of the Strait of Juan de Fuca Crescent Bay, and Vancouver Island in Canada. The 196–acre Park includes upland forests, rocky bluffs, rocky tide pools, a sand beach, and access to Salt Creek. The site was used during World War II as a harbor defense military base called Camp Hayden. The remnants of World War II Camp Hayden are preserved on the site – two concrete bunkers which housed 16" cannons and several smaller bunkers. Most of the campsites have a view of the water. The campground has two distinct sections: the first is in a relatively open area, and the second is in a forested area.

Reservations

Reserve sites 16–39, 50–68, and 71–73 (25 and 73 are host sites) online at *www.clallam.net/Parks/SaltCreek.html* or via email at *ParksReservations@co.clallam.wa.us*. The remaining sites are first come, first serve. In November and December all sites are first come, first serve. See Appendix B for details.

Season

Open all year

Activities

Beachcombing, Bird watching, Ball fields, Fishing and shellfish gathering, Hiking, Kayaking, Mountain biking, Scuba diving, Tide pooling at Tongue Point Marine Sanctuary, Volleyball.

Cost

$25 – standard site
$30 – utility site
$5 – extra vehicle
Residents of Clallam County receive a $3 discount.

Limitations

No alcohol allowed.
See Appendix A for camping regulations.

Contact

Clallam County
3506 Camp Hayden Road
Port Angeles, WA 98363
Phone: 360–928–3441
Email: *ccpsc@olypen.com*
Web: *www.clallam.net/Parks/SaltCreek.html*

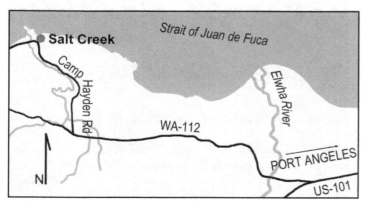

Driving Directions

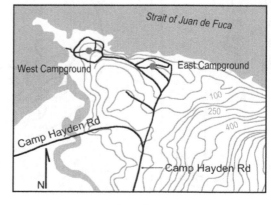

Location

Steamed Clams

Fresh clams keep well for a day in a bag covered with ice. We like to eat local food when possible and clams are a great addition to a seashore meal.

Ingredients

1½ to 2 pounds of live, small steamer clams
1 stalk of celery, chopped
1 clove garlic, mashed
¼ cup onion, chopped
¼ cup tomatoes, chopped
2 tablespoons butter

Preparation

Add ⅓ cup of non–iodized salt to a gallon of water. Soak clams for 30 minutes. (Salt with iodine will kill the clams and you don't want that yet.)

After the soaking, but before cooking, scrub the clams' outer shell with a stiff vegetable brush or scrubbing pad. Let them sit in cold unsalted water for a few minutes to remove sand and dirt. Rinse with fresh water.

Do not over–cook; the clams will get tough and rubbery. Throw away any clams that do not open or have cracked shells.

Put clean clams in a large pan with a tight-fitting lid (add no other liquid). Sprinkle with onions, garlic, celery, tomatoes, and place pat of butter on top. Cover and cook over medium heat until the clams open (about 5 minutes for fresh clams).

The seafood vendor at our local farmer's market taught us to cook clams in a dry pot. As the clams open, they release the nectar (broth) so no other liquid is needed. Remove clams from pan and eat using a fork. Enjoy the buttery broth with hunks of French bread. Servings – 2

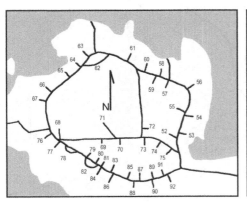

Salt Creek West Campground

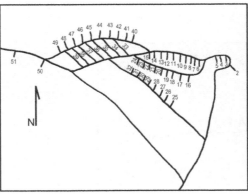

Salt Creek East Campground

Happy Campers

33 Lyre River
Department of Natural Resources

Directions

Start at the intersection of US–101 and WA–112 five miles west of Port Angeles. Travel west on WA–112 for 7.4 miles. Turn right onto East Lyre River Road and travel for 0.5 mile. Turn left into Lyre River.

N48°09'05" – W123°49'58"   Elevation – 50 feet

Lyre River Campsite

Features

The campground is fronted by the Lyre River with several campsites along the river. The campground has a kitchen shelter.

Reservations

None, all campsites are first–come, first–serve.

Season

Open all year, reduced services in winter

Activities

Fishing, Hiking.

Cost

No cost

Limitations

Maximum trailer length is 20 feet.
Maximum stay is 7 days in a 30–day period.
A Washington State Discover Pass is required.
See Appendix A for camping regulations.

Contact

WA Department of Natural Resources, Olympic Region
Phone: 360–374–2800
Web: *www.dnr.wa.gov*

Facilities

11 standard sites
Vault/pit toilets
Potable water
Garbage service
Shelter
Accessible toilet, water, and campsite

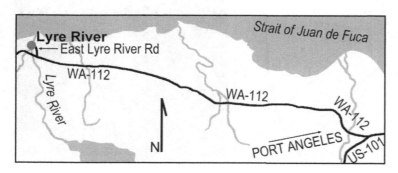

Driving Directions

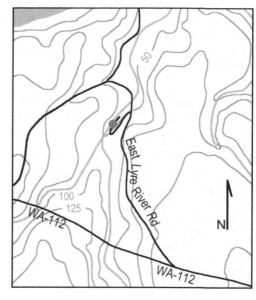

Location

34 Fairholme
Olympic National Park

Directions

Start at the intersection of US–101 and WA–112 west of Port Angeles. Travel south on US–101 for 21.1 miles. Turn right on Camp David Jr. Road and travel for 0.3 mile. Turn right to Fairholme.

N48°04'13" – W123°55'04"   Elevation – 580 feet.

Facilities

88 standard sites
Pull–through sites
Flush toilets
Potable water
Garbage service
Animal–proof storage lockers
RV dump station
Accessible toilet, water and campsite

Features

At the west end of Lake Crescent, Fairholme campground has several lakeside campsites. The glacially carved lake is cold, clear and deep. Several trails surround the Lake Crescent area, but the Spruce Railroad Trail is nearest the campground and allows pets and bicycles.

Reservations

None, all campsites are first–come, first–serve.

Season

Opens early April through late October

Activities

Boating, Fishing, Hiking.

Cost

$20
See Appendix C for available discounts.

Limitations

Maximum recommended RV length is 21 feet.
Pets and bicycles are not permitted on trails, except on the Spruce Railroad Trail.
Alcohol and glass are not permitted on public beaches.
See Appendix A for camping regulations.

Contact

Olympic National Park
600 East Park Avenue
Port Angeles, WA 98362–6798
Visitor Information: 360–565–3130,
TTY: 800–833–6388
Road & Weather Hotline: 360–565–3131

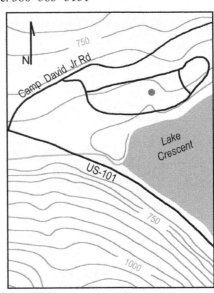

Location

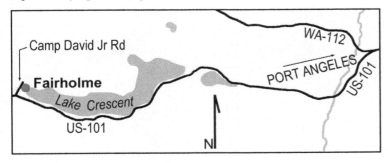

Driving Directions

35 Sol Duc
Olympic National Park

Directions

Start at the intersection of US–101 and WA–112 west of Port Angeles. Travel south on US–101 for 22.8 miles. Turn left onto Sol Duc Hot Springs Road and travel for 12.5 miles to campground.

N47°57'53" – W123°51'21"   Elevation – 1680 feet

Facilities

82 standard sites
Pull–through sites
Flush toilets and potable water in summer
Pit toilets and no water from November to early April
Garbage service
Animal–proof storage lockers
RV dump station
ADA toilet, water, and campsite (on Loop A)

Features

The Sol Duc campground is in a beautiful forest setting among huge old–growth trees. Riverside campsites are along the Sol Duc River. The campground provides access to several day hikes: Sol Duc Falls, Lover's Lane, Ancient Groves, Mink Lake, and Deer Lake. Eagle Ranger Station is intermittently staffed, but ranger programs are offered in summer.

Sol Duc Hot Springs Resort, a private concession near the campground, has cabins, an RV park, swimming pool, hot mineral pools, restaurant, and a shop. It is closed in winter.

Reservations

None, all campsites are first–come, first–serve.

Season

Open all year, but Sol Duc Road may close in winter due to snow or ice.

Activities

Hiking.

Cost

$20
See appendix C for available discounts.

Limitations

Maximum recommended vehicle length is 21 feet, although some sites can handle up to 35 feet.
Pets and bicycles are not permitted on any trails.
See Appendix A for camping regulations.

Contact

Olympic National Park
600 East Park Avenue
Port Angeles, WA 98362–6798
Visitor Information: 360–565–3130, TTY: 800–833–6388
Road & Weather Hotline: 360–565–3131

Sol Duc Campsite

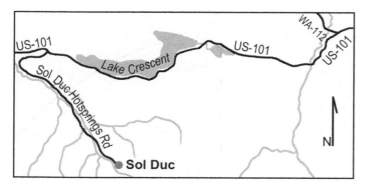

Driving Directions

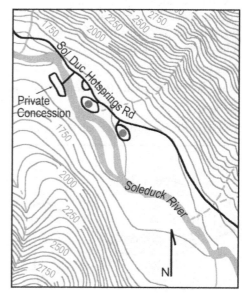

Location

36 Klahowya
Olympic National Forest

Directions

Start at the intersection of US–101 and WA–112 west of Port Angeles. Travel south on US–101 for 30.2 miles. Turn right into Klahowya.

OR

Start at the intersection of US–101 and WA–113 north of Forks. Travel north on US–101 for 8.1 miles. Turn left into Klahowya.

N48°03'57" – W124°06'52"   Elevation – 760 feet

Facilities

56 total sites: 54 standard sites, 2 electric sites
Pull–through sites
Walk–in sites
Flush and vault toilets
Potable water
Garbage service
River–boat ramp
Accessible toilet and campsite

Features

The Klahowya campground is nestled in the rainforest with a lush understory. The Sol Duc River encircles the majority of the campground providing many riverside campsites. Campsites can accommodate large recreation vehicles and vehicles pulling trailers. Interpretive programs are conducted during summer. Pioneer Path is an accessible interpretive trail located in the campground.

Reservations

None, all campsites are first–come, first–serve.

Season

Open May 15 through September 30

Activities

Biking, Fishing, Hiking, River boat/tubing.

Cost

$17
$5 extra vehicle
See Appendix C for available discounts.

Limitations

Recommended maximum vehicle length is 30 feet, however, some sites can accommodate 40 foot vehicles.
Maximum capacity is 5 persons per campsite.
See Appendix A for camping regulations.

Contact

Olympic National Forest – Pacific District North
437 Tillicum Lane
Forks , WA 98331
Phone: 360–374–6522, TDD: 360–374–6522

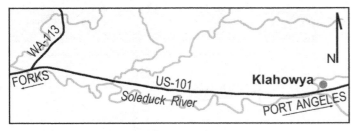

Driving Directions

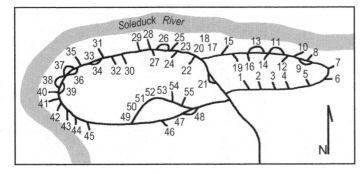

Campground

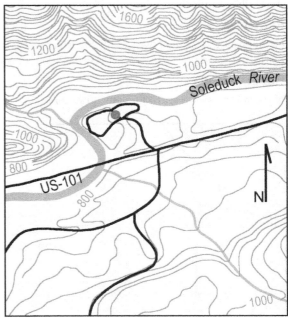

Location

37 Bear Creek
Department of Natural Resources

Directions

Start at the intersection of US–101 and WA–112 five miles west of Port Angeles. Travel south on US–101 for 36.3 miles. Turn left into Bear Creek.

OR

Start at the intersection of US–101 and WA–113 near Sappho. Travel north on US–101 for 2.0 miles. Turn right into Bear Creek.

N48°03'57" W124°14'26"   Elevation – 560 feet

Bear Creek Campsite

Facilities

16 standard sites
Pull–through sites
Vault/pit toilets
No water, bring your own
Pack out garbage
Accessible campsites

Features

Campground is fronted by the Sol Duc River with a viewing platform looking over the river. There are two accessible sites.

Reservations

None, all campsites are first–come, first–serve.

Season

Open all year

Activities

Bird watching, Fishing, Hiking.

Cost

No cost

Limitations

Maximum stay is 7 days in a 30–day period.
A Washington State Discover Pass is required.
See Appendix A for camping regulations.

Contact

WA Department of Natural Resources, Olympic Region
Phone: 360–374–2800
Web: *www.dnr.wa.gov*

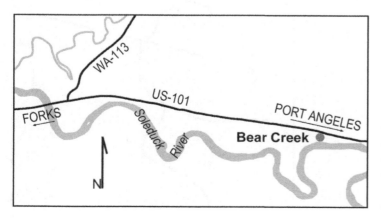

Driving Directions

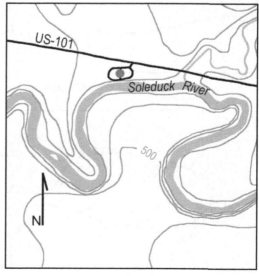

Location

38 Ozette
Olympic National Park

Directions

Start at the intersection of WA–113 and WA–112 south of Clallam Bay. Travel west on WA–112 for 10.6 miles. Turn left on Hoko–Ozette Road and travel for 21.4 miles. Turn left to Ozette.

N48°09'09" – W124°40'04"   Elevation – 40 feet

Lake Ozette

Facilities

15 standard sties
Vault/pit toilets
No water, bring your own
Animal–proof storage lockers
Garbage service
Accessible toilet (near the Ranger Station 400 feet from campground), water, and campsite.

Features

The campground is situated on the northern edge of Lake Ozette, Some sites overlook the lake. Ozette Ranger Station usually opens daily from May through September. Off season hours are intermittent.

Reservations

None, all campsites are first–come, first–serve.

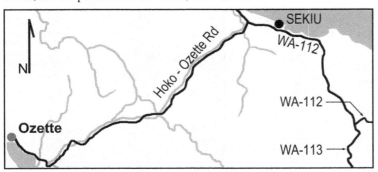

Driving Directions

Season

Open all year

Activities

Boat launch, Boating, Fishing, Hiking.

Cost

$20
See Appendix C for available discounts.

Limitations

High water covers most of the campground in winter.
Maximum recommended vehicle length is 21 feet.
Pets are not permitted on park trails and must be on leash at all times.
See Appendix A for camping regulations.

Contact

Olympic National Park
600 East Park Avenue
Port Angeles, WA 98362–6798
Visitor Information: 360–565–3130, TTY: 800–833–6388
Road & Weather Hotline: 360–565–3131

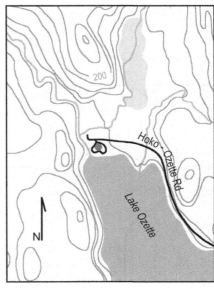

Location

39 Klahanie
Olympic National Forest

Directions

Start at the intersection of US–101 and WA–110 near Forks. Travel north on US–101 for 0.2 mile. Turn right onto Sitkum Sol Duc Road (Forest Service Road 29) and travel for 5.4 miles. Turn right to Klahanie.

N47°57'48" – W124°18'20"   Elevation – 360 feet

Facilities

20 standard sites
Vault toilets
No water, bring your own
Pack out garbage

Features

Klahanie campground is located on the South Fork Calawah River in a rainforest. The rainforest has old growth spruce over 8 feet in diameter, hanging mosses and an understory of wildflowers, ferns, mosses and shrubs. A half mile "adventure" trail is open to bicycles and a quarter mile "discovery" loop trail provides fishing access and is open to foot traffic.

Reservations

None, all campsites are first–come, first–serve.

Season

Open mid May 15 through late September

Activities

Biking, Fishing, Hiking.

Cost

$10
See Appendix C for available discounts.

Limitations

Maximum vehicle length is 21 feet.
Closely supervise children around the river. The river bank has eroded and may collapse. Stay three feet back from the edge.
See Appendix A for camping regulations.

Contact

Olympic National Forest – Pacific District North
437 Tillicum Lane
Forks, WA 98331
Phone: 360–374–6522, TDD: 360–374–6522

Klahanie Campsite

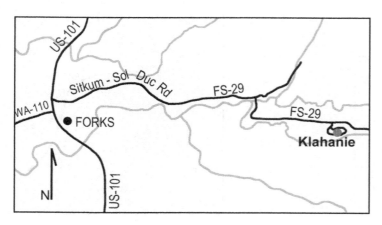

Driving Directions

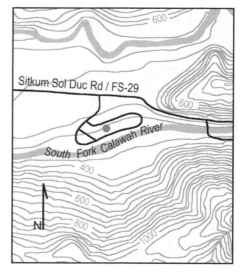

Location

40 Mora
Olympic National Park

Directions

Start at the intersection of US–101 and WA–110 in Forks. Travel west on WA–110 for 7.8 miles. Turn right onto Mora Road and travel for 3.4 miles. Turn left into campground.

N47°55'05" – W124°36'27"   Elevation – 32 feet

Foaming Surf Near Mora

Facilities

94 standard sites
Pull–through sites
Walk–in site
Flush toilets
Potable water
Garbage service
RV dump station
Accessible toilet, water, and campsites (Loop B)
Boat launch

Features

Mora campground lies in coastal forest two miles from Rialto Beach and the Pacific Ocean. Some riverside campsites on Loops D and E overlook the Quillayute River. The Mora Ranger Station is open intermittently in summer.

Reservations

None, all campsites are first–come, first–serve.

Season

Open all year

Activities

Beach combing, Bird watching, Boating, Fishing or shellfish harvesting, Hiking.

Cost

$20
See Appendix C for available discounts.

Limitations

Maximum recommended vehicle length is 21 feet, although some sites can handle up to 35 feet.

Pets are not allowed on the wilderness coast beaches or on any park trails.

Pets are allowed on Rialto Beach, to Ellen Creek only, and must be leashed at all times.

The Dickey River Boat Ramp (west of the campground) is not accessible at low tide.

See Appendix A for camping regulations.

Contact

Olympic National Park
600 East Park Avenue
Port Angeles, WA 98362–6798
Visitor Information: 360–565–3130, TTY: 800–833–6388
Road & Weather Hotline: 360–565–3131

Mora Campsite

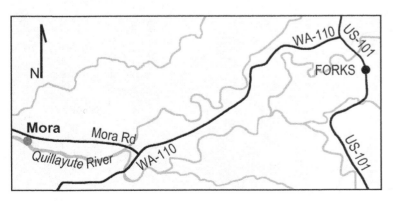

Driving Directions

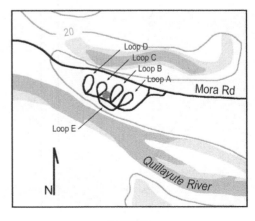

Location

41 Bogachiel
Washington State Parks

Directions

Start at the intersection of US–101 and WA–110 near Forks. Travel south on US–101 for 7.3 miles. Turn right into park.

N47°53'38" – W124°21'44"   Elevation – 200 feet

Bogachiel Restrooms and Kitchen

Facilities

35 sites: 26 standard sites, 6 partial–utility sites
Pull–through sites
Flush toilets
Potable water
Hot showers
Garbage service
RV dump station
Accessible toilet, drinking water, and campsite

Features

Bogachiel State Park lies along the banks of the Bogachiel River. Thickly forested, the park is on the tip of the Hoh Rainforest, where rainfall (140–160 inches per year) creates lush vegetation. Some campsites are on the river and a covered kitchen is available.

Reservations

None, all campsites are first–come, first–serve.

Season

Open all year

Activities

Bird watching, Fishing, Hiking.

Cost

$12 primitive site
Peak season: mid May – mid September
$22 – $35 standard site
$30 – $40 partial utility site
$35 – $45 full utility site
Off–peak season
$20 – $30 standard site
$25 – $35 partial utility site
$30 – $40 full utility site
$10 extra vehicle (all year)
See Appendix C for available discounts.

Limitations

Maximum site length is 40 feet.
See Appendix A for camping regulations.

Contact

Phone: 360–374–6356
Web: *www.parks.state.wa.us*

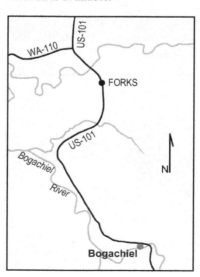

Driving Directions

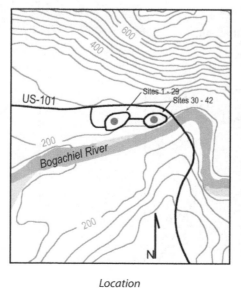

Location

Bee Is For Bogachiel

42 Minnie Peterson
Department of Natural Resources

Directions

Start at the intersection of US–101 and WA–110 near Forks. Travel south on US–101 for 14.9 miles. Turn left onto Upper Hoh Road and travel for 4.8 miles. Turn left to Minnie Peterson.

N47°49'07" – W124°10'25"   Elevation – 280 feet

Minnie Peterson Campsite

Facilities

9 standard sites
Vault/pit toilet
No water, bring your own
Pack out garbage
Accessible toilet and campsite

Features

The Hoh River is across the Upper Hoh Road from the campground.

Reservations

None, all campsites are first–come, first–serve.

Season

Open all year

Activities

Fishing, Hiking.

Cost

No cost

Limitations

Maximum stay is 7 days in a 30–day period.
A Washington State Discover Pass is required.
See Appendix A for camping regulations.

Contact

WA Department of Natural Resources, Olympic Region
Phone: 360–374–2800
Web: *www.dnr.wa.gov*

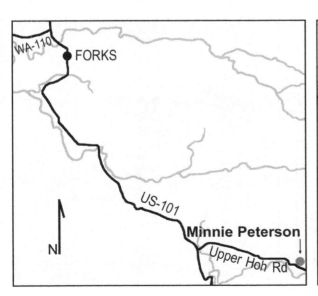

Driving Directions

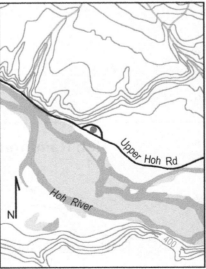

Location

Minnie Peterson Restroom

43 Hoh Rain Forest
Olympic National Park

Directions

Start at the intersection of US–101 and WA–110 near Forks. Travel south on US–101 for 14.9 miles. Turn left onto Upper Hoh Road and travel for 18.1 miles. Turn right into campground.

N47°51'28" – W123°56'08"   Elevation – 600 feet

Facilities

Hoh River Campsite

88 standard sites
Pull–through sites
Flush toilets
Potable water
Garbage service
Animal–proof storage lockers
RV dump station
Accessible toilet, water, and campsites (Loop A)

Features

The Hoh Rain Forest campground is located in old growth, temperate rainforest with several riverside campsites along the Hoh River. The Visitor Center is open daily in summer, and Friday through Sunday the rest of year. A boat launch is located east of the Park entrance station.

Reservations

None, all campsites are first–come, first–serve.

Season

Open all year

Activities

Fishing, Hiking.

Cost

$20
See appendix C for available discounts.

Limitations

Do not approach elk! They can hurt you.
Swimming and boating on the Hoh River can be extremely dangerous and are not recommended.
Maximum recommended vehicle length is 21 feet.

No pets on trails. In other areas, pets must be on a leash at all times.
See appendix A for camping regulations.

Contact

Olympic National Park
600 East Park Avenue
Port Angeles, WA 98362–6798
Visitor Information: 360–565–3130, TTY: 800–833–6388
Road & Weather Hotline: 360–565–3131

Hoh Rain Forest Lushness

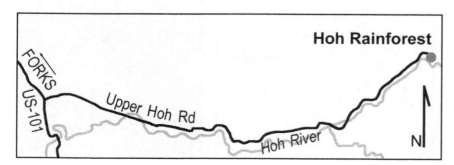

Driving Directions

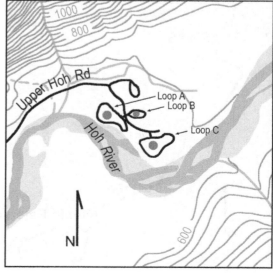

Location

44 Hoh–Oxbow
Department of Natural Resources

Directions
Start at the intersection of US–101 and WA–110 near Forks. Travel south on US–101 for 15.7 miles. Turn left into Hoh–Oxbow.

N47°48'40" – W124°14'58"   Elevation – 200 feet

Hoh–Oxbow Campsite

Facilities
8 standard sites
Vault/pit toilet
No water, bring your own
Pack out garbage
Accessible toilet and campsite
Boat launch (hand launch only)

Features
Hoh–Oxbow campground is along the Hoh River.

Reservations
None, all campsites are first–come, first–serve.

Season
Open all year

Activities
Fishing, Hiking.

Cost
No cost

Limitations
Maximum site length is 21 feet.
Maximum stay is 7 days in a 30–day period.
A Washington State Discover Pass is required.
See Appendix A for camping regulations.

Contact
WA Department of Natural Resources, Olympic Region
Phone: 360–374–2800
Web: *www.dnr.wa.gov*

Hoh River View From Campground

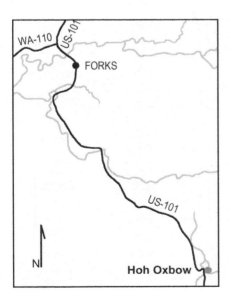

Driving Directions

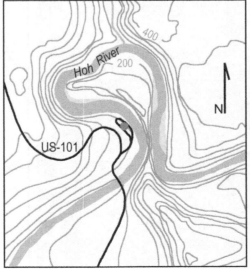

Location

Puff–Ball Mushrooms

45 Cottonwood
Department of Natural Resources

Directions

Start at the intersection of US–101 and WA–110 in Forks. Travel south on US–101 for 15.2 miles. Turn right onto Oil City Road and travel for 2.4 miles. Turn left onto H–4060 Road (gravel) and travel for 0.9 mile to Cottonwood.

N47°46'42" W124°17'33"   Elevation – 80 feet

Facilities

10 standard sites
Vault/pit toilet
No water, bring your own
Pack out garbage
Accessible toilet and campsite
Boat launch (hand launch only)

Features

Cottonwood campground is in a wooded setting along the Hoh River.

Reservations

None, all campsites are first–come, first–serve.

Season

Open all year

Activities

Fishing, Hiking.

Cost

None

Limitations

Maximum stay is 7 days in a 30–day period.
A Washington State Discover Pass is required.

Cottonwood Campsite

See Appendix A for camping regulations.

Contact

WA Department of Natural Resources, Olympic Region
Phone: 360–374–2800
Web: *www.dnr.wa.gov*

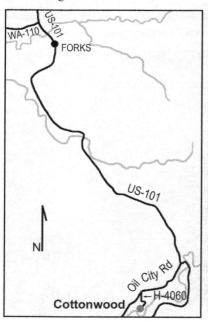

Driving Directions

Cottonwood Restroom

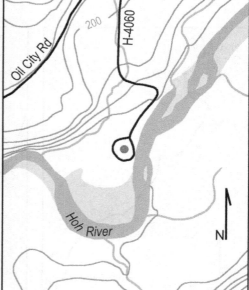

Location

46 Coppermine Bottom
Department of Natural Resources

Directions

Start at the intersection of US–101 and WA–110 in Forks. Travel south on US–101 for 44.8 miles. Turn left onto Clearwater Road (also called the Hoh Mainline Road) and travel for 12.6 miles. Turn right onto C–1010 Road (gravel one lane with turn–outs) and travel for 1.5 miles. Turn left into Coppermine Bottom.

N47°39'22" – W124°11'49"   Elevation – 240 feet

Facilities

11 standard sites
Vault/pit toilets
No water, bring your own
Pack out garbage
Shelter
Accessible toilet and campsite
Boat launch (hand launch only)

Features

The campground is along the Clearwater River and has is a kitchen shelter.

Reservations

None, all campsites are first–come, first–serve.

Season

Open all year

Activities

Fishing, Hiking.

Cost

No cost

Limitations

Maximum stay is 7 days in a 30–day period.
A Washington State Discover Pass is required.
See Appendix A for camping regulations.

Contact

WA Department of Natural Resources, Olympic Region
Phone: 360–374–2800
Web: *www.dnr.wa.gov*

Cherry Pies
Ingredients

1 package of refrigerator biscuits
1 (10 ounce) can of cherry pie filling
1 stick butter
½ tablespoon cinnamon
½ tablespoon sugar

Preparation

Press individual biscuit dough pieces with fingers until about 5 inches in diameter. Put a large spoonful of cherry pie filling on one side of the biscuit. Fold the dough over the filling and pinch the edges together to seal. Fry the pie in a skillet with melted butter over medium heat until it is golden brown and crispy. Place on paper towels and dust with cinnamon and sugar. Cool before eating.

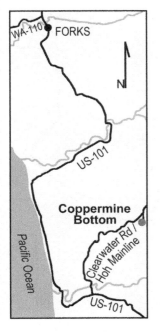

Driving Directions

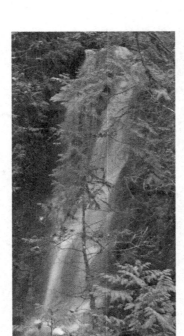

Roadside Waterfall

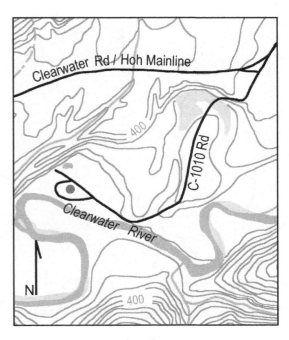

Location

47 Upper Clearwater
Department of Natural Resources

Directions

Start at the intersection of US–101 and WA–110 near Forks. Travel south on US–101 for 44.8 miles. Turn left onto Clearwater Road (also called Hoh Mainline Road) and travel for 12.9 miles. Turn right onto C–3000 Road (one lane gravel with turnouts) and travel 3.2 miles. Turn right into Upper Clearwater.

N47°40'44" W124°07'03"   Elevation – 360 feet

Facilities

6 standard sites
Vault/pit toilet
No water, bring your own
Pack out garbage
Boat launch (hand launch only)
Shelter

Features

Campground is fronted by the Clearwater River.

Reservations

None, all campsites are first–come, first–serve.

Season

Open all year

Activities

Fishing, Hiking.

Cost

No cost

Tenting Tonight

Limitations

Maximum stay is 7 days in a 30–day period.
A Washington State Discover Pass is required.
See Appendix A for camping regulations.

Contact

WA Department of Natural Resources, Olympic Region
Phone: 360–374–2800
Web: *www.dnr.wa.gov*

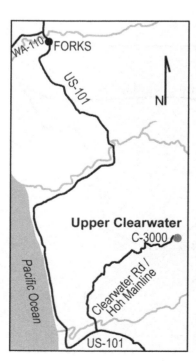

Driving Directions

So Many Flowers – So Little Time

Location

48 Kalaloch
Olympic National Park

Directions

Start at the intersection of US–101 and WA–110 near Forks. Travel south on US–101 for 34.8 miles. Turn right into Kalaloch.

OR

Start at the intersection of US–101 and WA–109 in Hoquiam. Travel north on US–101 for 69.8 miles. Turn left into Kalaloch.

N47°36'43" – W124°22'31"   Elevation – 160 feet

Facilities

170 standard sites
Flush toilets
Potable water
Garbage service
Animal–proof storage lockers
RV dump station
Accessible toilet, water, and campsites

Features

Kalaloch campground is one of the most visited areas of Olympic National Park. Campsites on the bluff overlooking the Pacific Ocean have incredible sunset views. The ranger station is open daily in summer and campfire programs are offered in summer only. Kalaloch Lodge is near the campground. It is open year round and offers cabins, rooms, restaurant, coffee shop, dining room, camp store, gasoline, and a group campsite.

Reservations

Reservations are recommended for "Peak Season" (between mid June through early September) Reserve sites at *www.recreation.gov* or by phone at 1–877–444–6777.

Reservations must be made 3 days ahead of arrival and can be made up to 6 months in advance. See Appendix B for details.

Season

Open all year

Activities

Beachcombing, Bird watching, Fishing and shellfish harvesting, Hiking.

Cost

$22
See Appendix C for available discounts.

Limitations

Maximum recommended vehicle length is 21 feet, although some sites can handle up to 35 feet.
Camping limit is 14 days in the park per year. During the peak season, the camping limit is 7 days.
Pets are allowed on Kalaloch area beaches, but they must be leashed at all times.
See Appendix A for camping regulations.

Contact

Olympic National Park
600 East Park Avenue
Port Angeles, WA 98362–6798
Visitor Information: 360–565–3130, TTY: 800–833–6388
Road & Weather Hotline: 360–565–3131

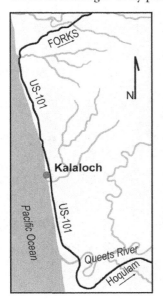

Driving Directions

Location

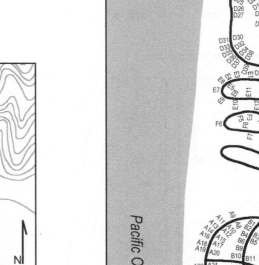

Campground

49 South Beach
Olympic National Park

Directions

Start at the intersection of US–101 and WA–110 in Forks. Travel south on US–101 for 38.5 miles. Turn right into South Beach.

OR

Start at the intersection of US–101 and WA–109 in Hoquiam. Travel north on US 101 for 66.6 miles. Turn left into South Beach.

N47°34'04" – W124°21'41"   Elevation – 20 feet

Facilities

50 standard sites
Flush toilets
No potable water, bring your own
Garbage service
Animal–proof storage lockers

Features

South Beach campground is an open field with little shade or privacy, however, it offers a panoramic view of the Pacific Ocean and a short walk to the beach. Kalaloch Ranger Station opens daily in summer only. Kalaloch Lodge is near the campground. It is open year round and offers cabins, rooms, restaurant, coffee shop, dining room, camp store, gasoline, and a group campsite.

Reservations

None, all campsites are first–come, first–serve.

Season

Open from late May to September

Activities

Beach combing, Bird watching, Hiking.

Cost

$15
See Appendix C for available discounts.

Limitations

Maximum recommended vehicle length is 21 feet, although some sites can handle up to 35 feet.
Pets are allowed on Kalaloch area beaches, but they must be leashed at all times.
See Appendix A for camping regulations.

Contact

Olympic National Park
600 East Park Avenue
Port Angeles, WA 98362–6798
Visitor Information: 360–565–3130, TTY: 800–833–6388
Road & Weather Hotline: 360–565–3131

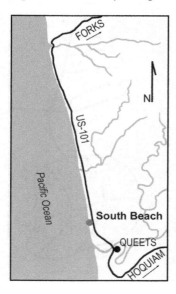

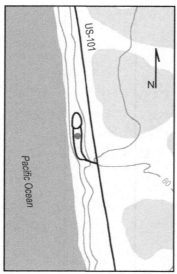

Driving Directions

Location

Shore Plants

50 Queets
Olympic National Park

Directions

Start at the intersection of US–101 and WA–110 in Forks. Travel south on US–101 for 55.4 miles. Turn left onto West

Boundary (becomes Forest Service Road 21) and travel for 8.3 miles. Turn left on Forest Service Road 2180–010/Q2100 and travel for 2.7 miles. Turn right onto Queets River Road and travel for 2.6 miles to campground.

OR

Start at the intersection of US–101 and WA–109 in Hoquiam. Travel north on US–101 for 49.8 miles. Turn right onto West Boundary (becomes Forest Service Road 21) and travel for 8.3 miles. Turn left on Forest Service Road 2180–010/Q2100 and travel for 2.7 miles. Turn right onto Queets River Road and travel for 2.6 miles to campground.

N47°37'39" – W124°01'06"   Elevation – 280 feet

Facilities

20 primitive sites
Pit toilets
No potable water, bring your own
Animal–proof storage lockers
Garbage containers when fully open, pack out otherwise
Accessible toilet
Boat launch

Features

Queets campground lies in a rain forest valley and offers some riverside campsites. The Queets River is fed from glaciers and melting snow on Mount Olympus.

Reservations

None, all campsites are first–come, first–serve.

Season

Open all year, with reduced service in winter.

Activities

Fishing, Hiking.

Cost

$15
See Appendix C for available discounts.

Limitations

Queets River Road is a narrow, gravel road and not recommended for RVs and trailers.
Use of boat launch depends on river level and erosion damage.
Queets Ranger Station is not staffed. There is no phone.
Pets must be leashed and are not allowed on trails.
See Appendix A for camping regulations.

Contact

Olympic National Park
600 East Park Avenue
Port Angeles, WA 98362–6798
Visitor Information: 360–565–3130, TTY: 800–833–6388
Road & Weather Hotline: 360–565–3131

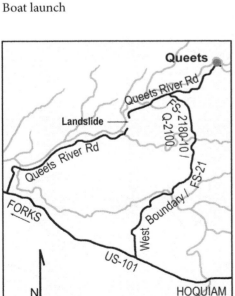

Driving Directions

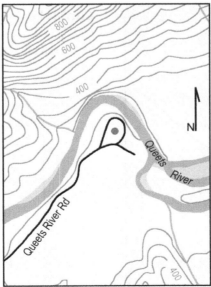

Location

Olympic Peninsula Stream

51 Willaby
Olympic National Forest

Directions

Start at the intersection of US–101 and WA–109 in Hoquiam. Travel north on US–101 for 37.8 miles. Turn right onto South Shore Road and travel for 1.6 miles. Turn Left into Willaby.

OR

Start at the intersection of US–101 and WA–110 in Forks. Travel south on US 101 for 66.9 miles. Turn left onto South Shore Road and travel for 1.6 miles. Turn left into Willaby.

N47°27'45" – W123°51'28"   Elevation – 200 feet

Facilities

21 sites: 19 standard sites, 2 walk–in sites
Flush toilets
Potable water
Garbage service
Shelter
Accessible toilet, water, and campsite
Boat launch

Features

Willaby campground is located on the south shore of Quinault Lake in the rainforest with dense shade. The forest floor has lush rainforest plants: moss, ferns, false lily–of–the–valley and oxalis. Some sites are in wooded areas, others are not. While only some sites are on the lake, most have a view of the lake. Hiking trails and many waterfalls are within walking distance of the campground.

Reservations

Reserve online at *www.recreation.gov* or call 1–877–444–6777 (5 am to 9 pm Pacific time), 518–885–3639, or TDD 1–877–833–6777.
See Appendix B for details.

Season

Open all year

Activities

Boating, Fishing, Hiking, Sailing, Swimming.

Willaby Campsite

Cost

$25
$7 extra vehicle
See appendix C for available discounts.

Limitations

Maximum vehicle length is 16 feet.
Lake Quinault is part of the Quinault Indian Nation. As such, a Tribal Fishing Permit and Boat Decal are required. Both may be purchased at local merchants.
See Appendix A for camping regulations.

Contact

Olympic National Forest – Pacific District South
353 South Shore Road – PO Box 9
Quinault, WA 98575
Phone: 360–288–2525, TDD: 360–288–2525

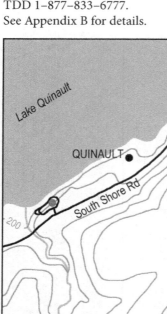

Driving Directions   *Location*

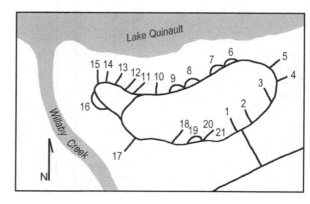

Campground

52 Falls Creek
Olympic National Forest

Directions

Start at the intersection of US–101 and WA–109 in Hoquiam. Travel north on US–101 for 37.8 miles. Turn right onto South Shore Road and travel for 2.4 miles. Turn Left to Falls Creek.

OR

Start at the intersection of US–101 and WA–110 in Forks. Travel south on US–101 for 66.9 miles. Turn left onto South Shore Road and travel for 2.4 miles. Turn left to Falls Creek.

N47°28'11" – W123°50'47"   Elevation – 200 feet

Facilities

31 sites: 21 standard sites, 10 walk–in tent sites
5 overflow RV sites
Flush toilets
Potable water
Garbage service
Shelter
Accessible toilet, water, and campsite
Boat launch

Features

On the south shore of Quinault Lake, Falls Creek campground is located along Falls Creek in temperate rain forest and lush understory. Several campsites are along the creek, most have a view of the lake. The campground provides access to the Quinault National Recreation Trail System. Lake Quinault

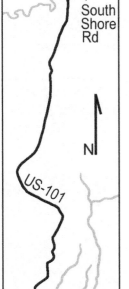

Lodge is near the campground. It has lodging, swimming pool, and a restaurant. The main lodge, with dining and retail, closes in winter. Other area resorts have cabins, motel units, restaurants and store.

Reservations

Reserve online at *www.recreation.gov* or call 1–877–444–6777 (5 am to 9 pm Pacific time), 518–885–3639, or TDD 1–877–833–6777. See Appendix B for details.

Season

Generally open May through September, however, call Pacific Ranger District, Quinault for possible closure dates.

Activities

Boating, Fishing, Hiking, Sailing, Swimming.

Cost

$25 – drive–in sites
$20 – walk–in sites
$7 extra vehicle
See Appendix C for available discounts.

Limitations

Maximum vehicle length is 16 feet.
Lake Quinault is part of the Quinault Indian Nation. As such, a Tribal Fishing Permit and Boat Decal are required. They may be purchased at local merchants.
See Appendix A for camping regulations.

Contact

Olympic National Forest – Pacific District South
353 South Shore Road – PO Box 9
Quinault, WA 98575
Phone: 360–288–2525, TDD: 360–288–2525

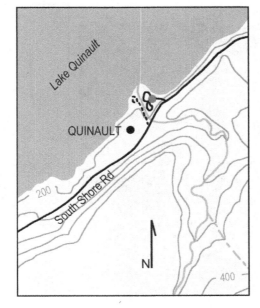

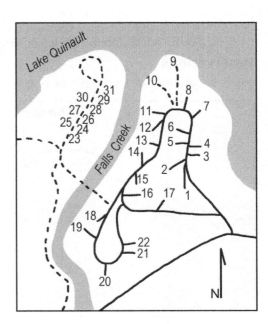

Driving Directions   *Location*   *Campground*

53 North Fork
Olympic National Park

Directions

Start at the intersection of US–101 and WA–110 in Forks. Travel south on US–101 for 63.3 miles. Turn left onto North Shore Road and travel for 18 miles to campground.

OR

Start at the intersection of US–101 and WA–109 in Hoquiam. Travel north on US–101 for 40.9 miles. Turn right onto North Shore Road and travel for 18 miles to campground.

N47°34'09" – W123°39'21"   Elevation – 520 feet

Looking Across Lake Quinault Toward North Fork

Facilities

9 primitive sites
Pit toilet at trailhead
No water, bring your own
Animal–proof storage lockers
Garbage service when fully open, pack out otherwise
Accessible toilet

Features

North Fork campground is located along the shores of the North Fork Quinault River in the Quinault Rain Forest. Trails from the North Fork trailheads offer long hikes.

Reservations

None, all campsites are first–come, first–serve.

Season

Normally open all year, may close in winter contingent on weather

Activities

Hiking.

Cost

$15
See Appendix C for available discounts.

Limitations

North Shore Road is a narrow, gravel road and not suitable for trailers or RVs.
Elk can be aggressive. Do not approach.
Wilderness permits, required for all overnight backpacking, are available at the Olympic National Forest and Park Information Station on the south shore of Lake Quinault, or in Port Angeles or Forks.
See Appendix A for camping regulations.

Contact

Olympic National Park
600 East Park Avenue
Port Angeles, WA 98362–6798
Visitor Information: 360–565–3130, TTY: 800–833–6388
Road & Weather Hotline: 360–565–3131

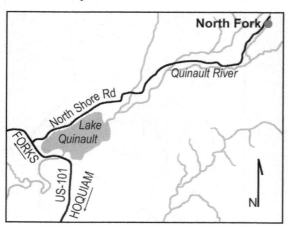

Driving Directions

You Can See the Forest

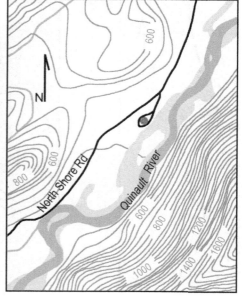

Location

54 Graves Creek
Olympic National Park

Directions

Start at the intersection of US–101 and WA–110 near Forks. Travel south on US–101 for 66.9 miles. At Quinault Lake turn left onto South Shore Road (becomes Graves Creek Road) and travel for 23.0 miles to campground.

OR

Start at the intersection of US–101 and WA–109 in Hoquiam. Travel north on US–101 for 37.0 miles. At Quinault Lake, turn right on South Shore Road (becomes Graves Creek Road) and travel for 23.0 miles to campground.

N47°34'24" – W123°34'36"   Elevation – 540 feet.

Quinault River at Graves Creek

Facilities

30 standard sites
Vault/pit toilets
Potable water in summer only
Garbage service in summer. Pack out garbage in winter
Animal–proof storage locker
Accessible toilet

Features

Located in the Quinault Rain Forest, the campground lies along Graves Creek. Trails from the Graves Creek offer long hikes to Anderson Pass and Sundown Pass.

Reservations

None, all campsites are first–come, first–serve.

Season

Open all year, but pit toilet and no water in off–season.

Activities

Hiking.

Cost

$20
See Appendix C for available discounts.

Limitations

Graves Creek Road becomes a narrow gravel road not suitable for trailers or large RVs.
Maximum recommended vehicle length is 21 feet.
Do not approach elk in the area. They can be aggressive.
Wilderness permits are required for all overnight backpacking.
See Appendix A for camping regulations.

Contact

Olympic National Park
600 East Park Avenue
Port Angeles, WA 98362–6798
Visitor Information: 360–565–3130, TTY: 800–833–6388
Road & Weather Hotline: 360–565–3131

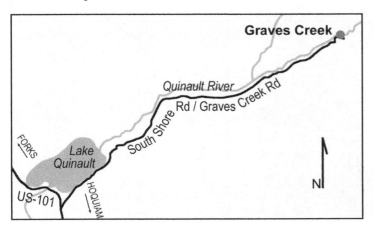

Driving Directions

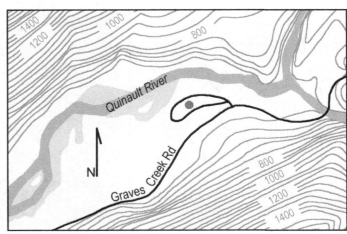

Location

55 Campbell Tree Grove
Olympic National Forest

Directions

Start at the intersection of US–101 and WA–109 in Hoquiam. Travel north on US–101 for 24.8 miles. Turn right onto Donkey Creek Road (Forest Service Road 22) and travel for 8.2 miles. Turn left on Forest Service Road 2204 and travel for 13.8 miles. (At junction with Forest Service Road 2208, bear left to remain on Forest Service Road 2204.) Turn right to Campbell Tree Grove.

OR

Start at the intersection of US–101 and South Shore Road at Quinault Lake. Travel south on US–101 for 13 miles. Turn left onto Donkey Creek Road (Forest Service Road 22) and travel for 8.2 miles. Turn left on Forest Service Road 2204 and travel for 13.8 miles. (At the junction with Forest Service Road 2208, bear left to remain on Forest Service Road 2204.) Turn right to Campbell Tree Grove.

N47°28'48" – W123°41'13"   Elevation – 1060 feet

Facilities

21 total sites: 11 standard sites, 10 walk–in sites
Vault toilets
No potable water
Garbage service
Accessible toilet

Features

Campbell Tree Grove campground is near the West Fork Humptulips River in temperate rain forest. Towering old growth trees provide dense shade for this beautiful setting. The forest floor is covered with lush rain forest plants. The campground has limited facilities. Access to the West Fork Humptulips Trail is adjacent to the campground.

Reservations

None, all campsites are first–come, first–serve.

Season

Open late May through early September

Activities

Fishing, Hiking.

Cost

No cost

Limitations

Maximum vehicle length is 16 feet.
A Northwest Forest Pass, Golden Age/Access Pass, or Interagency Pass is required on all vehicles parked at trailheads. Day and Annual Passes are available at Forest Service offices and vendors, but not available at trailheads.
See Appendix A for camping regulations.

Contact

Olympic National Forest – Pacific District South
353 South Shore Road – PO Box 9
Quinault, WA 98575
Phone: 360–288–2525, TDD: 360–288–2525

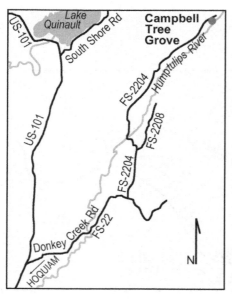

Driving Directions

Moss

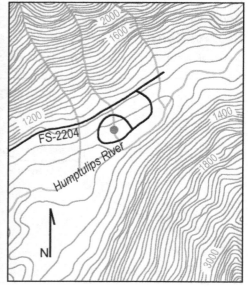

Location

56 Coho
Olympic National Forest

Directions

Start one mile west of Montesano on US–12 and take the Wynoochee Valley Road Exit. Travel for 33.8 miles on the Wynoochee Valley Road (becomes Forest Service Road 22). After 33.5 miles, turn left at a major intersection to remain on Forest Service Road 22 and travel another 0.3 mile. Turn right onto Forest Service Road 2294 and travel 1.4 miles to Coho.

OR

Start at the intersection of US–101 and WA–102 (Dayton–Airport Road) north of Shelton. Travel west on WA–102 for 5 miles. Turn right onto Dayton–Matlock Road and travel for 9.4 miles to the town of Matlock. Continue straight at the junction on Matlock–Deckerville Road (becomes Boundary Road) and travel for 8.8 miles. Turn right onto Cougar–Smith Road and travel for 5.5 miles to Forest Service Road 22. Turn right on Forest Service Road 22 and travel for 15 miles to a major intersection. Turn left at the intersection to remain on Forest Service Road 22 and travel another 0.3 mile. Turn right on Forest Service Road 2294 and travel 1.4 miles to Coho.

N47°23'25" – W123°36'18"   Elevation – 820 feet

Facilities

54 campsites: 46 standard sites, 8 walk–in sites
Flush toilets
Potable water
Garbage service
RV dump station on FS Rd 2294
Accessible toilets
Boat launch

Features

Coho Campground is located on the west shore of Wynoochee Lake. Access to the Working Forest Interpretive Trail and Wynoochee Lake Shore Trail are in the campground. Tacoma Power has a day–use area with picnicking and swimming facilities next to the campground. There is a public telephone at the Tacoma Power day–use entrance.

Reservations

Reserve online at *www.recreation.gov* or call 1–877–444–6777 (5 am to 9 pm Pacific time), 518–885–3639, or TDD 1–877–833–6777. See Appendix B for details.

Season

Open from May to late September

Activities

Boating, Fishing, Hiking, Hunting, Swimming.

Cost

$20 – for drive–in sites
$16 – for walk–in sites
$5.00 extra vehicle
See Appendix C for available discounts.

Limitations

Maximum vehicle length is 36 feet.
There are no commercial services. Motorists should have enough fuel for the return trip. The closest services are in Montesano – 35 miles away.
Use extreme caution on Cougar–Smith Road and yield to logging truck traffic.
See Appendix A for camping regulations.

Contact

Olympic National Forest – Hood Canal District
295142 Highway 101 S. – PO Box 280
Quilcene, WA 98376
Phone: 360–765–2200, TDD: 360–765–2200
For general lake information: 800–502–8690

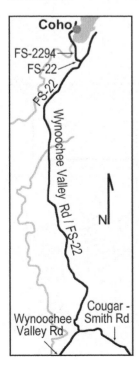

Driving Directions

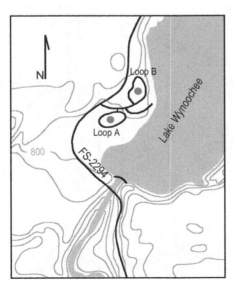

Location

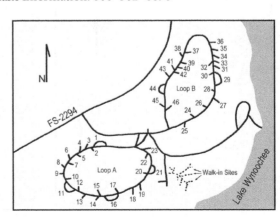

Campground

57 Pacific Beach
Washington State Parks

Directions

Start at the intersection of US–101 and WA–109 near Hoquiam. Travel north on WA–109 for 29.7 miles. Turn left onto Ocean Beach Road and travel for 0.2 mile. Turn left onto 2nd Street and travel 0.2 mile to park.

N47°12'18" – W124°12'08"   Elevation – 10 feet

Facilities

60 sites: 42 partial utility sites, 18 standard sites
Flush toilets
Potable water
Showers
Garbage
RV dump station
Accessible toilet, water, utility campsite, and showers

Features

A small park, Pacific Beach is on the coast of the Pacific Ocean. The park offers spectacular sunset views. The 26 campsites along the beach are not shaded. Sites 1–6, 32–33, 44–56, and 58 are standard sites. Sites 7–31, 34–43, and 59–64 have electricity.

Reservations

Sites may be reserved online at *www.parks.state.wa.us* or by telephone 1–888–CAMPOUT (1–888–226–7688).
See Appendix B for details.

Season

Open all year

Activities

Beachcombing, Bird watching, Fishing and shellfish gathering, Kite flying, and Winter–storm watching.

Cost

$12 primitive site
Peak season: mid May – mid September
$22 – $35 standard site
$30 – $40 partial utility site
$35 – $45 full utility site
Off–peak season
$20 – $30 standard site
$25 – $35 partial utility site
$30 – $40 full utility site
$10 extra vehicle (all year)
See Appendix C for available discounts.

Limitations

Maximum site length is 60 feet.
NOTE: Campfires are allowed only on the beach. No campfires or portable fire pits are allowed in the campground. Charcoal and propane barbecues are allowed.
Strong rip currents and floating logs may pose hazards.
Vehicle traffic is allowed seasonally on the uppermost hard–packed sand: speed limit is 25 mph.
No ATVs in park, on beach, or in dune area.
See Appendix A for camping regulations.

Contact

Phone: 360–276–4297
Web: *www.parks.state.wa.us*

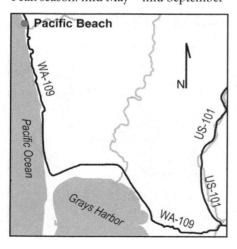

Driving Directions

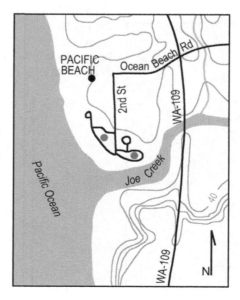

Location

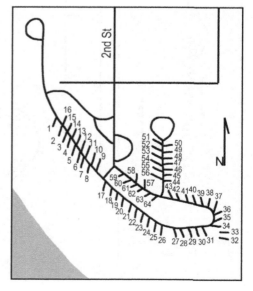

Campground

58 Ocean City
Washington State Parks

Directions

Start at the intersection of US–101 and WA–109 near Hoquiam. Travel north on WA–109 for 16.3 miles. Turn left onto WA–115 and travel for 1.0 mile. Turn right into park.

N47°01'57" – W124°09'54"   Elevation – 20 feet

Facilities

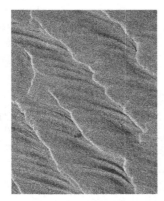

178 sites: 149 standard sites,
29 utility sites
Flush toilets
Potable water
Hot showers
Garbage service
RV dump station
Accessible water and utility
campsite
Interpretive center

Features

Ocean City State Park is on the shore of the Pacific Ocean and offers beach, dunes, and dense thickets of shore pine. The park is an excellent example of coastal wetlands and dune succession. There are four camping loops: Loops 1 and 2 have grassy areas for badminton, croquet and volleyball. Sites 138–156 and 164–173 are utility sites. Interpretive signs are available throughout the park.

The area is part of the Pacific Flyway for migratory birds and is adjacent to the migratory route of gray whales and other sea mammals. Annual average rainfall is 100 inches.

Reservations

Sites may be reserved online at *www.parks.state.wa.us* or by telephone 1–888–CAMPOUT (1–888–226–7688). See Appendix B for details.

Season

Open all year

Activities

Beachcombing, Bird watching, Badminton and volleyball courts, Fishing and clamming, Hiking, Kite flying, Metal detecting, Surfing, Winter–storm watching.

Cost

$12 primitive site
Peak season: mid May – mid September
$22 – $35 standard site
$30 – $40 partial utility site
$35 – $45 full utility site
Off–peak season
$20 – $30 standard site
$25 – $35 partial utility site
$30 – $40 full utility site
$10 extra vehicle (all year)
See Appendix C for available discounts.

Limitations

Maximum site length is 50 feet.
Strong rip currents and floating logs may pose hazards.
Vehicle traffic is allowed seasonally on the uppermost hard–packed sand: speed limit is 25 mph.
No ATVs in park, on beach, or in dune area.
See Appendix A for camping regulations.

Contact

Phone: 360–289–3553
Web: *www.parks.state.wa.us*

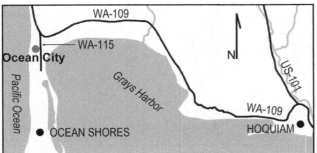

Driving Directions

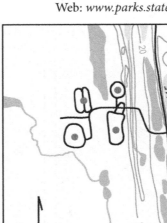

Location

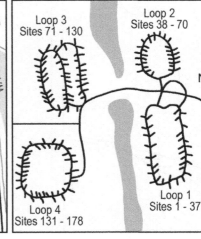

Campground

59 Lake Sylvia
Washington State Parks

Directions

Start at the intersection of US–12 and WA–107 near Montesano. Travel north on WA–107 for 0.9 mile. Turn left onto Spruce Road and travel for 0.1 mile. Turn right onto North 3rd Street (becomes Lake Sylvia Road) and travel for 1.3 miles to park.

N46°59'53" – W123°35'25"   Elevation – 120 feet

Facilities

39 sites: 31 standard sites, 4 partial utility, and 4 primitive sites
Pull–through sites
Flush toilets
Potable water
Hot showers
Garbage service
Accessible toilets, water, showers, campsite
Boat launch

Features

Lake Sylvia State Park is a quiet park. Originally a logging camp, the park has a rustic charm with interesting displays of old logging gear and curiosities. Park trails connect to the 37–miles of Montesano City trails. You won't starve: the lake has good fishing and a local pizza company delivers to the campsites – ask the ranger which one.

The area is rich with logging lore and history. Huge, old–growth stumps are everywhere. You will find a giant wooden ball carved from a single log by a local logging legend. Story has it, the logger could stand atop the floating ball and "walk it" from one end of the lake to the other. When logging ceased in 1930, the dam was used to generate electricity for the town of Montesano. In 1936, Montesano donated the land to state parks for conservation.

Reservations

Sites may be reserved from April 1 through September 30 online at *www.parks.state.wa.us* or by telephone 1–888–CAMPOUT (1–888–226–7688). See Appendix B for reservation details.

Season

Open all year

Activities

Bird watching, Boat rentals (kayaks and canoes), Boating (non–motorized only), Fishing, Hiking, Metal detecting, Swimming.

Cost

$12 primitive site
Peak season: mid May – mid September
$22 – $35 standard site
$30 – $40 partial utility site
$35 – $45 full utility site
Off–peak season
$20 – $30 standard site
$25 – $35 partial utility site
$30 – $40 full utility site
$10 extra vehicle (all year)
See Appendix C for available discounts.

Limitations

Maximum site length is 30 feet.
No internal–combustion engines permitted on Lake Sylvia. See Appendix A for camping regulations.

Contact

Phone: 360–249–3621
Web: *www.parks.state.wa.us*

Driving Directions

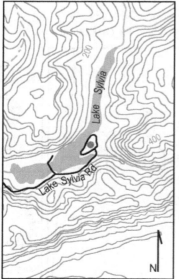

Location

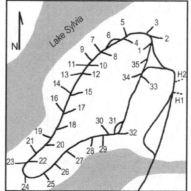

Campground

60 Schafer
Washington State Parks

Directions

Start at the intersection of US–12 and WA–107 near Montesano. Travel east on US–12 for 5.1 miles. Turn left onto Monte–Brady Road (becomes Middle Satsop Road, then Shelton–Matlock–Brady Road) and travel for 8.0 miles. Turn right onto Schafer Park Road and travel 1.3 miles to park.

OR

Start at the intersection of US–101 and WA–8 near Olympia. Travel west on WA–8 (becomes US–12) for 27.4 miles. Turn right onto Monte–Brady Road (becomes Middle Satsop Road, then Shelton–Matlock–Brady Road) and travel for 8.0 miles. Turn right onto Schafer Park Road and travel 1.3 miles to park.

N47°05'50" – W123°28'06"   Elevation – 40 feet

Facilities

41 sites: 27 standard sites, 9 partial utility sites, 1 primitive site, 4 walk–in sites
Flush toilets
Potable water
Hot showers
Garbage service
RV dump station
Accessible campsite

Features

Schafer State Park stretches along the Satsop River and is known for its fishing (sea–run cutthroat trout in summer, salmon in the fall and steelhead in late winter). Buildings are constructed from native stone. The park store is a nice amenity.

Reservations

Sites may be reserved online at *www.parks.state.wa.us* or by telephone 1–888–CAMPOUT (1–888–226–7688).
See Appendix B for details.

Season

Park open all year, but campground closed October 1 through April 30

Activities

Bird watching, Fishing, Hiking, Horseshoes, Metal detecting and Swimming.

Cost

$12 primitive site
Peak season: mid May – mid September
$22 – $35 standard site
$30 – $40 partial utility site
$35 – $45 full utility site
Off–peak season
$20 – $30 standard site
$25 – $35 partial utility site
$30 – $40 full utility site
$10 extra vehicle (all year)
See Appendix C for available discounts.

Limitations

Maximum site length is 40 feet.
See Appendix A for camping regulations.

Contact

Phone: 360–482–3852
Web: *www.parks.state.wa.us*

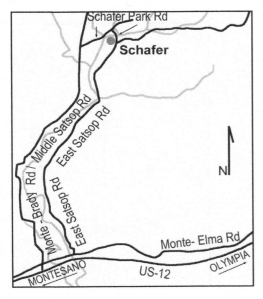

Driving Directions

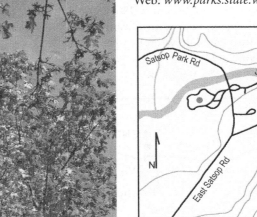

Autumn Colors

Location

61 Friends Landing
Port of Grays Harbor

Facilities

29 partial utility sites: 18 designated as RV sites
Flush toilets
Potable water
Hot showers
Garbage service
RV dump station
Accessible toilets, water, campsites, showers
Boat launch

Features

Friends Landing is one of only a very few "All Accessible" recreation area's in the USA. Friends Landing is a private/public partnership. Columbia–Pacific Resource Conservation and Economic Development District and Grays Harbor County funded the project and provided volunteers. The park has one-mile of Chehalis River frontage, a 32–acre man–made lake, Lake Quigg, and is 35 miles from the ocean beaches.

Reservations

Reservations are suggested, especially for holiday weekends, call 360–249–5117.

Season

Park open all year, but campground open from mid March to mid November.

Activities

Fishing, Hiking, Playground.

Cost

$30 – Trailers or RVs discounted to $25 for seniors or disabled
$15 – Tent

Contact

Friends Landing
300 Katon Rd
Montesano, WA
Phone: 360–486–1600
Web: *friendslanding.org*

Directions

Start at the intersection of WA–8 and US–101 west of Olympia. Travel west on WA–8 (becomes US–12) for 32.0 miles. Take the third Montesano exit to Devonshire Road and travel for 1.5 miles. Turn left onto Katon Road and travel for 1.1 miles to Friends Landing.

N46°56'54" – W123°38'14"   Elevation – 100 feet

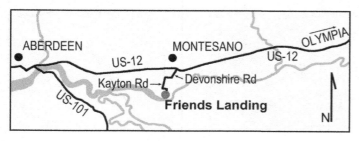

Driving Directions

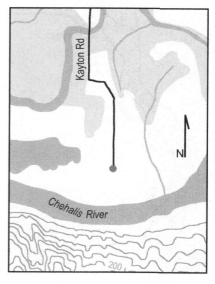

Location

62 Twin Harbors
Washington State Parks

Directions

Start at the intersection of US–101 and WA–105 near Aberdeen. Travel south on WA–105 for 18.3 miles. Turn left into park.

N46°51'26" – W124°06'29"   Elevation – 10 feet

Facilities

161 sites: 115 standard sites, 42 utility sites, 4 primitive sites
Flush toilets
Potable water
Hot showers
Garbage service
RV dump station
Accessible toilet, water, campsite, and showers
Interpretive center

Features

Twin Harbors State Park is on the Pacific Ocean coast and offers lots of beach activities. Campsites 192 – 284 are on the beach side of WA–105. Sites 1 – 49 are utility sites.

Reservations

Sites may be reserved online at *www.parks.state.wa.us* or by telephone 1–888–CAMPOUT (1–888–226–7688).
See Appendix B for details.

Season

Open all year

Activities

Beachcombing, Bird watching, Fishing or shellfish harvesting, Hiking, Horseshoes, and Metal detecting.

Cost

$12 primitive site
Peak season: mid May – mid September
$22 – $35 standard site
$30 – $40 partial utility site
$35 – $45 full utility site
Off–peak season
$20 – $30 standard site
$25 – $35 partial utility site
$30 – $40 full utility site
$10 extra vehicle (all year)
See Appendix C for available discounts.

Limitations

Maximum site length is 35 feet.
See Appendix A for camping regulations.

Contact

Phone: 360–268–9717
Web: *www.parks.state.wa.us*

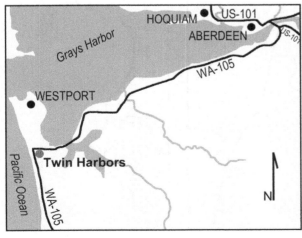

Driving Directions

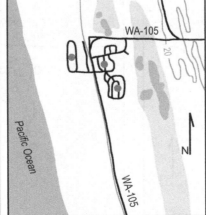

Location

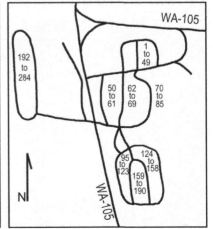

Campground

63 Grayland Beach
Washington State Parks

Directions

Start at the intersection of US–101 and WA–105 near Aberdeen. Travel south on WA–105 for 22.9 miles. Turn right onto Cranberry Beach Road and travel 0.1 mile. Turn left into park.

N46°47'30" – W124°05'35"   Elevation – 15 feet

Facilities

99 sites: 55 utility sites, 36 partial utility sites, 4 standard sites, and 4 primitive sites
Flush toilets
Potable water
Hot showers
Garbage service
RV dump station
Accessible water and campsite

Features

Grayland Beach has spectacular ocean frontage offering campsites that are within easy walking distance of the ocean. The park was named for Captain Robert Gray, an American sea captain.

Reservations

Sites may be reserved online at *www.parks.state.wa.us* or by telephone 1–888–CAMPOUT (1–888–226–7688). See Appendix B for details.

Season

Open all year

Activities

Beachcombing, Bird watching, Fishing or shellfish harvesting, Hiking, Swimming.

Cost

$12 primitive site
Peak season: mid May – mid September
$22 – $35 standard site
$30 – $40 partial utility site

$35 – $45 full utility site
Off–peak season
$20 – $30 standard site
$25 – $35 partial utility site
$30 – $40 full utility site
$10 extra vehicle (all year)
See Appendix C for available discounts.

Life Is Good At Grayland

Limitations

Maximum site length is 60 feet (limited availability). See Appendix A for camping regulations.

Contact

Phone: 360–267–4301
Web: *www.parks.state.wa.us*

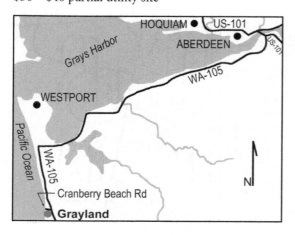

Driving Directions

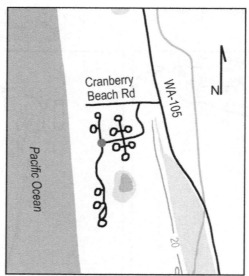

Location

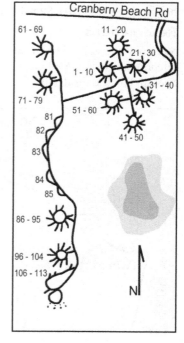

Campground

64 Bruceport County Park
Pacific County

Directions

Start at the intersection of US–101 and WA–105 in Raymond. Travel south on US–101 for 11.0 miles. Turn right into Bruceport.

N46°41'10" – W123°53'16"   Elevation – 160 feet

Reservations

Campsites are first–come, first–serve.

Season

Open May 15 through September 30

Activities

Beachcombing, Bird watching, Fishing, Hiking.

Cost

$20 – standard site
$25 – utility site
$15 – hikers and bikers

Contact

Phone: 360–875–9368

Facilities

40 sites: 32 standard sites, 1 partial utility site W/E, and 7 utility sites
Flush toilets
Potable water
Hot showers
Garbage service

Features

Campground has a view of Willapa Bay and a trail leading to the water's edge. Historically, there was a small native village on this 42 acre site called Wa–Hoot–San.

Bruceport Campsite

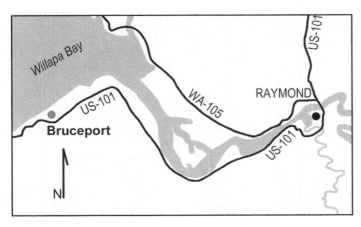

Driving Directions

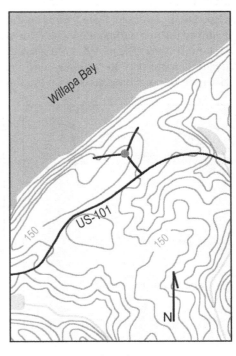

Location

65 Cape Disappointment
Washington State Parks

Directions

Start at the intersection of US–101 and WA–100 Loop (also called Spruce Street) in Ilwaco. Drive west on WA–100 Loop for 3.4 miles. Turn right into park.

N46°17'26" – W124°04'21"   Elevation – 20 feet

Cape Disappointment Campsite

Facilities

215 sites: 137 standard sites, 18 partial utility sites, 60 utility sites
Flush toilets
Potable water
Hot showers
Garbage service
RV dump station
Accessible toilets, water, and campsite
Boat launch (freshwater with 135' dock)
Interpretive center/museum

Features

Cape Disappointment State Park is on the Long Beach Peninsula with breathtaking views of the Pacific Ocean and Columbia River. The park has old–growth forest, lakes, freshwater and saltwater marshes, and streams and tidelands along the ocean. Some sites are on the shore of a freshwater lake and others are near the Pacific Ocean. The park has a camp store in summer.

Reservations

Sites may be reserved from May 13 through September 14 online at *www.parks.state.wa.us* or by telephone 1–888–CAMPOUT (1–888–226–7688). See Appendix B for details.

Season

Open all year

Activities

Beachcombing, Bird watching, Ball fields, Fishing, Hiking, Horseshoes, Mountain biking, Volleyball courts.

Cost

$12 primitive site
Peak season: mid May – mid September
$22 – $35 standard site
$30 – $40 partial utility site
$35 – $45 full utility site
Off–peak season
$20 – $30 standard site
$25 – $35 partial utility site
$30 – $40 full utility site
$10 extra vehicle (all year)
See Appendix C for available discounts.

Limitations

Maximum site length is 45 feet.
Saltwater swimming is not recommended due to strong currents.
See Appendix A for camping regulations.

Contact

Phone: 360–642–3078
Web: *www.parks.state.wa.us*

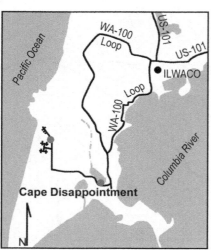

Driving Directions

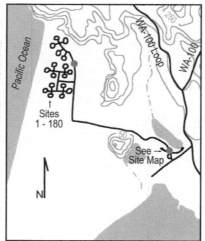

Location

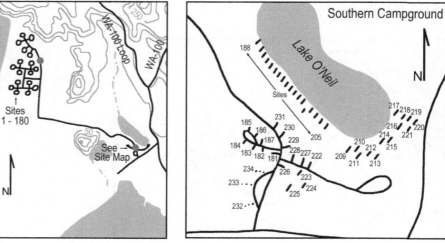

Campground

Woody's Mussels

Woody is a carpenter friend who gets an A+ for his mussels. When dining on his sailboat, they are always a treat. We find them equally easy to prepare at the campsite.

Ingredients

4 quarts mussels, cleaned and de–bearded
2 cloves garlic, minced
½ onion, chopped
½ cup fresh parsley or basil, chopped
1 bay leaf
1 cup white wine
3 tablespoons butter, divided
3 Roma (plum) tomatoes, chopped
Salt and pepper to taste

Preparation

Scrub mussels. Pull off the beards (the tuft of fibers that cling to each shell). Discard the mussels that do not close when you handle them and any with broken shells. Set cleaned mussels aside.

Combine onion, garlic, half of the parsley or basil, bay leaf, wine, and 2 tablespoons butter in large pot. Bring to boil to reduce sauce (about 10 minutes). Lower heat.

Mussels Beginning to Open

Add mussels, and cover. Cook just until shells open (3 to 4 minutes). Do not overcook. (The FDA recommends cooking seafood to 140°F.) Remove mussels from sauce, and place in bowls.

Remove bay leaf. Add chopped tomatoes and remaining butter. Heat until butter melts and tomatoes are warmed. Season to taste with salt and pepper. Pour sauce over mussels.

Serve over linguine or just pour sauce over mussels in a bowl. Sop sauce with hunks of crusty bread.

Woody Bringing Home the Mussels

81

66 Skamokawa Vista Park
Port of Wahkiakum County

Directions

Start at intersection of I–5 and WA–4 (exit 39) in Kelso. Travel west on WA–4 for 33.7 miles. Turn left to Skamokawa.

OR

Start at the intersection of US–101 and WA–4 north of Naselle. Travel east on WA–4 for 24.3 miles. Turn right into Skamokawa.

N46°16'15" – W123°27'32"   Elevation – 18 feet

Facilities

51 sites
Flush toilets
Potable water
Hot showers
Garbage service
RV dump station
Boat launch

Features

The Columbia River fronts the park, which offers large, open play–fields and a playground. A number of sites provide full hook–ups (water, electricity, and sewer) in addition to cable TV. Some sites have electricity, and some sites have no utilities.

Reservations

Call 360–795–8605. Cancellations must be made 2–days in advance.

Season

Open all year
Office closed Sunday from October 1 to May 1

Activities

Ball fields, Beachcombing, Bird watching, Boating, Fishing, Hiking.

Cost

$30 – utility site
$27 – partial utility site, electricity
$23 – standard site
$18 – tent site
Fees do not include taxes.

Contact

Skamokawa Vista Park
Phone: 360–795–8605
Email: *vistapark@vista–park.org*
Web: *www.vista–park.org*

View of Columbia River from Skamokawa Vista

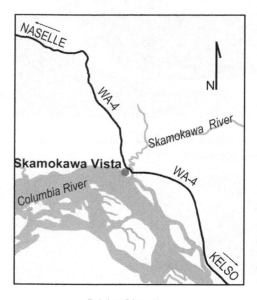

Driving Directions

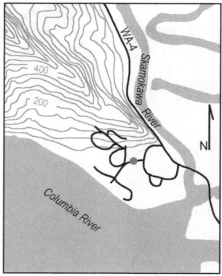

Location

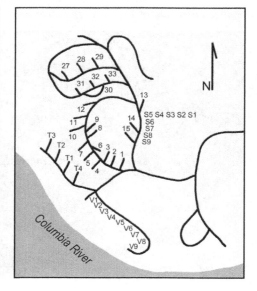

Campground

67 County Line
Port of Wahkiakum County

Directions

Start at intersection of I–5 and WA–4 (exit 39) in Kelso. Travel west on WA–4 for 17.0 miles. Turn left into County Line.

N46°10'28" – W123°13'08"   Elevation – 20 feet

Facilities

21 total sites: 18 partial utility sites (electrical), 3 walk–in sites
Flush toilets
Potable water
Garbage service

County Line Campsite

Features

County Line Park is located off Washington State Route 4 (Ocean Beach Highway) at the "county line" of Wahkiakum County and Cowlitz County. RV sites 4 – 21 front the Columbia River. There is a fishing platform. The campground is very close to the highway.

Reservations

Reserve sites by phone at 360–795–8605. Summer office hours from May 1st through September 30th are 9 am to 5 pm Monday through Friday and 10 am to 3 pm on Sunday. Winter office hours from October 1st through April 30th are 11 am to 2 pm Monday through Friday. There is a $10 non–refundable charge for all cancellations, however cancellations less than 7 days prior are charged a one night fee.

Season

None listed

Activities

Bird watching, Fishing.

Cost

$23 – partial utility site
$13 – walk–in sites

Limitations

Two sites can accommodate 53 foot RVs. Maximum length on other sites is 35 feet. Maximum stay is 10 days.

Contact

Phone: 360–795–8605
Email: *vistapark@vista–park.org*
Web: *www.countyline.vista–park.org*

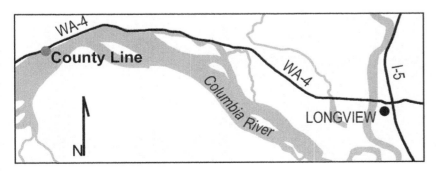

Driving Directions

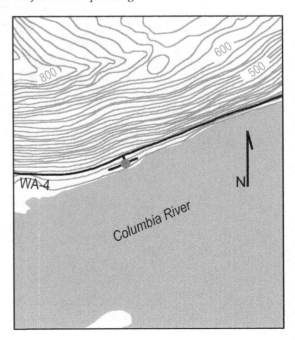

Location

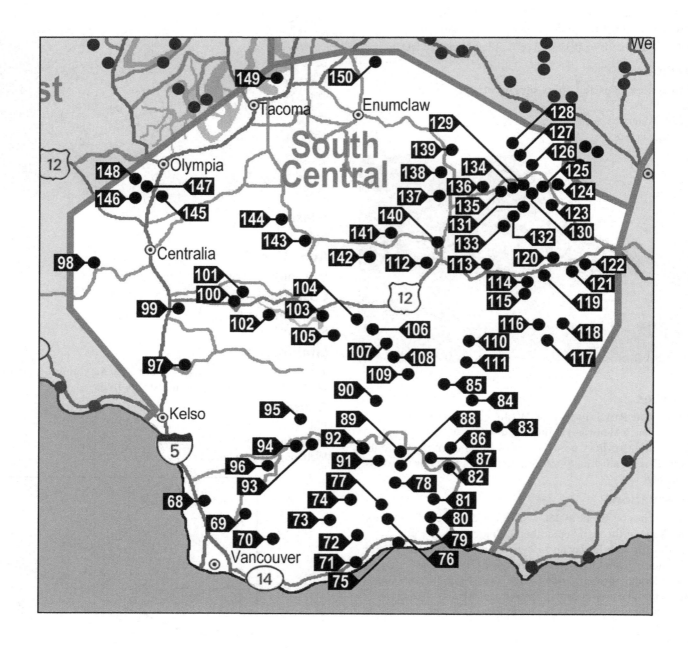

Chapter 3   South Central Region

68 Paradise Point
Washington State Parks

Directions

Start at the intersection of I–5 and NW LaCenter Road (exit 16) north of Vancouver. Travel east on NW LaCenter Road for less than 0.1 mile. Turn north on the I–5 frontage road (also called NW Paradise Park Road) and travel 0.3 mile into park.

N45°51'59" – W122°42'19"   Elevation – 100 feet

Facilities

76 total sites: 58 standard, 18 partial utility (W/E)
Flush toilets
Potable water
Hot showers
Garbage service
RV dump station
Accessible toilet, water, shower, campsite

Features

Paradise Point State Park is located along the Lewis River immediately east of the interstate. Some of the campsites are in a grassy area. The nine primitive sites are in the woods. The park has a small apple orchard. Named for its original peacefulness, the park has lost some of its reputation for quiet since the freeway went in. Still, the area possesses great natural beauty and the noise of I–5 can be avoided by using the woodland campsites.

Reservations

Sites may be reserved from May 13 through September 14 online at *www.parks.state.wa.us* or by telephone 1–888–CAMPOUT (1–888–226–7688). See Appendix B for details.

Season

Open all year

Activities

Bird watching, Boating, Fishing, Hiking, Horseshoe pits, Swimming, Volleyball.

Cost

$12 primitive site
Peak season: mid May – mid September
$22 – $35 standard site
$30 – $40 partial utility site
$35 – $45 full utility site
Off–peak season
$20 – $30 standard site
$25 – $35 partial utility site
$30 – $40 full utility site
$10 extra vehicle (all year)
See Appendix C for available discounts.

Limitations

Maximum site length is 40 feet.
See Appendix A for camping regulations.

Contact

Phone: 360–263–2350
Web: *www.parks.state.wa.us*

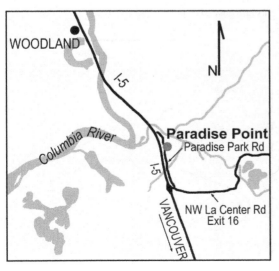

Driving Directions

Planning Ahead

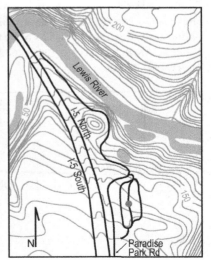

Location

69 Battle Ground Lake
Washington State Parks

Directions

Start at the intersection of I–5 and WA–502 (exit 9 near Battle Ground). Travel east on WA–502 for 9.2 miles (also called NE 219th Street which becomes Main Street which becomes NE 219th Street again). Turn left onto NE 182nd Avenue (which becomes NE Crawford Road) and travel for 1.6 miles. Turn left onto 249th Street and travel for 0.1 mile and then continue straight ahead into the park.

N45°48'09" – W122°29'31"   Elevation – 540 feet

Facilities

40 total sites: 6 partial utility (W/E), 25 standard,
15 walk–in
Some pull–through sites
Flush toilets
Potable water
Hot showers
Garbage service
RV dump station
Boat launch
Accessible toilet, water, campsite

Battle Ground Campsite

Features

Battle Ground Lake Park offers beautiful evergreen–forested campsites and a lake whose origin is volcanic, like Crater Lake in Oregon. It is believed that the crater that formed Battle Ground Lake came from an explosion of steam caused by hot lava or magma coming into contact with underground water. Around the lake are 5 miles of equestrian trails, which are shared with mountain bikes, and a horse camp with a separate primitive camping area. Annual average rainfall is 35 inches

Reservations

Sites may be reserved from May 13 through September 14 online at *www.parks.state.wa.us* or by telephone 1–888–CAMPOUT (1–888–226–7688). See Appendix B for reservation details.

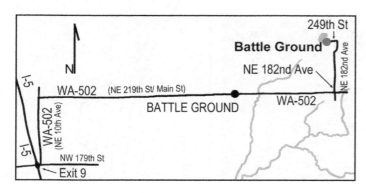

Driving Directions

Season

Open all year

Activities

Badminton, Bird watching, Ball fields, Boating, Equestrian trail riding, Fishing, Hiking, Horseshoes, Mountain biking, Scuba diving, Swimming, Volleyball.

Cost

$12 primitive site
Peak season: mid May – mid September
$22 – $35 standard site
$30 – $40 partial utility site
$35 – $45 full utility site
Off–peak season
$20 – $30 standard site
$25 – $35 partial utility site
$30 – $40 full utility site
$10 extra vehicle (all year)
See Appendix C for available discounts.

Limitations

Children under 4–years old are not allowed in the swimming area.
See Appendix A for camping regulations.

Contact

Phone: 360–687–4621
Web: *www.parks.state.wa.us*

Fishing With Father

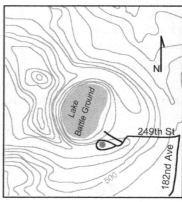

Location

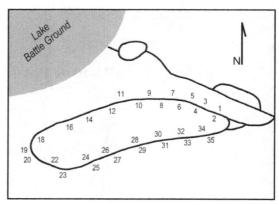

Campground

70 Cold Creek
Department of Natural Resources

Directions

Start at the intersection of I–5 and I–205 north of Vancouver. Travel south on I–205 for 4.2 miles. Exit at NE Padden Parkway (exit 32). Turn left (east) onto NE Padden Parkway and travel 4.4 miles. Bear left onto NE Ward Road and travel 3.3 miles (becomes NE 182nd Avenue the last mile). Turn right onto NE 139th Street and travel 2.5 miles. Bear left at the 'Y' onto Rawson Road and travel 4.0 miles (after 2.0 miles the pavement ends and the road becomes L–1400). Turn left onto L–1000 Road and travel 3.2 miles. Turn left onto L–1300 Road and travel 0.8 mile to Cold Creek.

N45°45'41" – W122°20'27"   Elevation – 960 feet

Facilities

8 standard sites
Vault/pit toilet
Potable water
Garbage service
Shelter
Accessible toilet, campsite, shelter

Reservations

None, all campsites are first–come, first–serve.

Season

Open all year

Activities

Hiking, Mountain biking.

Cost

No cost

Limitations

A Washington State Discover Pass is required.
See Appendix A for camping regulations.

Contact

Department of Natural Resources, Pacific Cascade Region
Phone: 360–577–2025
Web: *www.dnr.wa.gov*

Features

Cold Creek campground lies along Cedar Creek and offers a kitchen shelter.

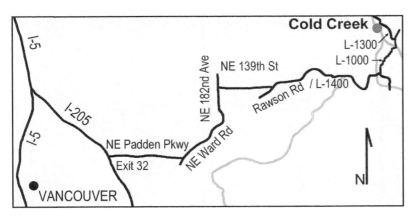

Driving Directions

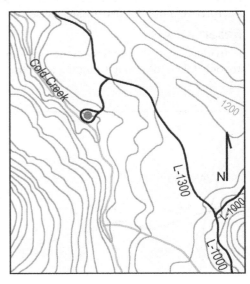

Location

71 Beacon Rock
Washington State Parks

Directions

Start at the intersection of I–205 and WA–14 in Vancouver. Travel east on WA–14 for 28.5 miles. Turn right into lower campground near the Columbia River or continue for another 0.7 mile and turn left into the access road for the upper campground.

N45°37'18" – W122°01'17"   Elevation – 80 feet

Facilities

33 total sites: 5 utility (W/E/S), 28 standard
Flush toilets
Potable water
Hot showers
Garbage service
RV dump station
Accessible toilet
Shelter
Boat launch
Boat dock (916 feet)
Marine pump–out
Shelter

Features

Beacon Rock State Park takes its name from a monolithic rock named, not surprisingly, "Beacon Rock" by Lewis and Clark on their expedition to the Pacific Ocean on October 31, 1805. It was near Beacon Rock that they first measured tidal influences from the ocean on the Columbia River. The park has two campgrounds. The main campground, with 26 campsites, is located upland of the rock in a heavily forested area with over 20 miles of roads and trails open to hiking, mountain biking and equestrian use. Woodard Creek Campground, with 5 utility and 2 standard sites, is near the shoreline of the Columbia River and access to water activities. A one-mile, ADA accessible interpretive trail is located at the Doetsch day–use area.

Reservations

Individual campsites are first–come, first–serve. Reservations are only taken for Group Camping and other park facilities.

Season

The park and Woodard Creek Campground are open all year, however, the main campground closes seasonally.

Activities

Beachcombing, Bird watching, Boating, Equestrian trail riding, Fishing, Hiking, Interpretive trail, Mountain biking, Rock climbing, Water skiing.

Cost

$12 primitive site
Peak season: mid May – mid September
$22 – $35 standard site
$30 – $40 partial utility site
$35 – $45 full utility site
Off–peak season
$20 – $30 standard site
$25 – $35 partial utility site
$30 – $40 full utility site
$10 extra vehicle (all year)
See Appendix C for available discounts.

Limitations

The main campground has a limited number of sites that accommodate RVs over 20 feet.
Woodard Creek Campground has a maximum site length of 40 feet.
See Appendix A for camping regulations.

Contact

Phone: 509–427–8265
Web: *www.parks.wa.gov*

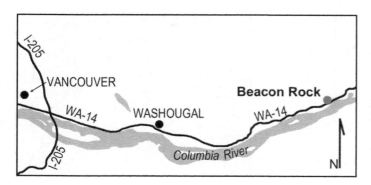

Driving Directions

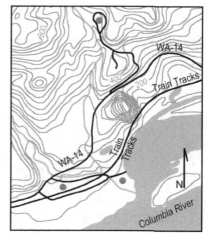

Location

72 Dougan Creek
Department of Natural Resources

Directions

Start at the intersection of I–205 and WA–14 near Vancouver. Travel east on WA–14 for 10.4 miles. Turn left onto Washougal River Road and travel 17.7 miles. Turn left into Dougan Creek.

In order to stay on Washougal River Road DNR advises – once on Washougal River Road, travel 1.4 miles and bear right. Travel 7.5 miles and bear left, then right for 1.3 miles. Bear left for 6.0 miles.

N45°40'25" – W122°09'21"   Elevation – 760 feet

Dougan Creek Campsite

Facilities

7 standard sites
Vault/pit toilet
Potable water
Garbage service

Features

Dougan Creek campground is in a forest setting near the Washougal River. The picnic area has a view of Dougan Falls making this is a scenic area for photography.

Reservations

None, all campsites are first–come, first–serve.

Season

Open all year

Activities

Bird watching, Fishing, Hiking.

Cost

No cost

Limitations

Maximum stay allowed is 7–days every 30 days.
A Washington State Discover Pass is required.
See Appendix A for camping regulations.

Contact

Department of Natural Resources, Pacific Cascade Region
Phone: 360–577–2025
Web: *www.dnr.wa.gov*

Dougan Creek Campsite

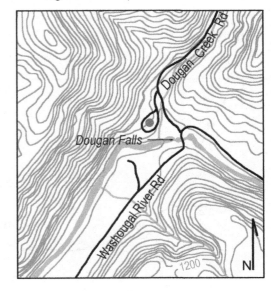

Location

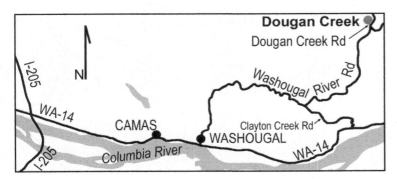

Driving Directions

73 Sunset Falls
Gifford–Pinchot National Forest

Directions

Start at the intersection of Yacolt Road and North Railroad Avenue in the town of Yacolt. Turn south on Railroad Avenue and travel for 2.5 miles. Turn left onto NE Sunset Falls Road (Forest Service Road 42) and travel 7.3 miles to Sunset Falls.

N45°49'06" – W122°15'07"   Elevation – 1,014 feet

Sunset Falls Campsite

Cost

$12
$5 extra vehicle
See Appendix C for available discounts.

Limitations

Maximum vehicle length is 22 feet.
See Appendix A for camping regulations.

Contact

Gifford Pinchot National Forest
Mt. Adams Ranger District
2455 Hwy 141
Trout Lake, WA 98650
Phone: 509–395–3400, TTY: 360–891–5003,
Fax: 509–395–3424

Facilities

18 total sites:
10 standard sites,
8 walk–in sites
Pull through sites
Vault toilet
No water, bring your own
Accessible toilet

Features

At the edge of the National Forest, Sunset Falls campground lies along the East Fork of the Lewis River. A paved road to the campground and paved level sites provide easy RV access. It is a popular local campground and day–use site. There is an accessible short trail to Sunset Falls.

Reservations

Reserve online at *www.recreation.gov* or call 1–877–444–6777, 518–885–3639, or TDD 1–877–833–6777. Reservations must be made at least 4 days ahead of arrival and can be made up to 6 months in advance. See Appendix B for details.

Season

Open all year, depending on weather

Activities

Berry picking, Fishing, Hiking, White–water rafting.

Sunset Falls with Autumn Flow

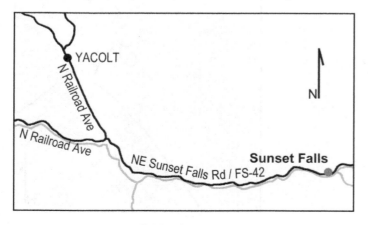

Driving Directions

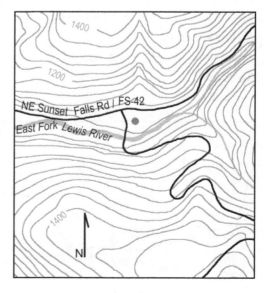

Location

74 Canyon Creek
Gifford–Pinchot National Forest

Directions

Start at the intersection of WA–503 and Healy Road (becomes Forest Service Road 54) in Chelatchie. Travel east on Forest Service Road 54 for 9.1 miles. Bear right continuing on Forest Service Road 54 for an additional 2.1 miles. Turn right onto Forest Service Road 53 for less than 0.1 mile. Turn left (sharp turn) onto Forest Service Road 37. Travel approximately 0.3 mile and turn left onto Forest Service Road 3701 to Canyon Creek.

  N45°54'54" – W122°12'10"   Elevation – 1,145 feet

Facilities

8 tent–only sites
Vault toilet
No water, bring your own
Pack out garbage
Accessible toilet

Features

The campground is hidden away in dense forest near Canyon Creek. There is no sign marking the campground entrance.

Reservations

None, all campsites are first–come, first–serve.

Season

Closed in winter

Cost

$5
See Appendix C for available discounts.

Limitations

Maximum vehicle size is 22 feet. The camp loop has tight turns. If pulling a trailer, it is best to leave it at a pullout on Forest Service Road 54 and find the campground first. Do not continue up Forest Service Road 3701. It is not maintained and is narrow and brushy. There is no chance to turn around if the entrance is missed.
See Appendix A for camping regulations.

Contact

Gifford Pinchot National Forest
Mount St. Helens National Volcanic Monument
42218 N.E. Yale Bridge Rd
Amboy, WA 98601
Phone: 360–449–7800, TTY: 360–891–5003

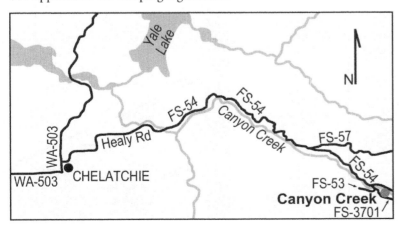

Driving Directions

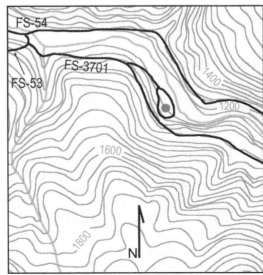

Location

75 Home Valley Park
Skamania County

Directions

Start at the intersection of US–97 and WA–14 near Maryhill. Travel west on WA–14 for 33.8 miles. Turn left into Home Valley Park.

Or

Start at the intersection of I–205 and WA–14 in Vancouver. Travel east on WA–14 for 44.7 miles. Turn right into Home Valley Park.

N45°42'33" – W121°46'32"   Elevation – 240 feet

Columbia River from Home Valley Park

Facilities

24 standard sites
Vault/pit toilets
Potable water
Showers
Garbage service
Shelter

Features

Home Valley Campground offers rustic campsites suitable for tents, cab–over campers and small RV's. While electricity and water hookups are not available, a beautiful view, scenic trails and access to the Columbia River make this campground a real treat.

Reservations

None, all campsites are first–come, first–serve.

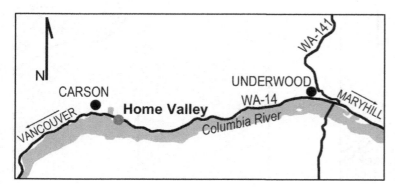

Driving Directions

Activities

Ball fields, Bird watching, Horseshoe pits, Sailboard beach, Swimming.

Cost

$20
$5 extra vehicle
Cost discounted for residents of Skamania County – see Appendix C.

Limitations

Recommend tents or small RVs only.
See Appendix A for camping regulations.

Contact

Phone: 509–427–3980
Web: *www.skamaniacounty.org/facilities–rec/*

Home Valley Campsite

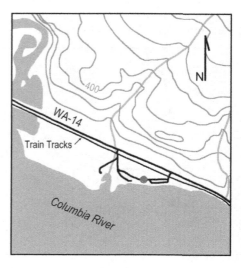

Location

76 Panther Creek
Gifford–Pinchot National Forest

Directions

Start at the intersection of I–205 and WA–14 in Vancouver. Travel east on WA–14 for 42 miles. Near Carson, turn left onto Wind River Road and travel for 5.9 miles. Turn right onto Old State Road and travel for 0.1 mile. Turn left onto Panther Creek Road (Forest Service Road 65 (paved 1.5 lanes with pullouts) for 2.7 miles. Turn right to campground.

Or

Start at the intersection of US–197 and WA–14, north of The Dalles, Oregon. Travel west on WA–14 for 36.4 miles. Near Carson, turn right onto Wind River Road and travel for 5.9 miles. Turn right onto Old State Road and travel for 0.1 mile. Turn left onto Panther Creek Road (Forest Service Road 65 (paved 1.5 lanes with pullouts) for 2.7 miles. Turn right to campground.

N45°49'13" – W121°52'39"   Elevation – 912 feet

Facilities

33 standard sites
Pull through site
Vault/pit toilets
Potable water
Garbage service
Accessible toilet

Features

Lightly used, Panther Creek campground is situated in deep forest along Panther Creek. Several sites are along the creek. Panther Creek Falls are about four miles north of the campground on Forest Road 65. The Pacific Crest Trail, which spans 2,663 miles from Mexico to Canada, can be accessed from the campground. The road to the campground is paved and it is easy to park in the well defined campsites.

Reservations

Reserve online at *www.recreation.gov* or call 1–877–444–6777, 518–885–3639, or TDD 1–877–833–6777. Reservations must be made at least 4 days ahead of arrival and can be made up to 6 months in advance. See Appendix B for details.

Season

Open mid May through mid September

Activities

Berry picking, Equestrian trail riding, Fishing, Hiking, Hunting, Mountain biking.

Cost

$18 per night
$9 extra vehicle
See Appendix C for available discounts.

Limitations

Maximum vehicle length is 25 feet.
See Appendix A for camping regulations.

Contact

Gifford Pinchot National Forest
Mt. Adams Ranger District
2455 Hwy 141
Trout Lake, WA 98650
Phone: 509–395–3400, TTY: 360–891–5003,
Fax: 509–395–3424

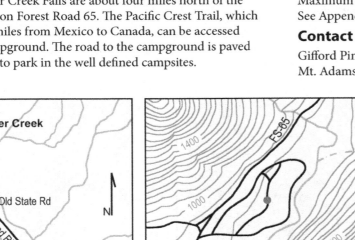

Driving Directions

Location

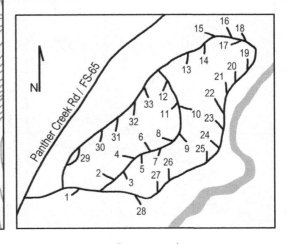

Campground

77 Beaver
Gifford–Pinchot National Forest

Directions

Start at the intersection of I–205 and WA–14 in Vancouver. Travel east on WA–14 for 42 miles. Near the town of Carson, turn left onto Wind River Road (Forest Service Road 30) for 13.1 miles. Turn left into Beaver.

Or

Start at the intersection of US–197 and WA–14 north of The Dalles, Oregon. Travel west on WA–14 for 36.4 miles. Near the town of Carson, turn right onto Wind River Road (Forest Service Road 30) and travel for 13.1 miles. Turn left into Beaver.

N45°51'12" – W121°57'19"   Elevation – 1,053 feet

Facilities

23 standard sites
Vault toilets
Potable water
Garbage service
Accessible toilet, campsite

Features

Located in the Columbia River Gorge, Beaver campground is nestled in large old maple and cottonwood trees along the Wind River. Some sites are along the river. This popular campground has paved sites for easy RV parking and a large grassy day use area.

Reservations

Reserve online at *www.recreation.gov* or call 1–877–444–6777, 518–885–3639, or TDD 1–877–833–6777. Reservations must be made at least 4 days ahead of arrival and can be made up to 6 months in advance. See Appendix B for details.

Season

Open mid May to mid September

Activities

Berry picking, Boating (non–motorized), Fishing, Hiking.

Cost

$20 per night
$10 extra vehicle
See Appendix C for available discounts.

Limitations

Maximum vehicle length is 25 feet.
See Appendix A for camping regulations.

Contact

Gifford Pinchot National Forest
Mt. Adams Ranger District
2455 Hwy 141
Trout Lake, WA 98650
Phone: 509–395–3400, TTY: 360–891–5003,
Fax: 509–395–3424

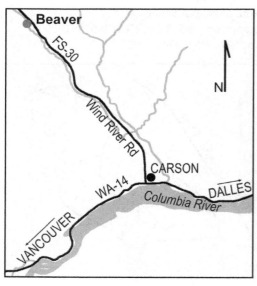

Driving Directions

Toilet Facility

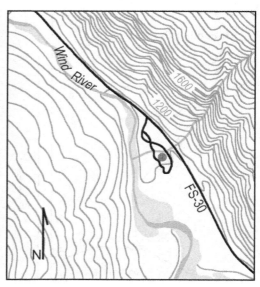

Location

78 Goose Lake
Gifford–Pinchot National Forest

Directions

Start at the intersection of I–205 and WA–14 in Vancouver. Travel east on WA–14 for 57.1 miles. Turn left on WA–141 Alternative (becomes Carson–Guler Road and Forest Service Road 24) and travel for 29.5 miles. Continue straight onto Forest Service Road 60 (still Carson–Guler Road) and travel 5.5 miles. Turn right to Goose Lake.

Or

Start at the intersection of US–197 and WA–14 north of The Dalles, Oregon. Travel west on WA–14 for 20.2 miles. Turn right on WA–141 Alternative (becomes Carson–Guler Road and Forest Service Road 24) and travel for 29.5 miles. Continue straight onto Forest Service Road 60 (still Carson–Guler Road) and travel 5.5 miles. Turn right to Goose Lake.

N45°56'23" – W121°45'30"   Elevation – 3,123 feet

Facilities

19 tent sites (many are walk–in)
Vault toilets
No water, bring your own
Garbage service
Boat launch

Features

Goose Lake campground is located among large pine and fir trees. There are many walk in campsites, however, only a few have good parking. All campsites have a view of the lake.

Reservations

Reserve online at *www.recreation.gov* or call 1–877–444–6777, 518–885–3639, or TDD 1–877–833–6777. Reservations must be made at least 4 days ahead of arrival and can be made up to 6 months in advance. See Appendix B for details.

Season

Closed in winter

Goose Lake Campsite

Activities

Boating, Fishing, Hiking.

Cost

$10 per night
$5 extra vehicle
See Appendix C for available discounts.

Limitations

RVs are not recommended. However, several spots located off Carson–Guler Road can accommodate small RVs and have trail access to the lake. These sites are not part of the official campground.

Access to campground is via approximately eight miles of gravel road.

See Appendix A for camping regulations.

Contact

Gifford–Pinchot National Forest
Mt. Adams Ranger District
2455 Hwy 141
Trout Lake, WA 98650
Phone: 509–395–3400, TTY: 360–891–5003,
Fax: 509–395–3424

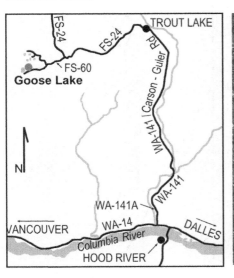

Driving Directions

Fishing on Goose Lake

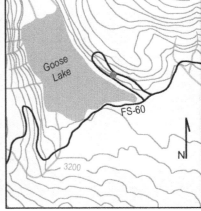

Location

79 Moss Creek
Gifford–Pinchot National Forest

Directions

Start at the intersection of I–205 and WA–14 in Vancouver. Travel east on WA–14 for 53.7 miles. Turn left onto Cook–Underwood Road and travel for 5.1 miles. Turn left onto Willard Road and travel for 1.6 miles. Bear right onto Oklahoma Road and travel for 1.0 mile. Turn right to Moss Creek.

Or

Start at the intersection of US–197 and WA–14 north of The Dalles, Oregon. Travel west on WA–14 for 27.5 miles. Turn right onto Cook–Underwood Road and travel for 5.1 miles. Turn left onto Willard Road and travel for 1.6 miles. Bear right onto Oklahoma Road and travel for 1.0 mile. Turn right to Moss Creek.

N45°47'42" – W121°38'04"   Elevation – 1,299 feet

Facilities

17 standard sites
Pull through sites
Vault/pit toilets
Potable water
Garbage service

Features

Moss Creek campground is bordered on two sides by the Little White Salmon River north of the Columbia River Gorge. Campsites are small, but useable by smaller RVs. The road to the campground is paved.

Reservations

Reserve online at *www.recreation.gov* or call 1–877–444–6777, 518–885–3639, or TDD 1–877–833–6777. Reservations must be made at least 4 days ahead of arrival and can be made up to 6 months in advance. See Appendix B for details.

Moss Creek Campsite

Season

Open May 8 through September 14

Activities

Fishing, Hiking.

Cost

$16
$8 extra vehicle
See Appendix C for available discounts.

Limitations

Maximum vehicle length is 32 feet.
See Appendix A for camping regulations.

Contact

Gifford Pinchot National Forest
Mt. Adams Ranger District
2455 Hwy 141
Trout Lake, WA 98650
Phone: 509–395–3400, TTY: 360–891–5003,
Fax: 509–395–3424

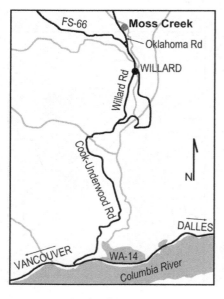

Driving Directions

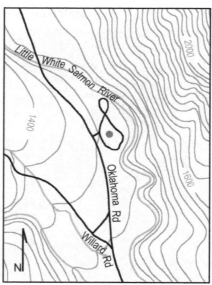

Location

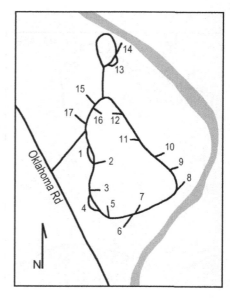

Campground

80 Big Cedars
Skamania County

Directions

Start at the intersection of US–197 and WA–14 north of The Dalles, Oregon. Travel west on WA–14 for 27.5 miles. Turn right onto Cook–Underwood Road and travel 5.1 miles. Turn left onto Willard Road and travel 1.6 miles. Bear right onto Oklahoma Road and travel 1.6 miles. Turn left into Big Cedars.

Or

Start at the intersection of I–205 and WA–14 in Vancouver. Travel east on WA–14 for 53.7 miles. Turn left onto Cook–Underwood Road and travel 5.1 miles. Turn left onto Willard Road and travel 1.6 miles. Bear right onto Oklahoma Road and travel 1.6 miles. Turn left into Big Cedars.

N45°48'07" – W121°38'36"   Elevation – 1,360 feet

Columbia River on the way to Big Cedars

Facilities

29 standard sites
Flush toilets
Potable water
Garbage service

Features

Big Cedars campground offers rustic campsites suitable for tents, cab–over campers, and small RV's. While electricity and water hookups are not available, scenic trails and access to nearby creeks and wilderness make this campsite worth visiting. The Little White Salmon River runs through the park.

Big Cedars Restroom

Reservations

None, all campsites are first–come, first–serve.

Activities

Hiking.

Cost

$20
$5 extra vehicle
Cost discounted for residents of Skamania County – see Appendix C for details.

Limitations

See Appendix A for camping regulations.

Contact

Phone: 509–427–3980
Web: *www.skamaniacounty.org/facilities-rec/*

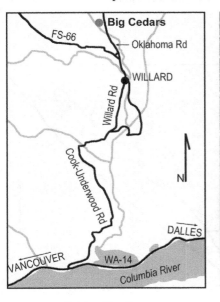

Driving Directions

Big Cedars Campsite

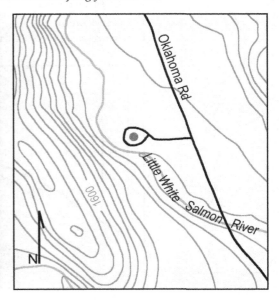

Location

81 Oklahoma
Gifford–Pinchot National Forest

Directions

Start at the intersection of I–205 and WA–14 in Vancouver. Travel east on WA–14 for 53.7 miles. Turn left onto Cook–Underwood Road and travel for 5.1 miles. Turn left onto Willard Road and travel for 1.6 miles. Bear right onto Oklahoma Road and travel for 7.7 miles. Bear left to campground.

Or

Start at the intersection of US–197 and WA–14 north of The Dalles, Oregon. Travel west on WA–14 for 27.5 miles. Turn right onto Cook–Underwood Road and travel for 5.1 miles. Turn left onto Willard Road and travel for 1.6 miles. Bear right onto Oklahoma Road and travel for 7.7 miles. Bear left to campground.

N45°52'16" – W121°37'28"   Elevation – 1,683 feet

Facilities

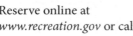

15 standard sites
Pull through sites
Vault/pit toilets
Potable water
Garbage service
Accessible toilet

Features

Oklahoma campground is nestled among large pine and fir trees along the Little White Salmon River. Several sites are along the river. The campground is fairly flat with some open meadow space. Big Lava Bed is located just west of the campground. There is a paved road to the campground and easy RV parking, however, the parking spurs are unpaved and may be lumpy. Fantastic displays of mushrooms pop up in fall.

Reservations

Reserve online at *www.recreation.gov* or call

1–877–444–6777, 518–885–3639, or TDD 1–877–833–6777. Reservations must be made at least 4 days ahead of arrival and can be made up to 6 months in advance. See Appendix B for details.

Season

Open mid May through mid September

Activities

Fishing, Hiking, Mountain biking.

Cost

$16
$8 extra vehicle
See Appendix C for available discounts.

Limitations

Maximum vehicle length is 22 feet.
Campsites 9 through 15 may be closed due to hazardous trees.
See Appendix A for camping regulations.

Contact

Gifford Pinchot National Forest
Mt. Adams Ranger District
2455 Hwy 141
Trout Lake, WA 98650
Phone: 509–395–3400, TTY: 360–891–5003,
Fax: 509–395–3424

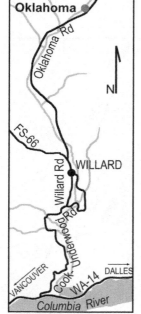

Driving Directions

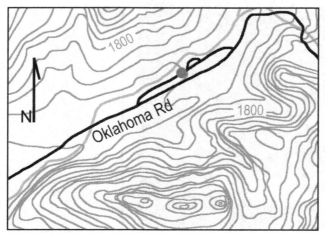

Location

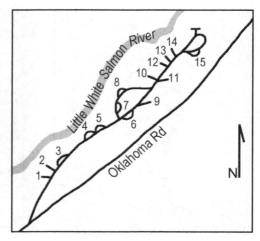

Campground

82   Guler–Trout Lake
Klickitat County

Directions

Start at the intersection of US–197 and WA–14 north of The Dalles, Oregon. Travel west on WA–14 for 20.2 miles. Turn right onto WA–141 Alternate and travel 21.6 miles. Turn left onto Jennings Road and travel 0.1 mile. Turn right onto Park Road and travel 0.2 mile. Turn left into park. (WA–141 Alternate is a few miles west of WA–141 and provides a more direct route to the park.)

Or

Start at the intersection of I–205 and WA–14 in Vancouver. Travel east on WA–14 for 58.3 miles. Turn left onto WA–141 Alternate and travel 21.6 miles. Turn left onto Jennings Road and travel 0.1 mile. Turn right onto Park Road and travel 0.2 mile. Turn left into park.

N45°59'54" – W121°31'39"   Elevation – 1,940 feet

Facilities

40 sites: some partial utility (W or W/E)
Flush toilets
Potable water
Hot showers
Garbage service
RV dump station

Features

Campground is adjacent to the town of Trout Lake. Bear Creek meanders through the campground. All sites have water service and some sites provide electrical hook–up. You can see a peek–a–boo view of Mt. Adams through the trees.

Reservations

None, all campsites are first–come, first–serve.

Activities

Hiking.

Cost

$18 standard site
$24 partial utility
$9 extra vehicle
See Appendix C for available discounts.

Limitations

See Appendix A for camping regulations.

Contact

Phone: 509–773–4616
Web: *www.klickitatcounty.org/195/Guler–Trout–Lake–Park*

Peek–A–Boo View of Mt. Adams from Campground

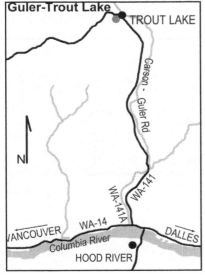

Driving Directions

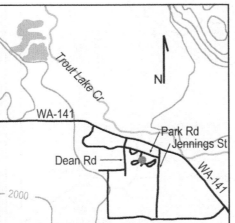

Location

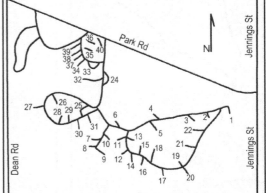

Campground

83 Bird Creek
Department of Natural Resources

Directions

Start at the intersection of WA–14 and WA–141 Alternate east of While Salmon. Travel north on WA–141 Alternate for 2.2 miles. Turn left onto WA–141 and travel for 7.8 miles. Turn right onto Glenwood Road (becomes BZ Glenwood Hwy) and travel for 14.7 miles. Turn left to continue on BZ Glenwood Hwy for 4.8 miles to Glenwood. Turn left onto Main Street and travel 0.3 mile. Turn right onto Bird Creek Road and travel 0.9 mile. Turn left onto Scott Road followed by an immediate half right turn to stay on Bird Creek Road (K–3000) and travel for 1.2 miles. Turn right onto S–4000 Road and travel 1.3 miles. Turn left onto K–4000 Road/BIA 285 and travel 1.0 mile. Turn left to stay on K–4000 Road/BIA 285 and travel 0.7 mile. Turn right into Bird Creek.

N46°03'50" – W121°20'15"   Elevation – 2,540 feet

Facilities

9 standard sites
Vault/pit toilet
No water, bring your own
Pack out garbage
Shelter
Accessible toilet, campsite

Features

Campground is on a forest stream. Site has a kitchen shelter.

Reservations

None, all campsites are first–come, first–serve.

Season

Open all year

Activities

ATV/ORV riding, Hiking, Hunting.

Cost

No cost

Limitations

A Washington State Discover Pass is required.
See Appendix A for camping regulations.

Contact

Department of Natural Resources, Southeast Region
Phone: 509–925–8510
Web: *www.dnr.wa.gov*

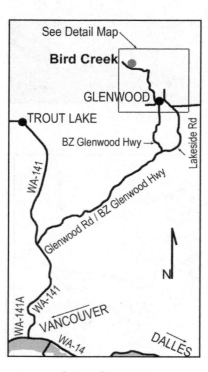

Driving Directions

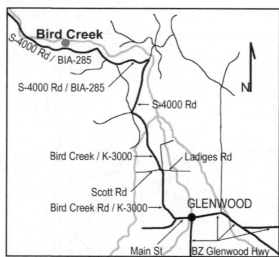

Driving Directions Detail

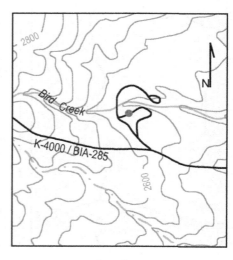

Location

84 Morrison Creek
Gifford–Pinchot National Forest

Directions

Start at the intersection of I–205 and WA–14 in Vancouver. Travel east on WA–14 for 58.3 miles. Turn left onto WA–141 Alternate for 21.1 miles to Trout Lake. Note: Mileage taken to WA–141 Alternate and not WA–141, which runs through town of Bingen. In Trout Lake, turn right onto Mt. Adams Road (also called Mt. Adams Recreation Highway) and travel 1.9 miles. Bear left onto Forest Service Road 80 and travel 3.7 miles. Bear right onto Forest Service Road 8040 (becomes FS Road 500) and travel 5.4 miles to Morrison Creek.

Or

Start at the intersection of US–197 and WA–14 north of The Dalles, Oregon. Travel west on WA–14 for 20.2 miles. Turn right onto WA–141 Alternate and travel for 21.1 miles to Trout Lake. Note: Mileage taken to WA–141 Alternate and not WA–141, which runs through town of Bingen. In Trout Lake, turn right onto Mt. Adams Road (also called Mt. Adams Recreation Highway) and travel for 1.9 miles. Bear left onto Forest Service Road 80 and travel 3.7 miles. Bear right onto Forest Service Road 8040 (becomes FS Road 500) and travel 5.4 miles to Morrison Creek.

N46°07'45" – W121°30'58"   Elevation – 4,665 feet

Facilities

12 primitive sites
Vault toilet
No water, bring your own
Accessible toilet

Features

Morrison Creek campground was burned in the Cascade Creek Fire of 2012. Several primitive campsites are available – some along Morrison Creek. The campground has access to several hiking trails.

Reservations

None, all campsites are first–come, first–serve.

Season

Closed in winter

Cost

No cost

Limitations

Access road is rough and not recommended for trailers or motor homes.
See Appendix A for camping regulations.

Contact

Gifford Pinchot National Forest
Mt. Adams Ranger District
2455 Hwy 141
Trout Lake, WA 98650
Phone: 509–395–3400, TTY: 360–891–5003,
Fax: 509–395–3424

Hamburger

They are quick. They are easy. They could be as American as any other food.

It's as simple as forming the patty. Salt and pepper to taste. Grill until done and serve with your favorite side dishes.
Yum!

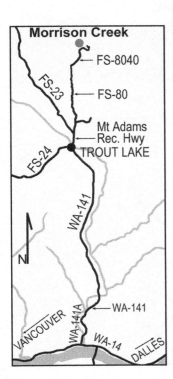

Driving Directions

Hamburger Perfection

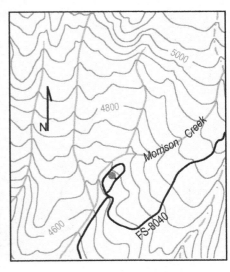

Location

85 Takhlakh Lake
Gifford–Pinchot National Forest

Directions

Start at the intersection of US–12 and WA–131 in Randle. Travel south on WA–131 for 1.0 mile. Bear left at the "Y" onto Forest Service Road 23 (Cispus Road) for 30.4 miles (the last 7 miles are gravel). Turn left onto Forest Service Road 2329 for 0.8 mile. Bear right at junction with Forest Service Road 5601 and continue on Forest Service Road 2329 for 0.7 mile. Turn right into Takhlakh Lake.

N46°16'41" W121°36'01"   Elevation – 4,400 feet

Facilities

54 total sites: 44 standard,
10 tent–only
Vault/pit toilets
No water, bring your own
Garbage service
Boat launch
Accessible toilet

Features

The campground is quiet and shaded on the shores of Takhlakh Lake at the base of Mt. Adams. Campers have breathtaking views of Mt. Adams, Mt. Rainier, and Mt. Saint Helens. There is easy access for RVs and outstanding quiet boating. The Takhlakh Loop Trail, a moderately difficult accessible trail, originates in the campground and encircles the lake.

Reservations

Reserve online at *www.recreation.gov* or call 1–877–444–6777, 518–885–3639, or TDD 1–877–833–6777. Reservations must be made at least 4 days ahead of arrival and can be made up to 6 months in advance. See Appendix B for details.

Season

Open from late June through late September

Activities

Boating, Fishing, Hiking, Hunting, Mountain biking.

Cost

$18
$9 extra vehicle
See Appendix C for available discounts.

Limitations

Maximum vehicle length is 22 feet. Parking spurs varying from 15 to 40 feet.
See Appendix A for camping regulations.

Contact

Gifford Pinchot National Forest
Cowlitz Valley Ranger District
10024 US Hwy 12, PO Box 670
Randle, WA 98377
Phone: 360–497–1100, TTY: 360–497–1101,
Fax: 360–497–1102

Takhlakh Lake Campsite

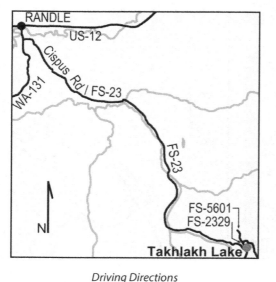

Driving Directions

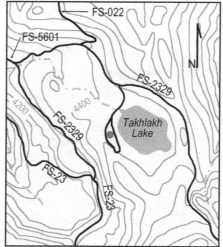

Location

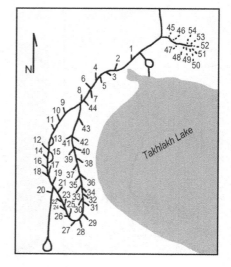

Campground

86 Trout Lake Creek
Gifford–Pinchot National Forest

Directions

Start at the intersection of I–205 and WA–14 in Vancouver. Travel east on WA–14 for 58.3 miles. Turn left onto WA–141 Alternate and travel for 23.1 miles. Note: Mileage taken from WA–141 Alternate, not from WA–141 in town of Bingen. Turn right onto Forest Service Road 88 (Trout Creek Road) and travel for 4.6 miles. Turn right onto Forest Service Road 8810 and travel for 1.2 miles. Turn right onto Forest Service Road 8810–010 and travel for 0.3 mile. Turn right into campground.

Or

Start at the intersection of US–197 and WA 14 north of the Dalles, Oregon. Travel west for 20.2 miles. Turn right onto WA–141 Alternate and travel for 23.1 miles. Note: Mileage taken from WA–141 Alternate, not from WA–141 in town of Bingen. Turn right onto Forest Service Road 88 (Trout Creek Road) and travel for 4.6 miles. Turn right onto Forest Service Road 8810 and travel for 1.2 miles. Turn right onto Forest Service Road 8810–010 and travel for 0.3 mile. Turn right into campground.

N46°02'42" – W121°35'50"   Elevation – 2,080 feet

Facilities

17 primitive sites
Vault/pit toilet
No water, bring your own
Garbage service

Features

The campground is located next to Trout Lake Creek. Some of the campsites are along the banks of the creek.

Reservations

None, all campsites are first–come, first–serve.

Season

Not maintained in off season, but camping permitted.

Activities

Fishing.

Cost

$10
$5 extra vehicle
See Appendix C for available discounts.

Limitations

Access road is rough, steep, and narrow and not recommended for trailers or motor homes.
See Appendix A for camping regulations.

Contact

Gifford Pinchot National Forest
Mt. Adams Ranger District
2455 Hwy 141
Trout Lake, WA 98650
Phone: 509–395–3400, TTY: 360–891–5003,
Fax: 509–395–3424

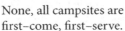

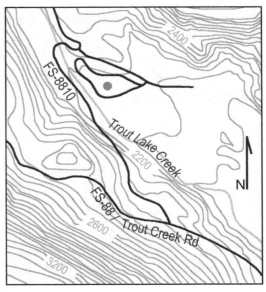

Driving Directions   *Trout Lake Creek Campsite*   *Location*

87 Peterson Prairie
Gifford–Pinchot National Forest

Directions

Start at the intersection of I–205 and WA–14 in Vancouver. Travel East on WA–14 for 58.3 miles. Turn left onto WA–141 Alternate (becomes Forest Service Road 24) and travel for 29.3 miles. NOTE: mileage taken from WA–141 Alternate, not from WA–141 in town of Bingen. Turn left into Peterson Prairie.

Or

Start at the intersection of US–197 and WA–14 north of the Dalles, Oregon. Travel West on WA–14 for 20.2 miles. Turn right onto WA–141 Alternate (becomes Forest Service Road 24) and travel for 29.3 miles. Turn left into Peterson Prairie.

N45°58'07" – W121°39'34"   Elevation – 2,976 feet

Facilities

35 standard sites
Pull through sites
Vault/pit toilets
Potable water
Garbage service

Features

Peterson Prairie campground offers well shaded and secluded campsites near large huckleberry fields, making this a popular camping spot during the fall huckleberry season. The rest of the year, use is light. The paved road to the campground and the level graveled sites provide easy RV parking. Popular tourist spots, Natural Bridges and Ice Caves, are nearby.

Peterson Prairie Campsite

518–885–3639, or TDD 1–877–833–6777. Reservations must be made at least 4 days ahead of arrival and can be made up to 6 months in advance. See Appendix B for details.

Season

Open mid May through mid September

Activities

Berry picking, Fishing, Hiking, Mountain biking, Mushroom picking.

Cost

$16
$8 extra vehicle
See Appendix C for available discounts.

Limitations

Maximum vehicle length is 32 feet.
See Appendix A for camping regulations.

Reservations

Reserve online at *www.recreation.gov* or call 1–877–444–6777,

Contact

Gifford Pinchot National Forest
Mt. Adams Ranger District
2455 Hwy 141
Trout Lake, WA 98650
Phone: 509–395–3400, TTY: 360–891–5003,
Fax: 509–395–3424

Driving Directions

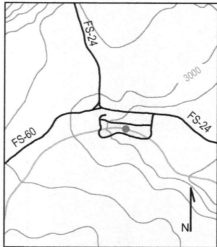

Location

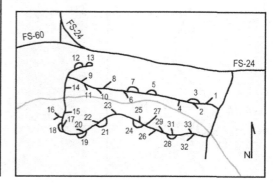

Campground

88 Forlorn Lakes
Gifford–Pinchot National Forest

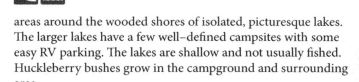

Directions

Start at the intersection of I–205 and WA–14 in Vancouver. Travel east on WA–14 for 58.3 miles. Turn left onto WA–141 Alternate and travel 29.5 miles. (WA–141A becomes Forest Service Road 24 also called Carson–Guler Road). Note: Mileage taken to WA–141 Alternate not WA–141, which runs through town of Bingen. Turn left onto Forest Service Road 60 (Carson–Guler Road) and travel 3.6 miles. Turn right onto Forest Service Road 6030 (Forlorn Lakes Road) and travel 0.2 mile. Continue straight onto Forest Service Road 6035 (still Forlorn Lakes Road) and travel 1.8 miles. Turn left onto Forest Service Road 6040 and travel approximately 1.8 miles to Forlorn Lakes.

Or

Start at the intersection of US–197 and WA–14 north of The Dalles, Oregon. Travel west on WA–14 for 20.2 miles. Turn right onto WA–141 Alternate and travel for 29.5 miles. (WA–141A becomes Forest Service Road 24 also called Carson–Guler Road). Note: Mileage taken to WA–141 Alternate and not WA–141, which runs through town of Bingen. Turn left onto Forest Service Road 60 (Carson–Guler Road) and travel 3.6 miles. Turn right onto Forest Service Road 6030 (Forlorn Lakes Road) and travel 0.2 mile. Continue straight onto Forest Service Road 6035 (still Forlorn Lakes Road) and travel 1.8 miles. Turn left onto Forest Service Road 6040 and travel approximately 1.8 miles to Forlorn Lakes.

N45°57'39" – W121°45'17"   Elevation – 3,717 feet

Facilities

25 standard sites
Vault/pit toilets
No water, bring your own
Accessible toilet

Features

Forlorn Lakes campground offers a series of small camping areas around the wooded shores of isolated, picturesque lakes. The larger lakes have a few well–defined campsites with some easy RV parking. The lakes are shallow and not usually fished. Huckleberry bushes grow in the campground and surrounding area.

Reservations

None, all campsites are first–come, first–serve.

Season

Opens with snow melt, usually mid June through early October

Activities

Berry picking, Fishing, Swimming.

Cost

$10
$5 extra vehicle
See Appendix C for available discounts.

Limitations

Maximum vehicle length is 18 feet.
Do not camp where there is no defined site.
Only small, non–motorized watercraft are allowed on the lakes.
Access is via nearly seven miles of dirt and gravel roads on gentle terrain.
See Appendix A for camping regulations.

Contact

Gifford Pinchot National Forest
Mt. Adams Ranger District
2455 Hwy 141
Trout Lake, WA 98650
Phone: 509–395–3400, TTY: 360–891–5003,
Fax: 509–395–3424

Driving Directions

Forlorn Lakes Campsite

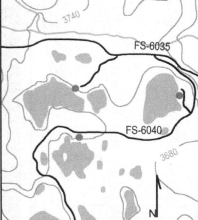

Location

89 Cultus Creek
Gifford–Pinchot National Forest

Directions

Start at the intersection of I–205 and WA–14 in Vancouver. Travel east on WA–14 for 58.3 miles. Turn left onto WA–141 Alternate and travel for 29.5 miles (WA–141A becomes Forest Service Road 24 also called Carson–Guler Road). Note: Mileage taken to WA–141 Alternate and not WA–141, which runs through town of Bingen. Turn right onto Forest Service Road 24 and travel for 9 miles to Cultus Creek.

Or

Start at the intersection of US–197 and WA–14 north of The Dalles, Oregon. Travel west on WA–14 for 20.2 miles. Turn right on WA–141 Alternate and travel for 29.5 miles. (WA–141A becomes Forest Service Road 24 also called Carson–Guler Road). Note: Mileage taken to WA–141 Alternate and not WA–141, which runs through town of Bingen. Turn right onto Forest Service Road 24 and travel for 9 miles to Cultus Creek.

N46°02'49" – W121°45'20"   Elevation – 3,996 feet

Facilities

50 standard sites
Vault/pit toilets
No water, bring your own
Accessible toilet

Features

Cultus Creek campground is popular during the fall huckleberry season. Use is light the rest of the year. Campsites are graveled and level offering easy RV parking. There are nice trees on gentle terrain. Indian Heaven and Cultus Creek wilderness trails start at the campground.

Reservations

None, all campsites are first–come, first–serve.

Season

Open after snow melt, historically by mid June through late October.

Activities

Berry picking, Hiking.

Cost

$10 per night
$5 extra vehicle
See Appendix C for available discounts.

Limitations

Maximum vehicle length is 32 feet.
Wilderness permits are required to use trails and are self–issued at trailheads.
The road to the campground has at least seven miles of gravel surface.
See Appendix A for camping regulations.

Contact

Gifford Pinchot National Forest
Mt. Adams Ranger District
2455 Hwy 141
Trout Lake, WA 98650
Phone: 509–395–3400, TTY: 360–891–5003,
Fax: 509–395–3424

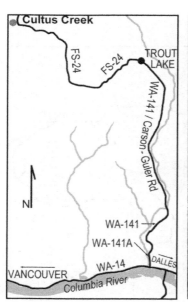

Driving Directions

Cultus Creek

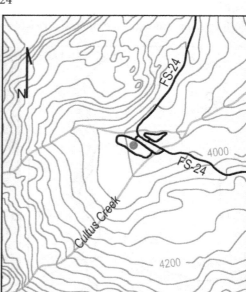

Location

90 Lower Falls
Gifford–Pinchot National Forest

Directions

Start at the intersection of I–5 and WA–503 (exit 21) in Woodland. Follow WA–503 South (at "Y" WA–503 South becomes WA–503 East) and travel for 23.4 miles. Continue straight on WA–503 Spur, which becomes Forest Service Road 90 (also called Hwy 90) and travel 37.9 miles. Turn right onto Forest Service Road 9054 to campground.

N46°09'24" – W121°52'43"   Elevation – 1,535 feet

Facilities

43 standard sites
Pull through sites
Composting toilets
Potable water
Accessible toilet

Features

Lower Falls campground is located along the North Fork Lewis River with views of picturesque waterfalls. Paved sites in a forest of large fir trees on gently slopping terrain provide easy RV parking. Campsites are large and very private. Motorcycle trails are near–by, although ATVs are not allowed in the campground. Lewis River Trail is accessible.

Reservations

Reserve online at *www.recreation.gov* or call 1–877–444–6777, 518–885–3639, or TDD 1–877–833–6777. Reservations must be made at least 4 days ahead of arrival and can be made up to 6 months in advance. See Appendix B for details.

Season

Open May through November, weather permitting

Activities

ATVs, Equestrian trail riding, Fishing, Hiking, Mountain biking.

Cost

$15
$35 premium site #21
$5 extra vehicle
See Appendix C for available discounts.

Limitations

Maximum vehicle length is 60 feet.
The road to the campground is paved except the last mile, which is a rough, gravel road from an old wash–out.
CAUTION: the calm water in the river looks deceivingly safe just above the huge falls. Trails go along dangerous cliffs.
See Appendix A for camping regulations.

Contact

Gifford Pinchot National Forest
Mount St. Helens National Volcanic Monument Headquarters
42218 N.E. Yale Bridge Rd
Amboy, WA 98601
Phone: 360–449–7800, TTY: 360–891–5003

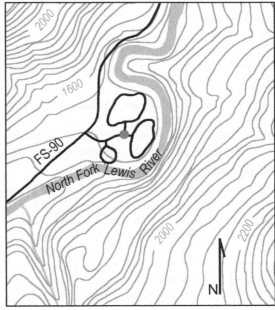

Location

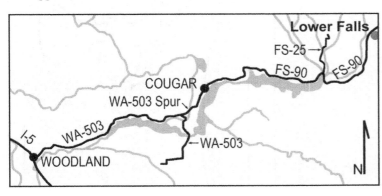

Driving Directions

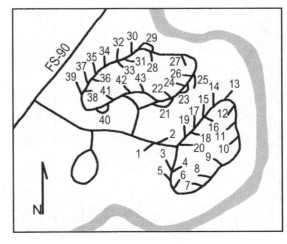

Campground

91 Paradise Creek
Gifford–Pinchot National Forest

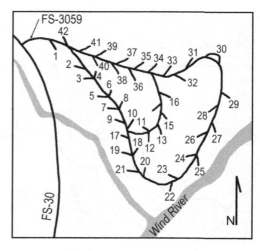

Paradise Creek Campsite

Directions

Start at the intersection of I–205 and WA–14 in Vancouver. Travel east on WA–14 for 42 miles. Near Carson, turn left onto Wind River Road (becomes Forest Service Road 30) and travel for 20.4 miles. Turn right onto Forest Service Road 3059 to Paradise Creek.

Or

Start at the intersection of US–197 and WA–14 north of The Dalles, Oregon. Travel west on WA–14 for 36.4 miles. Near Carson, turn right onto Wind River Road (becomes Forest Service Road 30) and travel for 20.4 miles. Turn right onto Forest Service Road 3059 to Paradise Creek.

N45°56'57" – W121°56'06"   Elevation – 1,539 feet

Facilities

42 standard sites
Vault/pit toilets
Potable water
Garbage service
Accessible toilet

Features

Heavily shaded by old growth forest, Paradise Creek campground is situated at the confluence of Paradise Creek and Wind River. Several sites are along the river. The road to the campground is paved and campsites offer easy RV parking.

Reservations

Reserve online at *www.recreation.gov* or call 1–877–444–6777, 518–885–3639, or TDD 1–877–833–6777. Reservations must be made 4 days ahead of arrival and can be made up to 6 months in advance. See Appendix B for details.

Season

Closed in winter

Activities

Berry picking, Fishing, Hiking, Hunting, Mountain biking.

Cost

$18
$9 extra vehicle
See Appendix C for available discounts.

Limitations

Maximum vehicle length is 25 feet.
See Appendix A for camping regulations.

Contact

Gifford Pinchot National Forest
Mt. Adams Ranger District
2455 Hwy 141
Trout Lake, WA 98650
Phone: 509–395–3400, TTY: 360–891–5003,
Fax: 509–395–3424

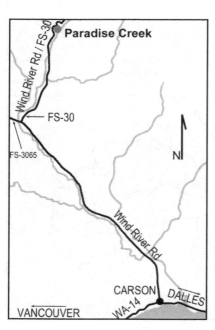

Driving Directions

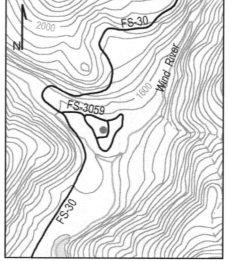

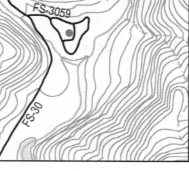

Location

Campground

92 Swift Forest Camp
Pacificorp Power

Directions

Start at the intersection of I–5 and WA–503 (exit 21) in Woodland. Follow WA–503 South (at "Y" WA–503 South becomes WA–503 East) and travel for 23.4 miles. Continue straight on WA–503 Spur, which becomes Forest Service Road 90 (also called Hwy 90) and travel 23.1 miles. Turn right into Swift Forest Camp.

N46°03'11" – W122°02'25"   Elevation – 1,030 feet

Facilities

93 standard sites
Some pull–through sites
Flush toilets
Potable water
Garbage service
RV dump station
Boat launch

Features

Swift Forest Camp lies along the Swift Reservoir. Campsites are large with paved spurs.

Reservations

Reservations are required between Memorial Day weekend and September 30. Phone 360–238–5251 or email *recreation@Pacificorp.com* or online at *http://www.pacificorp.com/about/or/washington.html*. See Appendix B for details.

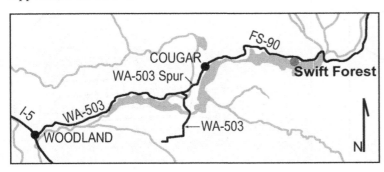

Driving Directions

Season

Open the Friday before the last Saturday in April (when fishing season starts) until the end of November.

Activities

Boating, Fishing, Hiking, Playground, Swimming.

Cost

$18
$5 extra vehicle

Limitations

See Appendix A for camping regulations.

Contact

Phone: 503–813–6666
Web: *http://www.pacificorp.com/about/or/washington.html*

Swift Forest Campsite

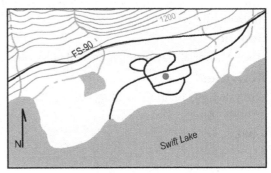

Location

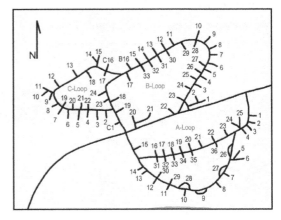

Campground

93 Beaver Bay
Pacificorp Power

Directions

Start at the intersection of I–5 and WA–503 (exit 21) in Woodland. Follow WA–503 South (at "Y" WA–503 South becomes WA–503 East) and travel for 23.4 miles. Continue straight onto WA–503 Spur and travel 7.8 miles. Turn right into Beaver Bay.

N46°03'41" – W122°16'08"   Elevation – 520 feet

Facilities

63 standard sites
Some pull–through sites
Flush toilets
Potable water
Hot showers
Garbage service
Boat launch
Accessible toilet, shower

Features

Beaver Bay campground lies along Yale Lake. Several sites are near the lake. The sites can accommodate RVs, however, there are no hook–ups.

Reservations

Reservations are required between Memorial Day weekend and September 30. Phone 360–238–5251 or email *recreation@Pacificorp.com* or online at *http://www.pacificorp.com/about/or/washington.html*. See Appendix B for details.

Season

Open Memorial Day through the end of September

Activities

Bird watching, Boating, Fishing, Hiking, Playground, Swimming.

Cost

$21
$5 extra vehicle

Limitations

See Appendix A for camping regulations.

Yale Lake

Contact

Phone: 503–813–6666
Web: *http://www.pacificorp.com/about/or/washington.html*

Location

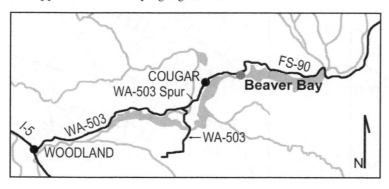

Driving Directions

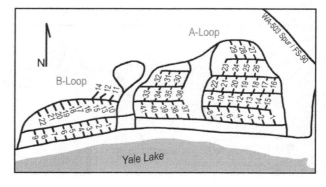

Campground

94 Cougar Park
Pacificorp Power

Directions

Start at the intersection of I–5 and WA–503 (exit 21) in Woodland. Follow WA–503 South (at the "Y" WA–503 South becomes WA–503 East) and travel for 23.4 miles. Continue straight on WA–503 Spur and travel 5.6 miles. Turn right into campground.

N46°03'15" – W122°17'22"   Elevation – 517 feet

Contact

Phone: 503–813–6666
Web: *http://www.pacificorp.com/about/or/washington.html*

Mount Saint Helens

Facilities

45 tent–only sites
Some walk–in sites
Flush toilets
Potable water
Hot Showers
Garbage service
Boat launch
Accessible toilet, shower

Features

Cougar Park is on the shore of Yale Lake and offers several lakeside campsites. The walk–in campsites are on the lake's edge. Cougar Creek runs through park.

Reservations

Reservations are required between Memorial Day weekend and September 30. Phone 360–238–5251 or email *recreation@Pacificorp.com* or online at *http://www.pacificorp.com/about/or/washington.html*. See Appendix B for details.

Season

Open Memorial Day weekend until September 4

Activities

Boating, Fishing, Hiking, Playground, Swimming.

Cost

$21
$5 extra vehicle

Limitations

See Appendix A for camping regulations.

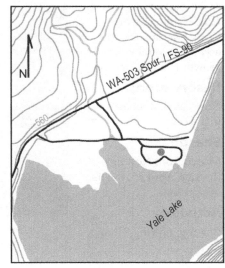

Location

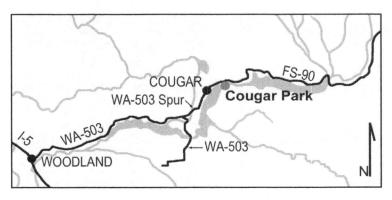

Driving Directions

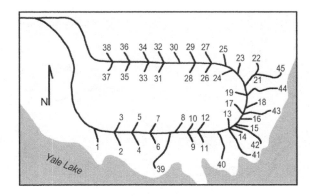

Campground

95 Merrill Lake
Department of Natural Resources

Directions

Start at the intersection of I–5 and WA–503 East (exit 21) in Woodland (also called Lewis River Road). Follow WA–503 South (at "Y" WA–503 South becomes WA–503 East) and travel for 23.4 miles. Continue straight onto WA–503 Spur and travel 4.5 miles. Turn left onto Merrill Lake Road (also called Forest Service Road 8100) and travel 4.8 miles. Turn left into campground (access road is unpaved and steep).

N46°05'40" – W122°19'13"   Elevation – 1,560 feet

Facilities

11 standard sites, tent–only
Vault/pit toilet
Potable water
Pack out garbage
Boat launch
Accessible toilet, campsite

Features

Merrill Lake campground is fronted by Merrill Lake and is part of the Merrill Lake Natural Resources Conservation area. The area has several huge, old–growth Douglas fir trees.

Reservations

None, all first–come, first–serve.

Season

Closed from November 15 through April 15, weather depending

Activities

Boating, Fishing, Hiking.

Merrill Lake Boat Launch

Merrill Lake Campground

Cost

No cost

Limitations

The campground is subject to flooding in winter and spring.
Maximum stay is 7–days every 30–days.
A Washington State Discover Pass is required.
See Appendix A for camping regulations.

Contact

Department of Natural Resources, Pacific Cascade Region
Phone: 360–577–2025
Web: *www.dnr.wa.gov*

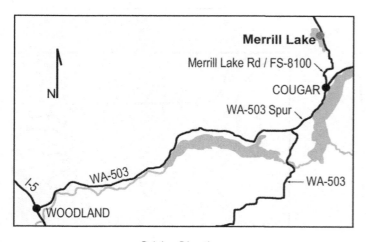

Driving Directions

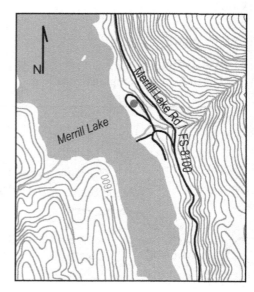

Location

96 Cresap Bay
Pacificorp Power

Directions

Start at the intersection of I–5 and WA–503 (exit 21) in Woodland. Follow WA–503 South (at "Y" WA–503 South becomes WA–503 East) and travel for 23.4 miles. At the intersection of WA–503 Spur and WA–503, turn right to stay on WA–503 and travel 2.9 miles. Turn right into Cresap Bay.

N45°58'07" – W122°23'08"   Elevation – 260 feet

Facilities

58 total sites: 51 standard, 7 walk–in
Pull–through sites
Flush toilets
Potable water
Hot showers
Garbage service
RV dump station
Boat launch

Features

Cresap Bay campground is located at the east end of Merwin Reservoir on the Lewis River in the shadow of Mount St. Helens. Several sites are along the reservoir. The park offers a marina for use by overnight guests at the campground.

Cresap Bay Boat Launch

Reservations

Reservations are required between Memorial Day weekend and September 30. Phone 360–238–5251 or email *recreation@Pacificorp.com* or online at *http://www.pacificorp.com/about/or/washington.html*. See Appendix B for details.

Season

Open the Friday before Memorial Day through end of September

Activities

Boating, Fishing, Hiking, Playground, Swimming.

Cost

$21
$5 extra vehicle

Limitations

See Appendix A for camping regulations.

Contact

Phone: 503–813–6666
Web: *http://www.pacificorp.com/about/or/washington.html*

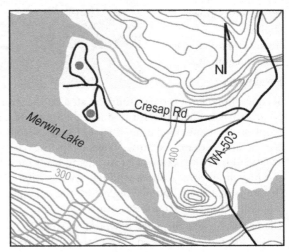

Location

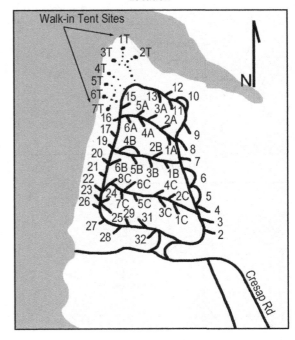

Campground

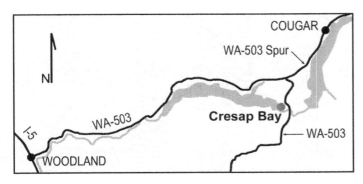

Driving Directions

97 Seaquest
Washington State Parks

Directions

Start at the intersection of I–5 and WA–504 (exit 49) near Castle Rock. Travel east on WA–504 for 5.5 miles. Turn left into park.

N46°17'52" – W122°49'22"   Elevation – 500 feet

Facilities

88 total sites: 55 standard, 33 utility
Some pull–through sites
Flush toilets
Potable water
Hot showers
Garbage service
RV dump station
Shelter
Accessible toilet, water, shower, campsite

Features

Seaquest State Park is beautifully forested on the shoreline of Silver Lake, which was formed when a Mount St. Helens eruption permanently dammed Silver Creek. Silver Lake is a shallow wetland lake only 10 feet deep. The park offers a wetland trail and six miles of woodland trails for hiking and bicycling with excellent wildlife viewing. There are also children's play areas and playing fields. The north, south and mid–camp loops are in forest settings.

The major draw to this park is Mount St. Helens. The visitor center, located across the road from the park entrance, focuses on information about the volcano and features a first–rate exhibition hall and a 15–minute film presentation of the 1980 eruption. An ADA–compliant trail opens to a view across Silver Lake of Mount St. Helens.

Reservations

Sites may be reserved online at *www.parks.wa.state.us* or by telephone 1–888–CAMPOUT (1–888–226–7688). See Appendix B for details.

Season

Open all year

Activities

Ball fields, Bird watching, Fishing, Hiking, Horseshoe pits, Interpretive center, Playground.

Cost

$12 primitive site
Peak season: mid May – mid September
$22 – $35 standard site
$30 – $40 partial utility site
$35 – $45 full utility site
Off–peak season
$20 – $30 standard site
$25 – $35 partial utility site
$30 – $40 full utility site
$10 extra vehicle (all year)
See Appendix C for available discounts.

Limitations

Maximum site length is 50 feet.
See Appendix A for camping regulations.

Contact

Phone: 360–274–8633
Web: *www.parks.state.wa.us*

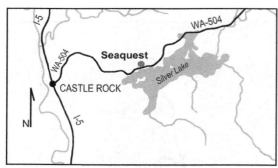

Driving Directions

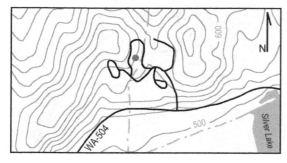

Location

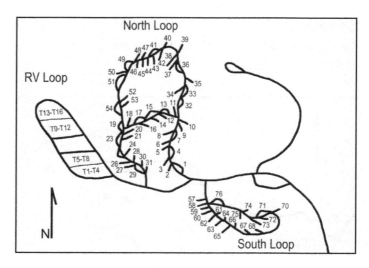

Campground

98 Rainbow Falls
Washington State Parks

Directions

Start at the intersection of I–5 and WA–6 (exit 77) near Chehalis. Travel west on WA–6 for 17.1 miles. Turn right onto Chandler Road and travel 0.3 mile. Turn right onto Leudinghaus Road and travel 0.8 mile. Turn right into the park.

N46°38'00" – W123°14'06"   Elevation – 280 feet

Facilities

50 total sites: 39 standard, 8 partial utility (W/E), 3 primitive
Some pull–through sites
Flush toilets
Potable water
Hot showers
Garbage service
RV dump station
Shelter
Boat launch (hand only)

Features

Rainbow Falls State Park is located along the Chehalis River in stands of old–growth forest. Visitors can take a self–guided nature walk through the forest and view the lovely waterfall and small fuchsia garden. The park and several log structures were built by the Civilian Conservation Corps in 1935. Primitive sites are for hiker/biker use.

Reservations

None, all campsites are first–come, first–serve.

Season

Open all year

Activities

Bird watching, Ball fields, Equestrian trail riding, Fishing, Hiking, Horseshoe pits, Swimming.

Cost

$12 primitive site
Peak season: mid May – mid September
$22 – $35 standard site
$30 – $40 partial utility site
$35 – $45 full utility site
Off–peak season
$20 – $30 standard site
$25 – $35 partial utility site
$30 – $40 full utility site
$10 extra vehicle (all year)
See Appendix C for available discounts.

Limitations

Maximum site length is 60 feet.
See Appendix A for camping regulations.

Contact

Phone: 360–291–3767
Web: *www.parks.state.wa.us*

Rainbow Falls Campsite

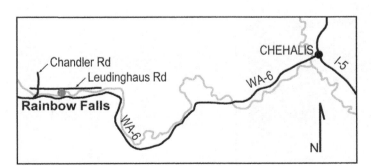

Driving Directions

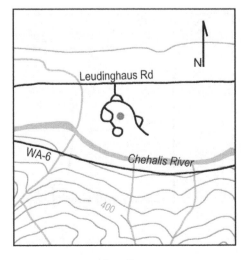

Location

99 Lewis and Clark
Washington State Parks

Directions

Start at the intersection of I–5 and US–12 (exit 68) south of Chehalis. Travel east on US–12 for 2.7 miles. Turn right onto Jackson Hwy and travel for 1.7 miles. Turn right into park.

N46°31'13" – W122°48'58"   Elevation – 400 feet

Facilities

40 total sites: 25 standard, 9 utility (W/E/S), 6 walk–in
Flush toilets
Potable water
Hot showers
Garbage service
Accessible water, campsite

Features

Lewis and Clark State Park is situated in one of the last major stands of old–growth forest in the state. A self–guided half–mile interpretive trail features information about the forest. The park has coniferous trees, streams, wetlands, dense vegetation and wet prairie. Five of the primitive sites are for equestrians; the sixth is a hiker/biker site. The park, which is separate from the Lewis and Clark Trail, began as a "public camp" for automobile tourists in 1922. Two years later, visitation had grown to more than 10,000 people.

The north spur of the pioneer Oregon Trail extended from the Cowlitz River to the city of Tumwater and passed directly through the present park site. Ramps were built over some of the downed logs (six to nine feet in diameter) to allow egress since there were no saws capable of cutting the giants.

The nearby John R. Jackson House, built in 1845, was the first

American pioneer home built north of the Columbia River. The original house deteriorated completely. The current log cabin was built by the Civilian Conservation Corps in the 1930s. The Jackson family donated some original pioneer artifacts for display at the cabin. Jackson House tours are available throughout the year by appointment. Call 360–864–2643.

Reservations

None, all campsites are first–come, first–serve.

Season

Closed October 1 through May 1

Activities

Ball fields, Equestrian trail riding, Hiking, Horseshoes, Interpretive center, Metal detecting, Mountain biking, Wading pool, Volleyball.

Cost

$12 primitive site
Peak season: mid May – mid September
$22 – $35 standard site
$30 – $40 partial utility site
$35 – $45 full utility site
Off–peak season
$20 – $30 standard site
$25 – $35 partial utility site
$30 – $40 full utility site
$10 extra vehicle (all year)
See Appendix C for available discounts.

Limitations

Maximum site length is 60 feet.
See Appendix A for camping regulations.

Contact

Phone: 360–864–2643
Web: *www.parks.state.wa.us*

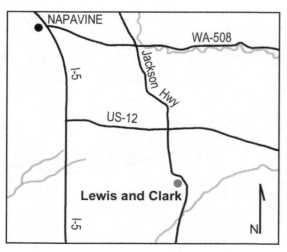

Driving Directions

Campground Entrance

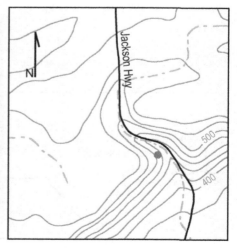

Location

100 Mayfield Lake Park
Tacoma Power and Light

Directions

Start at intersection of I–5 and US–12 south of Chehalis. Travel east on US–12 for 17.4 miles. Turn left onto Beach Road and travel 0.4 mile to park.

N46°32'08" – W122°33'21"   Elevation – 460 feet

Facilities

54 partial utility sites (W/E)
Some pull through sites
Flush toilets
Potable water
Hot showers
Garbage service
RV dump station
Boat launch
Accessible toilet

Boat Launch

Season

Open April 15 through October 15

Activities

Beach combing, Bird watching, Boating, Fishing, Hiking, Horseshoes, Playground, Swimming, Volleyball court, Water skiing.

Cost

$33 partial utility W/E
$37 premium water sites
$10 extra vehicle
See Appendix C for available discounts.

Limitations

Maximum vehicle length is 60 feet.
See Appendix A for camping regulations.

Contact

Phone: 360–985–2364

Mayfield Lake Campsite

Features

Mayfield campground offers nicely shaded campsites along Mayfield Lake. Several sites are shoreside.

Reservations

Reserve online at the WA State Parks website: *www.parks.state.wa.us* or phone 888–502–8690. Reservations are available May 15 through Sept 15. Individual sites are first come, first served from April 15 through May 14 and September 16 through October 15. See Appendix B for details.

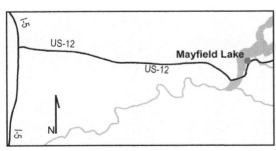

Driving Directions

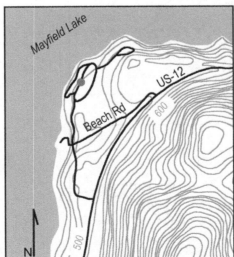

Location

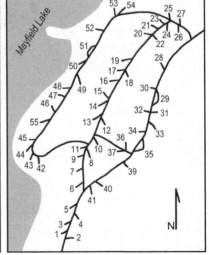

Campground

101 Ike Kinswa
Washington State Parks

Directions

Start at the intersection of I–5 and US–12 (exit 68) south of Chehalis. Travel east on US–12 for 14.0 miles. Turn left onto WA–122 East and travel 4.1 miles. Turn right into park.

N46°33'03" – W122°31'37"   Elevation – 360 feet

Facilities

103 total sites: 31 standard, 31 partial utility (W/E), 41 utility (W/E/S)

Some pull–through sites
Flush toilets
Potable water
Hot showers
Garbage service
Boat launch and dock
RV dump station
Accessible water, campsite

Features

Ike Kinswa State Park is on the north shore of Mayfield Lake. The campsites are forested and available year–round. The park provides good fishing, recreational boating and opportunities for swimming.

Reservations

Sites may be reserved online at *www.parks.state.wa.us* or by telephone 1–888–CAMPOUT (1–888–226–7688). See Appendix B for more details.

Season

Open all year

Activities

Beachcombing, Bird watching, Boating, Canoe access, Fishing, Hiking, Horseshoes, Metal detecting, Mountain biking, Personal watercraft access, Sail boarding, Swimming, Water skiing.

Cost

$12 primitive site
Peak season: mid May – mid September
$22 – $35 standard site
$30 – $40 partial utility site
$35 – $45 full utility site
Off–peak season
$20 – $30 standard site
$25 – $35 partial utility site
$30 – $40 full utility site
$10 extra vehicle (all year)
See Appendix C for available discounts.

Limitations

Maximum site length is 60 feet (limited availability). See Appendix A for camping regulations.

Contact

Phone: 360–983–3402
Web: *www.parks.state.wa.us*

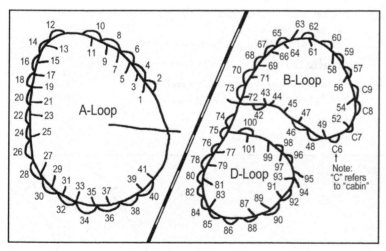

Campground

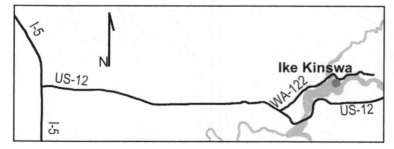

Driving Directions

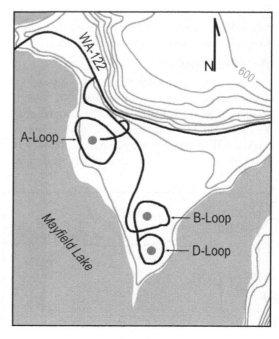

Location

102 Mossyrock Park
Tacoma Power and Light

Directions

Start at intersection of I–5 and US–12 south of Chehalis. Travel east on US–12 for 20.6 miles. Turn right onto Williams Street and travel 0.4 mile. Turn left onto State Street (becomes Mossyrock Road E) and travel 2.7 miles. Bear left at "Y" onto Aj Lune Road and travel 0.5 mile to park.

N46°30'57" – W122°24'51"   Elevation – 800 feet

Facilities

152 total sites: 64 standard, 76 partial utility (W/E), 12 walk–in

Some pull–through sites
Flush toilets
Potable water
Hot showers
Garbage service
RV dump station
Boat launch
Food Service (seasonal)
Laundry
Accessible toilet, campsite

Features

Mossyrock campground lies along Riffe Lake. Individual campsites may be reserved in one of three areas: Main Campground, Cascade Loop or Bird's Eye View. Campsites are among large deciduous trees, have great open spaces, and overlook the lake. The park offers laundry facilities. A store and a fast food concession stand are open seasonally. The campground offers a half–mile trail and a 3.5–mile loop trail.

Reservations

Reserve online at the WA State Parks website: *www.parks.state.wa.us* or phone 888–502–8690. Reservations are available May 15 through Sept 15. Sites are first come, first serve the rest of the year. See Appendix B for details.

Season

Closed December 20 through January 1

Activities

Beach combing, Bird watching, Bicycling (bicycle course), Boating, Fishing, Hiking, Playground, Swimming, Water skiing.

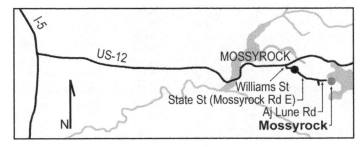

Driving Directions

Cost

$20 walk–in sites
$26 standard sites
$33 partial utility sites W/E
$10 extra vehicle
See Appendix C for available discounts.

Limitations

See Appendix A for camping regulations.

Contact

Phone: 360–983–3900

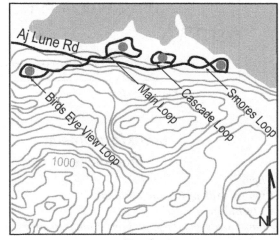

Location

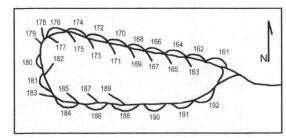

Birds Eye Loop

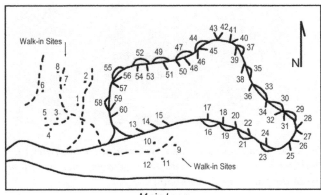

Main Loop
Continued On Next Page

Continued From Preceeding Page

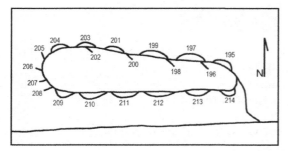

Mossyrock Park – Cascade Loop

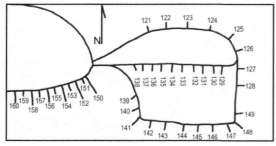

Mossyrock Park – Smores Loop

Breakfast Omelet

Ingredients

4 Eggs
1 Ounce Milk or Cream (optional)
4 Tbs Butter, divided
Almost any vegetables you have (onions, peppers, or mushrooms are a good start)
Almost any kind of cheese you have, sliced

Preparation

Cut up the vegetables into small pieces like shown below.

Place 2 Tbs butter in a skillet over medium heat. After the butter begins to bubble, sauté the vegetables. Remove them from the pan after they are done.

Crack four eggs into a bowl and add a little milk or cream, if desired (about 1 ounce). Beat together with a fork until blended. Add 2 tablespoons of butter to a skillet over medium heat. When the butter is melted as above, add the egg mixture. Cover the pan to help the top surface of the egg cook quicker.

Cut cheese slices and lay over half the omelet once the egg has begun to solidify.

Add the vegetable mixture to the top of the cheese and recover the skillet.

When the cheese has begun to melt, the egg is mostly set, and the bottom of the omelet has begun to brown, use a spatula to fold the empty half omelet over onto the half that has the vegetables.

Let cook for a couple more minutes until the egg is totally set, then serve. Sour cream or salsa is always good on top.

103 Taidnapam Park
Tacoma Power and Light

Directions

Start at intersection of I–5 and US–12 south of Chehalis. Travel east on US–12 for 36.8 miles. Turn right on Kosmos Road and travel for 0.1 mile. Turn left on Champion Haul Road and travel for 3.9 miles to park.

N46°28'06" – W122°09'51" Elevation – 800 feet

Facilities

163 total sites: 43 partial utility (W/E), 96 utility (W/E/S), 24 walk–in
Some pull–through sites
Flush toilets
Potable water
Hot showers
Garbage service
RV dump station
Shelter
Boat launches (2)
Fishing bridge
Accessible toilet, campsite

Features

Taidnapam campground offers wooded campsites along Riffe Lake. The walk–in sites are separated from the other campsites for privacy and quiet. The campground offers easy RV parking and accommodations.

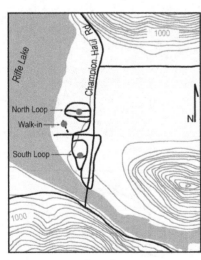
Location

Reservations

Reserve online at the WA State Parks website: *www.parks.state.wa.us* or phone 888–502–8690. Reservations are available May 15 through Sept 15.

Season

Closed December 20 to January 1

Activities

Beach combing, Bird watching, Boating, Fishing, Hiking, Horseshoes, Playground, Swimming, Water skiing.

Cost

$20 walk–in site
$33 partial utility site W/E
$35 utility site W/E/S
$10 extra vehicle
See Appendix C for available discounts.

Limitations

See Appendix A for camping regulations.

Contact

Phone: 360–497–7707

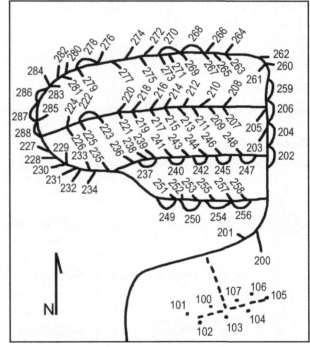
North Loop

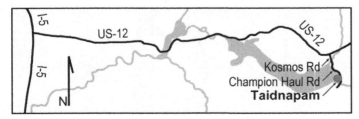
Driving Directions

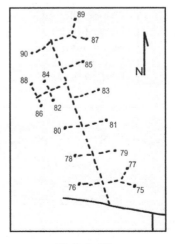
Walk–in Sites

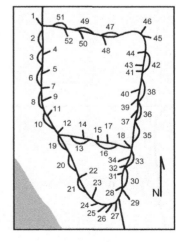
South Loop

104 Cowlitz Falls
Leonard Allen Park
Lewis County PUD

Directions

Start at the intersection of I–5 and US–12 south of Chehalis. Travel east on US–12 for 45.0 miles. Turn right onto Savio Road and travel 1.1 miles. Turn right onto Kiona Road (becomes Peters Road) and travel 3.0 miles. Turn right into Cowlitz Falls.

N46°30'10" – W122°0'56"   Elevation – 880 feet

Facilities

100 total sites: 60 standard, 40 partial utility (W/E)
Some pull–through sites
Flush toilets
Potable water
Hot showers
Garbage service
RV dump station
Shelter
Boat launch

Features

The campground lies along the Cowlitz River and, despite the name, there are no falls.

Reservations

Reservations can not be made for more than 14 consecutive days. Weekends, Holidays and special events require a 2 night minimum stay. See Appendix B for reservation details.

Cowlitz Falls Shelter

Cost

$20 standard site
$32 partial utility site
$6 extra vehicle
See Appendix C for available discounts.

Limitations

See Appendix A for camping regulations.

Contact

Phone 360–345–1484
Web: *https://www.lcpud.org/recreation/campground/*

Season

Closed September 10 through May 19

Activities

Ball fields, Bird watching, Boating, Fishing, Hiking, Horseshoe pit, Mountain biking, Playground, Soccer field, Volleyball.

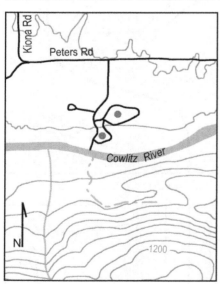

Location

A Campsite Just Like Home

Driving Directions

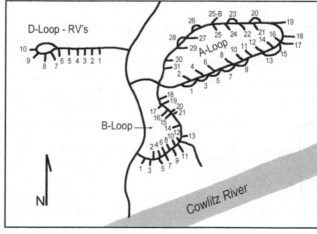

Campground

105 Iron Creek
Gifford–Pinchot National Forest

Directions

Start at the intersection of US–12 and WA–131 in Randle. Travel south on WA–131 (becomes Forest Service Road 25) for 9.8 miles. Turn left to Iron Creek.

N46°25'51" – W121°59'11"   Elevation – 1,083 feet

Facilities

98 total sites: 80 standard,18 double
Pull through sites
Vault toilets
Potable Water
Garbage service
Shelter
Accessible toilet, water, shelter

Features

Iron Creek campground is located along the confluence of Iron Creek and Cispus River. The campsites are nestled in old growth trees, secluded from one another on basically flat terrain. Several sites are along the river. There is paved road with gravel patches leading to the campground. Paved level parking spurs allow easy RV parking. A creekside accessible trail, Iron Creek Campground Loop, encircles the campground. It is a good place to camp for those visiting the east side of Mt. St. Helens.

Reservations

Reserve online at *www.recreation.gov* or call 1–877–444–6777, 518–885–3639, or TDD 1–877–833–6777. Reservations must be made at least 4 days ahead of arrival and can be made up to 6 months in advance. See Appendix B for details.

Season

Open mid May through mid September.

Activities

Fishing, Hiking.

Cost

$20
$38 double site
$10 extra vehicle
See Appendix C for available discounts.

Limitations

See Appendix A for camping regulations.

Contact

Gifford Pinchot National Forest
Cowlitz Valley Ranger District
10024 US Hwy 12, PO Box 670
Randle, WA 98377
Phone: 360–497–1100, TTY: 360–497–1101,
Fax: 360–497–1102

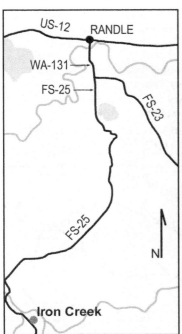

Driving Directions

Iron Creek

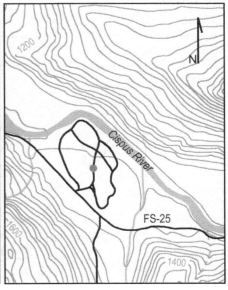

Location

106 Tower Rock
Gifford–Pinchot National Forest

Directions

Start at the intersection of US–12 and WA–131 in Randle. Travel south on WA–131 for 1.0 mile. Bear left on Forest Service Road 23 (Cispus Road) for 8.3 miles. Turn right onto Forest Service Road 28 (still called Cispus Road) for 1.4 miles. Turn right onto Forest Service Road 76 (still called Cispus Road) for 1.5 miles. Turn right onto Forest Service Road 073 for 0.3 mile to Tower Rock.

N46°26'45" – W121°52'02"   Elevation – 1,224 feet

Facilities

21 standard sites
Pull through sites
Vault/pit toilets
Potable water
Garbage service
Accessible toilet

Features

Tower Rock campground,
with nicely wooded campsites, was adjacent to the Cispus River but the river course has changed. A privately–owned trout pond is nearby. There is easy access on paved roads for RVs. It is conveniently located for those visiting the east side of Mt. St. Helens.

Reservations

Reserve online at *www.recreation.gov* or call 1–877–444–6777, 518–885–3639, or TDD 1–877–833–6777. Reservations must be made at least 4 days ahead of arrival and can be made up to 6 months in advance. See Appendix B for details.

Season

Open late May through late September

Activities

Fishing.

Cost

$18
$9 extra vehicle
See Appendix C for available discounts.

Limitations

Maximum vehicle length is 22 feet.
See Appendix A for camping regulations.

Contact

Gifford Pinchot National Forest
Cowlitz Valley Ranger District
10024 US Hwy 12, PO Box 670
Randle, WA 98377
Phone: 360–497–1100, TTY: 360–497–1101,
Fax: 360–497–1102

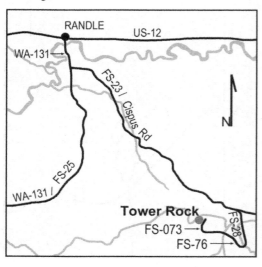

Driving Directions

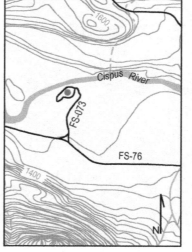

Location

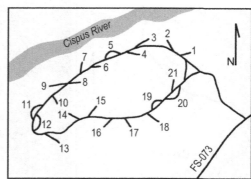

Campground

107 North Fork
Gifford–Pinchot National Forest

Directions

Start at the intersection of WA–12 and WA–131 in Randle. Travel south on WA–131 for 1.0 mile. Bear left at "Y" onto Forest Service Road 23 (Cispus Road) and travel for 10.8 miles. Turn left into North Fork.

N46°27'06" – W121°47'20"   Elevation – 1,400 feet

Facilities

8 standard sites
Pull through sites
Vault/pit toilet
Potable water
Garbage service
Accessible toilet

Features

North Fork campground is along the North Fork of the Cispus River and offers quiet, shaded and well–defined campsites. Some sites are along the river. There is good access on paved Forest Service Road 23 (gravel patches) and easy RV parking. Parking spurs range from 20 to 40 feet in length. Two trails, River and North Fork, are accessed from the campground. OHV trails and other hiking trails are nearby.

Reservations

Reserve online at *www.recreation.gov* or call 1–877–444–6777, 518–885–3639, or TDD 1–877–833–6777. Reservations must be made at least 4 days ahead of arrival and can be made up to 6 months in advance. See Appendix B for details.

Season

Open late May through late September

Activities

Fishing, Hiking, Hunting, Mountain biking, OHV riding.

Cost

$18
$9 extra vehicle
See Appendix C for available discounts.

Limitations

Maximum vehicle length is 28 feet.
See Appendix A for camping regulations.

Contact

Gifford Pinchot National Forest
Cowlitz Valley Ranger District
10024 US Hwy 12, PO Box 670
Randle, WA 98377
Phone: 360–497–1100, TTY: 360–497–1101,
Fax: 360–497–1102

North Fork Campsite

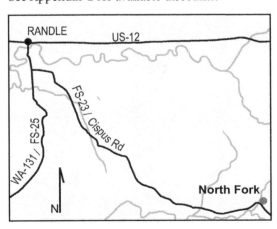

Driving Directions

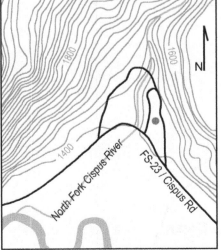

Location

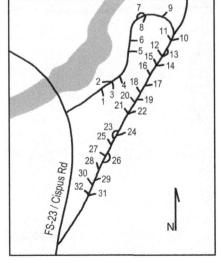

Campground

108 Blue Lake Creek
Gifford–Pinchot National Forest

Directions

Start at the intersection of WA–12 and WA–131 in Randle. Travel south on WA–131 for 1.0 mile. Bear left at "Y" onto Forest Service Road 23 (Cispus Road) and travel for 15.3 miles. Turn left to campground.

N46°24'14" – W121°44'09"   Elevation – 1,814 feet

Facilities

11 standard sites
Vault toilet
No water, bring your own
Garbage service

Features

Blue Lake Creek campground is quiet and well shaded, and offers easy RV parking. The sites are typically open and grassy. This campground is popular with Off–Highway–Vehicle users and can become noisy when ATV/ORVs come and go from the adjacent Blue Lake Off–Road Vehicle Area, although ATV/ORVs are not allowed in the campground. The heavily used motorized trail, Valley Trail, is accessed from the campground. A hiker only trail, High Log Trail, is directly across from the campground.

Reservations

Reserve online at *www.recreation.gov* or call 1–877–444–6777, 518–885–3639, or TDD 1–877–833–6777. Reservations must be made at least 4 days ahead of arrival and can be made up to 6 months in advance. See Appendix B for details.

Season

Open mid May through mid September

Activities

ATV/ORV riding, Fishing, Hiking, Hunting, Mountain biking.

Blue Lake Creek Campsite

Cost

$12
$8 extra vehicle
See Appendix C for available discounts.

Limitations

Recommended maximum length for RV/trailers is 22 feet. The sites are all back–in with parking spurs varying from 20 to 30 feet.
See Appendix A for camping regulations.

Contact

Gifford Pinchot National Forest
Cowlitz Valley Ranger District
10024 US Hwy 12, PO Box 670
Randle, WA 98377
Phone: 360–497–1100, TTY: 360–497–1101,
Fax: 360–497–1102

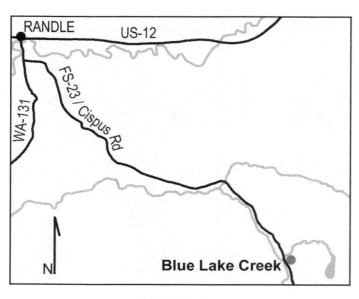

Driving Directions

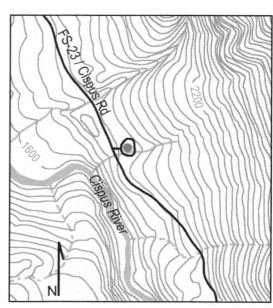

Location

109 Adams Fork
Gifford–Pinchot National Forest

Directions

Start at the intersection of WA–12 and WA–131 in Randle. Travel south on WA–131 for 1.0 mile. Bear left at "Y" onto Forest Service Road 23 (Cispus Road) and travel for 17.6 miles. Bear left at "Y" onto Forest Service Road 21 and travel for 4.6 miles. Turn right onto Forest Service Road 56 and travel for 0.2 mile to Adams Fork.

N46°20'21" – W121°38'48"   Elevation – 2,543 feet

Facilities

24 standard sites
Pull–through sites
Vault/pit toilets
Potable water
Garbage service
Accessible toilet

Features

Adams Fork campground lies in a forest of tall trees near the Cispus River. Camp sites are small but still usable by RVs. Several are along the river. The campground contains historic basket trees used by the Upper Cowlitz Tribe with related interpretive signage. The area is popular with ORV riders. Expect riders going out of the campground to ORV trails close by.

Reservations

Reserve online at *www.recreation.gov* or call 1–877–444–6777, 518–885–3639, or TDD 1–877–833–6777. Reservations must be made at least 4 days ahead of arrival and can be made up to 6 months in advance. See Appendix B for details.

Season

Open early May through late September

Activities

Fishing, ATV–ORV riding.

Cost

$16 standard site
$8 extra vehicle
See Appendix C for available discounts.

Limitations

Maximum vehicle length is 22 feet.
Forest Service Roads 23 and 21 are paved with gravel patches.
See Appendix A for camping regulations.

Contact

Cowlitz Valley Ranger District
10024 US Hwy 12 PO Box 670
Randle, WA 98377
Phone: 360–497–1100, TTY 360–497–1101,
Fax: 360–497–1102

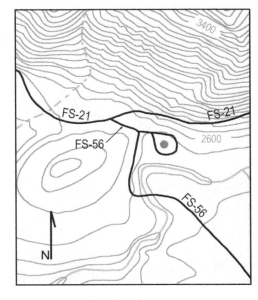

Adams Fork Campsite

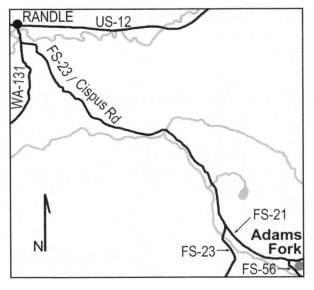

Driving Directions

Location

110 Walupt Lake
Gifford-Pinchot National Forest

Directions

Start at the town of Packwood's town center on US–12. Travel west on US–12 for 2.9 miles. Turn left onto Forest Service Road 21 and travel for 16.1 miles. Turn left onto Forest Service Road 2160 and travel 4.8 miles to Walupt Lake.

N46°25'25" – W121°28'26"   Elevation – 3,930 feet

Facilities

42 total sites: 36 standard, 6 tent-only
Vault toilets
Potable water
Garbage service
Boat ramp
Accessible toilet, campsite

Features

Located at the west end of Walupt Lake, the campground has stunning views of Mt. Adams and Goat Rocks Wilderness Area. The primitive boat ramp provides lake access for small motorboats and non–motorized boats. Several tent–only campsites are lakeside with small beach areas. There are numerous trails for hiking, biking and horseback riding. A horse camp is adjacent to the campground.

Reservations

Reserve online at *www.recreation.gov* or call 1–877–444–6777, 518–885–3639, or TDD 1–877–833–6777. Reservations must be made at least 4 days ahead of arrival and can be made up to 6 months in advance. See Appendix B for details.

Season

Open end of May through end of September

Activities

Boating, Equestrian trail riding, Fishing, Hiking, Mountain biking, Swimming.

Cost

$18
$9 extra vehicle
See Appendix C for available discounts.

Limitations

Recommended maximum length for vehicles is 22 feet.
Boat speed may not exceed 10 mph.
See Appendix A for camping regulations.

Contact

Gifford Pinchot National Forest
Cowlitz Valley Ranger District
10024 US Hwy 12, PO Box 670
Randle, WA 98377
Phone: 360–497–1100, TTY: 360–497–1101,
Fax: 360–497–1102

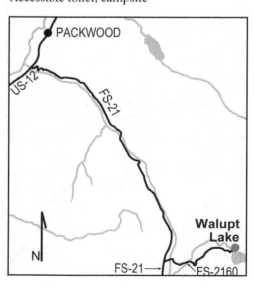

Driving Directions

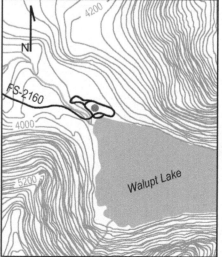

Location

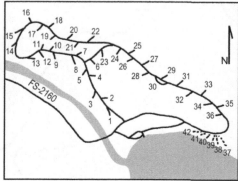

Campground

111 Horseshoe Lake
Gifford–Pinchot National Forest

Priceless Night Sky View

Features

Horseshoe Lake is a popular but rustic campground situated on a very picturesque high mountain lake. Most of the campsites have a view of the lake, which offers excellent, quiet boating. Mt. Adams Wilderness Area is nearby as are numerous trails.

Reservations

None, all campsites are first–come, first–serve.

Season

Open late June through mid September

Activities

Boating (rentals available), Fishing, Hiking, Mountain biking.

Cost

$12
$6 extra vehicle
See Appendix C for available discounts.

Limitations

Maximum vehicle length is 16 feet.
Only electric motors are allowed on the lake.
There are at least twelve miles of gravel road to campground.
Horses are not allowed in the campground or the lake.
See Appendix A for camping regulations.

Contact

Gifford Pinchot National Forest
Cowlitz Valley Ranger District
10024 US Hwy 12, PO Box 670
Randle, WA 98377
Phone: 360–497–1100, TTY: 360–497–1101,
Fax: 360–497–1102

Directions

Start at the intersection of US–12 and WA–131 in Randle. Travel south on WA–131 for 1.0 mile. Bear left at the "Y" onto Forest Service Road 23 (Cispus Road) for 30.4 miles (the last 7 miles are gravel). Turn right onto Forest Service Road 2329 (gravel) and travel for 6.8 miles. Turn left onto Forest Service Road 078 (gravel) for 1.4 miles to Horseshoe Lake.

N46°18'35" – W121°34'0"   Elevation – 4,150 feet

Facilities

10 standard sites
Vault/pit toilet
No water, bring your own
Accessible toilet

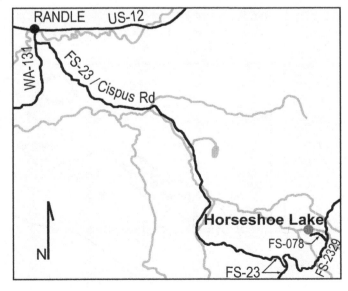

Driving Directions

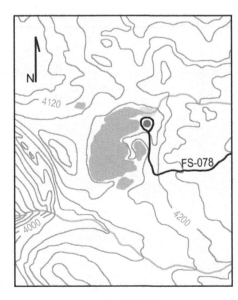

Location

112 La Wis Wis
Gifford–Pinchot National Forest

Directions

Start at the intersection of US–12 and Skate Creek Road South in Packwood. Travel east on US–12 for 6.6 miles. Turn left into entrance road and travel 0.6 mile to La Wis Wis.

Or

Start at the intersection of WA–123 and US–12. Travel east on US–12 for 0.7 mile. Turn right into entrance road and travel 0.6 mile to La Wis Wis.

N46°40'27 – W121°35'15"   Elevation – 1,243 feet

Facilities

122 standard sites
Some pull through sites
Vault/pit toilets
Potable water (see limitations)
Garbage service
Accessible site, toilet

Features

La Wis Wis campground is located at the junction of the Clear Fork of the Cowlitz and Ohanapecosh Rivers in an old growth forest. All sites are ideal for tents, car campers, and truck campers. Some sites in H loop are large enough for bigger RVs. Several campsites are along the river. Purcell Falls Trail and Blue Hole trail originate from the campground. Interpretive programs are given in the amphitheater.

Reservations

Reserve online at *www.recreation.gov* or call 1–877–444–6777, 518–885–3639, or TDD 1–877–833–6777. Reservations must be made at least 4 days ahead of arrival and can be made up to 6 months in advance. See Appendix B for details.

Season

Open mid May through mid September (weather permitting)

Activities

Bird watching, Fishing, Hiking, Mountain biking.

Cost

$20
$10 extra vehicle
See Appendix C for available discounts.

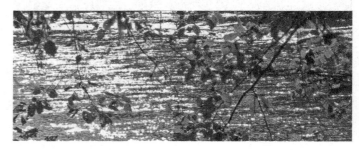

Limitations

Maximum stay is 14 days
Maximum vehicle length is 24 feet.
CAUTION: Campground loop roads have sharp turns and large, close trees. Do not enter loops that are too small for your vehicle. (Perhaps walk the loop before entering with your vehicle.)
The Hatchery Loop (H Loop) does NOT have water; water is available in the main La Wis Wis campground.
Selective fishing gear rules apply. See Washington Department of Fish and Wildlife Sport Fishing Rules for more information. See Appendix A for camping regulations.

Contact

Gifford Pinchot National Forest
Cowlitz Valley Ranger District
10024 US Hwy 12, PO Box 670
Randle, WA 98377
Phone: 360–497–1100, TTY: 360–497–1101,
Fax: 360–497–1102

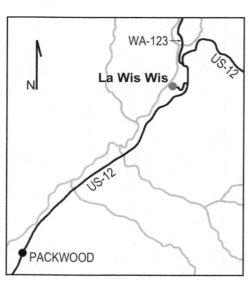

Driving Directions

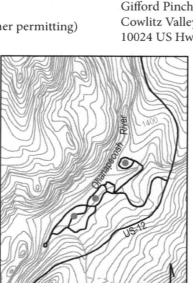

Location

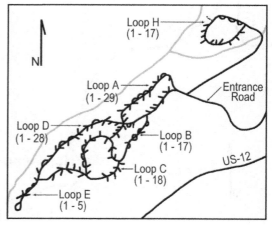

Campground

113 Dog Lake
Okanogan–Wenatchee National Forest

Directions

Start at the intersection of US–12 and WA–123 east of Packwood. Travel east on US–12 for 14.6 miles. Turn left into Dog Lake.

Or

Start at the intersection of US–12 and WA–410 north of Naches. Travel west on US–12 for 32.1 miles. Turn right into Dog Lake.

N46°39'18" – W121°21'37"   Elevation – 3,400 feet

Facilities

8 standard sites
Vault/pit toilet
No water, bring your own
Garbage service
Boat launch

Features

Dog Lake campground overlooks the lake. The picnic area is on the lake near the boat launch; the turning radius is limited. Dog Lake is a popular fishing lake. Motors are allowed.

Reservations

None, all campsites are first–come, first–serve

Season

Open from mid May through the end of October. Boat launch is closed and gate locked on October 31.

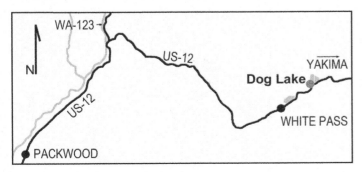

Driving Directions

Dog Lake Campsite

Activities

Boating, Fishing, Hiking.

Cost

$8
$5 extra vehicle
See Appendix C for available discounts.

Limitations

Maximum recommended trailer and vehicle length is 20 feet and a maximum RV length is 24 feet.
See Appendix A for camping regulations.

Contact

Okanogan–Wenatchee National Forest
Naches Ranger District
10237 Highway 12
Naches, WA 98937
Phone: 509–653–1401, Fax: 509–653–2638

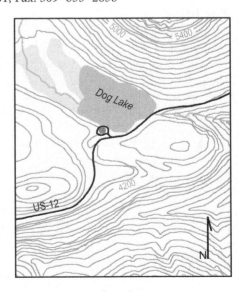

Location

114 Clear Lake North
Okanogan–Wenatchee National Forest

Directions

Start at the intersection of US–12 and WA–123 east of Packwood. Travel east on US–12 for 20.1 miles. Turn right onto Tieton Reservoir Road (Forest Service Road 1200) and travel 0.4 mile. Turn left into access road to Clear Lake North.

Or

Start at the intersection of US–12 and WA–410 north of Naches. Travel west on US–12 for 26.7 miles. Turn left onto Tieton Reservoir Road (Forest Service Road 1200) for 0.4 mile. Turn left into access road to Clear Lake North.

N46°38'01" – W121°15'0"   Elevation – 3,100 feet

Facilities

33 standard sites
Vault toilet
No water, bring your own or get at Clear Lake South campground
Garbage service

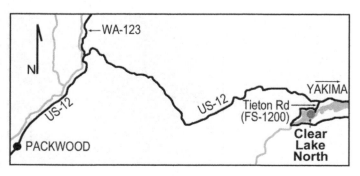

Driving Directions

Features

The Clear Creek North campground offers large campsites on both sides of the access road. Some campsites are along the North Fork Tieton River. Clear Lake North access road intersects with Forest Service Road 746 and access to Clear Lake South campground. Access to the lake is via Clear Creek South's boat launch.

Reservations

None, campsites are first–come, first–serve

Season

Open year around, but no services or fees after October 31

Activities

Boating, Fishing.

Cost

$10
$5 extra vehicle
See Appendix C for available discounts

Limitations

Maximum recommended vehicle length is 22 feet.
See Appendix A for camping regulations.

Contact

Okanogan–Wenatchee National Forest
Naches Ranger District
10237 Highway 12
Naches, WA 98937
Phone: 509–653–1401 (Voice/TTY), Fax: 509–653–2638

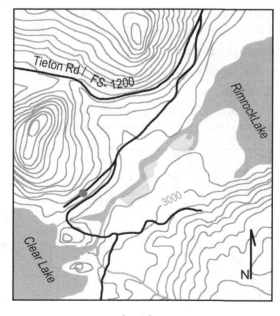

Location

115 Clear Lake South
Okanogan–Wenatchee National Forest

Directions

Start at the intersection of US–12 and WA–123 east of Packwood. Travel east on US–12 for 20.1 miles. Turn right onto Tieton Reservoir Road (Forest Service Road 1200) and travel 3.9 miles. Turn left onto Forest Service Road 740 and travel 0.5 mile to Clear Creek South.

Or

Start at the intersection of US–12 and WA–410 north of Naches. Travel west on US–12 for 26.7 miles. Turn left onto Tieton Reservoir Road (Forest Service Road 1200) for 3.9 miles. Turn left onto Forest Service Road 740 for 0.5 mile to campground.

N46°37'44" – W121°16'05"   Elevation – 3,100 feet

Facilities

22 standard sites
Vault toilets
Potable water
Garbage service
Boat launch

Features

Clear Lake South campground lies along Clear Lake. The campground offers large shaded campsites.

Reservations

None, campsites are first–come, first–serve.

Season

Open all year, but no services or fees after October 31

Activities

Boating, Fishing.

Cost

$10
$5 extra vehicle
See Appendix C for available discounts.

Limitations

Maximum recommended vehicle length is 22 feet.
See Appendix A for camping regulations.

Contact

Okanogan–Wenatchee National Forest
Naches Ranger District
10237 Highway 12
Naches, WA 98937
Phone: 509–653–1401 (Voice/TTY), Fax: 509–653–2638

Clear Lake Boat Launch

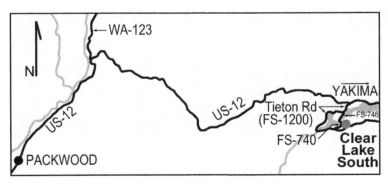

Driving Directions

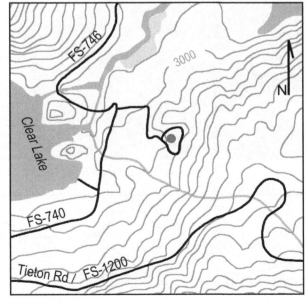

Location

116 Clover Flats
Department of Natural Resources

Directions

Start at the intersection of I–82 and East Valley Mall Blvd. (exit 36) near Yakima. Travel west on East Valley Mall Blvd. for 0.5 mile. Turn left onto Longfibre Avenue and travel south for 0.2 mile. Turn right onto W Ahtanum Road and travel 18.0 miles. In Tampico, turn right onto Ahtanum North Fork Road (A–2000 Road) and travel for 8.9 miles. Passing Ahtanum Camp the pavement ends (one lane with turn–outs). Continue on A–2000 Road for an additional 9.2 miles. Turn left into Clover Flats.

Note: The last 3.4 miles are very steep (12 – 13%).

N46°30'26" – W121°10'37"   Elevation – 6,320 feet

Facilities

9 standard sites
Vault/pit toilet
Potable water
Pack out garbage

Features

Clover Flats campground is in a sub–alpine area. Campground water may be turned off; always be prepared and bring a supply.

Reservations

None, all campsites are first–come, first–serve.

Season

Open all year

Activities

Hiking.

Cost

No Cost

Limitations

A Washington State Discover Pass is required.
See Appendix A for camping regulations.

Contact

Department of Natural Resources, Southeast Region
Phone: 509–925–8510
Web: *www.dnr.wa.gov*

Pine Forest Near Clover Flats

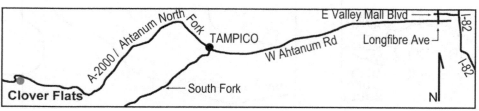

Driving Directions

Location

117 Tree Phones
Department of Natural Resources

Directions

Start at the intersection of I–82 and East Valley Mall Blvd. (exit 36) near Yakima. Travel west on East Valley Mall Blvd. for 0.5 mile. Turn left onto Longfibre Avenue and travel south for 0.2 mile. Turn right onto West Ahtanum Road and travel west for 18.0 miles. In Tampico, turn right onto Ahtanum North Fork Road (A–2000 Road) and travel for 8.9 miles. Passing Ahtanum Camp the pavement ends (one lane with turn–outs). Continue on A–2000 Road for an additional 5.8 miles. Turn left into Tree Phones (0.1 mile).

N46°29'49" – W121°07'17"   Elevation – 4,860 feet

Facilities

14 standard sites
Vault/pit toilets
Potable water
Pack out garbage
Shelter
Accessible toilet, campsite, shelter

Features

Tree Phones campground is near a forest stream. Campground water supply may be turned off; always be prepared and bring a supply. The facility has a snow shelter and provides access to the 23 mile Grey Rock Equestrian Trail.

Reservations

None, all campsites are first–come, first–serve.

Season

Open all year

Activities

Equestrian trail riding, Hiking, Hunting, Mountain biking.

Cost

No cost

Limitations

A Washington State Discover Pass is required.
See Appendix A for camping regulations.

Contact

Department of Natural Resources, Southeast Region
Phone: 509–925–8510
Web: *www.dnr.wa.gov*

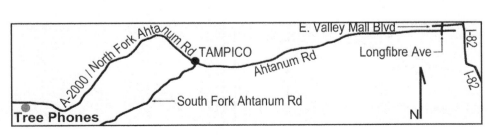

Driving Directions

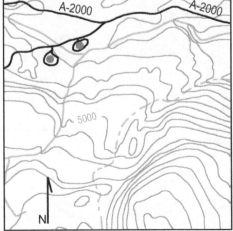

Location

118 Ahtanum Camp
Department of Natural Resources

Directions

Start at the intersection of I–82 and East Valley Mall Blvd. (exit 36) near Yakima. Travel west on East Valley Mall Blvd. for 0.5 mile. Turn left onto Longfibre Avenue and travel south for 0.2 mile. Turn right onto West Ahtanum Road and travel west for 18.0 miles. In Tampico, turn right onto Ahtanum North Fork Road (A–2000 Road) and travel 8.9 miles. Turn left into Ahtanum Camp.

N46°30'59" – W121°01'01"   Elevation – 3,160 feet

Facilities

12 standard sites
Vault/pit toilet
Potable water
Pack out garbage
Accessible toilet, water, campsite

Features

Ahtanum Camp is near a forest stream. Water in the campground may be turned off; always be prepared and bring a supply.

Reservations

None, all campsites are first–come, first–serve.

Season

Open all year

Activities

ATV/ORV riding, Hiking, Hunting, Snowmobiling.

Cost

No cost

Limitations

Ahtanum is a working forest with high volumes of heavy truck traffic during the week. Please use caution.

A Discover Pass is required at all times. A Sno–Park Permit is required during the winter.
See Appendix A for camping regulations.

Contact

Department of Natural Resources, Southeast Region
Phone: 509–925–8510
Web: *www.dnr.wa.gov*

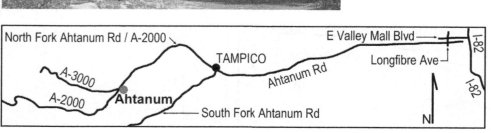

Driving Directions

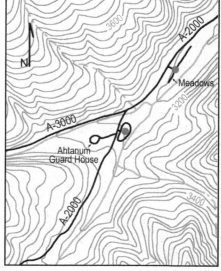

Location

119 Indian Creek
Okanogan–Wenatchee National Forest

Directions

Start at the intersection of US–12 and WA–123 near Packwood. Travel east on US–12 for 20.7 miles. Turn right into Indian Creek.

Or

Start at the intersection of US–12 and WA–410 North of Naches Travel west on US–12 for 25.9 miles. Turn left into Indian Creek.

N46°38'41" – W121°14'32"   Elevation – 3,000 feet

Facilities

34 standard sites
Vault/pit toilets
Potable water
Garbage service
Shelter

Features

Indian Creek campground is along the shore of Rimrock Lake and near Clear Lake. It offers many activities including swimming at nearby Minneapolis Beach. Summer temperatures typically get into the 80s. The parking spurs are paved.

Reservations

Reserve online at *www.recreation.gov* or call 1–877–444–6777 (5 am to 9 pm Pacific Time), 518–885–3639, or TDD 1–877–833–6777. Reservations must be made at least 4 days in advance. There is a 3 night minimum on holidays. Sites that are not reserved are available first–come, first–serve. See Appendix B for details.

Season

Open from mid May through mid September

Activities

Biking, Boating, Fishing, Hiking, Swimming, Whitewater paddling.

Cost

$18
$9 extra vehicle
See Appendix C for available discounts.

Limitations

Maximum recommended vehicle length is 32 feet. The reservation system lists the maximum vehicle length for

individual campsites.
See Appendix A for camping regulations.

Contact

Okanogan–Wenatchee National Forest
Naches Ranger District
10237 Highway 12
Naches, WA 98937
Phone: 509–653–1401 (Voice/TTY), Fax: 509–653–2638

Indian Creek Campsite

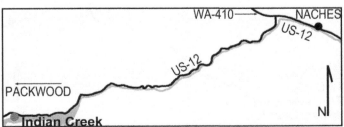

Driving Directions

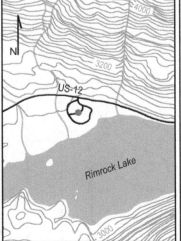

Location

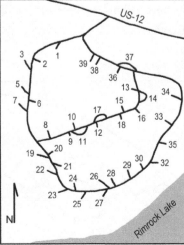

Campground

120 Hause Creek
Okanogan–Wenatchee National Forest

Directions

Start at the intersection of US–12 and WA–123 east of Packwood. Travel east on US–12 for 30.0 miles. Turn right into Hause Creek.

Or

Start at the intersection of US–12 and WA–410 north of Naches. Travel west on US–12 for 17.1 miles. Turn left into Hause Creek.

N46°40'29" – W121°04'48"   Elevation – 2,500 feet

Facilities

42 total sites: 37 standard, 5 walk–in
Some pull–through sites
Flush toilets
Potable water
Garbage service
Accessible campsite

Features

Hause Creek campground lies along the Tieton River. There are several riverside sites (9 – 20, 40 and 41). Summer temperatures reach into the 70s.

Reservations

Reserve online at *www.recreation.gov* or call 1–877–444–6777 (5 am to 9 pm Pacific Time), 518–885–3639, or TDD 1–877–833–6777. Reservations must be made at least 4 days in advance. There is a 3 night minimum on holidays. Sites that are not reserved are available first–come, first–serve. See Appendix B for details.

Season

Open from mid May through mid September. Campground will remain open with services (no water available after October 31) and reduced fees through mid November.

Activities

Fishing, Hiking, Whitewater paddling.

Cost

$18
$9 extra vehicle

See Appendix C for available discounts.

Limitations

Maximum recommended vehicle length is 30 feet. The reservation system lists the maximum vehicle length for individual campsites.
See Appendix A for camping regulations.

Contact

Okanogan–Wenatchee National Forest
Naches Ranger District
10237 Highway 12
Naches, WA 98937
Phone: 509–653–1401 (Voice/TTY), Fax: 509–653–2638

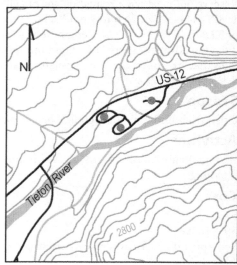

Location

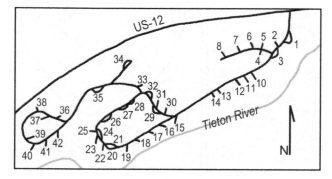

Campground

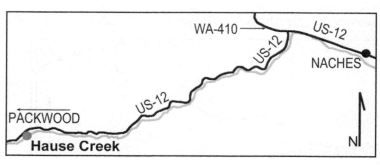

Driving Directions

121 Willows
Okanogan–Wenatchee National Forest

Directions

Start at the intersection of US–12 and WA–123 east of Packwood. Travel east on US–12 for 31.9 miles. Turn right into Willows.

Or

Start at the intersection of US–12 and WA–410 north of Naches. Travel west on US–12 for 15.1 miles. Turn left into Willows.

N46°40'21" – W121°02'24"   Elevation – 2,400 feet

Facilities

16 standard sites
Vault/pit toilet
Potable water
Garbage service

Features

Willows campground lies along the Tieton River and is surrounded by spectacular Jump Off Lookout. The campground has several riverside sites (5, 6, 7, 9, 11, and 13). Nearby hiking includes Little Wildcat, Ironstone Mountain and Grey Rock trails.

Willows Campsite

Reservations

Reserve online at *www.recreation.gov* or call 1–877–444–6777 (5 am to 9 pm Pacific Time), 518–885–3639, or TDD 1–877–833–6777. Reservations must be made at least 4 days in advance. There is a 3 night minimum on holidays. Sites that are not reserved are available first–come, first–serve. See Appendix B for details.

Season

Open from mid May through mid September

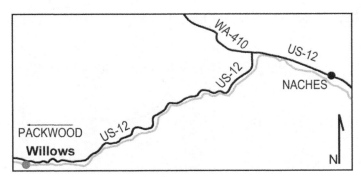

Driving Directions

Activities

Fishing, Hiking, Whitewater rafting.

Cost

$14
$7 extra vehicle
See Appendix C for available discounts.

Limitations

Maximum recommended vehicle length is 20 feet. The reservation system lists the maximum vehicle length for individual campsites.
See Appendix A for camping regulations.

Contact

Okanogan–Wenatchee National Forest
Naches Ranger District
10237 Highway 12
Naches, WA 98937
Phone: 509–653–1401 (Voice/TTY), Fax: 509–653–2638

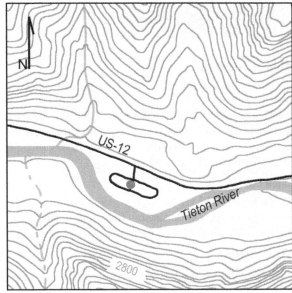

Location

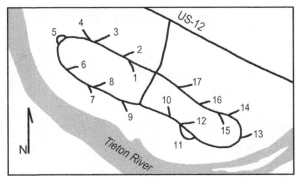

Campground

122 Windy Point
Okanogan–Wenatchee National Forest

Directions

Start at the intersection of US–12 and WA–123 east of Packwood. Travel east on US–12 for 39 miles. Turn right into Windy Point.

Or

Start at the intersection of US–12 and WA–410 north of Naches. Travel west on US–12 for 8.1 miles. Turn left into Windy Point.

N46°41'32" – W120°54'26" Elevation – 2,000 feet

Facilities

15 standard sites
Vault/pit toilet
Potable water
Garbage service

Features

Windy Point campground lies along the Tieton River. Nearby hiking includes Frost Mountain Lookout, Keenan Meadows and Grey Rock trails.

Reservations

Reserve online at *www.recreation.gov* or call 1–877–444–6777 (5 am to 9 pm Pacific Time), 518–885–3639, or TDD 1–877–833–6777. Reservations must be made at least 4 days in advance. There is a 3 night minimum on holidays. Sites that are not reserved are available first–come, first–serve. See Appendix B for details.

Season

Open from mid May through mid September. Campground will remain open with services (no water available after October 31) and reduced fees through mid November.

Activities

Fishing, Hiking, Whitewater paddling.

Cost

$14
$7 extra vehicle
See Appendix C for available discounts.

Limitations

Maximum recommended vehicle length is 22 feet. The reservation system lists maximum vehicle lengths for individual campsites.
See Appendix A for camping regulations.

Contact

Okanogan–Wenatchee National Forest
Naches Ranger District
10237 Highway 12
Naches, WA 98937
Phone: 509–653–1401 (Voice/TTY), Fax: 509–653–2638

Running the Tieton River

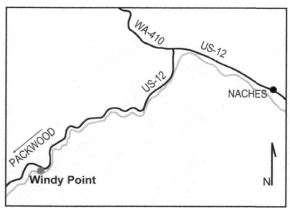

Driving Directions

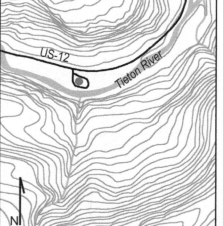

Location

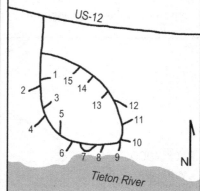

Campground

123 Cottonwood
Okanogan–Wenatchee National Forest

Directions

Start at the intersection of US–12 and WA–410 north of Naches. Travel west on WA–410 for 17.9 miles. Turn left into Cottonwood.

N46°54'25" – W121°01'33"   Elevation – 2,300 feet

Facilities

9 total sites: 5 standard sites, 4 tent–only sites
Pull–through sites (3,9)
Vault/pit toilet
Potable water
Garbage service

Features

Cottonwood Campground lies along the scenic Naches River. Sites 6, 7, 8, 9, 14, and 16 are located on the river, which offers excellent fishing. Summer temperatures are in the 70s.

Reservations

Reserve at *www.recreation.gov* or call 1–877–444–6777 (5 am to 9 pm Pacific Time), 518–885–3639, or TDD 1–877–833–6777. Reservations must be made at least 4 days in advance. There is a 2 night minimum on weekends and a 3 night minimum on holidays. Sites that are not reserved are available first–come, first–serve. See Appendix B for details.

Season

Open from mid May through the end of September. Campsites may remain open with full services and reduced fees through mid November, weather dependent.

Activities

Fishing.

Cost

$16
$8 extra vehicle
See Appendix C for available discounts.

Limitations

Maximum recommended vehicle length is 22 feet. The reservation system list the maximum vehicle length for individual campsites.
See Appendix A for camping regulations.

Watching the Campfire

Contact

Okanogan–Wenatchee National Forest
Naches Ranger District
10237 Highway 12
Naches, WA 98937
Phone: 509–653–1401 (Voice/TTY), Fax: 509–653–2638

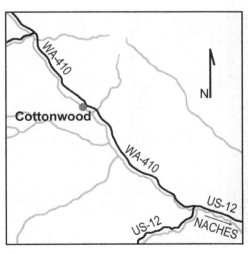

Driving Directions

Fire–Fighter Tribute in Naches

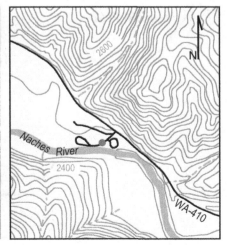

Location

124 Sawmill Flat
Okanogan–Wenatchee National Forest

Directions

Start at the intersection of US–12 and WA–410 north of Naches. Travel west on WA–410 for 23.9 miles. Turn left into Sawmill Flat.

N46°55'04" – W121°14'09"   Elevation – 2,500 feet

Facilities

23 total sites: 18 standard, 5 walk–in
Vault/pit toilet
Potable water
Garbage service
Shelter
Accessible toilet

Features

Sawmill Flat campground is located on the Naches River. Campsites are large, with sites 8, 9, and 14 –19 along the river. There is a Civilian Conservation Corp Shelter with fireplace and tables in the day use area. The campground is a great base camp for a variety of activities in the area. Nearby hiking includes Frost Mountain Lookout and Kaner Flat trails as well as whitewater paddling on the American River. Summer temperatures range in the 70s.

Activities

Hiking, Whitewater paddling.

Cost

$18
$5 extra vehicle
See Appendix C for available discounts.

Reservations

Reserve online at *www.recreation.gov* or call 1–877–444–6777 (5 am to 9 pm Pacific Time), 518–885–3639, or TDD 1–877–833–6777. Reservations must be made at least 4 days in advance. There is a 2 night minimum on weekends and a 3 night minimum on holidays. Sites that are not reserved are available first–come, first–serve. See Appendix B for details.

Limitations

Maximum recommended vehicle length is 24 feet. The reservation system lists the maximum vehicle length for individual campsites.
See Appendix A for camping regulations.

Contact

Okanogan–Wenatchee National Forest
Naches Ranger District
10237 Highway 12
Naches, WA 98937
Phone: 509–653–1401 (Voice/TTY), Fax: 509–653–2638

Season

Open from mid May through the end of September. Campground will remain open with services (no water available after October 31) and reduced fees through mid November.

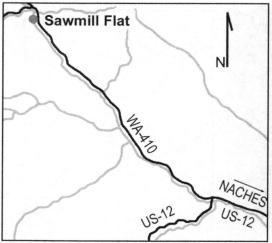

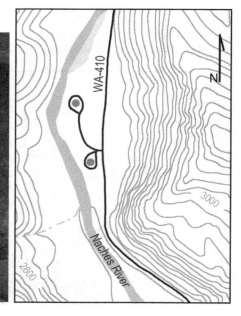

Driving Directions   *Campfire on a Cool Evening*   *Location*

125 Halfway Flat
Okanogan–Wenatchee National Forest

Naches River

Directions

Start at the intersection of US–12 and WA–410 north of Naches. Travel west on WA–410 for 20.9 miles. Turn left onto Old River Road (Forest Service Road 1704) and travel 3.0 miles. Turn right into Halfway Flat.

N46°56'46" – W121°05'45"   Elevation – 2,500 feet

Facilities

8 standard sites
3 double sites
Vault toilet
Potable water
Garbage service
Accessible toilet

Features

Halfway Flat campground is along the Little Naches River. The campground is popular with motorcyclists and jeep enthusiasts, although non–street legal motorized vehicle use is prohibited in the campground. There is an active gold mining claim along the river.

Reservations

None, all campsites are first–come, first–serve.

Season

Open late May through early September

Activities

Fishing, Hiking, Motorcycle riding.

Cost

$10–$18
$5 extra vehicle
See Appendix C for available discounts.

Limitations

Maximum vehicle length is 30 feet.
See Appendix A for camping regulations.

Contact

Okanogan–Wenatchee National Forest
Naches Ranger District
10237 Highway 12
Naches, WA 98937
Phone: 509–653–1401 (Voice/TTY), Fax: 509–653–2638

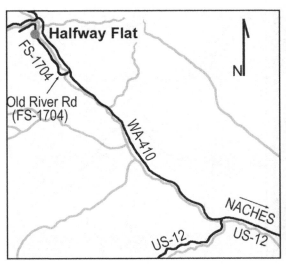

Driving Directions

Naches River

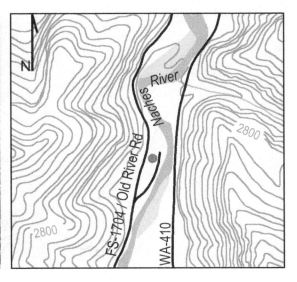

Location

126 Little Naches
Okanogan–Wenatchee National Forest

Directions

Start at the intersection of US–12 and WA–410 north of Naches. Travel west on WA–410 for 25.2 miles. Turn right onto Little Naches Road (Forest Service Road 19) for 0.1 mile. Turn left to campground.

N46°54'25" – W121°01'33"   Elevation – 2,562 feet

Facilities

18 standard sites
3 double sites
Vault/pit toilets
Potable water
Garbage service
Accessible campsite

Features

Little Naches campground is on the Little Naches River. Several sites are along the river. Frost Mountain Lookout and Kaner Flat trails are nearby, as well as American River for whitewater paddling. Summertime temperatures in the 70s make this campground an ideal place to spend a couple days or a two week vacation. The campground is 24 miles from Mount Rainier National Park.

Reservations

Reserve online at *www.recreation.gov* or call 1–877–444–6777 (5 am to 9 pm Pacific Time), 518–885–3639, or TDD 1–877–833–6777. Reservations must be made at least 4 days in advance. There is a 2 night minimum on weekends and a 3 night minimum on holidays. Sites that are not reserved are available first–come, first–serve. See Appendix B for details.

Season

Open from mid May through mid September

Activities

Hiking, Whitewater paddling.

Little Naches Campsite

Cost

$14
$7 extra vehicle
See Appendix C for available discounts.

Limitations

Maximum recommended vehicle length is 20 feet; however, some campsites can handle vehicles up to 32 feet. The reservation system lists the maximum vehicle length for individual campsites.
See Appendix A for camping regulations.

Contact

Okanogan–Wenatchee National Forest
Naches Ranger District
10237 Highway 12
Naches, WA 98937
Phone: 509–653–1401 (Voice/TTY), Fax: 509–653–2638

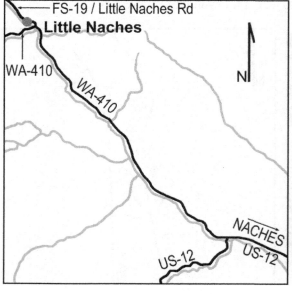

Driving Directions

Little Naches Flower

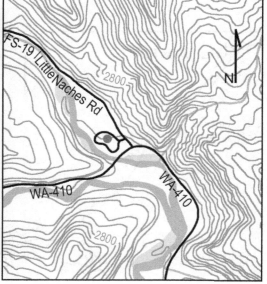

Location

127 Kaner Flat
Okanogan–Wenatchee National Forest

Directions

Start at the intersection of US–12 and WA–410 north of Naches. Travel west on WA–410 for 24.2 miles. Turn right onto Little Naches Road (Forest Service Road 19) and travel 1.8 miles. Continue straight onto Forest Service Road 70 for another 0.6 mile. Turn right into Kaner Flat.

N47°00'39" – W121°07'49"   Elevation – 2,678 feet

Kaner Flat Campsite

Facilities

43 standard sites
6 double sites
Some pull–through sites
Vault toilets
Potable water
Garbage service
Accessible toilet, campsite

Features

Kaner Flat campground is near the Little Naches River. Several sites are along the river. The campground has an RV loop and is popular with motorcyclists and jeep enthusiasts.

Reservations

None, all campsites are first–come, first–serve.

Season

Open from mid May through end of October, weather depending. Garbage service and vault toilets will be available until November 15, weather depending.

Activities

ATV/ORV riding.

Cost

$12 per night
$5 extra vehicle
See Appendix C for available discounts.

Limitations

Maximum vehicle length is 30 feet.
Non–street legal motorized vehicle use is prohibited in campground.
See Appendix A for camping regulations.

Contact

Okanogan–Wenatchee National Forest
Naches Ranger District
10237 Highway 12
Naches, WA 98937
Phone: 509–653–1401 (Voice/TTY), Fax: 509–653–2638

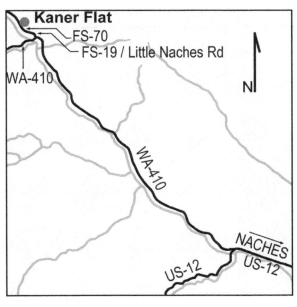

Driving Directions

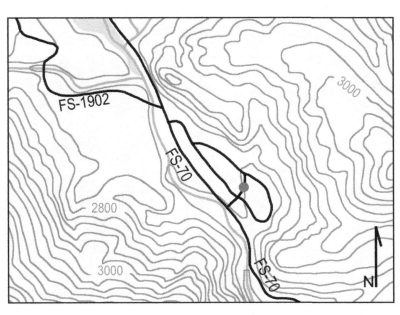

Location

128 Crow Creek
Okanogan–Wenatchee National Forest

Facilities

15 standard sites
Vault/pit toilet
No water, bring your own
Garbage service

Features

Crow Creek campground is at the fork of the Little Naches River and Crow Creek. A Civilian Conservation Corp shelter is available. This area is popular for motorcycle riding.

Reservations

None, campsites are filled first–come, first–serve.

Season

Open from mid May through end of September, weather permitting

Activities

Motorcycle riding.

Cost

$10
$5 extra vehicle
See Appendix C for available discounts.

Limitations

Maximum vehicle length is 30 feet.
See Appendix A for camping regulations.

Contact

Okanogan–Wenatchee National Forest
Naches Ranger District
10237 Highway 12
Naches, WA 98937
Phone: 509–653–1401 (Voice/TDD), Fax: 509–653–2638

Directions

Start at the intersection of US–12 and WA–410 north of Naches. Travel west on WA–410 for 24.2 miles. Turn right onto Little Naches Road (Forest Service Road 19) for 1.8 miles. Continue straight onto Forest Service Road 70 for another 0.9 mile. Turn left onto Forest Service Road 1902 for 0.5 mile. Turn right into campground.

   N47°00'59" – W121°08'23"   Elevation – 2,900 feet

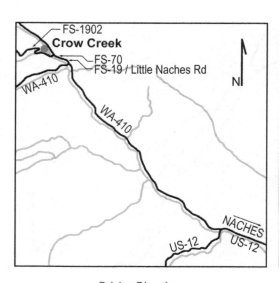

Driving Directions

Cascade Flower

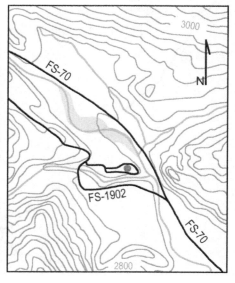

Location

129 American Forks
Okanagon–Wenatchee National Forest

Directions

Start at the intersection of US–12 and WA–410 north of Naches. Travel west on WA–410 for 28.9 miles. Turn left onto Bumping River Road (Forest Service Road 1800) for 0.1 mile. Turn left into campground.

N46°58'35" – W121°09'45"   Elevation – 2,900 feet

Facilities

16 standard sites
Vault/pit toilet
No water, bring your own
Garbage service

Features

American Forks campground is located on the Bumping River. A Civilian Conservation Corp Shelter is available.

Reservations

None, all sites are first–come, first–served.

Season

Season is from mid May to mid September, weather permitting

Cost

$10
$5 extra vehicle
See Appendix C for available discounts.

Limitations

Maximum vehicle length is 30 feet.
See Appendix A for camping regulations.

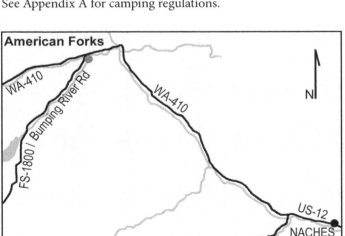

Bumping River

Contact

Okanogan–Wenatchee National Forest
Naches Ranger District
10237 Highway 12
Naches, WA 98937
Phone: 509–653–1401 (Voice/TDD), Fax: 509–653–2638

French Toast

French Toast for American Forks–ooh la la. The first time we had this French toast we were on a sailboat anchored in Hanalei Bay in the Hawaiian Islands. We were skeptical about the pepper but after tasting, it immediately became our favorite. Be brave.

Ingredients

4 eggs
1 cup milk
½ teaspoon pepper
1 teaspoon vanilla
1 teaspoon cinnamon
12 slices of day–old rustic French bread
Butter
Maple syrup, fresh berries, or jam

Preparation

Break eggs into a wide, shallow bowl or pie plate and beat lightly with a fork. Stir in pepper, vanilla, cinnamon, and milk.

Heat a griddle or skillet and coat with a little butter. Soak the bread slices in the egg mixture – about 30 seconds on each side. Soak only as many slices as you will be cooking at one time.

Fry the soaked bread until bottom is golden brown, flip and brown the other side. Serve with butter and top with syrup, berries or jam, or all three!

Serves 4

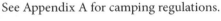

Driving Directions

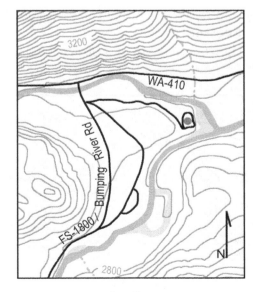

Location

130 Cedar Springs
Okanogan–Wenatchee National Forest

Directions

Start at the intersection of US–12 and WA–410 north of Naches. Travel west on WA–410 for 28.9 miles. Turn left onto Bumping River Road (Forest Service Road 1800) and travel for 0.5 mile. Turn left into Cedar Springs.

N46°58'17" – W121°09'49"   Elevation – 2,800 feet

Facilities

14 standard sites
Some pull-through sites
Vault toilet
Potable water
Garbage service

Features

Cedar Springs Campground is located along the Bumping River. Sites 1 – 4, 6, 7, 9, 10 and 11 are located on the river. The campground makes a great base camp for activities, such as hiking along the Quartz Creek Trail, whitewater paddling on the Little Naches River, or bike riding and site seeing. Summer highs in the 70s make this a pleasant summer camping experience.

Reservations

Reserve online at *www.recreation.gov* or call 1–877–444–6777 (5 am to 9 pm Pacific Time), 518–885–3639, or TDD 1–877–833–6777. Reservations must be made at least 4 days in advance. There is a 2 night minimum on weekends and a 3 night minimum on holidays. Sites that are not reserved are available first–come, first–serve. See Appendix B for details.

Season

Open from mid May through mid September

Activities

Hiking, Mountain biking, Whitewater paddling.

Cost

$16 per night
$8 extra vehicle
See Appendix C for available discounts.

Limitations

Maximum recommended vehicle length is 22 feet. The reservation system and campground manager list maximum vehicle length for individual campsites.
See Appendix A for camping regulations.

Contact

Okanogan–Wenatchee National Forest
Naches Ranger District
10237 Highway 12
Naches, WA 98937
Phone: 509–653–1401 (Voice/TTY), Fax: 509–653–2638

Cedar Springs Campsite

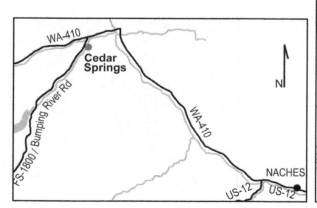

Driving Directions

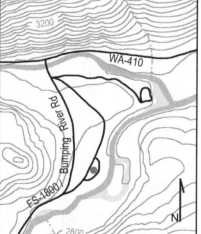

Location

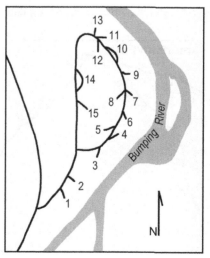

Campground

131 Soda Springs
Okanogan–Wenatchee National Forest

Directions

Start at the intersection of US–12 and WA–410 north of Naches. Travel west on WA–410 for 28.9 miles. Turn left onto Bumping River Road (Forest Service Road 1800) and travel for 4.8 miles. Turn left to Soda Springs.

N46°55'32" – W121°12'53"   Elevation – 3,100 feet

Facilities

26 standard sites
Pull–through sites
Vault toilets
Potable water
Garbage service

Features

Soda Springs campground sits along the Bumping River and offers a great view of Old Scab Mountain. Sites 6, 11 through 15, 19 and 20 are along the river. The campground has two Conservation Corp Picnic shelters/kitchens in the day use area. American River and Bumping River provide good whitewater paddling. The campground offers access to the William O Douglas Wilderness and many hiking trails that include: Goat Creek Trail, Nile Ridge Trail and the Richmond Mine Trail.

Reservations

Reserve online at *www.recreation.gov* or call 1–877–444–6777 (5 am to 9 pm Pacific Time), 518–885–3639, or TDD 1–877–833–6777. Reservations must be made at least 4 days in advance. There is a 2 night minimum on weekends and a 3 night minimum on holidays. Sites that are not reserved are available on a first–come, first–serve basis. See Appendix B for details.

Season

Open from mid May through end of September. Campground will remain open with services (no water available after October 31) and reduced fees through mid November.

Activities

Hiking, Whitewater paddling.

Cost

$18 per night
$9 extra vehicle
See Appendix C for available discounts.

Limitations

Recommended maximum vehicle length is 30 feet; however, the reservation system lists lengths for individual campsites.
See Appendix A for camping regulations.

Contact

Okanogan–Wenatchee National Forest
Naches Ranger District
10237 Highway 12
Naches, WA 98937
Phone: 509–653–1401 (Voice/TTY), Fax: 509–653–2638

Soda Springs Shelter and Campsite

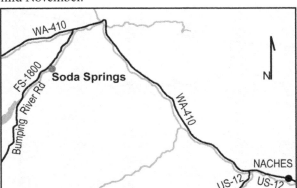

Driving Directions

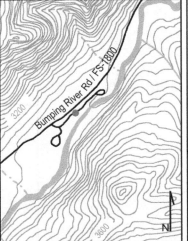

Location

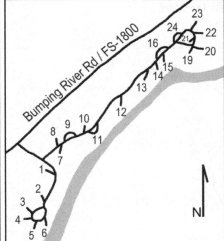

Campground

132 Cougar Flat
Okanogan–Wenatchee National Forest

Directions

Start at the intersection of US–12 and WA–410 north of Naches. Travel west on WA–410 for 28.9 miles. Turn left onto Bumping River Road (Forest Service Road 1800) and travel for 5.8 miles. Turn left into Cougar Flat.

N46°54'58" – W121°13'51"   Elevation – 3,100 feet

Facilities

12 total sites: 8 standard,
4 walk in
Vault/pit toilet
Potable water
Garbage service

Features

Cougar Flat campground lies along Bumping River with sites 1, 6 and 7 on the river. You can make out Old Scab Mountain from the campground. Goose Prairie and Goat Creek trails are nearby. Summertime temperatures in the 70s make an enjoyable summer experience.

Reservations

Reserve online at *www.recreation.gov* or call 1–877–444–6777 (5 am to 9 pm Pacific time), 518–885–3639, or TDD 1–877–833–6777. Reservations must be made at least 4 days in advance. There is a 2 night minimum on weekends and a 3 night minimum on holidays. Sites that are not reserved are available first–come, first–serve. See Appendix B for details.

Season

Open from mid May through mid September

Activities

Hiking.

Cost

$16 per night
$8 extra vehicle
See Appendix C for available discounts.

Limitations

Maximum length recommended for vehicles is 20 feet. The reservation system and the campground manager list the maximum vehicle length for individual campsites. See Appendix A for camping regulations.

Contact

Okanogan–Wenatchee National Forest
Naches Ranger District
10237 Highway 12
Naches, WA 98937
Phone: 509–653–1401 (Voice/TTY), Fax: 509–653–2638

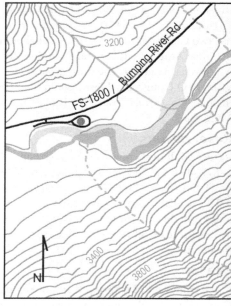

Location

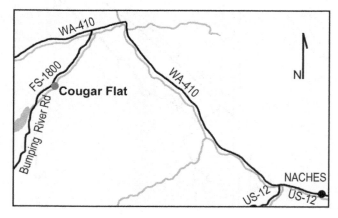

Driving Directions

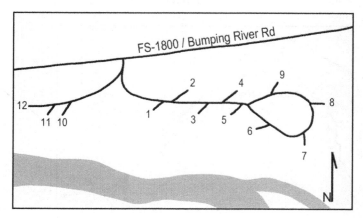

Campground

133 Bumping Lake
Okanogan–Wenatchee National Forest

Directions

Start at the intersection of US–12 and WA–410 north of Naches. Travel west on WA–410 for 28.9 miles. Turn left onto Bumping River Road (Forest Service Road 1800) and travel for 11.1 miles. Turn right to campground access road and travel for 0.2 mile.

46°51'41"N – 121°18'03"W   Elevation – 3,300 feet

Facilities

45 standard sites
Some pull–through sites (Lower Bumping)
Flush toilets
Vault toilets
Potable water
Garbage service
Boat launch
Accessible toilet, campsite

Features

Bumping Lake Campground sits just off the shores of Bumping Lake in the Cascade Mountains. Sites 43, 44, and 45 are situated along the lake. The Day area also has lake access and a boat launch. Temperatures commonly reach the 70s in summer. We thought this was a great RV camping spot on a stunningly beautiful lake and a good place for kids to ride bikes on the paved roads through–out the campground.

Reservations

Reserve online at *www.recreation.gov* or call 1–877–444–6777 (5 am to 9 pm Pacific Time), 518–885–3639, or TDD 1–877–833–6777. Reservations must be made at least 4 days in advance. There is a 2 night minimum on weekends and a 3 night minimum on holidays. Sites that are not reserved are available first–come, first–serve. See Appendix B for details.

Season

Upper Bumping is open from mid May through the end of September, weather permitting. Lower Bumping may remain open with full services and reduced fees through mid November, weather depending.

Activities

Boating, Fishing, Hiking, Hunting, Mountain Biking, Whitewater paddling.

Cost

$20 Upper Bumping
$10 extra vehicle
$18 Lower Bumping
$9 extra vehicle
See Appendix C for available discounts.

Limitations

Maximum recommended vehicle length is 30 feet for the Upper Bumping campsites and 50 feet for the Lower Bumping campsites. The reservation system and the campground manager list the maximum vehicle length for individual campsites.
See Appendix A for camping regulations.

Contact

Okanogan–Wenatchee National Forest
Naches Ranger District
10237 Highway 12
Naches, WA 98937
Phone: 509–653–1401 (Voice/TTY), Fax: 509–653–2638

(continued on next page)

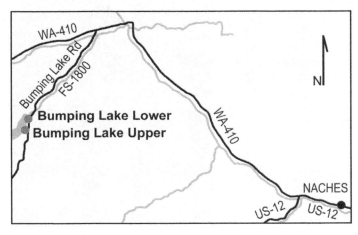

Driving Directions

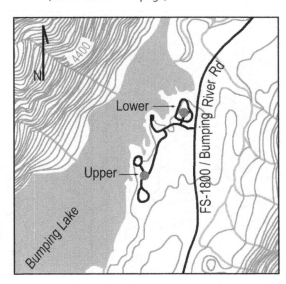

Location

Better Browns Breakfast

We love breakfast and especially when camping, we want bacon and eggs and love hash brown potatoes. Unfortunately, we are on a reduced carbohydrate diet. That prompted us to create Better Browns – a frittata variation but with fewer eggs.

Ingredients

½ head of cauliflower, grated
1 small zucchini, grated
½ onion, chopped
2 mushrooms, chopped
½ red pepper, chopped
1 jalapeño chili, finely chopped
6 green onions, thinly sliced
Salt and pepper to taste
2 tablespoons of olive oil or 1 tablespoon oil and 1 tablespoon butter
2 eggs
2 dollops sour cream

Preparation

At Home – *It may be easiest to do the grating and cutting at home and then transport to the campground in a sealed plastic bag or container in the cooler. Grate the cauliflower and zucchini and put into a sealable storage container. Dice the remaining vegetables with a knife, add them to the container, and stir well to mix.*

At the Campsite – *A good friend says that everything tastes better with bacon. In his honor, fry 2 pieces of bacon per person and set aside to drain. To complete a breakfast for two people, break two eggs*

into a bowl, add salt and pepper to taste, and stir with a fork until mixed. Add about 1 ½ cups of the vegetable mixture and stir to mix. Reseal the remaining vegetables for another day. (The two of us normally can eat for three days from one batch.)

In a skillet, add oil and/or butter and heat to just bubbling. Add egg/vegetable mixture to the hot skillet and flatten with a spatula. Cook until the bottom side browns.

Turn mixture over to brown the second side. (We cut the

patty in half or quarters to make flipping easier). After vegetables are turned, place the cooked bacon on top to reheat. Cook until the vegetables are

done and nicely browned. On cold days we put a lid on the skillet to help keep the heat in and make cooking faster. Place on a plate and top with a dab of sour cream.

(continued from previous page)

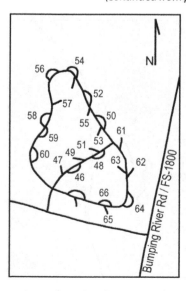

Lower Bumping Campground

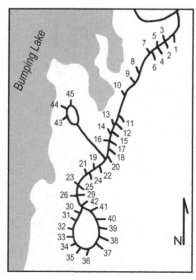

Upper Bumping Campground

Bumping Lake Better Browns

134 Hell's Crossing
Okanogan–Wenatchee National Forest

Directions

Start at the intersection of US–12 and WA–410 north of Naches. Travel west on WA–410 for 33.3 miles. Turn right into Hell's Crossing.

N46°57'56" – W121°15'51"   Elevation – 3,250 feet

Facilities

18 total sites: 16 standard sites, 2 double sites
Vault/pit toilets
Potable water (Westside only)
Garbage service

Features

Hells Crossing campground lies along the American River. The campground is in two sections, one section is on the east side of the river and one is on the west side with many riverside sites (1, 2, 5, 10, 13, 15, and 18). The nearby Goat Creek Trail offers hiking. A breathtaking view of Goat Peak can be seen from the campground. Summer temperatures reach into the 70s.

Reservations

Reserve online at *www.recreation.gov* or call
1–877–444–6777 (5 am to 9 pm Pacific Time), 518–885–3639, or TDD 1–877–833–6777. Reservations must be made at least 4 days in advance. There is a 2 night minimum on weekends and a 3 night minimum on holidays. Sites that are not reserved are available first–come, first–serve. See Appendix B for details.

Season

Season for Eastside campground is from mid May through the end of September. Westside campground may remain open with full services and reduced fees through the end of October, and with reduced services (no water) until mid November.

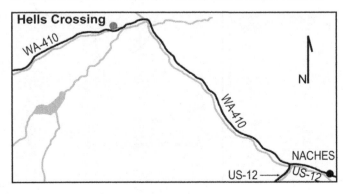

Driving Directions

Activities

Fishing, Hiking, Swimming.

Cost

$14
$7 extra vehicle
See Appendix B for available discounts.

Limitations

Maximum recommended vehicle length is 20 feet. The reservation system lists the maximum vehicle length for individual campsites.
See Appendix A for camping regulations.

Contact

Okanogan–Wenatchee National Forest
Naches Ranger District
10237 Highway 12
Naches, WA 98937
Phone: 509–653–1401 (Voice/TTY), Fax: 509–653–2638

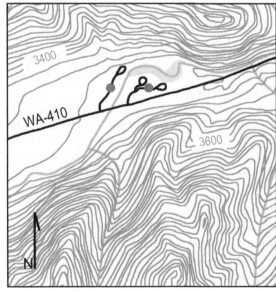

Location

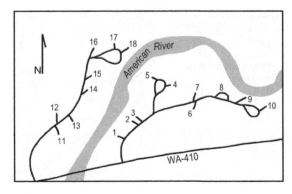

Campground

153

135 Pleasant Valley
Okanogan–Wenatchee National Forest

Directions

Start at the intersection of US–12 and WA–410 north of Naches. Travel west on WA–410 for 37.2 miles. Turn left into Pleasant Valley.

N46°56'34" – W121°19'32"   Elevation – 3,300 feet

Facilities

16 standard sites
Vault/pit toilet
Potable water
Garbage service
Shelter

Features

Pleasant Valley campground lies along the American River. The campground has a Civilian Conservation Corp shelter with tables and fireplace. Nearby hiking trails include Crow Lake trail, Swamp Lake trail, Cougar Valley trail and Union Creek trail. Our observation was that the campground was far enough off WA–410 to eliminate most road noise.

Reservations

Reserve online at *www.recreation.gov* or call 1–877–444–6777 (5 am to 9 pm Pacific Time), 518–885–3639, or TDD 1–877–833–6777. Reservations must be made at least 3 days in advance. There is a 3 night minimum on holidays. Sites that are not reserved are available first–come, first–serve. See Appendix B for details.

Season

Open from mid May through mid September. Campground will remain open with full services and reduced fees through the end of October.

Activities

Fishing, Hiking, Swimming, Whitewater paddling.

Cost

$16
$8 extra vehicle
See Appendix C for available discounts.

Limitations

Maximum recommended vehicle length is 32 feet. The reservation system lists the maximum vehicle length for individual campsites.
See Appendix A for camping regulations.

Contact

Okanogan–Wenatchee National Forest
Naches Ranger District
10237 Highway 12
Naches, WA 98937
Phone: 509–653–1401 (Voice/TTY), Fax: 509–653–2638

Pleasant Valley Shelter

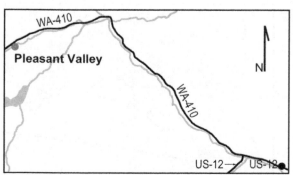

Driving Directions

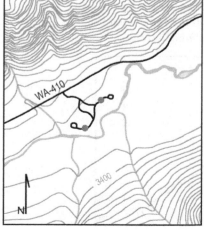

Location

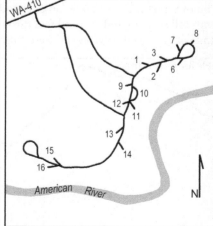

Campground

136 Lodgepole
Okanogan–Wenatchee National Forest

Directions

Start at the intersection of US–12 and WA–410 north of Naches. Travel west on WA–410 for 40.8 miles. Turn right into Lodgepole.

N46°54'59" – W121°23'03"   Elevation – 3,500 feet

Facilities

34 standard sites
Pull–through sites
Vault/pit toilets
Potable water
Garbage service

Features

Lodgepole campground lies along the American River. The campground has several riverside sites (12, 15, 16, 25, 26, 28, 32 – 34). Summer temperatures reach into the 70s. Nearby are Crow Lake trail, Swamp Lake trail, Cougar Valley trail and Union Creek trail.

Reservations

Reserve online at *www.recreation.gov* or call 1–877–444–6777 (5 am to 9 pm Pacific Time), 518–885–3639, or TDD 1–877–833–6777. Reservations must be made at least 4 days in advance. There is a 3 night minimum on holidays. Sites that are not reserved are available first–come, first–serve. See Appendix B for details.

Season

Open from mid May through mid September. Campground will remain open with full services and reduced fees through the end of October.

Activities

Fishing, Hiking, Swimming, Whitewater paddling.

Cost

$18
$9 extra vehicle
See Appendix C for available discounts.

Limitations

Maximum recommended vehicle length is 20 feet. The reservation system lists the maximum vehicle length for individual campsites.
See Appendix A for camping regulations.

Contact

Okanogan–Wenatchee National Forest
Naches Ranger District
10237 Highway 12
Naches, WA 98937
Phone: 509–653–1401
Fax: 509–653–2638

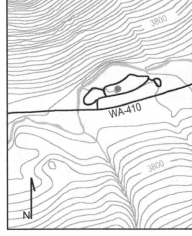

Location

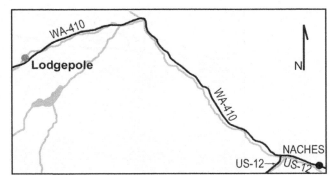

Driving Directions

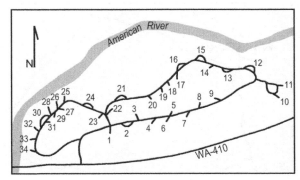

Campground

137 White River
Mt. Rainier National Park

Directions

Start at the intersection of US–12 and WA–410 north of Naches. Travel west on WA–410 for 55.4 miles. Turn left onto Sunrise Access Road and travel for 5.3 miles. Turn left onto campground road and travel for 1.0 mile.

N46°54'09" – W121°38'30"   Elevation – 4,400 feet

Facilities

112 standard sites
Some pull–through sites
Flush toilets
Potable water
Garbage service

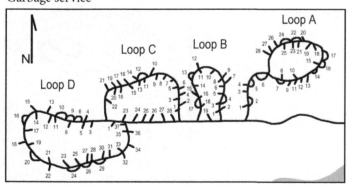

Campground

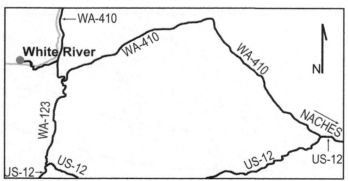

Driving Directions

Features

White River campground lies in a forest of exceptionally large trees, with a few campsites along the White River. Several trails are accessible from the campground: Wonderland Trail, Sunrise Trail, Glacier Basin Trail, Emmons Moraine Trail, Burroughs Mt. Trail, and Glacier Basin Camp. There are abundant wildflowers, even in September.

Reservations

None, campsites filled first–come, first–serve.

Season

Open from late June to late September

Activities

Hiking.

Cost

$20
See Appendix C for available discounts.

Limitations

Maximum RV length is 27 feet and trailer length is 18 feet. Camping is limited to 14 consecutive days and no more than 28 days total in any designated campground within the calendar year.
See Appendix A for camping regulations.

Contact

Mount Rainier National Park
55210 238th Avenue East
Ashford, WA 98304
Park Headquarters: 360–569–2211, TDD 360–569–2177
Park Information: 360–569–2211 ext. 3314

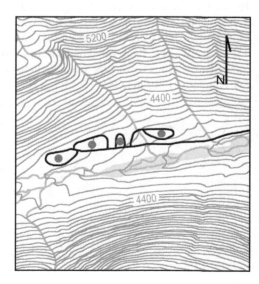

Location

138 Silver Springs
Mt. Baker–Snoqualmie National Forest

Directions

Start at the intersection of WA–164 (Griffin Avenue) and WA–410 in Enumclaw. Travel east on WA–410 (Roosevelt Avenue) towards Mount Rainier National Park for 31.5 miles. Turn right to Silver Springs.

N46°59'45" – W121°31'56"   Elevation – 2,560 feet

Facilities

56 standard sites
Pull through site
Vault toilets
Potable water
Garbage service
Shelter
Accessible toilets, campsite, shelter

Features

Silver Springs campground borders the White River in a beautiful section of old growth forest just outside the North Arch entrance to Mt. Rainier National Park. A natural spring flows through the center of the campground. Several hiking trails are available in the Crystal Mountain basin area, a short drive from the campground.

Reservations

Reserve online at *www.recreation.gov* or call 1–877–444–6777 (5 am to 9 pm Pacific time), 518–885–3639, or TDD 1–877–833–6777. Reservations must be made at least 4 days ahead of arrival and may be made up to 12 months in advance. See Appendix B for details.

Season

Open early May through late September

Activities

Fishing, Hiking.

Cost

$20
$10 extra vehicle
See Appendix C for available discounts.

Limitations

The Silver Creek Guard Station provides visitor information. See Appendix A for camping regulations.

Contact

Mt. Baker–Snoqualmie National Forest
Snoqualmie Ranger District
902 SE North Bend Way, Bldg. 1
North Bend, WA 98045
Phone: 425–888–1421
Enumclaw Office: 360–825–6585

Silver Springs Campsite

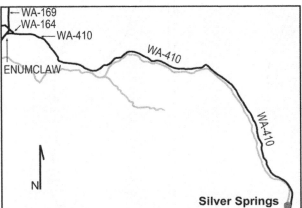

Driving Directions

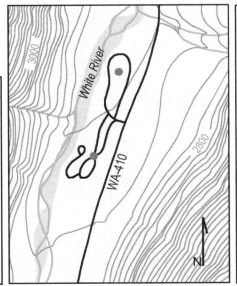

Location

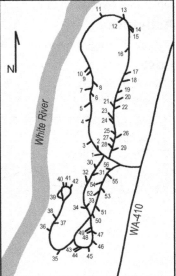

Campground

139 The Dalles
Mt. Baker–Snoqualmie National Forest

Directions

Start at the intersection of WA–164 (Griffin Avenue) and WA–410 in Enumclaw. Travel east on WA–410 (Roosevelt Avenue) towards Mount Rainier National Park for 25.5 miles. Turn right to The Dalles.

N47°04'15" – W121°34'41"   Elevation – 2,160 feet

Facilities

45 standard sites, 1 walk–in site
Vault toilets
Potable water
Garbage service
Accessible toilet, campsite

Features

The Dalles campground borders the White River in old growth forest. Several sites are along the river. The John Muir Nature Trail starts by the historic picnic shelter near the entrance. "Big Tree," a 9 foot diameter old growth Douglas–fir tree over 700 years old, is an amazing sight. Several trails are available within a short drive.

Reservations

Reserve online at *www.recreation.gov* or call 1–877–444–6777 (5 am to 9 pm Pacific time), 518–885–3639, or TDD 1–877–833–6777. Reservations must be made at least 4 days ahead of arrival and may be made up to 12 months in advance. See Appendix B for details.

Season

Open mid May through mid September

Activities

Fishing, Hiking, Interpretive Trail.

Cost

$18 – $20
$9 extra vehicle

See Appendix C for available discounts.

Limitations

A Recreation Pass is required to park at trailheads in the Snoqualmie Ranger District.
The Silver Creek Visitor Center, located 7 miles east of the campground, has information on local sites and attractions.
See Appendix A for camping regulations.

Contact

Mt. Baker–Snoqualmie National Forest
Snoqualmie Ranger District
902 SE North Bend Way, Bldg. 1
North Bend, WA 98045
Phone: 425–888–1421
Enumclaw Office: 360–825–6585

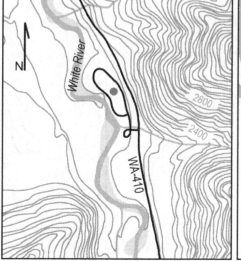

The Dalles Campsite

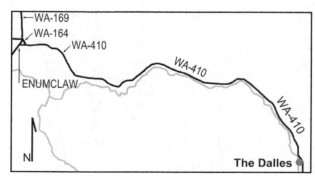

Driving Directions

Location

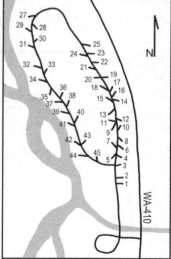

Campground

140 Ohanapecosh
Mt. Rainier National Park

Directions

Start at the intersection of WA–7 and WA–706 in Elbe. Travel east on WA–706 for 29.4 miles. Turn right on Ohanapecosh–Paradise Bypass Road (open June to October) and travel for 19.1 miles. Turn right on WA–123 and travel for 1.8 miles. Turn right into campground.

N46°44'04" – W121°34'07"   Elevation – 1914 feet

Facilities

188 standard sites
Some walk–in sites
Flush toilets
Potable water
Garbage service
RV dump station

Features

On the southeast side of the park, Ohanapecosh Campground is surrounded by an old–growth forest with an exceptionally beautiful snow–fed river running through it. Some campsites are along the Ohanapecosh river. Most campsites are large and open with little or no underbrush. Popular hikes to Silver Falls and the Grove of the Patriarchs are close to the campground. Ranger–led walks, talks, and campfire programs are scheduled daily from mid–June to early September.

Reservations

Reserve sites at *www.recreation.gov* or by phone at 1–877–444–6777. Reservations must be made at least 4 days ahead of arrival and can be made up to 6 months in advance. See Appendix B for details.

Season

Open late May to late September

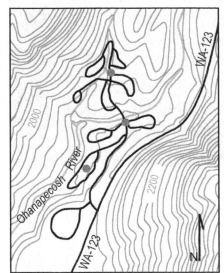

Location

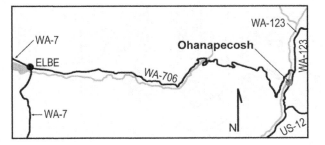

Driving Directions

Activities

Hiking.

Cost

$20
See Appendix C for available discounts.

Limitations

Maximum RV length is 32 feet and trailer length is 27 feet. Ohanapecosh campground is closed to generator use at all times.

Camping is limited to 14 consecutive days and no more than 28 days total in any designated campground within the calendar year.

See Appendix A for camping regulations.

Contact

Mount Rainier National Park
55210 238th Avenue East
Ashford, WA 98304
Park Headquarters: 360–569–2211, TDD: 360–569–2177
Park Information: 360–569–2211 ext. 3314

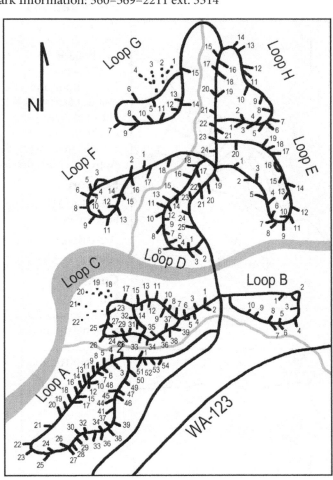

Campground

141 Cougar Rock
Mt. Rainier National Park

Directions

Start at the intersection of WA–7 and WA–706 in Elbe. Travel east on WA–706 for 22.3 miles. Turn left into campground.

N46°46'03 – W121°47'36"   Elevation – 3,180 feet

Facilities

173 standard sites
Some pull–through sites
Flush toilets
Potable water
Garbage service
RV dump station

Features

Cougar Rock campground lies in a forest of large trees and offers private campsites. The campground is near the Paradise area, which is the most popular destination in the park with a lodge and visitor center, many miles of hiking trails, and a commanding view of the mountain. Ranger–led walks, talks, and campfire programs are scheduled daily from mid–June to early September.

Reservations

Reserve sites at *www.recreation.gov* or by phone at 1–877–444–6777. Reservations must be made at least 4 days ahead of arrival and can be made up to 6 months in advance. See Appendix B for details.

Season

Open late May to late September

Activities

Hiking.

Cost

$20
See Appendix C for available discounts.

Limitations

Motor homes over 35 feet and trailers over 27 feet are not allowed to enter the campground! Turns on loop roads are tight and vehicles are likely to be damaged.

Loop E of Cougar Rock is closed to generator use at all times. This area is subject to sudden and severe geological hazards such as flooding, landslides, and rock fall.

Camping is limited to 14 consecutive days and no more than 28 days total in any designated campground within the calendar year.

See Appendix A for camping regulations.

Contact

Mount Rainier National Park
55210 238th Avenue East
Ashford, WA 98304
Park Headquarters: 360–569–2211, TDD: 360–569–2177
Park Information: 360–569–2211 ext. 3314

Mt. Rainier

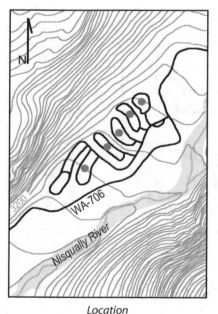

Location

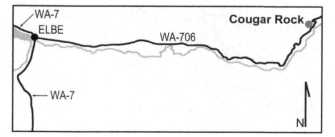

Driving Directions

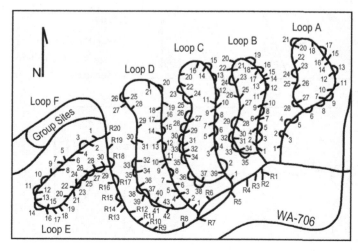

Campground

142 Big Creek
Gifford–Pinchot National Forest

Directions

Start at the intersection of WA–7 and WA–706 in Elbe. Travel east on WA–706 for 10.2 miles. Turn right onto Kernaham Road (becomes Skate Creek Road N and Forest Service Road 52) and travel for 1.9 miles. Turn right to Big Creek.

N48°44'04" – W121°58'09"   Elevation – 1,818 feet

Big Creek Campsite

Facilities

29 standard sites
Pull through sites
Vault toilets
Potable water
Garbage service

Features

Big Creek campground is 6 miles from the west entrance to Mt. Rainier National Park and nestled in large first and second growth trees. Thick undergrowth provides private campsites, a few of which are along the banks of Big Creek. Some parking spurs are paved; others are native moss and dirt. The campground is near Glacier View Wilderness and the Sawtooth Trail system, including High Rock Lookout Trail.

Reservations

Reserve online at www.recreation.gov or call 1–877–444–6777, 518–885–3639, or TDD 1–877–833–6777. Reservations must be made at least 4 days ahead of arrival and can be made up to 6 months in advance. See Appendix B for details.

Season

Open mid May through mid September

Activities

Equestrian trail riding, Fishing, Hiking, Mountain biking.

Cost

$18
$9 extra vehicle
See Appendix C for available discounts.

Limitations

Because of the tight turning radius for vehicles, the maximum length recommended for RV/trailers is 22 feet.
See Appendix A for camping regulations.

Contact

Gifford Pinchot National Forest
Cowlitz Valley Ranger District
10024 US Hwy 12, PO Box 670
Randle, WA 98377
Phone: 360–497–1100, TTY: 360–497–1101,
Fax: 360–497–1102

Big Creek Campsite

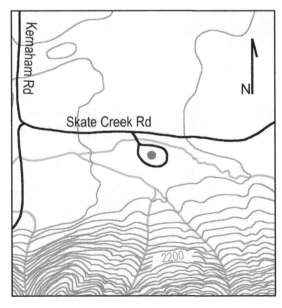

Location

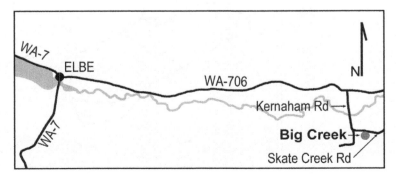

Driving Directions

143 Alder Lake, Rocky Point
Tacoma Power and Light

Directions

Start at intersection of I–5 and WA–512 (exit 127) south of Tacoma. Travel east on WA–512 for 2.2 miles. Turn right on WA–7 South (Pacific Avenue) and travel 34.5 miles. Turn right into Rocky Point.

N46°46'28" – W122°13'15"   Elevation – 1,260 feet

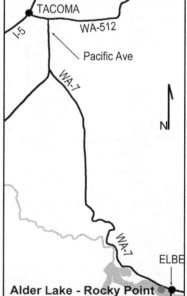

Alder Lake

Facilities

25 partial utility sites (W/E)
Some pull through sites
Vault toilets
Potable water
Garbage service
RV dump at main campground
Boat launch (when the reservoir water is not too low)

Features

Rocky Point is along Alder Lake, four miles east of the main Alder Lake Park. Several sites are along the water. The campground has paved sites.

Reservations

Reserve online at the WA State Parks website: *www.parks.state.wa.us* or phone 888–502–8690. Reservations are available May 15 through Sept 15. See Appendix B for details.

Season

Closed December 20 to January 1

Activities

Boating, Fishing.

Cost

$33 partial utility
$10 extra vehicle
See Appendix C for available discounts.

Limitations

See Appendix A for camping regulations.

Contact

Park Office : 360–569–2778

Rocky Point Campsite

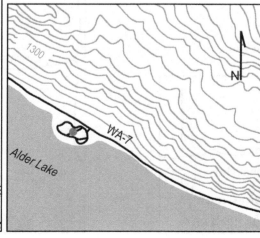

Driving Directions

Location

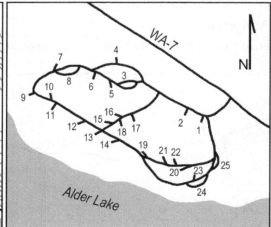

Campground

144 Alder Lake Park
Tacoma Power and Light

Directions

Start at intersection of I–5 and WA–512 (exit 127) south of Tacoma. Travel east on WA–512 for 2.2 miles. Turn right on WA–7 South (Pacific Avenue) and travel for 30.1 miles. Turn right into Alder Lake Park.

N46°48'01" – W122°17'53"   Elevation – 1,260 feet

Facilities

148 total sites: 26 standard, 49 partial utility (W/E), 37 utility (W/E/S), 36 walk–in
Some pull–through sites
Flush toilets
Potable water
Hot showers
Garbage service
RV dump station
Boat launch
Moorage
Accessible toilet

Alder Lake Campsite

Features

Alder Lake campground lies along Alder Lake. The park offers good shade and paved sites for easy RV parking.

Reservations

Reserve online at the WA State Parks website: *www.parks.state.wa.us* or phone 888–502–8690. Reservations are available May 15 through Sept 15. Sites are first come, first serve the rest of the year. See Appendix B for details.

Season

Closed December 20 to January 1

Activities

Beach combing, Bird watching, Boating, Fishing, Hiking, Swimming.

Cost

$24 standard site
$33 partial utility
$35 utility
$10 extra vehicle
See Appendix C for available discounts.

Limitations

See Appendix A for camping regulations.

Contact

Park Office: 360–569–2778

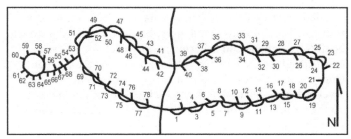

Main Campground

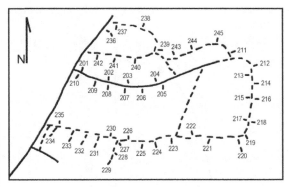

Walk–In Campground

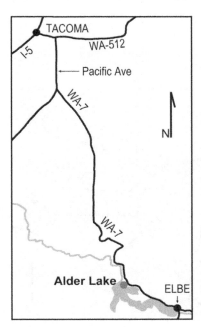

Driving Directions

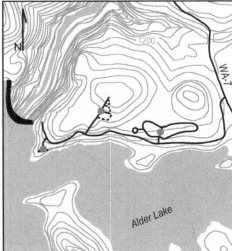

Location

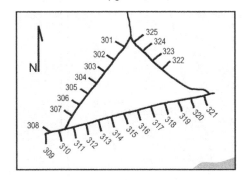

Elk Plain Campground

163

145 Millersylvania
Washington State Parks

Directions

Start at the intersection of I–5 and WA–121 (exit 95) south of Olympia. Travel north on WA–121 (also called Maytown Road) for 2.7 miles. Turn left to continue on WA–121 (now called Tilly Road) and travel for 0.7 mile. Turn left into park.

N46°54'39" – W122°54'42"   Elevation – 220 feet

Facilities

172 total sites: 120 standard, 48 partial utility (W/E),
4 primitive
Flush toilets
Potable water
Hot showers
Garbage service
Boat launch and dock
RV dump station
Accessible toilet, water, campsite

Features

Located on Deep Lake, Millersylvania State Park offers many trails and broad stands of old–growth forest. Deep Lake attracts boaters, swimmers and fishermen. The park buildings were constructed almost entirely by hand in 1935 by the Civilian Conservation Corps. Relics of a narrow–gauge railroad and several skid roads used in the 1800s by the loggers remain on the grounds. Stumps of trees still carry notch scars where springboards were secured.

Reservations

Sites may be reserved from May 13 through September 14 online at *www.parks.state.wa.us* or by telephone 1–888–CAMPOUT (1–888–226–7688). See Appendix B for details.

Activities

Bird watching, Boat rental, Boating, Concession stand, Fishing, Fitness trail, Hiking, Interpretive center, Horseshoe pits, Metal detecting, Mountain biking, Scuba diving, Swimming.

Cost

$12 primitive site
Peak season: mid May – mid September
$22 – $35 standard site
$30 – $40 partial utility site
$35 – $45 full utility site
Off–peak season
$20 – $30 standard site
$25 – $35 partial utility site
$30 – $40 full utility site
$10 extra vehicle (all year)
See Appendix C for available discounts.

Limitations

Maximum site length is 60 feet. Standard sites have a maximum vehicle length of 35 feet.
See Appendix A for camping regulations.

Contact

Phone: 360–753–1519
Web: *www.parks.state.wa.us*

Season

Open all year

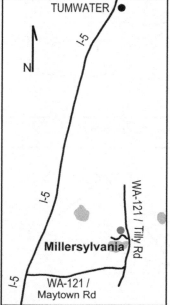

Driving Directions

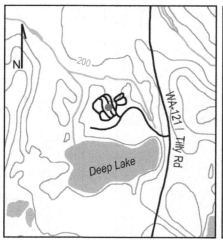

Location

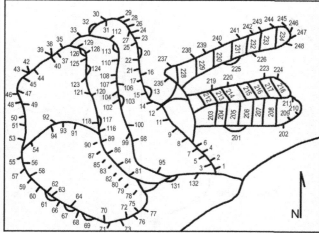

Campground

146 Fall Creek
Department of Natural Resources

Directions

Start at the intersection of I–5 and WA–121 (exit 95) near Maytown. After exiting, continue onto Maytown Road going west (toward Littlerock) for 2.8 miles. Continue straight onto Littlerock Road for 0.1 mile. Bear right onto 128th Avenue SW and travel 0.2 mile. Turn right onto Waddell Creek Road SW and travel 4.1 miles. Turn left at Sherman Valley Road SW and travel 1.3 miles. Bear left at Capital Peak Road/C–Line Road and travel for 1.9 miles. Turn left onto C–6000 and travel 2.5 miles. Turn right to Fall Creek.

N46°56'33" – W123°07'41"   Elevation – 600 feet

Facilities

8 standard sites
Vault toilet
No water, bring your own
Pack out garbage
Accessible toilet

Features

Fall Creek campground lies along Fall Creek on the south side of Little Larch Mountain. The campground provides a horse corral.

Reservations

None, first–come, first–serve

Season

Closed seasonally from December 1 to April 30

Activities

Equestrian trail riding, Hiking, Mountain biking.

Cost

No Cost

Limitations

Maximum stay is 7 days each year.
A Washington State Discover Pass is required.
See Appendix A for camping regulations.

Contact

Department of Natural Resources, South Puget Sound Region
Phone: 360–825–1631
Web: *www.dnr.wa.gov*

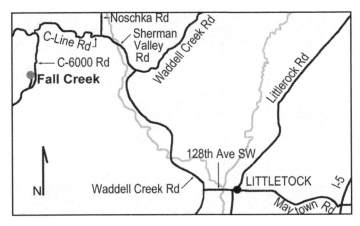

Driving Directions

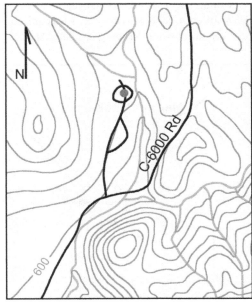

Location

147 Margaret McKenny
Department of Natural Resources

Directions

Start at the intersection of I–5 and WA–121 (exit 95) near Maytown. Travel west on WA–121 (becomes Maytown Road) toward town of Littlerock for 2.8 miles. Where Littlerock Road intersects from the right, continue straight. Maytown Road becomes 128th Avenue SW. Travel on 128th Avenue SW for 0.8 mile. Turn right into Waddell Creek Road and travel for 2.5 miles. Turn left into Margaret McKenny.

N46°55'30" – W123°03'38"   Elevation – 320 feet

Facilities

24 standard sites
Vault/pit toilets
No water, bring your own
Garbage service
Accessible campsites

Features

Margaret McKenny campground is in a lovely forest setting near Waddell Creek. The campground and trailhead are popular among horseback riders.

Reservations

None, all campsites are first–come, first–serve.

Season

Closed seasonally December 1 through April 30

Activities

Equestrian trail riding, Mountain biking.

Cost

No cost

Limitations

Maximum stay is 10–days each year.
A Washington State Discover Pass is required.
See Appendix A for camping regulations.

Contact

Department of Natural Resources, South Puget Sound Region
Phone: 360–825–1631
Web: *www.dnr.wa.gov*

Margaret McKenny Campsite

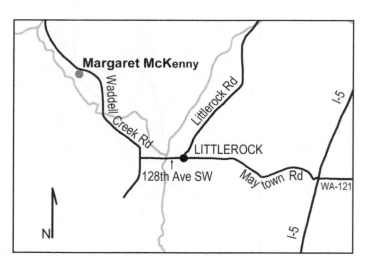

Driving Directions

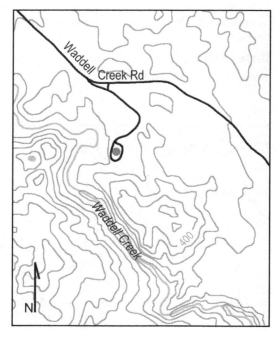

Location

148 Middle Waddell
Department of Natural Resources

Directions

Start at the intersection of I–5 and WA–121 (exit 95) near Maytown. Travel west on WA–121 (becomes Maytown Road) toward town of Littlerock for 2.8 miles. Where Littlerock Road intersects from the right, continue straight. Maytown Road becomes 128th Avenue SW. Travel on 128th Avenue SW for 0.8 mile. Turn right onto Waddell Creek Road SW and travel for 3.6 miles. Turn left into Middle Waddell.

N46°55'21" – W123°04'36"   Elevation – 240 feet

Facilities

24 standard sites
Some pull–through sites
Vault/pit toilets
No water, bring your own
Pack out garbage
Accessible campsites

Features

Middle Waddell campground is in a forest setting near Waddell Creek and offers access to Capitol State Forest's 89 miles of motorized trails.

Reservations

None, all campsites are first–come, first–serve.

Season

Closed seasonally from December 1 through April 30

Activities

Hiking, Mountain biking, Motorcycle Riding/ORV/ATVs.

Cost

No Cost

Limitations

Maximum stay is 10–days each year.
A Washington State Discover Pass is required.
See Appendix A for camping regulations.

Contact

Department of Natural Resources, South Puget Sound Region
Phone: 360–825–1631
Web: *www.dnr.wa.gov*

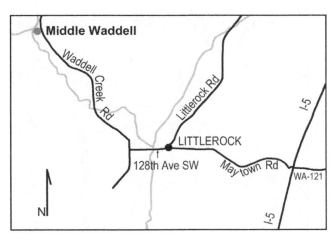

Driving Directions

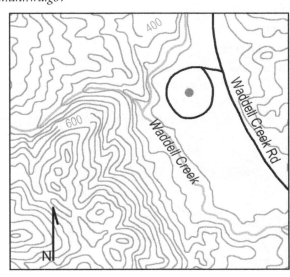

Location

149 Dash Point
Washington State Parks

Directions

Start at the intersection of I–5 and 272nd Street (Exit 147) near Federal Way. Travel west on 272nd Street for 0.6 mile. Turn left onto WA–99 and travel 1.5 miles. Turn right onto WA–509 South (also called Dash Point Road) and travel 6.1 miles. Turn left into park.

N47°18'58" – W122°24'40"   Elevation – 120 feet

Facilities

141 total sites: 114 standard, 27 partial utility (W/E)
Flush toilets
Potable water
Hot showers
Garbage service
RV dump station
Accessible toilet, water, campsite

Features

Dash Point State Park is located on the shoreline of Puget Sound.
The beach provides unobstructed views of the Sound with excellent opportunities for sea–life study and a variety of water activities. Interpretive events are held June through August. They include evening amphitheater programs and day walks. (Times and subjects are posted.) The park offers 10 miles of easy hiking trails that are shared with bikers. Sites 1–8, 29, 30, 32, 34, and 37–51 are partial utility sites.

Reservations

Sites may be reserved online at *www.parks.state.wa.us* or by telephone 1–888–CAMPOUT (1–888–226–7688).
See Appendix B for details.

Season

Open all year

Activities

Beachcombing, Bird watching, Canoe access, Fishing or shellfish gathering, Hiking, Metal detecting, Mountain biking, Scuba diving, Swimming.

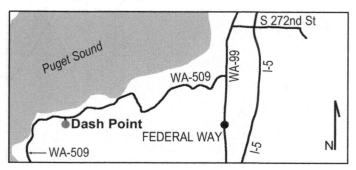

Driving Directions

Cost

$12 primitive site
Peak season: mid May – mid September
$22 – $35 standard site
$30 – $40 partial utility site
$35 – $45 full utility site
Off–peak season
$20 – $30 standard site
$25 – $35 partial utility site
$30 – $40 full utility site
$10 extra vehicle (all year)
See Appendix C for available discounts.

Limitations

Alcohol is allowed only in the campground by registered campers of legal age and only at their campsites. It is not allowed in any other area of the park. Maximum site length is 40 feet.
See Appendix A for camping regulations.

Contact

Phone: 253–661–4955
Web: *www.parks.state.wa.us*

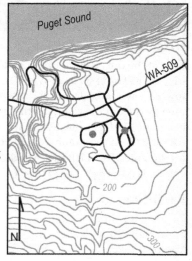

Location

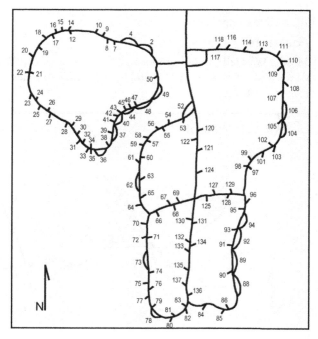

Campground

150 Kanaskat–Palmer
Washington State Parks

Directions

Start at the intersection of WA–18 and WA–169 near Maple Valley. Travel south on WA–169 (also called Maple Valley Highway) and travel for 2.9 miles. Turn left onto WA–516 (also called SE Kent–Kangley Road) and travel 3.5 miles. Bear right at the "Y" onto Retreat Kanaskat Road and travel 3.1 miles. Turn right onto Cumberland–Kanaskat Road and travel 1.9 miles. Turn right into park.

Or

Start at the intersection of WA–410 and WA–164 near Enumclaw. Travel east on WA–410 for 0.8 mile. Turn left onto 284th Avenue (which changes names to Vealzie–Cumberland Road and then to Cumberland–Kanaskat Road) and travel 8.9 miles. Turn left into park.

N47°19'09" – W121°54'17"   Elevation – 780 feet

Facilities

44 total sites: 25 standard, 19 partial utility (W/E)
Many pull–through sites
Flush toilets
Potable water
Hot showers
Garbage service
RV dump station
Shelter
Boat launch
Accessible water, utility campsite

Features

Kanaskat–Palmer State Park is on a small, low plateau in a natural forest setting along the Green River. The campsites are large and well shaded. A kitchen shelter is near the boat launch. Boat and raft launching is by hand only. River rafting and kayaking down the Green River Gorge is for expert–level enthusiasts only. Shoreline activities include nature appreciation, trout fishing and picnicing.

Reservations

Sites may be reserved for camping dates May 13 through September 14 online at *www.parks.state.wa.us* or by phone 1–888–CAMPOUT (1–888–226–7688). See Appendix B for reservation details.

Season

Open all year

Activities

Boating, Fishing, Hiking, Horseshoes, Whitewater paddling.

Cost

$12 primitive site
Peak season: mid May – mid September
$22 – $35 standard site
$30 – $40 partial utility site
$35 – $45 full utility site
Off–peak season
$20 – $30 standard site
$25 – $35 partial utility site
$30 – $40 full utility site
$10 extra vehicle (all year)
See Appendix C for available discounts.

Limitations

Maximum site length is 50 feet
CAUTION: River rafting is rated a Category 4 below the campground.

See Appendix A for camping regulations.

Contact

Phone: 360–886–0148
Web: *www.parks.state.wa.us*

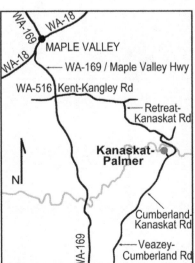

Driving Directions

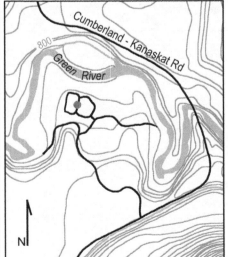

Location

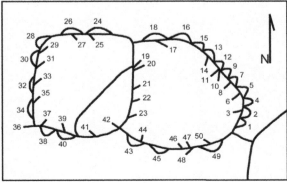

Campground

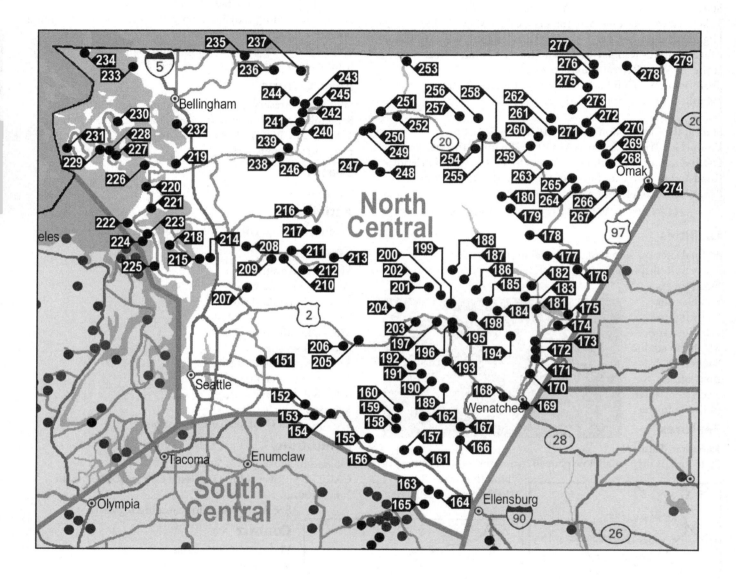

Chapter 4   North Central Region

151 Tolt–MacDonald Park
King County

Directions

Start at the intersection of US–2 and WA–203 in Monroe. Travel south on WA–203 for 18.7 miles. Turn right onto NE 40th Street in Carnation and travel 0.2 mile to Tolt–MacDonald Park.

N47°38'33" – W121°55'28"   Elevation – 60 feet

Facilities

38 total sites:
11 standard, 16 partial utility (W/E), 11 walk–in
Some pull–through sites
Flush toilets
Potable water
Hot showers
Garbage service

Features

Tolt–MacDonald Park and Campground is located at the confluence of the Tolt and Snoqualmie Rivers in Snoqualmie Valley. The park features stunning views of the Snoqualmie River and Cascade Foothills. Just 40 minutes from downtown Seattle and a short drive from Redmond, the park is a favorite site for mountain biking and provides access to an extensive network of trails on the Ames Lake Plateau. Walk–in sites are across a suspension foot–bridge, but the camp hosts have a loaner wheelbarrow. Two of the walk–in sites have three–sided cabins for shelter.

Tolt–MacDonald Campsite

Reservations

Sites can be reserved up to one year in advance, with at least a one week notice and a two night minimum booking, by calling 206–477–6149. All sites not reserved are first–come, first–serve. See Appendix B for details.

Season

Open all year

Activities

Ball fields, Boating (non–motorized), Hiking, Mountain biking.

Cost

$25 standard site
$35 partial utility site
$20 walk–in site
See Appendix C for available discounts.

Limitations

See Appendix A for camping regulations.

Contact

King County Parks and Recreation
201 South Jackson Street, KSC–NR–0700
Seattle, WA 98104
Phone: 206–477–4527
Web: _www.kingcounty.gov/recreation/parks/rentals/camping.aspx_

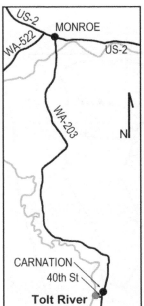

Driving Directions

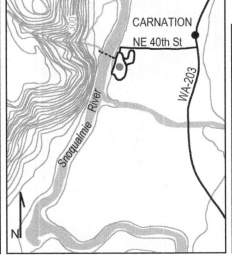

Location

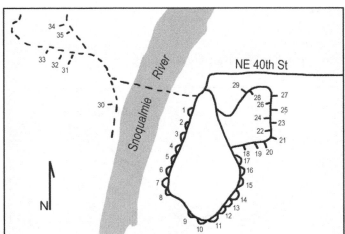

Campground

152 Middle Fork
Mount Baker–Snoqualmie National Forest

Directions

Start at the intersection of I–90 and WA–202 near North Bend. Travel east on I–90 for 4.4 miles. Leave the interstate at exit 34, turn left onto 468th Avenue and travel 0.6 mile. Turn right onto SE Middle Fork Road (Forest Service Road 56) and travel approximately 12 miles. The campground is on the left 0.5 mile past the Middle Fork Trail Trailhead.

N47°32'37" – W121°32'18"   Elevation – 1,030 feet

Facilities

38 total sites: 34 standard,
4 walk–in
Vault toilets
Potable water
Garbage service

Features

Middle Fork campground lies along the Taylor River. The campground has a nature and interpretative trail. The Middle Fork Trailhead and Middle Fork of the Snoqualmie River are nearby.

Middle Fork Campsite

Limitations

Campground will not accommodate larger RVs in any of the campsites; allowable trailer length is 35 feet.
Proceed carefully on the 9.5 miles of gravel and sometimes potholed road.
See Appendix A for camping regulations.

Reservations

Reserve online at *www.recreation.gov* or call 1–877–444–6777 (5 am to 9 pm Pacific time), 518–885–3639, or TDD 1–877–833–6777. Reservations must be made at least 4 days ahead of arrival and may be made up to 12 months in advance. See Appendix B for details.

Contact

Mt. Baker–Snoqualmie National Forest
2930 Wetmore Ave., Suite 3A
Everett, WA 98201
Phone: 425–783–6000, 800–627–0062
Outdoor Recreation Information: 206–470–4060

Season

Open late May to early September

Activities

Hiking.

Cost

$14 single site
$7 extra vehicle
See Appendix C for available discounts.

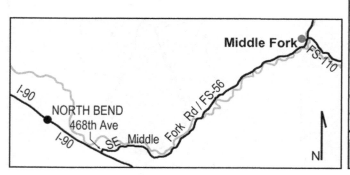

Driving Directions

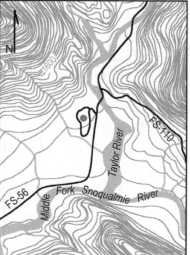

Location

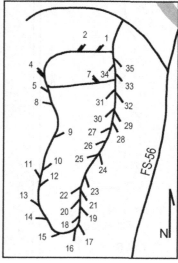

Campground

153 Tinkham
Mount Baker–Snoqualmie National Forest

Directions

Start at the intersection of I–90 and WA–18 near Snoqualmie. Travel east on I–90 for 16.7 miles and leave the interstate at exit 42 (Tinkham Road). Turn right on Tinkham Road and travel 1.9 miles. Turn left into campground.

N47°24'10" – W121°34'04"   Elevation – 1,520 feet

Facilities

47 campsites
Vault toilets
Potable water
Garbage service
Accessible toilet, campsite

Features

Tinkham campground is located along the South Fork of the Snoqualmie River with several sites near the river. Trails for hiking and fishing are within close driving distance. The campground is quite near the interstate and its ensuing noise.

Reservations

Reserve online at *www.recreation.gov* or call 1–877–444–6777 (5 am to 9 pm Pacific time), 518–885–3639, or TDD 1–877–833–6777. Reservations must be made at least 4 days ahead of arrival and may be made up to 12 months in advance. See Appendix B for details.

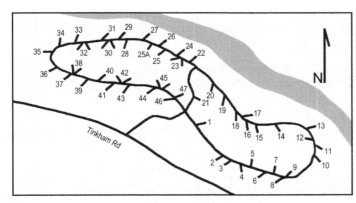

Campground

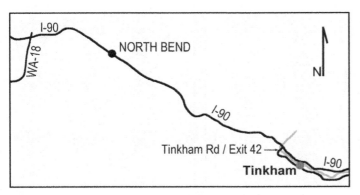

Driving Directions

Season

Open from mid May through the end of September

Activities

Fishing, Hiking.

Cost

$16 single site
$18 water view
$8 extra vehicle
See Appendix C for available discounts.

Limitations

A Recreation Pass is required to park at trailheads in the Snoqualmie Ranger District. Passes are available at Snoqualmie Pass Visitor Center. The visitor Center is located just 5 miles from the campground at Snoqualmie Pass.
See Appendix A for camping regulations.

River at Tinkham

Contact

Mt. Baker–Snoqualmie National Forest
2930 Wetmore Ave., Suite 3A
Everett, WA 98201
Phone: 425–783–6000, 800–627–0062
Outdoor Recreation Information: 206–470–4060

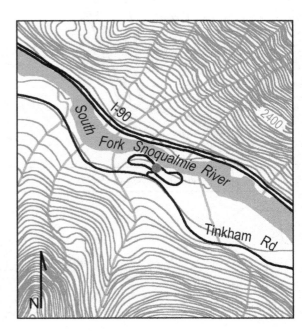

Location

154 Denny Creek
Mount Baker–Snoqualmie National Forest

Directions

Start at the intersection of I–90 and WA–18 near Snoqualmie. Travel east on I–90 for 21.7 miles and take exit 47 to Denny Creek/Asahel Curtis Road. Turn left onto Asahel Curtis Road (Forest Service Road 55) and travel 0.1 mile. Turn right onto Forest Service Road 9034 and travel 0.3 mile. Turn left onto Denny Creek Road (Forest Service Road 5800) and travel 2.1 miles. Turn left into campground.
NOTE: The bridge restrictions to the campground are five–ton single axle or six–ton double axle. (For an alternate route take exit 52 turning north on Forest Service Road 9041 and travel 0.1 mile. Turn left onto Forest Service Road 58 and travel 2.7 miles. Turn right into campground.)

N47°24'35" – W121°26'34"   Elevation – 2,160 feet

Facilities

33 total sites: 23 standard, 10 partial utility (E)
Pull–through sites
Flush toilets
Potable water
Garbage service
Accessible toilet, water, campsite

Features

One of the oldest Forest Service campgrounds, Denny Creek campground lies at the junction of the South Fork Snoqualmie River and Denny Creek and is bounded by I–90 corridors. Although the campground gets some freeway noise, thick forest muffles much of the sound. Several sites are riverside. Nearby Wagon Road Trail, Franklin Falls Trail and Denny Creek Trail, which enters the Alpine Lakes Wilderness, are within walking distance.

Reservations

Reserve online at *www.recreation.gov* or call 1–877–444–6777 (5 am to 9 pm Pacific time), 518–885–3639, or TDD 1–877–833–6777. Reservations must be made at least 4 days ahead of arrival and may be made up to 12 months in advance. See Appendix B for details.

Season

Open from early May through late September, dependent on snow melt

Activities

Biking, Hiking.

Cost

$20 single site
$24 partial utility
$10 extra vehicle
See Appendix C for available discounts.

Limitations

Stay limit is 14 days.
See Appendix A for camping regulations.

Contact

Mt. Baker–Snoqualmie National Forest
2930 Wetmore Ave., Suite 3A
Everett, WA 98201
Phone: 425–783–6000, 800–627–0062
Outdoor Recreation Information: 206–470–4060

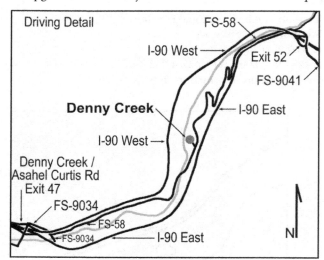

Driving Directions Detail

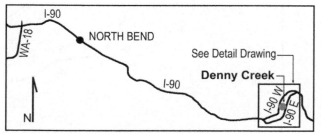

Driving Directions

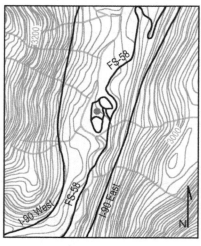

Location

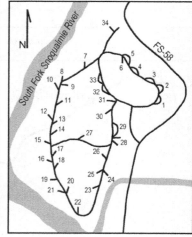

Campground

155 Kachess
Okanogan–Wenatchee National Forest

Directions

Start at the intersection of I–90 and Kachess Lake Road (exit 62) north of Easton and approximately 27 miles from Cle Elum. Travel north on Kachess Lake Road for 5.1 miles. Bear right at "Y" onto Baker Lane and travel 0.9 mile to Kachess.

N47°21'18" – W121°14'36"   Elevation – 2,300 feet

Facilities

152 standard campsites
Some pull–through sites
Flush toilets
Vault toilet
Potable water
Garbage service
Boat launches (2)
The south boat launch is paved and the north boat launch is maintained gravel.

Features

Kachess campground is located on the northwest shore of Kachess Lake with Little Kachess Lake to the immediate north. Set in a dense old–growth forest and surrounded by high mountains, the campground is considered one of the most beautiful in the Cle Elum Ranger District.

Reservations

Reserve online at *www.recreation.gov* or call 1–877–444–6777 (5 am to 9 pm Pacific Time), 518–885–3639, or TDD 1–877–833–6777. See Appendix B for details.

Season

Open from mid–May through mid–September, weather permitting

Activities

Boating, Fishing, Hiking, Mountain Biking, Swimming, Water Skiing; in Winter, Skiing, Snowshoeing, and Snowmobiling.

Cost

$21 standard site
$42 double site
$8 extra vehicle
See Appendix C for available discounts.

Limitations

Water levels in Kachess Lake and Little Kachess Lake will vary during the summer as water is drawn to provide irrigation for the lower valleys.
See Appendix A for camping regulations.

Beach at Kachess

Contact

Okanogan–Wenatchee National Forest
Cle Elum Ranger District
803 W. 2nd Street
Cle Elum, WA 98922
Phone: 509–852–1100,
Fax: 509–674–3800

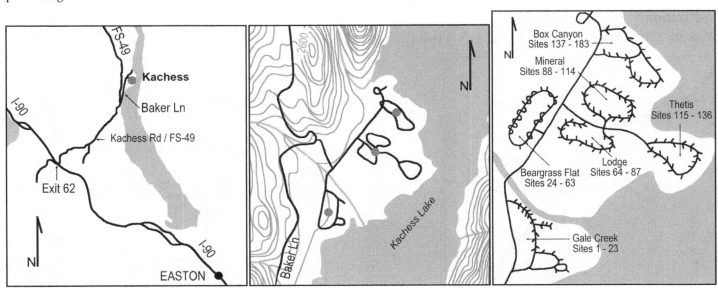

Driving Directions   *Location*   *Campground*

156 Lake Easton
Washington State Parks

Directions

Start at the intersection of I–90 and Exit 70 east of Stampede Pass. Turn south after exiting and travel 0.6 mile. Turn right into park. (There is a private RV campground very near the state park entrance.)

N47°15'12" – W121°11'42"   Elevation – 2,200 feet

Facilities

137 total sites: 45 utility, 90 standard sites, 2 walk–in sites
Some pull–through sites
Flush toilets
Potable water
Hot showers
Garbage service
RV dump
Boat launch
Accessible toilet, water, campsite

Features

Lake Easton State Park, located in a glacial valley in the Cascade Mountain foothills, lies along the shores of Lake Easton and offers beautiful mountain views. Most of the standard sites are near the Yakima River and most of the utility sites are near Lake Easton. Year–round recreational opportunities include swimming and boating in summer and cross country skiing (with 5 miles of groomed trails) and snowmobiling in winter. The snowmobile trails tie into other area trails.

Reservations

Sites may be reserved online at *www.parks.state.wa.us* or via telephone 1–888–CAMPOUT (1–888–226–7688). See Appendix B for more details.

Season

Open all year

Activities

Basketball, Bird watching, Boating, Cross–country skiing,

Fishing, Hiking, Horseshoes, Mountain biking, Snowmobiling, Swimming.

Cost

$12 primitive site
Peak season: mid May – mid September
$22 – $35 standard site
$30 – $40 partial utility site
$35 – $45 full utility site
Off–peak season
$20 – $30 standard site
$25 – $35 partial utility site
$30 – $40 full utility
$10 extra vehicle (all year)
See Appendix C for available discounts.

Limitations

Maximum site length is 60 feet.
See Appendix A for camping regulations.

Contact

Phone: 509–656–2230
Web: *www.parks.state.wa.us*

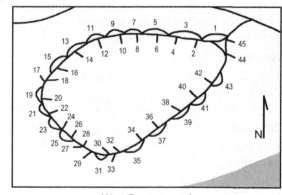

West Campground

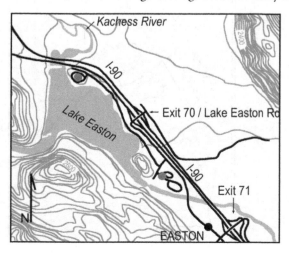

Driving Directions and Location

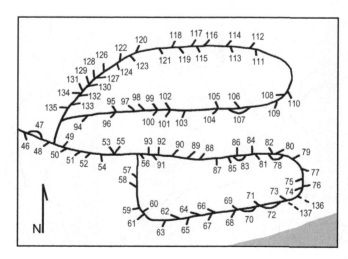

East Campground

157 Wish Poosh
Okanogan–Wenatchee National Forest

Directions

Start at the intersection of I–90 and Bullfrog Road (exit 80), west of Cle Elum. Travel north on Bullfrog Road for 2.7 miles. As you drive around the rotary, follow WA–903 (Salmon la Sac Road) north and travel 7.7 miles. Turn left into Wish Poosh.

N47°16'38" – W121°05'05"   Elevation – 2,400 feet

Facilities

34 standard campsites
Flush toilets
Potable water
Garbage service
Boat launch

Features

Located near the southeastern shore of Cle Elum Lake, Wish Poosh campground has spacious sites and a wide sandy beach nearby. The Pacific Crest Trail can be accessed near the campground.

Reservations

Reserve online at *www.recreation.gov* or call 1–877–444–6777 (5 am to 9 pm Pacific Time), 518–885–3639, or TDD 1–877–833–6777. Reservations must be made at least 4 days ahead of arrival and can be made up to 6 months in advance. See Appendix B for details.

Season

Open from mid May through mid September, weather permitting

Activities

Boating, Fishing, Hiking, Swimming.

Cost

$20 single site
$8 extra vehicle; however, no additional vehicles are allowed if the primary vehicle fills the parking pad.
See Appendix C for available discounts.

Limitations

Cle Elum Lake is an irrigation reservoir and water levels vary during the summer to provide water for the lower valleys. The boat ramp at Wish Poosh is often high–and–dry by mid–July. See Appendix A for camping regulations.

Contact

Okanogan–Wenatchee National Forest
Cle Elum Ranger District
803 W. 2nd Street
Cle Elum, WA 98922
Phone: 50– 852–1100,
Fax: 509–674–3800

Lake Cle Elum

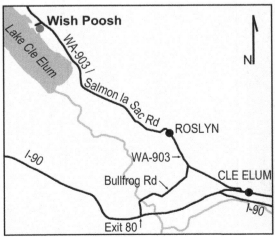

Driving Directions

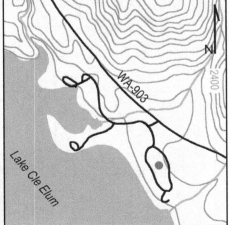

Location

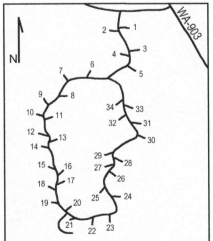

Campground

158 Cle Elum River
Okanogan–Wenatchee National Forest

Directions

Start at the intersection of I– 90 and Bullfrog Road (exit 80) west of Cle Elum. Travel north on Bullfrog Road for 2.7 miles. As you drive around the rotary, follow WA–903 (Salmon la Sac Road) north and travel 13 miles. Turn left into Cle Elum River.

N47°20'56" – W121°06'16"   Elevation – 2,200 feet

Facilities

23 standard sites
Vault toilets
No water, bring your own
Pack out garbage

Features

Cle Elum River campground is located at the head of Lake Cle Elum and offers waterside campsites. The campground is surrounded by mountains and thick forest. Summer temperatures average 70–80 degrees.

Reservations

None, all campsites are first–come, first–serve.

Season

Open from mid–May through mid–September, weather permitting

Activities

Fishing, Hiking.

Cost

$18 standard site
$7 extra vehicle
See Appendix C for available discounts.

Cle Elum River Campsite

Limitations

See Appendix A for camping regulations.

Contact

Okanogan–Wenatchee National Forest
Cle Elum Ranger District
803 W. 2nd Street
Cle Elum, WA 98922
Phone: 509–852–1100,
Fax: 509–674–3800

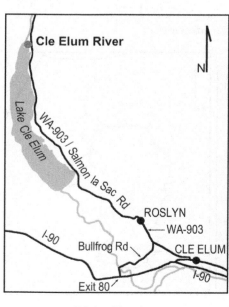

Driving Directions

Cle Elum River Campsite

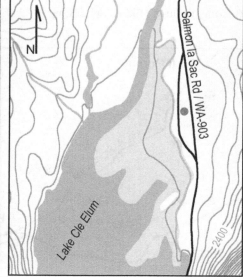

Location

159 Red Mountain
Okanogan–Wenatchee National Forest

Cle Elum River at Red Mountain

Directions

Start at the intersection of I–90 and Bullfrog Road (exit 80) west of Cle Elum. Travel north on Bullfrog Road for 2.7 miles. As you drive around the rotary, follow WA–903 (Salmon la Sac Road) north and travel 13.9 miles. Turn left into Red Mountain.

N47°21'60" – W121°06'08"   Elevation – 2,200 feet

Facilities

10 standard sites
Vault toilet
No potable water, bring your own
Pack out garbage

Features

Red Mountain campground lies along the Cle Elum River and offers some riverside campsites.

Reservations

None, all campsites are first–come, first–serve.

Season

Open from mid–May through mid–September, weather permitting

Activities

Fishing, Hiking.

Cost

$14 standard site
$6 extra vehicle
Fees end Sept 28. Campground remains available for use with no services until snow prevents access. Pack out your trash.
See Appendix C for available discounts.

Limitations

See Appendix A for camping regulations.

Contact

Okanogan–Wenatchee National Forest
Cle Elum Ranger District
803 W. 2nd Street
Cle Elum, WA 98922
Phone: 509–852–1100,
Fax: 509–674–3800

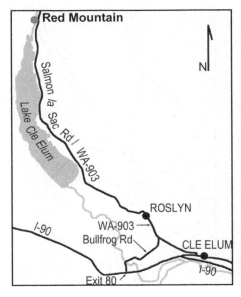

Driving Directions

Red Mountain Campsite

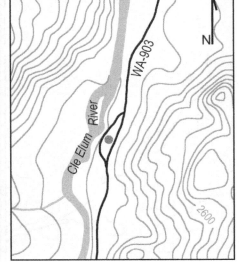

Location

160 Salmon la Sac
Okanogan–Wenatchee National Forest

Directions

Start at the intersection of I–90 and Bullfrog Road (exit 80) west of Cle Elum. Travel north on Bullfrog Road for 2.7 miles. As you drive around the rotary, follow WA–903 (Salmon la Sac Road) north and travel 16.7 miles. Turn left into Salmon la Sac.

N47°24'04" – W121°06'01"   Elevation – 2,400 feet

Shelter

Facilities

69 standard campsites
Some pull through sites
Flush toilets
Vault toilets
Potable water
Garbage service
Shelter

Features

Salmon La Sac Campground lies between the Cle Elum River and the Cooper River in the Wenatchee National Forest. The campground has spacious sites – several are riverside. The Salmon La Sac Trail is within driving distance of the campground. The campground offers a day–use community kitchen.

Reservations

Reserve online at *www.recreation.gov* or call 1–877–444–6777 (5 am to 9 pm Pacific Time), 518–885–3639, or TDD 1–877–833–6777. Reservations must be made at least 4 days ahead of arrival and can be made up to 6 months in advance. See Appendix B for details.

Season

Open from mid May through mid September, weather permitting

Activities

Fishing, Hiking, Mountain biking, Swimming.

Cost

$21 standard site
$8 extra vehicle; however, no additional vehicles are allowed if the primary vehicle fills the parking pad.
See Appendix C for available discounts.

Limitations

See Appendix A for camping regulations.

Contact

Okanogan–Wenatchee National Forest
Cle Elum Ranger District
803 W. 2nd Street
Cle Elum, WA 98922
Phone: 509–852–1100,
Fax: 509–674–3800

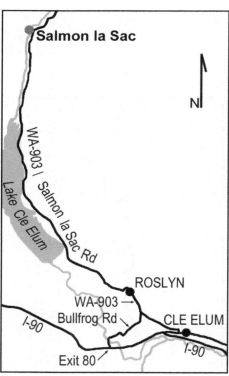

Driving Directions

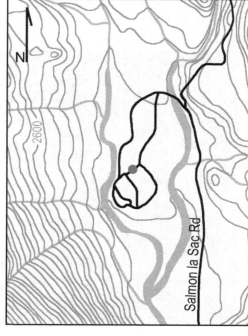

Location

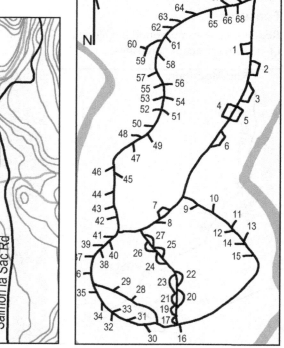

Campground

161 Indian Camp
Department of Natural Resources

Directions

Start at the intersection of I–90 and WA–970 (exit 85) near Cle Elum. Travel east on WA–970 for 6.9 miles. Turn left onto Teanaway Road and travel 7.3 miles. Turn left onto West Fork Teanaway Road and travel 0.6 mile. Turn right onto Middle Fork Teanaway Road and travel 3.9 miles. Turn left into Indian Camp.

N47°17'25" – W120°57'20"   Elevation – 2,520 feet

Stream at Indian Camp

Facilities

611standard sites
Vault toilets
No water, bring your own
Pack out garbage

Features

Indian Camp campground is located on the Middle Fork Teanaway River.

Reservations

None, first–come, first–serve

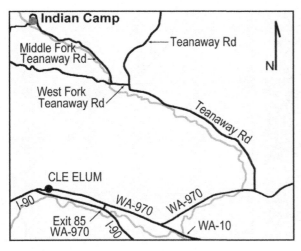

Driving Directions

Season

Open all year

Activities

Fishing, Hiking.

Cost

No cost

Limitations

A Washington State Discover Pass is required.
See Appendix A for camping regulations.

Contact

Department of Natural Resources, Southeast Region
Phone: 509–925–8510
Web: *www.dnr.wa.gov*

Tuscan Salad

You might not be camping in Tuscany but many parts of eastern Washington look like it.
Go ahead and enjoy the salad – you know it sounds good.

Ingredients

Yellow Pepper; sliced
Red Pepper; sliced
Mushrooms; sliced
1 tablespoon Capers
½ cup Kalamata Olives; sliced
1 small can Artichoke hearts
⅓ cup Balsamic vinegar
⅓ cup olive oil
Salt and pepper to taste
¼ to ½ teaspoon garlic powder

Preparation

Mix and serve

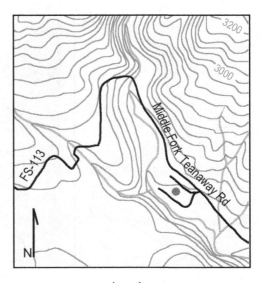

Location

162 Beverly
Okanogan–Wenatchee National Forest

Mushrooms Emerge

Directions

Start at the intersection of I–90 and Exit 85 east of Cle Elum. Travel north from the exit on an unnamed access road for 0.4 mile to the intersection with WA–970. Turn right onto WA–970 and travel for 6.5 miles. Turn left onto Teanaway Road and travel 7.3 miles. Continue straight on North Fork Teanaway Road and travel 5.8 miles. At the end of the pavement, turn right onto Forest Service Road 9737 and travel 4 miles. Turn left into Beverly.

N47°22'39" – W120°52'58"   Elevation – 3,080 feet

Facilities

14 standard campsites
Vault toilet
No water, bring your own
Pack out garbage
Boat launch

Features

Beverley campground is located along the North Teanaway Creek.

Reservations

None, all campsites are first–come, first–serve.

Season

Open from mid May through mid September, weather permitting

Activities

Fishing, Hiking.

Cost

$8 single campsite
See Appendix C for available discounts.

Limitations

Large RVs are not recommended.
See Appendix A for camping regulations.

Contact

Okanogan–Wenatchee National Forest
Cle Elum Ranger District
803 W. 2nd Street
Cle Elum, WA 98922
Phone: 509–852–1100,
Fax: 509–674–3800

Driving Directions

Looking Up

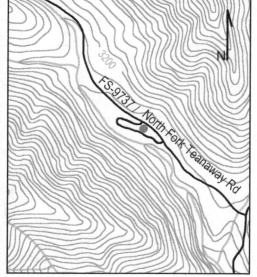

Location

163 Icewater Creek
Okanogan–Wenatchee National Forest

Directions

Start at intersection of I–90 and Thorp Hwy. (exit 101) west of Ellensburg. Turn south on South Thorp Hwy. and travel for 0.7 mile. Turn right onto Thorp Cemetery Road and travel 4.7 miles. Bear straight onto West Taneum Road (becomes Forest Service Road 33) and travel 8.5 miles. Turn left to Icewater Creek.

N47°06'48" – W120°54'09"   Elevation – 2,500 feet

Facilities

14 standard campsites
Vault toilet
No water, bring your own
Garbage service

Wind Farm On The Way To Icewater Creek

Features

Icewater Creek campground is forested with many of the campsites along the creek. The North Fork Taneum Trail, #1377, is accessed from the campground. A beginners motorcycle loop trail originates in the campground.

Reservations

None, all campsites are first–come, first–serve.

Season

Open from mid May through mid September, weather permitting. After September, campground remains open with no fees until snow prevents access.

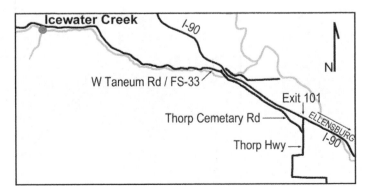

Driving Directions

Icewater Creek Campsite

Activities

Hiking, Motorcycle/ATV riding.

Cost

$18 single site
$7 extra vehicle, however, no additional vehicles are allowed if the primary vehicle fills the parking pad.
See Appendix C for available discounts.

Limitations

See Appendix A for camping regulations.

Contact

Okanogan–Wenatchee National Forest
Cle Elum Ranger District
803 W. 2nd Street
Cle Elum, WA 98922
Phone: 509–852–1100,
Fax: 509–674–3800

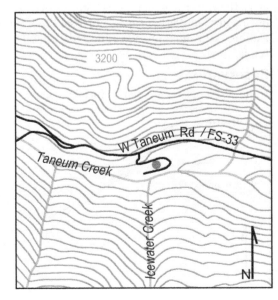

Location

183

164 Taneum
Okanogan–Wenatchee National Forest

Directions

Start at the intersection of I–90 and Thorp Hwy. (exit 101) west of Ellensburg. Travel south on Thorpe Hwy. for 0.6 mile. Turn right onto Thorp Cemetary Road, which becomes West Taneum Road, and travel for 11.3 miles. Turn left into campground.

N47°06'31" W120°51'24"   Elevation – 1,920 feet

Facilities

13 standard campsites
Vault toilets
Boil water from spigots/hydrants prior to human consumption (as of August 2015)
Garbage service
Shelter

Taneum Campsite

Season

Open from mid May through mid September, weather permitting

Activities

Equestrian riding, Fishing, Hiking.

Cost

$18 single site
$6 extra vehicle, however no additional vehicles are allowed if the primary vehicle fills the parking pad.
See Appendix C for available discounts.

Limitations

See Appendix A for camping regulations.

Contact

Okanogan–Wenatchee National Forest
Cle Elum Ranger District
803 W. 2nd Street
Cle Elum, WA 98922
Phone: 509–852–1100,
Fax: 509–674–3800

Taneum Creek

Features

Taneum campground lies along Taneum Creek in a forested area. The entrance road crosses a stream that is shallow during dry months but can be impassable during wet months. Additional facilities include a covered eating shelter and a horse stable.

Reservations

None, all campsites are first–come, first–serve.

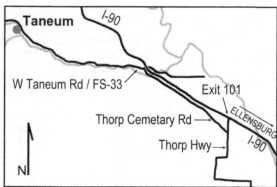

Driving Directions

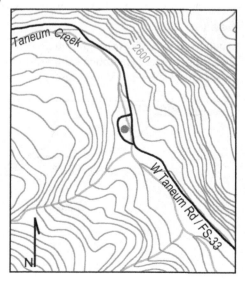

Location

165 Manastash Camp
Okanogan–Wenatchee National Forest

Directions

Start at the intersection of I–90 at South Thorp Hwy. (exit 101) near Thorp. Travel south on South Thorp Hwy. for 2 miles. Turn right onto Cove Road and travel 4.2 miles. Turn right onto Manastash Road (becomes Forest Service Road 31) and travel 17.6 miles. Turn left onto on Forest Service Road 3104. Manastash Camp access is on the immediate right.

N47°02'11" – W120°57'01"   Elevation – 4,400 feet

Facilities

14 standard campsites
Vault toilet
Potable water
Garbage service

Reservations

None, all campsites are first–come, first–serve.

Season

Open from mid May through mid September, weather permitting. After September, campground remains open with no fees until snow prevents access.

Activities

Equestrian riding, Hiking, Motorcycle, Jeep and ATV riding.

Cost

$5 single campsite
NW Forest Pass Required at trailhead
See Appendix C for available discounts.

Limitations

See Appendix A for camping regulations.

Contact

Okanogan–Wenatchee National Forest
Cle Elum Ranger District
803 W. 2nd Street
Cle Elum, WA 98922
Phone: 509–852–1100,
Fax: 509–674–3800

Zippy Chili Verde
A good meal doesn't have to be difficult.

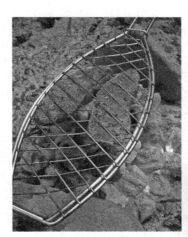

Preparation
Grill a pork loin chop.

Place it in a puddle of warmed canned Verde sauce and add a dollop of sour cream.
Include a side salad – Yum!.

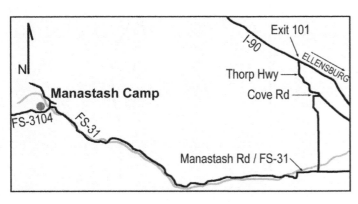

Driving Directions

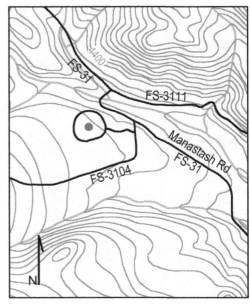

Location

166 Mineral Springs
Okanogan–Wenatchee National Forest

Directions

Start at the intersection of I–90 and Exit 85, east of Cle Elum. Travel north from the exit on an unnamed access road for 0.4 mile to the intersection with WA–970. Turn right onto WA–970 and travel for 10.3 miles. Continue straight onto US–97 and travel 6.4 miles. Turn left into campground.

N47°17'13" – W120°42'21"   Elevation – 2,700 feet

Cost

$18

$7 extra vehicle; however, no additional vehicles are allowed if the primary vehicle fills the parking pad.

See Appendix C for available discounts.

Limitations

See Appendix A for camping regulations.

Contact

Okanogan–Wenatchee National Forest
Cle Elum Ranger District
803 W. 2nd Street
Cle Elum, WA 98922
Phone: 509–852–1100,
Fax: 509–674–3800

Facilities

6 standard campsites
Vault/pit toilet
Potable water
Garbage service

Features

Mineral Springs campground is located at the confluence of Swauk Creek and Medicine Creek in forested and mountainous terrain. Daytime temperatures range from 70 – 80 degrees in the summer. Mineral Springs Resort, a full service restaurant and lounge, is across the highway and walking distance from the campground.

Reservations

None, all campsites are first–come, first–serve.

Season

Open from mid–May through mid–September, weather permitting

Activities

Hiking, Rock hounding on Teanaway Ridge.

Mineral Springs Campsite

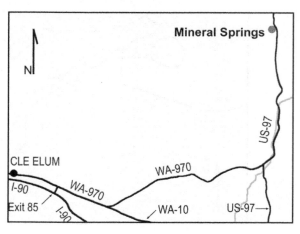

Driving Directions

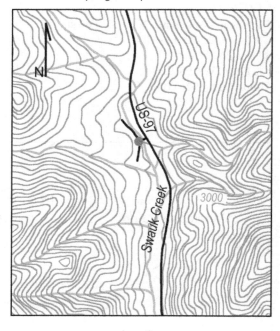

Location

167 Swauk
Okanogan–Wenatchee National Forest

Directions

Start at the intersection of I–90 and Exit 85, east of Cle Elum. Travel north from the exit on an unnamed access road for 0.4 mile to the intersection with WA–970. Turn right onto WA–970 and travel for 10.3 miles. Continue straight on US–97 and travel 10.3 miles. Turn right into campground.

N47°19'48" – W120°40'03"   Elevation – 3,200 feet

Facilities

22 standard campsites
Some pull–through sites
Vault toilets
Potable water
Garbage service
Shelter

Features

Swauk campground is located along Swauk Creek and nestled in a grove of large trees. There is a community kitchen shelter in the day–use area.

Reservations

None, all campsites are first–come, first–serve.

Season

Open from mid May through mid September, weather permitting

Activities

Bird watching, Hiking, Horseshoe pit.

Cost

$18 single site
$7 extra vehicle; however, no additional vehicles are allowed if the primary vehicle fills the parking pad.

See Appendix C for available discounts.

Limitations

See Appendix A for camping regulations.

Contact

Okanogan–Wenatchee National Forest
Cle Elum Ranger District
803 W. 2nd Street
Cle Elum, WA 98922
Phone: 509–852–1100,
Fax: 509–674–3800

Swauk Shelter

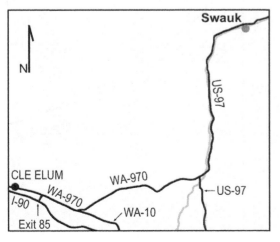

Driving Directions

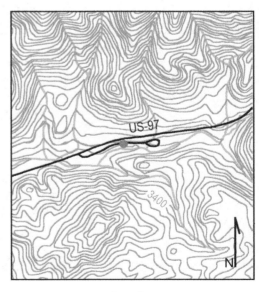

Location

168 Wenatchee River
Chelan County

Directions

Start at intersection of US–2 and WA–285 west of Wenatchee. Travel west on US–2 for 3.6 miles. Turn left onto the frontage road and travel 0.2 mile. Turn left into the park.

N47°28'57" – W120°24'57"   Elevation – 640 feet

Facilities

49 total sites: 2 standard, 4 partial utility (W/E), 43 full utility (W/E/S)
Some pull–through sites
Flush toilets
Potable water
Hot showers
Garbage service
RV dump
Store
Laundry

Features

Wenatchee River County Park lies along the Wenatchee River. The campground has lovely grassy areas and large shade trees.

Several sites are near the river. The campground also provides free Wi–Fi, exercise equipment, and a playground.

Reservations

Reserve sites online at *www.wenatcheeriverpark.org*. Reservations require a non–refundable deposit equal to the first night's fee. See Appendix B for more information.

Season

Open April 1 through October 31

Activities

Basketball, Bicycling, Bird watching, Hiking, Golfing cage, Ping Pong, Volleyball.

Cost

$28 standard site
$33 partial utility (W/E)
$38 full utility (W/E/S)
$5 extra vehicle

Limitations

No tents allowed in campground.
No fishing allowed.
See Appendix A for camping regulations.

Contact

Wenatchee River County Park
2924 US Hwy 2/97
Monitor, WA 98836
Phone: 509–667–7503
Web: *www.wenatcheeriverpark.org*

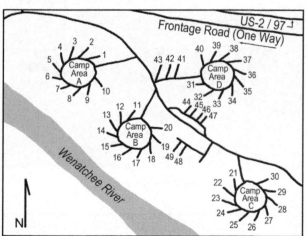

Campground

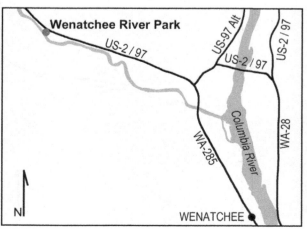

Driving Directions

River at Park

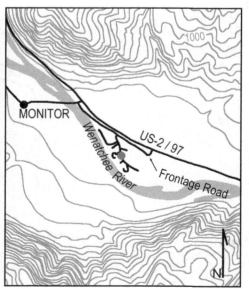

Location

169 Wenatchee Confluence
Washington State Parks

Directions

Start at the intersection of US–2 and US–97 east of Leavenworth. Travel east on US–2/97 for 14.7 miles. Take the right exit toward Euclid Avenue and travel 0.4 mile. Turn right onto Euclid Avenue and travel an additional 0.4 mile. Turn left to remain on Euclid Avenue (becomes Olds Station Road) and travel 0.4 mile. Turn left into park.

N47°27'32" – W120°19'42"   Elevation – 620 feet

Facilities

59 total sites: 8 standard sites, 51 utility sites (W/E/S)
Some pull–through sites
Flush toilets
Potable water
Hot showers
Garbage service
RV dump
Boat launch
Accessible toilet, campsite

Features

Wenatchee Confluence Park is at the confluence of the Wenatchee and Columbia Rivers. This grassy park is shaded by deciduous trees and fronted by the two rivers. The park is divided into two areas, North and South Confluence. The North Confluence is urban and recreational. It offers a roped–off swimming beach and play equipment for children. The South Confluence was designated a natural environment and wetlands (Horan Natural Area). You might see muskrat and beaver in the rivers. Footpaths and a pedestrian bridge over the Wenatchee River lead to the interpretive kiosks and an interpretive trail. Bicycles are permitted on footpaths, but are prohibited in the natural area. The climate is dry and summer temperatures are in the 80s and 90s. Rock climbing and winter skiing opportunities are nearby.

Reservations

Sites may be reserved online at *www.parks.state.wa.us* or by telephone 1–888–CAMPOUT (1–888–226–7688). See Appendix B for details.

Season

Open all year

Activities

Ball fields, Basketball, Biking, Bird watching, Boating, Fishing, Hiking, Horseshoes, Swimming, Tennis, Volleyball, Water skiing.

Cost

$12 primitive site
Peak season: mid May – mid September
$22 – $35 standard site
$30 – $40 partial utility site
$35 – $45 full utility site
Off–peak season
$20 – $30 standard site
$25 – $35 partial utility site
$30 – $40 full utility site
$10 extra vehicle (all year)
See Appendix C for available discounts.

Limitations

Maximum site length is 65 feet.
See Appendix A for camping regulations.

Contact

Phone: 509–664–6373
Web: *www.parks.state.wa.us*

Campsite

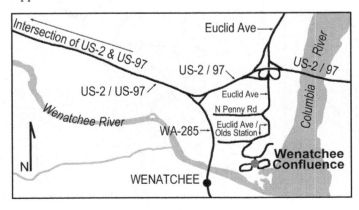

Driving Directions

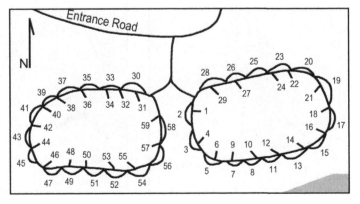

Campground

170 Lincoln Rock
Washington State Parks

Directions

Start at the intersection of US–97 and WA–28 near East Wenatchee. Travel north on US–97 for 4.7 miles. Turn left into park.

N47°32'24" – W120°17'01"   Elevation – 720 feet

Facilities

96 total sites: 27 standard, 69 utility sites
Some pull–through sites
Flush toilets
Potable water
Hot showers
Garbage service
RV dump
Boat launch and dock
Accessible campsite

Features

Lincoln Rock State Park is located on the east side of Lake Entiat (created by Rocky Reach Dam blocking the flow of the Columbia River) north of Wenatchee. Expansive lawns and shade trees break up the brown, rocky terrain of the scablands and provide respite from the hot sun.

The park offers boat rentals and a 630 foot boat dock. Average annual rainfall is 15 inches, with 10 inches of snowfall in winter. Park staff offer interpretive programs on most Saturdays from Memorial Day through Labor Day.

Reservations

Sites may be reserved from May 13 through September 14 online *www.parks.state.wa.us* or telephone 1–888–CAMPOUT (1–888–226–7688). See Appendix B for reservation details.

Season

Closed for camping October 31 through March 15

Activities

Ball fields, Basketball, Bird watching, Boating, Fishing, Hiking, Horseshoes, Metal detecting, Swimming, Tennis, Volleyball, Water skiing.

Cost

$12 primitive site
Peak season: mid May – mid September
$22 – $35 standard site
$30 – $40 partial utility site
$35 – $45 full utility site
Off–peak season
$20 – $30 standard site
$25 – $35 partial utility site
$30 – $40 full utility site
$10 extra vehicle (all year)
See Appendix C for available discounts.

Limitations

Maximum site length is 65 feel.
See Appendix A for camping regulations.

Contact

Phone: 509–884–8702
Web: *www.parks.state.wa.us*

Lincoln Rock Campsite

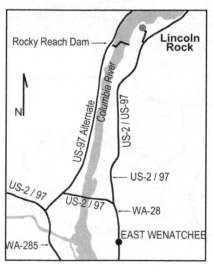

Driving Directions

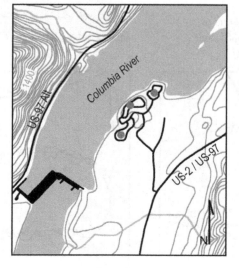

Location

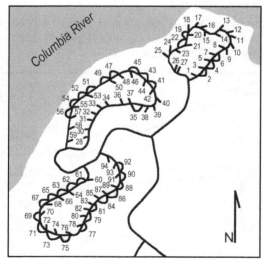

Campground

171 Entiat City Park
City of Entiat

Directions

Start at intersection of US–97 Alternate and WA–971 south of Chelan. Travel south on US–97 Alternate for 8.4 miles. Turn left into Entiat Park.

N47°40'21" – W120°12'37"   Elevation – 740 feet

Facilities

57 total sites: 29 utility, 2 partial utility, 26 standard
Flush toilets
Potable water
Hot showers
Garbage service
RV dump
Boat launch

Features

Entiat City Park lies along the shore of the Columbia River. The park opened in May 2015 and was built by the Chelan Public Utilities District. Families will enjoy the nice playground.

Reservations

Reservations are accepted by Entiat City Hall by phone at 509–784–1500.
See Appendix B for reservation details.

Season

Closed October 1 through April 15

Activities

Bird watching, Boating, Fishing, Swimming.

Cost

Summer Season: May 1 to Labor Day
$40 utility site
$35 partial utility site
$30 standard site

Off Season: After Labor Day to April 30
$20 utility and partial utility site
$15 standard site
$2 extra vehicle
See Appendix C for available discounts.

Entiat Campsite

Limitations

Water and sewer are not available during the off season.
See Appendix A for camping regulations.

Contact

City of Entiat
PO Box 228
Entiat, WA 98822
Phone: 509–784–1500

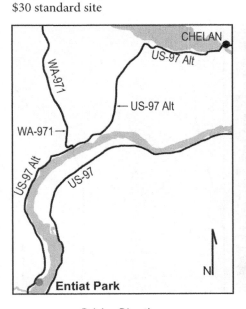
Driving Directions

Entiat Park Playground

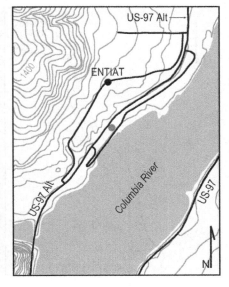
Location

172 Orondo River Park
Port of Douglas County

Directions

Start at the intersection of US–97 and WA–128 near East Wenatchee. Travel north on US–97 for 12.1 miles. Turn left into park.

N 47º39'25" – W 120º12'57"   Elevation – 720'

Facilities

38 total sites: 25 standard sites, 13 partial utility (W/E)
Flush Toilets
Potable water
Showers
RV dump station
Boat launch
Boat docks
Boat fuel
Food concession

Features

This park is located on the Columbia River. The campground has shade trees and lawn.

Reservations

Sites may be reserved online at *www.orondoriverpark.com* or by phoning 509–784–5818. See Appendix B for details.

Season

Open all year

Activities

Boating, Fishing, Hiking, Playground, Swimming, Volleyball.

Cost

$28 – $33

Limitations

See Appendix A for camping regulations.

Trees and Campsites at Orondo

Contact

Phone: 509–784–5818
Web: *www.orondoriverpark.com*

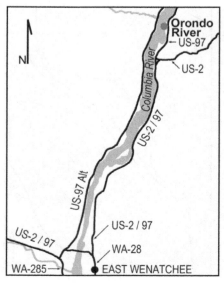

Driving Directions

Orondo on the Columbia River

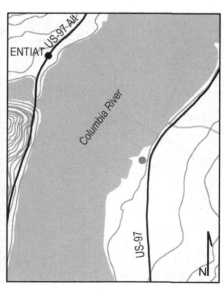

Location

173 Daroga
Washington State Parks

Directions

Start at the intersection of US–97 and WA–28 near East Wenatchee. Travel north on US–97 for 16.1 miles. Turn left into park.

N47°42'33" – W120°12'01"   Elevation – 760 feet

Facilities

45 total sites: 28 partial utility (W/E), 17 walk–in
Flush toilets
Potable water
Hot showers
Garbage service
RV dump
Accessible toilet, water, campsite

Features

Daroga State Park has 1.5 miles of Columbia River shoreline on the elevated edge of the desert scablands. Lots of sunshine combine with water activities to make this desert park a delight. Nationally recognized, Desert Canyon Golf Course is two miles away.

Reservations

None, all campsites are first–come, first–serve.

Season

Open April 1 through September 30

Activities

Ball fields, Bird watching, Boating, Canoeing, Fishing, Hiking, Metal detecting, Sailing, Soccer, Swimming, Tennis, Water skiing.

Cost

$12 primitive site
Peak season: mid May – mid September
$22 – $35 standard site
$30 – $40 partial utility site
$35 – $45 full utility site
Off–peak season
$20 – $30 standard site
$25 – $35 partial utility site
$30 – $40 full utility site
$10 extra vehicle (all year)
See Appendix C for available discounts.

Limitations

See Appendix A for camping regulations.

Contact

Phone: 509–784–0229
Web: *www.parks.state.wa.us*

Alyssa's Quick Chili

Alyssa is one of the busier people we know which is why she has a way of making quick, but yummy, chili.

Ingredients

1 teaspoon cumin
1 ½ teaspoons chili powder
1 clove garlic, chopped
1 onion, chopped
¼ teaspoon coriander, powder
2 mild peppers, chopped
1 tablespoon jalapeño pepper, chopped
2 tablespoons oil
1 (15 ounce) can of pinto beans
1 (30 ounce) can of diced tomatoes

Preparation

Sauté cumin, chili powder, garlic, onion, coriander, peppers, and jalapeño in oil.
Add beans and tomatoes – heat until warm.
Top with shredded cheese and chopped onion.

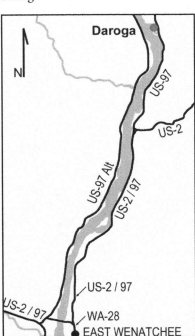

Driving Directions

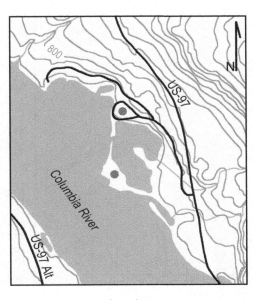

Location

174 Beebe Bridge
Chelan County PUD

Directions

Start at intersection of US–97 and end of WA–28 in East Wenatchee. Travel north on US–97 for 31.4 miles. Turn left into Beebe Bridge campground.

N47°48'25" – W119°58'27"   Elevation – 720 feet

Facilities

46 partial utility sites
Some pull–through sites
Flush toilets
Potable water
Hot showers
Garbage service
RV dump
Boat launch

Features

Beebe Bridge campground offers lovely grassy campsites with large shade trees. All sites have a view of the Columbia River.

Reservations

None, all campsites are first–come, first–serve.

Season

Open April 1 through October 31, depending on weather

Activities

Ball fields, Bird watching, Boating, Fishing, Hiking, Horseshoes, Soccer, Swimming, Tennis, Volleyball.

Beebe Bridge Campsite

Cost

$30 partial utility site
See Appendix C for available discounts.

Limitations

Alcohol is not allowed in the park.
See Appendix A for camping regulations.

Contact

Phone: 509–661–4551
Web: *https://www.chelanpud.org/parks–and–recreation/our–parks/parks–with–camping/beebe–bridge–park*

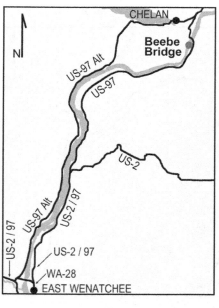

Driving Directions

Beebe Bridge Dock

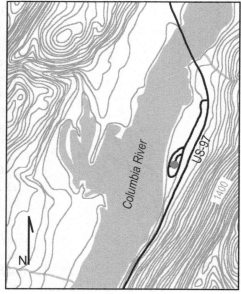

Location

175 Lakeshore RV Park
City of Chelan

Directions

Start at intersection of US–97 Alternate and WA–150 near Chelan. Travel west on WA–150 for 4.6 miles. Turn left into Lakeshore RV Park.

N47°50'45" – W120°01'39"   Elevation – 1,120 feet

Facilities

163 full utility sites
Flush toilets
Potable water
Hot showers
Garbage service
RV dump
Boat launch
Accessible toilet, shower

Features

Lakeshore RV Park lies along Lake Chelan. Although primarily an RV park, 22 sites have tent pads. The campground provides Cable TV at each site and an internet hotspot at the office. Adjacent to park are a basketball court, skateboard park, tennis court, marina, 18–hole golf putting course, and volleyball court.

Reservations

Reservations may only be made by phone 9 months in advance by calling 509–682–8023. See Appendix B for reservation details.

Season

Open all year

Activities

Boating, Fishing, Hiking, Swimming, Water skiing.

Cost

January 1 through March 31:
$30 RV $24 tent
April 1 through May 31, excluding Memorial weekend:
$35 RV $27 tent

Peak Season: Friday, Saturday and Sunday of Memorial weekend and June 1st through the 2nd Saturday of September:
$49 RV $39 tent.
Peak Season Prime sites in ares D and E:
$60 RV   no tent camping allowed.
Fall Season: 2nd Sunday of September through September 30:
$40 RV $27 tent
October 1 through December 31:
$40 RV $$24 tent
See Appendix C for available discounts.

Limitations

Maximum vehicle length is 40 feet.
No dogs allowed the 3 days of Memorial Weekend and July 1st through Labor day weekend.
See Appendix A for camping regulations.

Contact

City of Chelan
619 W Manson HWY
Chelan, WA 98816
Phone: 509–682–8023
Web: *www.cityofchelan.com*

Lakeshore Playground

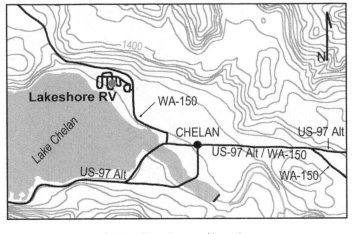

Driving Directions and Location

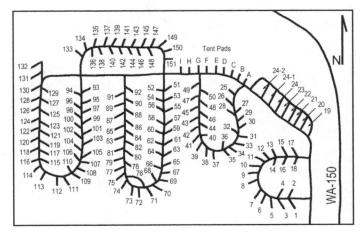

Campground

176 Alta Lake
Washington State Parks

Directions

Start at the intersection of US–97 and WA–153 near Pateros. Drive north on WA–153 for 1.7 miles. Turn left onto Alta Lake Road and travel 1.8 miles to park.

N48°01'39" – W119°56'19"   Elevation – 1,200 feet

Facilities

125 total sites: 32 partial utility, 93 standard
Some pull–through sites
Flush toilets
Potable water
Hot showers
Garbage service
RV dump station
Shelter
Boat launch
Accessible toilet, campsite

Features

The 174 acres Alta Lake State Park is at the juncture of mountainous pine forests and desert. The campground loops are located along Alta Lake. The lake, which is about two miles long and a half mile wide, offers good trout fishing during summer months. Sailboards are popular on the lake. The camp store opens in summer.

Activities

Bird watching, Boating, Fishing, Hiking, Horseshoes, Sailboarding, Scuba diving, Swimming, Volleyball.

Cost

$12 primitive site
Peak season: mid May – mid September
$22 – $35 standard site
$30 – $40 partial utility site
$35 – $45 full utility site
Off–peak season
$20 – $30 standard site
$25 – $35 partial utility site
$30 – $40 full utility site
$10 extra vehicle (all year)
See Appendix C for available discounts.

Limitations

Maximum site length is 38 feet, limited availability.
See Appendix A for camping regulations.

Contact

Phone: 509 923–2473
Web: *www.parks.state.wa.us*

Reservations

Sites may be reserved from April 1 through October 31 online at *www.parks.state.wa.us* or by telephone 1–888–CAMPOUT (1–888–226–7688). See Appendix B for reservation details.

Season

Open April 1 through October 31

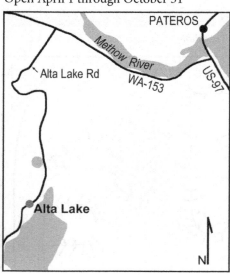

Driving Directions

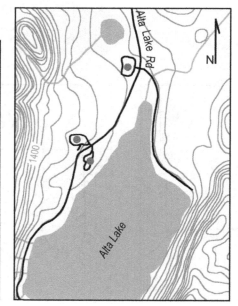

Location

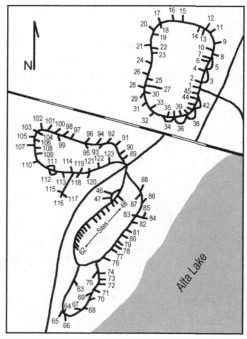

Campground

177 Foggy Dew
Okanogan–Wenatchee National Forest

Directions

Start at the intersection of WA–20 and WA–153 near Twisp. Travel south on WA–153 for 11.7 miles. Turn right onto Gold Creek Loop (Okanogan County Road 1029) and travel 1.6 miles. Turn right onto Gold Creek Road (Okanogan County Road 1034, which becomes Forest Service Road 4340) and travel 5.0 miles. Bear left onto Forest Service Road 200 and travel less than 190 feet. Turn left into Foggy Dew.

N48°12'20" – W120°11'46"   Elevation – 2,100 feet

Facilities

12 standard sites
Vault toilet
No water, bring your own
Pack out garbage
Accessible toilet

Features

Foggy Dew campground is located at the confluence of the North Fork Gold Creek and Foggy Dew Creek. Most sites are creekside. Several multi–use trails are near the campground; refer to the Sawtooth Backcountry Recreational Trail Brochure.

Reservations

None, all campsites are first–come, first–serve.

Season

Open April through October

Activities

Fishing, Hiking, Mountain biking, Motorcycle/Off Highway Vehicle access.

Cost

$8
$5 extra vehicle (limit 2)
See Appendix C for available discounts.

Limitations

Maximum stay is 14 days.
Maximum site length is 25 feet. The campground is best for tents or camping trailers.
Off Highway Vehicle (OHV) use is not allowed in the campground.
Rattlesnakes are occasionally seen in the area.
See Appendix A for camping regulations.

Contact

Okanogan–Wenatchee National Forest
Methow Valley Ranger District
24 West Chewuch Road
Winthrop, WA 98862
Phone: 509–996–4003
Fax: 509–996– 2208

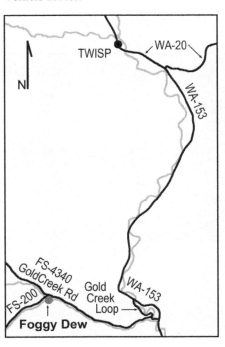

Driving Directions

Autumn Colors

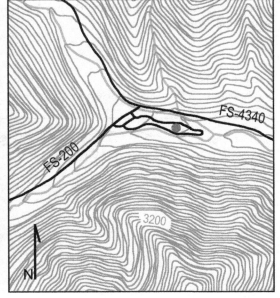

Location

178 Black Pine Lake
Okanogan–Wenatchee National Forest

Directions

Start at the intersection of WA–20 and Twisp River Road in Twisp. The Twisp River Road, also called Okanogan County Road 9114, becomes Forest Service Road 44. Travel west on Twisp River Road for 10.8 miles. Turn left onto West Buttermilk Road (Okanogan County Road 1090) and travel for 0.3 mile crossing the Twisp River. Bear left at the "Y" onto East Buttermilk Road for 0.5 mile. Turn right onto Forest Service Road 43 and travel 6.7 miles. Turn left into Black Pine Lake.

N48°18'49" – W120°16'29"   Elevation – 4,200 feet

Boat Launch

Facilities

23 standard sites
Vault/pit toilets
Potable water in summer
Garbage service
Boat launch and docks
Accessible toilet

Features

Black Pine Lake campground lies along Black Pine Lake and offers majestic landscape views. There are several tent–only campsites by the lake near the interpretative trail.

Reservations

None, all campsites are first–come, first–serve.

Season

Normally open from May through October

Activities

Boating (non–motorized), Fishing, Hiking, Interpretive trail, Swimming, Wildlife viewing.

Cost

$12
$5 extra vehicle
See Appendix C for available discounts.

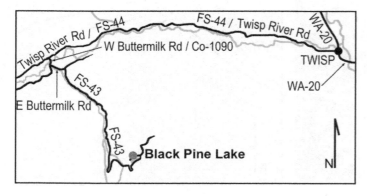

Driving Directions

Limitations

Maximum site length is 30 feet. Most campsites are suitable for tents or camping trailers.
Maximum stay limit is 14 days.
See Appendix A for camping regulations.

Contact

Okanogan–Wenatchee National Forest
Methow Valley Ranger District
24 West Chewuch Road
Winthrop, WA 98862
Phone: 509–996–4003
Fax: 509–996– 2208

Black Pine Lake Campsite

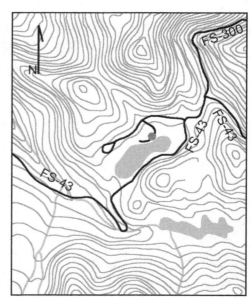

Location

179 War Creek
Okanogan–Wenatchee National Forest

Twisp River

Directions

Start at the intersection of WA–20 and Twisp River Road in Twisp. Travel west on Twisp River Road (Okanogan County road 9114, which becomes Forest Service Road 44) for 14.4 miles. Turn left into War Creek.

N48°22'04" – W120°23'55"   Elevation – 2,400 feet

Facilities

10 standard sites
Vault toilet
Potable water
Pack out garbage
Accessible toilet

Features

War Creek campground, located near the confluence of War Creek and Twisp River, has two sections. The section that stretches along the seasonal War Creek has sites that are well suited for recreational vehicles with a few in a small grassy meadow. The other section of the campground is small and just off the roadway. It is best suited for smaller vehicles as well as tent campers. A thick middle and understory in both sections provide good privacy between some sites. Four back–packing trails are nearby; War Creek, South Fork War Creek, Eagle Creek, and Oval Creek trails.

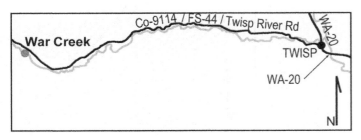

Driving Directions

Reservations

None, all campsites are first–come, first–serve.

Season

Open May through October

Activities

Fishing, Hiking.

Cost

$8
$5 extra vehicle
See Appendix C for available discounts.

Limitations

Maximum length of some sites is 25 feet.
Maximum stay limit is 14 days.
Rattlesnakes are occasionally seen near area.
See Appendix A for camping regulations.

War Creek Campsite

Contact

Okanogan–Wenatchee National Forest
Methow Valley Ranger District
24 West Chewuch Road
Winthrop, WA 98862
Phone: 509–996–4003
Fax: 509–996– 2208

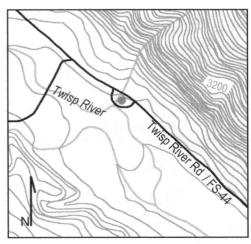

Location

180 Poplar Flat
Okanogan–Wenatchee National Forest

Directions

Start at the intersection of WA–20 and Twisp River Road in Twisp. Travel west on Twisp River Road (Okanogan County road 9114, which becomes Forest Service Road 44) for 18.2 miles. Bear right at "Y" onto Forest Service Road 4440 and travel for 2.0 miles. Turn left to Poplar Flats.

N48°25'18" – W120°29'56"   Elevation – 2,900 feet

Facilities

16 standard sites
Vault toilets
Potable water in summer
Garbage service
Accessible toilet

Features

Poplar Flat campground is located along the Twisp River. The campground offers a covered community kitchen with fireplace and a small group campsite/picnic site for up to 12 people. Campers have access to the Twisp River Trail and other trailheads nearby.

Shelter

Cost

$12
$5 extra vehicle
See Appendix C for available discounts.

Limitations

Maximum length of some sites is 30 feet.
Maximum stay limit is 14 days.
See Appendix A for camping regulations.

Contact

Okanogan–Wenatchee National Forest
Methow Valley Ranger District
24 West Chewuch Road
Winthrop, WA 98862
Phone: 509–996–4003
Fax: 509–996–2208

Poplar Flat Campsite

Reservations

None, all campsites are first–come, first–serve.

Season

April through October

Activities

Fishing, Hiking, Wildlife viewing.

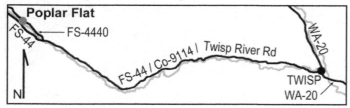

Driving Directions

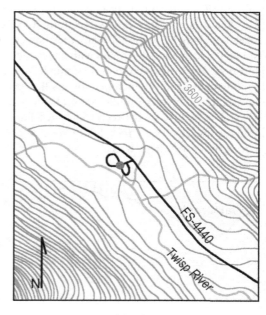

Location

181 Lake Chelan
Washington State Parks

Directions

Start at the intersection of US–97 Alternate and WA–971 southwest of Chelan. Travel west on WA–971 (also called South Lakeshore Road) for 5.9 miles. Turn right into park.

N47°52'24" – W120°11'52"   Elevation – 1,120 feet

Facilities

144 total sites: 109 standard sites, 18 partial utility sites (W/E), 17 full utility sites
Flush toilets
Potable water
Hot showers
Garbage service
Boat launch and dock
Mooring buoys
Food service
RV dump
Accessible water

Features

Lake Chelan State Park lies on the forested south shore of Lake Chelan. The lake was created by two glaciers, the Chelan Glacier and the continental ice sheet. The park offers lakeside views, a large sandy beach, and expansive lawns for strolling or playing. Many of the beach campsites have a very short walk to the lake and come with boat dock space.

Reservations

Sites may be reserved from April 1 through September 29 online at *www.parks.state.wa.us* or by telephone 1–888–CAMPOUT (1–888–226–7688). See Appendix B for reservation details.

Season

Open February 2 through October 31

Activities

Ball fields, Beachcombing, Bird watching, Boating, Cross–country skiing, Fishing, Hiking, Horseshoes, Interpretive monuments, Metal detecting, Personal watercraft, Sailboarding, Scuba diving, Swimming, Volleyball, Water skiing.

Cost

$12 primitive site
Peak season: mid May – mid September
$22 – $35 standard site
$30 – $40 partial utility site
$35 – $45 full utility site
Off–peak season
$20 – $30 standard site
$25 – $35 partial utility site
$30 – $40 full utility site
$10 extra vehicle (all year)
See Appendix C for available discounts.

Limitations

See Appendix A for camping regulations.

Contact

Phone: 509–687–3710
Web: *www.parks.state.wa.us*

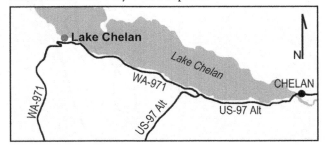

Driving Directions

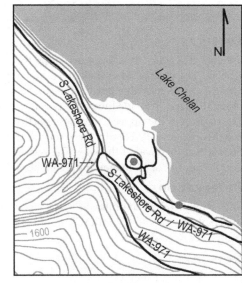

Location

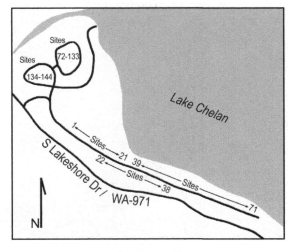

Campground

182 Twenty–five Mile Creek
Washington State Parks

Directions

Start at the intersection of US–97 Alternate and WA–971 near Chelan. Travel north on WA–971 for 6.0 miles. Continue straight onto South Lakeshore Road (WA–971 turns left – don't do it) and travel 10.1 miles. Turn right into park.

N47°59'33" – W120°15'41"   Elevation – 1,180 feet

Facilities

67 total sites: 46 standard sites, 8 partial utility sites (W/E), 13 utility sites (W/E/S)
Flush toilets
Potable water
Hot showers
Garbage service
RV dump
Boat launch and ramps
Marina
Store, seasonal
Accessible toilet

Features

Twenty–five Mile Creek Park lies along the south shore of Lake Chelan. The park is set in rocky terrain, with forested areas along Twenty–five Mile Creek. The smaller shaded campsites along the creek provide limited access for larger RVs. Boat exploration of the upper wilderness portions of Lake Chelan is a favorite activity. Nearby ferry service travels each day to Stehekin at the head of the lake. The region receives an average annual rainfall of 11 inches and 39 inches of snow.

Reservations

Sites may be reserved online at *www.parks.state.wa.us* or by telephone 1–888–CAMPOUT (1–888–226–7688). See Appendix B for details.

Season

Open April 1 through October 31

Activities

Beachcombing, Bird watching, Boating, Fishing, Hiking, Personal watercraft, Metal detecting, Mountain biking, Scuba diving, Swimming, Water skiing.

Cost

$12 primitive site
Peak season: mid May – mid September
$22 – $35 standard site
$30 – $40 partial utility site
$35 – $45 full utility site
Off–peak season
$20 – $30 standard site
$25 – $35 partial utility site
$30 – $40 full utility site
$10 extra vehicle (all year)
See Appendix C for available discounts.

Limitations

Maximum site length is 30 feet; larger RVs not recommended.
See Appendix A for camping regulations.

Contact

Phone: 509–687–3610
Web: *www.parks.state.wa.us*

Campsite

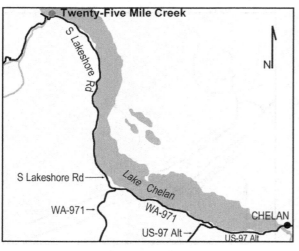

Driving Directions

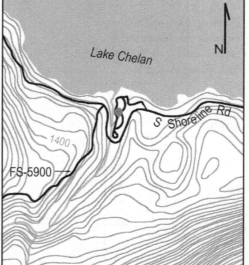

Location

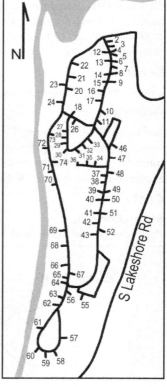

Campground

183 Snowberry Bowl
Okanogan–Wenatchee National Forest

Directions

Start at the intersection of US–97 Alternate and WA–971 near Chelan. Travel north on WA–971 for 6.0 miles. Where US–97A turns left, continue straight onto South Lakeshore Road and travel 10.5 miles. Turn left onto Shady Pass Road (Forest Service Road 5900) and travel 2.6 miles. Turn left onto Forest Service Road 8410 (a gravel 1 ½ lane road with pullouts) and travel 0.8 mile to campground.

N47°57'30" – W120°17'30"   Elevation – 2,000 feet

Toilet and Campsite

Facilities

7 standard campsites
Vault toilet
Potable water
Garbage service
Accessible campsite

Features

Snowberry campground is located close to Lake Chelan and its associated recreational activities. The campground offers a picnic shelter and access to several day hikes: Pot Peak, Lone Peak, and Stormy Mountain.

Reservations

None, all campsites are first–come, first–serve.

Activities

Hiking.

Cost

$10 single campsite
See Appendix C for available discounts.

Limitations

See Appendix A for campground regulations.

Snowberry Bowl Campsite

Contact

Okanogan–Wenatchee National Forest
Chelan Ranger District
428 W. Woodin Avenue
Chelan, WA 98816–9724
Phone: 509–682–4900 (Voice/TTY)
Fax: 509–682–9004

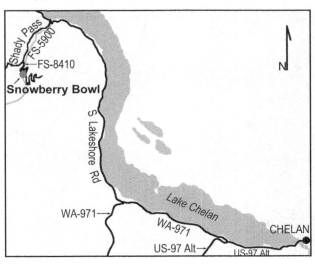

Driving Directions

Campsite

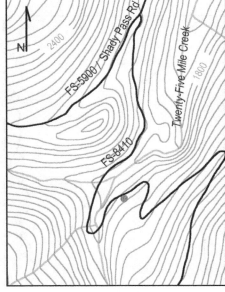

Location

184 Fox Creek
Okanogan–Wenatchee National Forest

Directions

Start at the intersection of US–97 Alternate and WA–971 south of Chelan. Travel south on US–97 Alternate for 8.9 miles. Turn right onto Entiat River Road (Forest Service Road 5100) and travel 27 miles. Turn left into Fox Creek. (Paved road to campground.)

Or

Start at the intersection of US–2/97 and US–97 Alternate in Wenatchee. Travel north on US–97 Alternate for 14.6 miles. Turn left onto Entiat River Road (Forest Service Road 5100) and travel 27 miles. Turn left into Fox Creek. (Paved road to campground.)

N47°55'25" – W120°31.09"   Elevation – 2,000 feet

Entiat River

Facilities

16 standard sites
Pit toilet
Potable water
Garbage service
Accessible toilet

Features

Fox Creek campground lies along the Entiat River with several campsites overlooking the river.

Reservations

None, all campsites are first–come, first–serve.

Season

Open from the end of April through mid October. Walk–in access is allowed in winter with no services; pack out garbage.

Activities

Hiking, Mountain biking.

Cost

$10
$8 extra vehicle
See Appendix C for available discounts.

Limitations

Maximum trailer length is 28 feet.
See Appendix A for camping regulations.

Contact

Okanogan–Wenatchee National Forest
Entiat Ranger District
2108 Entiat Way
P.O. Box 476
Entiat, WA 98822
Phone: 509–784–1511 (Voice/TTY)
Fax: 509–784–1150

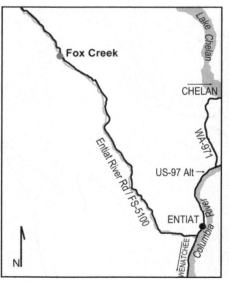

Driving Directions

Fox Creek Campsite with Snow Dusting

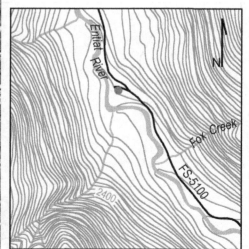

Location

185 Lake Creek
Okanogan–Wenatchee National Forest

Directions

Start at the intersection of US–97 Alternate and WA–971 south of Chelan. Travel south on US–97 Alternate for 8.9 miles. Turn right onto Entiat River Road (Forest Service Road 5100) and travel 27.7 miles. Turn left to Lake Creek. (Paved road to campground.)

Or

Start at the intersection of US–2/97 and US–97 Alternate in Wenatchee. Travel north on US–97 Alternate for 14.6 miles. Turn left onto Entiat River Road (Forest Service Road 5100) and travel 27.7 miles. Turn left to Lake Creek. (Paved road to campground.)

N47°56'19" – W120°30'21"   Elevation – 2,200 feet

Facilities

18 standard campsites
Vault/pit toilet
Potable water
Garbage service
Accessible toilet

Features

Lake Creek campground lies at the intersection of the Entiat River and Lake Creek. Several campsites are along the water. Box Canyon is near the campground (29 miles up the Entiat River Road from US–97A) and offers a view of the canyon cut through solid rock by the river. Lake Creek Trailhead is nearby.

Reservations

None, all campsites are first–come, first–serve.

Season

Open from the end of April through mid October. Walk–in access is allowed in winter with no services; pack out garbage.

Activities

Hiking, Mountain biking.

Cost

$10
$8 extra vehicle
See Appendix C for available discounts.

Limitations

Maximum trailer length is 20 feet.
See Appendix A for camping regulations.

Contact

Okanogan–Wenatchee National Forest
Entiat Ranger District
2108 Entiat Way
P.O. Box 476
Entiat, WA 98822
Phone: 509–784–1511 (Voice/TTY)
Fax: 509–784–1150

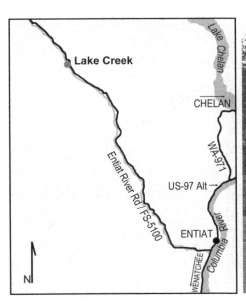

Driving Directions

Toilet at Lake Creek

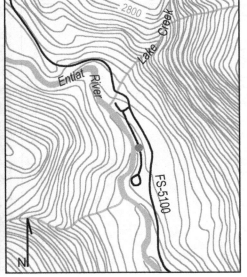

Location

186 Silver Falls
Okanogan–Wenatchee National Forest

Directions

Start at the intersection of US–97 Alternate and WA–971 south of Chelan. Travel south on US–97 Alternate for 8.9 miles. Turn right onto Entiat River Road (Forest Service Road 5100) and travel 29.4 miles. Turn left into Silver Falls. (Paved road to campground.)

Or

Start at the intersection of US–2/97 and US–97 Alternate in Wenatchee. Travel north on US–97 Alternate for 14.6 miles. Turn left onto Entiat River Road (Forest Service Road 5100) and travel 29.4 miles. Turn left into Silver Falls. (Paved road to campground.)

N47°57'30"N – W120°32'16"   Elevation – 2,400 feet

Facilities

29 standard sites
Vault/pit toilets
Potable water
Garbage service
Accessible toilet

Features

Silver Falls campground lies along the Entiat River and several sites overlook the river. The campground offers a 1.25 mile riverside ecosystem trail and viewing platforms. Before reaching Silver Falls campground, Box Canyon viewpoint provides a view of the canyon cut by the river through solid rock. Across the road from the campground is Silver Falls, a 150 foot natural waterfall. Entiat Falls, just beyond the campground (approximately 32 miles up Entiat River Road), is a 25 foot natural waterfall.

Reservations

None, all campsites are first–come, first–serve.

Season

Open from the end of April through mid October. Walk–in access is allowed in winter with no services; pack out garbage.

Activities

Fishing (see Limitations below), Hiking.

Cost

$12
$10 extra vehicle
See Appendix C for available discounts.

Limitations

Maximum vehicle length is 30 feet.
The Entiat River adjacent to campground is closed to fishing, however, fishing is allowed on the river above the Entiat River Falls, about 2.5 miles up river from the campground.
See Appendix A for camping regulations.

Contact

Okanogan–Wenatchee National Forest
Entiat Ranger District
2108 Entiat Way
P.O. Box 476
Entiat, WA 98822
Phone: 509–784–1511 (Voice/TTY)
Fax: 509–784–1150

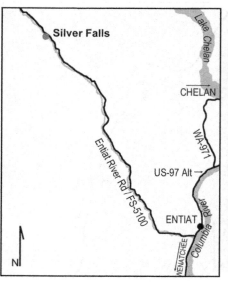

Driving Directions

Silver Falls Campsite

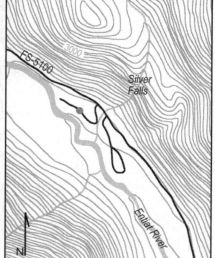

Location

187 North Fork
Okanogan–Wenatchee National Forest

Directions

Start at the intersection of US–97 Alternate and WA–971 south of Chelan. Travel south on US–97 Alternate for 8.9 miles. Turn right onto Entiat River Road (Forest Service Road 5100) and travel 32.6 miles. Turn left into North Fork. (Pavement ends about 0.4 mile before campground.)

Or

Start at the intersection of US–2/97 and US–97 Alternate in Wenatchee. Travel north on US–97 Alternate for 14.6 miles. Turn left onto Entiat River Road (Forest Service Road 5100) and travel 32.6 miles. Turn left into North Fork. (Pavement ends about 0.4 mile before campground.)

N47°59'20" – W120°34'52"   Elevation – 2,680 feet

Facilities

8 tent-only sites
Vault/pit toilet
Potable water
Garbage service

Features

North Fork campground lies along the Entiat River with several riverside sites. Entiat Falls, a 25 foot natural waterfall, is just prior to the campground with a viewpoint having an 8–car parking area.

Reservations

None, all campsites are first–come, first–serve.

Season

Open from the end of April through mid October. Walk–in access is allowed in winter with no services; pack out garbage.

Activities

Fishing, Hiking, Mountain biking.

Cost

$10
$8 extra vehicle
See Appendix C for available discounts.

Limitations

Maximum trailer length is 28 feet.
See Appendix A for camping regulations.

Contact

Okanogan–Wenatchee National Forest
Entiat Ranger District
2108 Entiat Way
P.O. Box 476
Entiat, WA 98822
Phone: 509–784–1511 (Voice/TTY)
Fax: 509–784–1150

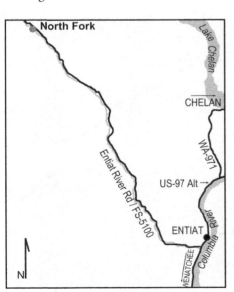
Driving Directions

Autumn Flower

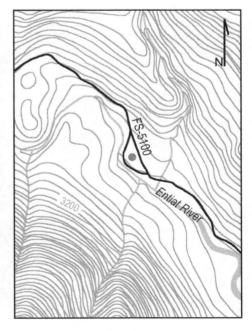
Location

188 Cottonwood
Okanogan–Wenatchee National Forest

Directions

Start at the intersection of US–97 Alternate and WA–971 south of Chelan. Travel south on US–97 Alternate for 8.9 miles. Turn right onto Entiat River Road (Forest Service Road 5100) and travel approximately 38 miles. Turn left into Cottonwood. (Pavement ends on the Entiat River Road at mile post 34.)

Or

Start at the intersection of US–2/97 and US–97 Alternate in Wenatchee. Travel north on US–97 Alternate for 14.6 miles. Turn left onto Entiat River Road (Forest Service Road 5100) and travel approximately 38 miles. Turn left into Cottonwood. (Pavement ends on the Entiat River Road at mile post 34.)

N48°01'21" – W120°38'10"   Elevation – 3,100 feet

Facilities

25 standard sites
Vault/pit toilets
Potable water
Garbage service

Features

Cottonwood campground lies along the Entiat River. Several sites are riverside. Cottonwood Cabin is adjacent the campground and may be reserved through the reservation system. The horse corral, which must be reserved in advance through the Ranger Station, is available for an extra charge for a maximum of 4 stock. A stock tank and feed bunk are provided but visitors need to bring their own weed–free hay or pellet–style feed for their livestock.

Reservations

None, all campsites are first–come, first–serve.

Season

Open from the end of April through mid October. Walk–in access allowed in winter with no services; pack out garbage.

Activities

Equestrian trail riding, Fishing, Hiking, Hunting.

Cost

$10
$8 extra vehicle
See Appendix C for available discounts.

Limitations

Maximum vehicle length is 20 feet.
See Appendix A for camping regulations.

Contact

Okanogan–Wenatchee National Forest
Entiat Ranger District
2108 Entiat Way
P.O. Box 476
Entiat, WA 98822
Phone: 509–784–1511 (Voice/TTY)
Fax: 509–784–1150

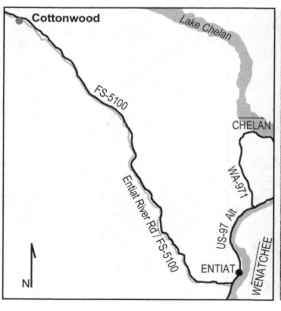

Driving Directions

Mushroom Emerging

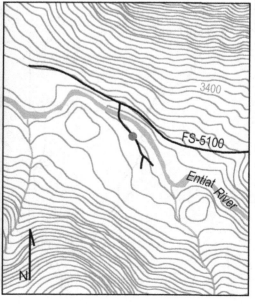

Location

189 Eight–Mile
Okanogan–Wenatchee National Forest

Directions

Start at the intersection of US–2 and US–97 east of Leavenworth. Travel west on US–2 for 5.4 miles. Turn left onto Icicle Road (Forest Service Road 76) and travel 7.1 miles. Turn left on Forest Service Road 112 to Eight–Mile campground.

N47°33'03" – W120°45'54"   Elevation – 1,800 feet

Facilities

45 total sites:
41 standard sites,
4 double sites
Vault toilets
Potable water
Garbage service

Features

Eight–Mile campground lies near Icicle Creek, approximately eight miles south of the town of Leavenworth. Several campsites are along the creek. The campground has large sites and a paved parking lot. Summer temperatures range from the high 70s to low 90s.

Reservations

None, campsites are filled first–come, first–serve.

Season

Open all year. The gate is closed in mid October, but visitors may park outside the gate (without blocking it) for walk–in camping. No fees are charged during the winter months, although campers must bring drinking water, toilet paper and pack out garbage.

Activities

Hiking, Biking.

Cost

$22 standard site
$44 double site
$14 extra vehicle
See Appendix C for available discounts.

Limitations

Recommended maximum vehicle length is 50 feet. See Appendix A for camping regulations.

Contact

Okanogan–Wenatchee National Forest
Wenatchee River Ranger District
600 Sherbourne
Leavenworth, WA 98826
Phone: 509–548–2550
Fax: 509–548–5817

Eight–Mile Campsite

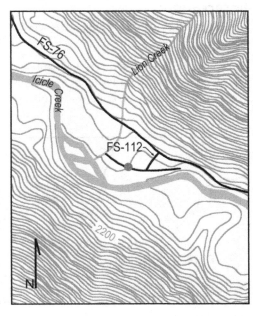

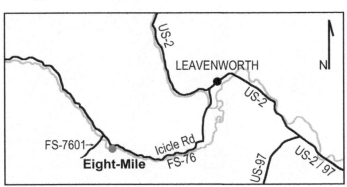

Driving Directions

Location

190 Bridge Creek
Okanogan–Wenatchee National Forest

Directions

Start at the intersection of US–2 and US–97 east of Leavenworth. Travel west on US–2 for 5.4 miles. Turn left onto Icicle Road (Forest Service Road 76) and travel 8.6 miles. Turn left onto Forest Service Road 7601 for 0.1 mile to Bridge Creek.

N47°33'50" – W120°46'56"   Elevation – 1,900 feet

Activities

Biking, Hiking.

Cost

$19
$12 extra vehicle
See Appendix C for available discounts.

Limitations

Recommended maximum vehicle length is 19 feet.
See Appendix A for camping regulations.

Contact

Okanogan–Wenatchee National Forest
Wenatchee River Ranger District
600 Sherbourne
Leavenworth, WA 98826
Phone: 509–548–2550
Fax: 509–548–5817

Facilities

6 standard sites
Vault toilet
Potable water
Garbage service

Features

Bridge Creek campground is located near the confluence of Bridge Creek and Icicle Creek. There are several sites along the water. Summer temperatures range from the high 70s to low 90s.

Reservations

None, campsites are first–come, first–serve

Season

Open all year. In mid October, there are no fees and no services; the campground is often inaccessible because of snow. Campers must bring drinking water, toilet paper and pack out garbage.

Bridge Creek Campsite

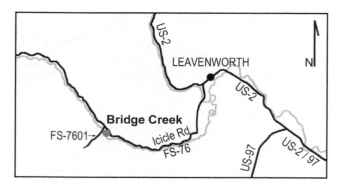

Driving Directions

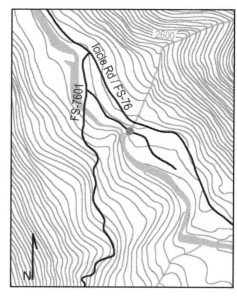

Location

191 Johnny Creek
Okanogan–Wenatchee National Forest

Johnny Creek Campsite

Directions

Start at the intersection of US–2 and US–97 east of Leavenworth. Travel west on US–2 for 5.4 miles. Turn left onto Icicle Road (Forest Service Road 76) and travel 11.6 miles. Turn left into Lower Johnny Creek campground. Upper Johnny Creek campground is 0.1 mile further, with the campground access road on the right side of Icicle Road.

Upper: N47°36'09" – W120°49'13"
Lower: N47°35'53" – W120°49'03"   Elevation – 2,300 feet

Facilities

65 total sites:
56 standard sites
9 double sites
Vault toilets
Potable water
Garbage service
Accessible campsite at lower campground

Features

Johnny Creek campground has two separate sites. Lower Johnny Creek campground is located at the confluence of Icicle Creek and Johnny Creek and offers some campsites along Icicle Creek. Upper Johnny Creek campground is on the mountain side of the road near Johnny Creek.

Reservations

None, campsites are first–come, first–serve.

Season

Open all year. In mid October, there are no fees and no services; the campground is often inaccessible because of snow. Campers must bring drinking water, toilet paper and pack out garbage.

Activities

Hiking, Biking.

Cost

$22 Lower Johnny Creek standard site
$44 Lower Johnny Creek double site
$14 Lower Johnny Creek extra vehicle
$19 Upper Johnny Creek standard site
$38 Upper Johnny Creek double site
$12 Upper Johnny Creek extra vehicle
See Appendix C for available discounts.

Limitations

Maximum trailer length is 50 feet.
See Appendix A for camping regulations.

Contact

Okanogan–Wenatchee National Forest
Wenatchee River Ranger District
600 Sherbourne
Leavenworth, WA 98826
Phone: 509–548–2550
Fax: 509–548–5817

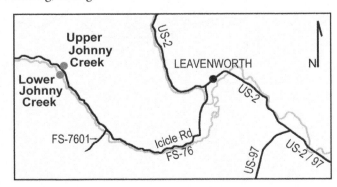

Driving Directions

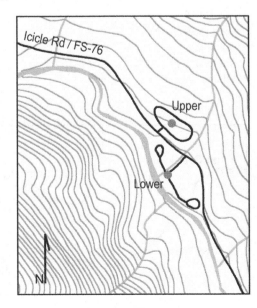

Location

192 Ida Creek
Okanogan–Wenatchee National Forest

Directions

Start at the intersection of US–2 and US–97 east of Leavenworth. Travel west on US–2 for 5.4 miles. Turn left onto Icicle Road (Forest Service Road 76) and travel 13.1 miles. Turn left into Ida Creek.

N47°36'25" – W120°50'52"   Elevation – 2,500 feet

Facilities

10 standard sites
Vault toilet
Potable water
Garbage service

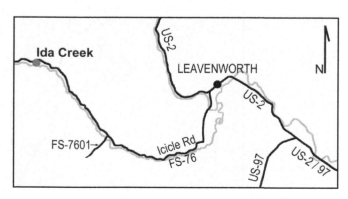

Driving Directions

Features

Ida Creek campground is located at the confluence of Ida Creek and Icicle Creek, with some sites along Icicle Creek.

Reservations

None, campsites are first–come, first–serve.

Season

Open all year. In mid October, there are no fees and no services; the campground is often inaccessible because of snow. Campers must bring drinking water, toilet paper and pack out garbage.

Activities

Hiking, Biking.

Cost

$19
$9 extra vehicle
See Appendix C for available discounts.

Limitations

Recommended maximum trailer length is 30 feet.
See Appendix A for camping regulations.

Contact

Okanogan–Wenatchee National Forest
Wenatchee River Ranger District
600 Sherbourne
Leavenworth, WA 98826
Phone: 509–548–2550
Fax: 509–548–5817

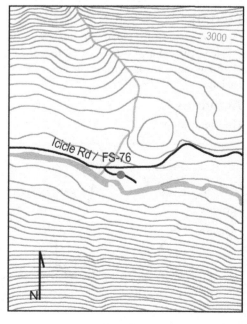

Location

193 Tumwater
Okanogan–Wenatchee National Forest

Directions

Start at the intersection of US–2 and US–97 east of Leavenworth. Travel west on US–2 for 14.1 miles. Turn right to Tumwater.

N47°40'41" – W120°43'57"   Elevation – 2,050 feet

Facilities

86 total sites:
84 standard sites
2 double sites
Flush toilets
Potable water
Garbage service
Shelter
Accessible toilet, campsite

Features

Tumwater campground is located at the confluence of the Wenatchee River and Chiwaukum Creek in Tumwater Canyon. Some sites are along the river. The campground offers a shelter and a covered picnic area.

Reservations

None, campsites are first–come, first–serve.

Season

Closed for the winter

Activities

Biking, Hiking.

Cost

$23 single site
$46 double site
$14 extra vehicle
See Appendix C for available discounts.

Limitations

Maximum recommended length for trailers is 50 feet.
See Appendix A for camping regulations.

Contact

Okanogan–Wenatchee National Forest
Wenatchee River Ranger District
600 Sherbourne
Leavenworth, WA 98826
Phone: 509–548–2550
Fax: 509–548–5817

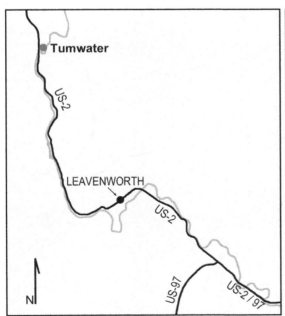

Driving Directions

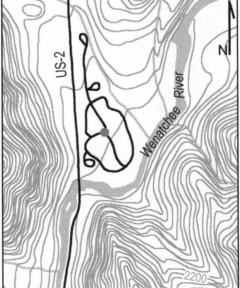

Location

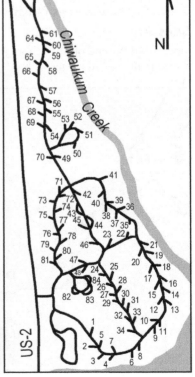

Campground

194 Pine Flats
Okanogan–Wenatchee National Forest

Directions

Start at the intersection of US–97 Alternate and WA–971, south of Chelan. Travel south on US–97 Alternate for 8.9 miles. Turn right on Entiat River Road (Forest Service Road 5100) and travel 9.9 miles. Turn left onto Mad River Road and travel 2.0 miles. Turn right onto Forest Service Road 5700 (one lane paved road with turnouts) and travel 1.8 miles. Turn left at Pine Flats entrance, which is a gravel road.

Or

Start at the intersection of US–2/97 and US–97 Alternate in Wenatchee. Travel north on US–97 Alternate for 14.6 miles. Turn left on Entiat River Road (Forest Service Road 5100) and travel 9.9 miles. Turn left onto Mad River Road and travel 2.0 miles. Turn right onto Forest Service Road 5700 (one lane paved road with turnouts) and travel 1.8 miles. Turn left at Pine Flats entrance, which is a gravel road.

N47°45'31" – W120°25'34   Elevation – 1,600 feet

Facilities

6 tent–only campsites
Vault/pit toilet
Potable water
Pack out garbage

Features

Pine Flats campground is located along the Mad River. The campground is near the Mad River Trailhead.

Reservations

None, all campsites are first–come, first–serve.

Season

Open from the end of April through mid October. Walk–in access is allowed in winter with no services.

Pine Flats Campsite

Activities

Hiking, Motorcycle riding/ORVs on designated trails only.

Cost

$8
See Appendix C for available discounts.

Limitations

Maximum trailer length is 20 feet.
Mad River is closed to fishing.
Livestock are not allowed in campground, but a hitching rail is available for stock users taking Mad River Trail #1409.
See Appendix A for camping regulations.

Contact

Okanogan–Wenatchee National Forest
Entiat Ranger District
2108 Entiat Way
P.O. Box 476
Entiat, WA 98822
Phone: 509–784–1511 (Voice/TTY)
Fax: 509–784–1150

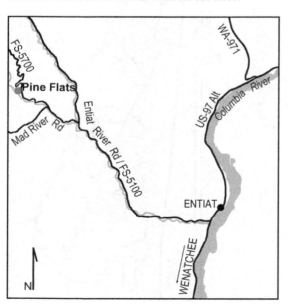

Driving Directions

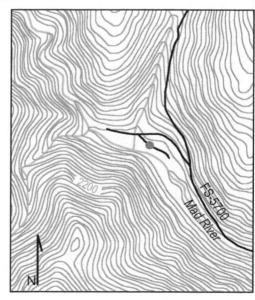

Location

195 Nason Creek
Okanogan–Wenatchee National Forest

Directions

Start at the intersection of US–2 and WA–207 north of Leavenworth. Travel north on WA–207 for 3.6 miles. Turn left onto Cedar Brae Road for 0.1 mile. Nason Creek campground is on both sides of the road.

N47°47'58"N – W120°42'53"   Elevation – 1,800 feet

Facilities

73 total sites:
70 single sites
3 double sites
Some pull–through sites
Flush toilets
Potable water
Garbage service
Accessible campsite, toilet, water

Features

Nason Creek campground is located on the southeastern end of Lake Wenatchee on both sides of Cedar Brae Road. Some sites are along a creek. Canoeing in the creek is a popular activity and a golf course is nearby.

Reservations

None, campsites are first–come, first–serve.

Season

Closed in winter

Activities

Biking, Boating (non–motorized), Hiking.

Cost

$23
$14 extra vehicle

See Appendix C for available discounts.

Limitations

See Appendix A for camping regulations.

Nason Creek Campsite

Contact

Okanogan–Wenatchee National Forest
Wenatchee River Ranger District
600 Sherbourne
Leavenworth, WA 98826
Phone: 509–548–2550
Fax: 509–548–5817

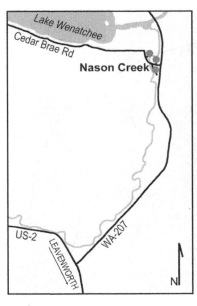

Driving Directions

Nason Creek Fish Counter

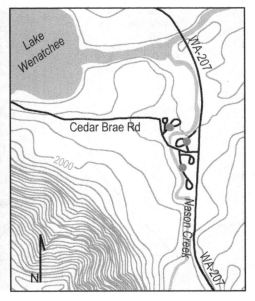

Location

196 Lake Wenatchee
Washington State Parks

Potable water
Hot showers
Garbage service
Boat launch
RV dump
Food service

Directions

Start at the intersection of US–2 and WA–207 near Leavenworth. There are two camping areas. To get to the southern campground, travel north on WA–207 for 3.6 miles. Turn left onto Cedar Brae Road and travel 0.3 mile to the park. To get to the northern campground, travel north on WA–207 for 4.4 miles. Continue as the road becomes Lake Wenatchee Highway and travel 0.3 mile. Turn left into park.

N47°48'38" – W120°43'21   Elevation – 1,880 feet

Facilities

197 total sites: 155 standard sites, 42 partial utility sites
Some pull–through sites
Flush toilets

Features

Lake Wenatchee State Park lies along glacier–fed Lake Wenatchee and the Wenatchee River. The Wenatchee River bisects the park into two distinct areas: South Park (with camping, swimming and horseback riding) and North Park, located in a less developed forested section that is a quarter–mile walk from the lake.

More than five miles of equestrian trails are in and around the park. A concession offers horses for rent for day rides or overnight pack trips. No public stables are available. The park offers year–round recreation opportunities, including swimming, boating and hiking in summer and cross–country skiing, snowshoeing and sledding in winter.

Reservations

Sites may be reserved May 13 through September 14 online at *www.parks.state.wa.us* or telephone 1–888–CAMPOUT (1–888–226–7688). See Appendix B for reservation details.

Season

Most sites are closed from October 1 through April 1, although, some camping sites in the southern campground are open all year.

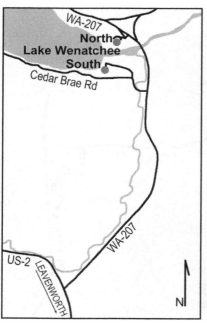

Driving Directions

Lake Wenatchee Playground

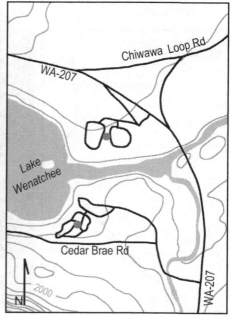

Location

Activities

Bird watching, Boating, Cross country skiing, Equestrian trail riding, Fishing, Hiking, Interpretive center, Mountain biking, Personal watercraft, Scuba diving, Snowshoeing, Sledding, Swimming, Wind surfing.

Cost

$12 primitive site
Peak season: mid May – mid September
$22 – $35 standard site
$30 – $40 partial utility site
$35 – $45 full utility site
Off–peak season
$20 – $30 standard site
$25 – $35 partial utility site
$30 – $40 full utility site
$10 extra vehicle (all year)
See Appendix C for available discounts.

Limitations

Maximum site length is 60 feet.
Mosquitoes may be prevalent May to early July. Repellant is recommended.
The park is a natural wildlife area, watch for bears and other natural dangers.
See Appendix A for camping regulations.

Contact

Phone: 509–763–3101
Web: *www.parks.state.wa.us*

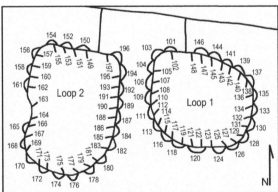

North Campground

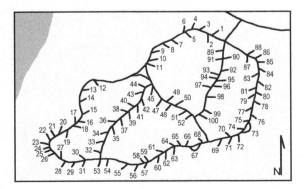

South Campground

Eggs Saratoga

We have made this delicious breakfast for years and look forward to having it while camping. Excellent by itself (like most things) it's always better with bacon.

Ingredients

*4 strips bacon
2 tsp cooking oil
3 eggs, beaten
3 tsp milk
3 green onions, chopped
¼ cup cream cheese, cut into small chunks
salt and pepper*

Preparation

Begin by frying the bacon until done to your liking. Set bacon aside and clean the pan.

Add cooking oil and heat over medium high heat. (Some people would use the leftover bacon fat to cook the eggs. We like to use oil because it helps the fresh flavor of the onions and cream cheese come through.) Beat milk into eggs and pour into skillet when heated. Turn heat down to medium so the eggs won't scorch. Add green onions and cream cheese. Stir like scrambled eggs.

When eggs are done and cheese has started melting, turn heat off, lay cooked bacon on top of eggs to rewarm, and put lid on pan for a few minutes. Put onto plates and enjoy.

197 Glacier View
Okanogan–Wenatchee National Forest

Directions

Start at the intersection of US–2 and WA–207 north of Leavenworth. Travel north on WA–207 for 3.6 miles. Turn left onto Cedar Brae Road (the road takes a sharp left after 0.3 mile) and travel for 3.5 miles. Cedar Brae Road becomes Forest Service Road 6607, a one–lane, gravel road. Travel on this road for 1.2 miles to Glacier View.

N47°49'26" – W120°48'21"   Elevation – 1,900 feet

Glacier View

Facilities

23 total sites: 7 standard, 16 walk–in
Vault toilets
Potable water
Garbage service
Boat launch

Features

Glacier View campground is located on the south side of Lake Wenatchee. The walk–in sites are located along the lakeshore.

Reservations

None, campsites are first–come, first–serve.

Season

Open all year. However, in winter, there are no fees and no services and campers must bring drinking water, toilet paper and pack out garbage.

Glacier View Campsite

Activities

Boating, Fishing.

Cost

$18
$10 extra vehicle
See Appendix C for available discounts.

Limitations

Vehicles limited to cars, vans and pickups.
Maximum trailer length is 15 feet.
Watercraft may not exceed 3 mph.
See Appendix A for camping regulations.

Contact

Okanogan–Wenatchee National Forest
Wenatchee River Ranger District
600 Sherbourne
Leavenworth, WA 98826
Phone: 509–548–2550
Fax: 509–548–5817

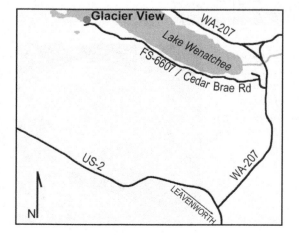

Driving Directions

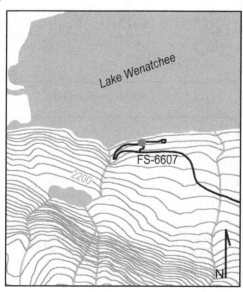

Location

198　Goose Creek
Okanogan–Wenatchee National Forest

Directions

Start at the intersection of US–2 and WA–207 north of Leavenworth. Travel north on WA–207 for 4.4 miles. Turn right onto Chiwawa Loop Road and travel 1.3 miles. Turn left onto Chiwawa River Road (Forest Service Road 62) and travel 3.3 miles. Turn right onto Forest Service Road 6208 and travel 0.1 mile. Turn right onto Forest Service Road/County Road 6100 and travel 0.6 mile. Turn right to Goose Creek.

N47°50'20" – W120°38'53"　Elevation – 2,200 feet

Facilities

29 standard sites
Vault toilets
Potable water
Garbage service

Features

Goose Creek campground is located along Goose Creek, near the Chiwawa River. The campground provides access to motorcycle trails.

Reservations

None, campsites are first–come, first–serve.

Season

Closed in winter

Activities

Motorcycle riding.

Cost

$14
$10 extra vehicle
See Appendix C for available discounts.

Limitations

See Appendix A for camping regulations.

Contact

Okanogan–Wenatchee National Forest
Wenatchee River Ranger District
600 Sherbourne
Leavenworth, WA 98826
Phone: 509–548–2550
Fax: 509–548–5817

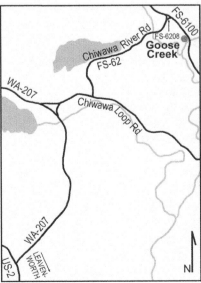

Driving Directions

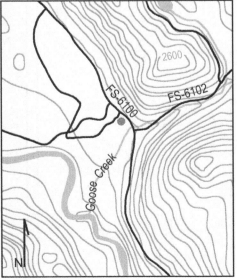

Location

199 Riverbend
Okanogan–Wenatchee National Forest

Directions

Start at the intersection of US–2 and WA–207 north of Leavenworth. Travel north on WA–207 for 4.4 miles. Turn right onto Chiwawa Loop Road and travel 1.3 miles. Turn left onto Chiwawa River Road (Forest Service Road 62) and travel 14.5 miles. The road becomes single lane, paved with turnouts, with the last 2.1 miles becoming a single lane, gravel road with turnouts. Turn left to Riverbend.

N47°57'43" – W120°47'16"   Elevation – 2,500 feet

Facilities

6 standard sites
Vault toilet
No water, bring your own
Pack out garbage

Features

Riverbend campground is located along the Chiwawa River and provides river access. Some of the sites are along the river.

Reservations

None, campsites are first–come, first–serve.

Season

Open all year. During the winter months, when there is snow on the roads, the campground is inaccessible to wheeled motor vehicles.

Activities

Fishing.

Cost

$14
$10 extra vehicle
See Appendix C for available discounts.

Limitations

Maximum vehicle length is 30 feet.
See Appendix A for camping regulations.

Contact

Okanogan–Wenatchee National Forest
Wenatchee River Ranger District
600 Sherbourne
Leavenworth, WA 98826
Phone: 509–548–2550
Fax: 509–548–5817

Driving Directions   *Location*

200 Schaefer Creek
Okanogan–Wenatchee National Forest

Directions

Start at the intersection of US–2 and WA–207 north of Leavenworth. Travel north on WA–207 for 4.4 miles. Turn right onto Chiwawa Loop Road and travel 1.3 miles. Turn left onto Chiwawa River Road (Forest Service Road 62) and travel 15.4 miles (road becomes a single lane, paved road with turnouts and a single lane, gravel road with turnouts the last 3.0 miles). Turn left to Schaefer Creek.

N47°58'30" – W120°48'11"   Elevation – 2,500 feet

Facilities

10 standard sites
Vault toilet
No water, bring your own
Pack out garbage

Features

Schaefer Creek campground provides access to the Chiwawa River.

Reservations

None, campsites are first–come, first–serve.

Season

Open all year. During the winter months, when there is snow on the roads, the campground is inaccessible to wheeled motor vehicles.

Activities

Fishing.

Cost

$14 standard site

Chiwawa River

$10 extra vehicle
See Appendix C for available discounts.

Limitations

Maximum vehicle length is 30 feet.
See Appendix A for camping regulations.

Contact

Okanogan–Wenatchee National Forest
Wenatchee River Ranger District
600 Sherbourne
Leavenworth, WA 98826
Phone: 509–548–2550
Fax: 509–548–5817

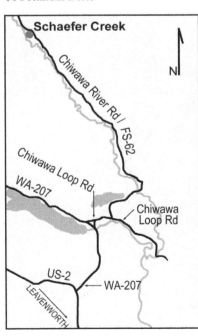

Driving Directions

Schaefer Creek Toilet

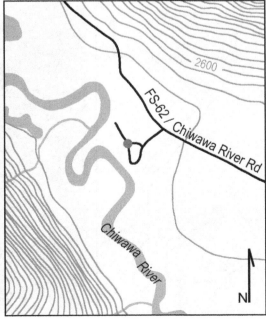

Location

201 Atkinson Flats
Okanogan–Wenatchee National Forest

Directions

Start at the intersection of US–2 and WA–207 north of Leavenworth. Travel north on WA–207 for 4.4 miles. Turn right onto Chiwawa Loop Road and travel 1.3 miles. Turn left onto Chiwawa River Road (Forest Service Road 62) and travel 17.1 miles (becomes a single lane, paved road with turnouts and a single lane, gravel road with turnouts the last 4.7 miles). Turn left to Atkinson Flats.

N47°59'58" – W120°49'00"   Elevation – 2,550 feet

Facilities

7 standard sites
Vault toilet
No water, bring your own
Pack out garbage

Features

Atkinson Flats campground provides access to the Chiwawa River.

Reservations

None, campsites are first–come, first–serve.

Season

Open all year. During the winter months, when there is snow on the roads, the campground is inaccessible to wheeled motor vehicles.

Activities

Fishing.

Cost

$14 standard site
$10 extra vehicle
See Appendix C for available discounts.

Limitations

Maximum vehicle length is 20 feet.
See Appendix A for camping regulations.

Contact

Okanogan–Wenatchee National Forest
Wenatchee River Ranger District
600 Sherbourne
Leavenworth, WA 98826
Phone: 509–548–2550
Fax: 509–548–5817

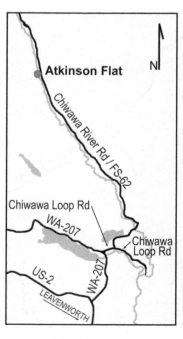

Driving Directions

Chiwawa River

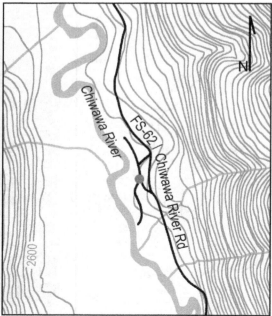

Location

202 Phelps Creek
Okanogan–Wenatchee National Forest

Directions

Start at the intersection of US–2 and WA–207 north of Leavenworth. Travel north on WA–207 for 4.4 miles. Turn right onto Chiwawa Loop Road and travel 1.3 miles. Turn left onto Chiwawa River Road (Forest Service Road 62) and travel 24.6 miles (becomes a single lane, paved road with turnouts for 12.4 miles, then becomes a single lane, gravel road with turnouts for 12.2 miles). Turn left to Phelps Creek.

N48°04'10" – W120°51'04"   Elevation – 2,800 feet

Chiwawa River at Phelps Creek

Facilities

13 standard sites
Vault toilet
No water, bring your own
Pack out garbage

Features

Phelps Creek campground is located near the confluence of Phelps Creek and the Chiwawa River. The campground provides access to the river and offers additional campsites (6) dedicated to equestrian use.

Reservations

None, campsites are first–come, first–serve.

Season

Open all year. During the winter months, when there is snow on the roads, the campground is inaccessible to wheeled motor vehicles.

Activities

Equestrian trail riding, Fishing.

Cost

$14 standard site
$10 extra vehicle
See Appendix C for available discounts.

Limitations

Maximum trailer length is 30 feet.
See Appendix A for available discounts.

Contact

Okanogan–Wenatchee National Forest
Wenatchee River Ranger District
600 Sherbourne
Leavenworth, WA 98826
Phone: 509–548–2550
Fax: 509–548–5817

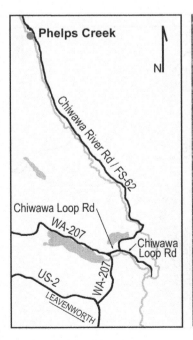

Driving Directions

Phelps Creek Campsite

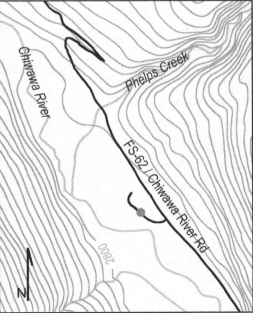

Location

203 Rainy Creek
Okanogan–Wenatchee National Forest

Directions

Start at the intersection of US–2 and WA–207 north of Leavenworth. Travel north on WA–207 (becomes Lake Wenatchee Highway) for 10.7 miles. Turn left onto Little Wenatchee Road (Forest Service Road 6500) and travel 6.1 miles. Turn left onto Smithbrook–Rainy Creek Road (Forest Service Road 6700) and travel 0.5 mile. Bear right at "Y" onto Forest Service Road 6701 and travel 0.7 mile. Turn right into Rainy Creek.

N47°51'11" – W120°57'44"   Elevation – 2,000 feet

Little Wenatchee River

Facilities

10 standard sites
Some pull–through sites
Vault toilet
No water, bring your own
Pack out garbage

Features

Rainy Creek campground is located at the confluence of Rainy Creek and the Wenatchee River.

Reservations

None, campsites are first–come, first–serve.

Season

Open all year. During the winter months when there is snow on the roads, the campground is inaccessible to wheeled motor vehicles.

Activities

Fishing.

Cost

No cost

Limitations

Maximum trailer length is 30 feet. See Appendix A for camping regulations.

Rainy Creek

Contact

Okanogan–Wenatchee National Forest
Wenatchee River Ranger District
600 Sherbourne
Leavenworth, WA 98826
Phone: 509–548–2550
Fax: 509–548–5817

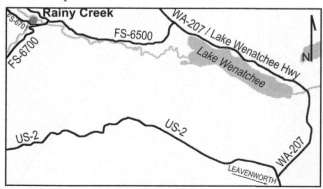

Driving Directions

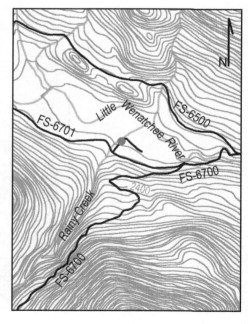

Location

204 Lake Creek
Okanogan–Wenatchee National Forest

Directions

Start at the intersection of US–2 and WA–207 north of Leavenworth. Travel north on WA–207 for 4.4 miles. WA–207 (becomes Lake Wenatchee Highway). Continue on the highway for 5.9 miles. Turn left onto Little Wenatchee Road (Forest Service Road 6500) and travel 10.7 miles. Turn left to Lake Creek. The road becomes a single–lane, paved road with pullouts approximately five miles before the campground.

N47°52'32" – W121°0'49"   Elevation – 2,300 feet

Facilities

8 standard sites
Vault toilet, bring toilet paper
No water, bring your own
Pack out garbage

Features

Lake Creek campground is located at the confluence of the Little Wenatchee River and Lake Creek. The campground offers river access.

Reservations

None, campsites are first–come, first–serve.

Season

Open year around. During the winter months when there is snow on the roads, the campground is inaccessible to wheeled motor vehicles.

Activities

Fishing.

Cost

No Cost

Limitations

Due to a washout that severely narrowed Forest Service Road 6500 between Soda Springs and Lake Creek, large vehicles and trailers are not advised to travel beyond the junction of Forest Service Road 6500 and Smithbrook–Rainy Creek Road (Forest Service Road 6700).

See Appendix A for camping regulations.

Contact

Okanogan–Wenatchee National Forest
Wenatchee River Ranger District
600 Sherbourne
Leavenworth, WA 98826
Phone: 509–548–2550
Fax: 509–548–5817

Lake Creek Campsite

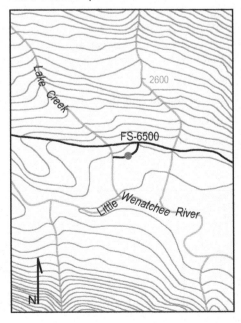

Location

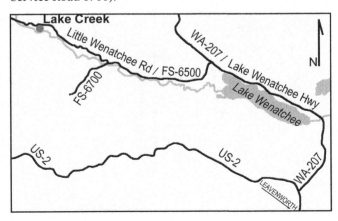

Driving Directions

205 Beckler River
Mount Baker–Snoqualmie National Forest

Directions

Start at the intersection of US–2 and WA–203 in Monroe. Travel east on US–2 for 34.5 miles. Pass through the town of Skykomish and turn left onto Beckler Road (Forest Service Road 6500) and travel 1.5 miles. Turn left into Beckler River campground.

Or

Start at the intersection of US–2 and WA–207 near Lake Wenatchee. Travel west on US–2 for 35.1 miles. Near the town of Skykomish turn right onto Beckler Road (Forest Service Road 6500) and travel 1.5 miles. Turn left into Beckler River campground.

N47°44'05" – W121°19'59"   Elevation – 1,020 feet

Facilities

27 standard campsites
Pull–through sites
Vault/pit toilets
Potable water
Garbage service
Accessible toilet, campsite

Features

Beckler campground lies on the banks of Beckler River, less than 1.5 miles from US Highway 2 and the outskirts of the town of Skykomish. The campground's dense surrounding forest and river noise create private and peaceful sites, several of which are along the river. Good jump–off point for recreational activities in the North Fork Skykomish and West Fork Foss River areas.

Reservations

Reserve online at *www.recreation.gov* or call 1–877–444–6777 (5 am to 9 pm Pacific time), 518–885–3639, or TDD 1–877–833–6777. Reservations must be made at least 4 days ahead of arrival and may be made up to 12 months in advance. See Appendix B for details.

Season

Open from mid May through mid September

Activities

Fishing, Hiking.

Beckler River Campsite

Cost

$16
$8 extra vehicle
See Appendix C for available discounts.

Limitations

See Appendix A for camping regulations.

Contact

Mt. Baker–Snoqualmie National Forest
2930 Wetmore Ave., Suite 3A
Everett, WA 98201
Phone: 425–783–6000, 800–627–0062
Outdoor Recreation Information: 206–470–4060

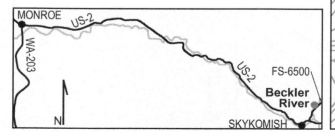

Driving Directions

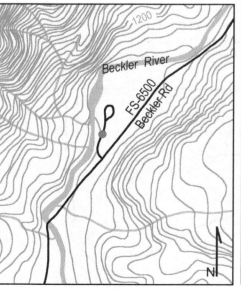

Location

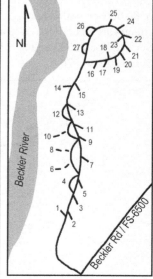

Campground

206 Money Creek
Mount Baker–Snoqualmie National Forest

Directions

Start in Monroe at the intersection of US 2 and WA 203. Travel east on US 2 for 30.9 miles. Before the town of Skykomish turn right onto Money Creek Road and travel 0.1 mile. Money Creek is on both sides of the road.

Or

Start near Lake Wenatchee at the intersection of US 2 and WA 207. Travel west on US 2 for 38.9 miles. After the town of Skykomish turn left onto Money Creek Road and travel 0.1 mile. Money Creek is on both sides of the road.

N47°43'44" – W121°24'31"   Elevation – 860 feet

Facilities

25 standard campsites
Pull–through sites
Vault/pit toilets
Potable water
Garbage service
Accessible toilet, campsite

Features

Money Creek campground lies on the banks of South Fork Skykomish River. It is tucked between busy Highway 2 and the BNSF railway tracks so the traffic noise can be heavy at times. Several sites are riverside. Majestic old growth trees surround the campground.

Reservations

Reserve online at *www.recreation.gov* or call 1–877–444–6777 (5 am to 9 pm Pacific time), 518–885–3639, or TDD 1–877–833–6777. Reservations must be made at least 4 days ahead of arrival and may be made up to 12 months in advance. See Appendix B for details.

Season

Open from May through late September

Activities

Fishing, Hiking.

Cost

$18 – $20
$9 extra vehicle

See Appendix C for available discounts.

Limitations

See Appendix A for camping regulations.

Contact

Mt. Baker–Snoqualmie National Forest
2930 Wetmore Ave., Suite 3A
Everett, WA 98201
Phone: 425–783–6000, 800–627–0062
Outdoor Recreation Information: 206–470–4060

Money Creek View

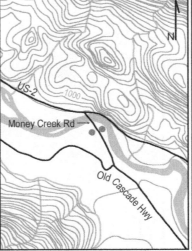

Driving Directions

Location

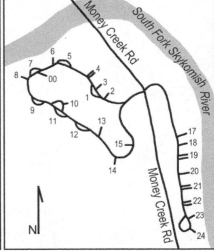

Campground

207 Flowing Lake Park
Snohomish County

Directions

Start at the intersection of US–2 and WA–203 near Monroe. Travel west on US–2 for 4.9 miles. Turn right onto 100th Street SE (also called Westwick Road) and travel 1.9 miles. Bear left as road becomes 171st Avenue SE and travel 3.2 miles. Turn right onto 48th Street SE and travel 0.5 mile to park.

N 47°57'09" – W 121°59'19"   Elevation – 560 feet

Facilities

31 total sites: 7 standard, 24 partial utility (W/E)
Flush toilets
Potable water
Hot showers
Garbage service
Boat launch
Accessible campsites

Features

Flowing Lake Park lies along the shore of Flowing Lake and offers many water activities such as swimming (although no life–guard is on duty), boating, and fishing from the fishing pier.

Reservations

Reservations may be made online at *https://snoco.usedirect.com/snohomishweb/* or by telephone at 425–388–6600. Telephone reservation requests go to a voicemail box and may take up to 3 days to receive a call back. See Appendix B for reservation details.

Season

Open all year, no campsite water hook–ups in winter

Activities

Beachcombing, Biking, Bird watching, Boating, Fishing, Playground, Swimming, Walking, Water skiing.

Flowing Lake

Cost

$28 standard site
$35 partial utility site
$40 premium site (sites 15 – 17 and 23)
$10 extra vehicle
See Appendix C for available discounts.

Limitations

See Appendix A for camping regulations.

Contact

Flowing Lake Park
17900 48th SE
Snohomish, WA 98290
Phone: 360–568–2274
Web: *snohomishcountywa.gov/200/Parks–Recreation–Tourism*

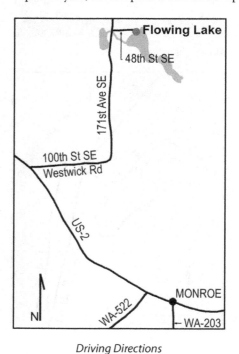

Driving Directions

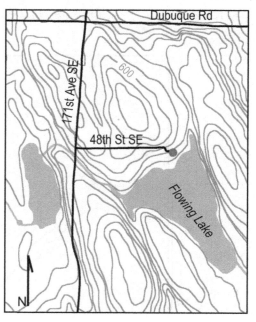

Location

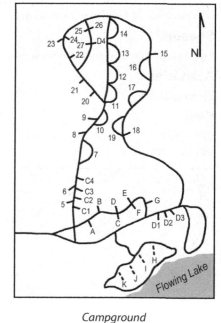

Campground

208 River Meadows Park
Snohomish County

Directions

Start at the intersection of WA–9 and WA–530 in Arlington. Travel east on WA–530 for 1.1 miles. Turn right onto Arlington Heights Road and travel for 0.9 mile. Turn right onto Jordan Road and travel 2.9 miles. Turn right into River Meadows Park.

N48°10'47" – W122°04'54"   Elevation – 100 feet

Facilities

14 total sites:
10 standard, 4 walk–in
Pull–through sites
Flush toilets
Potable water
Garbage service
Shelters

Features

River Meadows Park offers large open meadows and forests along the banks of the Stillaguamish River. The park is a popular rafting location.

Reservations

Reservations can be made online at *https://snoco.usedirect.com/snohomishweb/* or by telephone at 425–388–6600. Telephone reservation requests go to a voicemail box and it sometimes takes up to 3 days to receive a call back. Weekend reservations require a 2–night stay. See Appendix B for reservation details.

Season

Open all year

Activities

Bird watching, Boating (non–motorized), Fishing, Hiking.

Cost

$28
$10 extra vehicle
See Appendix C for available discounts.

Limitations

Maximum site length is 42 feet.
See Appendix A for camping regulations.

Contact

River Meadows Park
20416 Jordan Road
Arlington, WA 98223
Phone: 360–435–3441
Web: *snohomishcountywa.gov/200/Parks–Recreation–Tourism*

River Float Entry Point

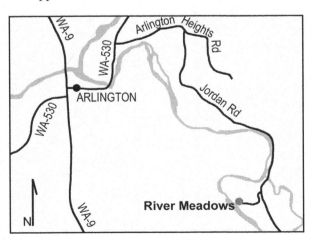

Driving Directions

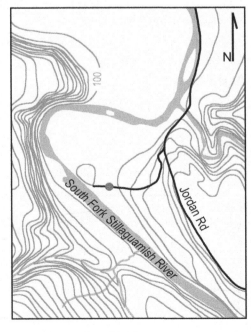

Location

209 Turlo
Mount Baker–Snoqualmie National Forest

Directions

Start at the intersection of WA–9 and WA–92 northwest of Lake Stevens. Travel east on WA–92 (Granite Falls Hwy) for 8.6 miles. In the town of Granite Falls, turn left onto Mountain Loop Hwy (also called Alder Road for a short distance) and travel 10.8 miles. Turn right to Turlo.

N48°05'32" – W121°47'07"   Elevation – 920 feet

Limitations

See Appendix A for camping regulations.

Contact

Mt. Baker–Snoqualmie National Forest
2930 Wetmore Ave., Suite 3A
Everett, WA 98201
Phone: 425–783–6000, 800–627–0062
Outdoor Recreation Information: 206–470–4060

Facilities

18 standard sites
Vault toilet
No water, bring your own
Garbage service
Accessible toilet, campsite

Features

Turlo campground is across the Mt Loop Highway from the Verlot Public Service Center and nestled in old growth forest. The campground drops down from the highway to the south fork of the Stillaguamish River. Several sites are riverside. Mt. Dickerman Trail, close to the campground, offers stunning views from the 5,723 foot summit.

Reservations

Reserve online at *www.recreation.gov* or call 1–877–444–6777 (5 am to 9 pm Pacific time), 518–885–3639, or TDD 1–877–833–6777. Reservations must be made at least 4 days ahead of arrival and may be made up to 12 months in advance. See Appendix B for details.

Season

All year, weather permitting

Activities

Fishing, Swimming, Tubing.

Cost

$16
$8 extra vehicle
See Appendix C for available discounts.

Turlo Toilet

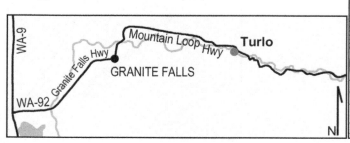

Driving Directions

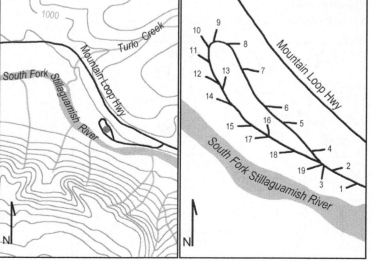

Location   *Campground*

210 Verlot
Mount Baker–Snoqualmie National Forest

Directions

Start at the intersection of WA–9 and WA–92 northwest of Lake Stevens. Travel east on WA–92 (Granite Falls Hwy) for 8.6 miles. In the town of Granite Falls, turn left onto Mountain Loop Hwy (also called Alder Road for a short distance) and travel 11.1 miles. Turn right to Verlot.

N48°05'23" – W121°46'41"   Elevation – 960 feet

Facilities

25 standard sites
Flush toilets
Potable water
Garbage service
Accessible toilet, water, campsite

Features

Verlot campground is located across the Mt Loop Highway from the Verlot Public Service Center along the South Fork Stillaguamish River. The tree canopy is open allowing sunny campsites suitable for tents and trailers. Although just off the highway, the campground is relatively quiet. Many sites border either the South Fork Stillaguamish River or Benson Creek. Mt. Dickerman Trail, close to the campground, offers stunning views from the 5,723 foot summit.

Reservations

Reserve online at *www.recreation.gov* or call 1–877–444–6777 (5 am to 9 pm Pacific time), 518–885–3639, or TDD 1–877–833–6777. Reservations must be made at least 4 days ahead of arrival and may be made up to 12 months in advance. See Appendix B for details.

Season

All year, weather permitting

Activities

Fishing, Hiking.

Cost

$18 – 24 single site
$9 extra vehicle
See Appendix C for available discounts.

Limitations

See Appendix A for camping regulations.

Contact

Mt. Baker–Snoqualmie National Forest
2930 Wetmore Ave., Suite 3A
Everett, WA 98201
Phone: 425–783–6000, 800–627–0062
Outdoor Recreation Information: 206–470–4060

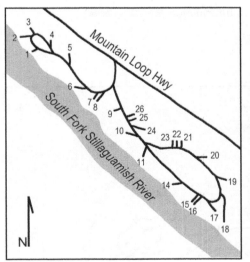

Campground

Verlot Campsite

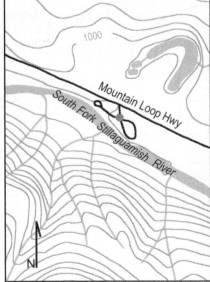

Location

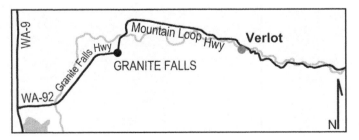

Driving Directions

211 Gold Basin
Mount Baker–Snoqualmie National Forest

Directions

Start at the intersection of WA–9 and WA–92 northwest of Lake Stevens. Travel east on WA–92 (Granite Falls Hwy) for 8.6 miles. In the town of Granite Falls, turn left onto Mountain Loop Hwy (also called Alder Road for a short distance) and travel 13.5 miles. Turn left into Gold Basin.

N48°04'42" – W121°44'13"   Elevation – 1,082 feet

Restrooms and Showers

Facilities

93 total sites: 83 standard, 10 tent–only
Pull–through sites
Flush and vault toilets
Potable water
Hot showers
Garbage service
Accessible toilet, campsite

Features

Located east of Verlot Public Service Center, Gold Basin campground is the largest on the Mountain Loop Highway and offers the most developed and accessible camping. Several sites are along the Stillaguamish River. Campsites are suitable for tents and trailers. The campground has a large open field. Across the road from the campground is a salmon fry viewing area, Gold Basin Pond, with a 1/2–mile accessible boardwalk and benches on the viewing platforms.

Reservations

Reserve online at *www.recreation.gov* or call 1–877–444–6777 (5 am to 9 pm Pacific time), 518–885–3639, or TDD 1–877–833–6777. Reservations must be made at least 4 days ahead of arrival and may be made up to 12 months in advance. See Appendix B for details.

Season

Open from mid May through the end of September

Activities

Hiking, Swimming, Tubing.

Cost

$22 single site
$11 extra vehicle
See Appendix C for available discounts.

Limitations

See Appendix A for camping regulations.

Contact

Mt. Baker–Snoqualmie National Forest
2930 Wetmore Ave., Suite 3A
Everett, WA 98201
Phone: 425–783–6000, 800–627–0062
Outdoor Recreation Information: 206–470–4060

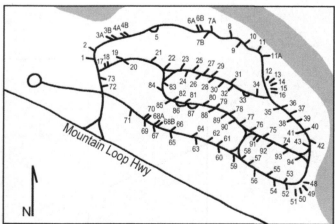

Campground

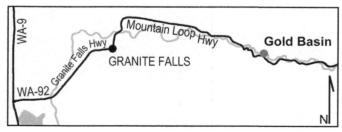

Driving Directions

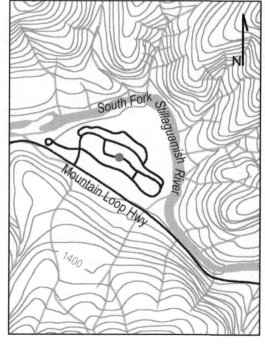

Location

212 Red Bridge
Mount Baker–Snoqualmie National Forest

Directions

Start at the intersection of WA–9 and WA–92 northwest of Lake Stevens. Travel east on WA–92 (Granite Falls Hwy) for 8.6 miles. In the town of Granite Falls, turn left onto Mountain Loop Hwy (also called Alder Road for a short distance) and travel 18.2 miles. Turn right to Red Bridge.

N28°04'12" – W121°39'09"   Elevation – 1,280 feet

Facilities

14 standard sites
Vault toilet
No water, bring your own
Garbage service
Accessible toilet, campsite

Features

Red Bridge campground is 7.1 miles east of Verlot Public Service Center on the Mountain Loop Highway. The campground is nestled among old–growth forest along the south fork Stillaguamish River and has very private sites. A large river bar, close by, offers riverside activities.

Reservations

Reserve online at *www.recreation.gov* or call 1–877–444–6777 (5 am to 9 pm Pacific time), 518–885–3639, or TDD 1–877–833–6777. Reservations must be made at least 4 days ahead of arrival and may be made up to 12 months in advance. See Appendix B for details.

Season

Open from mid May through mid September

Activities

Fishing

Cost

$14 single site
$7 extra vehicle
See Appendix C for available discounts.

Limitations

See Appendix A for camping regulations.

Contact

Mt. Baker–Snoqualmie National Forest
2930 Wetmore Ave., Suite 3A
Everett, WA 98201
Phone: 425–783–6000, 800–627–0062
Outdoor Recreation Information: 206–470–4060

Red Bridge Campsite

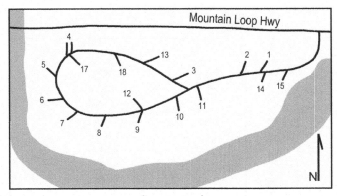

Campground

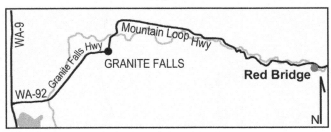

Driving Directions

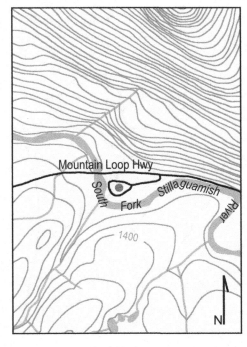

Location

213 Bedal
Mount Baker–Snoqualmie National Forest

Directions

Start at the intersection of WA–530 and WA–9 in Arlington. Travel north on WA–530/WA–9 for 0.1 mile. Turn east on WA–530 (also called W. Burke Avenue) and travel 27.9 miles to Darrington. Turn right onto Mountain Loop Road (Forest Service Road 20/Forest Service Road 40) and travel 16.2 miles. Turn right into Bedal.

N48°05'47" – W121°23'14   Elevation – 1,240 feet

Facilities

21 standard sites
Pull–through sites
Vault toilets
No water, bring your own
Garbage service
Shelter
Boat launch
Accessible toilet, campsite

Features

Bedal campground lies along the Sauk River in old growth forest on the Mountain Loop Highway. It offers a more primitive experience – off the main road and away from traffic noise. The river can be heard from most of the campsites, many of which are riverside. The campground has a large Adirondack shelter built of old growth timber.

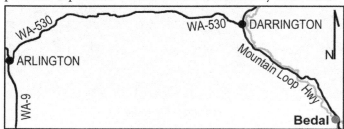

Driving Directions

Reservations

Reserve online at *www.recreation.gov* or call 1–877–444–6777 (5 am to 9 pm Pacific time), 518–885–3639, or TDD 1–877–833–6777. Reservations must be made at least 4 days ahead of arrival and may be made up to 12 months in advance. See Appendix B for details.

Season

Open from mid May through mid September

Activities

Fishing, Hiking, Mountain biking.

Cost

$14 single site
$7 extra vehicle
See Appendix C for available discounts.

Limitations

Large motor homes and trailers are not recommended.
Dogs allowed on leash only.
See Appendix A for camping regulations.

Contact

Mt. Baker–Snoqualmie National Forest
2930 Wetmore Ave., Suite 3A
Everett, WA 98201
Phone: 425–783–6000, 800–627–0062
Outdoor Recreation Information: 206–470–4060

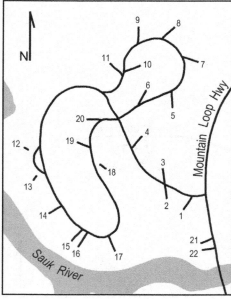

Campground

Balancing Act

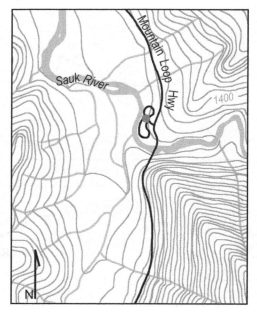

Location

214 Wenberg County Park
Snohomish County

Directions

Start at the intersection of I–5 and WA–531 (exit 206). Travel west on WA–531 for 4.8 miles. Turn left onto East Lake Goodwin Road (the continuation of WA–531) and travel 1.5 miles. Turn right into Wenberg County Park.

N48°08'11" – W122°17'16"   Elevation – 420 feet

Facilities

70 total sites: 41 standard, 29 partial utility (W/E)
Some pull–through sites
Flush toilets
Potable water
Hot showers
Garbage service
RV dump
Shelter
Boat launch
Accessible campsites

Features

Located on the shore of Lake Goodwin, Wenberg County Park offers a lovely fresh–water beach area. While there is a swimming area, there is no lifeguard. The park has a concession stand during the summer season. Wi–Fi is available.

Reservations

Reservations may be made online at https://snoco.usedirect.com/snohomishweb/ or by telephone at 425–388–6600. Telephone reservation requests go to a voicemail box and may take up to 3 days to receive a call back. See Appendix B for reservation details.

Season

Open all year

Activities

Bird watching, Boating, Fishing, Hiking, Swimming.

Cost

$28 standard
$35 partial utility (W/E)
$10 extra vehicle
See Appendix C for available discounts.

Limitations

See Appendix A for camping regulations.

Contact

Wenberg County Park
15430 E Lake Goodwin Rd
Stanwood, WA 98292
Phone: 360–652–7417
Web: *snohomishcountywa.gov/200/Parks–Recreation–Tourism*

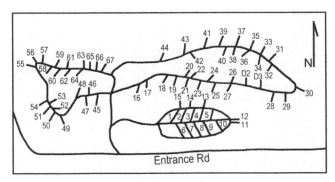

Campground

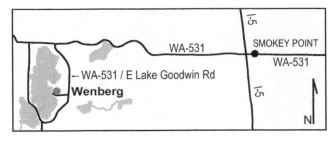

Driving Directions

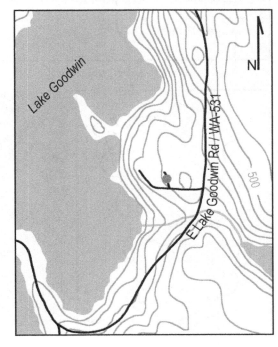

Location

215 Kayak Point
Snohomish County

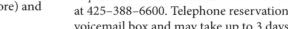

Directions

Start at the intersection of I–5 and WA–531 (exit 206). Travel west on WA–531 for 4.8 miles. At the 4.8 mile point, WA–531 turns south onto East Lake Godwin Rd – do not turn – continue straight ahead onto Warm Beach Road and travel 3.5 additional miles. Turn left onto Marine Drive and travel 0.7 mile. Turn right onto 176th Street NW and travel 0.2 mile. Turn left onto Marine Drive (yes, the same name as before) and travel 1.3 miles. Turn right into park.

N48°08'20" – W122°21'31"   Elevation – 100 feet

Facilities

30 partial utility sites (E only)
Some pull–through sites
Flush toilets
Potable water
Hot showers
Garbage service
Shelter
Boat launch
Accessible campsites

Features

Kayak Point County Park is located along the shore of Point Susan on Puget Sound. With a fishing pier that extends 300' into the water, visitors have access to good fishing and crabbing. The park has a swimming area, although no lifeguard. The county operates Kayak Golf Course which is nearby.

Reservations

Reservations may be made online at *https://snoco.usedirect.com/snohomishweb/* or by telephone at 425–388–6600. Telephone reservation requests go to a voicemail box and may take up to 3 days to receive a call back. See Appendix B for reservation details.

Season

Open all year

Activities

Beachcombing, Bird watching, Boating, Crabbing, Fishing, Hiking, Playground, Scuba diving, Swimming.

Cost

$28 standard site
$35 partial utility site
$40 premium site (sites 7, 9, 13, and 15)
$10 extra vehicle
See Appendix C for available discounts.

Limitations

Maximum site length is 35 feet.
See Appendix A for camping regulations.

Contact

Kayak Point County Park
15610 Marine Drive
Stanwood WA 98292
Phone: 360–652–7992
Web: *snohomishcountywa.gov/200/Parks–Recreation–Tourism*

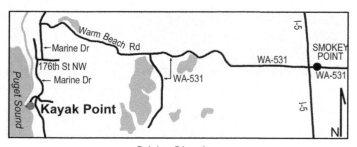

Driving Directions

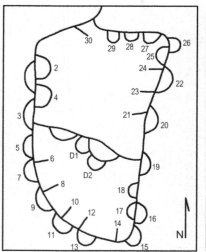

Campground

Kayak Point Campsite

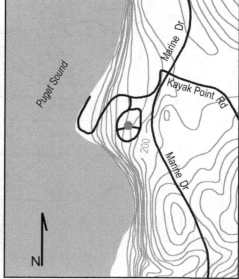

Location

216 Squire Creek Park
Snohomish County

Directions

Start at the intersection of I–5 and WA–530 (exit 208) near Arlington. Travel east on WA–530 for 28.4 miles. Turn left into Squire Creek Park.

N48°16'20" – W121°40'28"   Elevation – 460 feet

Squire Creek Restrooms

Facilities

33 standard sites
Some pull–through sites
Flush toilets
Potable water, in summer
Garbage service
Shelters

Features

Squire Creek Park is located among beautiful moss–laden trees of an old growth forest with access to Squire Creek. There are covered picnic shelters near the creek. Mt Baker – Snoqualmie National Forest, Boulder River Wilderness and Whitehorse Mountain are nearby.

Reservations

Reservations can be made online at *https://snoco.usedirect.com/snohomishweb/* or by telephone at 425–388–6600. Telephone reservation requests go to a voicemail box and it sometimes takes up to 3 days to receive a call back. Weekend reservations require a 2–night stay. See Appendix B for reservation details.

Season

Open all year; restrooms are closed in the winter, although sanicans are provided. Water spigots are also turned off in the winter. Bring your own water.

Activities

Hiking.

Cost

$28 standard site
$10 extra vehicle
See Appendix C for available discounts.

Limitations

See Appendix A for camping regulations.

Contact

Squire Creek Park
41415 State Road 530
Arlington, WA 98223
Phone: 360–435–3441
Web: *snohomishcountywa.gov/200/Parks–Recreation–Tourism*

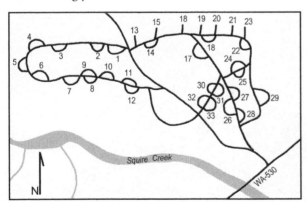

Campground

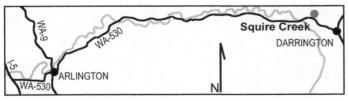

Driving Directions

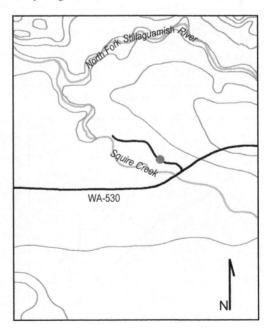

Location

217 Clear Creek
Mount Baker–Snoqualmie National Forest

Directions

Start at the intersection of WA–530 and WA–9 in Arlington. Travel north on WA–530/WA–9 for 0.1 mile. Turn east onto WA 530 (also called W. Burke Avenue) and travel 27.9 miles to Darrington. Turn right onto Mountain Loop Road (Forest Service Road 20/Forest Service Road 40) and travel 2.9 miles. Turn left into Clear Creek.

   N48°13'14" – W121°34'22"   Elevation – 640 feet

Facilities

13 standard sites
Pull–through sites (10–13)
Vault toilet
No water, bring your own
Garbage service
Accessible toilet, campsite

Features

Clear Creek campground is located along the Sauk River 3.5 miles south of Darrington on the Mountain Loop Highway. The undergrowth is relatively sparse, although the campground has stately old fir trees. Several sites are riverside. Nearby are the one–mile long Frog Lake Nature Trail and the three–mile Old Sauk Trail.

Reservations

Reserve online at *www.recreation.gov* or call 1–877–444–6777 (5 am to 9 pm Pacific time), 518–885–3639, or TDD 1–877–833–6777. Reservations must be made at least 4 days ahead of arrival and may be made up to 12 months in advance. See Appendix B for details.

Season

Open from mid May through late September

Activities

Fishing, Hiking, Mountain biking.

Cost

$14
$7 extra vehicle
See Appendix C for available discounts.

Limitations

See Appendix A for camping regulations.

Contact

Mt. Baker–Snoqualmie National Forest
2930 Wetmore Ave., Suite 3A
Everett, WA 98201
Phone: 425–783–6000, 800–627–0062
Outdoor Recreation Information: 206–470–4060

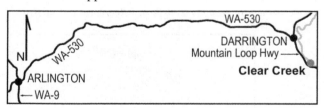

Driving Directions

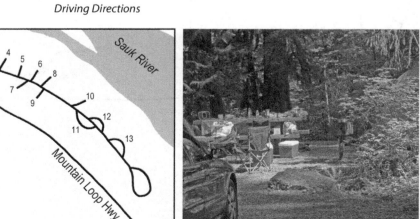

Campground

Campsite

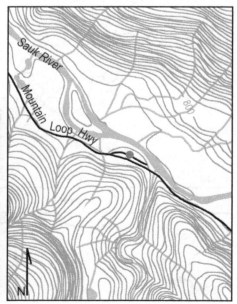

Location

238

218 Camano Island
Washington State Parks

Directions

Start at the intersection of I–5 and WA–532 (exit 212) near Arlington. Travel west on WA–532 for 9.8 miles. Bear left onto East Camano Drive and travel 6.2 miles. Continue straight onto Elger Bay Road and travel 1.9 miles. Turn right onto Mountain View Road and travel 1.7 miles. Turn left onto Lowell Point Road and travel 0.8 mile to park.

N48°07'45" – W122°30'04"   Elevation – 100 feet

Facilities

88 standard sites
Flush toilets
Potable water
Hot showers
Garbage service
RV dump
Boat launch
Accessible toilet

Features

Camano Island State Park offers more than a mile of rocky shoreline and beach on Puget Sound with sweeping views of the Sound, the Olympic Mountains and Mount Rainer. Volunteers host summer interpretive programs. The upper campground loop is better for RVs. A golf course is nearby.

Reservations

None, all campsites are first–come, first–serve.

Season

Open all year

Activities

Ball fields, Beachcombing, Bird watching, Boating, Fishing and shellfish harvesting, Hiking, Interpretive center, Mountain biking, Sailing, Sail–boarding, Scuba diving.

Cost

$12 primitive site
Peak season: mid May – mid September
$22 – $35 standard site
$30 – $40 partial utility site
$35 – $45 full utility site
Off–peak season
$20 – $30 standard site
$25 – $35 partial utility site
$30 – $40 full utility site
$10 extra vehicle (all year)
See Appendix C for available discounts.

Limitations

Maximum site length is 40 feet.
See Appendix A for camping regulations.

Contact

Phone: 360–387–3031
Web: *www.parks.state.wa.us*

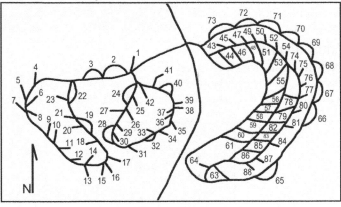

Campground

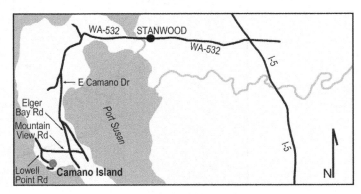

Driving Directions

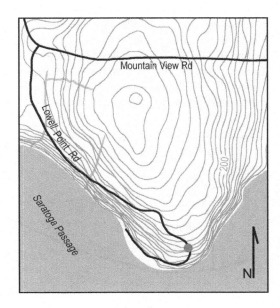

Location

219 Bayview
Washington State Parks

Directions

Start at the intersection of I–5 and WA–20 near Burlington. Travel west on WA–20 for 6.4 miles. Turn right onto Bayview–Edison Road and travel 3.6 miles. Turn right into park.

N48°29'17" – W122°28'47"   Elevation – 50 feet

Sunset from Bayview

Facilities

75 total sites: 46 standard sites, 29 partial utility sites (W/E)
Flush toilets
Potable water
Hot showers
Garbage service
Accessible water, campsite

Features

Bay View State Park has 1,285 feet of saltwater shoreline on Padilla Bay with views of the San Juan Islands and Olympic Mountains to the west and Mt. Rainier to the south. Sites 1 – 9 are partial utility sites with a view and premium price, sites 10 – 30 are partial utility sites, and sites 31 – 76 are standard sites. Over 11,000 acres of Padilla Bay are designated as a National Estuarine Sanctuary, one of 28 existing national marine estuaries. Breazeale Padilla Bay Interpretive Center is a half mile north of the park. When the tide is high and the breeze is up, sail–boarding is popular. The beach area is good for swimming, but no lifeguards are on–site.

Reservations

Sites may be reserved from May 13 through September 29 online at *www.parks.state.wa.us* or by telephone 1–888–CAMPOUT (1–888–226–7688). See Appendix B for reservation details.

Season

Open all year

Activities

Beach walking, Bird watching, Boating, Fishing (shellfish harvesting is closed), Hiking, Horseshoes, Sail–boarding, Scuba diving, Swimming, Water skiing, Volleyball.

Cost

$12 primitive site
Peak season: mid May – mid September
$22 – $35 standard site
$30 – $40 partial utility site
$35 – $45 full utility site
Off–peak season
$20 – $30 standard site
$25 – $35 partial utility site
$30 – $40 full utility site
$10 extra vehicle (all year)
See Appendix C for available discounts.

Limitations

Maximum site length is 50 feet with limited availability.
NOTE: A public boat launch is three blocks from the park. Be advised Padilla Bay is heavily influenced by tidal action and the

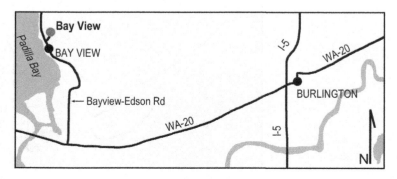

Driving Directions

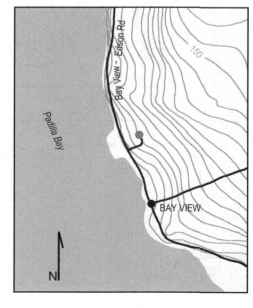

Location

bay becomes a large mud flat during low tides. Skagit County Parks provides a boat launch eight miles west of the park, just off WA–20 under the Swinomish Channel Bridge. The launch is useable under various tide conditions.

See Appendix A for camping regulations.

Contact

Phone: 360–757–0227
Web: *www.parks.state.wa.us*

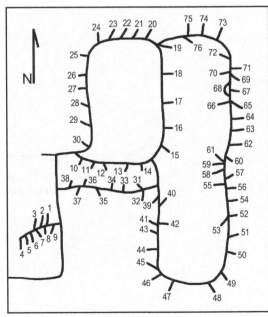

Campground

Oysters

Be sure to buy your oysters from a commercial outlet or check with local authorities about safety before eating oysters picked up from the shore. Discard broken or bad looking oysters.

Ingredients

Oysters, in their shell
Butter, melted
Onion, chopped fine
Garlic, chopped fine
Your favorite hot sauce
Parmesan cheese, grated

Preparation

Place the oysters on a grill over a hot bed of coals with the flatter shell half up. When juice begins to ooze from between the shell halves (about 3 – 5 minutes), put on a pair of old work gloves (to keep from burning your hands) and place each oyster in turn on you palm. Using an oyster knife pry the shell open. Be very careful not to hurt yourself with the knife. As the oyster begins to open, use the knife to cut its connection to the shell. Discard the flatter shell half.

Return the deeper shell half, with the oyster, open side up to the grill.

Add a little butter, onion, garlic, hot sauce, and cheese to the oyster and let cook until the butter begins to bubble. The oyster is done. Slurping is allowed.

220 Deception Pass
Washington State Parks

Directions

Start at the intersection of I–5 and WA–20 near Burlington. Travel west on WA–20 for 11.8 miles. Turn left to continue on WA–20 and travel 6.9 miles. Turn right into park.

N48°23'58" – W122°39'34"   Elevation – 60 feet

Bridge Over Deception Pass

Facilities

315 total sites: 143 partial utility sites (W/E), 167 standard sites, and 5 bicycle–in sites
Flush toilets
Potable water
Hot showers
Garbage service
RV dump
Marina
Boat launch
Mooring buoys
Park store and commissary
Accessible toilet, water, campsite

Features

Deception Pass State Park offers spectacular views of the surrounding waters, mountains, and islands. Rugged cliffs drop to meet the turbulent waters of Deception Pass. Old–growth forests, sand dunes, saltwater shoreline, and three lakes are home to abundant wildlife; 174 varieties of bird have been seen. Scuba dive to explore the underwater park. The interpretive center at Bowman Bay is open from mid May through Labor Day for individuals and all year by appointment for group tours. Contact 360– 675–3767 for hours. An observation deck overlooks the Cranberry Lake wetlands on the west–beach sand–dunes interpretive trail. The Maiden of Deception Pass story pole, on Rosario Beach in the northern section of the park, depicts a Samish Indian Nation story. The outdoor amphitheater hosts frequent lectures and slide shows on weekend evenings. The schedule of planned events is posted at the ranger station.

Deception Pass Swimming Area

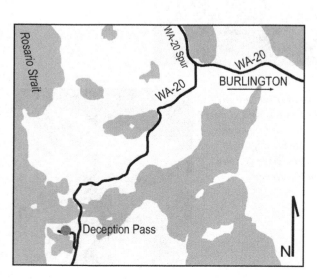

Driving Directions

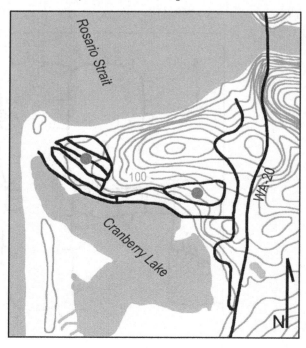

Location

Good Dog

Reservations

Sites may be reserved on *www.parks.state.wa.us* or by telephone 1–888–CAMPOUT (1–888–226–7688). See Appendix B for more details.

Season

Open all year

Activities

Beachcombing, Bird Watching, Boat rentals, Boating, Equestrian trail riding, Fishing and shellfish harvesting, Hiking, Interpretative center, Mountain biking, Scuba diving, Swimming.

Cost

$12 primitive site
Peak season: mid May – mid September
$22 – $35 standard site
$30 – $40 partial utility site
$35 – $45 full utility site
Off–peak season
$20 – $30 standard site
$25 – $35 partial utility site
$30 – $40 full utility site
$10 extra vehicle (all year)
See Appendix C for available discounts.

Limitations

Maximum sites length is 60 feet.
See Appendix A for camping regulations.

Contact

Phone: 360–675–3767
Web: *www.parks.state.wa.us*

Deception Pass Campsite

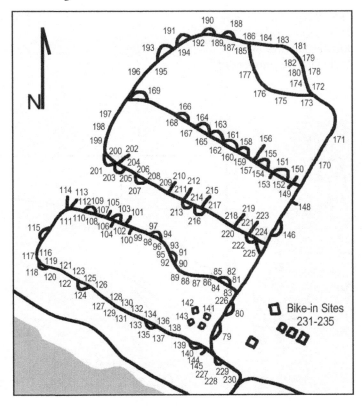

West Campground

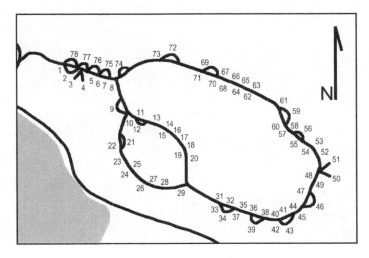

East Campground

221 Staysail Park
City of Oak Harbor

Directions

Start at intersection of I–5 and WA–20 near Burlington. Travel west on WA–20 for 11.8 miles. Turn left to remain on WA–20 and continue for 16.4 miles, where WA–20 turns right in Oak Harbor. Instead of turning, continue straight into Staysail Park.

N48°16'29" – W122°38'03"   Elevation – 60 feet

Facilities

82 total sites: 26 standard, 56 full utility (W/E/S)
Flush toilets
Potable water
Hot showers
Garbage service
RV dump
Boat launch

Features

Staysail RV Park is located in downtown Oak Harbor on the waterfront at 1600 S Beeksma Drive. Along the shore of Puget Sound, the park offers walking trails, a swimming lagoon, wading pools, picnicking, and playgrounds. The park is part of the larger Windjammer Park which has many of the activities listed in addition to an exercise course, basketball, soccer, and baseball fields, playgrounds, and volleyball courts.

Reservations

None, all campsites are first–come, first–serve.

Activities

Ball fields, Beachcombing, Bird watching, Boating, Fishing, Hiking, Swimming.

Cost

$12 standard site
$25 full utility site

Limitations

Maximum site length is 40 feet.
As of this writing, portions of the park are closed to facilitate a city construction project. Please check on site availability.
See Appendix A for camping regulations.

Contact

Oak Harbor Parks and Recreation
865 SE Barrington Drive
Oak Harbor, WA 98277
Phone: 360–279–4756
Web: *www.oakharbor.org*

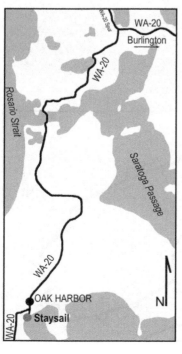

Driving Directions

Staysail Campsites

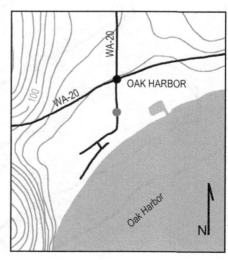

Location

222 Fort Ebey
Washington State Parks

Directions

Start at the intersection of I–5 and WA–20 near Burlington. Travel west on WA–20 for 11.8 miles. Turn left to remain on WA–20 and travel 22.5 miles. Turn right onto Libbey Road and travel 0.9 mile. Turn left onto Hill Valley Drive and travel 0.7 mile. Turn right into park.

N48°13'22" – W122°45'48"   Elevation – 100 feet

Facilities

50 total sites: 39 standard sites, 11 partial utility sites (W/E)
Some pull–through sites
Flush toilets
Potable water
Hot showers
Garbage service
Accessible toilet, water, and campsite

Features

Fort Ebey State Park, on the west shore of Whidbey Island, offers panoramic views of the Strait of Juan de Fuca, the Olympic Mountains and sunsets. The park features saltwater shoreline, Lake Pondilla, and miles of hiking and biking trails.

Reservations

Sites may be reserved up to nine months in advance for camping dates from May 15 through September 15 online at *www.parks.state.wa.us* or phone 1–888–CAMPOUT (1–888–226–7688). See Appendix B for reservation details.

Season

Open all year

Boats from Picnic Area

Activities

Beachcombing, Bird watching, Fishing, Hiking, Para–gliding, Mountain biking.

Cost

$12 primitive site
Peak season: mid May – mid September
$22 – $35 standard site
$30 – $40 partial utility site
$35 – $45 full utility site
Off–peak season
$20 – $30 standard site
$25 – $35 partial utility site
$30 – $40 full utility site
$10 extra vehicle (all year)
See Appendix C for available discounts.

Limitations

Maximum site length is 60 feet.
See Appendix A for camping regulations.

Contact

Phone: 360–678–4636
Web: *www.parks.state.wa.us*

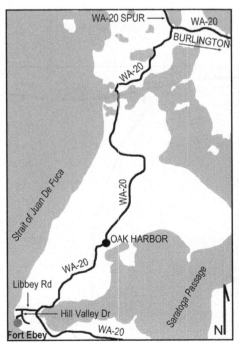

Driving Directions

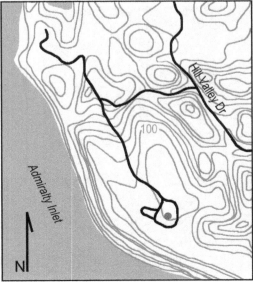

Location

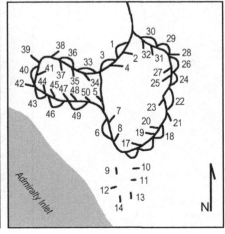

Campground

223 Rhododendron Park
Island County

Directions

Start at the intersection of I–5 and WA–20 near Burlington. Travel west on WA–20 for 11.8 miles. Turn left to remain on WA–20 and travel for 27.5 miles. Turn right into park.

N48°12'07" – W122°39'18"   Elevation – 200 feet

Facilities

15 standard sites
Vault toilet
Potable water
Garbage service

Features

Rhododendron Park lives up to its name; there are lots of wild rhododendron bushes as well as a lovely forest.

Reservations

None, all campsites are first–come, first–serve.

Season

Open April 1 to October 31

Activities

Bird watching, Hiking.

Cost

$15 standard site

Limitations

Maximum stay is 7 days in each 30 days.
See Appendix A for camping regulations.

Contact

Phone: 360–679–7335
Web: *https://www.islandcountywa.gov/PublicWorks/Parks/Pages/rhododendron-park.aspx*

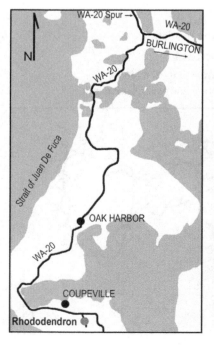

Driving Directions

Rhododendron Campsite

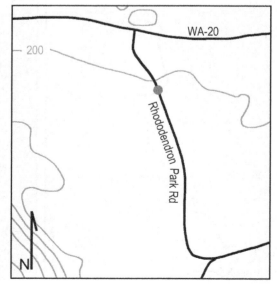

Location

224 Fort Casey
Washington State Parks

Directions

Start at the intersection of I–5 and WA–20 near Burlington. Travel west on WA–20 for 11.8 miles. Turn left to remain on WA–20 and continue for 26 miles. Turn right onto South Main Street (becomes South Engle Road) in Coupeville, and travel 3.6 miles. Turn right into park.

N48°09'31" – W122°40'30"   Elevation – 10 feet

Facilities

35 total sites:
22 standard,
13 utility
Flush toilets
Potable water
Hot showers
Garbage service
Boat launch
Accessible water, campsite, boating

Features

Fort Casey State Park campground lies on Puget Sound with many of the campsites along the shoreline. The park has sweeping views of Admiralty Inlet and the Strait of Juan de Fuca, and includes Keystone Spit. The park offers a protected dive area and a large field suitable for kite flying. Nearby are Seattle Pacific University Conference Center and the Washington State Ferry Terminal with service to Port Townsend.

The park is the site of Admiralty Head lighthouse, which has an interpretive center open seasonally. Tours can be arranged by contacting lighthouse staff at 360–678–4519.

Reservations

Sites may be reserved online at *www.parks.state.wa.us* or via telephone 1–888–CAMPOUT (1–888–226–7688). See Appendix B for more details.

Season

Open all year

Activities

Beachcombing, Bird watching, Boating, Fishing or shellfish harvesting, Hiking, Interpretive center, Kite flying, Scuba diving.

Cost

$12 primitive site
Peak season: mid May – mid September
$22 – $35 standard site
$30 – $40 partial utility site
$35 – $45 full utility site
Off–peak season
$20 – $30 standard site
$25 – $35 partial utility site
$30 – $40 full utility site
$10 extra vehicle (all year)
See Appendix C for available discounts.

Limitations

Maximum site length is 40 feet.
See Appendix A for camping regulations.

Contact

Phone: 360–678–4519
Web: *www.parks.state.wa.us*

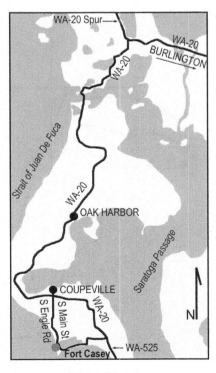

Driving Directions

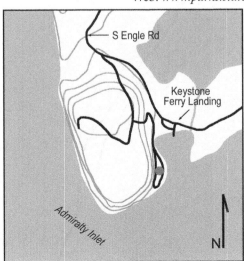

Location

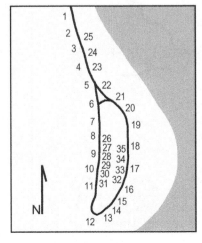

Campground

225 South Whidbey
Washington State Parks

Directions

Start at the intersection of I–5 and WA–20 near Burlington. Travel west on WA–20 for 11.8 miles. Turn left to continue on WA–20 and travel 31.4 miles. Continue straight ahead onto WA–525 (WA–20 turns right – don't) and travel 4.7 miles. Turn right onto Smugglers Cove Road and travel 4.4 miles. Turn right into park.

N48°03'48" – W122°35'59"   Elevation – 120 feet

Facilities

57 total sites: 46 standard sites, 8 partial utility sites (W/E), 3 walk–in sites
Some pull through sites
Flush toilets
Potable water
Hot showers
Garbage service
RV dump
Shelter
Store, in season
Accessible campsite

Features

South Whidbey Park is on the shore of Admiralty Inlet.

The park features old–growth forest, tidelands for crabbing and clamming, and breathtaking views of the Puget Sound and Olympic Mountains. The lush forest undergrowth creates secluded campsites. The 3 primitive sites are for hiker/biker use.

Reservations

Sites may be reserved online at *www.parks.state.wa.us* or by telephone 1–888–CAMPOUT (1–888–226–7688). See Appendix B for details.

Season

Open all year

Activities

Beachcombing, Bird watching, Fishing and shellfish harvesting, Hiking.

Cost

$12 primitive site
Peak season: mid May – mid September
$22 – $35 standard site
$30 – $40 partial utility site
$35 – $45 full utility site
Off–peak season
$20 – $30 standard site
$25 – $35 partial utility site
$30 – $40 full utility site
$10 extra vehicle (all year)
See Appendix C for available discounts.

Limitations

As of this writing, the campground temporarily closed due to some hazardous trees in the campground. Please check the park's website for current conditions.
Maximum site length is 50 feet.
See Appendix A for camping regulations.

Contact

Phone: 360–331–4559
Web: *www.parks.state.wa.us*

Driving Directions

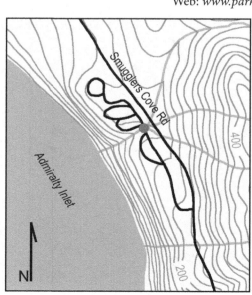

Location

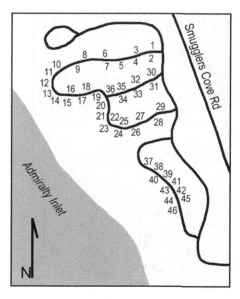

Campground

226 Washington Park
City of Anacortes

Directions

Start at intersection of US–20 and US–20 Spur east of Anacortes. Travel west on US–20 Spur for 2.7 miles. Turn right to remain on US–20 Spur (becomes Commercial Avenue) and travel 1.4 miles. Turn left to remain on US–20 Spur (becomes 12th Street) and travel 3.1 miles. Bear left at Y onto Sunset Ave and travel 0.7 mile to Washington Park.

N48°29'54" – W122°41'39   Elevation – 100 feet

Facilities

68 total sites: 22 standard, 46 partial utility (W/E)
Some pull–through sites
Flush toilets
Potable water
Hot showers
Garbage service
RV dump
Shelter
Boat launch
Laundry
Accessible campsites

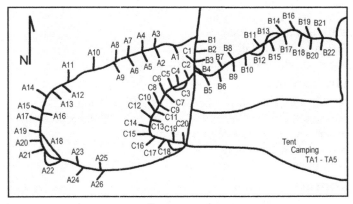

Campground

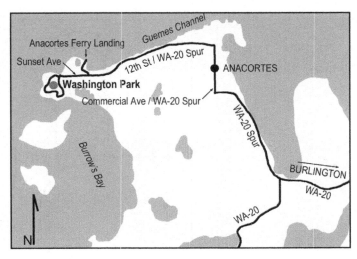

Driving Directions

Features

Washington Park, with 220 acres, sits on a peninsula that juts into Rosario Strait on the western edge of Fidalgo Island. A scenic 2.2–mile loop road winds through the park's forested hills and meadows with views of the San Juan Islands and Olympic Mountains and provides access to several shoreline areas. The loop road is used by cars, joggers, bicyclists and walkers.

Reservations

39 sites may be reserved online at *cityofanacortes.org*. Please see Appendix B for reservation details. All other sites are first–come, first–serve.

Season

Open all year

Activities

Beachcombing, Bird watching, Boating, Fishing or shellfish gathering, Hiking, Playground, Scuba diving.

Cost

$20 standard site
$26 partial utility

Limitations

The maximum stay limit is 14 days.
See Appendix A for camping regulations.

Contact

Anacortes Parks and Recreation
904 6th Street/P.O. Box 547
Anacortes WA, 98221
Phone: 360–293–1918
Park Information Line: 360–293–1927, option 4, gives recorded information on campground availability and is updated 3 times a day during the summer season.

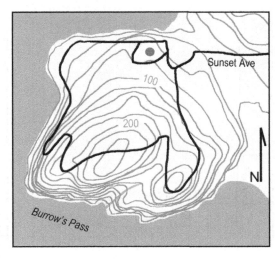

Location

227 Spencer Spit
Washington State Parks

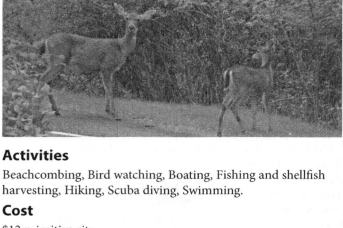

Directions

Exit the Washington State Ferry (from Anacortes to Lopez Island) on Lopez Island. Travel straight on Ferry Road for 2.1 miles. Turn left onto Center Road and travel 0.7 mile. Turn left onto Cross Road and travel 0.5 mile. Turn right onto Port Stanley Road and travel 0.3 mile. Turn left onto Bakersview Road and travel 0.5 mile into park.

N48°32'16" – W122°51'45"   Elevation – 160 feet

Facilities

50 total sites: 37 standard sites, 13 walk–in sites
Some pull–through sites
Flush toilets
Potable water
RV dump
Mooring buoys

Features

Spencer Spit State Park is on Lopez Island in the Strait of Juan de Fuca and is named for the lagoon–enclosing sand spit on which it rests. The park has a reputation for excellent crabbing, clamming and "car–top boating." Please note: there are no showers or garbage service. The tent sites are large and private. Six hiker/biker walk–in sites are available, as well as the seven Cascadia Marine Trail walk–in beach sites, which have limited privacy. Kayak and bike rentals are available.

Reservations

Sites may be reserved online at *www.parks.state.wa.us* or by telephone 1–888–CAMPOUT (1–888–226–7688). See Appendix B for details.

Season

Closed October 30 through March 3

Activities

Beachcombing, Bird watching, Boating, Fishing and shellfish harvesting, Hiking, Scuba diving, Swimming.

Cost

$12 primitive site
Peak season: mid May – mid September
$22 – $35 standard site
$30 – $40 partial utility site
$35 – $45 full utility site
Off–peak season
$20 – $30 standard site
$25 – $35 partial utility site
$30 – $40 full utility site
$10 extra vehicle (all year)
See Appendix C for available discounts.

Limitations

NOTE: The schedule for the Anacortes ferry changes seasonally. Call 888–808–7977 or 800–843–3779 or check on line at *www.wsdot.com/ferries/schedule*
Maximum site length is 35 feet.
See Appendix A for camping regulations.

Contact

Phone: 360–468–2251
Web: *www.parks.state.wa.us*

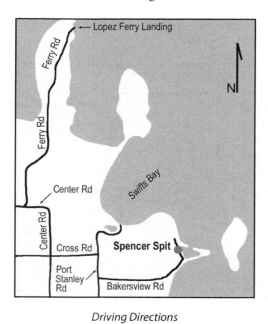

Driving Directions

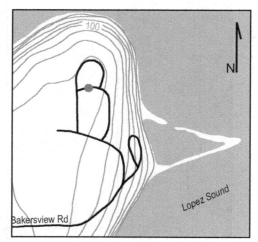

Location

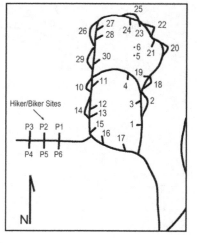

Campground

228 Odlin County Park
San Juan County

Directions

Exit the Washington State Ferry from Anacortes to the Lopez terminal on Lopez Island. Travel south on Ferry Road for 1.2 miles. Turn right into Odlin County Park.

N48°33'20" – W122°53'36"   Elevation – 20 feet

Facilities

30 total sites:
24 standard, 6 walk–in
Vault toilets
Potable water
Garbage service
Shelter
Boat launch
Mooring buoy

Features

Odlin County Park is on the west side of Lopez Island and looks onto Upright Channel. It offers lovely open spaces and a sandy beach. Sites 1 through 10 can accommodate RVs (sites 6, 8, and 10 a maximum vehicle length of 30 feet with the the balance of the 10 accommodating maximum vehicle lengths of 22 feet). Sites 11 through 17, 19, 21, 23, and 24 are tent–only sites. Sites 25 through 30 are walk–in only tent camping. The park is part of the Cascadia Marine Trail system.

Reservations

Reservations, strongly recommended in summer, may be made online at *sanjuanco.com*. See Appendix B for reservation details.

Season

Open all year with reduced fees and services during winter (November 1–March 31), when all sites are on a first–come, first–served basis only.

Activities

Ball fields, Beachcombing, Bird watching, Boating, Fishing and shellfish gathering, Hiking, Scuba diving.

Cost

All fees are for 4 people and 1 vehicle with a maximum of 8 people per site.
$27 waterside campsites
$22 landside campsites
$20 walk–in campsites (no vehicle)
$10 mooring buoy
$5 extra child
$8 extra adult
$10 extra vehicle

Washington Ferry from Odlin Park

Limitations

NOTE: The schedule for the Anacortes ferry changes seasonally. Call 888–808–7977 or 800–843–3779 or check on line at www.wsdot.com/ferries/schedule
Maximum site length is 30 feet.
See Appendix A for camping regulations.

Contact

San Juan County Parks
350 Court Street #8
Friday Harbor, WA 98250
Phone: 360–378–8420
Email: *parks@sanjuanco.com*
Web: *www.sanjuanco.com*

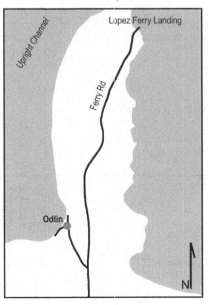

Driving Directions

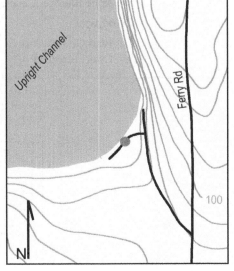

Location

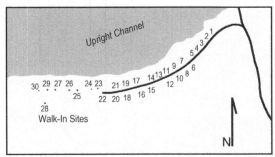

Campground

229 Shaw Island Park
San Juan County

Directions

Exit the Washington State Ferry from Anacortes to Shaw Island onto Blind Bay Road. Travel for 1.1 miles. Turn left onto Squaw Bay Road and travel for 0.6 mile. Turn left into Shaw Island County Park.

N48°33'53" – W122°56'16"   Elevation – 20 feet

Facilities

11 standard sites
Vault toilet
Potable water, summer only
Garbage service
Shelter
Boat launch
Accessible toilet

Features

Shaw Island County Park is located on Indian Cove on the southeast shore of Shaw Island overlooking Canoe Island. The park is part of the Cascadia Marine Trail system. The island only has one small grocery store by the ferry landing and the only public access on the island is this campground. Residents protect their privacy.

Reservations

Reservations, strongly recommended in summer, may be made online at *sanjuanco.com*. See Appendix B for reservation details.

Season

Open all year with reduced fees and services during winter (November 1–March 31), when all sites are on a first-come, first-served basis only.

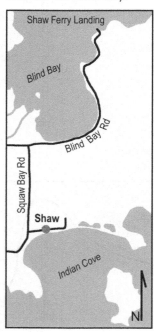

Driving Directions

Activities

Beachcombing, Bird watching, Boating, Fishing and shellfish gathering.

Cost

Fee covers 4 people and 1 vehicle per site, with a maximum of 6 people.
$20 waterfront sites
$15 wooded sites
$5 extra child
$8 extra adult
$8 extra vehicle

Riding the Ferry

Limitations

NOTE: The schedule for the Anacortes ferry changes seasonally. Call 888–808–7977 or 800–843–3779 or check online at www.wsdot.com/ferries/schedule
RVs and trailers are not recommended.
From November 1 through March 31 you must bring your own water supply. The park turns off the water and there are no other sources of running water available on the island.
See Appendix A for camping regulations.

Contact

San Juan County Parks
350 Court Street #8
Friday Harbor, WA 98250
Phone: 360–378–8420
Email: *parks@sanjuanco.com*
Web: *www.sanjuanco.com*

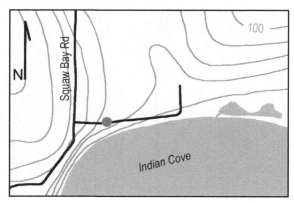

Location

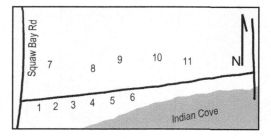

Campground

230 Moran
Washington State Parks

Directions

Exit the Washington State Ferry (from Anacortes to Orcas Island) in Orcas Landing. Turn left onto Orcas Road and travel 8.6 miles. Bear right onto Mt Baker Road (which changes names to Olga Road) and travel 5.0 miles into park.

N48°39'06" – W122°50'59"   Elevation – 400 to1000 feet

Facilities

166 total sites: 151 standard sites, 15 primitive, walk–in sites

Flush toilets
Potable water
Hot showers
Garbage service
RV dump
Boat launch
Snack bar
Accessible toilet

Features

Moran State Park features more than 30 miles of trails, five lakes and several waterfalls, an old growth forest and a lodge pole pine forest. There are five campgrounds throughout the park. Northend is closest to the entrance, across the road from the day–use and swim beach area. Midway has several sites along the Cascade Lake shoreline. Southend is the most popular camp area with almost all of the sites located along Cascade Lake. Mountain Lake, a mile up Mount Constitution Road, has sites along the shores of the largest lake in the park. The primitive campsites on the road to Mount Constitution are for hikers and bikers. Atop the 2,409–foot high Mt. Constitution (the highest point on the San Juan Islands) stands a stone observation tower that offers panoramic views of the surrounding islands, the Cascade Mountains, and the Olympic Mountains. There is a short, self–guided interpretive trail near the kitchen shelter in the day–use area and interpretive displays in the observation tower on Mount Constitution. Camp Moran, the Environmental Learning Center, is available for group and family rentals by calling 800–360–4240 or 360–902–8600.

Reservations

Sites may be reserved from May 13 through September 14 online at *www.parks.state.wa.us* or telephone 1–888–CAMPOUT (1–888–226–7688). See Appendix B for reservation details.

Season

Open all year

Activities

Bird watching, Boating (non–motorized), Equestrian trail riding, Fishing, Hiking, Metal detecting, Mountain biking, Swimming.

Cost

$12 primitive site
Peak season: mid May – mid September
$22 – $35 standard site
$30 – $40 partial utility site
$35 – $45 full utility site
Off–peak season
$20 – $30 standard site
$25 – $35 partial utility site
$30 – $40 full utility site
$10 extra vehicle (all year)
See Appendix C for available discounts.

(continued on next page)

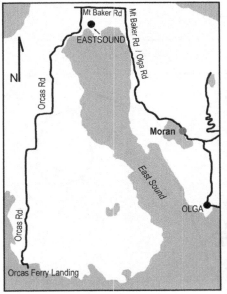

Driving Directions

South End Campsite

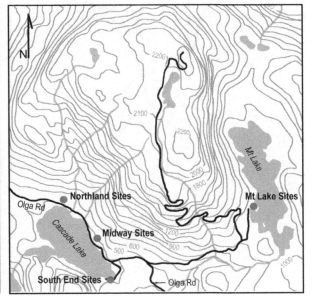

Location

View from Mt. Constitution at Moran

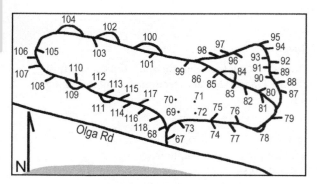

Northland Campground

Limitations

NOTE: The schedule for the Anacortes ferry changes seasonally. Call 888–808–7977 or 800–843–3779 or check on line at *www.wsdot.com/ferries/schedule*

Maximum site length is 45 feet. Some areas and campsites can not accommodate large RVs.

See Appendix A for camping regulations.

Contact

Phone: 360–376–2326
Web: *www.parks.state.wa.us*

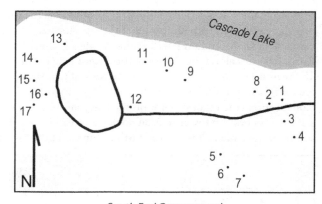

South End Campground

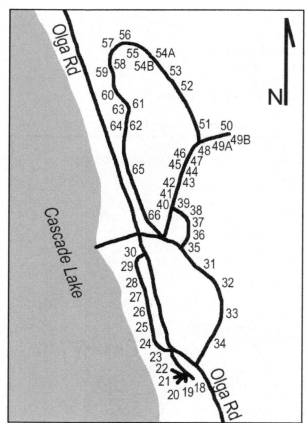

Midway Campground

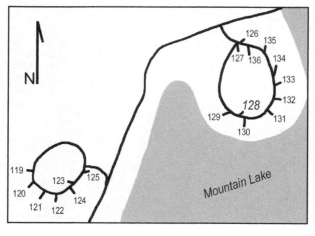

Mountain Lake Campground

231 San Juan County Park
San Juan County

Directions

Exit the Washington State Ferry from Anacortes to Friday Harbor. Turn right onto Front Street and travel 0.1 mile. Turn left onto Spring Street and travel 0.1 mile. Turn right onto Second Avenue and travel 6.9 miles (becomes Guard Street, Beaverton Valley Road and West Valley Road). Turn left onto Mitchell Bay Road and travel for 1.3 miles. Turn left onto West Side Road and travel for 1.8 miles. Turn right into park.

N 48°32'32" – W123°09'39"   Elevation – 20 feet

Facilities

26 standard sites (16 accommodate RVs or trailers, 10 are tent–only)

Flush toilets
Potable water
Garbage service
Boat launch
Accessible campsite

Features

San Juan County campground overlooks Haro Strait with several campsites along the water. Small Pox Bay, a small inlet encompassed by the campground, offers a gravel beach. The campground is part of the Cascadia Marine Trail system. Lucky visitors may see Orca whales swimming by in the summer. Sites 2, 4H, 12, 13, 14, and 16 through 20 are tent–only sites.

Reservations

Reservations, strongly recommended in summer and may be made online at *www.sanjuanco.com*. See Appendix B for reservation details.

Season

Open all year with reduced fees and services during winter (November 1–March 31), when all sites are on a first–come, first–served basis only.

Activities

Beachcombing, Bird watching, Boating, Fishing and shellfish gathering.

Cost

All fees are for 4 people and 1 vehicle with a maximum of 8 people per site.

$32 sites 2 through 14, 17, 19, and 20
$40 sites 15 and 16
$45 site 18
$5 extra child
$8 extra adult
$20 extra vehicle
$10 per person for hikers, bikers, and kayakers

Limitations

NOTE: The schedule for the Anacortes ferry changes seasonally. Call 888–808–7977 or 800–843–3779 or check on line at *www.wsdot.com/ferries/schedule*
Maximum RV length is 25 feet; maximum trailer length is 20 feet.
See Appendix B for camping regulations.

Contact

San Juan County Parks
350 Court Street #8
Friday Harbor, WA 98250
Phone: 360–378–8420
Email: *parks@sanjuanco.com*
Web: *www.sanjuanco.com*

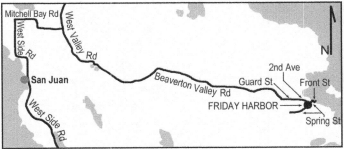

Driving Directions

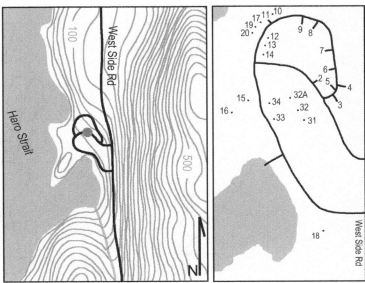

Location

Campground

255

232 Larrabee
Washington State Parks

Directions

Start at the intersection of I–5 and WA–11 (exit 231) near Burlington. Travel north on WA–11 (also called Chuckanut Drive) for 15.9 miles. Turn left into park.

N48°39'20" – W122°29'28"   Elevation – 140 feet

Facilities

85 total sites: 51 standard sites, 26 utility sites, 8 walk–in sites
Some pull–through sites
Flush toilets
Potable water
Hot showers
Garbage service
RV dump
Boat launch
Accessible toilet, water, campsite

Features

Larrabee State Park lies along the shoreline of Samish Bay near Bellingham. The park is primarily forested with coniferous trees and dense vegetation. It has marshlands, wetlands, streams, and Chuckanut Mountain. The park also features two freshwater lakes and saltwater tide pools to explore. Sunsets are gorgeous. Sites T1–T26 provide full utilities. A variety of non–motorized, multiple–use trails wind through the park.

Reservations

Sites may be reserved from May 15 through September 15 online *www.parks.state.wa.us* or telephone 1–888–CAMPOUT (1–888–226–7688). See Appendix B for reservation details.

Activities

Beachcombing, Bird watching, Boating, Fishing or shellfish harvesting, Hiking, Metal detecting, Mountain biking, Scuba diving.

Cost

$12 primitive site
Peak season: mid May – mid September
$22 – $35 standard site
$30 – $40 partial utility site
$35 – $45 full utility site
Off–peak season
$20 – $30 standard site
$25 – $35 partial utility site
$30 – $40 full utility site
$10 extra vehicle (all year)
See Appendix C for available discounts.

Limitations

Maximum site length is 60 feet.
See Appendix A for camping regulations.

Contact

Phone :360–676–2093
Web: *www.parks.state.wa.us*

Season

Open all year

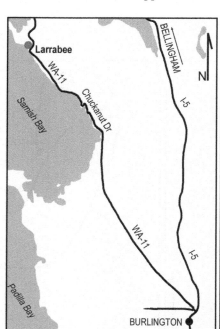

Driving Directions

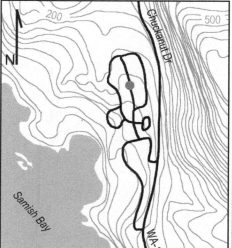

Location

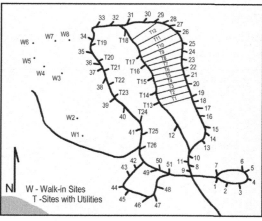

W - Walk-in Sites
T -Sites with Utilities

Campground

233 Birch Bay
Washington State Parks

Directions

Start at the intersection of I–5 and WA–548 West north of Bellingham. Travel west on WA–548 for 6.1 miles. Continue west on Grandview Road (at the rotary) and travel 1.0 mile. Turn right onto Jackson Road and travel 0.7 mile. Turn left onto Helweg Road and travel 0.6 mile to park.

N48°54'14" – W122°45'52"   Elevation – 20 feet

Facilities

167 total sites: 147 standard sites, 20 partial utility sites (W/E)
Some pull–through sites
Flush toilets
Potable water
Hot showers
Garbage service
RV dump
Boat launch
Accessible toilet, campsite

Features

Birch Bay State Park offers panoramic views of the Cascade Mountains and Canadian Gulf Islands and nearly two miles of beach on Birch Bay, a popular destination for harvesting hard shell clams and Dungeness crabs. The park also offers freshwater shoreline on Terrell Creek. Terrell Creek Marsh is one of the few remaining saltwater/freshwater estuaries in north Puget Sound. The park also hosts an active summer interpretive program, interpretive signs, and an interpretive trail in Terrell Marsh. A natural game sanctuary is at the park's north end. A marina and a golf course are also near the park. Personal watercraft may be used in the saltwater.

Reservations

Sites may be reserved from May 13 through September 14 online at *www.parks.state.wa.us* or by telephone 1–888–CAMPOUT (1–888–226–7688). See Appendix B for details.

Season

Open all year

Activities

Basketball, Beachcombing, Bird watching, Boating, Fishing or shellfish harvesting, Hiking, Interpretive center, Metal detecting, Scuba diving, Swimming.

Cost

$12 primitive site
Peak season: mid May – mid September
$22 – $35 standard site
$30 – $40 partial utility site
$35 – $45 full utility site
Off–peak season
$20 – $30 standard site
$25 – $35 partial utility site
$30 – $40 full utility site
$10 extra vehicle (all year)
See Appendix C for available discounts.

Limitations

Maximum site length is 60 feet.
See Appendix A for camping regulations.

Contact

Phone: 360–371–2800
Web: *www.parks.state.wa.us*

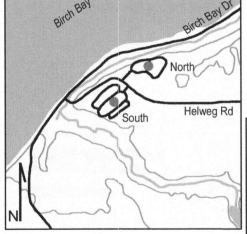

Location

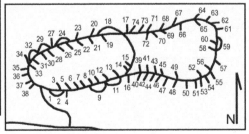

North Campground

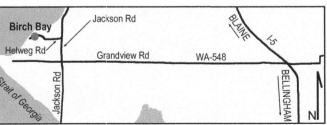

Driving Directions

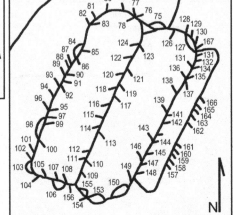

South Campground

234 Lighthouse Marine
Whatcom County

Directions

Start at the intersection of I–5 and the Canadian Border Crossing. Travel north into Canada on BC–99 (I–5 becomes BC–99 in Canada) for 16.9 miles. Turn left onto BC–17 and travel 4.8 miles. Turn left onto 56th Street and travel 2.8 miles to the US Border Crossing. Continue straight ahead on Tyee Drive and travel 2.9 miles. (Tyee Drive becomes Marina Drive and then becomes Edwards Drive.) Turn left into park.

N48°58'25" – W123°04'59"   Elevation – 9 feet

Facilities

30 standard sites
Flush toilets
Potable water
Hot showers
Garbage service
Boat launch

Features

Located on a peninsula on the Salish Sea, Lighthouse Marine Park can only be accessed by the rest of the county by water or through Canada. The Oregon Treaty of 1846 fixed the boundary between the United States and Canada at 49 degrees north latitude, isolating Point Roberts from the rest of the United States. A portion was reserved for a lighthouse station that was never built. This area became Lighthouse Marine Park. The area is a historic gathering place for the Native Straits Salish people; for hundreds of generations this has been a sockeye salmon harvesting area. Orca whales are often seen from the beach, particularly in summer months when members of the three local pods frequently pass close by these shores.

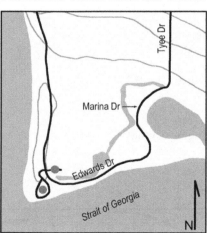

Location

Reservations

Call 360–945–4911 to reserve a campsite. Weekend reservations require a two–night stay. Non–county residents may begin reserving for the current year beginning on March 1.

Season

Open March 1 through October 31

Activities

Beachcombing, Bird watching, Boating, Fishing and shellfish gathering, Scuba diving.

Cost

$25 standard site
See Appendix C for available discounts.

Limitations

See Appendix A for camping regulations.

Contact

Lighthouse Marine Park
811 Marine Drive
Point Roberts, WA 98281
Phone: 360–945–4911
Email: *lthouse@pointroberts.net*
Web: *www.co.whatcom.wa.us/1787/Parks–Recreation*

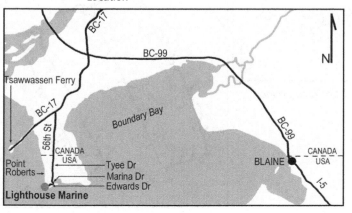

Driving Directions

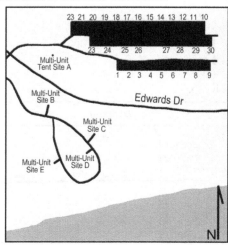

Campground

235 Silver Lake Park
Whatcom County

Directions

Start at the intersection of I–5 and WA–542 (exit 255) in Bellingham. Travel east on WA–542 for 26.2 miles. Turn left onto Silver Lake Road in Maple Falls and travel 3.5 miles. Turn right into park.

N48°58'06" – W122°04'24"   Elevation – 800 feet

Facilities

61 total sites: 27 standard, 34 partial utility (W/E)

Flush and vault toilets
Potable water
Hot showers
Garbage service
RV dump
Boat launch
Shelter

Features

Nestled in a scenic mountain valley, Silver Lake Park is situated on the shore of the lake. The main attraction is the lake itself and the associated water–related activities. Rowboats, canoes, and pedal–boat rentals are available as well as cabins and a day lodge. Campers can visit Gerdrum Historical House and Black Mountain Forestry Center for some insight into early Whatcom County. A Horse Camp with campsites, kitchen shelters, and stables with tie stalls for park users' horses, provides access to many miles of trails.

Reservations

Reservations are available by calling Silver Lake Park at 360–599–2776.
See Appendix B for details.

Season

Open all year, although some sites may not have water in winter.

Activities

Ball fields, Bird watching, Boating (non–motorized), Equestrian trail riding, Fishing, Hiking, Interpretive center, Swimming.

Cost

$25 standard site
$31 partial utility site
See Appendix C for available discounts.

Limitations

See Appendix A for camping regulations.

Contact

Whatcom County Parks and Recreation
Silver Lake Park
9006 Silver Lake Road
Maple Falls, WA 98266
Phone: 360–599–2776
Web: *www.co.whatcom.wa.us/1787/Parks–Recreation*

North Campground

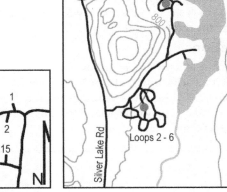

Location

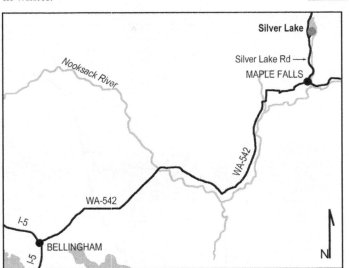

Driving Directions

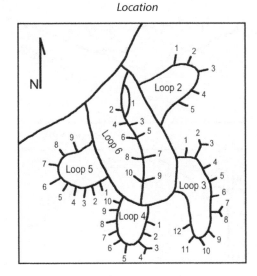

South Campground

236 Douglas Fir
Mount Baker–Snoqualmie National Forest

Directions

Start at the intersection of I–5 and WA–542 (exit 255) in Bellingham. Travel east on WA–542 for 35.9 miles. Turn left into Douglas Fir.

N48°54'10" – W121°54'52"   Elevation – 1,050 feet

Facilities

29 standard sites
Vault toilets
Potable water
Garbage service
Shelter
Accessible toilet, campsites

Features

Douglas Fir campground is situated along the North Fork Nooksack River in a heavily forested setting. Several sites are along the river. The campground has an historic CCC built day-use picnic shelter and provides access to Horseshoe Bend Trail. There is a launch site for rafts and kayaks under the highway bridge near the campground.

Reservations

Reserve online at *www.recreation.gov* or call 1–877–444–6777 (5 am to 9 pm Pacific time), 518–885–3639, or TDD 1–877–833–6777. Reservations must be made at least 4 days ahead of arrival and may be made up to 12 months in advance. See Appendix B for details.

Season

Open from late–May to late September

Activities

Fishing, Hiking, River rafting/kayaking.

Cost

$18 – 20 standard site
$9 extra vehicle
See Appendix C for available discounts.

Limitations

See Appendix A for camping regulations.

Contact

Mt. Baker–Snoqualmie National Forest
2930 Wetmore Ave., Suite 3A
Everett, WA 98201
Phone: 425–783–6000, 800–627–0062
Outdoor Recreation Information: 206–470–4060

Douglas Fir Campsite

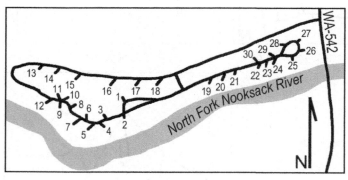

Campground

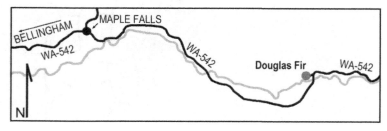

Driving Directions

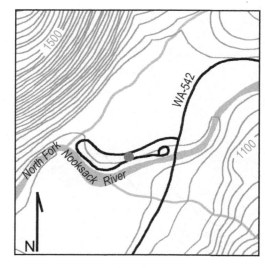

Location

237 Silver Fir
Mount Baker–Snoqualmie National Forest

Directions

Start at the intersection of I–5 and WA–542 (exit 255) in Bellingham. Travel east on WA–542 for 48.7 miles. Turn right into Silver Fir.

N48°54' 16" – W121°41' 48"   Elevation – 2,008 feet

Facilities

20 standard sites
Vault toilets
Potable water
Garbage service
Shelter
Accessible campsite

Features

Silver Fir Campground is situated along the North Fork Nooksack River. Most of the sites are a short walk to the river with a gravel bar between the campground and the river. A CCC built historic, day–use picnic shelter is located in the campground.

Reservations

Reserve online at *www.recreation.gov* or call 1–877–444–6777 (5 am to 9 pm Pacific time), 518–885–3639, or TDD 1–877–833–6777. Reservations must be made at least 4 days ahead of arrival and may be made up to 12 months in advance. See Appendix B for details.

Season

Open from late May through late September

Activities

Fishing, Hiking, River rafting/kayaking.

Cooking At Silver Fir

Cost

$16 standard single site
$8 extra vehicle
See Appendix C for available discounts.

Limitations

See Appendix A for camping regulations.

Contact

Mt. Baker–Snoqualmie National Forest
2930 Wetmore Ave., Suite 3A
Everett, WA 98201
Phone: 425–783–6000, 800–627–0062
Outdoor Recreation Information: 206–470–4060

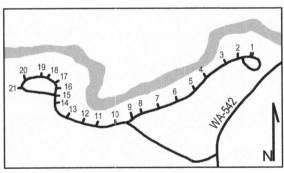

Campground

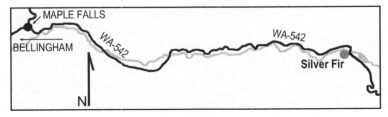

Driving Directions

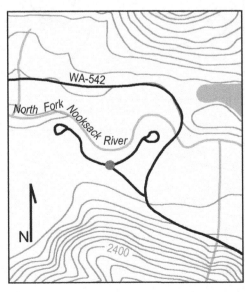

Location

238 Rasar
Washington State Parks

Directions

Start at the intersection of WA–20 and WA–530 near Rockport. Travel west on WA–20 for 14.9 miles. Turn left onto Russell Road and travel 0.8 mile. Turn right onto Cape Horn Road and travel 1.3 miles. Turn left into park.

N48°31'02" – W121°54'58"   Elevation – 120 feet

Facilities

49 total sites: 18 standard sites, 20 partial utility sites (W/E), 11 walk–in/primitive sites

Some pull–through sites
Flush toilets
Potable water
Hot showers
Garbage service
RV dump
Shelter
Store
Accessible toilet, campsite

Features

Rasar State Park offers low–bank riverfront along the Skagit River and second–growth evergreen forests. All sites are paved. Three of the primitive sites are for hiker/biker use. The park offers a playground area for children and 3.7 miles of hiking trails for wildlife viewing. Eagles can be seen, particularly in early fall and winter. Staff present interpretive and Junior Ranger programs on weekends from Memorial Day to Labor Day.

Reservations

Sites may be reserved from May 13 through September 14 online at *www.parks.state.wa.us* or by telephone 1–888–CAMPOUT (1–888–226–7688). See Appendix B for details.

Season

Open all year

Activities

Bird watching, Fishing, Hiking, Metal–detecting.

Cost

$12 primitive site
Peak season: mid May – mid September
$22 – $35 standard site
$30 – $40 partial utility site
$35 – $45 full utility site
Off–peak season
$20 – $30 standard site
$25 – $35 partial utility site
$30 – $40 full utility site
$10 extra vehicle (all year)
See Appendix C for available discounts.

Rasar Campsite

Limitations

Maximum site length is 40 feet.
See Appendix A for camping regulations.

Contact

Phone: 360–826–3942
Web: *www.parks.state.wa.us*

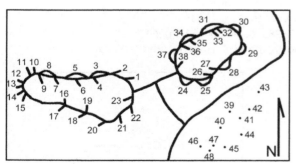

Campground

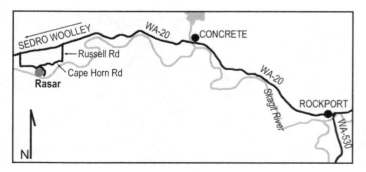

Driving Directions

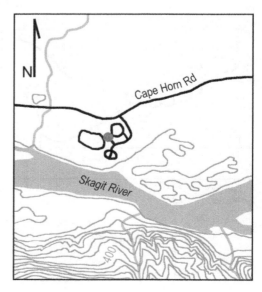

Location

239 Grandy Lake
Skagit County

Grandy Lake Campsite

Cost

$7 standard sites
$5 extra vehicle

Limitations

Maximum stay is 14 days
See Appendix A for camping regulations.

Grandy Lake Campsite

Directions

Start at the intersection of WA–9 North and WA–20 near Sedro Woolley. Travel east on WA–20 for 16.5 miles. Turn left onto Baker Lake Road (Forest Service Road 11) and travel 4.8 miles. Turn right into Grandy Lake.

> N48°33'58" – W121°48'19"   Elevation – 800 feet

Facilities

32 primitive sites
Portable restrooms
No water, bring your own
Pack out garbage
Boat launch

Features

Although off Baker Lake Road, all these campsites are along Grandy Lake. The launch is gravel and can accommodate car top boats and small trailer boats.

Reservations

All campsites are first–come, first–serve.

Season

Open all year

Activities

Bird watching, Boating, Fishing, Hiking.

Contact

Phone 360–416–1350
Web: *www.skagitcounty.net*

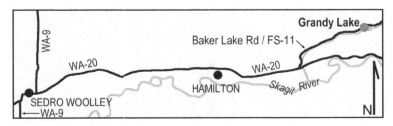

Driving Directions

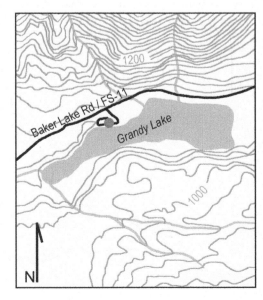

Location

240 Kulshan
Puget Sound Energy

Directions

Start at the intersection of WA–9 North and WA–20 East near Sedro Woolley. Travel east on WA–20 for 16.5 miles. Turn left onto Baker Lake Road (Forest Service Road 11) and travel 13.8 miles. Turn right onto Forest Service Road 1106 (with signs to dam) and travel 0.9 mile. Turn left into Kulshan campground.

N48°39'17" – W121°41'37"   Elevation – 720 feet

Baker Lake at Kulshan

Facilities

108 total sites: 28 standard sites, 80 partial utility sites (W/S)
Some pull–through sites
Flush toilets
Potable water
Garbage service
RV dump
Boat launch

Features

Kulshan campground lies near the south end of Baker Lake and provides both a shady, forested area and a level, grassy field for campers. Baker Lake, a very short distance from the campsites, is nearly 10 miles long and offers fishing, water skiing and swimming. Day hikers can enjoy the nearby trails with breath–taking vistas of Mount Baker and Mount Shuksan.

Reservations

None, all campsites are first–come, first–serve.

Season

Open all year

Activities

Bird watching, Boating, Fishing, Hiking.

Cost

$22 per site: standard site or utility site
Free after Labor Day weekend until Memorial Day weekend.

Limitations

See Appendix A for camping regulations.

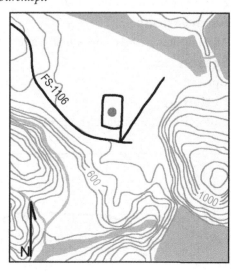

Kulshan Campsite

Contact

Phone: 360–853–8341 (Baker Visitor Center)
Web: *https://pse.com/inyourcommunity/ToursandRecreation/Pages/Baker–Lake–Tours.aspx*

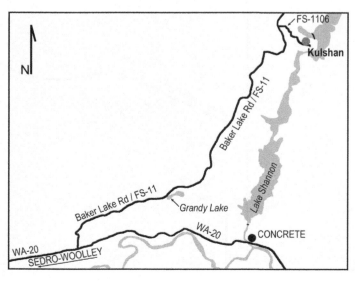

Driving Directions

Location

241 Horseshoe Cove
Mount Baker–Snoqualmie National Forest

Directions

Start at the intersection of WA–9 North and WA–20 in Sedro Woolley. Travel east on WA–20 for 16.5 miles. Turn left onto Baker Lake Road (Forest Service Road 11) and travel 15.2 miles. Turn right onto Forest Service Road 1118 and travel 1.8 miles to Horseshoe Cove.

N48°40'16" – W121°40'40"   Elevation – 760 feet

Facilities

35 standard sites
Some pull–through sites
Flush and vault toilets
Potable water
Outdoor cold showers
Garbage service
Boat launch
Accessible toilet, campsite

Features

Horseshoe Cove Campground is situated on the western shore of Baker Lake. Several sites are lakeside. The campsites are large and most sites can easily accommodate RVs. The campground has a swimming area and boat rentals are available during the summer season.

Reservations

Reserve online at *www.recreation.gov* or call 1–877–444–6777 (5 am to 9 pm Pacific time), 518–885–3639, or TDD 1–877–833–6777. Reservations must be made at least 4 days ahead of arrival and may be made up to 12 months in advance. See Appendix B for details.

Season

Open from mid May through late September

Activities

Boating (boat rentals available), Fishing, Hiking, Swimming.

Cost

$18 single
$9 extra vehicle
See Appendix C for available discounts.

Limitations

See Appendix A for camping regulations.

Contact

Mt. Baker–Snoqualmie National Forest
2930 Wetmore Ave., Suite 3A
Everett, WA 98201
Phone: 425–783–6000, 800–627–0062
Outdoor Recreation Information: 206–470–4060

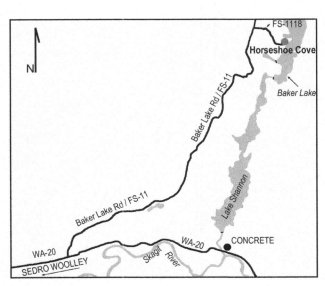

Driving Directions

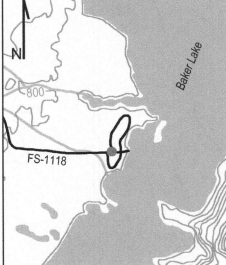
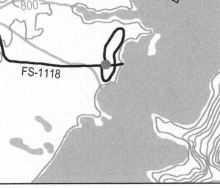

Location

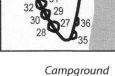

Campground

242 Boulder Creek
Mount Baker–Snoqualmie National Forest

Directions

Start at the intersection of WA–9 North and WA–20 in Sedro Woolley. Travel east on WA–20 for 16.5 miles. Turn left onto Baker Lake Road (Forest Service Road 11) and travel 18.0 miles. Turn right into Boulder Creek.

N48°42'48" – W121°41'29"   Elevation – 1,020 feet

Facilities

7 standard sites, 2 walk–in sites
Vault toilet
No water, bring your own
Garbage service

Features

Boulder Creek campground is situated along Boulder Creek, with most of the sites along the creek. Hiking opportunities are nearby. The Shadow of the Sentinels Trail begins just south of the campground. This accessible interpretive trail winds through a 500–year old forest. Displays along the path explain the dynamics of the forest. The trail is constructed of asphalt and boardwalks with grades no greater than 8%. Baker Lake is within walking distance.

Reservations

Reserve online at *www.recreation.gov* or call 1–877–444–6777 (5 am to 9 pm Pacific time), 518–885–3639, or TDD 1–877–833–6777. Reservations must be made at least 4 days ahead of arrival and may be made up to 12 months in advance. See Appendix B for details.

Season

Open late May through late September

Activities

Boating, non–motorized, Fishing, Hiking, Hunting.

Cost

$14
$7 extra vehicle
See Appendix C for available discounts.

Limitations

Because the campground's gravel road does not have any turn–around areas and the spurs are mostly short, it is better suited for tent camping and vehicles shorter than 24 feet.
See Appendix A for camping regulations.

Contact

Mt. Baker–Snoqualmie National Forest
2930 Wetmore Ave., Suite 3A
Everett, WA 98201
Phone: 425–783–6000, 800–627–0062
Outdoor Recreation Information: 206–470–4060

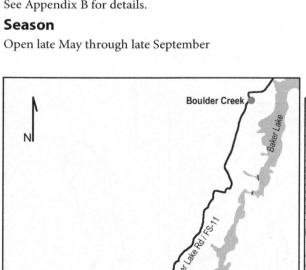

Driving Directions

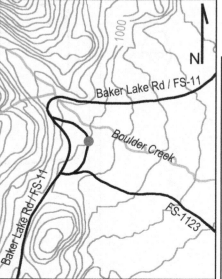

Location

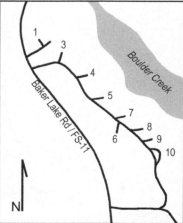

Campground

243 Panorama Point
Mount Baker–Snoqualmie National Forest

Directions

Start at the intersection of WA–9 North and WA–20 in Sedro Woolley. Travel east on WA–20 for 16.5 miles. Turn left onto Baker Lake Road (Forest Service Road 11) and travel 19.4 miles. Turn right past boat ramp to Panorama Point.

N48°43'21" – W121 40' 15"   Elevation – 760 feet

Facilities

15 standard sites
Vault toilet
Potable water
Garbage service
Boat launch
Accessible campsite

Features

Panorama Point campground is situated along the western shore of Baker Lake. All of the campsites are nestled in a forested setting either along Little Park Creek or Baker Lake. A boat ramp is adjacent to the campground.

Reservations

Reserve online at *www.recreation.gov* or call 1–877–444–6777 (5 am to 9 pm Pacific time), 518–885–3639, or TDD 1–877–833–6777. Reservations must be made at least 4 days ahead of arrival and may be made up to 12 months in advance. See Appendix B for details.

Season

Open from mid May through mid September

Activities

Boating, Fishing, Hiking.

Cost

$16 single
$8 extra vehicle
See Appendix C for available discounts.

Limitations

Drinking water is available but not for RV hose hookups. During Sockeye fishing season the gravel boat launch use is extremely heavy.
See Appendix A for camping regulations.

Contact

Mt. Baker–Snoqualmie National Forest
2930 Wetmore Ave., Suite 3A
Everett, WA 98201
Phone: 425–783–6000, 800–627–0062
Outdoor Recreation Information: 206–470–4060

Panorama Point Boat Launch

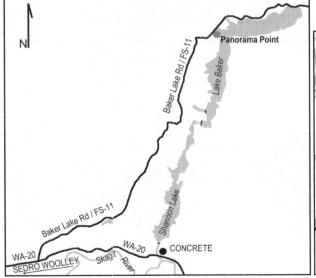

Driving Directions

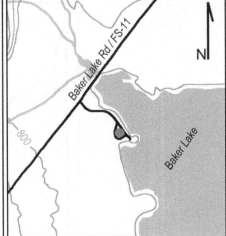

Location

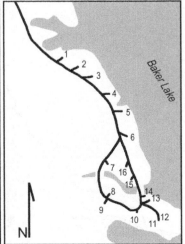

Campground

244 Park Creek
Mount Baker–Snoqualmie National Forest

Directions

Start at the intersection of WA–9 North and WA–20 in Sedro Woolley. Travel east on WA–20 for 16.5 miles. Turn left onto Baker Lake Road (Forest Service Road 11) and travel 20.0 miles. Turn left at Forest Service Road 1144 and travel 0.1 mile to Park Creek.

N48°44'06" – W121°39'59"   Elevation – 800 feet

Facilities

12 standard sites
Vault toilet
No water, bring your own
Garbage service

Features

Park Creek campground is situated in old growth forest along Park Creek. There is a boat launch nearby at Panorama Point Campground. The campground is within walking distance to the grocery store at Mt. Baker RV and Cabin Resort.

Reservations

Reserve online at *www.recreation.gov* or call 1–877–444–6777 (5 am to 9 pm Pacific time), 518–885–3639, or TDD 1–877–833–6777. Reservations must be made at least 4 days ahead of arrival and may be made up to 12 months in advance. See Appendix B for details.

Season

Open from mid May through mid September

Activities

Boating, Fishing, Hiking.

Park Creek

Cost

$12
$6 extra vehicle
See Appendix C for available discounts.

Limitations

See Appendix A for camping regulations.

Contact

Mt. Baker–Snoqualmie National Forest
2930 Wetmore Ave., Suite 3A
Everett, WA 98201
Phone: 425–783–6000, 800–627–0062
Outdoor Recreation Information: 206–470–4060

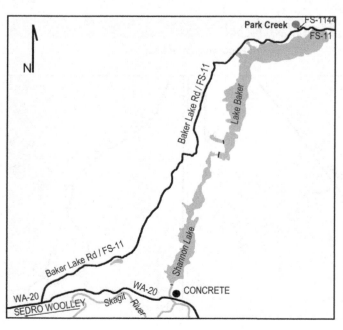

Driving Directions

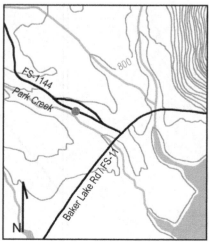

Location

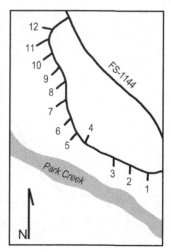

Campground

245 Shannon Creek
Mount Baker–Snoqualmie National Forest

Directions

Start at the intersection of WA–9 North and WA–20 in Sedro Woolley. Travel east on WA–20 for 16.5 miles. Turn left onto Baker Lake Road (Forest Service Road 11) and travel 23.4 miles. Turn right into Shannon Creek.

N48°44'20" – W121°35'59"   Elevation – 800 feet

Facilities

20 total campsites: 2 tent–only
Vault toilet
Potable water
Garbage service
Boat launch
Accessible toilet, campsite

Features

Shannon Creek campground is situated along the western shore of Baker Lake. The campground offers a boat ramp and swimming area. The views across the lake look toward the Noisy Creek drainage and the Noisy–Diobsud Wilderness Area.

Reservations

Reserve online at *www.recreation.gov* or call 1–877–444–6777 (5 am to 9 pm Pacific time), 518–885–3639, or TDD 1–877–833–6777. Reservations must be made 4 day(s) ahead of arrival and may be made up to 12 month(s) in advance. See Appendix B for details.

Season

Open from mid May to mid September

Activities

Boating, Fishing, Hiking, Swimming.

Cost

$14
$16 for sites on the lake
$7 extra vehicle
See Appendix C for available discounts.

Limitations

The gravel boat launch is not suitable for larger boats. During Sockeye fishing season boat ramp use is limited to Shannon Creek campers only.
See Appendix A for camping regulations.

Contact

Mt. Baker–Snoqualmie National Forest
2930 Wetmore Ave., Suite 3A
Everett, WA 98201
Phone: 425–783–6000, 800–627–0062
Outdoor Recreation Information: 206–470–4060

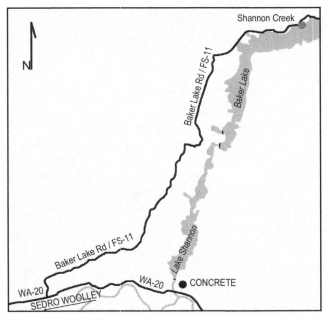

Driving Directions

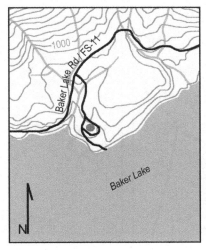

Location

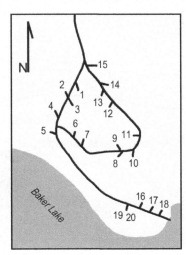

Campground

246 Howard Miller Steelhead Park
Skagit County

Directions

Start at the intersection of WA–20 and WA–530 near Rockport. Travel south on WA–530 for 0.2 mile. Turn right into park.

N48°29'03" – W121°35'54"   Elevation – 270 feet

Facilities

60 total sites: 50 partial utility (W/E), 10 walk–in

Some pull–through sites
Flush toilets
Potable water
Hot showers
Garbage service
RV dump
Shelter
Boat launch
Accessible campsite

Features

Howard Miller Steelhead Park lies along the Skagit River with large open, grassy areas and large shade trees. There are some riverside sites. The park offers an extensive trail system and houses the Skagit River Interpretive Center. Adjacent to the park is a small grocery store.

Reservations

Reservations are available by phoning 360–853–8808.
All non–reserved sites are first–come, first–serve.
See Appendix B for reservation details.

Season

Open all year

Activities

Ball fields, Bicycling, Bird watching, Boating, Equestrian trails,

Fishing, Hiking, Interpretive center, Playground, Rafting.

Cost

$30 partial utility sites (W/E)
$16 walk–in sites
$29 accessible site
$5 extra vehicle

Limitations

See Appendix A for camping regulations.

Contact

Howard Miller Steelhead Park
52804 Rockport Park Road
P.O. Box 127
Rockport, WA 98283
Phone: 360.853.8808
email: *hmsp@co.skagit.wa.us*

Howard Miller Campsite

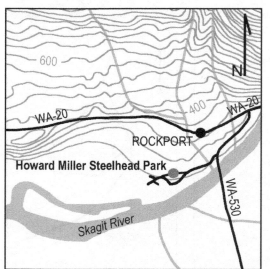

Driving Directions and Location

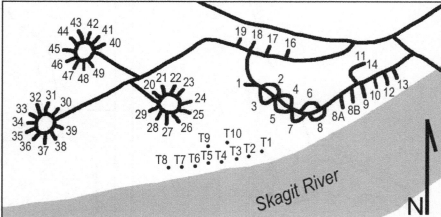

Campground

247 Marble Creek
Mount Baker–Snoqualmie National Forest

Directions

Start at the intersection of WA–20 and WA–530 near Rockport. Travel east on WA–20 for 8.4 miles. Bear right onto Cascade River Road (Forest Service Road 15) and travel 7.9 miles (last portion is a light duty, gravel road). Turn right into Marble Creek.

N48°31'46" – W121°16'34"   Elevation – 1,000 feet

Facilities

23 standard sites
Vault toilet
No water, bring your own
Garbage service
Boat ramp (hand only)
Accessible toilet, campsite

Cascade River

Features

Marble Creek campground is remote and nestled amongst giant Douglas fir and cedar trees adjacent to Marble Creek and the Cascade River. The campsites are large and private with several sites bordering the river.

Activities

Berry picking, Bird watching, Boating (canoeing, kayaking, tubing), Fishing, Hiking.

Reservations

Reserve online at *www.recreation.gov* or call 1–877–444–6777 (5 am to 9 pm Pacific time), 518–885–3639, or TDD 1–877–833–6777. Reservations must be made at least 4 days ahead of arrival and may be made up to 12 months in advance. See Appendix B for details.

Cost

$14 single
$7 extra vehicle
See Appendix C for available discounts.

Limitations

Come prepared, there is no cell phone coverage and no potable water.
See Appendix A for camping regulations.

Season

Open from mid May to mid September

Contact

Mt. Baker–Snoqualmie National Forest
2930 Wetmore Ave., Suite 3A
Everett, WA 98201
Phone: 425–783–6000, 800–627–0062
Outdoor Recreation Information: 206–470–4060

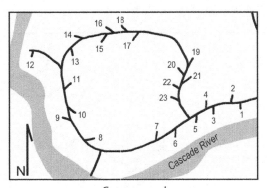

Campground

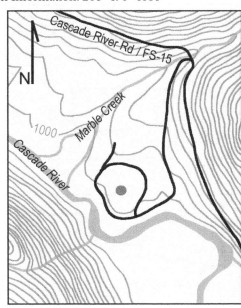

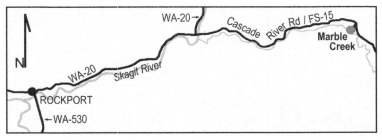

Driving Directions

Location

248 Mineral Park
Mount Baker–Snoqualmie National Forest

Directions

Start at the intersection of WA–20 and WA–530 near Rockport. Travel east on WA–20 for 8.4 miles. Bear right onto Cascade River Road (Forest Service Road 15) and travel 13.6 miles. Bear left at "Y" onto Saddle Point Road and travel 1.7 miles. Turn right into Mineral Park. (The last portion of Cascade River Road and Saddle Point Road are light duty, gravel roads.)

N48°27'48" – W121°09'56"   Elevation – 1,360 feet

Facilities

21 total sites: 20 standard, 1 walk–in
Pull–through sites
Vault toilets
No water, bring your own
Garbage service

Features

Mineral Park campground is situated near the confluence of the North and South Forks of the Cascade River. The campground has two sections: Mineral Park East with 7 standard sites and Mineral Park West with 14 standard sites. Many sites are riverside. Nearby are the North Cascades National Park and access to the National Forest trail system.

Reservations

Reserve online at *www.recreation.gov* or call 1–877–444–6777 (5 am to 9 pm Pacific time), 518–885–3639, or TDD 1–877–833–6777. Reservations must be made at least 4 days ahead of arrival and may be made up to 12 months in advance. See Appendix B for details.

Season

Open from mid May through mid September

Activities

Fishing.

Cost

$12 single site
$6 extra vehicle
See Appendix C for available discounts.

Limitations

The campground is better suited for tent and small trailer camping because the narrow, gravel road.
See Appendix A for camping regulations.

Contact

Mt. Baker–Snoqualmie National Forest
2930 Wetmore Ave., Suite 3A
Everett, WA 98201
Phone: 425–783–6000, 800–627–0062
Outdoor Recreation Information: 206–470–4060

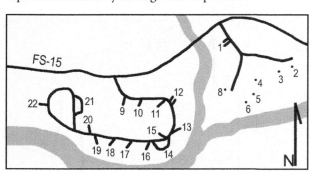

Campground

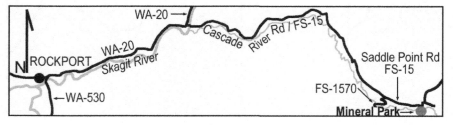

Driving Directions

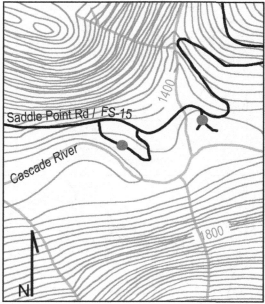

Location

249 Goodell Creek
North Cascades National Park

Directions

Start at the intersection of WA–20 and County Road 9137 (also called Bluff Road) in Winthrop. Travel west on WA–20 for 70.4 miles. Turn left into campground access road and travel for 0.2 mile to Goodell Creek.

Or

Start at the intersection of WA–20 and WA–530 in Rockport. Travel east on WA–20 for 21.9 miles. Turn right into campground access road and travel for 0.2 mile to Goodell Creek.

N48°40'24" – W121°16'00"   Elevation – 500 feet

Facilities

21 standard sites
Vault toilet
Potable water
Garbage service
Shelter
Boat launch (hand only)

Features

Goodell Creek campground is situated in lush, old growth forest on the banks of the Skagit River. Several sites are along the river. There is a covered picnic shelter, a raft/kayak launch, and fishing on the river and its tributaries.

Reservations

None, all campsites are first–come, first–serve.

Season

The whole campground is open from mid May through mid September with all services and fees. The main campground is open the remaining portion of the year with no services or fees. In winter, vault toilets are available but no garbage service – carry out all trash.

Activities

Fishing, Whitewater paddling.

Cost

$16
See Appendix C for available discounts.

Limitations

Campground is appropriate for tents and small RVs.
There is snow in campground at times and winter camping conditions may apply. Check on–line to see the status of the campground at: *http://www.nps.gov/noca/planyourvisit/ campground-status.htm.*
Gathering firewood is prohibited. Firewood can be purchased outside of the park.
See Appendix A for camping regulations.

Contact

North Cascades National Park
810 State Route 20
Sedro–Woolley, WA 98284
Visitor Information: 360–854–7200
Wilderness Information Center: 360–854–7245

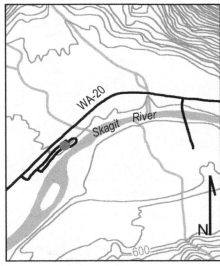

Location

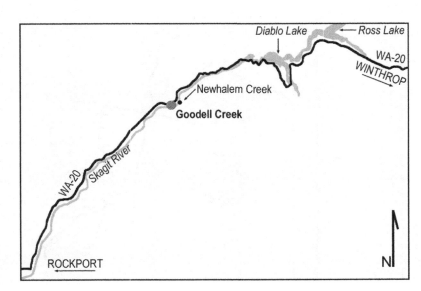

Driving Directions

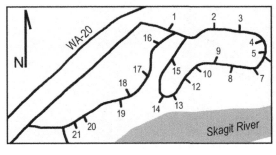

Campground

250 Newhalem Creek
North Cascades National Park

Directions

Start at the intersection of WA–20 and County Road 9137 (also called Bluff Road) in Winthrop. Travel west on WA–20 for 69.8 miles. Turn left at the Newhalem Creek Visitor sign and travel 1.2 miles to campground.

Or

Start at the intersection of WA–20 and WA–530 in Rockport. Travel east on WA–20 for 22.4 miles. Turn right at the Newhalem Creek Visitor sign and travel 1.2 miles to campground.

N48°40'15" – W121°15'39"   Elevation – 500 feet

Facilities

111 standard sites
Some pull–through sites
Several walk–in sites
Flush toilets
Potable water
Garbage and recycling
RV dump station
Accessible campsite

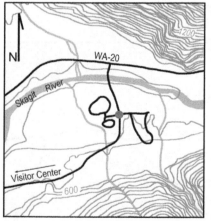

Location

Features

Newhalem campground is conveniently located between the town of Newhalem and the Newhalem Visitor Center on the banks of the Skagit River. Ranger programs are provided in the campground and at the visitor center during the summer. A series of short walks and interpretive trails link the campground to many natural and historic destinations: Sterling Munro, River Loop, "To Know a Tree," Rock Shelter, Trail of the Cedars, and Ladder Creek trails.

Reservations

Reservations are accepted for Loop C only. Reserve sites at *www.recreation.gov* or by phone at 1–877–444–6777. Reservations must be made 3 days ahead of arrival and can be made up to 12 months in advance. See Appendix B for details.

Season

Open end of May through mid September

Activities

Fishing, Hiking.

Cost

$16
See Appendix C for available discounts.

Limitations

Large RVs can be accommodated. For Loop C, the National Reservation System provides specific campsite driveway lengths.
Gathering firewood is prohibited. Firewood can be purchased outside of the park.
See Appendix A for camping regulations.

Contact

North Cascades National Park Complex
810 State Route 20
Sedro–Woolley, WA 98284
Visitor Information: 360–854–7200
Wilderness Information Center: 360–854–7245

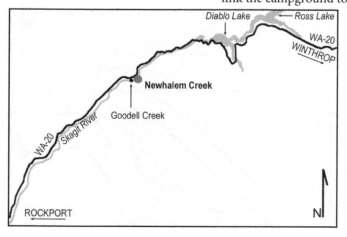

Driving Directions

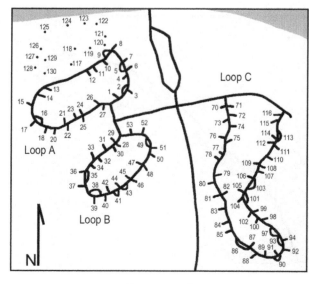

Campground

251 Gorge Lake
North Cascades National Park

Directions

Start at the intersection of WA–20 and County Road 9137 (also called Bluff Road) in Winthrop. Travel west on WA–20 for 66.8 miles. Turn right onto Diablo Street and travel 0.6 mile. Turn right into Gorge Lake.

Or

Start at the intersection of WA–20 and WA–530 in Rockport. Travel east on WA–20 for 28.2 miles. Turn left into Diablo Street and travel 0.6 mile. Turn right into Gorge Lake.

N48°42'58" – W121°09'04"   Elevation – 900 feet

Ross Lake

Diablo Dam

Facilities

6 standard sites
Vault toilet
No water, bring your own
Garbage service available from late May to September
Boat launch

Features

Gorge Lake campground is on the bank of Gorge Lake next to the cascading Stetattle Creek.

Reservations

None, all campsites are first–come, first–serve.

Season

Open all year with no water or services. Pack out all garbage.

Activities

Boating, Fishing, Hiking.

Cost

No cost

Limitations

There is snow in campground at times. Winter camping conditions may apply. Check status at: *http://www.nps.gov/noca/planyourvisit/campground–status.htm*
Gathering firewood is prohibited. Firewood can be purchased outside of the park.
See Appendix A for camping regulations.

Contact

North Cascades National Park
810 State Route 20
Sedro–Woolley, WA 98284
Visitor Information: 360–854–7200
Wilderness Information Center: 360–854–7245

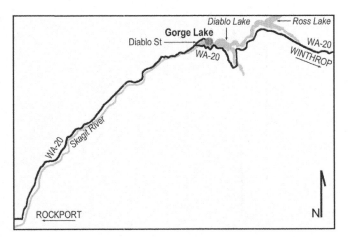

Driving Directions

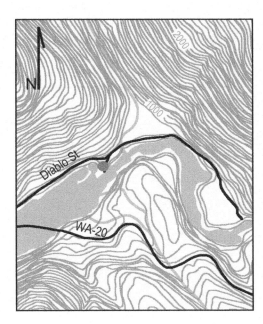

Location

252 Colonial Creek
North Cascades National Park

Directions

Start at the intersection of WA–20 and County Road 9137 (also called Bluff Road) in Winthrop. Travel west on WA–20 for 59.3 miles. Campground is on both sides of road.

Or

Start at the intersection of WA–20 and WA 530 in Rockport. Travel east on WA–20 for 30 miles. Campground is on both sides of the road.

N48°41'24" – W121°05'55"   Elevation – 1,200 feet

Facilities

142 standard sites
Some pull–through sites
Some walk–in sites
Flush toilets
Potable water
Garbage and recycling
RV dump station
Boat launch and dock
Accessible campsites

Colonial Creek Welcome

Features

Colonial Creek campground is on the shore of Diablo Lake in old growth forest at the base of glaciated Colonial Peak. The lovely campsites have substantial undergrowth for privacy. Great access to hiking on Thunder Creek, Thunder Woods Nature Walk, and Thunder Knob trails. There are evening ranger programs and weekend activities during the summer.

Reservations

None, all campsites are first–come, first–serve.

Season

From late May through late September. However, South Loop lakefront sites 64 – 73 are open during winter months with no water, services or fees. The area is not plowed in winter. Please carry out all trash.

Activities

Boating, Fishing, Hiking.

Cost

$16
See Appendix C for available discounts.

Limitations

Gathering firewood is prohibited. Firewood can be purchased outside of the park.
See Appendix A for camping regulations.

Contact

North Cascades National Park
810 State Route 20
Sedro–Woolley, WA 98284
Visitor Information: 360–854–7200
Wilderness Information Center: 360–854–7245

Fishing Dock

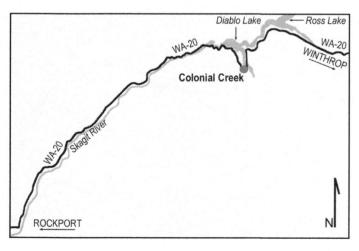

Driving Directions

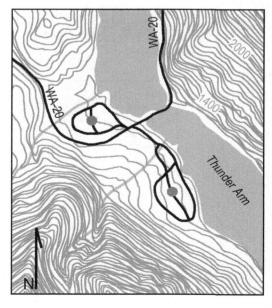

Location

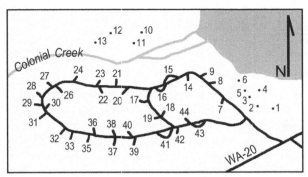

North Campground

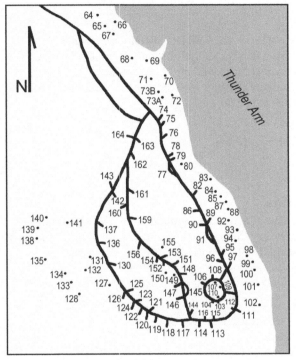

South Campground

National Park Beauty

Grilled Steak and Salad

Sometimes the easiest tastes the best.

A nice steak cooked outdoors.

A salad made from an assortment of fresh greens, vegetables, a little cheese and dinner is served.

If local corn is in season, it does very well cooking in the grill basket. Be careful turning the basket over. Don't loose the corn.

277

253 Hozomeen
North Cascades National Park

Directions

Start in Canada at the intersection of Canada Highway #1 and Silver/Skagit Road (exit 68) 2 miles (3 km) west of Hope, B.C., Canada. Travel south on Silver/Skagit Road for 40 miles (64 km) to Hozomeen.

N48°50'04" – W121°04'17"   Elevation – 1,600 feet

Facilities

75 designated standard sites with other camping areas
Vault/pit toilets
Potable water in summer
Pack out garbage
Boat launch and dock

Features

Deep in the mountains, Hozomeen campground is a primitive camp that sits near the US–Canadian border at the north end of Ross Lake. The campground is not accessible by road from the U.S. The Hozomeen Ranger Station is nearby. Interpretive programs are offered during the summer in the amphitheater.

Reservations

None, all campsites are first–come, first–serve.

Season

Open with water service until late September. Open with no service from late September through the end of October. Closed November 1 through mid May. Closed at border gate. Check status at: *http://www.nps.gov/noca/planyourvisit/campground-status.htm*

Activities

Boating, Fishing, Hiking.

Cost

No cost

Limitations

The Silver/Skagit Road is maintained but unpaved and often rough – carry a spare tire. For current road conditions refer to the road conditions report: *http://www.nps.gov/noca/planyourvisit/current-park-conditions.htm.*
See Appendix A for camping regulations.

Contact

North Cascades National Park Complex
810 State Route 20
Sedro–Woolley, WA 98284
Visitor Information: 360–854–7200
Wilderness Information Center: 360–854–7245

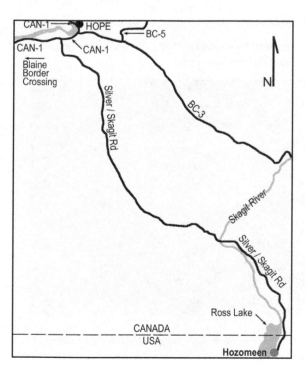

Driving Directions

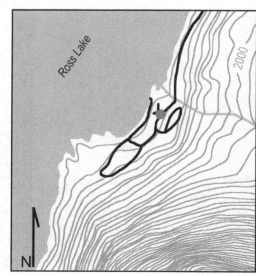

Location

254 Lone Fir
Okanogan–Wenatchee National Forest

Directions

Start at the intersection of WA–20 and Bluff Road (Okanogan County Road 9137) in Winthrop. Travel west on WA–20 for 20.8 miles. Turn left into Lone Fir.

N48°34'48" – W120°37'37"   Elevation – 3,640 feet

Facilities

27 standard sites
Some pull–through sites
Vault toilets
Potable water in summer
Garbage service
Accessible toilet

Features

Lone Fir campground lies near Early Winters Creek in a forested area with mountain views. Several sites are near the creek. The campground offers a good overnight spot for bicyclists. There is a short hiking trail in the campground and access to Lone Fir Trail and Cutthroat Lake trailheads are nearby.

Reservations

None, all campsites are first–come, first–serve.

Season

The normal camping season is June through October.

Activities

Hiking, Interpretive area.

Cost

$12
$5 extra vehicle
See Appendix C for available discounts.

Limitations

Campground is suitable for tents or smaller recreational vehicles; however, some sites lengths are 36 feet.

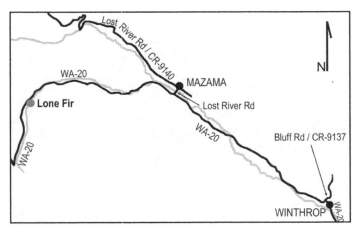

Driving Directions

Maximum stay limit is 14 days.
Early Winters Creek is closed to fishing – check the Washington State Fishing Regulations.
See Appendix A for camping regulations.

Contact

Okanogan–Wenatchee National Forest
Methow Valley Ranger District
24 West Chewuch Road
Winthrop, WA 98862
Phone: 509–996–4003
Fax: 509–996–2208

Lone Fir Toilet and Scenery

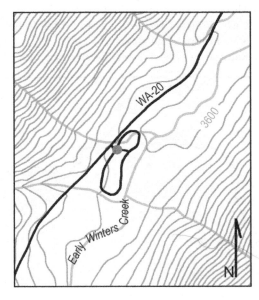

Location

279

255 Klipchuck
Okanogan–Wenatchee National Forest

Directions

Start at the intersection of WA–20 and Bluff Road (Okanogan County Road 9137) in Winthrop. Travel west on WA–20 for 17.8 miles. Turn right onto Forest Service Road 300 and travel 1.3 miles. Turn left to Klipchuck.

N48°35'49" – W120°30'48"   Elevation – 2,920 feet

Facilities

46 standard sites
Vault toilets
Potable water
Garbage service
Accessible toilet

Features

Klipchuck campground is near Early Winters Creek among majestic trees. Campsites may be combined to accommodate groups.

Reservations

None, all campsites are first–come, first–serve.

Season

The normal camping season is May through October.

Activities

Hiking.

Cost

$12
$5 extra vehicle
See Appendix C for available discounts.

Limitations

Maximum site length of five of the sites is 34 feet, the remaining sites are shorter.
Maximum stay limit is 14 days.
Early Winters Creek is closed to fishing – check the Washington State Fishing Regulations.
Rattlesnakes are occasionally seen near area.

Klipchuck Campsite

See Appendix A for camping regulations.

Contact

Okanogan–Wenatchee National Forest
Methow Valley Ranger District
24 West Chewuch Road
Winthrop, WA 98862
Phone: 509–996–4003
Fax: 509–996–2208

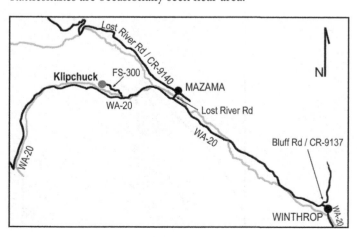

Driving Directions

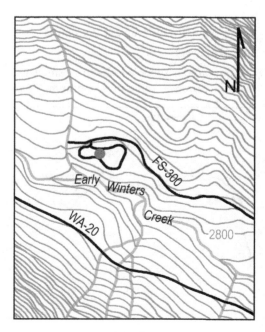

Location

256 Ballard
Okanogan–Wenatchee National Forest

Directions

Start at the intersection of WA–20 and Lost River Road near Mazama. Travel north on Lost River Road for 0.4 mile. Turn left onto Lost River Road (Okanogan County Road 9140 which becomes Forest Service Road 5400) and travel for 8.5 miles. Turn left into Ballard.

N48°39'32" – W120°32'40"   Elevation – 2,520 feet

Methow River

Activities

Fishing, Hiking.

Cost

$8
$5 extra vehicle
See Appendix C for available discounts.

Facilities

7 standard sites
Some pull–through sites
Vault toilet
No water, bring your own
Pack out garbage
Accessible toilet

Features

Ballard campground lies along the West Fork Methow River and provides access to nearby hiking trails: Robinson Creek, West Fork Methow and Lost River/Monument Creek.

Reservations

None, all campsites are first–come, first–serve.

Season

Open May through October

Limitations

Maximum vehicle length is 28 feet.
Maximum stay limit is 14 days.
See Appendix A for camping regulations.

Ballard Campsite

Contact

Okanogan–Wenatchee National Forest
Methow Valley Ranger District
24 West Chewuch Road
Winthrop, WA 98862
Phone: 509–996–4003
Fax: 509–996–2208

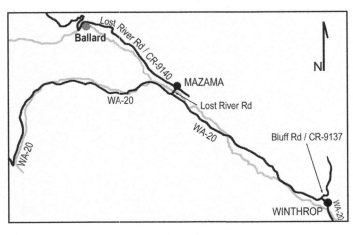

Driving Directions

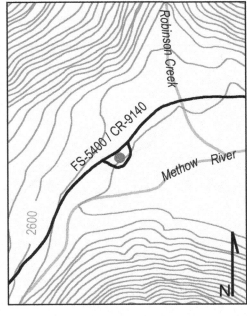

Location

257 Meadows
Okanogan–Wenatchee National Forest

Directions

Start at the intersection of WA–20 and Lost River Road near Mazama. Travel northeast on Lost River Road for 0.4 mile. Turn left to stay on Lost River Road (Okanogan County Road 9140) and travel 8.9 miles. Turn right on Forest Service Road 5400 and travel 9.7 miles. Turn left onto Forest Service Road 5400–500 and travel 1.0 mile. Turn left into Meadows.

N48°42'39" – W120°40'35"   Elevation – 6,200 feet

Facilities

14 standard sites
Vault toilet
No water, bring your own
Pack out garbage
Accessible toilet

Features

Meadows campground is located in the Lost River – Hart's Pass Area. The campground offers wonderful views and alpine meadows and provides access to the Pacific Crest National Scenic Trail.

Reservations

None, all campsites are first–come, first–serve.

Season

Open July through October, depending on weather.

Activities

Hiking.

Cost

$8
$5 extra vehicle
See Appendix C for available discounts.

Limitations

Trailers are prohibited on Forest Service Road 5400/Hart's Pass Road. The road is a narrow, windy mountain road with steep side cliffs in places. Yield to trucks.
See Appendix A for camping regulations.

Contact

Okanogan–Wenatchee National Forest
Methow Valley Ranger District
24 West Chewuch Road
Winthrop, WA 98862
Phone: 509–996–4003
Fax: 509–996–2208

Meadows Area

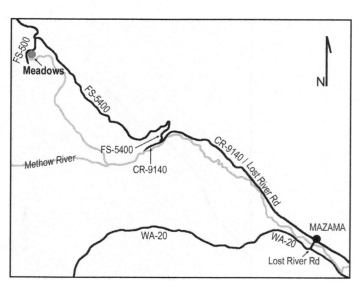

Driving Directions

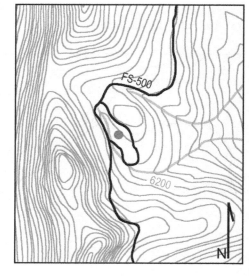

Location

258 Early Winters
Okanogan–Wenatchee National Forest

Directions

Start at the intersection of WA–20 and Bluff Street (Okanogan County Road 9137) in Winthrop. Travel west on WA–20 for 15.3 miles. Turn left or right to campground. (Early Winters campsites are on both sides of the highway.)

N48°35'51" – W120°26'46"   Elevation – 2,160 feet

Facilities

12 standard sites
Vault toilets
Potable water in summer
Garbage service
Accessible toilet

Features

Early Winters campground is located near the confluence of Early Winters Creek and the Methow River. Campsites are on the north and south sides of Highway 20. Several sites are located near the creek. The area has flat, open land with great views

Early Winters Creek

of Goat Wall. Cedar Creek Trail and Driveway Butte Trail are nearby, as is the town of Mazama.

Reservations

None, all campsites are first–come, first–serve.

Season

Open April through October, depending on snow conditions.

Activities

Hiking, Interpretive site.

Cost

$8
$5 extra vehicle
See Appendix C for available discounts.

Limitations

Maximum site length is 32 feet; maximum trailer length is 24 feet. Campground is appropriate for tents or smaller recreational vehicles.
Check Washington State Fishing Regulations – Early Winters Creek is closed to fishing.
Maximum stay limit is 14 days.
See Appendix A for camping regulations.

Contact

Okanogan–Wenatchee National Forest
Methow Valley Ranger District
24 West Chewuch Road
Winthrop, WA 98862
Phone: 509–996–4003
Fax: 509–996–2208

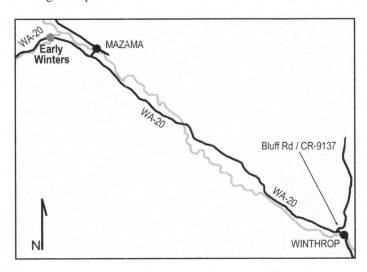

Driving Directions

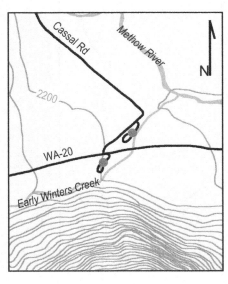

Location

259 Buck Lake
Okanogan–Wenatchee National Forest

Directions

Start at the intersection of WA–20 and Westside Chewuch Road (Okanogan County Road 1213) in Winthrop. Travel north on Westside Chewuch Road (becomes Forest Service Road 51) for 9.3 miles. Turn left onto Forest Service Road 5130, a paved road, and travel 0.6 mile. Turn left on Forest Service Road 5130–100 and travel 2.3 miles. Turn left to Buck Lake.

N48°36'20" – W120°12'08"   Elevation – 3,250 feet

Facilities

7 standard sites
Vault toilet
No water, bring your own
Pack out garbage
Boat landing for small craft
Accessible toilet

Buck Lake Campsite

Features

Buck Lake campground is a small quiet forested campground that offers good fishing early in the year in a stocked lake.

Reservations

None, all campsites are first–come, first–serve.

Season

Open May through October

Activities

Boating (non–motorized), Fishing, Mountain biking .

Cost

$8
$5 extra vehicle
See Appendix C for available discounts.

Limitations

Maximum vehicle length is 25 feet.
Maximum stay limit is 14 days.
Check Washington State Fishing Regulations.
See Appendix A for camping regulations.

Contact

Okanogan–Wenatchee National Forest
Methow Valley Ranger District
24 West Chewuch Road
Winthrop, WA 98862
Phone: 509–996–4003
Fax: 509–996–2208

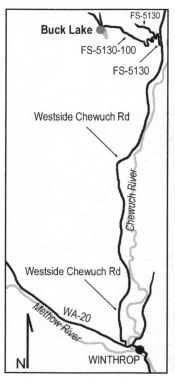

Driving Directions

Buck Lake

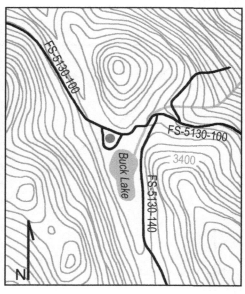

Location

260 Flat
Okanogan–Wenatchee National Forest

Directions

Start at the intersection of WA–20 and Westside Chewuch Road (Okanogan County Road 1213) in Winthrop. Travel north on Westside Chewuch Road (becomes Forest Service Road 51) for 9.3 miles. Turn left onto Forest Service Road 5130, a paved road, and travel 2.6 miles. Turn left into Flat campground.

N48°36'55" – W120°11'44"   Elevation – 2,850 feet

Facilities

12 standard sites
Vault toilet
Potable water in summer
Pack out garbage
Accessible toilet

Features

Flat campground is located along Eight–Mile Creek with some sites on the creek. The paved road allows easy access for trailers.

Reservations

None, all campsites are first–come, first–serve.

Season

Open May through October, contingent on snow conditions.

Activities

Fishing.

Cost

$8
$5 extra vehicle
See Appendix C for available discounts.

Limitations

Maximum vehicle length is 36 feet.
Bridge weight limit is 15 tons.
Maximum stay is 14 days.
See Appendix A for camping regulations.

Contact

Okanogan–Wenatchee National Forest
Methow Valley Ranger District
24 West Chewuch Road
Winthrop, WA 98862
Phone: 509–996–4003
Fax: 509–996–2208

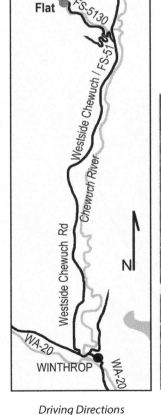

Driving Directions

Flat Campsite

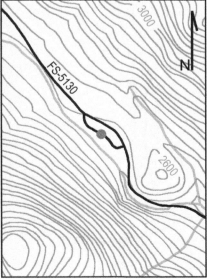

Location

261 Falls Creek
Okanogan–Wenatchee National Forest

Directions

Start at the intersection of WA–20 and Westside Chewuch Road (Okanogan County Road 1213) in Winthrop. Travel north on Westside Chewuch Road (becomes Forest Service Road 51) for 11.9 miles. Turn right to Falls Creek.

N48°38'07" – W120°09'21"   Elevation – 2,100 feet

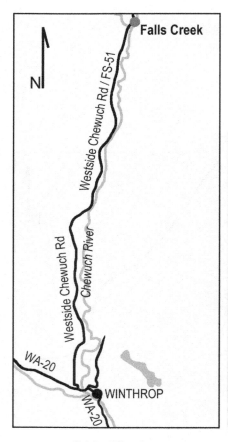

Facilities

7 standard sites
Vault toilet
Potable water in summer
Pack out garbage
Accessible toilet

Features

Falls Creek campground lies along the Chewuch River and Falls Creek. Some sites are riverside. There is a ¼ mile paved, wheelchair accessible, trail to scenic Falls Creek waterfalls.

Reservations

None, all campsites are first–come, first–serve.

Season

Open May through October

Activities

Fishing, Hiking, Swimming.

Cost

$8
$5 extra vehicle
See Appendix C for available discounts.

Limitations

Maximum vehicle length is 18 feet.
Check Washington State Fishing Regulations.
Maximum stay limit is 14 days.
See Appendix A for camping regulations.

Contact

Okanogan–Wenatchee National Forest
Methow Valley Ranger District
24 West Chewuch Road
Winthrop, WA 98862
Phone: 509–996–4003
Fax: 509–996–2208

Driving Directions

Falls Creek Campsite

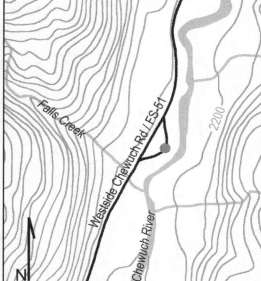

Location

262 Chewuch
Okanogan–Wenatchee National Forest

Directions

Start at the intersection of WA–20 and Westside Chewuch Road (Okanogan County Road 1213) in Winthrop. Travel north on Westside Chewuch Road (becomes USFS Road 51, a paved road) for 15.1 miles. Turn right to campground.

N48°40'43" – W120°07'56"   Elevation – 2,278 feet

Facilities

16 standard sites
Vault toilet
Potable water in summer
Garbage service
Accessible toilet

Features

Chewuch is a small, remote campground along the Chewuch River surrounded by Ponderosa Pine.

Reservations

None, all campsites are first–come, first–serve.

Season

Open May through October

Activities

Fishing, Mountain biking.

Cost

$12
$5 extra vehicle
See Appendix C for available discounts.

Limitations

Maximum length of some sites is 35 feet, the remaining sites are shorter.
Maximum stay limit is 14 days.
Check Washington State Fishing Regulations.
See Appendix A for camping regulations.

Contact

Okanogan–Wenatchee National Forest
Methow Valley Ranger District
24 West Chewuch Road
Winthrop, WA 98862
Phone: 509–996–4003
Fax: 509–996–2208

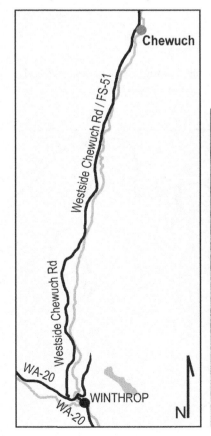

Driving Directions

Chewuch Campsite

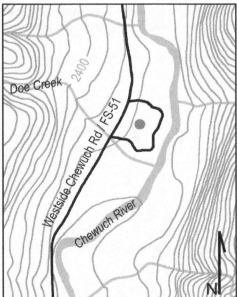

Location

263 Pearrygin Lake
Washington State Parks

Directions

Start at the intersection of WA–20 and County Road 9137 (also called Bluff Street) in Winthrop. Travel north on County Road 9137 for 1.7 miles. Turn right onto Bear Creek Road and travel 0.9 mile. Turn right into the West Campground or continue for an additional 0.8 mile. Turn right at the entrance road and travel 1.3 miles into the East Campground.

N48°29'32" – W120°09'23"   Elevation – 1,960 feet

Facilities

155 total sites: 76 standard sites, 50 utility sites (W/E/S), 27 partial utility sites (W/E), 2 walk–in sites

Some pull–through sites
Flush toilets
Potable water
Hot showers
Garbage service
RV dump
Boat launch and dock
Food service
Laundry
Accessible toilet, water, campsite, shower

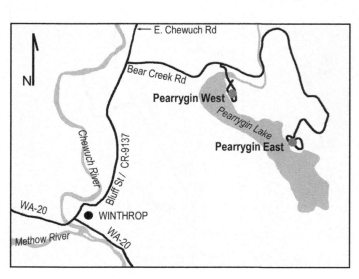

Features

Pearrygin Lake State Park features expansive green lawns, willow and ash trees for shade on hot summer days, and a sandy beach on Pearrygin Lake. The lake is a popular water recreation area offering swimming, fishing and boating. Park staff offer campfire programs on Tuesday and Thursday nights from June 15th through Labor Day and a Junior Ranger program.

Pearrygin Campsites

Temperatures may reach well below zero in winter, and up to the 80s and 90s in summer. Annual average rainfall is 11 inches. The annual average snowfall is six inches. Wildflowers color the landscape in spring and summer, with red–winged and yellow–headed blackbirds and marmots adding to the display.

Reservations

Sites may be reserved from April 15 through October 24 online at *www.parks.state.wa.us* or by telephone 1–888–CAMPOUT (1–888–226–7688). See Appendix B for details.

Season

Open April 8 through October 31

Activities

Bird watching, Boating, Fishing, Hiking, Horseshoes, Personal watercraft, Swimming, Water skiing, Volleyball.

Driving Directions

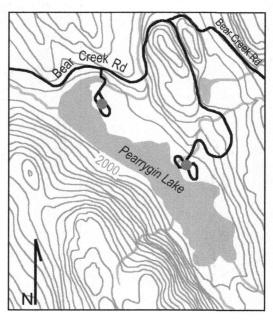

Location

Cost

$12 primitive site
Peak season: mid May – mid September
$22 – $35 standard site
$30 – $40 partial utility site
$35 – $45 full utility site
Off–peak season
$20 – $30 standard site
$25 – $35 partial utility site
$30 – $40 full utility site
$10 extra vehicle (all year)
See Appendix C for available discounts.

Pearrygin Swimming Area

Limitations

Maximum site length is 60 feet.
See Appendix A for camping regulations.

Contact

Phone: 509–996–2370
Web: *www.parks.state.wa.us*

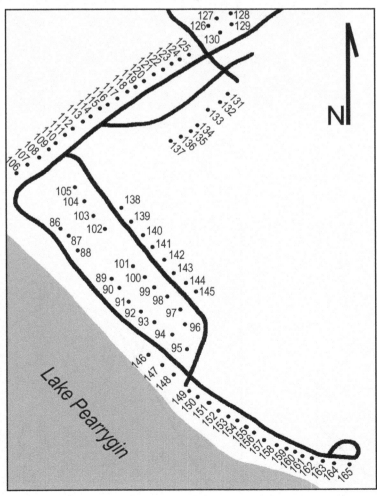

West Campground

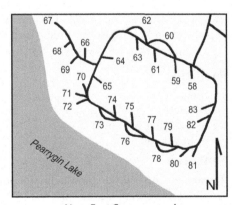

Near East Campground

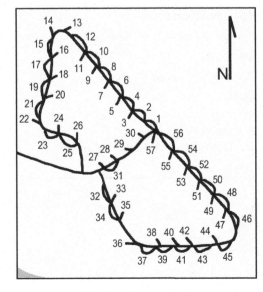

Far East Campground

264 JR
Okanogan–Wenatchee National Forest

Limitations

Maximum site length is 25 feet.
Maximum stay limit is 14 days.
See Appendix A for camping regulations.

Contact

Okanogan–Wenatchee National Forest
Methow Valley Ranger District
24 West Chewuch Road
Winthrop, WA 98862
Phone: 509–996–4003
Fax: 509–996–2208

JR Campsite

Directions

Start at the intersection of US–97 and WA–20 in Okanogan.
Travel west on WA–20 for 26.6 miles. Turn right into
campground.

Or

Start at the intersection of WA–153 and WA–20 in Twisp.
Travel east on WA–20 for 9.9 miles. Turn left into campground.

N48°23'15" – W119°54'04"   Elevation – 3,920 feet

Facilities

6 standard sites
Vault toilet
No water, bring your own
Pack out garbage

Features

JR campground is located in the Loup Loup area, alongside
WA–20. It is a great place to "just rest." (We thought this was
how it got named.)

Reservations

None, all campsites are first–come, first–serve.

Season

Open April through October

Cost

$8
$5 extra vehicle
See Appendix C for available discounts.

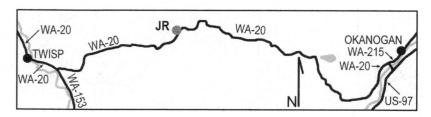

Driving Directions

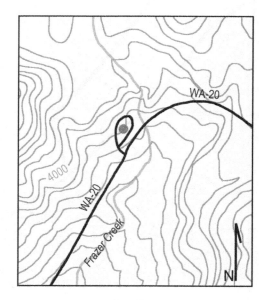

Location

265 Loup Loup
Okanogan–Wenatchee National Forest

Directions

Start at the intersection of US–97 and WA–20 in Okanogan. Travel west on WA–20 for 25.7 miles. Turn right onto Forest Service Road 42 and travel 0.5 mile. Turn sharply to the right (remaining on Forest Service Road 42) and travel an additional 0.6 mile. Turn left to Loup Loup.

Or

Start at the intersection of WA–153 and WA–20 in Twisp. Travel east on WA–20 for 10.8 miles. Turn left onto Forest Service Road 42 and travel 0.5 mile. Turn sharply to the right (remaining on Forest Service Road 42) and travel for an additional 0.6 mile. Turn left to Loup Loup.

N48°23'44" – W119°54'09"   Elevation – 4,200 feet

Loup Loup Campsite

Loup Loup Campsite

Facilities

25 standard sites
Vault toilets
Potable water in summer
Garbage service
Accessible toilet

Features

Loup Loup campground is located along Frazer Creek. The campground is a good location for large groups and offers access to mountain bike trails and scenic drives. The Loup Loup Ski area is nearby.

Reservations

None, all campsites are first–come, first–serve.

See Appendix C for available discounts.

Limitations

Maximum site length is 36 feet.
Maximum stay limit is 14 days.
See Appendix A for camping regulations.

Contact

Okanogan–Wenatchee National Forest
Methow Valley Ranger District
24 West Chewuch Road
Winthrop, WA 98862
Phone: 509–996–4003
Fax: 509–996–2208

Season

Open April through October

Activities

Hiking, Mountain biking.

Cost

$12
$5 extra vehicle

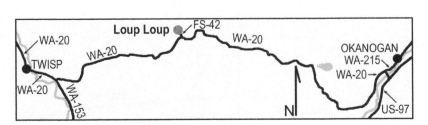

Driving Directions

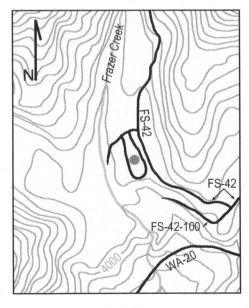

Location

266 Sportsman Camp
Department of Natural Resources

Directions

Start at the intersection of WA–20 and WA–215 near Okanogan. Travel west on WA–20 for 14.9 miles. (The road sign calls this Sweat Creek Campground.) Turn right onto Sweat Creek Road and travel 1.0 mile. Turn right into Sportsman Camp.

   N48°23'28" – W119°48'28"   Elevation – 3,270 feet

Facilities

6 standard sites
Vault toilet
No water, bring your own
Pack out garbage
Shelter

Features

Sportsman Camp lies along Sweat Creek and offers a kitchen shelter.

Reservations

None, all campsites are first–come, first–serve.

Season

Open all year, depending on weather

Activities

Hiking.

Cost

No cost

Limitations

A Washington State Discover Pass is required.
See Appendix A for camping regulations.

Contact

WA Department of Natural Resources, Northeast Region
Phone: 509–684–7474
Web: *www.dnr.wa.gov*

Sportsman Camp Shelter

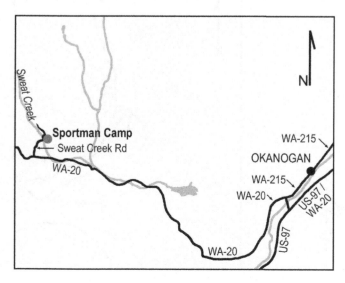

Driving Directions

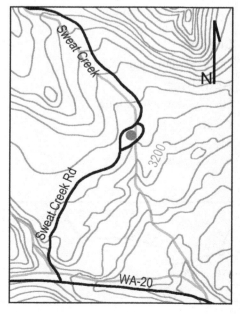

Location

267 Leader Lake
Department of Natural Resources

Directions

Start at the intersection of WA–20 and WA–215 near Okanogan. Travel west on WA–20 for 8.5 miles. Turn right onto Leader Lake Road and travel 0.4 mile to Leader Lake.

N48°21'36" – W119°41'39"   Elevation – 2,120 feet

Leader Lake

Facilities

16 standard sites
Vault toilet
No water, bring your own
Pack out garbage
Boat launch
Accessible toilets, campsites, fishing platform

Features

Leader Lake campground lies along photogenic Leader Lake.

Reservations

None, all campsites are first–come, first–serve.

Season

Open all year on plowed county road.

Activities

Boating, Fishing, Hiking.

Cost

No cost

Limitations

A Washington State Discover Pass is required.
See Appendix A for camping regulations.

Contact

WA Department of Natural Resources, Northeast Region
Phone: 509–684–7474
Web: *www.dnr.wa.gov*

Leader Lake Campsite

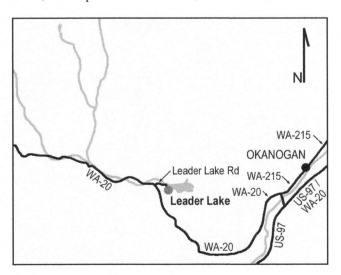

Driving Directions

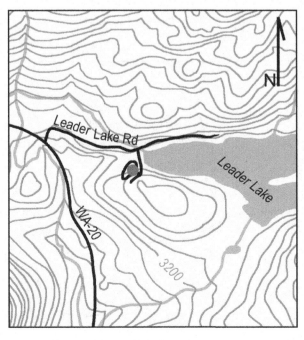

Location

268 Rock Creek
Department of Natural Resources

Directions

Start at the intersection of WA–20 and WA–215 near Okanogan. Travel west on WA–20 for 9.8 miles. Turn right onto Loup Loup Canyon Road (unpaved two lane) and travel 3.9 miles. Turn left into Rock Creek.

N48°24'20" – W119°45'32"   Elevation – 2,440 feet

Rock Creek Campsite

Facilities

8 standard sites
Vault toilet
Potable water
Pack out garbage
Shelter
Accessible toilet, water, campsite

Features

Rock Creek campground lies at the conjunction or Loup Loup Creek and Rock Creek.

Reservations

None, all campsites are first–come, first–serve.

Season

Open all year, depending on weather

Activities

Equestrian trail riding, Hiking, Mountain biking.

Cost

No cost

Limitations

A Washington State Discover Pass is required.
See Appendix A for camping regulations.

Contact

WA Department of Natural Resources, Northeast Region
Phone: 509–684–7474
Web: *www.dnr.wa.gov*

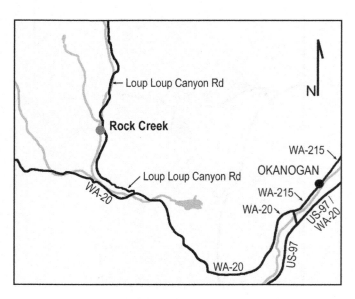

Driving Directions

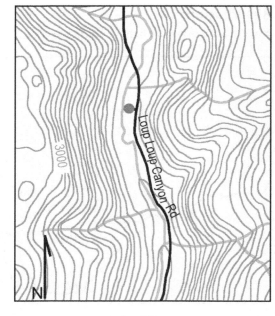

Location

269 Rock Lakes
Department of Natural Resources

Directions

Start at the intersection of WA–20 and WA–215 near Okanogan. Travel west on WA–20 for 9.8 miles. Turn right onto Loup Loup Canyon Road (unpaved two lane) and travel 4.8 miles. Turn left onto Rock Lake Road and travel 5.8 miles. Turn left onto access road and travel 0.3 mile to Rock Lakes.

N48°27'09" – W119°47'18"   Elevation – 3,800 feet

Facilities

8 standard sites
Vault toilet
No water, bring your own
Pack out garbage

Features

Rock Lakes campground lies at the southern edge of the forest lake.

Reservations

None, all campsites are first–come, first–serve.

Season

Open all year, depending on weather

Activities

Fishing, Hiking.

Cost

No cost

Limitations

A Washington State Discover Pass is required.
See Appendix A for camping regulations.

Contact

WA Department of Natural Resources, Northeast Region
Phone: 509–684–7474
Web: *www.dnr.wa.gov*

Rock Lakes Campsite

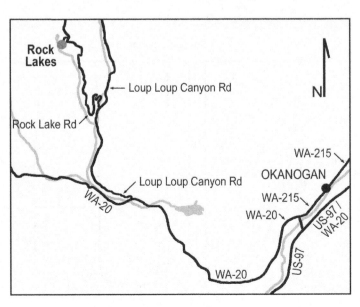

Driving Directions

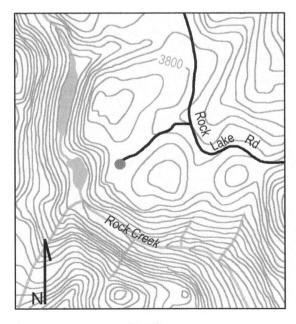

Location

270 Conconully
Washington State Parks

Directions

Start at the intersection of US–97/WA–20 and WA–155 in Omak. Travel north on US–97/WA–20 for 7.6 miles. Turn left onto Riverside Cutoff Road (in Riverside) and travel 5.1 miles. Turn right onto Conconully Road and travel 10 miles. Turn left onto Broadway Street and travel 0.1 mile. Turn left into park.

N48°33'24" – W119°45'03"   Elevation – 2,290 feet

Features

Considered a fisherman's paradise, Conconully State Park is located on Conconully Reservoir and has boat launches on the reservoir and Conconully Lake. The park is nestled between three mountains. Winter temperatures reach below zero. Summer temperatures are in the 80s and 90s. There is an annual average rainfall of 14 inches, with an average of 38.5 inches of snowfall.

Reservations

Sites may be reserved online at *www.parks.state.wa.us* or by telephone 1–888–CAMPOUT (1–888–226–7688). See Appendix B for details.

Season

Open April 1 through October 31

Activities

Bird watching, Boating, Canoeing, Fishing, Hiking, Horseshoes, Mountain biking, Personal watercraft, Sailing, Wading pool, Wind surfing.

Cost

$12 primitive site
Peak season: mid May – mid September
$22 – $35 standard site
$30 – $40 partial utility site
$35 – $45 full utility site
Off–peak season
$20 – $30 standard site
$25 – $35 partial utility site
$30 – $40 full utility site
$10 extra vehicle (all year)
See Appendix C for available discounts.

Facilities

59 total sites: 39 standard, 20 partial utility (W/E)
Flush toilets
Potable water
Hot showers
Garbage service
Boat launch and dock

Limitations

Maximum site length is 76 feet (limited availability)
See Appendix A for camping regulations.

Contact

Phone: 509–826–7408
Web: *www.parks.state.wa.us*

Conconully Campsite

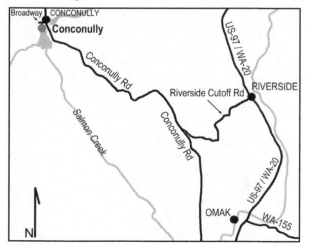

Driving Directions

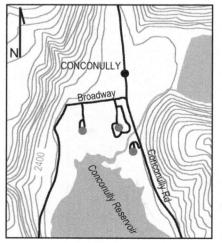

Location

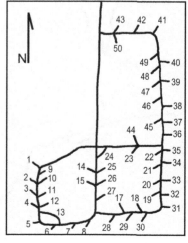

Campground

271 Oriole
Okanogan–Wenatchee National Forest

Directions

Start at the intersection of US–97/WA–20 and WA–155 in Omak. Travel north on US–97/WA–20 for 7.6 miles. Turn left onto Riverside Cutoff Road (in Riverside) and travel 5.1 miles. Turn right onto Conconully Road and travel 13.0 miles. (Conconully Road becomes Main Street in the town of Conconully and then becomes North Fork Salmon Creek Road, Okanogan County Road 2361, and Forest Service Road 38.) Turn left on Forest Service Road 3800–025 and travel for 0.3 mile. After crossing bridge turn left into Oriole.

N48°35'38" – W119°46'16"   Elevation – 2,900 feet

Facilities

10 standard sites
Vault toilet
Potable water
Garbage service

Features

Oriole campground is located along North Fork Salmon Creek.

Reservations

None, all campsites are first–come, first–serve.

Season

The normal camping season is May through October.

Activities

Fishing.

Cost

$8
$5 extra vehicle
See Appendix C for available discounts.

Limitations

See Appendix A for camping regulations.

Oriole Campsite

Contact

Okanogan–Wenatchee National Forest
Tonasket Ranger District
1 West Winesap
Tonasket, WA 98855
Phone: 509–486–2186
TTY: 509–486–5144
Fax: 509–486–1922

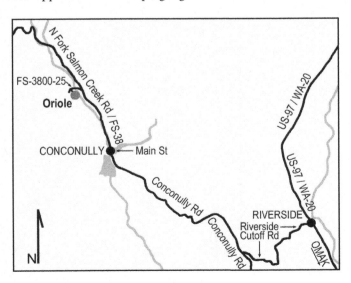

Driving Directions

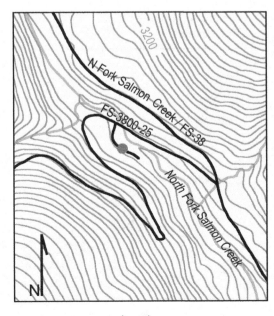

Location

272 Kerr
Okanogan–Wenatchee National Forest

Kerr Campsite

Directions

Start at the intersection of US–97/WA–20 and WA–155 in Omak. Travel north on US–97/WA–20 for 7.6 miles. Turn left onto Riverside Cutoff Road (in Riverside) and travel 5.1 miles. Turn right onto Conconully Road and travel 15.0 miles. (Conconully Road becomes Main Street in the town of Conconully and then becomes North Fork Salmon Creek Road, Okanogan County Road 2361, and Forest Service Road 38.) Turn left into campground.

N48°36'41" – W119°47'19"   Elevation – 3,100 feet

Facilities

13 standard sites
Vault toilet
No water, bring your own
Pack out garbage

Features

Kerr campground lies along the North Fork Salmon Creek. The campground tends to be best for tents or smaller recreational vehicles. Garbage service is located in Oriole campground to the south.

Reservations

None, all campsites are first–come, first–serve.

Season

Normally May through October

Activities

Fishing.

Cost

$8
$5 extra vehicle
See Appendix C for available discounts.

Limitations

See Appendix A for camping regulations.

Contact

Okanogan–Wenatchee National Forest
Tonasket Ranger District
1 West Winesap
Tonasket, WA 98855
Phone: 509–486–2186
TTY: 509–486–5144
Fax: 509–486–1922

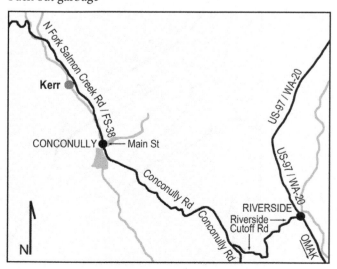

Driving Directions

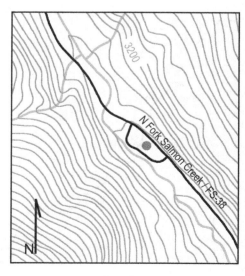

Location

273 Salmon Meadows
Okanogan–Wenatchee National Forest

Directions

Start at the intersection of US–97/WA–20 and WA–155 in Omak. Travel north on US–97/WA–20 for 7.6 miles. Turn left onto Riverside Cutoff Road (in Riverside) and travel 5.1 miles. Turn right onto Conconully Road and travel 15.0 miles. (Conconully Road becomes Main Street in the town of Conconully and then becomes North Fork Salmon Creek Road, Okanogan County Road 2361, and Forest Service Road 38.) Turn right into campground.

N48°39'31" – W119°50'30"   Elevation – 4,500 feet

Salmon Meadows

Facilities

8 standard sites
Vault toilet
Potable water
Pack out garbage
Shelter

Features

Salmon Meadows campground is located along Mutton Creek and offers a picnic gazebo built by the Civilian Conservation Corps. The name comes from the lovely meadow adjacent to the campground.

Reservations

None, all campsites are first–come, first–serve.

Season

Open May through October, weather permitting

Activities

Bird watching, Equestrian trail riding, Hiking, Wildlife viewing.

Cost

$8
$5 extra vehicle
See Appendix C for available discounts.

Limitations

Campsites best accommodate tents or smaller recreational vehicles.
See Appendix A for camping regulations.

Contact

Okanogan–Wenatchee National Forest
Tonasket Ranger District
1 West Winesap
Tonasket, WA 98855
Phone: 509–486–2186
TTY: 509–486–5144
Fax: 509–486–1922

Salmon Meadows Shelter and Livestock Pen

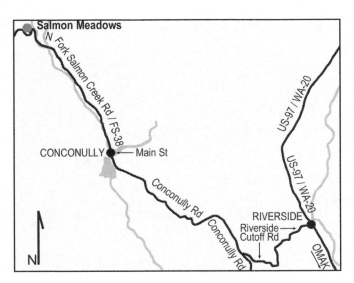

Driving Directions

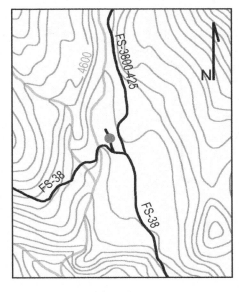

Location

274 Eastside Park
City of Omak

Directions

Start at the intersection of US–97 and WA–155 in Omak. Travel northwest on WA–155 (also called Omak Ave) for 0.3 mile. Turn right onto Columbia St and travel for 0.3 mile to Eastside Park.

N48°24'43" – W119°31'01"   Elevation – 840 feet

Facilities

68 full utility sites (W/E/S)
Some pull–through sites
Flush toilets
Potable water
Hot showers
Garbage service
Shelter

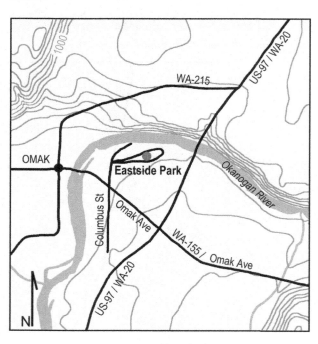

Driving Directions and Location

Features

Eastside Park, with its 76.6 acres, encompasses the shady Carl Precht Memorial RV Park and is located in East Omak – directly across the Okanogan River from the central business district. In addition to the RV campground, the park houses the Stampede Arena, a municipal pool, a variety of playground equipment, Veterans Memorial Garden, a Tourist Information Center, and a walking trail. Eastside Park also serves as the home of the Stampede Association which operates the annual rodeo and famous Suicide Race.

Reservations

None, all campsites are first–come, first–serve.

Season

Open all year – water and sewer are not available in winter.

Activities

Ball fields (baseball, soccer), Basketball courts, Swimming pool, Tennis courts, Dog park, and enclosed Skate park.

Cost

$25 full utility site
Winter rate: $20 partial utility (E)
$15 tent site
See Appendix C for available discounts.

Limitations

Maximum site length is 60 feet.
See Appendix A for camping regulations.

Contact

Omak City Parks
2 North Ash Street
Omak, WA 98841
Phone: 509–826–1170
Email: *kristim@omakcity.com*
Web: *www.omakcity.com/parks.html*

Eastside Park Campsites

275 Toats Coulee
Department of Natural Resources

Directions

Start at the intersection of US–97 and WA–20 in Tonasket. Travel northeast on US–97 (Whitcomb Avenue) for 0.1 mile. Turn left onto 4th Street and travel 0.3 mile. Turn right onto WA–7 and travel 5.2 miles. Continue straight onto Loomis–Oroville Road and travel 11.5 miles. Turn right to continue on Loomis–Oroville Road and travel 2.1 miles. Turn left onto Toats Coulee Road and travel 5.5 miles to the lower campground and 0.1 mile further to the upper campground.

N48°50'39" – W119°43'33"   Elevation – 1,240 feet

Facilities

9 standard sites
Vault toilet
No water, bring your own
Pack out garbage
Accessible toilet, campsite

Features

Toats Coulee campground is located along a forest stream.

Toats Coulee Campsite

Reservations

None, all campsites are first–come, first–serve.

Season

Open all year, depending on weather

Activities

Hiking.

Cost

No cost

Limitations

A Washington State Discover Pass is required.
Refer to Appendix A for camping regulations.

Contact

WA Department of Natural Resources, Northeast Region
Phone: 509–684–7474
Web: www.dnr.wa.gov

Toats Creek

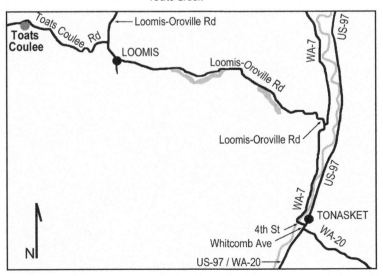

Driving Directions

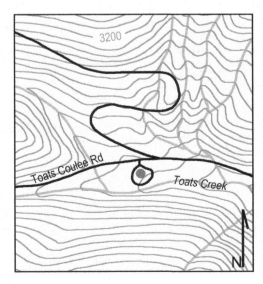

Location

276 Chopaka Lake
Department of Natural Resources

Directions

Start at the intersection of US–97 and WA–20 in Tonasket. Travel northeast on US–97 (Whitcomb Avenue) for 0.1 mile. Turn left onto 4th Street and travel 0.3 mile. Turn right onto WA–7 and travel 5.2 miles. Continue straight onto Loomis–Oroville Road and travel 11.5 miles. In the town of Loomis, turn right to continue on Loomis–Oroville Road and travel 2.1 miles. Turn left onto Touts Coulee Road and travel 1.4 miles. Turn right onto a one–lane road (no name and quite a steep climb) and travel 3.4 miles. Bear left and travel 1.7 miles. Turn right and travel 2.0 miles to Chopaka Lake campground.

N48°54'49" – W119°42'08"   Elevation – 2,900 feet

Facilities

16 standard sites
Vault toilet
Potable water
Pack out garbage
Shelter
Accessible toilet, campsite

Features

Chopaka Lake campground lies along Chopaka Lake. The entry road is a long, steep grade. Watch for cattle on the road. The area has a covered kitchen shelter for picnickers.

Reservations

None, all campsites are first–come, first–serve.

Season

Open all year, dependent on weather

Activities

Boating, Fishing.

Cost

No cost

Limitations

A Washington State Discover Pass is required.
See Appendix A for camping regulations.

Contact

WA Department of Natural Resources, Northeast Region
Phone: 509–684–7474
Web: *www.dnr.wa.gov*

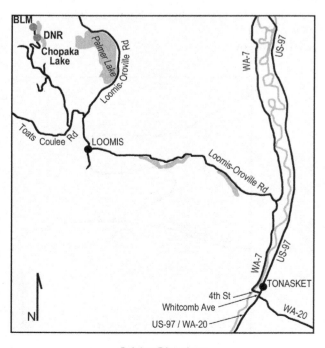

Driving Directions

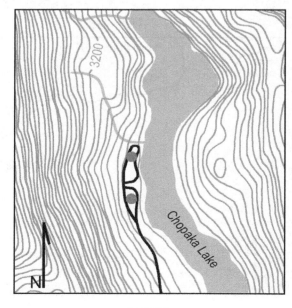

Location

277 Chopaka Lake
Bureau of Land Management

Directions

Start at the intersection of US–97 and WA–20 in Tonasket. Travel northeast on US–97 (Whitcomb Avenue) for 0.1 mile. Turn left onto 4th Street and travel 0.3 mile. Turn right onto WA–7 and travel 5.2 miles. Continue straight onto Loomis–Oroville Road and travel 11.5 miles. In the town of Loomis, turn right to continue on Loomis–Oroville Road and travel 2.1 miles. Turn left onto Touts Coulee Road and travel 1.4 miles. Turn right onto a one–lane road (no name and a steep grade up the mountain) and travel 3.4 miles. Bear left and travel 1.7 miles. Turn right and travel 2.0 miles to Chopaka Lake campground.

N48°54'58" – W118°42'09"   Elevation – 2,900 feet

Facilities

8 standard sites
Vault toilet
Bring your own water
Pack out garbage
Boat launch
Accessible toilet, campsite

Features

Chopaka Lake campground offers solitude and access to the nearby Chopaka Mountain Wilderness Study Area. Aspen groves and sagebrush line the shores for a scenic backdrop to lakeside activities. The BLM camping area is north of the Washington State Department of Natural Resources campground.

Reservations

None, all campsites are first–come, first–serve.

Season

Open all year. Road access is limited during winter months. Drive in access is approximately April 15 to November 15.

Activities

Boating, Fishing, Hiking, Hunting.

Cost

No cost

Limitations

Motor boats are prohibited.
Stay limit is 14 days.
See Appendix A for camping regulations.

Contact

Contact the office for directions, road conditions, accessible facilities, RV size limit, and recreation opportunities.
Bureau of Land Management
Spokane District Office
1102 N Francher, Spokane WA 99212
Phone: 509–536–1200
Web: *www.blm.gov/or*

View from Entry Road

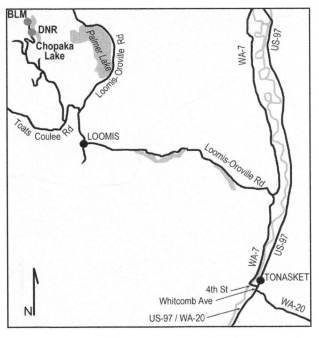

Driving Directions

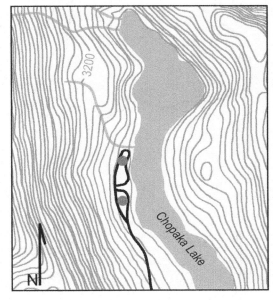

Location

278 Palmer Lake
Department of Natural Resources

Directions

Start at the intersection of US–97 and WA–20 in Tonasket. Travel northeast on US–97 (also called Whitcomb Avenue) for 0.1 mile. Turn left onto 4th Street and travel 0.3 mile. Turn right onto WA–7 and travel 5.2 miles. Continue straight onto Loomis–Oroville Road and travel for 11.5 miles. In Loomis, turn right to continue on Loomis–Oroville Road and travel for 8.3 miles to Palmer Lake. Turn left into campground.

N48°54'57" – W119°38'02"   Elevation – 1,200 feet

Features

Palmer Lake campground is located along the north shore of Palmer Lake. All sites are accessible. The lake is a scenic area for photography.

Reservations

None, all campsites are first–come, first–serve.

Season

Open all year

Facilities

7 standard sites
Vault toilet
No water, bring your own
Pack out garbage
Boat launch (hand launch only)
Accessible toilet, campsite

Activities

Boating, Fishing, Hiking.

Cost

No cost

Limitations

Maximum stay is 7 days in a 30–day period.
A Washington State Discover Pass is required.
Refer to Appendix A for camping regulations.

Contact

WA Department of Natural Resources, Northeast Region
Phone: 509–684–7474
Web: *www.dnr.wa.gov*

Palmer Lake Campsites

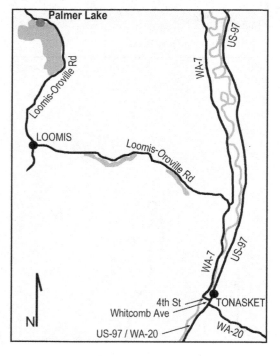

Driving Directions

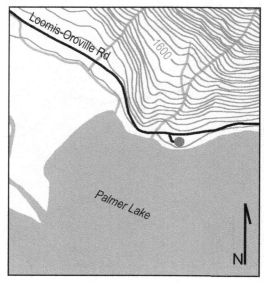

Location

279 Osoyoos Lake
City of Oroville

Directions

Start at intersection of US–97 and Chesaw Rd in downtown Oroville. Travel north on US–97 for 0.6 mile. Turn right into park.

N48°56'59" – W119°25'01"   Elevation – 930 feet

Facilities

86 total sites: 19 partial utility (W/E), 61 standard, 6 walk–in
Flush toilets
Potable water
Hot showers
Garbage service
RV dump
Boat launch
Accessible toilet, water, campsites

Features

Osooyos Lake Veterans Memorial Park lies along Osooyos Lake. The lake is 14 miles long and stretches into British Columbia, Canada. Cradled in the Okanogan River Valley, visitors enjoy a beautiful setting of green pastures and valley floor contrasted with rugged cliffs and glacial features. The park provides welcome respite from the hot and arid environment with its sandy shores, green lawns and shade trees. The park features a veteran's memorial.

Reservations

Reservation may be made 9 months in advance for all sites at: *orovillepark.goingtocamp.com*. There is a 2–night minimum stay on holiday weekends. See Appendix B for reservation details.

Season

Open March 1 through October 31

Activities

Bird watching, Boating, Fishing, Hiking, Horseshoe pit, Swimming, Volleyball.

Cost

$26 standard site
$33 partial utility site
$16 walk–in site
$10 Extra vehicle
Off–season:
$17 standard site
$10 walk–in site
See Appendix C for available discounts.

Limitations

See Appendix A for camping regulations.

Contact

City of Oroville
2207 Juniper
Oroville, Washington 98844
Phone: 509–476–3321
Web: *oroville-wa.com*

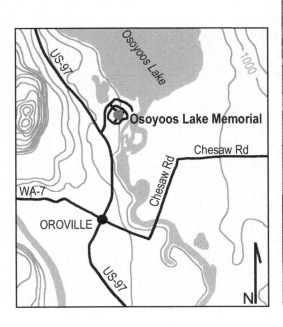

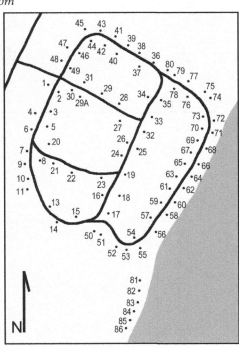

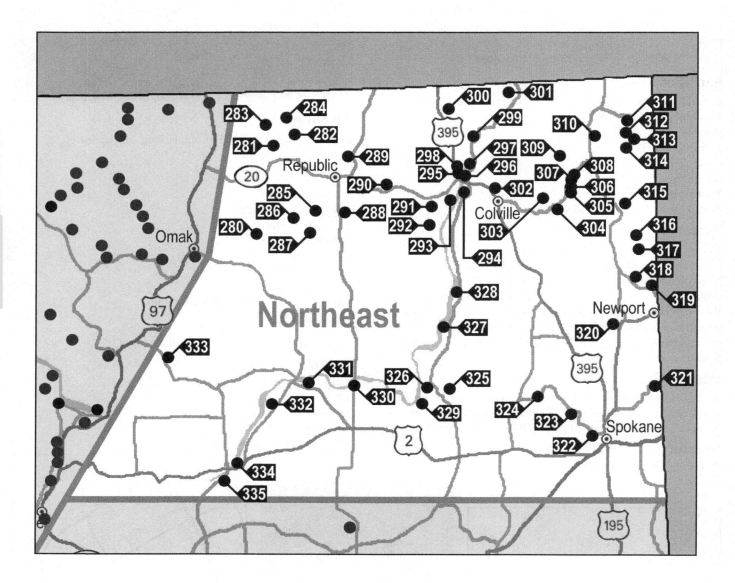

Chapter 5　Northeast Region

280　Crawfish Lake
Okanogan–Wenatchee National Forest

Directions

Start at the intersection of US–97/WA–20 and North Main Street in Riverside. Travel east on North Main Street for 0.8 mile. Turn left onto Tunk Valley Road crossing the Okanogan River. Turn left onto Tunk Creek Road (Okanogan County Road 9320) and travel east for 18 miles (this road changes from paved to gravel road). Okanogan County Road 9320 becomes Forest Service Road 30. Continue for 2.0 miles and turn right onto Forest Service Road 3000–1000 for 0.5 mile into campground.

N48°29'02" – W119°12'49"　Elevation – 4500 feet

Parade of Ducks

Facilities

19 standard sites
Vault toilets
No water, bring your own
Pack out garbage
Boat launch

Features

Crawfish Lake Campground is located on the northern end of Crawfish Lake. Eleven campsites border the lakeshore.

Reservations

None, all campsites are first–come, first–serve.

Season

Open May through October

Limitations

Campground is most suitable for tents or smaller recreational vehicles.
See Appendix A for camping regulations.

Contact

Okanogan–Wenatchee National Forest
Tonasket Ranger District
1 West Winesap
Tonasket, WA 98855
Phone: 509–486–2186
TTY: 509–486–5144
Fax: 509–486–1922

Activities

Boating, Fishing.

Cost

No Cost

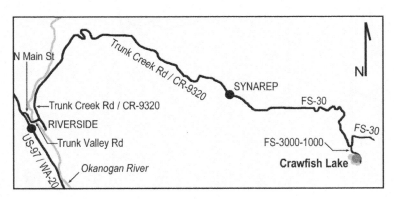

Driving Directions

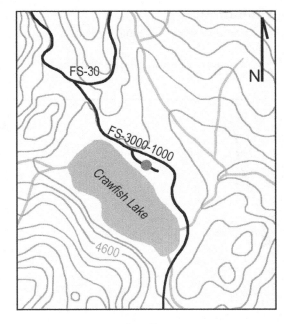

Location

281 Bonaparte Lake
Okanogan–Wenatchee National Forest

Directions

Start at the intersection of US–97 and WA–20 in Tonasket. Travel east on WA–20 for 20.3 miles to Bonaparte Recreation Area. Turn left onto Bonaparte Lake Road (Okanogan County Road 4953) and travel for 5.8 miles. Turn left into campground.

N48°47'33" – W119°03'28"   Elevation – 3600 feet

Contact

Okanogan–Wenatchee National Forest
Tonasket Ranger District
1 West Winesap
Tonasket, WA 98855
Phone: 509–486–2186
TTY: 509–486–5144
Fax: 509–486–1922

Facilities

24 standard sites,
3 walk–in sites
Flush and vault toilets
Potable water
Garbage service
Boat launch
Accessible toilet, water, fishing platform

Features

Bonaparte Lake campground lies along Bonaparte Lake with several lakeside sites. Some 30 foot sites were observed.

Reservations

None, all campsites are first–come, first–serve.

Season

Open May through October

Activities

Boating, Fishing, Hiking, Swimming.

Cost

$12
$5 extra vehicle
See Appendix C for available discounts.

Limitations

Campground is most suitable for tents or smaller recreational vehicles.
See Appendix A for camping regulations.

Bonaparte Lake Boat Launch and Fishing Platform

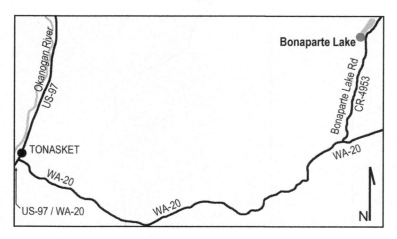

Driving Directions

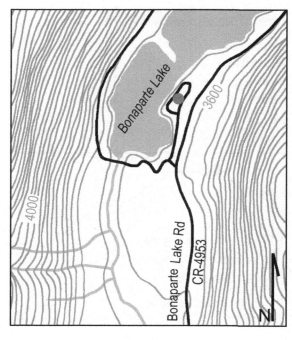

Location

282 Beaver Lake
Okanogan–Wenatchee National Forest

Directions

Start at the intersection of US–97 and WA–20 in Tonasket. Travel east on WA–20 for 20.3 miles to the Bonaparte Recreation Area. Turn left onto Bonaparte Lake Road (Okanogan County Road 4953) and travel for 8.5 miles. Bear right at "Y" onto Forest Service Road 32 for 3.2 miles. Turn left into campground.

N48°50'59" – W118°58'06"   Elevation – 2700 feet

Beaver Lake Campsite

Facilities

11 standard sites
Vault toilet
No water, bring your own
Garbage service
Boat launch

Features

Beaver Lake campground is located along the southern end of Beaver Lake. Access to the lakeshore is via a short trail near the day use area, which continues for 1.9 miles to Beth Lake.

Reservations

None, all campsites are first–come, first–serve.

Season

Open May through October

Activities

Boating, Fishing, Hiking (Beth Lake Trail).

Cost

$8
$5 extra vehicle
See Appendix C for available discounts.

Limitations

Campground is most suitable for tents or small trailers. Small boats can access the lake from a gravel boat launch. See Appendix A for camping regulations.

Contact

Okanogan–Wenatchee National Forest
Tonasket Ranger District
1 West Winesap
Tonasket, WA 98855
Phone: 509–486–2186
TTY: 509–486–5144
Fax: 509–486–1922

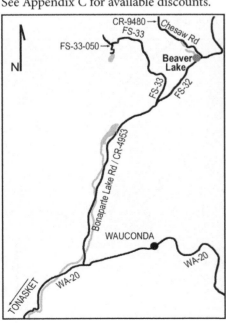

Driving Directions

Rope Swing

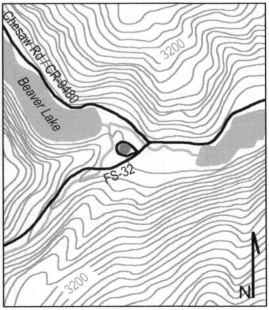

Location

283 Lost Lake
Okanogan–Wenatchee National Forest

Directions

Start at the intersection of US–97 and WA–20 in Tonasket. Travel east on WA–20 for 20.3 miles to the Bonaparte Recreation Area. Turn left onto Bonaparte Lake Road (Okanogan County road 4953 which becomes Forest Service Road 32) and travel for 8.5 miles. Bear left at "Y" onto Forest Service Road 33 for 5.3 miles. Turn left at the four corner junction onto Forest Service Road 33–50 for 0.5 mile. Turn right to campground. (Paved road to campground.)

N48°51'11" – W119°03'03"   Elevation – 3800 feet

Facilities

18 standard sites
Vault and Flush toilets
Potable water
Garbage service
Boat launch

Features

Lost Lake Campground is located on the northern end of Lost Lake. The campground offers hiking in the Big Tree Botanical Area, on the Strawberry Mountain Trail, and on Lost Lake Trail. An amphitheater is near the group campsite.

Reservations

None, all campsites are first–come, first–serve.

Season

Open May through October

Activities

Biking, Bird watching, Boating, Fishing, Hiking, Hunting, Swimming.

Cost

$12
$5 extra vehicle
See Appendix C for available discounts.

Limitations

Check Washington State Fishing Regulations.
See Appendix A for camping regulations.

Contact

Okanogan–Wenatchee National Forest
Tonasket Ranger District
1 West Winesap
Tonasket, WA 98855

Phone: 509–486–2186
TTY: 509–486–5144
Fax: 509–486–1922

Lost Lake Campsite

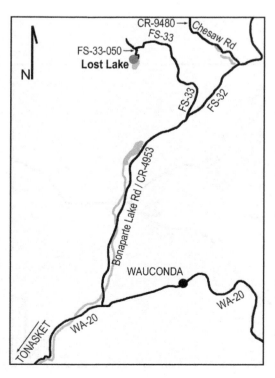

Driving Directions

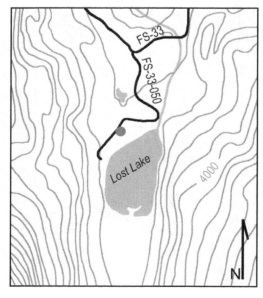

Location

284 Beth Lake
Okanogan–Wenatchee National Forest

Directions

Start at the intersection of US–97 and WA–20 in Tonasket. Travel east on WA–20 for 20.3 miles to the Bonaparte Recreation Area. Turn left onto Bonaparte Lake Road (Okanogan County Road 4953) and travel for 8.5 miles. Bear right at "Y" onto Forest Service Road 32 for 3.3 miles. Turn left onto Chesaw Road (Okanogan County Road 9480) for 1.1 miles. Turn left into campground.

N48°51'36" – W118°59'09"   Elevation – 2800 feet

Facilities

15 standard sites
Vault toilets
Potable water
Garbage service
Boat launch

Features

Beth Lake Campground lies between Beth Lake and Beaver Lake. Boat launches are on either end of the campground. The southern launch accesses Beaver Lake and the northern launch accesses Beth Lake. An earthen dam is near the northern boat launch and Beth Lake Trail.

Reservations

None, all campsites are first–come, first–serve.

Season

Open May through October

Beth Lake

Activities

Boating, Fishing, Hiking.

Cost

$8
$5 extra vehicle
See Appendix C for available discounts.

Limitations

Campground is most suitable for tents or smaller recreational vehicles.
See Appendix A for camping regulations.

Contact

Okanogan–Wenatchee National Forest
Tonasket Ranger District
1 West Winesap
Tonasket, WA 98855
Phone: 509–486–2186
TTY: 509–486–5144
Fax: 509–486–1922

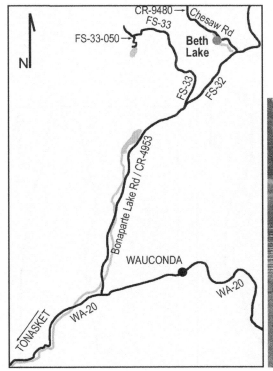

Driving Directions

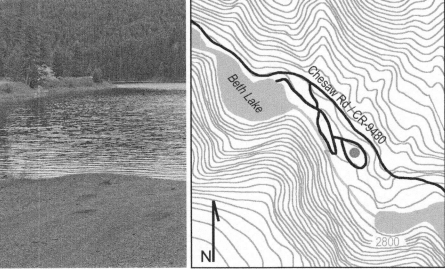

Boat Launch

Location

285 Ferry Lake
Colville National Forest

Directions

Start at the intersection of WA–20 and WA–21 south of Republic. Travel south on WA–21 for 6.7 miles. Turn right onto Scatter Creek Road (Forest Service Road 53) and travel 5.9 miles. Turn right onto Forest Service Road 5330 and travel 0.3 mile. Turn right onto Forest Service Road 100 and travel 0.9 mile. Turn left to Ferry Lake.

N48°31'23" – W118°48'38"   Elevation – 3,400 feet

Facilities

9 standard sites
Vault toilet
No water, bring your own
Garbage service (bear–proof cans)
Boat ramp

Features

Ferry Lake campground lies along Ferry Lake, which is located in forested mountains. Most campsites are shady, private, and near the lake.

Reservations

None, all campsites are first–come, first–serve.

Season

Open late May through early September, depending on weather

Activities

Boating, Fishing.

Ferry Lake

Cost

$6
See Appendix C for available discounts.

Limitations

Combustion engines are not allowed on Ferry Lake.
See Appendix A for camping regulations.

Contact

Colville National Forest
Republic Ranger District
765 South Main Street
Colville, WA 99114
Phone: 509–775–7400
Web: *http://www.fs.fed.us/r6/colville/*

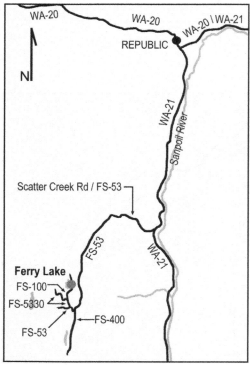

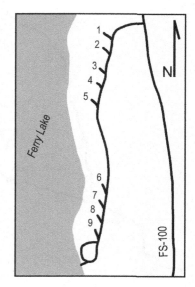

Driving Directions   *Location*   *Campground*

286 Swan Lake
Colville National Forest

Directions

Start at the intersection of WA–20 and WA–21 south of Republic. Travel south on WA–21 for 6.7 miles. Turn right onto Scatter Creek Road (Forest Service Road 53) and travel 7.2 miles to Swan Lake.

   N48°30'47" – W118°50'06"   Elevation – 3,680 feet

Facilities

32 total sites: 28 standard sites, 4 walk–in sites
Vault toilets
Potable water
Garbage service (bear–proof cans)
Shelter
Boat launch
Swim dock
Accessible toilet

Features

Swan Lake campground lies along Swan Lake in a mountain setting. The lake is very popular and, because the campground is heavily used, the former pull–through sites were divided to increase the number of campsites. Some of the standard campsites and all the walk–in sites are lakeside, although most of the sites have a lake view. There is a swimming area with a dock and access to trails. The road to the campground is paved.

Reservations

None, all campsites are first–come, first–serve.

Season

Open late May through early September, depending on weather

Activities

Boating, Fishing, Hiking, Swimming.

Cost

$10
$2 extra vehicle
See Appendix C for available discounts.

Limitations

See Appendix A for camping regulations.

Contact

Colville National Forest
Republic Ranger District
765 South Main Street
Colville, WA 99114
Phone: 509–775–7400
Web: *http://www.fs.fed.us/r6/colville/*

Swan Lake Boat Launch

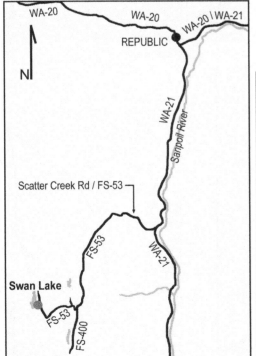

Driving Directions

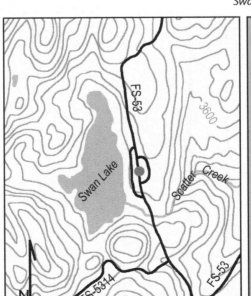

Location

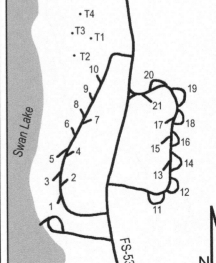

Campground

287 Long Lake
Colville National Forest

Directions

Start at the intersection of WA–20 and WA–21 south of Republic. Travel south on WA–21 for 6.7 miles. Turn right onto Scatter Creek Road (Forest Service Road 53) and travel 5.7 miles. Turn left onto Forest Service Road 400 and travel for 0.7 mile. Turn right into Long Lake.

N48°30'02" – W118°48'36"   Elevation – 3,280 feet

Facilities

12 standard sites
Vault toilets
Potable water
Garbage service
Boat ramp
Accessible toilet

Features

Long Lake campground lies along the northeast side of Long Lake in a setting of small lakes and forested mountains. The large, shaded campsites can accommodate large vehicles and most are along the lake. Visitors can hike on Long Lake trail.

Reservations

None, all campsites are first–come, first–serve.

Season

Open late May through early September, depending on weather

Activities

Boating, Fishing, Hiking.

Cost

$8
$2 extra vehicle
See Appendix C for available discounts.

Limitations

Long Lake is a fly–fishing only lake and no combustion boat engines are allowed.
See Appendix A for camping regulations.

Contact

Colville National Forest
Republic Ranger District
765 South Main Street
Colville, WA 99114
Phone: 509–775–7400
Web: *http://www.fs.fed.us/r6/colville/*

Long Lake Campsite

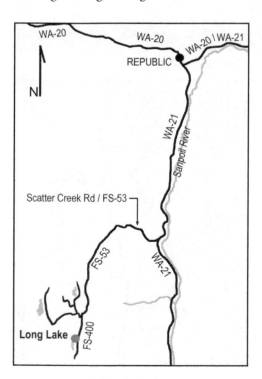

Driving Directions

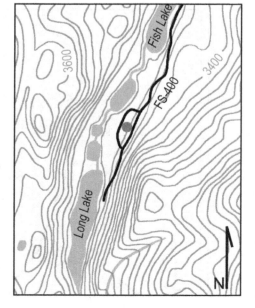

Location

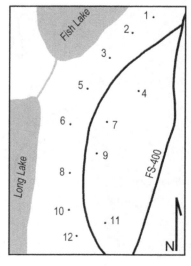

Campground

288 Ten Mile
Colville National Forest

Directions

Start at the intersection of WA–20 and WA–21 south of Republic. Travel south on WA–21 for 9.1 miles. Ten Mile campground is on both sides of the road.

N48°31'02" – W118°44'16"   Elevation – 2,133 feet

Facilities

9 standard sites
Vault toilet
No water, bring your own
Garbage service
Accessible toilet

Features

Lying at the confluence of Tenmile Creek and the San Poil River, Ten Mile campground has two loops, one on each side of the highway. The east loop and day–use area are along the San Poil River. The west loop is tucked into a hillside near the creek and the trailhead of Ten Mile Trail.

Reservations

None, all campsites are first–come, first–serve.

Season

Open late May through early September, depending on weather

Activities

Fishing, Hiking.

Cost

$6
$2 extra vehicle
See Appendix C for available discounts.

Limitations

Maximum vehicle length is 21 feet.
See Appendix A for camping regulations.

Contact

Colville National Forest
Republic Ranger District
765 South Main Street
Colville, WA 99114
Phone: 509–775–7400
Web: *http://www.fs.fed.us/r6/colville/*

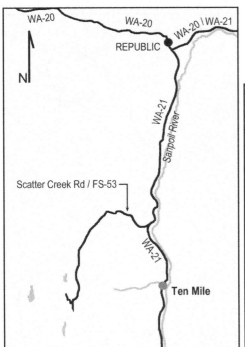

Driving Directions

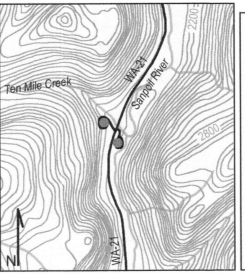

Location

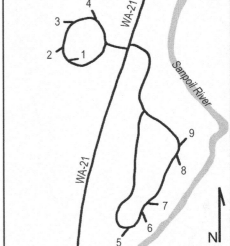

Campground

289 Curlew Lake
Washington State Parks

Directions

Start at the intersection of WA–21 and WA–20 east of Republic. Travel north on WA–21 for 6.0 miles. Turn left onto State Park Road and travel 0.7 mile to the park.

N48°43'16" – W118°39'38"   Elevation ~ 2360 feet

Facilities

84 total sites: 57 standard, 7 partial utility (W/E)
18 full utility (W/E/S), 2 primitive
Some pull–through sites
Flush toilets
Potable water
Hot showers
Garbage service
RV dump
Boat launch and dock (80 feet)
Accessible full utility site, toilet

Features

Curlew Lake Park lies along the eastern edge of Curlew Lake. The south camp area has ten campsites with eight sites overlooking the lake. There is a no–fee mooring dock and a sea plane dock, a restroom, but no showers for these sites. The main campground has 16 sites that overlook the lake. Most of the standard sites are walk–in tent sites. Site 7 is ADA. Sites 20 through 25 are full utility sites. If all sites are full, you may camp in an open area until a site becomes available.

Reservations

Sites may be reserved online at *www.parks.state.wa.us* or by telephone 1–888–CAMPOUT (1–888–226–7688). See Appendix B for details.

Season

Open April 1 – October 31

Activities

Bird watching, Boating, Fishing, Hiking, Personal watercraft, Swimming, Water skiing.

Cost

$12 primitive site
Peak season: mid May – mid September
$22 – $35 standard site
$30 – $40 partial utility site
$35 – $45 full utility site
Off–peak season
$20 – $30 standard site
$25 – $35 partial utility site
$30 – $40 full utility site
$10 extra vehicle (all year)

See Appendix C for available discounts.

Limitations

Maximum site length is 40 feet.
See Appendix A for camping regulations.

Contact

Phone: 509–775–3592
Web: *www.parks.state.wa.us*

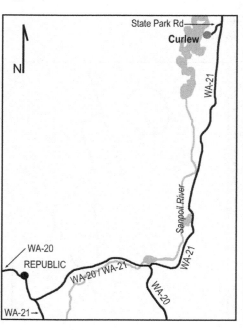

Driving Directions

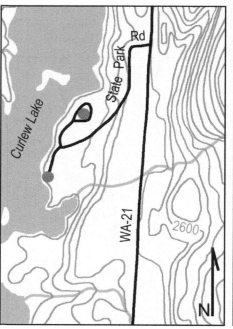

Location

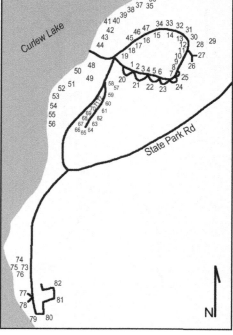

Campground

290 Sherman Pass
Colville National Forest

Directions

Start at the intersection where US–395 and WA–20 diverge west of Kettle Falls. Travel west on WA–20 for 23.9 miles. Turn right into the overlook.

N48°36'22" – W118°27'41"   Elevation – 1,550 feet

Facilities

9 standard sites
Vault toilet
No water, bring your own
Garbage service (bear–proof cans)
Accessible toilet

Features

Sherman Pass Overlook campground has private, wooded campsites. The overlook has commanding views of the surrounding hills and an interpretive forest trail with a scenic overlook. The campground provides access to the Kettle Crest Trailhead.

Reservations

None, all campsites are first–come, first–serve.

Season

Open season depends on weather

Activities

Hiking, Interpretive area.

Cost

$6
See Appendix C for available discounts.

Limitations

See Appendix A for camping regulations.

Contact

Colville National Forest
Three Rivers Ranger District (Kettle Falls)
765 South Main Street
Colville, WA 99114
Phone: 509–738–7700
Web: *http://www.fs.fed.us/r6/colville/*

View From Sherman Pass

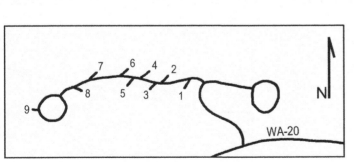

Campground

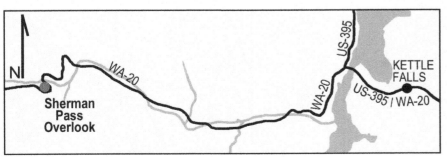

Driving Directions

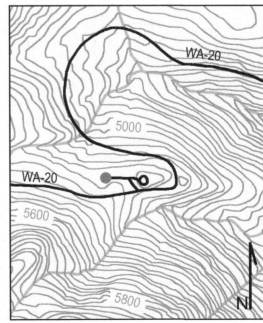

Location

291 Canyon Creek
Colville National Forest

Directions

Start at the intersection where US–395 and WA–20 diverge west of Kettle Falls. Travel west on WA–20 for 7.6 miles. Turn left onto Bangs Mountain Road and travel 0.1 mile. Bear right at "Y" to Canyon Creek.

N48°34'45" – W118°14'24"   Elevation – 2,200 feet

Facilities

12 standard sites
Vault toilets
No water, bring your own
Pack out garbage
Accessible toilet

Features

Canyon Creek campground is a large circular loop in a Lodgepole pine forest. Although the campground is just off Highway 20, there is minimal traffic noise. Campsites are large and private and a few are adjacent to Canyon Creek. The campground offers a 1.0 mile hiking trail along Canyon Creek to the Log Flume Heritage Site and platforms for bank fishing.

Reservations

None, all campsites are first–come, first–serve.

Season

Open season depends on weather

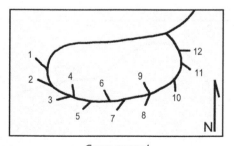

Campground

Activities

Fishing, Hiking.

Cost

$6
See Appendix C for available discounts.

Limitations

See Appendix A for camping regulations.

Contact

Colville National Forest
Three Rivers Ranger District (Kettle Falls)
765 South Main Street
Colville, WA 99114
Phone: 509–738–7700
Web: *http://www.fs.fed.us/r6/colville/*

Canyon Creek

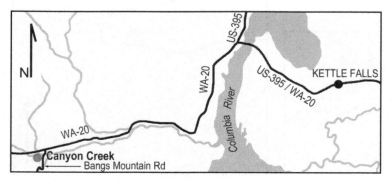

Driving Directions

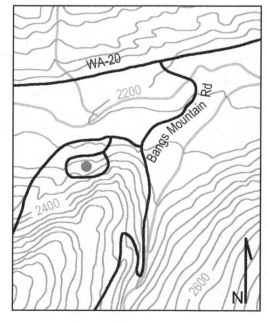

Location

292 Lake Ellen
Colville National Forest

Directions

Start at the intersection where US–395 and WA–20 diverge west of Kettle Falls Bridge. Travel west on WA–20 for 4.1 miles. Turn left onto Inchelium Highway and travel 4.5 miles. Turn right onto Paris Mitchell Road and travel 3.6 miles (no road name sign, but signed to Lake Ellen). Turn right onto Lake Ellen Road and travel 1.6 miles to east Lake Ellen campground. Continue on Lake Ellen Road and travel an additional 0.8 mile followed by a right turn into west Lake Ellen campground and boat launch.

N48°30'05" – W118°15'0"   Elevation – 2,300 feet

Facilities

15 standard sites
Vault toilets
No water, bring your own
Garbage service (bear–proof cans)
Boat launch
Fishing dock
Accessible toilet

Features

Lake Ellen campgrounds are along the east and west ends of Lake Ellen (a 75 acre lake). The popular lake is set among low dry hills covered with sagebrush and timber. It has a primitive boat launch on the west end. Campsites have good separation with a thick underbrush and offer privacy. There are 11 sites in the east campground and 4 sites in the west campground. Access is via a single lane, gravel road. The sites are approximately 30 feet in length.

Reservations

None, all campsites are first–come, first–serve.

Season

Open season depends on weather

Activities

Boating, Fishing, Swimming.

Cost

$6
See Appendix C for available discounts.

Limitations

See Appendix A for camping regulations.

Contact

Colville National Forest
Three Rivers Ranger District (Kettle Falls)
765 South Main Street
Colville, WA 99114
Phone: 509–738–7700
Web: *http://www.fs.fed.us/r6/colville/*

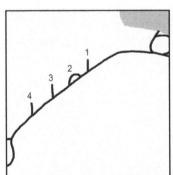

West Campground   East Campground

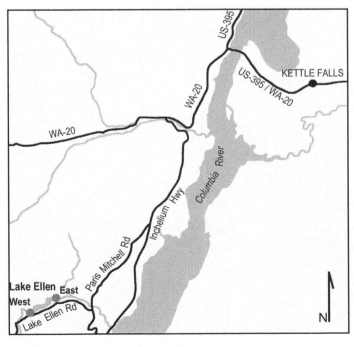

Driving Directions

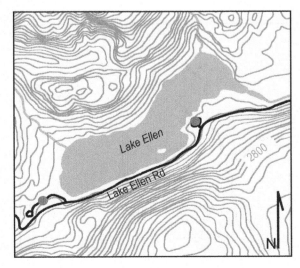

Location

293 Haag Cove
Lake Roosevelt National Recreation Area

Lake Roosevelt at Haag Cove

Directions

Start at the intersection where US–395 and WA–20 diverge west of Kettle Falls Bridge. Travel west on WA–20 for 4.1 miles. Turn left onto Inchelium Highway and travel 2.2 miles. Turn left onto Haag Road and travel 1.0 mile to campground.

N48°33'39" – W118°09'08"   Elevation – 1,320 feet

Facilities

16 standard sites
Vault toilets
Potable water (Seasonal)
Garbage Service
Boat dock

Features

Several of the shady campsites at Haag Cove campground are along Lake Roosevelt. Although there are no hook–ups, campsites will fit most large RVs and offer paved parking pads. When we visited, a frisky peacock was the official greeter.

Reservations

None, all campsites are first–come, first–serve.

Season

Open all year

Activities

Boating, Fishing.

Cost

$18 from May 1 – September 30
$9 from October 1 – April 30
See Appendix C for available discounts.

Limitations

Water may be turned off in the winter during low water levels. Check with the park for water availability.
See Appendix A for camping regulations.

Contact

Lake Roosevelt National Recreation Area
1008 Crest Drive
Coulee Dam, WA 99116
Park Headquarters: 509–633–9441
Kettle Falls Office: 509–738–6266

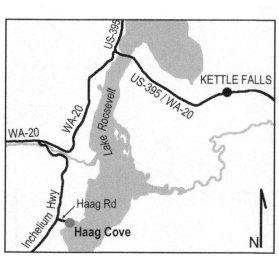

Driving Directions

Haag Cove Greeter

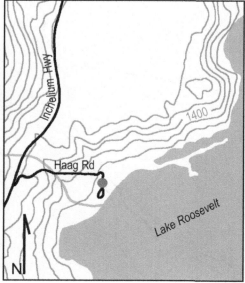

Location

294 Kettle Falls
Lake Roosevelt National Recreation Area

Directions

Start at the intersection of US–395 and WA–25 in Kettle Falls. Travel west on US–395 for 2.3 miles. Turn left onto Boise Road and travel 1.7 miles. Turn right into campground.

N48°36'05" – W118°07'25"   Elevation – 1,320 feet

Facilities

76 standard sites
Some pull–through sites
Flush and vault toilets
Potable water
Garbage service
RV dump
Boat launch and dock
Moorage

Features

Several sites in Kettle Falls campground overlook Lake Roosevelt. Although there are no hook–ups, the sites will fit most large RVs and have paved parking areas. Maximum vehicle lengths for individual sites are given on the reservation system. The boat launch and dock are open all year and can accommodate larger vessels. The campground has an amphitheater and a playground. A rocky decent from the campground to the lake makes swimming a bit of a challenge. The nearby marina offers moorage and fuel.

The original Kettle Falls are under approximately 80 feet of the backwaters of Grand Coulee Dam. The area has extensive Native American history dating back 9,000 years ago. Nearby are St. Paul's Mission and Fort Colville, the Hudson Bay Company post on the Upper Columbia.

Reservations

Sites may be reserved online at *www.recreation.gov* or by phone at 1–877–444–6777. Reserve or change reservations at least 7 days in advance. Reservations can be made up to 6 months in advance. See Appendix B for details.

Season

Open all year. Comfort station opens from mid April to mid October, weather permitting.

Activities

Boating, Fishing, Swimming, Water skiing.

Cost

$18 from May 1 – September 30
$9 from October 1 – April 30
See Appendix C for available discounts.

Limitations

See Appendix A for camping regulations.

Contact

Lake Roosevelt National Recreation Area
1008 Crest Drive
Coulee Dam, WA 99116
Park Headquarters: 509–633–9441
Kettle Falls Office: 509–738–6266

Kettle Falls Marina and Launch

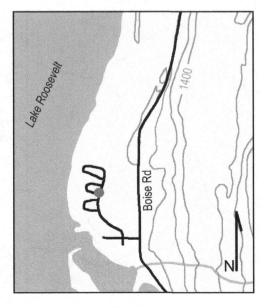

Location

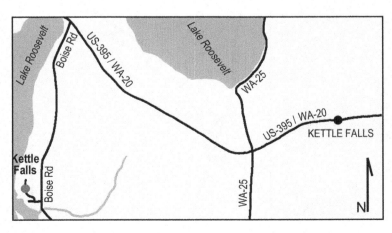

Driving Directions

295 Kamloops
Lake Roosevelt National Recreation Area

Directions

Start at the intersection of US–395 and WA–25 in Kettle Falls.
Travel west on US–395 for 6.2 miles. Turn right onto Northport
Flat Creek Road and travel 0.1 mile. Turn left into campground.

N48°40'44" – W118°07'02"   Elevation – 1,280 feet

Facilities

17 standard sites
Some pull–through sites
Vault toilets
Potable water (Seasonal)
Garbage service
Boat dock

Features

Kamloops campground is on Kamloops Island. Sites are on
a hill overlooking the Kettle River arm. Individual sites offer
paved parking with either pull–through or back–in pads
approximately 30 to 35 feet in length. There are no hook–ups.
A steep trail leads to the boat dock.

Reservations

None, all campsites are first–come, first–serve.

Season

Open all year

Activities

Boating, Fishing.

Cost

$18 from May 1 – September 30
$9 from October 1 – April 30
See Appendix C for available discounts.

Kamloops Campsite

Limitations

Water may be turned off in the winter during low water levels.
Check with the park for water availability.
See Appendix A for camping regulations.

Contact

Lake Roosevelt National Recreation Area
1008 Crest Drive
Coulee Dam, WA 99116
Park Headquarters: 509–633–9441
Kettle Falls Office: 509–738–6266

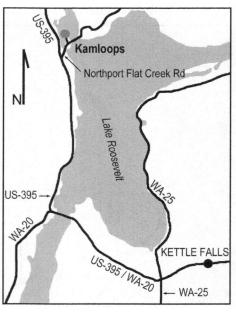

Driving Directions

Water Pump

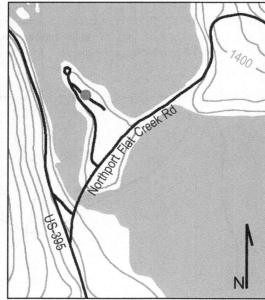

Location

296 Marcus Island
Lake Roosevelt National Recreation Area

Directions

Start at the intersection of WA–25 and US–395 near Kettle Falls. Travel north on WA–25 for 6.6 miles. Turn left onto the campground access road and travel 1.3 miles. (Access road is 1½ lane paved with pullouts.)

N48°40'09" – W118°03'26"   Elevation – 1,320 feet

Facilities

27 standard sites
Some pull–through sites
Vault toilets
Potable water (seasonal)
Garbage service
RV dump
Boat launch and dock

Features

Several sites at Marcus Island campground are along the Columbia River (16 through 25). Although there are no hook–ups, sites are large enough to fit most RVs. The campground is a great spot for kids with bikes and has a small swimming beach.

Reservations

None, all campsites are first–come, first–serve.

Season

Open all year

Activities

Boating, Fishing, Swimming.

Cost

$18 from May 1 – September 30
$9 from October 1 – April 30
See Appendix C for available discounts.

Marcus Island Campsite

Limitations

Water may be turned off in the winter during low water levels. Check with the park for water availability.
See Appendix A for camping regulations.

Contact

Lake Roosevelt National Recreation Area
1008 Crest Drive
Coulee Dam, WA 99116
Park Headquarters: 509–633–9441
Kettle Falls Office: 509–738–6266

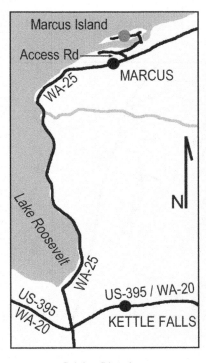

Driving Directions

Boat Launch Unusable When Lake Is Low

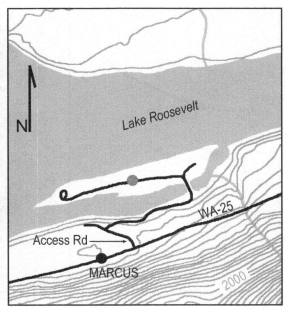

Location

297 Evans
Lake Roosevelt National Recreation Area

Directions

Start at the intersection of WA–25 and US–395 west of Kettle Falls. Travel north on WA–25 for 9.2 miles. Turn left at park entrance and travel 0.4 mile to campground.

N48°41'54" – W118°01'03"   Elevation – 1,280 feet

Facilities

42 standard sites
Vault and Flush toilets
Potable water (seasonal)
Garbage service
RV dump
Boat launch and dock
Accessible campsite

Features

Evans campground offers thick forests of ponderosa pine, Douglas fir and maple trees. There is abundant wildlife in the area, including moose, elk, deer, and bald eagles. The water in Lake Roosevelt originates from melting glaciers and snow in the high Canadian Rockies, although water temperatures are pleasant for swimming during summer. Several of the campsites border the lake. Although there are no hook–ups, the campsites will fit most large RVs and offer paved parking pads. The campground has a playground and Ranger–led activities in the summer season.

Reservations

None, all campsites are first–come, first–serve.

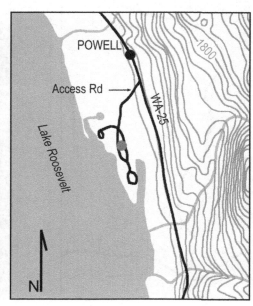

Evans Campsite

Season

Open all year. Comfort station open from mid April to mid October, weather permitting.

Activities

Boating, Fishing, Swimming, Water–skiing, Volleyball.

Cost

$18 from May 1 – September 30
$9 from October 1 – April 30
See Appendix C for available discounts.

Limitations

See Appendix A for camping regulations.

Contact

Lake Roosevelt National Recreation Area
1008 Crest Drive
Coulee Dam, WA 99116
Park Headquarters: 509–633–9441
Fort Spokane District Office: 509–633–9441
Kettle Falls Office: 509–738–6266

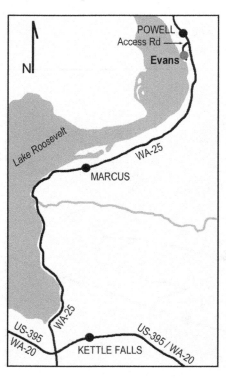

Driving Directions

Evans Campsite

Location

298 Kettle River
Lake Roosevelt National Recreation Area

Directions

Start at the intersection of US–395 and WA–25 in Kettle Falls. Travel west on US–395 for 8.9 miles. Turn right and cross the railroad tracks. Bear left at "Y" and travel 0.7 mile to entrance.

N48°42'55" – W118°07'18"   Elevation – 1,320 feet

Facilities

13 standard sites
Some pull–through sites (9, 10, and 11)
Vault toilets
Potable water (seasonal)
Garbage service
Boat dock

Features

Several sites at Kettle River campground are along Lake Roosevelt (6, 8, 10, 11, and 13). Although there are no hook–ups, campsites will fit most large RVs and offer paved pull–through or back–in parking pads. The nearest boat launch is at Napoleon Bridge, approximately 1 mile north on the Kettle River.

Reservations

None, all campsites are first–come, first–serve.

Season

Open all year

Activities

Boating, Fishing.

Cost

$18 from May 1 – September 30
$9 from October 1 – April 30
See Appendix C for available discounts.

Limitations

Water may be turned off in the winter during low water levels. Check with the park for water availability.
See Appendix A for camping regulations.

Kettle River Campsite

Contact

Lake Roosevelt National Recreation Area
1008 Crest Drive
Coulee Dam, WA 99116
Park Headquarters: 509–633–9441
Kettle Falls Office: 509–738–6266

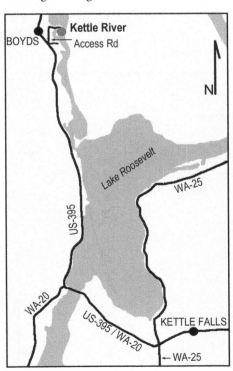

Driving Directions

View from Campground

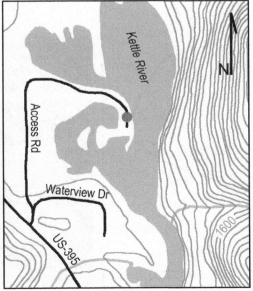

Location

299 North Gorge
Lake Roosevelt National Recreation Area

Directions

Start at the intersection of WA–25 and US–395 near Kettle Falls. Travel north on WA–25 for 16.4 miles. Turn left into campground.

N48°47'11" – W118°00'11"   Elevation – 1,320 feet

North Gorge Boat Launch

Facilities

12 standard sites
Vault toilet

Potable water (Seasonal)
Garbage service
Boat launch and dock

Features

At this lovely little campground, all camp sites overlook Lake Roosevelt. There is great RV access, but good tent camping also. The campground is along the train tracks and the train can be loud.

Reservations

None, all campsites are first–come, first–serve.

Season

Open all year

Activities

Boating, Fishing.

Cost

$18 from May 1 – September 30
$9 from October 1 – April 30
See Appendix C for available discounts.

Limitations

Water may be turned off in the winter during low water levels. Check with the park for water availability.
See Appendix A for camping regulations.

Contact

Lake Roosevelt National Recreation Area
1008 Crest Drive
Coulee Dam, WA 99116
Park Headquarters: 509–633–9441
Kettle Falls Office: 509–738–6266

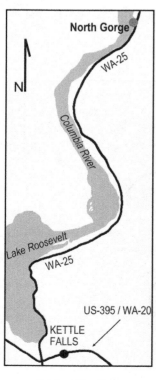

Driving Directions

North Gorge Campsite

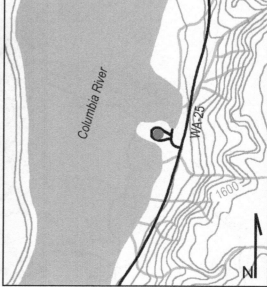

Location

300 Pierre Lake
Colville National Forest

Directions

Start at the intersection where US–395 and WA–20 diverge west of Kettle Falls. Travel west on US–395 for 11.3 miles. Turn right onto Barstow Bridge Road and travel 1.1 miles. Turn left onto Pierre Lake Road and travel 9 miles. Turn right into campground.

  N48°54'15" – W118°08'26"   Elevation – 2,040 feet

Facilities

15 standard sites
Vault toilets
Potable water
Pack out garbage
Boat launch
Fishing dock
Accessible toilet

Features

All of the campsites in Pierre Lake campground are lakeside. There are two sections to the campground. The north section has six sites that can accommodate a vehicle up to 30 feet but the south section has a tight "J" hook turn–around, so most sites can only accommodate pick–up campers or tents.

Reservations

None, all campsites are first–come, first–serve.

Season

Open season depends on weather

Activities

Boating, Fishing, Hiking.

Cost

$6
See Appendix C for available discounts.

Limitations

Maximum length of stay is 14 days.
See Appendix A for camping regulations.

Contact

Colville National Forest
Three Rivers Ranger District (Kettle Falls)
765 South Main Street
Colville, WA 99114
Phone: 509–738–7700
Web: *http://www.fs.fed.us/r6/colville/*

Driving Directions

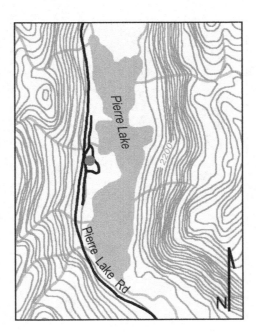

Location

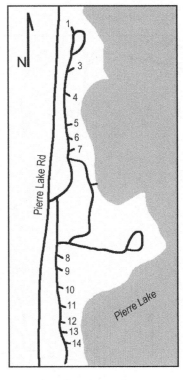

Campground

301 Sheep Creek
Department of Natural Resources

Directions

Start at the intersection of WA–25 and Aladdin Road in Northport. Travel north on WA–25 for 1.0 mile. Turn left onto Big Sheep Creek Road and travel for 4.3 miles (good gravel road). Turn right into campground.

N48°57'38" W117°50'06"   Elevation – 1,960 feet

Facilities

12 standard sites
Vault toilet
Potable water
Pack out garbage
Accessible toilet, campsite
Shelter
Stream viewing platform

Features

Sheep Creek Campground is on both sides of the stream at Sheep Creek and is surrounded by miles of forest. A kitchen shelter is available. In 2009, DNR looked at closing many campgrounds across the state due to serious budget cuts. Realizing that Sheep Creek Campground was one of the many facing closure, the Town of Northport (population 295) adopted it to keep it open for the public. DNR now maintains the campground.

Reservations

None, all campsites are first–come, first–serve.

Season

Open all year

Sheep Creek Scenery

Activities

Fishing, Hiking, Hunting.

Cost

No cost

Limitations

A Washington State Discover Pass is required.
See Appendix A for camping regulations.

Contact

WA Department of Natural Resources, Northeast Region
Phone: 509–684–7474
Web: *www.dnr.wa.gov*

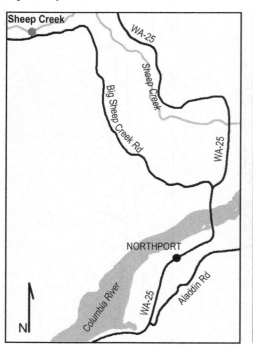

Driving Directions

Sheep Creek

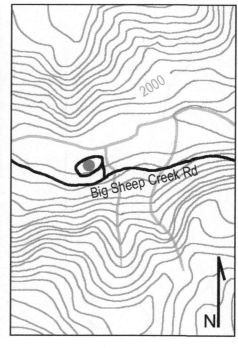

Location

302 Douglas Falls Park
Department of Natural Resources

Directions

Start at the intersection of US–395 and WA–20 in Colville. Travel east on WA–20 for 1.1 mile. Turn left onto Aladdin Road and travel for 2.0 miles. Turn left onto Douglas Falls Road and travel for 3.0 miles. Turn left into park.

N48°36'54" – W117°53'57"   Elevation – 1,800 feet

Facilities

9 standard sites
Vault toilet
Potable water
Shelter
Accessible toilet, water, viewing area

Features

Douglas Falls campground lies along Mill Creek and Douglas Falls. The viewing area for the falls is beside the parking area and easily accessed. Trailer use is not recommended in some areas.

Reservations

None, all campsites are first–come, first–serve.

Season

Unlisted

Activities

Ball fields, Fishing.

Cost

No cost

Limitations

A Washington State Discover Pass is required.
See Appendix A for camping regulations.

Douglas Falls Shelter

Contact

WA Department of Natural Resources, Northeast Region
Phone: 509–684–7474
Web :*www.dnr.wa.gov*

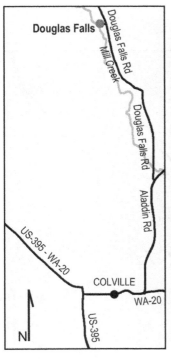

Driving Directions

Douglas Falls

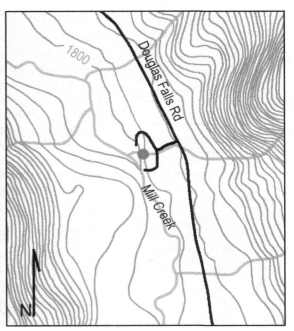

Location

303 Little Twin Lakes
Colville National Forest

Directions

NORTH CAMPGROUND: Start at the intersection of WA–20 and WA–31 south of Ione. Travel west on WA–20 for 23.6 miles. Turn right onto Little Twin Lakes Road (also County Road 4939) and travel 4.9 miles. Turn left to park entrance road (Forest Service Road 150) and travel 1.4 miles to Little Twin Lakes.

Or

Start at the intersection of WA–20 and US–395 in Colville. Travel east on WA–20 for 12.3 miles. Turn left onto Little Twin Lakes Road (also County Road 4939) and travel 4.9 miles. Turn left to park entrance road (Forest Service Road 150) and travel 1.4 miles to campground.

SOUTH CAMPGROUND: Start at the intersection of WA–20 and WA–31 south of Ione. Travel west on WA–20 for 23.6 miles. Turn right onto Little Twin Lakes Road (also County Road 4939) and travel 5.0 miles. Turn left to Little Twin Lakes.

Or

Start at the intersection of WA–20 and US–395 in Colville. Travel east on WA–20 for 12.3 miles. Turn left onto Little Twin Lakes Road (also County Road 4939) and travel 5.0 miles. Turn left to campground.

N48°34'30" – W117°38'44"   Elevation – 3,760 feet

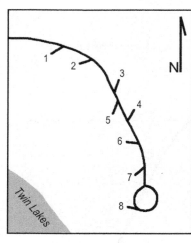

North Campground

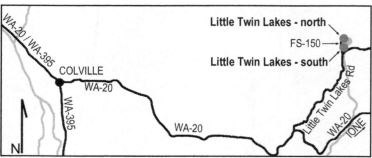

Driving Directions

Facilities

8 standard sites
Vault toilets
No water, bring your own
Pack out garbage
Boat launch
Fishing dock

Features

Little Twin Lakes campground is on both sides of the lake and provides large and private campsites. The 1½ lane road to the north campground entrance reduces to 1 lane. Most of the sites are less than

30 feet. The day–use area is a wildlife viewing area with a beautiful lake view.

Reservations

None, all campsites are first–come, first–serve.

Season

Open season depends on weather

Activities

Boating, Fishing.

Cost

No cost

Limitations

Maximum length of stay is 14 days.
See Appendix A for camping regulations.

Contact

Colville National Forest
Three Rivers Ranger District (Kettle Falls)
765 South Main Street
Colville, WA 99114
Phone: 509–738–7700
Web: *http://www.fs.fed.us/r6/colville/*

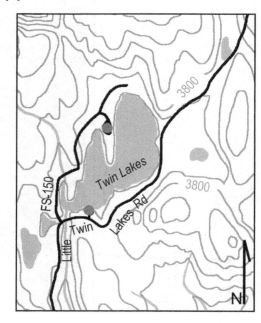

Location

304 Flodelle Creek
Department of Natural Resources

Directions

Start at the intersection of US–395 and WA–20 in Colville. Travel east on WA–20 for 19.4 miles. Turn right onto Tacoma Creek Road (two lane gravel) and travel 0.3 mile. Bear left and travel 0.1 mile to campground.

N48°32'43" – W117°34'17"   Elevation – 3,060 feet

Flodelle Creek Campsite

Facilities

8 standard sites
Vault toilet
Potable water
Pack out garbage
Accessible toilet, campsites

Features

Flodelle Creek campground lies between Pend Oreille River and Flodelle Creek. The creek meanders through some of the campsites. All sites are accessible. The US Forest Service operates a nearby winter snow park.

Reservations

None, all campsites are first–come, first–serve.

Season

Opens seasonally, weather dependent

Activities

Fishing, Hiking, Motorcycle riding/ATVs, Snowmobiling.

Cost

No cost

Limitations

A Washington State Discover Pass is required.
See Appendix A for camping regulations.

Contact

WA Department of Natural Resources, Northeast Region
Phone: 509–684–7474
Web: *www.dnr.wa.gov*

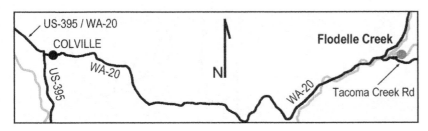

Driving Directions

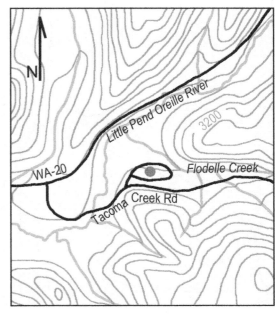

Location

305 Gillette
Colville National Forest

Directions

Start at the intersection of WA–20 and WA–31 south of Ione. Travel west on WA–20 for 11.8 miles. Turn left onto Little Pend Oreille Road and travel 0.6 mile. Turn right to Gillette campground.

Or

Start at the intersection of WA–20 and US–395 in Colville. Travel east on WA–20 for 24.6 miles. Turn right onto Little Pend Oreille Road and travel for 0.6 mile. Turn right to Gillette campground.

N48°36'45" – W117°32'07"   Elevation – 3,200 feet

Facilities

30 standard sites
Flush/Vault toilets
Potable water
Garbage service (bear–proof cans)
RV dump
Shelter
Accessible toilet, campsite

Features

Gillette campground is located within walking distance of Gillette Lake and offers large, open campsites. Look for the unusual shelter with a large tree trunk. The campground has access to Rufus Trail and Springboard Interpretive Trail.

Reservations

None, all campsites are first–come, first–serve.

Season

Open from mid May through early September

Activities

Boating, Fishing, Hiking, Interpretive trail.

Cost

$16
$8 extra vehicle
See Appendix C for available discounts.

Limitations

Maximum length of stay is 14 days.
Weight restriction of 20,000 lb. on Little Pend Oreille Road bridge.
See Appendix A for camping regulations.

Contact

Colville National Forest
Three Rivers Ranger District (Kettle Falls)
765 South Main Street
Colville, WA 99114
Phone: 509–738–7700
Web: *http://www.fs.fed.us/r6/colville/*

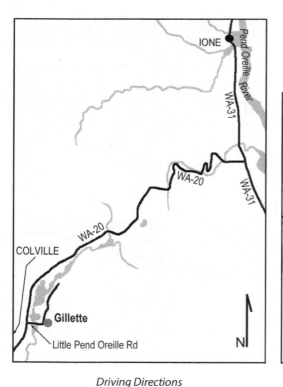

Driving Directions

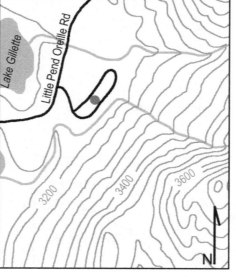

Location

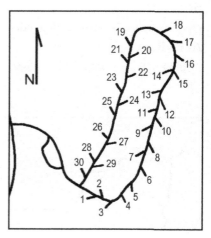

Campground

306 Lake Gillette
Colville National Forest

Directions

Start at the intersection of WA–20 and WA–31 south of Ione. Travel west on WA–20 for 11.8 miles. Turn left onto Little Pend Oreille Road and travel 0.5 mile. Turn left into Lake Gillette.

Or

Start at the intersection of WA–20 and US–395 in Colville. Travel east on WA–20 for 24.6 miles. Turn right onto Little Pend Oreille Road and travel 0.5 mile. Turn left into Lake Gillette.

N48°36'43" – W117°32'26"   Elevation – 3,160 feet

Facilities

14 standard sites
Vault toilets
Potable water
Garbage service
Boat launch and dock
Accessible campsite

Features

Gillette Lake campground, not surprisingly, lies along Gillette Lake – a very popular lake in a setting of low wooded hills. The campground offers spacious campsites with varying degrees of privacy and views of the lake. The lake is connected to three other lakes by water thoroughfares, which are accessible by small boats. The campground has a day–use area and access to Rufus Trail.

Reservations

None, all campsites are first–come, first–serve.

Season

Open from mid May through early September

Activities

Boating, Fishing, Hiking, Swimming, Water Skiing, Amphitheater.

Cost

$16 single site
$32 double site
$8 extra vehicle
See Appendix C for available discounts.

Limitations

Maximum length of stay is 14 days.
Weight restriction of 20,000 lb. on Little Pend Oreille Road bridge.
See Appendix A for camping regulations.

Lake Gillette Campsite

Contact

Colville National Forest
Three Rivers Ranger District
765 South Main Street
Colville, WA 99114
Phone: 509–738–7700
Web: *http://www.fs.fed.us/r6/colville/*

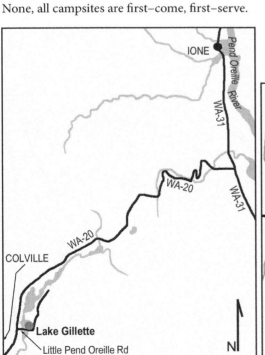

Driving Directions

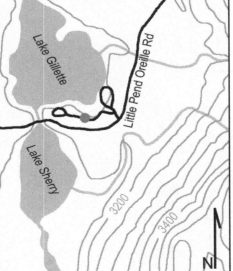

Location

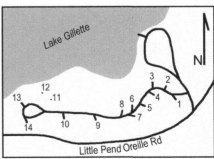

Campground

307 Lake Thomas
Colville National Forest

Directions

Start at the intersection of WA–20 and WA–31 south of Ione. Travel west on WA–20 for 11.8 miles. Turn left onto Little Pend Oreille Road and travel 1.3 miles. Bear left to Lake Thomas.

Or

Start at the intersection of WA–20 and US–395 in Colville. Travel east on WA–20 for 24.6 miles. Turn right onto Little Pend Oreille Road and travel 1.3 miles. Bear left to campground.

N48°37'26" – W117°32'10"   Elevation – 3,160 feet

Facilities

16 total sites: 6 standard sites, 10 walk–in sites
Vault toilets
Potable water
Garbage service (bear–proof cans)

Features

On a small hillside overlooking Lake Thomas, the campground offers private sites with a view of the lake. Most are tent sites and small trailer sites. Access to Rufus Trail is nearby.

Reservations

None, all campsites are first–come, first–serve.

Season

Open from mid May through early September

Activities

Boating, Fishing, Hiking.

Lake Thomas Campsite

Cost

$16
$8 extra vehicle
See Appendix C for available discounts.

Limitations

Maximum length of stay is 14 days.
Weight restriction of 20,000 lb. on Little Pend Oreille Road bridge.
See Appendix A for camping regulations.

Contact

Colville National Forest
Three Rivers Ranger District (Kettle Falls)
765 South Main Street
Colville, WA 99114
Phone: 509–738–7700
Web: *http://www.fs.fed.us/r6/colville/*

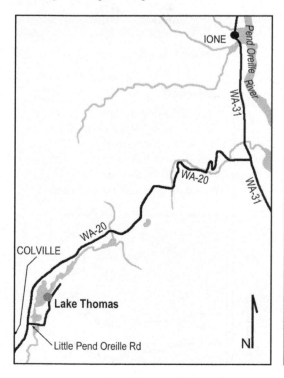

Driving Directions

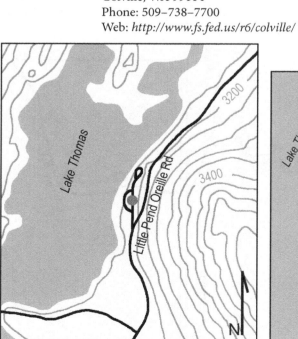

Location

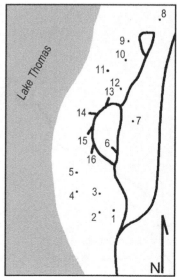

Campground

308 Lake Leo
Colville National Forest

Directions

Start at the intersection of WA–20 and WA–31 south of Ione. Travel west on WA–20 for 7.8 miles. Turn left and travel 0.3 mile to Lake Leo.

Or

Start at the intersection of WA–20 and US–395 in Colville. Travel east on WA–20 for 28.4 miles. Turn right and travel 0.3 mile to Lake Leo.

N48°38'53" – W117°29'59"   Elevation – 3,200 feet

Facilities

8 total sites: 7 standard sites, 1 walk–in site
Vault toilet
Potable water
Garbage service (bear–proof cans)
Boat launch

Features

Located on Lake Leo, the campground lies in a setting of low, wooded hills. Sites 1, 2, 4, 6, and 8 have lake views. The campground has no day–use facilities.

Reservations

None, all campsites are first–come, first–serve.

Season

Open for start of fishing season, weather permitting, in mid May through early September.

Activities

Boating, Cross–country skiing, Fishing, Hiking, Swimming.

Cost

$16
$8 extra vehicle
See Appendix C for available discounts.

Limitations

Most sites can accommodate vehicles up to 30 feet.
Maximum length of stay is 14 days.
See Appendix A for camping regulations.

Lake Leo Campsite

Contact

Colville National Forest
Three Rivers Ranger District
765 South Main Street
Colville, WA 99114
Phone: 509–738–7700
Web: *http://www.fs.fed.us/r6/colville/*

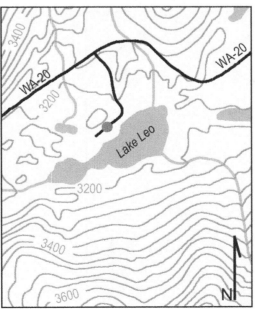

Driving Directions

Location

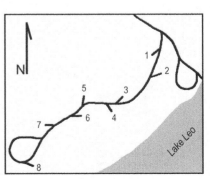

Campground

309 Big Meadow Lake
Colville National Forest

Directions

Start at the intersection of WA–20 and US–395 in Colville. Travel east on WA–20 for 1.1 miles. Turn left onto Aladdin Road and travel 19.6 miles. Turn right onto Meadow Creek Road (County Road 4702 which becomes County Road 2695) and travel 6.1 miles. Turn right at entrance drive and travel 0.2 mile to Big Meadow Lake.

> N48°43'33" – W117°33'47"   Elevation – 3,440 feet

Facilities

16 standard sites
Vault toilets
No water, bring your own
Pack out garbage
Boat launch
Fishing dock
Accessible toilet, campsite

Features

Nestled in a forested mountain setting, Big Meadow Lake campground is on a popular lake for fishing and wildlife viewing. The campground offers either lakeside campsites or private, wooded campsites. Each accommodate RVs and trailers. The 0.5 mile hiking trail through wetlands is accessible. A day–use area has a wildlife viewing area and trail parking. The Hess homestead cabin is nearby and available for anyone to use, first–come, first–serve.

Reservations

None, all campsites are first–come, first–serve.

Season

Open season depends on weather

Big Meadow Lake

Activities

Bird watching, Boating, Fishing, Hiking, Interpretive trail.

Cost

No cost

Limitations

Maximum length of stay is 14 days.
See Appendix A for camping regulations.

Contact

Colville National Forest
Three Rivers Ranger District (Kettle Falls)
765 South Main Street
Colville, WA 99114
Phone: 509–738–7700
Web: *http://www.fs.fed.us/r6/colville/*

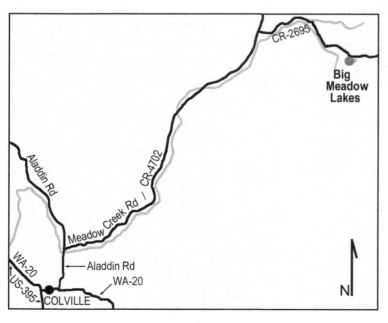

Driving Directions

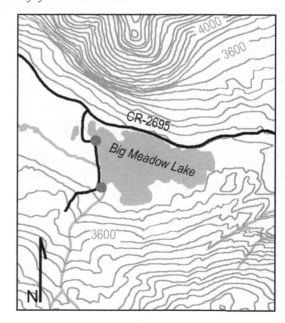

Location

310 Edgewater
Colville National Forest

Directions

Start at the intersection of WA–31 and Sullivan Lake Road in Ione. Travel east on Sullivan Lake Road for 0.4 mile. Turn left onto Box Canyon Road and travel 2.0 miles. Turn left onto Forest Service Road 1130 and travel 0.3 mile to Edgewater.

N48°45'23" – W117°24'31"   Elevation – 2,040 feet

Facilities

19 standard sites, 1 double site
Vault toilets
Potable water
Garbage service
Boat launch
Accessible toilet

Features

Edgewater campground lies along the Pend Oreille River. Most campsites can accommodate large RVs. All sites are private and have a view of the river.

Reservations

Reserve sites at *www.recreation.gov* or by phone at 1–877–444–6777. Reservations must be made 4 days ahead of arrival and can be made up to 6 months in advance. See Appendix B for details.

Season

Open with full services from mid May through early September

Activities

Boating, Fishing.

Cost

$16 single site
$32 double site
$8 extra vehicle
See Appendix C for available discounts.

Limitations

CAUTION: Edgewater campground gates are closed from 10pm to 6am.
See Appendix A for camping regulations.

Contact

Colville National Forest
Sullivan Lake Ranger District
765 South Main Street
Colville, WA 99114
Phone: 509–446–7500
Web: *http://www.fs.fed.us/r6/colville/*

Edgewater Campsite

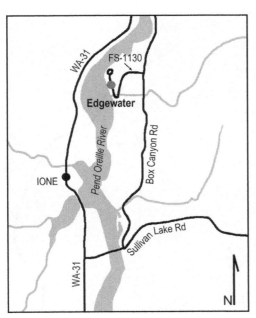

Driving Directions

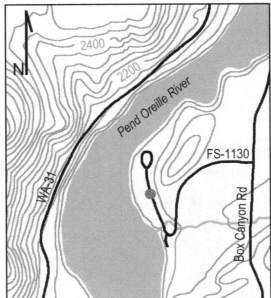

Location

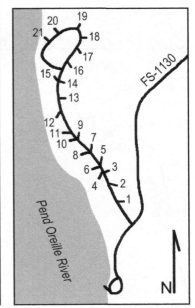

Campground

311 Mill Pond
Colville National Forest

Directions

Start at the intersection of WA–31 and Sullivan Lake Road (County Road 9345) northeast of Metaline Falls. Travel east on Sullivan Lake Road for 3.9 miles. Turn right to Mill Pond.

N48°51'14" – W117°17'30"   Elevation – 2,520 feet

Facilities

10 standard sites
Vault toilet
Potable water
Garbage service (bear–proof cans)
Unimproved small boat access
Accessible toilet

Features

Mill Pond campground is located at the confluence of Sullivan creek and Mill Pond in a forested area. The campsites are private and many are near the water. An accessible interpretive trail and picnic area are located at the Mill Pond Historic site at the west end of Mill Pond. A hiker–only trail circles Mill Pond and ties into the interpretive trail. Elk Creek Falls and Elk Creek trails are nearby.

Reservations

None, all campsites are first–come, first–serve.

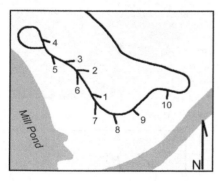

Campground

Activities

Boating, Fishing, Hiking, Interpretive trail.

Cost

$16
$8 extra vehicle
See Appendix C for available discounts.

Limitations

Boat use is restricted to electric motors due to the small size of the lake. Boat size is limited to those which can be carried the 50 feet from the edge of the parking area to the water.
See Appendix A for camping regulations.

Contact

Colville National Forest
Sullivan Lake Ranger District
765 South Main Street
Colville, WA 99114
Phone: 509–446–7500
Web: *http://www.fs.fed.us/r6/colville/*

Season

Open with full services mid May through early September and reduced services from early September through the end of October. Open for start of fishing season, weather permitting.

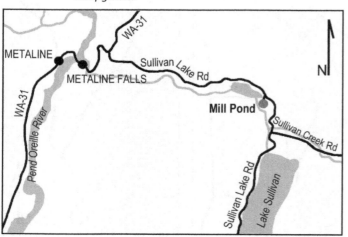

Driving Directions

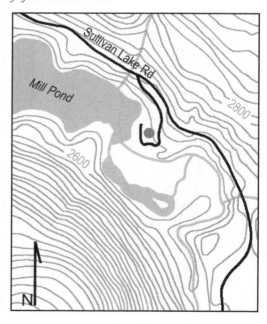

Location

312 West Sullivan
Colville National Forest

Directions

Start at the intersection of WA–31 and Sullivan Lake Road (County Road 9345) northeast of Metaline Falls. Travel east on Sullivan Lake Road for 5.2 miles. Turn left to West Sullivan campground.

N48°50'21" – W117°17'09"   Elevation – 2,600 feet

Facilities

10 standard sites
Vault toilet
Potable water
Garbage service
Shelter
Swimming dock
Accessible toilet

Features

West Sullivan campground is located along the north shore of Sullivan Lake in forested, mountain terrain. Campsites are large, but only suitable for tent camping and shorter trailers and RVs. The densely wooded terrain provides privacy and shade for warm summer days. The 4.2–mile Lakeshore Trail is a designated National Scenic Trail on the east side of Sullivan Lake. The day–use area has a buoyed off area for swimming and a floating swim platform, which is shared with West Sullivan campground. Other attractions include ice fishing and bighorn sheep viewing during the winter. Adjacent to the campground is a small, grass airstrip.

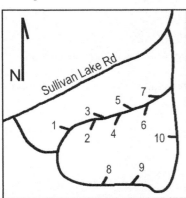

Campground

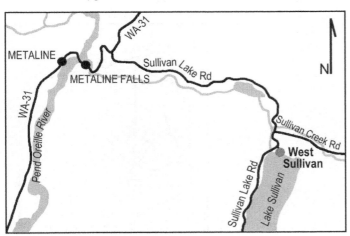

Driving Directions

Reservations

Reserve sites at *www.recreation.gov* or by phone at 1–877–444–6777. Reservations must be made 4 days ahead of arrival and can be made up to 6 months in advance. See Appendix B for details.

Season

Open mid May through mid September

Activities

Boating, Fishing, Hiking, Scuba Diving, Swimming.

Cost

$16
$8 extra vehicle
See Appendix C for available discounts.

Limitations

See Appendix A for camping regulations.
CAUTION: Bears and cougars frequent the area; keep all food in approved containers.

Contact

Colville National Forest
Sullivan Lake Ranger District
765 South Main Street
Colville, WA 99114
Phone: 509–446–7500
Web: *http://www.fs.fed.us/r6/colville/*

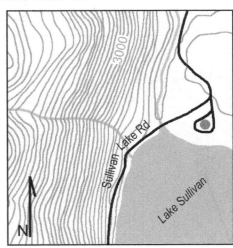

Location

313 East Sullivan
Colville National Forest

Directions

Start at the intersection of WA–31 and Sullivan Lake Road (County Road 9345) northeast of Metaline Falls. Travel east on Sullivan Lake Road for 4.8 miles. Turn left onto Sullivan Creek Road (Forest Service Road 22) and travel 0.4 mile. Turn right into East Sullivan Lake.

N48°50'24" – W117°16'52"   Elevation – 2,600 feet

Facilities

32 standard sites, 6 double sites
Some pull–through sites
Vault toilets
Potable water
Garbage service
RV dump
Boat launch
Accessible toilet, water, campsite

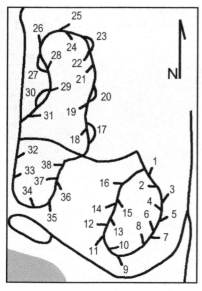

Campground

Features

East Sullivan campground is located along the northern shore of Sullivan Lake in forested, mountain terrain. Campsites can accommodate vehicles up to 55 feet in length and are a short walk to the lake. The densely wooded terrain provides privacy and shade for warm summer days. The 4.2–mile Lakeshore Trail is a designated National Scenic Trail on the east side of Sullivan Lake. The day–use area has a buoyed off area for swimming and a floating swim platform, which is shared with West Sullivan campground. Other attractions include ice fishing and bighorn sheep viewing during the winter. Adjacent to the campground is a small, grass airstrip.

Reservations

Reserve sites at *www.recreation.gov* or by phone at 1–877–444–6777. Reservations must be made 4 days ahead of arrival and can be made up to 6 months in advance. See Appendix B for details.

Season

Open mid May through mid September. The boat launch is open during off–season.

Activities

Boating, Fishing, Hiking, Scuba diving, Swimming, Whitewater paddling.

Cost

$16 single site
$32 double site
$8 extra vehicle
See Appendix C for available discounts.

Limitations

See Appendix A for camping regulations.
CAUTION: East Sullivan campground gates are closed from 10pm to 6am.
CAUTION: Bears and cougars frequent the area; keep all food in approved containers.

Contact

Colville National Forest
Sullivan Lake Ranger District
765 South Main Street
Colville, WA 99114
Phone: 509-446-7500
Web: *http://www.fs.fed.us/r6/colville/*

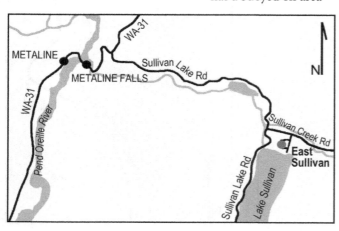

Driving Directions

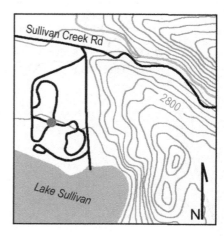

Location

314 Noisy Creek
Colville National Forest

Directions

Start at the intersection of WA–31 and Sullivan Lake Road in Ione. Travel east on Sullivan Lake Road for 8.4 miles. Turn right to Noisy Creek campground.

N48°47'26" – W117°17'03"   Elevation – 2,600 feet

Facilities

19 standard sites
Pull–through sites (15 and 16)
Vault toilets
Potable water
Garbage service (bear–proof cans)
Boat launch
Accessible toilet, campsite

Features

Noisy Creek campground is located at the confluence of Noisy Creek and Sullivan Lake on the southern shore of Sullivan Lake in a forested, mountain setting. Campsites are private, suitable for both tent and RV camping, and within walking distance of the lake. Swimming, boat launch and Lakeshore Trail are accessed from the day use area. Noisy Creek Trail and Hall Mountain Trail, a trail to the bighorn sheep winter feeding station, are nearby.

Reservations

Reserve sites at *www.recreation.gov* or by phone at 1–877–444–6777. Reservations must be made 4 days ahead of arrival and can be made up to 6 months in advance. See Appendix B for details.

Season

Open with full services mid May through mid September

Activities

Boating, Fishing, Hiking, Swimming.

Cost

$16
$8 extra vehicle
See Appendix C for available discounts.

Limitations

See Appendix A for camping regulations.
CAUTION: Noisy Creek campground gates are closed from 10pm to 6am.

Contact

Colville National Forest
Sullivan Lake Ranger District
765 South Main Street
Colville, WA 99114
Phone: 509–446–7500
Web: *http://www.fs.fed.us/r6/colville/*

Noisy Creek Campsite

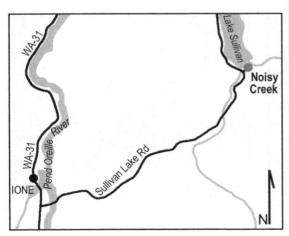

Driving Directions

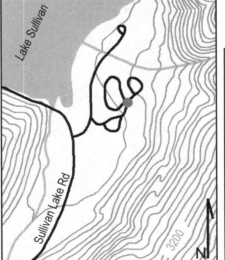

Location

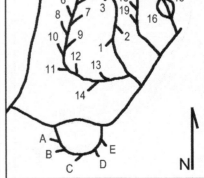

Campground

315 Panhandle
Colville National Forest

Directions

Start at the intersection of US–2 and WA–20 in Newport. Travel north on WA–20 for 15.9 miles. Turn right onto Kings Lake Road and travel 0.8 mile through the town of Usk. Take the first left after crossing the bridge onto Le Clerc Road North and travel 15.2 miles. Turn left into Panhandle.

N48°30'21" – W117°15'58"   Elevation – 2,040 feet

Facilities

11 standard sites
Vault toilet
Potable water
Garbage service
Boat launch

Features

Panhandle campground is set in a heavily forested area along the east shore of the Pend Oreille River with some riverside sites. Sites are suitable for tents and large RVs. Located next to the boat launch, a small wetland area provides visitors with the sights and sounds of the wetland environment.

Reservations

Reserve sites at *www.recreation.gov* or by phone at 1–877–444–6777. Reservations must be made 4 days ahead of arrival and can be made up to 6 months in advance. See Appendix B for details.

Season

Open from mid May through early September. The boat launch is open during the off season.

Activities

Boating, Fishing, Swimming.

Cost

$16
$8 extra vehicle
See Appendix C for available discounts.

Limitations

CAUTION: Bears and cougars frequent the area; keep all food in approved containers.
Maximum length of stay is 14 days.
See Appendix A for camping regulations.

Pend Oreille River

Contact

Colville National Forest
Newport Ranger District
765 South Main Street
Colville, WA 99114

Phone: 509–447–7300
Web: *http://www.fs.fed.us/r6/colville/*

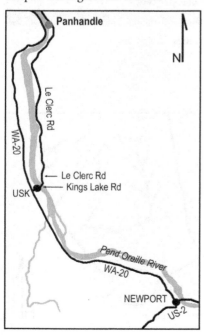

Driving Directions

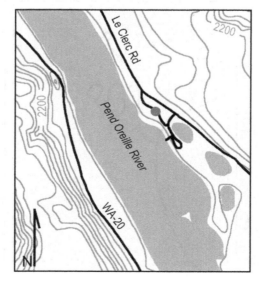

Location

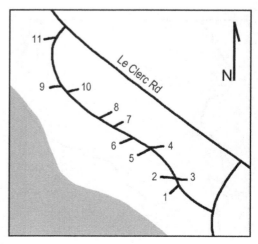

Campground

316 Browns Lake
Colville National Forest

Directions

Start at the intersection of WA–20 and US–2 in Newport. Travel north on WA–20 for 15.9 miles. Turn right onto Kings Lake Road (County Road 3389) and travel through the town of Usk and across the bridge. Travel for an additional 7.2 miles (the last 2.1 miles are gravel). Turn left on Half Moon Lake Road (County Road 5030, gravel) and travel 4.2 miles. Turn left into Browns Lake.

N48°26'09" – W117°11'47"   Elevation – 3,470 feet

Facilities

18 standard sites
Vault toilets
No water, bring your own
Garbage service
Boat launch
Accessible toilet

Features

Browns Lake campground is located in a setting of heavily forested mountains. The campground has a historical cabin built by the Civilian Conservation Corps. Campsites 6, 7, 9, and 10 overlook the lake. The Lake is a popular fly–fishing only lake with a primitive boat launch on the south end. An interpretive trail with a parking area and a viewing platform over a beaver pond is located 1 mile east of campground. This non–motorized only trail provides scenic viewpoints of the lake and passes through a grove of old growth cedar. Visitors come to view the cutthroat spawning run in spring from the platform.

Reservations

None, all campsites are first–come, first–serve.

Season

Open for start of fishing season, weather permitting, from mid May through early September and with reduced services from early September through the end of October.

Activities

Boating (non–motorized), Fly–fishing, Hiking, Interpretive trail.

Cost

$14
$8 extra vehicle
See Appendix C for available discounts.

Limitations

Browns Lake allows non–motorized boats only.
Half Moon Lake Road (County Road 5030) is a single–lane, gravel road with turnouts and not recommended for large RVs.
See Appendix A for camping regulations.

Contact

Colville National Forest
Newport Ranger District
765 South Main Street
Colville, WA 99114
Phone: 509–447–7300
Web: *http://www.fs.fed.us/r6/colville/*

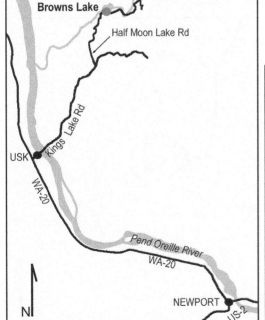

Driving Directions

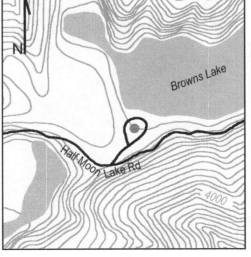

Location

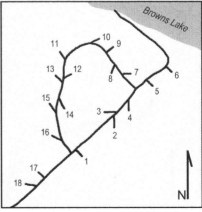

Campground

317 South Skookum Lake
Colville National Forest

Directions

Start at the intersection of WA–20 and US–2 in Newport. Travel north on WA–20 for 15.9 miles. Turn right onto Kings Lake Road (County Road 3389) and travel 8.7 miles, passing through the town of Usk and across the bridge. Bear right at "Y" onto County Road 5032 and travel 0.9 mile to South Skookum Lake. The last 3.6 miles are gravel road.

N48°23'37" – W117°11'09"   Elevation – 3,560 feet

Facilities

25 total sites: 16 standard sites, 9 walk–in sites
Vault toilets
Potable water
Garbage service (bear–proof cans)
Boat ramp
Accessible dock

Features

South Skookum Lake campground is located in a heavily forested area. Most campsites are private; some have a view of the lake. Two docks, one of which is ADA accessible, are located near the launch area and allow fishing for campers without boats. South Baldy Lookout, which is still staffed during the summer months, is visible from the campground and is a popular day trip. The trailhead for South Skookum Trail is next to the launch area.

Reservations

None, all campsites are first–come, first–serve.

Season

Open with full services mid May through early September

Activities

Boating, Fishing, Hiking.

Pedestrians Have the Right–of–Way

Cost

$16
$8 extra vehicle
See Appendix C for available discounts.

Limitations

South Skookum Lake is relatively small and is not suitable for boats larger than 20 feet or motors greater than 15 horsepower. In addition, the boat ramp is short and narrow.
See Appendix A for camping regulations.

Contact

Colville National Forest
Newport Ranger District
765 South Main Street
Colville, WA 99114
Phone: 509–447–7300
Web: *http://www.fs.fed.us/r6/colville/*

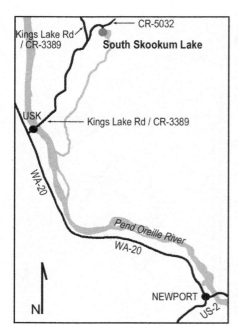

Driving Directions

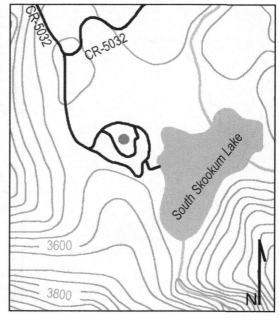

Location

318 Skookum Creek
Department of Natural Resources

Directions

Start at the intersection of WA–20 and WA–211 near Usk. Travel north on WA–20 for 0.4 mile. Turn right onto 5th Street (also called Kings Lake Road) and travel 0.9 mile. Turn right onto Le Clerc Road and travel for 2.3 miles. Turn left onto Bear Park Road (road off to right of this intersection is called Lenora Drive) and travel 0.1 mile. Turn left onto Skookum Creek access road and travel 0.3 mile to campground.

N48°17'30" – W117°13'35"   Elevation – 2,050 feet

Activities

Hiking.

Cost

No cost

Limitations

A Washington State Discover Pass is required. See Appendix A for camping regulations.

Contact

WA Department of Natural Resources, Northeast Region
Phone: 509–684–7474
Web *www.dnr.wa.gov*

Facilities

10 standard sites
Vault toilet
Potable water
Pack out garbage
Shelter

Features

Skookum Creek Campground lies near the South Fork of Skookum Creek. The sites are large, open, and private with good shade.

Reservations

None, first–come, first–serve

Season

Opens seasonally, weather dependent

Skookum Creek

Skookum Creek Shelter

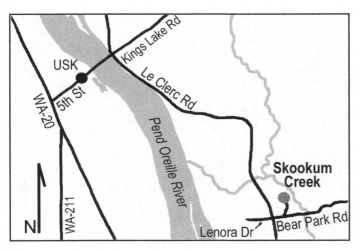

Driving Directions

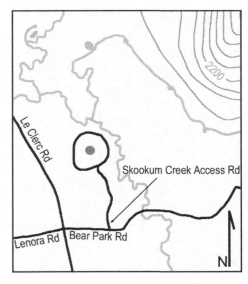

Location

319 Pioneer Park
Colville National Forest

Directions

Start at the intersection of US–2 and WA–20 in Newport and travel east on US–2 for 0.5 mile. Turn left onto Le Cleric Road, at the east end of the bridge over the Pend Oreille River, and travel 2.4 miles. (Crossing the bridge over the Pend Oreille River, you briefly enter Idaho, then return to Washington as you head north on Le Clerc Road.) Turn left into Pioneer Park.

N48°12'45" – W117°03'18"   Elevation – 2,080 feet

Facilities

14 standard sites
Vault toilets
Potable water
Garbage service
Shelter
Boat launch
Accessible toilet

Features

Pioneer campground is located on the east side of the Pend Oreille River and is surrounded by a forest of ponderosa pine, white pine, hemlock and grand fir trees. Campsites are suitable for both tent and RV camping. The Heritage Interpretive Trail, a 0.3 mile archeological interpretive trail about the Kalispell Tribe's historical use of the area, begins in the day–use area. The elevated boardwalk overlooks the Pend Oreille River and also provides glimpses of osprey and eagles.

Reservations

Reserve sites at *www.recreation.gov* or by phone at 1–877–444–6777. Reservations must be made 4 days ahead of arrival and can be made up to 6 months in advance. See Appendix B for details.

Season

Open with full services from mid May through mid September

Activities

Bird watching, Boating, Fishing, Hiking, Interpretative trail, Swimming.

Cost

$16
$8 extra vehicle
See Appendix C for available discounts.

Limitations

CAUTION: Bears/cougars frequent the area; keep all food in approved containers.
See Appendix A for camping regulations.

Contact

Colville National Forest
Newport Ranger District
765 South Main Street
Colville, WA 99114
Phone: 509–447–7300
Web: *http://www.fs.fed.us/r6/colville/*

Pioneer Park Campsite

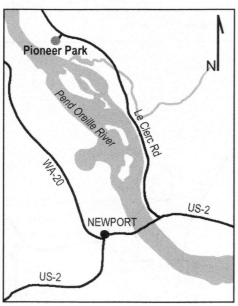

Driving Directions

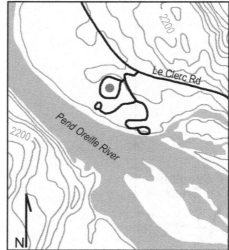

Location

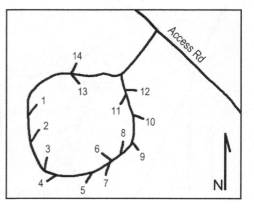

Campground

320 Pend Oreille Park
Pend Oreille County

Directions

Start at the intersection of US–2 and WA–291 in Spokane. Travel north on US–2 for 27.2 miles. Turn left into park.

N48°04'57" – W117°20'04"   Elevation – 2,280 feet

Facilities

25 standard sites
Flush toilets
Potable water
Hot showers
Pack out garbage

Features

Pend Oreille County Park features over 7 miles of hiking trails. About half of the campsites can accommodate an RV longer than 30–feet.

Reservations

None, all campsites are first–come, first–serve.

Season

Open from Memorial Day through Labor Day weekends

Activities

Hiking.

Cost

$10 per site

Limitations

No ATV's allowed.
Campfires not permitted after August 1st.

Pend Oreille Park Campsite

Contact

Phone: 509–447–4821
Web: *www.pendoreilleco.org/your–government/parks–and–recreation/*

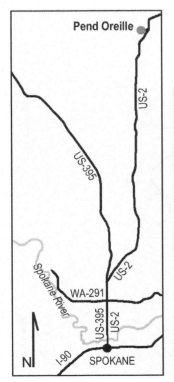

Driving Directions

Pend Oreille Park Restroom

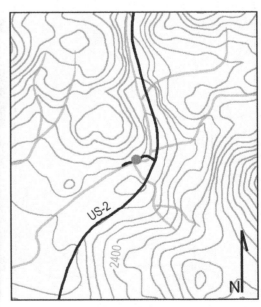

Location

321 Mount Spokane
Washington State Parks

Directions

Start at the intersection of I–90 and Argonne Road (exit 287) near Spokane. Travel north on Argonne Road for 8.5 miles (becomes Bruce Road). Turn right onto WA–206 and travel for 13.0 miles to Park's Visitor Center. Continue for an additional 3.1 miles. Turn left onto North Summit Road and travel for 0.9 mile. Turn right into campground.

N47°54'48" – W117°06'43"   Elevation – 5,120 feet

Facilities

8 standard sites
One pull–through site
Flush toilets
Potable water
Garbage service

Features

Mount Spokane contains over 13,000 acres, provides a wide variety of summer and winter activities, and features stands of old–growth trees and granite rock outcroppings. The park offers 100 miles of hiking and equestrian trails, 90 miles of biking trails, 15.5 miles of groomed cross–country ski trails, and a down–hill winter ski facility (which aptly uses the 300 inches of snow received annually).

Reservations

None, all campsites are first–come, first–serve.

Season

The park remains open all year. The campground closes Sept 15 and reopens July 1 (depending on snow conditions).

Activities

Bird watching, Cross–country skiing, Down–hill skiing, Equestrian trail riding, Hiking, Metal detecting, Mountain biking, Snowmobiling.

Cost

$12 primitive site
Peak season: mid May – mid September
$22 – $35 standard site
$30 – $40 partial utility site
$35 – $45 full utility site
Off–peak season
$20 – $30 standard site
$25 – $35 partial utility site
$30 – $40 full utility site
$10 extra vehicle (all year)
See Appendix C for available discounts.

Limitations

Maximum site length is 30 feet.
See Appendix A for camping regulations.

Contact

Phone: 509– 238–4258
Web: *www.parks.state.wa.us*

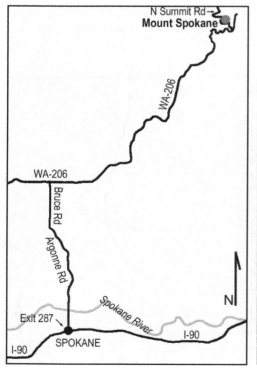

Driving Directions

Mount Spokane Campsite

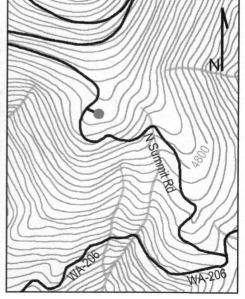

Location

322 Riverside
Washington State Parks

Directions

Start at the intersection of US–2 and WA–291 near Spokane. Travel west on WA–291 for 4.5 miles. Turn left onto Rifle Club Road and travel 0.4 mile. Turn left onto Aubrey L Parkway and travel for 2.0 miles. Bear right into park.

N47°41'40" – W117°29'36"   Elevation – 1,700 feet

Facilities

32 total sites: 16 standard, 14 partial utility, 2 full utility

Some pull through sites
Flush toilets
Potable water
Hot showers
Garbage service
RV dump
Store
Accessible campsite

Features

Riverside State Park offers 10,000 acres along the Spokane and Little Spokane rivers. At the Bowl and Pitcher Campground, sites 1–14 front the Spokane River. Sites 15 and16 are full utility sites. The campground has its own swinging bridge, a store, and the oldest log structure in Spokane County.

Reservations

Sites may be reserved online at *www.parks.state.wa.us* or by telephone 1–888–CAMPOUT (1–888–226–7688).
See Appendix B for details.

Season

The park is open all year, but only the upper campground is open during winter.

Activities

Bird watching, Canoeing, Equestrian trail riding, Fishing, Hiking, Interpretive Center, Mountain Biking, Snowmobiling, Swimming.

Cost

$12 primitive site
Peak season: mid May – mid September
$22 – $35 standard site
$30 – $40 partial utility site
$35 – $45 full utility site
Off–peak season
$20 – $30 standard site
$25 – $35 partial utility site
$30 – $40 full utility site
$10 extra vehicle (all year)
See Appendix C for available discounts.

Limitations

Maximum site length is 45 feet.
See Appendix A for camping regulations.

Contact

Phone: 509–465–5064
Web: *www.parks.state.wa.us*

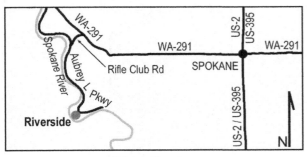

Driving Directions

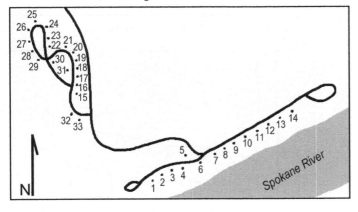

Campground

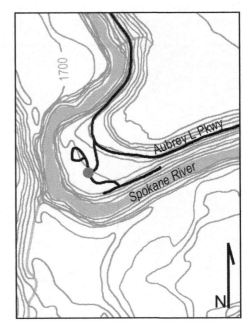

Location

323 Nine Mile Rec. Area
Washington State Parks

Directions

Start at the intersection of WA–291 and US–2 near Spokane. Travel west on WA–291 for 9.9 miles. Turn left onto Charles Road and travel for 1.3 miles. Turn right onto Nine Mile Recreation Road and travel for 0.5 mile to campground.

N47°47'37" – W117°33'54"   Elevation – 1,520 feet

Facilities

24 total sites
Flush toilets
Potable water
Hot showers
Garbage service
RV dump
Boat launch

Features

Riverside State Park offers 12,000 acres along the Spokane and Little Spokane rivers in Eastern Washington. The Nine Mile Recreation Area is a portion of this large park. The Civilian Conservation Corps developed the park between 1933 and 1936. This area was a major gathering site for Native American cultures.

Reservations

Sites may be reserved online at *www.parks.state.wa.us* or by telephone 1–888–CAMPOUT (1–888–226–7688).
See Appendix B for details.

Season

Camping is available May 15 – September 15

Activities

Bird watching, Boating, Canoeing, Fishing, Hiking, Kayaking, Swimming, Water skiing.

Cost

$12 primitive site
Peak season: mid May – mid September
$22 – $35 standard site
$30 – $40 partial utility site
$35 – $45 full utility site
Off–peak season
$20 – $30 standard site
$25 – $35 partial utility site
$30 – $40 full utility site
$10 extra vehicle (all year)
See Appendix C for available discounts.

Limitations

Maximum site length is 45 feet.
See Appendix A for camping regulations.

Contact

Phone: 509–465–5064
Web: *www.parks.state.wa.us*

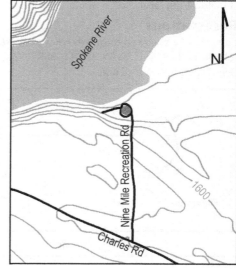

Location

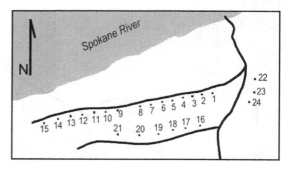

Campground

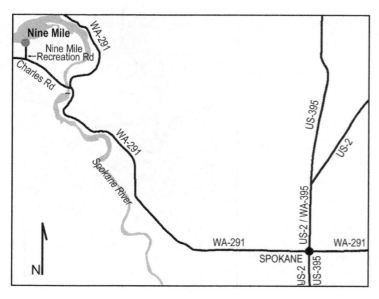

Driving Directions

324 Lake Spokane
Washington State Parks

Directions

Start at the intersection of US–2 and WA–231 in Reardan. Travel north on WA–231 for 14.2 miles. Turn right onto WA–291 and travel for 4.7 miles. Turn right into campground.

N47°50'08" – W117°45'56"   Elevation – 1,700 feet

Facilities

11 primitive sites
Vault toilet
Potable water
Pack out garbage
Shelter
Boat launch

Accessible toilets, water, campsite, shelter, view area

Features

Lake Spokane Campground lies on a ridge overlooking the lake which is created by a dam on the Spokane River. The campground has a kitchen shelter. A native paintings interpretive site is located across Long Lake Dam Road 0.1 mile past entrance to campground.

Reservations

Sites may be reserved online at *www.parks.state.wa.us* or by telephone 1–888–CAMPOUT (1–888–226–7688). The online system handles reservations for Lake Spokane through the Nine Mile Recreation Area location. See Appendix B for details.

Season

Open May 15 through September 15

Lake Spokane

Activities

Boating, Fishing, Hiking.

Cost

$12 primitive and water trail sites
$10 extra vehicle
See Appendix C for available discounts.

Limitations

No pets are allowed in the campground. See Appendix A for camping regulations.

Contact

Phone: 509–465–5064
Web: *www.parks.state.wa.us*

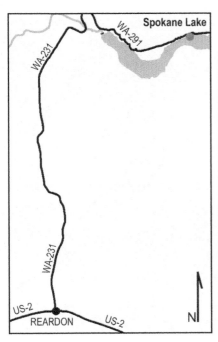

Driving Directions

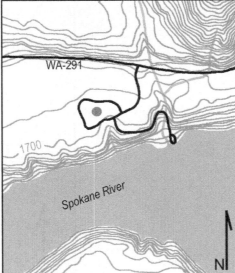

Location

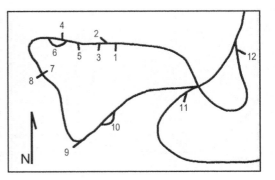

Campground

325 Porcupine Bay
Lake Roosevelt National Recreation Area

Directions

Start at the intersection of US–2 and WA–25 in Davenport. Travel north on WA–25 for 12.2 miles. Turn right onto Porcupine Bay Road and travel 6.1 miles to campground.

N47°53'45" – W118°10'35"   Elevation – 1,320 feet

Facilities

31 standard sites
Flush and vault toilets
Potable water
Garbage service
RV dump
Boat launch and dock

Features

Sites at the Porcupine Bay campground overlook the Spokane River. Individual sites have paved parking pads. Although there are no hook–ups, the campground has sites that will fit most large RVs. The park offers a grassy picnic area and designated swimming area.

Reservations

None, all campsites are first–come, first–serve.

Season

Open all year
Comfort Station is open from mid April to mid October, weather permitting.

Activities

Boating, Fishing, Swimming.

Cost

$18 from May 1 – September 30
$9 from October 1 – April 30
See Appendix C for available discounts.

Limitations

See Appendix A for camping regulations.

Contact

Lake Roosevelt National Recreation Area
1008 Crest Drive
Coulee Dam, WA 99116
Fort Spokane District Office: 509–633–9441
Park Headquarters: 509–633–9441

Spokane River at Porcupine Bay

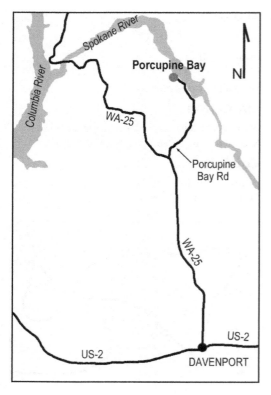

Driving Directions

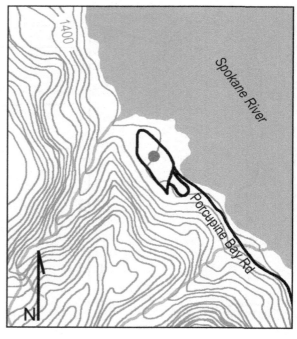

Location

326 Fort Spokane
Lake Roosevelt National Recreation Area

Directions

Start at the intersection of US–2 and WA–25 in Davenport. Travel north on WA–25 for 23.5 miles. The campground is on both sides of the road.

N47°54'32" – W118°18'36"   Elevation – 1,340 feet

Facilities

67 standard sites
Some walk–in sites
Some pull–through sites
Flush and vault toilets
Potable water (off in winter)
Garbage service
RV dump
Boat launch and dock
Accessible campsite

Features

Fort Spokane campground lies near the confluence of the Spokane River and the Columbia River (Lake Roosevelt) in a forest of ponderosa pines and shrubs. The campground sites will fit most large RVs with paved parking areas that are either pull–through or back–in pads. The boat launch and dock are open summer and winter. Fort Spokane Visitor Center and Museum offers exhibits about the military and the Indian boarding school from June through Labor Day (509–725–2715, extension 43 for information). Interpretive programs demonstrating military life happen throughout the summer.

Reservations

Sites may be reserved online at *www.recreation.gov* or by phone at 1–877–444–6777. Make or change reservations at least 7 days ahead of arrival. Reservations can be made up to 6 months in advance. See Appendix B for details.

Season

Open all year. Comfort station opens from mid April to mid October, weather permitting.

Activities

Birding, Boating, Fishing, Biking, Interpretive Center/Museum, Swimming.

Cost

$18 from May 1 – September 30
$9 from October 1 – April 30
See Appendix C for available discounts.

Limitations

See Appendix A for camping regulations.

Contact

Lake Roosevelt National Recreation Area
1008 Crest Drive
Coulee Dam, WA 99116
Fort Spokane District Office: 509–633–9441
Park Headquarters: 509–633–9441

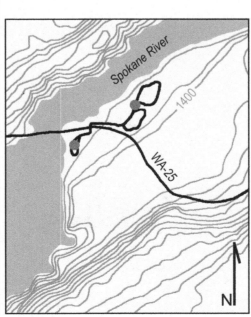

Driving Directions   *Location*

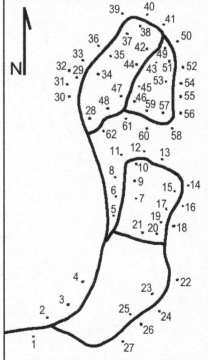

East Campground

327 Hunters
Lake Roosevelt National Recreation Area

Directions

Start at the intersection of US–2 and WA–25 in Davenport. Travel north on WA–25 for 42.3 miles. In the town of Hunters, turn left onto Hunters Campground Road and travel 1.5 miles to campground.

N48°07'29" – W118°13'54"   Elevation – 1,320 feet

Facilities

39 standard sites
Some pull–through sites
Flush and vault toilets
Potable water (Seasonal)
Garbage service
RV dump
Boat launch and dock

Features

Several of the campsites are along Lake Roosevelt and are shaded by a thick Ponderosa pine forest. The water in the lake originates from glaciers and snow in the Canadian Rockies, but during summer the temperatures are pleasant for swimming. Although there are no hook–ups, campsites will fit most large RVs and offer paved pull–through or back–in parking pads.

Reservations

None, all campsites are first–come, first–serve.

Season

Open all year

Activities

Biking, Boating, Fishing, Hiking, Hunting, Swimming.

Cost

$18 from May 1 – September 30
$9 from October 1 – April 30
See Appendix C for available discounts.

Limitations

Water may be turned off in the winter during low water levels. Check with the park for water availability.
See Appendix A for camping regulations.

Contact

Lake Roosevelt National Recreation Area
1008 Crest Drive
Coulee Dam, WA 99116
Park Headquarters: 509–633–9441
Fort Spokane District Office: 509–633–9441

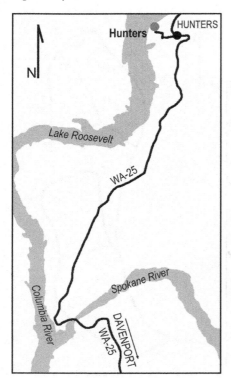

Driving Directions

Fishing on Lake Roosevelt

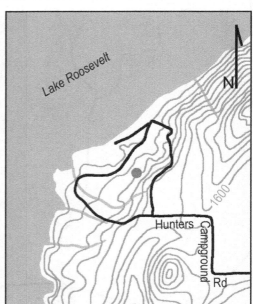

Location

328 Gifford
Lake Roosevelt National Recreation Area

Directions

Start at the intersection of US–395 and WA–25 near Kettle Falls. Travel south on WA–25 for 25.2 miles. Turn right to campground.

N48°17'09" – W118°08'33"   Elevation – 1,320 feet

Facilities

42 standard sites
Some pull–through sites
Flush and vault toilets
Potable water (Seasonal)
Outside swimming showers
Garbage service
RV Dump
Boat launch and dock
Marina

Features

Several of the campsites are along the Lake Roosevelt portion of the Columbia River. Although there are no hook–ups, the campsites will fit most large RVs and offer paved parking pads. The boat launch and dock are available in summer and winter.

Reservations

None, all campsites are first–come, first–serve.

Season

Open all year

Activities

Boating, Fishing, Hiking, Swimming.

Gifford Campsite

Cost

$18 from May 1 – September 30
$9 from October 1 – April 30
See Appendix C for available discounts.

Limitations

See Appendix A for camping regulations.

Contact

Lake Roosevelt National Recreation Area
1008 Crest Drive
Coulee Dam, WA 99116
Park Headquarters: 509–633–9441
Fort Spokane District Office, 509–633–9441
Kettle Falls Office: 509–738–6266

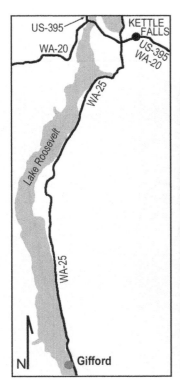

Driving Directions

Gifford Sunset

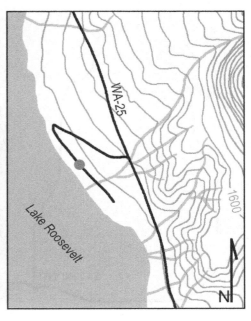

Location

355

329 Hawk Creek
Lake Roosevelt National Recreation Area

Directions

Start at the intersection of US–2 and WA–25 in Davenport. Travel north on WA–25 for 22.4 miles. Turn left onto Miles Creston Road and travel for 7.3 miles. Turn right onto Hawk Creek Road (1 ½ lane gravel road) and travel 1.0 mile to site.

N47°48'55" – W118°19'27"   Elevation – 1,320 feet

Facilities

21 standard sites
Vault toilets
Potable water (seasonal)
Garbage service
Boat launch and ramp

Features

Several of the campsites are along Hawk Creek Inlet. Although there are no hook–ups, campsites will fit most large RVs and offer paved parking pads. Driveway lengths appeared 35 to 37 feet long. The campground hosts a wonderful old apple orchard.

Reservations

None, all campsites are first–come, first–serve.

Season

Open all year

Activities

Boating, Fishing, Hiking.

Hawk Creek Boat Launch

Cost

$18 from May 1 – September 30
$9 from October 1 – April 30
See Appendix C for available discounts.

Limitations

Water may be turned off in the winter during low water levels. Check with the park for water availability.
See Appendix A for camping regulations.

Contact

Lake Roosevelt National Recreation Area
1008 Crest Drive
Coulee Dam, WA 99116
Park Headquarters: 509–633–9441
Fort Spokane District Office: 509–633–9441

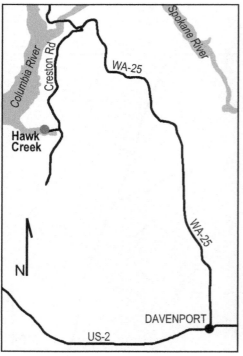

Driving Directions

Hawk Creek Campsite

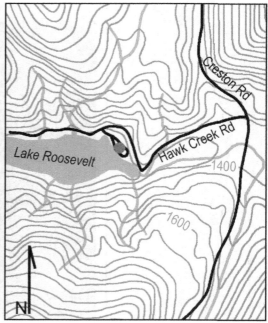

Location

330 Jones Bay
Lake Roosevelt National Recreation Area

Directions

Start at the intersection of US–2 and WA–21 in Wilbur. Travel north on WA–21 for 0.5 mile. Bear right to stay on WA–21 and travel 4.3 miles. Turn right onto Krause Road and travel 3.0 miles. Turn left onto Hanson Harbor Road and travel 6.6 miles. Bear right at "Y" onto Jones Bay Road North (partial gravel) and travel 2.9 miles to campground.

N47°55'11" – W118°34'56"   Elevation – 1,320 feet

Facilities

9 standard sites
Vault toilet
No potable water
Garbage service
Boat launch and dock

Features

Some sites at the campground are along Jones Bay inlet on the Columbia River. Although the park recommends tent only sites, the campground has sites that will accommodate some small RVs.

Reservations

None, all campsites are first–come, first–serve.

Season

Open all year

Activities

Boating, Fishing.

Cost

$18 from May 1 – September 30
$9 from October 1 – April 30
See Appendix C for available discounts.

Limitations

See Appendix A for camping regulations.

Jones Bay

Contact

Lake Roosevelt National Recreation Area
1008 Crest Drive
Coulee Dam, WA 99116
Park Headquarters: 509–633–9441
Fort Spokane District Office: 509–633–9441
Kettle Falls Office: 509–738–6266

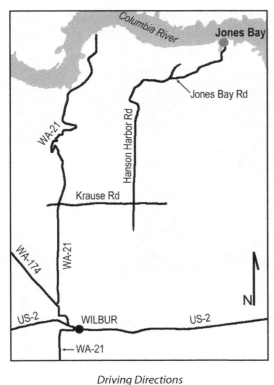

Driving Directions

Jones Bay Campsite

Location

331 Spring Canyon
Lake Roosevelt National Recreation Area

Directions

Start at the intersection of WA–155 and WA–174 in Grand Coulee. Travel east of WA–174 for 2.8 miles. Turn left onto Spring Canyon Campground Road and travel for 1.2 miles. Turn left into campground.

N47°55'57" – W118°56'20"   Elevation – 1,400 feet

Facilities

78 standard sites
Some pull–through sites
Flush and vault toilets
Potable water (Seasonal)
Garbage service
RV dump
Boat launch and dock

Features

Spring Canyon campground offers beautiful views of the Lake Roosevelt and the surrounding hills. Although there are no hook–ups, the sites will fit most large RVs and have paved parking areas. Maximum vehicle lengths for individual sites are given on the reservation system. The designated swimming area, a short walk of 300 yards from the camping area, also has a playground. Lake temperatures are comfortable for swimming during summer. The boat launch and dock are open all year. Bunchgrass Prairie Nature Trail offers a short walk through the sagebrush.

Reservations

Sites may be reserved online at *www.recreation.gov* or by phone at 1–877–444–6777. Reserve or change reservations at least 7 days in advance. Reservations can be made up to 6 months in advance. See Appendix B for details.

Season

Open all year. Comfort station opens from mid April to mid October, weather permitting.

Activities

Biking, Boating, Fishing, Hiking, Swimming.

Cost

$18 from May 1 – September 30
$9 from October 1 – April 30
See Appendix C for available discounts.

Limitations

Campfires are not allowed in upper loop sites 32–78.
Water is shut off during winter.
See Appendix A for camping regulations.

Contact

Lake Roosevelt National Recreation Area
1008 Crest Drive
Coulee Dam, WA 99116
Park Headquarters: 509–633–9441

Spring Canyon Campsite

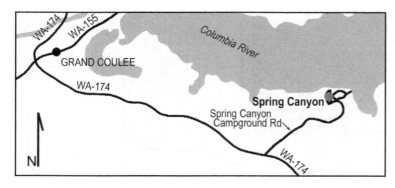

Driving Directions

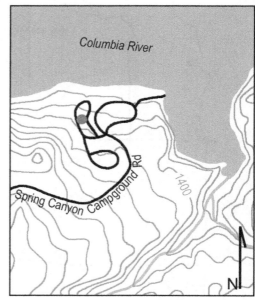

Location

332 Steamboat Rock
Washington State Parks

Directions

Start at the intersection of WA–174 and WA–155 near Grand Coulee. Travel south on WA–155 for 10.0 miles. Turn right into park entrance. Travel 2.0 miles to destination.

Or

Start at the intersection of US–2 and WA–155 near Coulee City. Travel north on WA–155 for 15.6 miles. Turn left into park entrance. Travel 2.0 miles to destination.

N47°51'21" – W119°07'42"   Elevation – 1,540 feet

Facilities

174 total sites: 26 standard, 136 full utility (W/E/S), 12 boat–in primitive – See Note in Features
Flush toilets
Potable water
Hot showers
Garbage service
Boat launch and dock (320 feet)
Store
Accessible toilet, water, campsite

Features

Steamboat Rock State Park lies on the north end of Banks Lake and dominates the landscape with its columnar, basaltic rock. Two main campground areas and a day–use area have sweeping green lawns and are protected from the winds by poplar trees. Primitive sites are accessible only by water. The surrounding area delights visitors with wildflowers that contrast with the gray–green brush of the Scablands. The park is an oasis in desert surroundings. A sandy swimming area and water activities give respite from the hot, summer sun (summer temperatures range between 80 to 100 degrees). The park offers a concession–operated store with fast food, basic groceries, firewood, ice, and fishing supplies. Grand Coulee Dam provides tours, a visitor's center, and a nightly laser–light show.

Note: Additional camping in the park includes 36 standard sites at Osborn Bay and 44 standard sites at Jones Bay. These have vault toilets, no water, and available first–come, first–serve.

(Continued on next page.)

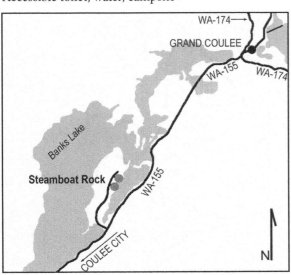

Driving Directions

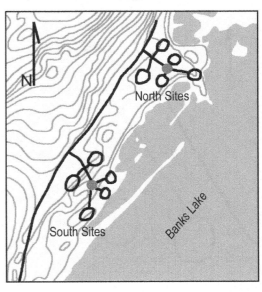

Location

Reservations

Sites may be reserved online at *www.parks.state.wa.us* or by telephone 1–888–CAMPOUT (1–888–226–7688). See Appendix B for details.

Season

Partially open all year. Water to individual campsites is shut off October 31 – March 31.

Activities

Beach combing, Bird watching, Boating, Cross–country skiing, Equestrian trail riding, Fishing, Hiking, Mountain Biking, Motorcycle riding/ATVs, Personal watercraft, Rock climbing, Scuba diving, Snowshoeing, Swimming, Volleyball, Water skiing, Winter ice climbing.

Cost

$12 primitive site
Peak season: mid May – mid September
$22 – $35 standard site
$30 – $40 partial utility site
$35 – $45 full utility site
Off–peak season
$20 – $30 standard site
$25 – $35 partial utility site
$30 – $40 full utility site
$10 extra vehicle (all year)
See Appendix C for available discounts.

Limitations

Maximum site length is 50 feet.
The park is closed to metal detecting indefinitely.
See Appendix A for camping regulations.

Contact

Phone: 509–633–1304
Web: *www.parks.state.wa.us*

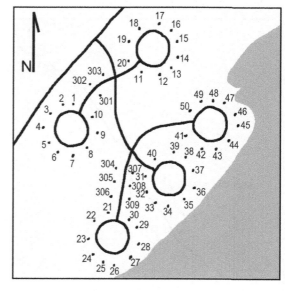

Steamboat Rock Campsite

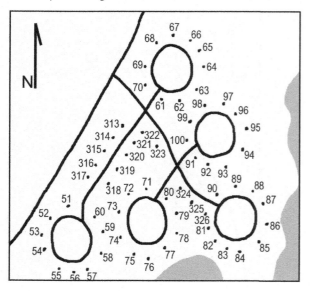

North Campground

South Campground

333 Bridgeport
Washington State Parks

Directions

Start at the intersection of US–97 and WA–17 near Brewster. Travel south on WA–17 for 8.1 miles. Turn left onto Half–Sun Way. Travel for 2.5 miles to the park.

N48°00'55" – W119°36'29"   Elevation – 960 feet

Facilities

34 total sites: 14 standard, 20 partial utility (W/E)
Flush toilets
Potable water
Hot showers
Garbage service
Boat launch and dock (240 feet)
Accessible toilet, water, utility site

Features

Bridgeport State Park lies along the shoreline on Rufus Woods Lake. The park provides 18 acres of lawn and some shade in the midst of a desert terrain. "Haystacks," (unusual volcanic formations resembling their name) are the park's most striking feature.

Located directly behind Chief Joseph Dam, Rufus Woods Lake is actually part of the Columbia River and contains rainbow trout, silvers and walleye. Most fishing is by boat. Shore fishing, outside of state park property, may require a Colville Tribe fishing license in addition to a state license. Colville Tribe fishing licenses can be purchased in the cities of Bridgeport or Brewster.

There is a golf course adjacent to campground.

Reservations

Sites may be reserved online from May 15 through October 15 at *www.parks.state.wa.us* or by telephone 1–888–CAMPOUT (1–888–226–7688). See Appendix B for details.

Season

Open April 1 – October 31

Activities

Bird watching, Boating, Canoeing, Fishing, Hiking, Personal watercraft, Scuba diving, Swimming, Water skiing.

Cost

$12 primitive site
Peak season: mid May – mid September
$22 – $35 standard site
$30 – $40 partial utility site
$35 – $45 full utility site
Off–peak season
$20 – $30 standard site
$25 – $35 partial utility site
$30 – $40 full utility site
$10 extra vehicle (all year)
See Appendix C for available discounts.

Limitations

Maximum site length is 45 feet.
See Appendix A for camping regulations.

Contact

Phone: 509–686–7231
Web: *www.parks.state.wa.us*

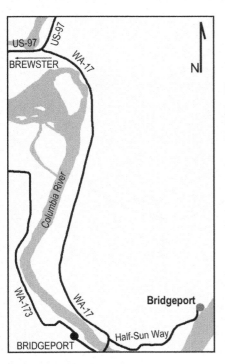

Driving Directions

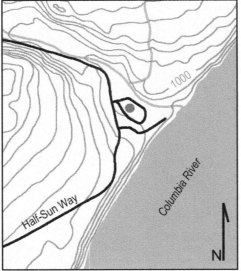

Location

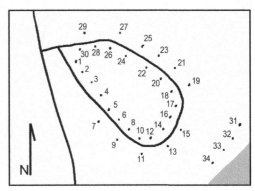

Campground

334 Coulee City Park
City of Coulee City

Directions

Start at the intersection of US–2 and WA–155 near Coulee City. Travel west on US–2 for 2.3 miles. Turn right into campground.

N47°37'0" – W119°17'29"   Elevation – 1,580 feet

Coulee City Park View

Facilities

100 total sites: 45 standard, 55 utility (W/E/S)
19 pull–through sites
Flush toilets
Potable water
Hot showers
Garbage service
RV dump station
Boat launch and dock
Accessible restroom, showers

Features

Coulee City Campground lies on the south end of Banks Lake. Most of the sites are shaded. The campground has a lovely playground and swimming area.

Reservations

None, all campsites are first–come, first–serve.

Season

Open all year. Showers and water hook–ups are available April through October.

Activities

Beachcombing, Bird watching, Boating, Fishing, Swimming.

Cost

$15 standard site
$30 utility site

Limitations

Maximum RV length is 35 feet

Contact

Coulee City
Phone: 509–632–5331
Email: *tcoulee@odessaoffice.com*

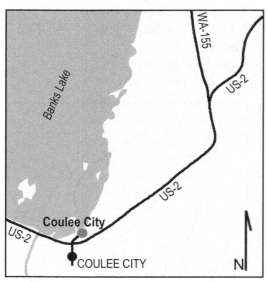

Driving Directions

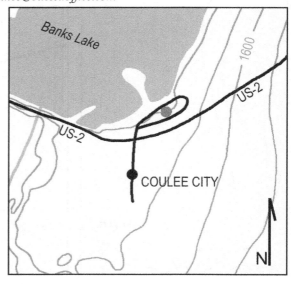

Location

335 Sun Lakes – Dry Falls
Washington State Parks

Directions

Start at the intersection of US–2 and WA–17 near Coulee City. Travel south on WA–17 for 4.0 miles. Turn left into park.

N47°35'33" – W119°23'46"   Elevation – 1,040 feet

Facilities

191 total sites: 152 standard, 39 full utility (W/E/S)
Flush toilets
Potable water
Hot showers
Garbage service
RV dump
Boat launch and rentals
Moorage
Food service
Store
Laundry
Accessible toilet, interpretive site, boating

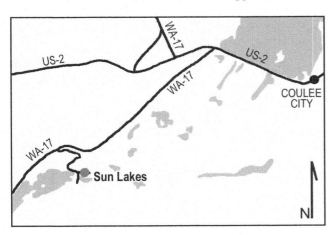

Features

Sun Lakes – Dry Falls State Park is located on the shoreline at the foot of Dry Falls. The park offers a variety of amenities and features seasonal boat rentals, a nine–hole golf course and a miniature golf course.

Dry Falls is one of the great geological wonders of North America. Carved by Ice Age floods that long ago disappeared, the former waterfall is now a stark cliff, 400 feet high and 3.5 miles wide. In its heyday, the waterfall was four times the size of Niagara Falls. Today it overlooks a desert oasis filled with lakes and wildlife, and is surrounded by natural formations.

Reservations

Sites may be reserved online at *www.parks.state.wa.us* or by telephone 1–888–CAMPOUT (1–888–226–7688). Reservations are advised for the summer months. See Appendix B for details.

Season

Open all year, though the campground is only partially open during winter.

Activities

Bird watching, Boating, Fishing, Golfing, Hiking, Horseshoes, Interpretative center, Mountain biking, Scuba diving, Swimming, Water skiing.

Cost

$12 primitive site
Peak season: mid May – mid September
$22 – $35 standard site
$30 – $40 partial utility site
$35 – $45 full utility site
Off–peak season
$20 – $30 standard site
$25 – $35 partial utility site
$30 – $40 full utility site
$10 extra vehicle (all year)
See Appendix C for available discounts.

Limitations

Maximum site length is 65 feet.
Be prepared for the possibility of high winds.
See Appendix A for camping regulations.

Contact

Phone: 509–632–5583
Web: *www.parks.state.wa.us*

Driving Directions

Location

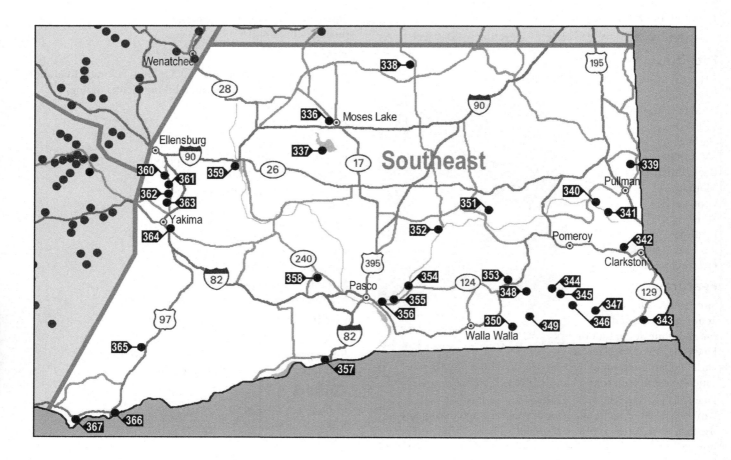

Chapter 6   Southeast Region

336 Cascade Park
City of Moses Lake

Directions

Start at intersection of I–90 and WA–17 in Moses Lake. Travel north on WA–17 for 3.9 miles and exit at Stratford Road. Turn left onto Stratford Road and travel 0.4 mile. Turn right onto Valley Road and travel 1.9 miles. Turn left into park.

N47°08'24" – W119°18'47"   Elevation – 1,050 feet

Facilities

83 total sites: 33 standard, 50 partial utility (W/E)
Flush toilets
Potable water
Hot showers
Garbage service
RV dump
Shelter
Boat launch and docks
Moorage
Accessible standard site

Features

Cascade Park campground lies along the Lewis Horn of Moses Lake. Several of the campsites are lakeside. The park has a playground and soccer fields. Ice and firewood are available for purchase during operational hours.

Reservations

Reservations for May through September dates can be made by phone at 509–764–3805 or by mail at Cascade Campground, P.O. Box 1579, Moses Lake, WA 98837. During the month of April, all campsites are first–come, first–served. See Appendix B for more information.

Season

Open April 1 through September 30

Activities

Bird watching, Boating, Fishing, Swimming, Water skiing.

Cost

$30 standard site plus $5 processing fee
$35 partial utility site plus $5 processing fee

Cascade Park Play Area and Shelter

Limitations

Minimum stay is two nights over weekends and three nights over holiday weekends.
Only one vehicle per camp site is allowed.
Each site allows a maximum of 6 people, including children.
See Appendix A for camping regulations.

Contact

City of Moses Lake
Parks & Recreation
411 S. Balsam Street
Moses Lake, WA 98837
Phone: 509–764–3805
Web: *www.cityofml.com*

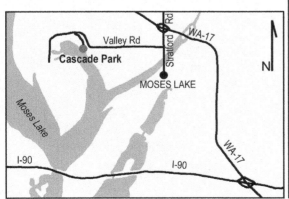

Driving Directions

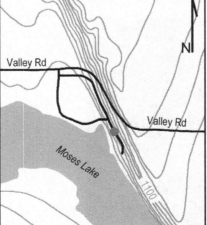

Location

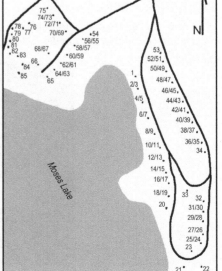

Campground

Huevos Rancheros

Ingredients

2 small tortillas (corn or wheat)
3 eggs
2 tablespoons milk or half and half
1 tablespoon olive oil
1 (7 ounce) can of salsa casera
1 small can of black beans
½ teaspoon of cumin
½ cup cheddar cheese (sliced or shredded)
½ avocado, peeled, pitted and thinly sliced
Sour cream
Salt and pepper to taste

Preparation

Crack eggs into bowl, add milk, and beat with a fork until frothy. Open beans, drain, and stir cumin into the drained beans. Preheat a skillet on the camp stove, briefly heat tortillas and put on a plate. (We often place a second inverted plate over the first plate to help keep the tortillas warm.)

Add olive oil to the skillet over medium heat. Pour in eggs. Cover briefly to set eggs (we are making an omlet).

Place cheese and slices of avocado on half of egg circle.

When top of eggs have set and the bottom has begun to brown, use a spatula and fold the omelet in half and move to one side of skillet.

Put beans and salsa on the empty side of the skillet to heat.

Place tortillas on top of everything and cover until omelet is done and beans are warm.

Put a tortilla on each plate. Cut the omelet (one half for each person). Put a half omlet piece on each tortilla. Spoon beans and salsa over the omelet and put a dollop of sour cream on top. Salt and pepper to taste. A sausage patty makes a nice addition. Life is good.

337 Potholes
Washington State Parks

Directions

Start at the intersection of I–90 and WA–17 near Moses Lake. Travel south on WA–17 for 10.1 miles. Turn right onto WA–262 and travel for 11.7 miles. Turn right into park.

N 46º58'48" – W 119º21'09"   Elevation – 1,050 feet

Facilities

121 total sites: 61 standard sites, 60 utility sites (W/E/S)

Potable water
Flush toilets
Hot showers
Garbage service
RV dump station
Boat launch

Features

A series of Ice Age floods carved depressions that are the main geologic feature of this park which combine with O'Sullivan Dam to create hundreds of tiny islands surrounded by pothole lakes. The terrain is desert with freshwater marshes.

Reservations

Sites may be reserved online at *www.parks.state.wa.us* or by telephone 1–888–CAMPOUT (1–888–226–7688). See Appendix B for details.

Season

Open all year

Activities

Boating, Fishing, Hiking, Metal detecting, Personal watercraft, Volleyball courts.

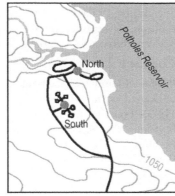

Location

Cost

$12 primitive site
Peak season: mid May – mid September
$22 – $35 standard site
$30 – $40 partial utility site
$35 – $45 full utility site
Off–peak season
$20 – $30 standard site
$25 – $35 partial utility site
$30 – $40 full utility site
$10 extra vehicle (all year)
See Appendix C for available discounts.

Limitations

Maximum site length is 50 feet.
See Appendix A for camping regulations.

Contact

Phone: 509–346–2759
Web: *www.parks.state.wa.us*

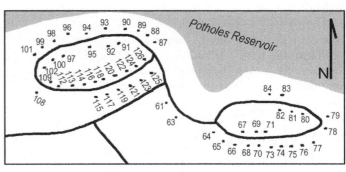

North Campground

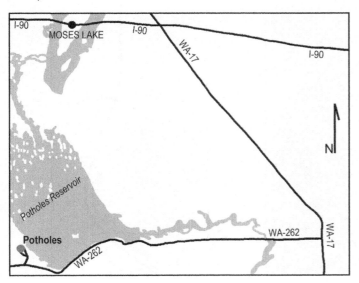

Driving Directions

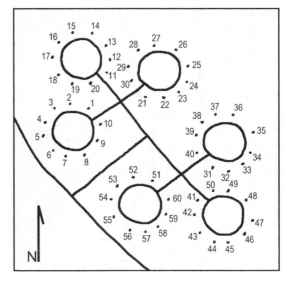

South Campground

338 Pacific Lake
Lakeview Ranch
Bureau of Land Management

Directions

Start at the intersection of WA–28 and WA–21 in Odessa. Travel north on WA–21 for 2.8 miles. Turn left onto Lakeview Ranch Loop Road North and travel 2.3 miles (you are forced to make a right turn after about 1 mile). Turn left to continue on Lakeview Ranch Loop Road North and travel 1.0 mile. Turn right to continue on Lakeview Ranch Loop Road North and travel for 1.1 miles. Turn right into campground.

N47°24'16" – W118°44'29"   Elevation – 1,650 feet

Facilities

6 standard sites
Vault toilet
No water, bring your own
Pack out garbage

Features

Lakeview Ranch campground is a short distance east of the Lakeview Ranch buildings and has views of, now dry, Pacific and Walter Lakes. Hiking trails in the area include the 12.5 mile Odessa to Pacific Lake Trail that winds through shrub–steppe uplands and Lake Creek Canyon between the town of Odessa and Lakeview Ranch.

The north end of the area has approximately seven miles of linked two–track roads and is designated as LIMITED motorized use. Motorized use is restricted to the road so no off–road motorized use is allowed. The area boasts unique geological features, such as the Odessa Craters area which is 5 miles north of Odessa off WA–21.

Campsite View

Reservations

None, all campsites are first–come, first–serve.

Season

Open all year

Activities

Bird watching, Equestrian trail riding, Hiking, Hunting, Motorcycle riding/ATVs, Mountain biking.

Cost

No cost

Limitations

Stay limit is 14 days.
Caution, rattlesnakes are in the area.
See Appendix A for camping regulations.

Contact

Bureau of Land Management
Spokane District Office
1102 N Francher Road
Spokane WA 99212
Phone: 509–536–1200
Web: *www.blm.gov/or*

Driving Directions

Campsite

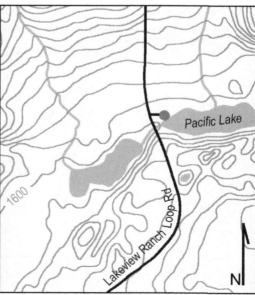

Location

339 Kamiak Butte Park
Whitman County

Directions

Start at the intersection of WA–270 and WA–27 in Pullman. Travel north on WA–27 (also called N Grand Ave) for 11.6 miles. Turn left onto Clear Creek Road and travel 0.4 miles. Bear left onto Fugate Road and travel for 0.7 miles. Turn left onto Kamiak Butte Park Road and travel 1.0 mile to the park.

N46°51'45" – W117°10'01"   Elevation – 2,900 feet

Facilities

7 sites
Restrooms available year round
Water available between April 15th and October 15th

Features

Kamiak Butte is recognized as a Natural National Landmark. It has over 5–miles of hiking trails and offers a panoramic view of the Palouse region.

Reservations

None, all campsites are first–come, first–serve.

Season

Park open year round

Activities

Hiking, Bird watching.

Cost

$15 per site
$5 for extra vehicles

Limitations

This is a gated park with no access in or out of the park from dusk until 7:00 am.
Campsites are limited to vehicles 18' or shorter though the upper parking area is available for overnight accommodations.

Contact

Whitman County Parks and Recreation
310 North Main Street
Colfax, WA 99111
Phone: 509–397–6238
Web: *whitmancounty.org*

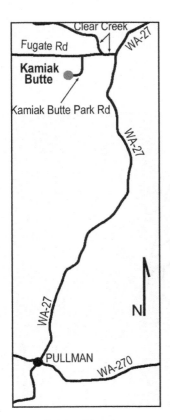

Driving Directions

Palouse

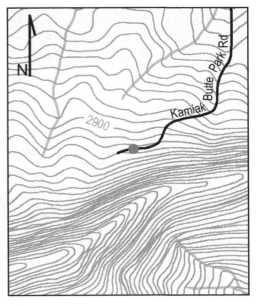

Location

340 Boyer Park and Marina
Port of Whitman County

Directions

Start at the intersection of US–195 and WA–194 in Pullman. Travel west on WA–194 for 21.1 miles. At the end of the road, turn left onto Lower Granite Dam Road and travel for 1.4 miles. Turn right into park.

N46º41'05" – W117º26'55"   Elevation – 640 feet

Facilities

48 total sites: 12 standard sites, 16 partial utility sites (W/E), 20 utility sites (W/E/S)
Flush toilets
Showers
Garbage service
RV dump station
Marina
Convenience store

Features

From the awe inspiring river views at the top of Almota grade to the green shady lawns and campsites of the park itself, Boyer Park is a lovely spot located on the Snake River. While owned by the Corps of Engineers, the park is managed by the Port of Whitman County through a private vendor.

Reservations

Reservations are available by telephone at 509–397–3208. See Appendix B for additional information.

Season

Open all year

Activities

Boating, Fishing, Hiking, Water skiing, Swimming.

Cost

$18 – $40

Limitations

Please see Appendix A for camping regulations.

Contact

Phone: 509–397–3208

Boyer Campsite

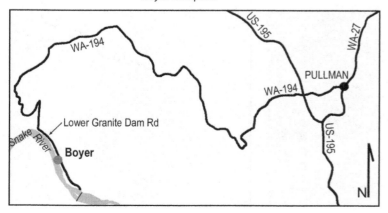

Driving Directions

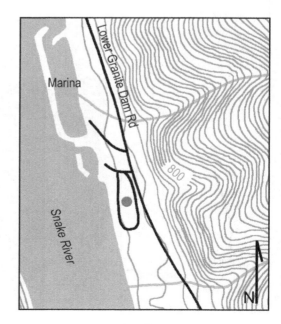

Location

341 Wawawai County Park
Whitman County

Directions

Start at the intersection of US–195 and WA–194 in Pullman. Travel west on WA–194 for 2.7 miles. Turn left onto Wawawai–Pullman Road and travel for 7.5 miles. Turn right onto Wawawai Road and travel for 5.4 miles. Turn right into park.

N46º38'06" – W117º22'33"   Elevation – 240 feet

Facilities

9 sites total: 4 pull through
Restroom available year round
Water between mid–April and mid–October
Garbage service

Features

Located in the Snake River Canyon, the park has a nearby boat launch. Motorized boating is allowed on the Snake River but only non–motorized is allowed on the lagoon located in the park.

Reservations

None, all campsites are first–come, first–serve.

Season

Open year round

Activities

Boating, Fishing, Hiking, Bird watching.

Cost

$15 per site
$5 for extra vehicle

Limitations

This is a gated park with no access in or out between dusk and 7:00 am.
Campfires are only permitted in the off–season (between October 11 and June 9). Between June 10 and October 10, only charcoal briquettes or gas grills are permitted due to the high fire danger.

Contact

Whitman County Parks and Recreation
310 North Main Street
Colfax, WA 99111
Phone: 509–397–6238
Web: *whitmancounty.org*

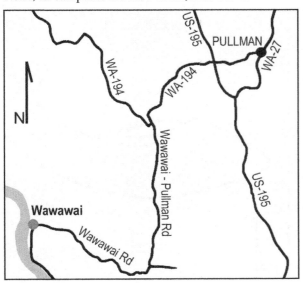

Driving Directions

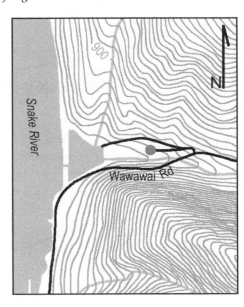

Location

342 Chief Timothy Park
US Army Corps of Engineers

Directions

Start at the intersection of US–12 and WA–128 in Clarkston. Travel west on US–12 for 3.5 miles. Turn right onto Silcott Road and into park.

N46°25'04" – W117°11'42"   Elevation – 600 feet

Facilities

66 total sites: 17 standard sites, 16 tent only sites, 8 partial utility (W/E), 25 utility sites (W/E/S)

Flush toilets
Potable water
Showers
Garbage service
RV dump station
Boat launch
Boat docks

Features

This park is located on an island in the Snake River. The campground has shade trees and lawn. The Army Corps of Engineers contracts with a private management company to operate the park.

Reservations

Sites may be reserved online at https://www.sunrisereservations.com/campground/Chief+Timothy+Park

Season

Open April – October

Activities

Boating, Fishing, Hiking, Playground, Swimming, Volleyball.

Cost

$29 – $44

Limitations

Maximum recommended vehicle length is 40 feet.

Contact

Phone: 509–758–9580
Web: https://www.sunrisereservations.com/campground/Chief+Timothy+Park

Chief Timothy Swimming Area

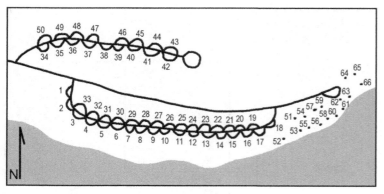

Campground

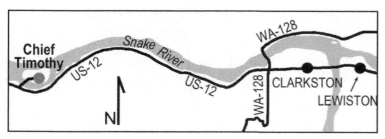

Driving Directions

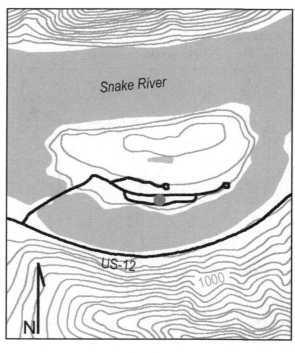

Location

343 Fields Spring
Washington State Parks

Directions

Start at the intersection of US–12 and WA–129 in Clarkston. Travel south on WA–129 (Sixth St) for 29.1 miles. (The road changes names several times but remains WA–129.) Turn left into park.

N46º04'55" – W117º10'12"   Elevation – 3,960 feet

Facilities

20 total sites
Potable water
Flush toilets
Kitchen shelter
Garbage services
RV dump station

Features

This park is nestled in the folds of the Blue Mountains in the southeastern corner of the state and offers spectacular scenery. It has two environmental learning centers.

Reservations

Reservations can be made online at *www.parks.state.wa.us* or by calling 888–CAMPOUT (888–226–7688). See Appendix B for details.

Season

Open all year

Cost

$12 primitive site
Peak season: mid May – mid September
$22 – $35 standard site
$30 – $40 partial utility site
$35 – $45 full utility site
Off–peak season
$20 – $30 standard site
$25 – $35 partial utility site
$30 – $40 full utility site
$10 extra vehicle (all year)
See Appendix C for available discounts.

Limitations

The maximum site length is 30 feet.
A Sno–Park permit is required between December 1 and April 30.
See Appendix A for camping regulations.

Contact

Phone: 509–256–3332
Web: *www.parks.state.wa.us*

Activities

Hiking, Metal detecting area, Horseshoe pits, Winter sledding, Snowshoeing.

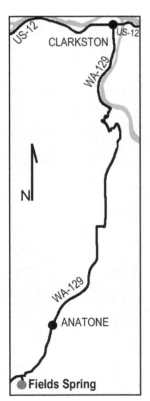

Driving Directions

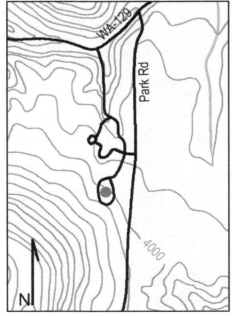

Location

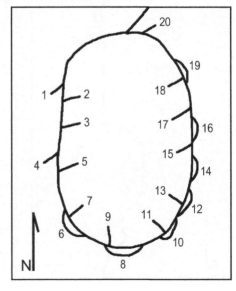

Campground

344 Forest Boundary
Umatilla National Forest

Directions

Start at the intersection of US–12 and WA–128 in Clarkston. Travel west on US–12 for 29.2 miles. Turn left onto 15th Street in Pomeroy (which becomes Peola Road). Continue straight onto Mountain Road (becomes Forest Service Road 40). Travel for 15.2 miles. Turn left into campground.

Or

Start at the intersection of US–12 and WA–127 west of Pomeroy. Travel east on US–12 for 13.2 miles. Turn right onto 15th Street in Pomeroy (which becomes Peola Road). Continue straight onto Mountain Road (which becomes Forest Service Road 40). Travel for 15.2 miles. Turn left into campground.

N46º17'34" – W117º33'28"   Elevation – 4,480 feet

Forest Boundary Campsite

Facilities

7 standard sites
Vault toilet
No water, bring our own

Features

The campground has a great view overlooking Scoggin's Ridge with lovely sunsets. The campground is near Boundary Snow Park, Wooten State Wildlife Area, and the Arbothknott Canyon. ATV trailheads for the North and South trails are located close by.

Reservations

None, all campsites are first–come, first–serve.

Season

Open all year

Activities

Hiking, ATV trail riding.

Cost

No cost

Limitations

There is a limit of 14 nights stay every 30 days. See Appendix A for camping regulations.

Contact

Umatilla National Forest
Pomeroy Ranger District
71 West Main
Pomeroy, WA 99347
Phone: 509–843–1891

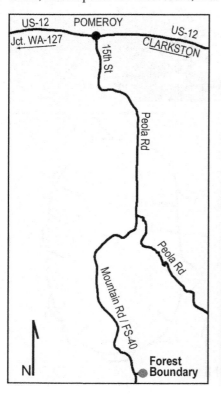
Driving Directions

Forest Boundary Toilet

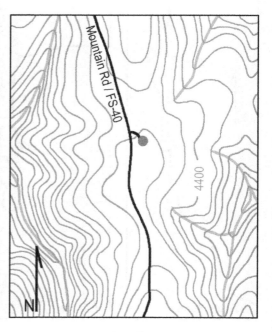
Location

345 Big Springs
Umatilla National Forest

Directions

Start at the intersection of US–12 and WA–128 in Clarkston. Travel west on US–12 for 29.2 miles. Turn left onto 15th Street in Pomeroy (which becomes Peola Road) Continue straight onto Mountain Road (which becomes Forest Service Road 40). Travel for 23.3 miles. Turn left onto Forest Service Road 42 and travel for 3.0 miles. Turn left into campground.

Or

Start at the intersection of US–12 and WA–127 west of Pomeroy. Travel east on US–12 for 13.2 miles. Turn right onto 15th Street in Pomeroy (which becomes Peola Road) Continue straight onto Mountain Road (which becomes Forest Service Road 40). Travel for 23.3 miles. Turn left onto Forest Service Road 42 and travel for 3.0 miles. Turn left into campground.

N46º13'49" – W117º32'38"   Elevation – 5,000 feet

Facilities

10 standard sites
Vault toilet
No water, bring our own
Shelter

Features

There is a spring which flows through part of the campground. This, and it's location, contribute to it having a cooler temperature than surrounding areas – a benefit on hot summer days.

Reservations

None, all campsites are first–come, first–serve.

Season

Open all year

Activities

Hiking, Hunting (in season).

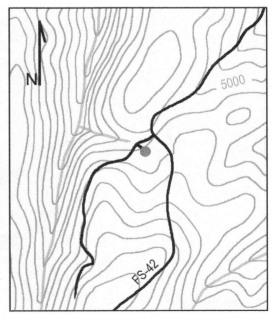

Range Cattle

Cost

No cost

Limitations

There is a limit of 14 nights stay every 30 days. See Appendix A for camping regulations.

Contact

Umatilla National Forest
Pomeroy Ranger District
71 West Main
Pomeroy, WA 99347
Phone: 509–843–1891

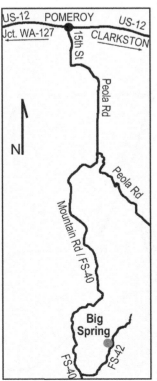

Driving Directions

Big Spring Campground

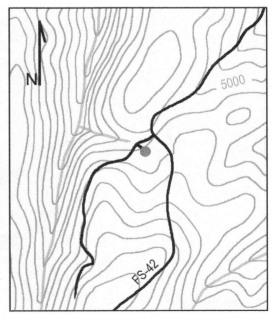

Location

346 Teal Spring
Umatilla National Forest

Directions

Start at the intersection of US–12 and WA–128 in Clarkston. Travel west on US–12 for 29.2 miles. Turn left onto 15th Street in Pomeroy (which becomes Peola Road). Continue straight onto Mountain Road (which becomes Forest Service Road 40). Travel for 24.0 miles. Turn right onto Forest Service Road 200 and travel for 0.3 miles to campground.

Or

Start at the intersection of US–12 and WA–127 west of Pomeroy. Travel east on US–12 for 13.2 miles. Turn right onto 15th Street in Pomeroy (which becomes Peola Road). Continue straight onto Mountain Road (which becomes Forest Service Road 40). Travel for 24.0 miles. Turn right onto Forest Service Road 200 and travel for 0.3 miles to campground.

N46º11'20" – W117º34'24"   Elevation – 5,600 feet

Facilities

7 standard sites
Vault toilet
No water, bring our own
Warming cabin

Features

There are campsites on a bluff that have incredible views of the valley.

Teal Spring View Campsite

Reservations

None, all campsites are first–come, first–serve.

Season

Open all year

Activities

Hiking, OHV opportunities.

Cost

No cost

Limitations

Weed–free feed is required for stock animals.
See Appendix A for camping regulations.

Contact

Umatilla National Forest
Pomeroy Ranger District
71 West Main
Pomeroy, WA 99347
Phone: 509–843–1891

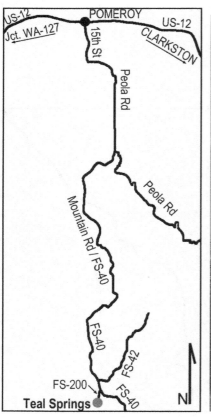

Driving Directions

Fire Watch Tower Near Teal Spring

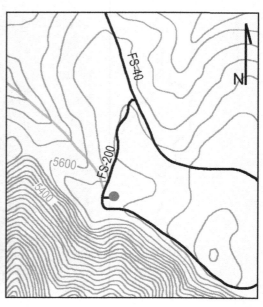

Location

347 Wickiup
Umatilla National Forest

Directions

Start at the intersection of US–12 and WA–128 in Clarkston. Travel west on US–12 for 29.2 miles. Turn left onto 15th Street in Pomeroy (which becomes Peola Road). Continue straight onto Mountain Road (which becomes Forest Service Road 40). Travel for 30.9 miles. Bear left at the "Y" onto Forest Service Road 44 and travel 3.1 miles. Turn right onto Forest Service Road 43 and travel 0.1 mile. Turn left into campground.

Or

Start at the intersection of US–12 and WA–127 west of Pomeroy. Travel east on US–12 for 13.2 miles. Turn right onto 15th Street in Pomeroy (which becomes Peola Road). Continue straight onto Mountain Road (which becomes Forest Service Road 40). Travel for 30.9 miles. Bear left at the "Y" onto Forest Service Road 44 and travel 3.1 miles. Turn right onto Forest Service Road 43 and travel 0.1 mile. Turn left into campground.

N46º08'11" – W117º26'10"   Elevation – 5,100 feet

Facilities

7 standard sites
Vault toilet
No water, bring our own

Features

This campground has several nearby ridges and a cold water spring within 100 yards.

Reservations

None, all campsites are first–come, first–serve.

Season

Open all year

Activities

Hiking, Fishing (within 5–miles at Ranger Creek).

Cost

No cost

Limitations

There is a limit of 14 days stay out of every 30 days. See Appendix A for camping regulations.

Contact

Umatilla National Forest
Pomeroy Ranger District
71 West Main
Pomeroy, WA 99347
Phone: 509–843–1891

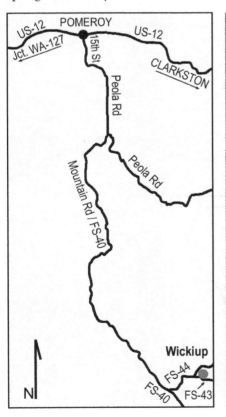

Driving Directions

Umatilla Forest

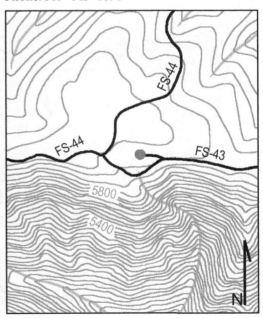

Location

348 Tucannon
Umatilla National Forest

Directions

Start at the intersection of US–12 and WA–261 north of Dayton. Travel west on US–12 for 1.6 miles. Turn left onto Tucannon Road (signed for Camp Wooten and becomes Forest Service Road 47). Travel for 28.6 miles. Turn left onto Forest Service Road 4700–160 (at the Camp Wooten sign). Tucannon campground is just after the bridge that is immediately crossed on the Camp Wooten access road.

   N46º14'34" – W117º41'17"   Elevation – 2,600 feet

Facilities

18 standard sites
Vault toilet
No water, bring our own

Features

The campground is located along the Tucannon River. There are several stocked ponds nearby.

Reservations

None, all campsites are first–come, first–serve.

Season

Open all year

Activities

Hiking, Fishing.

Cost

$8 standard site
$5 extra vehicle
No cost during winter

See Appendix C for details.

Limitations

There is a limit of 14 days stay out of every 30 days.
See Appendix A for camping regulations.

Contact

Umatilla National Forest
Pomeroy Ranger District
71 West Main
Pomeroy, WA 99347
Phone: 509–843–1891

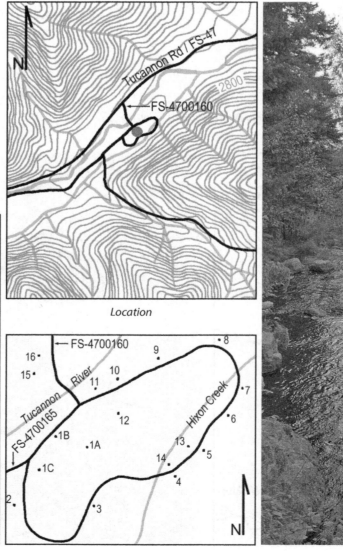

Driving Directions

Campground

Location

Tucannon Stream

349 Lady Bug
Umatilla National Forest

Directions

Start at the intersection of US–12 and WA–261 north of Dayton. Travel west on US–12 for 1.6 miles. Turn left onto Tucannon Road (signed for Camp Wooten and becomes Forest Service Road 47). Travel for 32.4 miles. Bear left onto Forest Service Road 4712 and travel 2.0 miles to campground.

N46°11'49" – W117°40'12"   Elevation – 4,700 feet

Facilities

7 standard sites
Vault toilet
No water, bring our own

Features

This campground is near the Wenaha–Tucannon Wilderness Area.

Reservations

None, all campsites are first–come, first–serve.

Season

Open all year

Activities

Hiking.

Cost

$8 standard site
$5 extra vehicle
No cost during the winter

Limitations

Vehicles requiring high clearance not recommended.
There is a limit of 14 days stay out of every 30 days.
See Appendix A for camping regulations.

Contact

Umatilla National Forest
Pomeroy Ranger District
71 West Main
Pomeroy, WA 99347
Phone: 509–843–1891

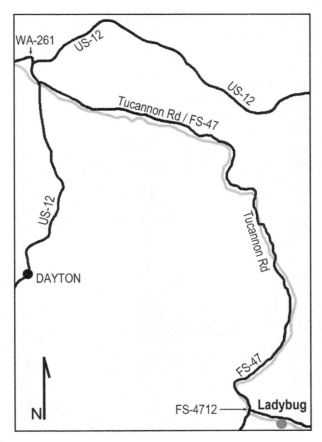

Driving Directions

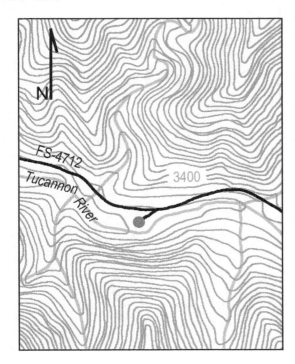

Location

350 Godman
Umatilla National Forest

Directions

Start at the intersection of US–12 and WA–261 north of Dayton. Travel west on US–12 for 14.8 miles. Turn left onto South 4th Street (becomes North Touchet Road) and travel for 5.0 miles. Turn left onto Hartley Gulch Road and travel 4.4 miles. Turn right onto Kendall Skyline Road and travel 5.9 miles. Turn right to stay on Kendall Skyline Road (becomes Forest Service Road 46) and travel 11.7 miles. Turn right into campground.

N46°06'00" – W117°47'10"   Elevation – 6,050 feet

Facilities

8 standard sites
Vault toilet
No water, bring our own
Shelter

Features

This campground offers nice views and great sunsets.

Reservations

None, all campsites are first–come, first–serve.

Season

Open all year

Activities

Hiking, Fishing, Bicycling.

North of Umatilla National Forest

Cost

No cost

Limitations

There is a limit of 14 days stay out of every 30 days.
Wilderness restrictions apply: no motorized or mechanized equipment on trail.
Weed–free feed is required for stock animals.
See Appendix A for camping regulations.

Contact

Umatilla National Forest
Pomeroy Ranger District
71 West Main
Pomeroy, WA 99347
Phone: 509–843–1891

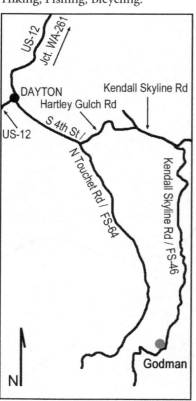

Driving Directions

Moon Rise

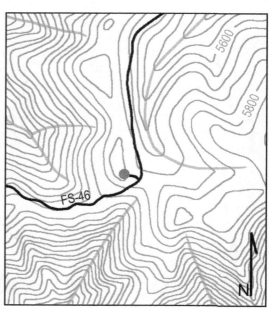

Location

351 Palouse Falls
Washington State Parks

Directions

Start at the intersection of US–12 and WA–261 north of Dayton. Travel north on WA–261 for 20.7 miles. Turn right onto Palouse Falls Road and travel for 2.0 miles into park.

N46º39'51" – W118º13'28"   Elevation – 725 feet

Facilities

11 total sites
Pit toilet
Potable water available
April to October

Features

This is a small park with a unique geology and history. It offers a dramatic view of a 198 foot tall waterfall with high volumes of water in the spring and early summer.

Reservations

All sites are first–come, first–served.

Season

Open all year

Activities

Hiking, Viewing site, Interpretive site.

Cost

$12 primitive site
Peak season: mid May – mid September
$22 – $35 standard site
$30 – $40 partial utility site
$35 – $45 full utility site

Off–peak season
$20 – $30 standard site
$25 – $35 partial utility site
$30 – $40 full utility site
$10 extra vehicle (all year)
See Appendix C for available discounts.

Limitations

Parking in the park is very limited. Expect long waits on weekends and holidays. RVs and trailers will not be permitted to enter the park because turn–arounds do not exist.
See Appendix A for camping regulations.

Contact

Phone: 509–646–9218
Web: *www.parks.state.wa.us*

Palouse Falls

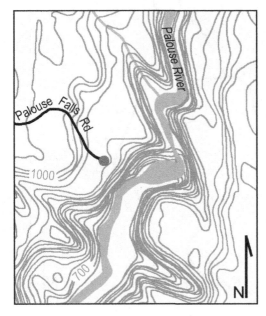

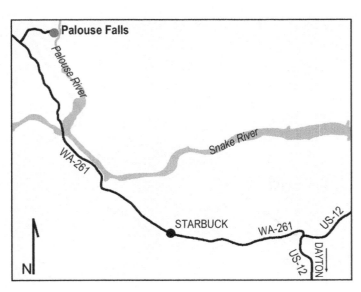

Driving Directions

Location

352 Windust
US Army Corps of Engineers

Directions

Start at the intersection of WA–260 and WA–263 in the town of Kahlotus. Travel south on WA–263 for 0.7 miles. Continue straight onto Pasco–Kahlotus Road and travel for 3.2 miles. Turn left onto Wallace Walker Road and travel for 6.1 miles. Turn right onto Burr Canyon Road and travel for 0.1 mile. Turn left into park.

N46º32'05" – W118º34'43"   Elevation – 500 feet

Facilities

24 total sites
Flush toilets
No water, bring your own
RV dump station
Boat launch

Features

The park is located on the shore of the Snake River. The park has wide–open vistas with few trees and an arid climate.

Reservations

All sites are first–come, first–serve.

Season

Open May – early September

Activities

Boating, Fishing, Hiking, Water skiing, Swimming.

Cost

$10 – $24
$5 extra vehicle
See Appendix C for available discounts.

Arrival

Limitations

Alcoholic beverages are prohibited.
See Appendix A for camping regulations.

Contact

Phone: 509–547–2048
Web: *http://www.nww.usace.army.mil/Missions/Recreation/Ice–Harbor–Dam–Lake–Sacajawea/Windust–Park/*

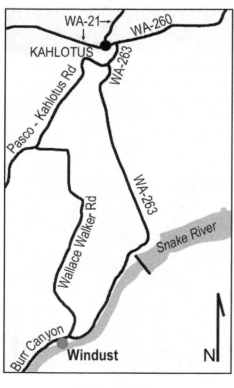

Driving Directions

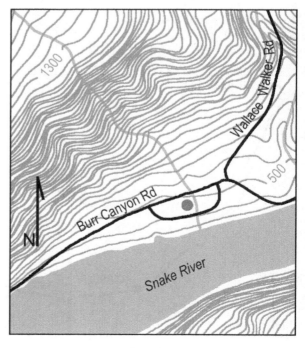

Location

353 Lewis and Clark Trail
Washington State Parks

Directions

Start at the intersection of US–12 and WA–124 near Waitsburg. Travel east on US–12 for 4.4 miles. Turn left into park.

N46°17'19" – W118°04'20"   Elevation – 1,400 feet

Facilities

24 full total sites
Flush toilets
Potable water
Garbage service
Kitchen shelter

Features

This park is a 37–acre camping park with shoreline on the Touchet River. It is a forested "oasis" in the middle of arid grassland.

Reservations

Reservations can be made online at *www.parks.state.wa.us* or by calling 888–CAMPOUT (888–226–7688). See Appendix B for details.

Season

Camping open April 1 – October 31

Activities

Fishing, Hiking, Swimming, Stream tubing, Badminton, Volleyball, Winter snowshoeing.

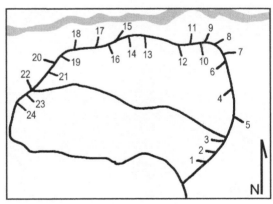

Campground

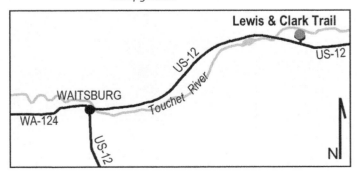

Driving Directions

Lewis and Clark Trail Campsite

Cost

$12 primitive site
Peak season: mid May – mid September
$22 – $35 standard site
$30 – $40 partial utility site
$35 – $45 full utility site
Off–peak season
$20 – $30 standard site
$25 – $35 partial utility site
$30 – $40 full utility site
$10 extra vehicle (all year)
See Appendix C for available discounts.

Limitations

The maximum site length is 32 feet.
See Appendix A for camping regulations.

Contact

Phone: 509–337–6457
Web: *www.parks.state.wa.us*

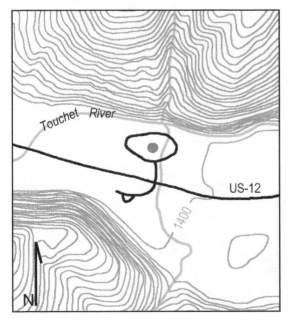

Location

354 Fishhook Park
US Army Corps of Engineers

Directions

Start at the intersection of US–12 and WA–124 near Pasco. Travel east on WA–124 (Ice Harbor Road) for 16.2 miles. Turn left onto Fishhook Park Road and travel 4.5 miles to park.

N46°18'48" – W118°45'59"   Elevation – 450 feet

Facilities

52 total sites: 41 sites partial utility (E), 11 walk–in tent sites
Flush toilets
Potable water
Hot showers
Garbage service
RV dump station
Playground
Boat launch

Activities

Boating, Fishing, Hiking, Hunting, Swimming, Water skiing.

Cost

$10 – $24
$12 – $30 (partial utility)
$5 extra vehicle
See Appendix C for available discounts.

Limitations

Alcoholic beverages are prohibited.
See Appendix A for camping regulations.

Contact

Phone: 509–547–2048

Snake River from Fishhook Park

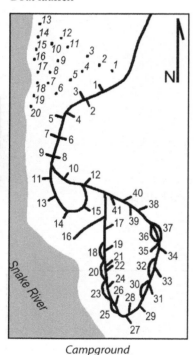

Campground

Features

Fishhook is located on the shore of the Snake River and has several large shade trees.

Reservations

Sites may be reserved at *www.recreation.gov* or at 1–877–444–6777. Reserve or change reservations at least 2 days in advance. Reservations can be made up to 6 months in advance. See Appendix B for details.

Season

Open
May – early September

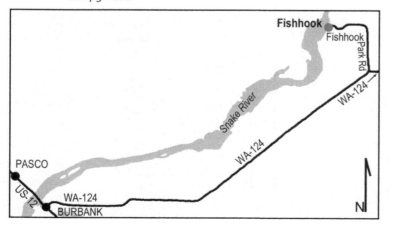

Driving Directions

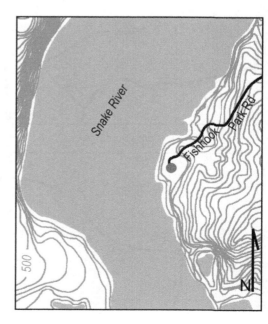

Location

355 Charbonneau Park
US Army Corps of Engineers

Directions

Start at the intersection of US–12 and WA–124 near Pasco. Travel east on WA–124 (Ice Harbor Road) for 8.6 miles. Turn left onto Sun Harbor Drive and travel 1.2 miles. Turn right onto Harbor Blvd and travel 0.4 mile. Turn left onto Charbonneau Road and travel 1.0 mile to park.

N46°13'03" – W119°00'39"   Elevation – 470 feet

Facilities

52 total sites: all with electric hookups

Flush toilets
Potable water
Hot showers
Garbage service
RV dump station
Playground
Boat launch
Marina

Features

The park is located on the shore of the Snake River and was named one of America's Top 100 Family Campgrounds. The park has open grassy areas dotted with a few large shade trees.

Reservations

Sites may be reserved online at *www.recreation.gov* or by phone at 1–877–444–6777. Reserve or change reservations at least 2 days in advance. Reservations can be made up to 6 months in advance. See Appendix B for details.

Season

Open May – early September

Activities

Boating, Fishing, Hiking, Swimming, Volleyball, Water skiing.

Cost

$12 – $30
$5 extra vehicle (all year)
See Appendix C for available discounts.

Limitations

Alcoholic beverages are prohibited.

Maximum site length is 45 feet.
See Appendix A for camping regulations.

Contact

Phone: 509–547–2048

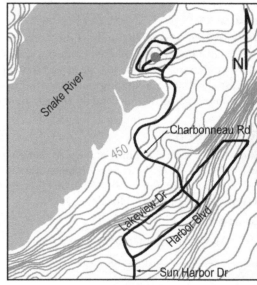

Location

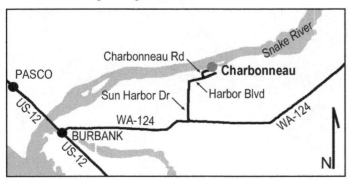

Driving Directions

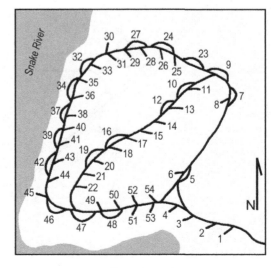

Campground

356 Hood Park
US Army Corps of Engineers

Directions

Start at the intersection of US–12 and WA–124 near Pasco. Travel east on WA–124 (Ice Harbor Road) for 0.1 mile. Turn left onto Hood Park Road and travel 0.2 mile into campground.

N46º13'03" – W119º00'39"   Elevation – 350 feet

Facilities

67 total sites with electrical hookup: 24 pull–through sites

Flush toilets
Potable water
Hot showers
Garbage service
RV dump station
Playground
Boat launch
Shelter

Features

The park is located on the shore of the Snake River in a section that is just upriver from where it joins the Columbia River. The McNary National Wildlife Refuge is next to the park which provides habitat for migrating waterfowl and resident wildlife. The refuge has nature trails and an environmental learning center.

Reservations

Sites may be reserved online at *www.recreation.gov* or by phone at 1–877–444–6777. Reserve or change reservations at least 2 days in advance. Reservations can be made up to 6 months in advance. See Appendix B for details.

Season

Open May – early September

Activities

Boating, Fishing, Hiking, Basketball, Horseshoe pit, Swimming, Water skiing.

Cost

$12 – $26
$5 extra vehicle (all year)
See Appendix C for available discounts.

Limitations

Alcoholic beverages are prohibited.
See Appendix A for camping regulations.

Contact

Phone: 509–547–2048

Riverfront at Hood Park

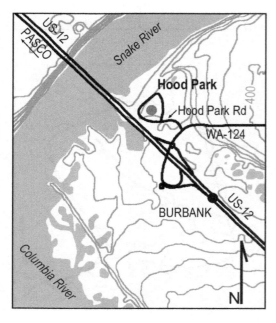

Driving Directions and Location

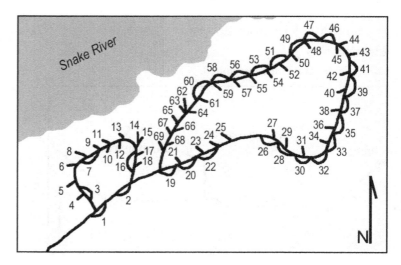

Campground

Coconut Ice Cream

Southeastern Washington can be very warm in the summer. On hot evenings, there is no better way to cool the troops than to have ice cream. When you are at a campground with electricity available, it is even easy to make. We found a used ice cream freezer at a thrift store for $5 and it is still churning after 6 years.

Ingredients

1 cup milk
15 oz can sweetened coconut milk
1 ½ cup heavy cream
1 cup coconut flakes, toasted
fresh fruit, sliced (optional)
1 large bag of crushed party ice
1 ½ cup ice cream freezer rock salt

Preparation

Toast the coconut flakes in a dry frying pan over medium heat. Stir constantly. Place flakes into a separate bowl when lightly browned since it will continue to cook if left in the pan.

Place milk and coconut milk in the ice cream freezer's can and stir vigorously until thoroughly mixed. Add and gently stir heavy cream and coconut flakes into the milk mixture.
Place the freezer's stir paddle into the can with the milk mixture. Put the can's lid into place, feeding the paddle's drive stem through the hole in the lid.
Place the freezer can into the center of the ice cream maker's bucket and mount the freezer motor on the top. (There is usually a little bulge on the can's bottom that fits into a dimple in the bucket's bottom.) Be careful to align the paddle top into the motor's gear drive. Do not force. It should go in easily when aligned. Plug the motor into an electrical outlet and verify the can is revolving freely before proceeding.

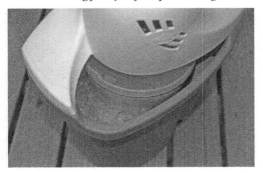

As the freezer can rotates, add a layer of ice chips into the bucket (surrounding the can), After adding a couple inches of ice, add a couple tablespoons of rock salt. Follow with more ice and then more salt until the bucket is full. Do not pile ice higher than the lid of the can since salty ice water can get into your ice cream.
When this ice has melted down about 1/4 of the can height, add more ice and a little more rock salt.

Keep this up until the motor begins to labor or after about 45 minutes. After unplugging the motor, take off the motor without letting the can raise out of the ice. Remove the lid to get a peek at the ice cream. If it appears semi-solid, it's done. Remove the can from the bucket and wipe off the salt and ice from the outside. If it isn't solid, replace the lid and motor and continue running and add more ice and salt as needed.
Dish into serving bowls and eat immediately unless you have an RV freezer or like melted ice cream. If you have sliced fresh fruit, spoon it on top.

That cooled things down.

357 Plymouth
US Army Corps of Engineers

Directions

Start at the intersection of I–82 and WA–14 south of Kennewick and near the town of Plymouth. Travel west on WA–14 for 0.7 mile. Turn left onto South Plymouth Road and travel 1.1 miles. Bear right onto Christie Road and travel 0.1 mile. Turn left in the park.

N45º56'01" – W119º20'42"   Elevation – 290 feet

Facilities

32 total sites: 16 partial utility sites (W/E), 16 full utility sites

Flush toilets
Potable water
Hot showers
Garbage service
RV dump station
Playground
Laundry facilities
Boat Launch

Features

The park is located on the shore of the Columbia River in a section that is called Lake Umatilla. The surrounding area is high desert and shade from trees is limited.

Reservations

Sites may be reserved online at *www.recreation.gov* or by phone at 1–877–444–6777. Reserve or change reservations at least 2 days in advance. Reservations can be made up to 6 months in advance. See Appendix B for details.

Season

Open April – October

Activities

Boating, Fishing, Hunting, Water skiing.

Cost

$24 – $27
$5 extra vehicle (all year)
See Appendix C for available discounts.

Limitations

Maximum site length is 40 feet.
See Appendix A for camping regulations.

Contact

Plymouth Park
PO Box 823
Rufus, OR 97050
Phone: 541–506–4807

Plymouth Campsites

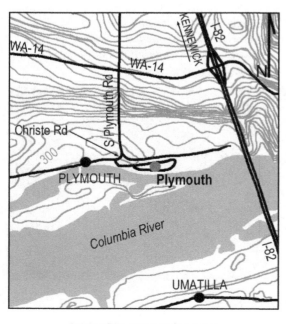

Driving Directions and Location

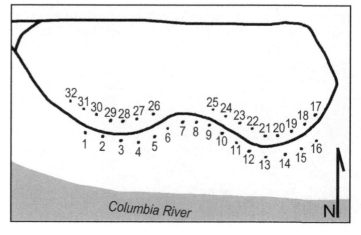

Campground

358 Horn Rapids Park
Benton County

Directions

Start at the intersection of WA–240 and WA–225 west of Richland, WA. Travel south on WA–225 (Horn Rd.) for 0.7 mile. Turn left into campground.

N46°21'48" – W119°26'48"   Elevation – 460 feet

Facilities

22 total sites: 16 partial utility (W/E), 6 standard

Pull–through sites
Flush toilets
Potable water
Garbage service
RV dump
Boat launch
Horse stable

Features

Horn Rapids Park is fronted by over four miles of Yakima River on one side and the public lands of the Hanford Reach National Monument, Rattlesnake Mountain Shooting Facility, and Rattlesnake Slope Wildlife Area on the other. Horn Rapids Park offers over 800 acres of transitional river–to–upland shrub–steppe habitat. The park has a campground, horse camp, model airplane facility, boat launch, tree collection, and miles of multi–use trails. It is a sanctuary for both the quantity and variety of dragonflies and birds.

Reservations

None, all campsites are first–come, first–serve.

Season

Open all year

Activities

Boating, Fishing, Hiking, Horse riding.

Cost

$25 – partial utility site
$15 – standard site

Horn Rapids Campsites

Limitations

No alcohol or campfires
No discharge of fire arms or fireworks in park
See Appendix A for camping regulations.

Contact

Park Ranger, Horn Rapids Park
7122 W. Okanogan Place
Building A
Kennewick, WA 99336
Phone: 509–531–7106
Email: *parks@co.benton.wa.us*
Web: *http://www.co.benton.wa.us*

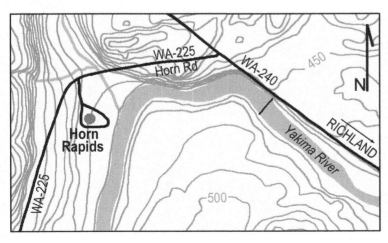

Driving Directions and Location

Horn Rapids Campsite

359 Wanapum
Washington State Parks

Directions

Start at the intersection of I–90 and Huntzinger Road (exit 136) near Vantage. Travel south on Huntzinger Road for 2.9 miles. Turn left into park.

N46º54'15" – W119º59'25"   Elevation – 600 feet

Facilities

50 full utility sites
Flush toilets
Potable water
Garbage service
Boat launch

Features

This park is part of the Wanapum Recreational Area which is adjacent to Ginkgo Petrified Forest State Park. Listed activities are for both parks. This campground is subject to high winds. Be sure to secure your tent.

The Ginkgo Petrified Forest Interpretive Center tells the geologic story of the Vantage Petrified Forest and displays one of the most diverse petrified wood collections in North America.

Reservations

Reservations can be made online at *www.parks.state.wa.us* or by calling 888–CAMPOUT (888–226–7688). See Appendix B for details.

Season

Open March 1 – October 31

Activities

Boating, Fishing, Hiking, Swimming.

Cost

$12 primitive site
Peak season: mid May – mid September
$22 – $35 standard site
$30 – $40 partial utility site
$35 – $45 full utility site
Off–peak season
$20 – $30 standard site
$25 – $35 partial utility site
$30 – $40 full utility site
$10 extra vehicle (all year)
See Appendix C for available discounts.

Limitations

The maximum site length is 60 feet.
Tenters may use the sites but must pay full fee.
See Appendix A for camping regulations.

Contact

Phone: 509–856–2700
Web: *www.parks.state.wa.us*

Wanapum Campsite

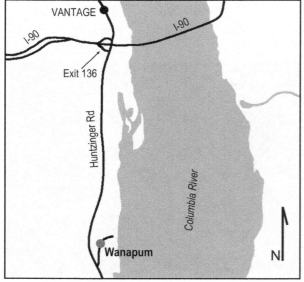

Driving Directions

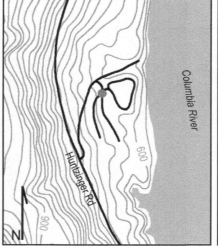

Location

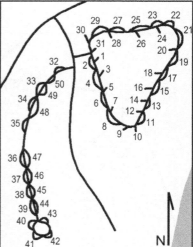

Campground

360 Umtanum
Bureau of Land Management

Directions

Start at the intersection I–82 and WA–821 (exit 26) near Yakima. Travel north on WA–821 for 16.4 miles and turn left into the campground.

Or

Start at the intersection I–90 and WA–821 (exit 109) in Ellensburg. Travel south on WA–821 for 12 miles and turn right into the campground.

N46°51'17"– W120°28'57"   Elevation – 1,300 feet

Facilities

6 standard sites
Vault toilet
No water, bring your own
Garbage service
Boat launch (undeveloped)
Accessible campsite, toilet

Features

The Umtanum recreation site is located in the Yakima River Canyon. The canyon cuts through massive basalt cliffs and rolling desert hills and offers excellent wildlife viewing. The drive through the canyon is designated a state scenic route. Campsites lie along the Yakima River and will easily accommodate RVs up to 37 feet.

A wooden footbridge crosses the Yakima River at this site, providing the only access to the west side of the river in the Yakima River Canyon. The west side of the river consists mainly of BLM and Washington Department of Fish and Wildlife managed lands.

Reservations

Reserve sites at *www.recreation.gov* or by phone at 1–877–444–6777 from May 15 through September 15. Reservations can be made up to six months in advance but not less than 48 hours of the desired arrival date. The rest of the year is first–come, first–serve. See Appendix B for more information.

Season

Open all year

Activities

Boating (non–motorized), Fishing, Hiking, Hunting, River rafting, Swimming, Wildlife viewing.

Cost

$15.00
See Appendix C for available discounts.

Limitations

Stay limit is 7 days.
See Appendix A for camping regulations.

Contact

Bureau of Land Management
Spokane District Office
1102 N Francher Road
Spokane WA 99212
Phone: 509–536–1200
Web: *www.blm.gov/or*

Driving Directions

Umtanum Boat Launch

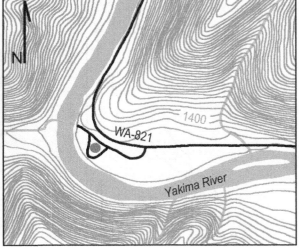

Location

361 Lmuma Creek
Bureau of Land Management

Directions

Start at the intersection I–82 and WA–821 (exit 26) near Yakima. Travel north on WA–821 for 12.5 miles and turn left into the campground.

Or

Start at the intersection I–90 and WA–821 (exit 109) in Ellensburg. Travel south on WA–821 for 15.9 miles and turn right into the campground.

N46°49'41" – W120°27'39"   Elevation – 1,300 feet

Facilities

7 standard sites
Vault toilet
No water, bring your own
Garbage service
Boat launch (undeveloped)
Accessible sites, toilet

Features

Lmuma Creek recreation site is located in the Yakima River Canyon. The canyon cuts through massive basalt cliffs and rolling desert hills and offers excellent wildlife viewing. The drive through the canyon is designated a state scenic route. Campsites lie along the Yakima River and will easily accommodate RVs up to 50 feet.

Lmuma Creek Campsite

Reservations can be made up to six months in advance but not less than 48 hours of the desired arrival date. The rest of the year is first–come, first–serve. See Appendix B for more information.

Season

Open all year

Activities

Boating (non–motorized), Fishing, Rafting, Swimming, Wildlife viewing.

Cost

$15.00
See Appendix C for available discounts.

Limitations

Stay limit is 7 days.
See Appendix A for camping regulations.

Contact

Bureau of Land Management
Spokane District Office
1102 N Francher Road
Spokane WA 99212
Phone: 509–536–1200
Web: *www.blm.gov/or*

Reservations

Reserve sites at *www.recreation.gov* or by phone at 1–877–444–6777 from May 15 through September 15.

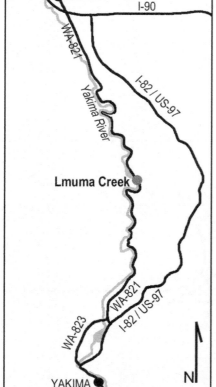

Driving Directions

Lmuma Creek Toilet

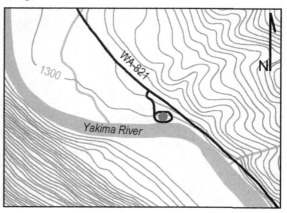

Location

362 Big Pines
Bureau of Land Management

Directions

Start at the intersection of I–82 and WA–821 (exit 26) near Yakima. Travel north on WA–821 for 9.6 miles and turn left into the campground.

Or

Start at the Intersection of I–90 and WA–821 (exit 109) in Ellensburg. Travel south on WA–821 for 18.8 miles and turn right into the campground.

N46°48'50" – W120°27'01"   Elevation – 1,280 feet

Facilities

41 total sites:
some walk–in tent sites,
some pull–through sites
Vault toilets
No water, bring own
Garbage service
Boat launch
Accessible toilets, hiking trails

View from Campground

Features

Big Pines recreation area is located in the Yakima River Canyon. The campsites lie along the Yakima River and can easily accommodate RVs up to 50 feet. The canyon cuts through massive basalt cliffs and rolling desert hills and offers excellent wildlife viewing. The canyon drive is designated a state scenic route. The northern edge of the site is adjacent to undeveloped hiking trails on lands managed by the Washington Department of Fish and Wildlife.

Reservations

Reserve sites at *www.recreation.gov* or by phone at 1–877–444–6777 from May 15 through September 15. Reservations can be made up to six months in advance but not less than 48 hours of the desired arrival date. The rest of the year is first–come, first–serve. See Appendix B for more information.

Season

Open all year

Activities

Boating (non–motorized), Fishing, Hiking, Equestrian trail riding, Mountain biking, River rafting, Swimming, Wildlife viewing.

Cost

$15.00
See Appendix C for available discounts.

Limitations

Stay limit is 7 days.
See Appendix A for camping regulations.

Contact

Bureau of Land Management
Spokane District Office
1102 N Francher Road
Spokane WA 99212
Phone: 509–536–1200
Web: *www.blm.gov/or*

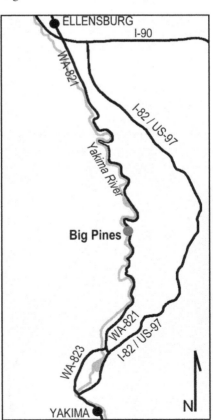

Driving Directions

Big Pines Campsite

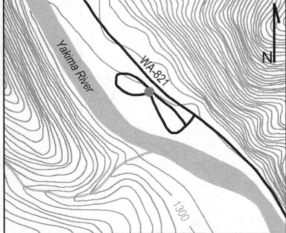

Location

363 Roza
Bureau of Land Management

Directions

Start at the intersection of I–82 and WA–821 (exit 26) near Yakima. Travel north on WA–821 for 7.2 miles and turn left into the campground.

Or

Start at the intersection I–90 and WA–821 (exit 109) in Ellensburg. Travel south on WA–821 for 21.2 miles and turn right into the campground.

N46°45'53" – W120°27'23"   Elevation – 1,260 feet

Facilities

6 total sites
Vault toilet
No water, bring own
Garbage service
Boat launch
Accessible toilets

Features

Roza is located in the scenic Yakima River Canyon which cuts through massive basalt cliffs and rolling desert hills. This canyon has been designated as a state scenic route and offers excellent wildlife viewing, fishing in a Blue Ribbon trout stream, family river rafting and camping. Campsites, which will easily fit RVs 50 feet long, are near trees for additional shade.

Roza is the main take–out for all river floaters, as it is located about 1½ mile above Roza Dam. Motorized vessels are permitted from the Roza boat launch down to Roza dam. Upstream of the Roza boat launch, the river is limited to non–motorized boats only. There is a concrete boat launch at the site to accommodate motorized boat users.

Reservations

Reserve sites at *www.recreation.gov* or by phone at 1–877–444–6777 from May 15 through September 15. Reservations can be made up to six months in advance but not less than 48 hours of the desired arrival date. The rest of the year is first–come, first–serve. See Appendix B for more information.

Season

Open all year

Activities

Boating (see Features section, above), Fishing, Hiking, River rafting, Swimming, Wildlife viewing.

Cost

$15.00
See Appendix C for available discounts.

Limitations

Stay limit is 7 days.
See Appendix A for camping regulations.

Contact

Bureau of Land Management
Spokane District Office
1102 N Francher Road
Spokane WA 99212
Phone: 509–536–1200
Web: *www.blm.gov/or*

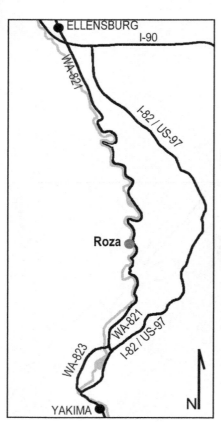

Driving Directions

Roza Boat Launch

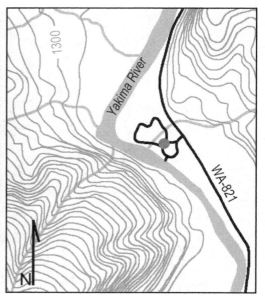

Location

364 Yakima Sportsman
Washington State Parks

Directions

Start at the intersection of I–82/US–12 and WA–24 near Yakima. Travel east on WA–24 for 1.3 miles. Turn left onto University Pkwy and travel for 1.0 mile. Turn left into park.

N46º35'30" – W120º27'28"   Elevation – 1,030 feet

Facilities

67 total sites: 30 standard sites, 37 utility sites (W/E/S)

Flush toilets
Potable water
Hot showers
Garbage service
RV dump station

Features

The park is located near the urban amenities of Yakima yet it attracts lots of birds to its riverfront location. The Yakima River flood plain contains wetland marshes, grasses, and ponds which host 140 bird species.

Reservations

Sites may be reserved online at *www.parks.state.wa.us* or by telephone 1–888–CAMPOUT (1–888–226–7688). See Appendix B for details.

Season

Park open all year but campground is closed October 16 – February 28.

Activities

Canoe access to river, Hiking, Birding, Horseshoe pit, Metal detecting, Volleyball.

Cost

$12 primitive site
Peak season: mid May – mid September
$22 – $35 standard site
$30 – $40 partial utility site
$35 – $45 full utility site
Off–peak season
$20 – $30 standard site
$25 – $35 partial utility site
$30 – $40 full utility site
$10 extra vehicle (all year)
See Appendix C for available discounts.

Limitations

Maximum site length is 60 feet.
See Appendix A for camping regulations.

Contact

Phone: 509–575–2774
Web: *www.parks.state.wa.us*

Yakima Sportsman Campsite

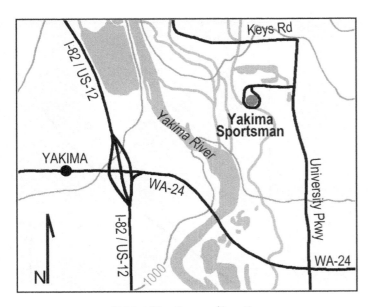

Driving Directions and Location

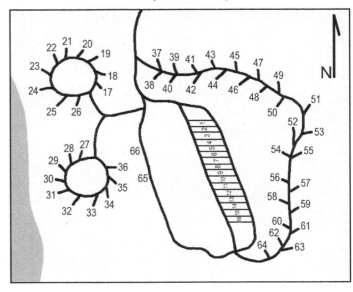

Campground

Pork and Peach Salad

Someone said that timing is everything. When it comes to eating fresh fruit while camping in eastern Washington, nothing is more true. We were skeptical when we first had this salad but after one bite we were sold. (One of us thinks the salad greens aren't even necessary, but that's another story.)

Ingredients

2 boneless center–cut pork chops
2 tablespoons balsamic vinegar
2 tablespoons lime juice
3 teaspoons thyme
½ teaspoon salt
½ teaspoon coarsely ground pepper
2 tablespoons balsamic vinegar (additional)
2 large, ripe peaches
Lettuce salad mixture

Preparation

Combine 2 tablespoons balsamic vinegar, lime juice, thyme, salt, and pepper in a small bowl. Reserve a little of the marinade for a salad dressing. Pour remaining marinade into a zip–top plastic bag and add the pork chops. Seal and put bag into an iced cooler for about an hour.

Cut peaches in half, remove pit, and peel. Place them on a plate and drizzle with the additional balsamic vinegar.

Take pork out of marinade bag and discard this marinade and the bag.

Put the pork in the grilling rack and cook over charcoal coals until done. USDA recommends an internal temperature of 145°F (about 3 – 8 minutes on each side depending on thickness and fire intensity). Set aside.

Put peaches in grill rack and cook until slightly browned (4 – 5 minutes on one side and 2 to 3 minutes on the back side).

While the peaches are cooking, thinly slice the cooked pork. After the peaches are cooked, cut them into smaller pieces. Divide lettuce mixture into servings and put onto plates. Add sliced pork and place grilled peaches on top. Drizzle with reserved marinade from initial step. (Do not reuse any marinade that was used to marinade the raw pork.)

While eating, be happy you chose ripe–peach–season to go camping.

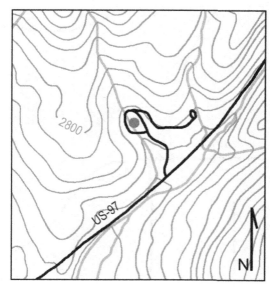

Brooks Memorial Location

365 Brooks Memorial
Washington State Parks

Directions

Start at the intersection of US–97 and WA–14 near Maryhill. Travel north on US–97 for 22.0 miles. Park is on both sides of US–97 but turn left for campground.

N45°57'06" – W120°39'58"   Elevation – 2,680 feet

Facilities

45 total sites: 22 standard, 23 utility
Flush toilets
Potable water
Hot showers
Garbage service
RV dump
Kitchen shelters

Features

This is a 700 acre park with a variety of natural environments. There are over 9 miles of hiking trails along the Little Klickitat River and up through Ponderosa Pine forests. At the top is a meadow with a panoramic view of Mount Hood.

Reservations

Reservations can be made online at *www.parks.state.wa.us* or by calling 888–CAMPOUT (888–226–7688). See Appendix B for details.

Season

Open all year

Activities

Hiking, Butterfly garden, Mountain biking, Softball field.

Cost

$12 primitive site
Peak season: mid May – mid September
$22 – $35 standard site
$30 – $40 partial utility site
$35 – $45 full utility site
Off–peak season
$20 – $30 standard site
$25 – $35 partial utility site
$30 – $40 full utility site
$10 extra vehicle (all year)
See Appendix C for available discounts.

Limitations

The maximum site length is 60 feet (limited availability)
See Appendix A for camping regulations.

Contact

Phone: 509–773–4611
Web: *www.parks.state.wa.us*

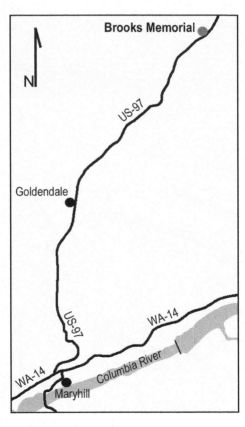

Driving Directions

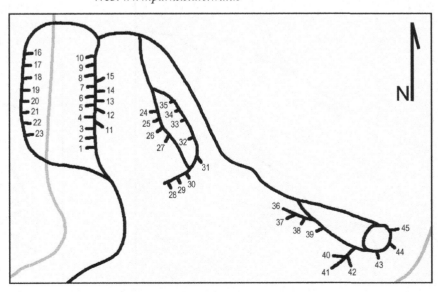

Campground

366 Maryhill
Washington State Parks

Directions

Start at the intersection of US–97 and WA–14 near Dallesport. Travel east on WA–14 for 13.1 miles. Turn right onto US–97. Travel 1.6 miles. Turn left into park. (There is an entrance to a private RV park adjacent to the State Park entrance.)

N45°40'57" – W120°49'36"   Elevation – 180 feet

Facilities

70 total sites: 20 standard, 50 utility

Flush toilets
Potable water
Showers
Garbage service
RV dump
Boat launch
Boat docks

Features

This park is fronted by the Columbia River and offers many waterborne activities.

Reservations

Reservations can be made online at *www.parks.state.wa.us* or by calling 888–CAMPOUT (888–226–7688). See Appendix B for details.

Season

Open all year

Activities

Boating, Fishing, Hiking, Personal watercraft, Sailboarding.

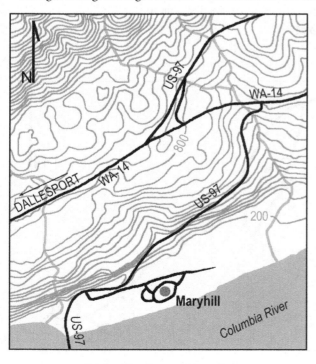

Driving Directions and Location

Cost

$12 primitive site
Peak season: mid May – mid September
$22 – $35 standard site
$30 – $40 partial utility site
$35 – $45 full utility site
Off–peak season
$20 – $30 standard site
$25 – $35 partial utility site
$30 – $40 full utility site
$10 extra vehicle (all year)
See Appendix C for available discounts.

Limitations

The maximum site length is 60 feet.
Potable water is turned off in the campground during winter but is available at the dump station at a labeled faucet.
See Appendix A for camping regulations.

Maryhill Campsite

Contact

Phone: 509–773–5007
Web: *www.parks.state.wa.us*

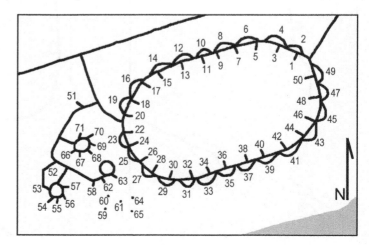

Campground

367 Columbia Hills
Washington State Parks

Directions

Start at the intersection of US–197 and WA–14 north of Dallesport. Travel east on WA–14 for 1.6 miles. Turn right into park.

N45º38'37" – W121º06'27"   Elevation – 200 feet

Facilities

18 total sites: 4 standard, 8 partial utility
Flush toilets
Potable water
Garbage service
RV dump

Features

This park is located with the Columbia River Gorge Scenic Area at your fingertips. There are a significant number of Native American pictographs and petroglyphs available for viewing with regularly scheduled guided ranger tours.

Reservations

Reservations can be made online at *www.parks.state.wa.us* or by calling 888–CAMPOUT (888–226–7688). See Appendix B for details.

Season

Open all year

Activities

Fishing, Hiking, Horseshoe pit, Rock climbing, Sailboarding.

Cost

$12 primitive site
Peak season: mid May – mid September
$22 – $35 standard site
$30 – $40 partial utility site
$35 – $45 full utility site
Off–peak season
$20 – $30 standard site
$25 – $35 partial utility site

$30 – $40 full utility site
$10 extra vehicle (all year)
See Appendix C for available discounts.

Limitations

The maximum site length is 60 feet (limited availability).
Be prepared for very windy conditions.
See Appendix A for camping regulations.

Contact

Phone: 509–767–1159
Web: *www.parks.state.wa.us*

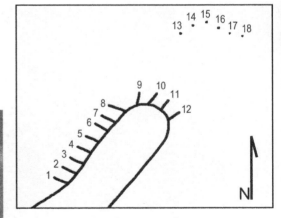

Campground

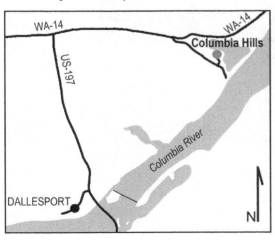

Driving Directions

Petroglyph

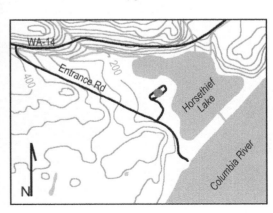

Location

Columbia River near Maryhill State Park

Appendix A Agency Information

As we look at general information about each campground's controlling agency, it is important to remember that the status can change quickly – budget issues, construction projects, and weather can cause campgrounds to close and reopen overnight. It is the camper's responsibility to contact the appropriate office to verify operational status and cost changes. If one campground is closed, there are many alternatives.

Although the number of public non–camping recreational areas in Washington State is greater, the ones that allow camping include: 3 National Parks, 1 National Recreation Area, parts of 6 National Forests, 6 Bureau of Land Management sites, 10 Army Corps of Engineers campgrounds, 73 Washington State Parks, 30 Department of Natural Resources sites, several county and city locations, 11 Public Power Utility District campgrounds, 4 Port Districts, and 1 Recreation District.

National Parks
Mount Rainier National Park

Mount Rainier National Park is located about two–thirds down the state in the Cascade Mountains. Surrounding Washington's tallest mountain, this park provides the opportunity to learn about glaciers, discover life in a rainforest, hike the Wonderland Trail, explore subalpine ecology, watch clouds form and shroud the mountain, visit a rustic historic building, or dream about climbing to the summit. You can study geology, experience a mountain meadow, or listen to a glacier crack.

Mount Rainier

Weather

Weather patterns at Mount Rainier are strongly influenced by the Pacific Ocean and the park's high elevation. The climate is generally cool and rainy, with summer highs often between 60°F and 70°F. While July and August are the sunniest months, visitors should be aware that mountain weather is very changeable – rain is possible any day, and is very likely in spring, fall, and winter. Snow will often remain at an elevation as low as 5,000 feet well into July. Hikers and mountain climbers should be prepared for changing weather and pay close attention to both short and long term weather forecasts, avalanche warnings, and special weather alerts. Visitors should carry extra clothing, rain gear, and a tent for protection against storms anytime of the year.

Regulations

- Campsites are limited to a maximum of 6 persons (or immediate family) and two tents. All vehicles must be parked within the designated campsite parking area and not beyond the barriers or on vegetation.
- A 14–day camping limitation applies to all camping.
- Do not collect firewood, branches, twigs or cones. As these materials decompose they nourish the trees and preserve the quality of the forest.
- Dogs, cats and other pets must be caged, on a leash (no longer than 6 feet), or otherwise under physical restraint at all times.
- Pets may not be left unattended or tied to trees.
- Pets are not permitted in amphitheaters, buildings, or on vegetated areas or trails. Pets are permitted only in parking lots and roads open to vehicles.
- Bicycles and motorbikes may be operated in the campground on roadways only in the same direction of travel as other vehicles.
- Motorcycles must be licensed for street use and drivers must have an operator's license. Travel on trails with a bicycle or motorbike is not permitted.
- The use of wheeled vehicles (such as skateboards, roller skates, roller blades, scooters, etc.) is not permitted in the park.
- To preserve the natural features of the park, driving nails into trees and creating ditches around tents are not permitted.
- Do not feed any wildlife (including birds) in the park. Human food can cause digestive problems and can result in an animal's death or in injury to you.
- Picking flowers and gathering plants is not permitted. Collecting rocks or other materials is also prohibited.
- RV sink drains must empty into containers which may be emptied into service sinks or toilets only.
- Do not use water fountains or spigots for cleaning purposes.
- Wash dishes in a container at your campsite. Dump used water in camp sink located at the restrooms.
- RV dump stations located at the Cougar Rock and Ohanapecosh campgrounds are available for your use at no cost.
- Quiet hours are between 9 pm and 7 am. Keep noise to a minimum at all times and show respect for others.
- Generators may only be used between the following hours: 8 am – 10 am, noon – 2 pm, and 5 pm – 7 pm.
- Loop E of Cougar Rock and Ohanapecosh campgrounds are closed to generator use at all times.

Fees

The entrance fee is $25 for a private vehicle or $20 for a motorcycle or $10 for each visitor 16 and older entering by bicycle, horseback, on foot, or for individuals traveling together as a non– commercial, organized group. These fees provide the visitor with a 7 day entrance permit for Mount Rainier National Park.

Campground fees are included in Chapters 2 – 6 which contain specific campground information.

Contact Information

Web: *www.nps.gov/mora*
Mail: Mount Rainier National Park
         55210 238th Avenue East
         Ashford, WA 98304
Phone: 360–569–2211
TTD: 360–569–2177
Fax: 360–569–2170

North Cascades National Park

Jagged peaks, deep valleys, cascading waterfalls, and over 300 glaciers adorn the North Cascades National Park Complex. The park is located at the extreme north end of the state's Cascade Mountains. Steep mountains and onshore weather systems influence a wide range of climate conditions depending on the season and location. While the park is open every day of the year, its visitor centers and the five car–accessible campgrounds are generally open from late May to late October. All are located along State Route 20 except for one campground that sits on the north end of Ross Lake, and is accessed from Canada on Canada's Highway 1.

Diablo Lake

Weather

From autumn to spring much of the park is buried under a thick layer of snow. The best weather is from mid–June to late September, when all but the highest trails are generally clear of snow.

The west slopes and high peaks catch the brunt of wet systems blowing in from the Pacific Ocean creating a more lush and temperate evergreen forest, while the shielded, lower east slopes tend to be warm and dry throughout the summer.

The differences between west and east are great. The western slopes receive an average of 76 more inches of rain and 407 more inches of snowfall annually. So much snow falls in the mountains that State Route 20 – the only road that traverses the park – is closed every winter for four or more months. During an average year heavy snow and continuous avalanches bury the highway from mid–November to April. No matter what time of year, visitors entering the North Cascades should remember that mountain weather is unpredictable and prone to sudden changes. Even in the summer, storms are common. Visitors who travel into the backcountry should be especially prepared for adverse conditions – warm, waterproof clothing is all but required year–round.

Regulations

- Dogs are allowed on a leash within the Ross Lake and Lake Chelan National Recreation Areas, as well as on most surrounding US Forest Service lands. Dogs must be leashed and in control at all times, including while in camp. Dogs are not allowed on trails in the National Park.

- Federal law allows people who can legally possess firearms under applicable federal, state, and local laws, to legally possess firearms in North Cascades National Park Complex which includes North Cascades National Park, Ross Lake National Recreation Area and Lake Chelan National Recreation Area. It is the responsibility of visitors to understand and comply with all applicable state, local, and federal firearms laws before entering this park. As a starting point, please visit Washington State's website.

- Federal law also prohibits firearms in certain facilities in this park; those places are marked with signs at all public entrances and generally include all NPS staffed offices open to the public.

- Hunting is not permitted within the National Park.

- Campfires are allowed only in designated fire grates and must be attended at all times. Firewood collecting is prohibited. Bring your own wood or buy it from a local vendor.

Fees

There is no entrance fee to this park. Campground fees are included in Chapters 2 – 6 which contain specific campground information.

Contact Information

Web: *www.nps.gov/noca*
Mail: North Cascades National Park
         810 State Route 20
         Sedro–Woolley, WA 98284
Phone: 360–854–7200
Fax: 360–856–1934

Olympic National Park

Olympic National Park is located in the extreme northwest corner of the state. Here you will find Pacific Ocean beaches, rain forest valleys, glacier–capped peaks and a stunning variety of plants and animals. Roads provide access to the outer edges of the park, but the heart of Olympic is wilderness; a primeval sanctuary for humans and wild creatures alike.

Weather

The Olympic Peninsula has a moderate marine climate with pleasant summers and mild, wet winters, but like everything else about Olympic, the weather is extremely variable. The temperate forests of west facing valleys are sustained by about twelve feet of annual rainfall. The east side of the mountains lies in a rain shadow, with only 25 inches of annual rainfall and much dryer conditions.

Hurricane Ridge

Summers tend to be fair and warm, with high temperatures between 65°F and 75°F. July, August and September are the driest months, with heavier precipitation during the rest of the year. While low elevation winter temperatures range in the 30's and 40's, snowfall can be heavy in the mountains – accumulations up to 10 feet are common. Come prepared with rain gear and layered clothing.

Tides

Don't get trapped by a rising tide! When hiking Olympic's coast, you need a topographic map showing the headlands that are only passable at lower tides. This map, along with your tide table (available at visitor centers and coastal ranger stations) and a watch, is essential to safely enjoying this rugged

Pacific Ocean near Mora Campground

wilderness. You must know when the tides will occur and plan your hike accordingly.

Additionally, strong winds or storms can significantly elevate tides and create hazardous conditions. Be attentive to your surroundings and never underestimate the power of the Pacific Ocean.

Regulations

• Pets are permitted on a leash (up to 6') in park campgrounds, picnic and parking areas, and Rialto (to Ellen Creek) and Kalaloch beaches only. Pets are prohibited in park buildings, on trails or in the back–country. Pet excrement must be collected and put in trash receptacles.

• Feeding wildlife is prohibited for animal health and your safety.

• Hunting or disturbing wildlife is prohibited in national parks.

• All fireworks and explosives are prohibited in the park.

• Visitors may possess firearms in the park in compliance with Washington State regulations. All firearm use, including target shooting and hunting, is prohibited within the park.

• There is an 8 person per campsite limit and vehicle wheels must be on paved pads where available.

• Camping limit is 14 days in the park per year. Kalaloch Campground limit is 7 days from June 15 to September 1.

• In campgrounds where wood is not available for sale by concession services, visitors may collect dead and down wood (smaller than 6" diameter) within 100 feet of campgrounds. Wood must be collected only below 3,500 feet.

• Campground quiet hours are 10 pm to 6 am.

• Vehicle camping is only allowed in authorized campgrounds in the park.

Fees

Single visit entrance fees are good for up to seven consecutive days at any Olympic National Park entrance and cost $25 for a private vehicle or $15 for a motorcycle or $10 for an individual on foot, bicycle or motorcycle.

Children less than 16 years of age are admitted free. An Olympic National Park Annual Pass costs $50 and is good at any Olympic National Park entrance station for one year from the month of purchase.

Hoh Fee Station

Campground fees are included in Chapters 2 – 6 which contain specific campground information.

Contact Information

Web: *www.nps.gov/olym*
Mail: Olympic National Park
        600 East Park Ave.
        Port Angeles, WA 98362
Phone: 360–565– 3130
TTY: 800–833–6388
Fax: 360–565–3015

Lake Roosevelt National Recreation Area

Lake Roosevelt National Recreation Area is located in the northeastern part of the state. The Columbia River has drawn people to its waters for over 9,000 years. Historically, the river offered a rich fishing ground. Today Lake Roosevelt's visitors continue to enjoy the river's recreational offerings of fishing, camping, hunting and boating. Administered by the National Park Service, Lake Roosevelt stretches north from the Grand Coulee Dam for 150 miles to just 25 miles south of the Canadian boarder. Goods and services are limited; however, there are a few towns within a 5 to 20 minute drive.

Weather

A dry, sunny climate predominates in the summer months. As you go further north, the weather becomes cooler and wetter. In the summer, temperatures range from 75°F to 100°F during the day and from 50°F to 60°F at night. Spring and fall are cooler but still pleasant. The weather can be dramatically different from one end of the lake to the other. Annual rainfall in the south averages 10 inches. Vegetation is characterized by shrub steppe species such as sagebrush and bitterbrush. To the north, precipitation is around 17 inches per year, which supports the ponderosa pine and Douglas–fir forests common to the area.

Regulations

- Check–Out time is Noon.
- No more than two vehicles per campsite. (For example, a truck and a boat trailer or an RV and a car, or two cars.)
- No more than ten people at each campsite.
- Vehicles must fit within the site pads provided or a designated parking space and not on the roadway or vegetation.
- While campsites accommodate most RVs, campgrounds do not provide hookups for recreational vehicles.
- Generators may only be used from 6 am to 10 pm.
- Do not attach wires, ropes, or nails to trees or shrubs.
- Digging, leveling, or other alterations of the ground is not permitted.
- Quiet Hours are from 10 pm to 6 am.
- Maximum stay within the recreation area is limited to 30 days within any calendar year and limited to 14 consecutive days per campground.
- Campgrounds are closed to the public from 11 pm to 5 am except to registered campers.
- Motorized vehicles, including but not limited to motorized foot scooters, motorized skateboards, mopeds, motorcycles, ATVs, motor assisted bicycles, golf carts, and other similar type devices not licensed by Washington State for highway use, are prohibited from being operated within the recreation area. Exemptions include electric wheelchairs and other motor–assisted limited mobility devices.
- Campsites may not be left unattended for more than 24 hours.
- Fires are permitted in campsites where fire grates are provided by the National Park Service. A UL approved portable propane campfire unit is permitted.
- Do not leave fires unattended. Fires must be completely extinguished with water, doused and stirred.
- Debris burning is not permitted.
- Fires are not permitted on exposed lakebed from May 2 – October 31.

Fishing on Lake Roosevelt

- During very hot and dry weather conditions, strong winds, and periods of extreme fire danger, or by order of the Area's Superintendent, fires of any type may not be allowed anywhere in the park. Visitors may contact the park headquarters office to check on current conditions.
- Dead and down wood may be collected for campfires in the park. Chainsaws cannot be used to gather wood.
- Pets must be kept on a leash six feet or less in length and may not be left unattended. Barking dogs are considered a nuisance. Owners must remove them from the campground.
- Do not leave pets locked in the car. On an 85°F day, the temperature inside a car can reach over 100°F within 10 minutes – even with the windows cracked open.
- Pet feces must be disposed of in a trash bin by the person responsible for the pet.

Lake Roosevelt Sunset

Fees

There is no entrance fee to this recreation area. Campground fees are included in Chapters 2 – 6 which contain specific campground information.

Contact Information

Web: www.nps.gov/laro
Mail: Lake Roosevelt National Recreation Area
         1008 Crest Drive
         Coulee Dam, WA 99116
Phone: 509–754–7800
Fax: 509–633–9332

National Forests
Colville National Forest

The Colville National Forest has 1.1 million acres in northeastern Washington and includes the Kettle River, Selkirk Mountain ranges, and the upper reaches of the Columbia River. Visitors enjoy the Colville National Forest's wild huckleberries, camping, 468 miles of hiking trails, its off highway vehicle (OHV) roads, mountain biking, horse trails, and its lakes, rivers, and streams. The forest also boasts exciting wildlife such as grizzly and black bears, cougars, bald eagles and the last remaining herd of caribou in the U.S.

You can take your pick of camping experiences in an array of settings from dry ponderosa pine forests to high-country subalpine fir. Dispersed camping is allowed in this national forest – be sure to follow the rules listed in the Dispersed Camping section of Chapter 1. If you are in the mood for a less rustic experience, stay at one of Colville National Forest's twenty–three developed campgrounds listed in this book.

Wherever you stay, remember that you are responsible for helping care for the land and facilities. Most non–fee campgrounds do not have garbage service, so please pack it out. Be sure to take your own water to campsites where water is not available.

Weather

Daytime summer temperatures vary widely in Colville National Forest from 70°F to 100°F depending on the day and elevation. Though considerably drier than the western part of the state, the northeast does get afternoon shower activity during the summer and can get quite a bit of snow in the winter with temperatures dipping well below freezing. Visitors need to bring adequate clothing and equipment to handle varied conditions.

Regulations

- Quiet hours are between 10 pm and 6 am.
- Campfires in developed fire pits only.
- Fireworks prohibited.
- Dogs must be on leash.
- OHV/ATV use prohibited in the campground.
- Maximum length of stay is 14 days.

Fees/Passes

There is no entrance fee, however, a Recreation Pass is required to use the many trailheads, picnic areas, boat launches and interpretive sites on national forests throughout Washington. Signs are posted at participating sites where Recreation Passes are required. Revenues from pass sales help maintain and improve trails, land and facilities – visit Pacific Northwest Recreation Passes or call 800–270–7504 for more information and to purchase.

Campground fees are included in Chapters 2 – 6 which contain specific campground information.

Contact Information

Web: *www.fs.fed.us/r6/colville*
Mail: Colville National Forest
         765 South Main Street
         Colville, WA 99114
Phone: 509–684–7000

Colville National Forest near Sherman Pass

Gifford Pinchot National Forest

The Gifford Pinchot National Forest is located in southern Washington in the Cascade Mountains. It is one of the oldest National Forests in the United States – included as part of the Mount Rainier Forest Reserve in 1897, this area was renamed the Gifford Pinchot National Forest in 1949. The Forest is 1,368,330 acres in size and includes the 110,300–acre Mount St. Helens National Volcanic Monument established by Congress in 1982.

Weather

Like other mountainous areas in the state, summer daytime temperatures generally range between 60°F and 80°F. July through September is the driest period with winter bringing much more rain and snow to the higher elevations. Check the weather forecast and be prepared with a variety of clothing and shelter options.

Mount Adams

Regulations

- Do not litter – take along a trash bag or other receptacle for collecting your trash, then deposit it in the proper trash receptacle.
- Make sure you are using the correct type of camping equipment permitted in that area. Check ahead of time for seasonal fire or camp stove restrictions.
- Don't camp in areas where you are not permitted. These areas have been declared off limits to protect wildlife, vegetation, or for your safety.
- Take precautions against camping in an area that may be prone to sudden flash floods.
- Check with a local forest ranger to find a safe and legal camping area.
- Check with a local Forest District office to see what precautions need to be taken in regard to storing food away from wildlife.

Yakima River

- Do not feed the local wildlife.
- Remember to take along non–perishable food that won't make you ill if it spoils.
- Be courteous and remember that you are sharing the Gifford Pinchot National Forest with other campers and visitors.
- Bring along extra safety items such as water, flashlights, maps, and a cell phone or radio.
- No ATVs or OHVs allowed in the campgrounds.
- All equipment must fit on the site pad.
- All vehicles must park in developed areas only.
- Horses are prohibited except in designated horse camps.
- Quiet hours are from 10 pm to 6 am.
- Pets must be leashed at all times.

Fees/Passes

There is no entrance fee, however, a Recreation Pass is required to use the many trailheads, picnic areas, boat launches and interpretive sites on national forests throughout Washington. Signs are posted at participating sites where Recreation Passes are required. Revenues from pass sales help maintain and improve trails, land and facilities – visit Pacific Northwest Recreation Passes or call 800–270–7504 for more information and to purchase.

Campground fees are included in Chapters 2 – 6 which contain specific campground information.

Contact Information

Web: *www.fs.fed.us/gpnf*
Mail: Gifford Pinchot National Forest
         501 E 5th Street, #404
         Vancouver, WA 98661
Phone: 360–891–5000
TTY: 360–891–5003
Fax: 360–891–5045

Mount Baker–Snoqualmie Nat'l Forest

Mount Baker–Snoqualmie National Forest is one of the most visited forests in the country, located east of Seattle on the west side of the Cascades between the Canadian border and Mount Rainier National Park. Here you will find glacier–covered peaks, spectacular mountain meadows and old–growth forests, rich in history and outdoor opportunities.

The forest offers year–round recreational as well as educational opportunities. You can tour the forest, visit one the lakes or rivers, go fishing, river rafting, bird watching, or for a change of pace try snowshoeing or skiing.

Weather

No matter what time of year, visitors should remember that mountain weather is unpredictable and prone to sudden changes. Even in the summer, storms are common. Backcountry visitors should be especially prepared for adverse conditions – warm, waterproof clothing is all but required year–round.

Regulations

- Dispersed camping is allowed in this national forest – be sure to follow the rules listed in the Dispersed Camping section of Chapter 1.
- Use picnic sites, swimming beaches, and other day use areas only between the hours of 6 am and 10 pm.
- Campgrounds and other recreation sites can be used only for recreation purposes. Permanent use or use as a principal residence without authorization is not allowed.

Nooksack Falls

- In campgrounds, camp only in those places specifically marked or provided.
- At least one person must occupy a camping area during the first night after camping equipment has been set up, unless permission has otherwise been granted by the Forest Ranger.
- Camping equipment cannot be left unattended for more than 24 hours without permission by the Forest Ranger. The Federal Government is not responsible for any loss or damage to personal property.
- Remove all personal property and trash when leaving.
- Depending on the location, fees may be charged for parking within the campground at picnic sites, boat launches, swimming areas and in campsites for day use. Some of the picnic sites are available through the reservation service. Fees are required if a reservation is made for these sites.
- Obey restrictions on fires. Fires may be limited or prohibited at certain times.
- In campgrounds, build a fire only in the fire rings, stoves, grills, or fireplaces provided for that purpose.
- You are responsible for keeping fires under control. Be sure your fire is completely extinguished before leaving.
- Pets must always be restrained or on a leash.
- Pets are not allowed in swimming areas.
- Saddle, pack, or draft animals are allowed only in authorized areas.
- Use of fireworks or other explosives is prohibited on all National Forest lands. Firing a gun is not allowed in or within 150 yards of a residence, building, campsite, developed recreation site, or occupied area. It is also not permitted to shoot on or across a road or body of water nor in any circumstance where any person may be injured or property damaged.

Fees/Passes

There is no entrance fee, however a Recreation Pass is required to use the many trailheads, picnic areas, boat launches and interpretive sites on national forests throughout Washington. Signs are posted at participating sites where Recreation Passes are required. Revenues from pass sales help maintain and improve trails, land and facilities – visit Pacific Northwest Recreation Passes or call 800–270–7504 for more information and to purchase a pass.

Individual campground fees are included in Chapters 2 – 6 which contain specific campground information.

Contact Information

Web: *www.fs.usda.gov/mbs*
Mail: Mount Baker–Snoqualmie National Forest
         2930 Wetmore Avenue
         Suite 3A
         Everett, WA 98201
Phone: 800–627–0062
         425–783–6000

Okanogan–Wenatchee National Forest

The Okanogan–Wenatchee National Forest is managed as one forest and encompasses more than 4–million acres in Washington. It stretches north to south from the Canadian border to just south of Mount Rainier National Park – a distance of about 180 miles. The forest lies east of the Cascade Crest, which defines its western boundary. The eastern edge of the forest is in the Okanogan highlands, then south along the Okanogan and Columbia Rivers, and then to the Yakima River valley.

Bumping Lake

Because of this wide geographic range, the forest is very diverse – from the high, glaciated alpine peaks in the Cascades, eastward through deep, lush valleys of old growth forest, to the dry and rugged shrub–steppe country at its eastern edge. The Okanogan–Wenatchee National Forest is noted for a wide range of recreation opportunities – there truly is something for everyone who likes to have fun in the outdoors.

Weather

Precipitation varies widely – from more than 70–inches along the crest to less than 10–inches at its eastern edge. This of course greatly affects the forest and vegetation types across the area. While quite a bit drier than the western slope of the Cascade Range, summer showers can still develop. Summer daytime temperatures vary from about 70°F at the higher elevations to high 90's as you descend toward Washington's central basin to the east. Like other areas, bring a variety of clothes, equipment, and a lot of sun screen. During the winter, snow and freezing temperatures are prevalent – though there are certainly more blue sky days than in the west.

Regulations

- Upon arrival check out the entire campground to find the site that best suites your needs. Are there special rules that will affect your recreation activities? Are some areas for day use only? Are some sites better suited to tents or trailers than other sites? Some sites allow saddle or pack animals; others do not.
- Set up your campsite only if you intend to stay; others may need to use the site.

- Is there plenty of room at the site you selected?
- Remember to keep your car and trailer on the surfaced area/ drive through/parking pad so no damage occurs to trees and their roots.
- Use a closed bucket or other similar receptacle for garbage from your trailer and campsite.
- Keep the faucet area clean because soap residues can build up under the faucet and hamper proper drainage.
- Take water back to your campsite for personal hygiene, cleaning fish, washing dishes, etc. or use special facilities when they are provided.
- Use the fire ring or fire pit provided.
- Please remember, be careful not to hurt or destroy any of the native plants in the area.
- If camping at a "pack–it–out" campground, please take your garbage with you; don't stash it in the toilets, as this fills them quickly and makes them impossible to pump and clean.
- Did you remember to take all your gear when leaving? Check the area – will the next camper to use the area think you were a good neighbor? A good rule of thumb is to leave the campsite looking better than it did when you arrived.

Suggestions

- Keep radios/music turned low; sound really carries outside.
- Run generators only when it won't disturb others or interfere with other campers' sleep. Encourage children to refrain from loud, boisterous play while near other campsites.
- Gather firewood only from designated areas, and then only dead and down wood.
- Pick up litter that other people leave; everyone has a stake in keeping the area beautiful.
- Keep pets under control at all times.
- Don't drive nails into or tie wire around trees. This opens the way for insects and other plant diseases.

Johnny Creek

- Drive vehicles cautiously through campgrounds.
- Ride motorcycles only where they are designated and where they do not disturb other campers' peace and quiet.

Fees/Passes

There is no entrance fee, however a Recreation Pass is required to use the many trailheads, picnic areas, boat launches and interpretive sites on national forests throughout Washington. Signs are posted at participating sites where Recreation Passes are required. Revenues from pass sales help maintain and improve trails, land and facilities – visit Pacific Northwest Recreation Passes or call 800–270–7504 for more information and to purchase.

Campground fees are included in Chapters 2 – 6 which contain specific campground information.

Contact Information

Web: *www.fs.fed.us/r6/wenatchee*
Mail: Okanogan–Wenatchee National Forest
          215 Melody Lane
          Wenatchee, WA 98801
Phone: 509–664–9200
TTY: 509–664–9201
Fax: 509–664–9208

Olympic National Forest

The Olympic National Forest is part of an emerald paradise. The Forest is located on the Olympic Peninsula in the northwest corner of the state. It is a unique geographic province consisting of five major landscape settings: temperate rainforest, rugged mountain terrain, large lowland lakes, cascading rivers, and saltwater beaches. Olympic National Forest has over 633,600 acres where recreational opportunities seem unlimited.

Weather

Influenced by mountains and sea, Olympic National Forest has a wide range of climate conditions. The temperate forests of west facing valleys are sustained by about twelve feet of annual rainfall. The east side of the mountains lies in a rain shadow, with only 25 inches of annual rainfall and much dryer conditions.

The Olympic Peninsula has a moderate marine climate with pleasant summers and mild, wet winters. Summer tends to be fair and warm, with high temperatures between 65°F and 75°F. July, August and September are the driest months, with heavier precipitation during the rest of the year. While low elevation winter temperatures range in the 30s and 40s, snowfall can be heavy in the mountains – accumulations up to 10 feet are common. Come prepared for a wide range of conditions, rain gear and layered clothing are essential.

Regulations

- When using campgrounds, please check the visitor information board at each site for current regulations pertaining to the use of Forest Service developed recreation facilities. The following is a partial list:
- Throw all garbage and litter in containers provided for this purpose or take it with you.

Collins

- Garbage containers, when provided, are reserved for visitors to the National Forest, not for visitors or owners of private lands or lands under permit.
- Wash food and personal items away from drinking water supplies. Use water faucets for drawing water only.
- Prevent pollution – keep garbage, litter, and foreign substances out of lakes, streams, and other water.
- Use toilets properly. Do not throw garbage, litter, fish cleanings, or other foreign substances in toilets and plumbing fixtures.
- Obey all traffic signs and posted speed limits. State traffic laws apply to the National Forests unless otherwise specified.
- When operating vehicles of any kind, do not damage the land or vegetation, or disturb wildlife.
- Within campgrounds and other recreation sites, use licensed vehicles such as motorbikes, motorcycles, or other motor vehicles only for entering or leaving, unless areas or trails are specifically marked for them. Vehicles are to be parked in marked areas only.
- For the safety and convenience of others, do not block, restrict, or interfere with the use of roads or trails.
- Operate trail bikes and other off–road vehicles to avoid damage to the Forest. Obey area and trail restrictions on such use.
- Obey restrictions on fires. Fires may be limited or prohibited at certain times.
- Within campgrounds and other recreation sites, build fires only in fire rings, stoves, grills, or fireplaces provided for that purpose.
- Keep flammable materials away from campfires.

- You are responsible for keeping fires under control. Be sure your fire is completely extinguished before leaving. Do not leave trash of any kind within the fire ring.
- Campgrounds and other recreation sites can be used only for recreation purposes. Permanent use or use as a principal residence without authorization is prohibited.
- Maximum stay is 14 days.
- In campgrounds, camp only in those places specifically marked or provided.
- At least one person must occupy a camping area during the first night after camping equipment has been set up unless permission has been granted by a Forest Service employee or campground host.
- Camping equipment cannot be left unattended for more than 24 hours. The Federal Government is not responsible for any loss or damage to personal property.
- Remove all personal property and trash when leaving.
- Pets must always be restrained (under physical control) or on a leash.
- Pets are prohibited in swimming areas.
- Saddle, pack, or draft animals are allowed only in authorized areas.
- Operate any audio device, such as a radio or musical instrument, only when it will not disturb others.
- Use of fireworks or other explosives is prohibited on National Forest lands.
- Firing a gun is prohibited in or within 150 yards of a residence, building, campsite, developed recreation site, or occupied area; or across or on a road or a body of water.

Fees/Passes

There is no entrance fee, however, a Recreation Pass is required to use the many trailheads, and picnic areas, boat launches interpretive sites on national forests throughout Washington. Signs are posted at participating sites where Recreation Passes are required.

Revenues from pass sales help maintain and improve trails, land and facilities – visit Pacific Northwest Recreation Passes or call 800–270–7504 for more information and to purchase.

Campground fees are included in Chapters 2 – 6 which contain specific campground information.

Contact Information

Web: *www.fs.fed.us/r6/olympic*
Mail: Olympic National Forest
          1835 Black Lake Blvd. SW
          Olympia, WA 98512
Phone: 360–956–2402
TTD: 360–956–2401

Umatilla National Forest

The Umatilla National Forest, located in the Blue Mountains of southeast Washington and northeast Oregon, covers 1.4 million acres of diverse landscapes and plant communities. The Forest has some mountainous terrain, but mostly consists of v–shaped valleys separated by narrow ridges or plateaus. The landscape includes heavily timbered slopes, grassland ridges, benches, and bold basalt outcroppings. Elevations range from 1,600 to 8,000 feet.

Tucannon River

Weather

Changes in weather are common, but summers are generally warm and dry with cool evenings. Winters are cold, snowy but mild temperatures are prevalent during spring and fall.

Regulations

- Overnight fees are charged at several campgrounds. Electric hookups are not available.
- Water may or may not be available. Most campgrounds have vault toilets.
- Additional occupancy and use regulations apply for several campgrounds in the Forest. You may camp a maximum of 14 days out of every 30 in the Forest.
- All campgrounds are available on a first–come, first–serve basis.
- Campfire permits are not required, but campfires may be restricted during extreme fire danger.
- The Forest Service administers and maintains all campsites.
- Camping is also allowed in most dispersed areas, up to 300 feet from an open road, throughout the Forest (see Dispersed Camping section in Chapter 1).

Fees

There is no entrance fee, however, a Recreation Pass is required to use the many trailheads, picnic areas, boat launches and interpretive sites on national forests throughout Oregon and Washington. Signs are posted at participating sites where Recreation Passes are required. Revenues from pass sales help maintain and improve trails, land and facilities – visit Pacific Northwest Recreation Passes or call 800–270–7504 for more information and to purchase.

Campground fees are included in Chapters 2 – 6 which contain specific campground information.

Contact Information

Web: *www.fs.usda.gov/umatilla*
Mail: Umatilla National Forest
　　　　72510 Coyote Road
　　　　Pendleton, OR 97801
Phone: 541– 278–3716

For specific information about the part of Umatilla Forest that lies in Washington, contact:

Mail: Umatilla National Forest
　　　　Pomeroy Ranger District
　　　　71 West Main
　　　　Pomeroy, WA 99347
Phone: 509–843–1891

Bureau of Land Management

The majority of BLM public lands in Washington are east of the Cascade crest in the central Columbia Basin and in the highlands of northeastern Washington along the Canadian border. BLM campgrounds operate on a first–come, first–serve basis. These areas are managed principally for their recreational, riparian, and wildlife values.

BLM lands offer a wide range of recreational opportunities – wildlife viewing, mountain biking, hiking, fishing, hunting, camping/picnicking, and horseback riding are just a few. Within the Spokane District there are various habitats, from pine forest to shrub–steppe and Palouse grassland. Other features include wetlands, meadows, and basalt cliffs. The Channeled Scablands, carved out during the glacial Lake Missoula floods roughly 12,000 years ago, is one of the unique landscapes managed by the district.

Regulations

- Plan your trip from start to finish at home.
- Inform a responsible party of your itinerary, and where to call in case of an emergency.
- Include a full account of who is in your party, where you are going, when you will be back, and the approximate location of each night's campsite.

Fires

Fire danger varies with weather conditions. Drought, heat, and wind help dry timber and other fuel, making it easier to ignite. Once a fire is burning, these same conditions help increase a fire's intensity. Please do your part to protect your forest from human–caused fire. Before each visit check with the Bureau of Land Management for current campfire restrictions, regulations, and campfire and camp stove permit requirements. Regulations governing campfires are specific to each area and change with elevations, weather conditions, and the seasons.

If you build a campfire remember to:

- Remove any burnable material within a 5–foot minimum radius in all directions.
- Build campfires away from overhanging branches, steep slopes, rotten stumps or logs, meadows, and dry grass and leaves.
- Reuse existing fire rings, or use a fire pan to contain coals and minimize fire scars. Keep the fire small.
- Never leave a fire unattended. Even a small breeze could quickly cause the fire to spread.
- Do not use a campfire to burn foil, plastic, or other trash; pack it out.
- Drown your fire with water to extinguish it. Thoroughly stir the mix to cool it off. Use your bare hands to feel all sticks, charred materials, coals, and ashes to make sure the fire is completely out.

Umtanum

Fees

Campground fees are included in Chapters 2 – 6 which contain specific campground information.

Contact Information

Web: *www.blm.gov/or*
Mail: Bureau of Land Management
　　　　Spokane District Office
　　　　1103 N. Fancher Road
　　　　Spokane, WA 99212
Phone: 509–536–1200
Fax: 509–536–1275

Army Corps of Engineers

The Army Corps of Engineers is the steward of the lands and waters at their water resource projects. Its mission is to manage and conserve those natural resources, consistent with ecosystem management principles, while providing quality public outdoor recreation experiences to serve the needs of present and future generations.

Geese at Chief Timothy

The Corps campgrounds included in this book are found along the Columbia and Snake Rivers. Some areas are managed directly by the Corps, while others are leased to state, or local agencies. Most campgrounds are found in the warmer and drier eastern basin of the state and are ideal locations for swimming, water skiing, fishing and enjoying the sun.

Regulations

- Only camp in designated areas.
- Limit camping, at any one water source, to 14 days in any 30 consecutive day period. Campsites must be occupied – no saving sites with just equipment.
- Do not dig or level the ground of any site in any way. Do not attempt to camp at a site with a Reserved sign.
- Campsites must be kept free of trash during occupancy.
- Fires may be built only in approved locations.
- All animals must be kept on a leash or otherwise confined.
- Quiet hours are between 10 pm and 6 am.

Fees

Campground fees are included in Chapters 2 – 6 which contain specific campground information.

Contact Information

The Corps campgrounds in Washington State are administered by three different districts.

Upper Columbia River campgrounds:
Mail: Corps of Engineers
        Seattle District Office
        PO Box 3755
        Seattle, WA 98124
Phone: 206–764–3742

Lower Columbia River campgrounds:
Mail: Corps of Engineers
        Portland District Office
        PO Box 2946
        Portland, OR 97208
Phone: 503–808–5150

Snake River campgrounds:
Mail: Corps of Engineers
        Walla Walla District
        201 North Third Ave
        Walla Walla, WA 99362
Phone: 509–527–7020

State of Washington

A Discover Pass is required for vehicle access or parking in recreation lands and water access sites managed by Washington State agencies. This includes heritage sites, wildlife and natural areas, trails and trailheads. A Discover Pass is not required if camping at a state park; although required if visiting nearby state recreational areas. The annual pass costs $30 and the one–day pass costs $10. Refer to: *discoverpass.wa.gov* for a complete list of exemptions.

Washington State Parks

Created from private land donations in 1913, Washington has the fourth oldest state park system in the country. The parks with camping that are included in this book represent all regions of the state and offer a wide variety of activities. Some parks offer a little of everything while others emphasize certain activities – for instance, Lake Wenatchee is geared toward the winter enthusiast as well as a full menu of summer fun.

Since the parks are located throughout the state, no one weather forecast is adequate. Like all camping areas it is important to prepare for the unexpected as well as for conditions anticipated.

Battle Ground State Park

Lighthouse at Fort Worden State Park with Mount Baker

Regulations

Please observe the following rules so that all park visitors may enjoy their visit:

- Report disturbances to park rangers; they are trained to help you resolve issues and concerns.
- Park hours vary depending on weather and season. However, all day–use areas close at dusk.
- Campers may enter parks until 10 pm.
- Campground check–in begins at 2:30 pm. Check–out is at 1 pm. Campsites cannot be held for someone who might arrive later.
- Quiet hours are from 10 pm to 6:30 am, unless otherwise noted at the park.
- Engine–driven electric generators may be operated only between the hours of 8 am and 9 pm.
- During summer months, the maximum length of stay in any one park is 10 days. From October 1 – March 31, the maximum stay is 20 days.
- One camping party is allowed per site, with a maximum of eight people per site.
- Please use the trash cans and dumpsters to help keep parks clean. Recycling is encouraged in all Washington State Parks. In parks with a pack–it–in/pack–it–out program, visitors must carry out everything they have brought in.
- Please do not harm wild plants or animals. Feeding of wildlife is strictly prohibited. Horses are allowed only in designated parks.
- Wildlife, plants and all park buildings, signs and tables and other structures are protected; removal or damage of any kind is prohibited.
- Pets are allowed in most state parks, but must be under physical control at all times on a leash no more than eight feet long. Owners are responsible for cleaning up after their pets. Pets are not permitted on designated swimming beaches.
- Smoking and pets are not allowed inside vacation houses, yurts, cabins or other rustic structures.
- Glass bottles or metal cans are not allowed on swimming beaches.
- Alcoholic beverages are permitted only in designated campground and picnic areas.
- Fireworks are prohibited on all state public lands, including state parks and beaches that front state park lands.
- All Washington state laws are enforced in Washington State Parks.

Fees

Campground fees are included in Chapters 2 – 6 which contain specific campground information.

Contact Information

Web: *www.parks.state.wa.us*
Mail: Washington State Parks and Recreation
PO Box 42650
Olympia, WA 98504–2650
Phone: 360–902–8844
TTY: 360–664–3133

Department of Natural Resources

The Department of Natural Resources is mandated to manage the state's forests. As a small part of that duty, they operate recreational facilities throughout the state. Though not their primary task, they do offer a wide variety of campgrounds. Many do not offer garbage pickup or provide potable water. In those instances, campers must be prepared to pack out their own trash and take an adequate fresh water supply with them.

Ahtanum

As with State Parks, DNR campgrounds are in all parts of Washington and no one weather forecast is adequate. Like all camping areas it is important to prepare for unexpected weather as well as for conditions anticipated.

Regulations

Unless posted otherwise, observe these rules at DNR campgrounds:

- Maximum length of stay is 10 nights on any DNR land in a 30 day period. No more than 8 people to a campsite.
- Tent pads or vegetation around tent pads must not be altered.
- Two passenger vehicles allowed per campsite.
- No discharge of firearms within 500 feet of campgrounds.
- All campsites are first–come, first–serve. Checkout time is 1 pm.
- Campsites can not be held for another party.
- Personal property must not be left unattended over–night.
- Residence camps not allowed without permission.
- Campfires are allowed in designated fire pits.
- Pets are allowed and must be leashed, unless other–wise posted or an area is closed to pets.

Fees

Campground fees are included in Chapters 2 – 6 which contain specific campground information.

Contact Information

Web: *www.dnr.wa.gov/Campsites*
Mail: Washington State Department of Natural Resources
         PO Box 47000
         Olympia, WA 98504
Phone: 360–902–1000

Public Utility Districts
Chelan County Public Utility District

The Chelan County PUD campgrounds listed in this book are located along the Columbia River in the eastern foothills of the Cascades. Generally warm and sunny during the summer, this area is perfect for outdoor activities.

Regulations

- Consumption of alcoholic beverages prohibited.
- Campers and extra vehicle must register prior to setting up camp.
- Quiet hours are from 10 pm to 6:30 am.
- Camping is allowed in designated areas only.
- Campers must vacate campsites by 1 pm or pay an additional day's fee.
- Speed limit is 5 mph.
- Vehicles shall park in designated parking areas only.
- Pets must be on leash at all times.
- Discharge of firearms or fireworks is prohibited.
- Swimming is allowed in designated areas only.
- Glass containers are not allowed on the beach.

Fees

Campground fees are included in Chapters 2 – 6 which contain specific campground information.

Contact Information

Web: *chelanpud.org*
Mail: Chelan County PUD
         PO Box 1231
         Wenatchee, WA 98807
Phone: 509–661–4551

Beebe Bridge

Lewis County Public Utility District

Lewis County Public Utility District has one campground listed in this book. It is centrally located to Mount St. Helens, Mount Rainier, and Gifford Pinchot National Forest on the western slopes of the Cascade Range. There is hiking, biking, golfing, fishing, boating, mountain climbing, kite flying and bird watching nearby. Also, it's a great place to just relax.

Weather

Like other mountainous areas in the state, summer daytime temperatures generally range between 60°F and 80°F. July through September is the driest period with winter bringing much more rain and snow to the higher elevations. Check the weather forecast and be prepared with a variety of clothing and shelter options.

Fees

Campground fees are included in Chapters 2 – 6 which contain specific campground information.

Contact Information

Web: *https://www.lcpud.org/recreation/campground/*
Mail: Lewis County PUD
       PO Box 330
       Chehalis, WA 98532
Phone: 360–497–7175 (May – September)

PacifiCorp Power

For more than 65 years, Pacific Power has provided public recreation opportunities along the Lewis River. Located south of Mount St. Helens on the western slope of the Cascade Range, Pacific Corp manages several campgrounds listed in this book.

Weather

Like other mountainous areas in the state, summer daytime temperatures generally range between 60°F and 80°F. July through September is the driest period with winter bringing much more rain and snow to the higher elevations. Check the weather forecast and be prepared with a variety of clothing and shelter options.

Regulations

- The speed limit is 10 miles per hour.
- Alcohol is not permitted in any Pacific Power campground or day use area.
- Parking is permitted in designated areas only.
- Use only designated roadways and paths (applies to bikes, hiking, etc.).
- The use of motorbikes, off–road vehicles and snowmobiles is not allowed in recreation areas.
- All applicable laws regarding public safety, illegal substances, sanitation, boating and fires will be enforced.
- All fires shall be confined to company fireplaces or manufactured grills. Fireworks and other flammable materials are not permitted.
- The discharge of firearms or other devices discharging

Mount St. Helens from near Cougar Park

projectiles within or near any recreation area is not permitted.

- Damage to trees, vegetation or facilities is not permitted.
- Wildlife is not to be disturbed.
- Operation of public address systems or other noise producing devices is not permitted except with prior written approval. Campsite quiet hours are from 10 pm to 8 am.
- Pets are to be under owner's control at all times and physically restrained by leashes no more than six feet in length. Pet owners are required to clean up and appropriately dispose of animal waste.
- Commercial use of the property, including offers of commercial services on or pertaining to recreation sites, is not permitted without prior written permission. Commercial use includes vending merchandise, site rentals, equipment sales or rentals, advertising, providing services, etc.
- Place bottles, cans, paper, garbage and other rubbish or refuse in receptacles for that purpose.
- Violators of policies are subject to removal and prosecution.
- Park users who violate rules will be asked to leave, and thereafter, will be subject to trespass and prosecution if they enter company property.
- Policies are subject to change without notice. We do not accept responsibility for the safety or well–being of recreation area guests.

Fees

Campground fees are included in Chapters 2 – 6 which contain specific campground information.

Contact Information

Web: *www.pacificorp.com/about/or/washington.html*
Mail: Pacific Power
       825 NE Multnomah St
       Portland, OR 97232
Phone: 503–813–6666

Puget Sound Energy

Puget Sound Energy operates one campground that is included in this book. Located south of the Canadian Border and Mount Baker on the western slopes of the Cascades, PSE also operates a visitor center, which houses an interpretive display and information on the adjacent fish management facilities. There is a fish trap viewing platform providing a place to watch salmon returning to spawn in the river watershed.

Near Kulshan

Weather

No matter what time of year, visitors should remember that mountain weather is unpredictable and prone to sudden changes. Even in the summer, storms are common – adequate rain gear and warm clothes are important.

Regulations

- There is a 2 vehicle limit per site.
- There is a 5 mph speed limit. No parking on the grass.
- Quiet hours are between 10 pm and 8 am.
- Parents are responsible for the safety and conduct of their children.
- Pets must be kept on a leash.
- Use of firearms is prohibited.
- Use of fireworks is prohibited.
- Do not damage the vegetation.
- Do not gather wood for fires.
- Fires are only allowed in designated places.
- Stays are limited to 14 days each 30 day period.
- Checkout time is 2 pm.

Fees

Campground fees are included in Chapters 2 – 6 which contain specific campground information.

Contact Information

Web: https://pse.com/inyourcommunity/ToursandRecreation/
       Pages/Baker-Lake-Tours.aspx
Mail: Puget Sound Energy
       PO Box 97034
       Bellevue, WA 98009
Phone: 360-853-8341

Tacoma Power

Tacoma Power operates four campgrounds listed in this book. They are located west of Mount Rainier on the western slope of the Cascade Range. There are a wide range of activities available at these sites with spectacular mountain views.

Weather

Like other mountainous areas in the state, summer daytime temperatures generally range between 60°F and 80°F. July through September is the driest period with winter bringing much more rain and snow to the higher elevations. Visitors should always check the weather forecast and be prepared with a variety of clothing and shelter options.

Regulations

- Keep it down! People like to sleep, so quiet hours are from 10 pm to 6 am.
- You may want your buddy in the site next to you, but keep in mind the site must be paid for and occupied with a tent or RV to hold it.
- You may be a kid at heart, but you can't be a kid to rent a campsite. We only rent to people who are at least 18 years old.
- We don't allow glass bottles in swimming beach areas.
- Park visits are limited to 10 consecutive days.
- We provide tent pads in each campsite for you to pitch your tent.
- Alcohol in kegs and other bulk containers is not allowed.
- Store and consume alcoholic beverages only in your site or group camp circle.
- You may purchase an unattended vehicle permit to park overnight in the day–use parking areas at Taidnapam and Mossyrock parks.
- Alcoholic beverages are not permitted in the day–use areas or on the Taidnapam Park fishing bridge.
- Your campsite fee includes only one vehicle. Additional or unattended vehicles, cost $10 each per night.
- Sorry, we don't allow overnight parking in the day–use and boat launch areas at Alder Lake and Mayfield Lake parks.
- Leave your gas and electric pocket bikes and motorized scooters at home. Only people with disabilities may operate unlicensed mobility devices in the parks.
- Please don't park or drive on vegetated areas.
- We provide fire pits or fire rings for your safety and don't allow campfires anywhere else.
- Using power saws is not allowed in campgrounds.
- You're not allowed to cut or burn live or downed trees. Each park may have additional rules about collecting branches and driftwood.
- Keep your pets under control in cages or on physical leashes no longer than eight feet. (Make sure someone is holding the other end of the leash.)

- At night, keep pets in a tent or enclosed vehicle.
- Scoop the poop. We provide bags to make it easier for you.
- Keep pets off the swimming beaches and the Taidnapam Park fishing bridge and out of restrooms and showers.
- Do not leave your pets unattended.
- You may not tie pets to trees or shrubs.
- We will ask that barking dogs be removed from the parks.
- Please do not feed the wildlife.
- Bringing livestock into the parks is not permitted.
- Boat launches close at dusk.
- Docks may not be used for skiing, swimming or diving.
- Alder Lake Park offers free moorage on a first–come, first–serve basis. Moorage is limited to 10 consecutive days, and overnight camping is not permitted on moored boats.
- Observe and follow state and local boating regulations.
- It is illegal to operate watercraft in excess of eight miles per hour in Lewis County and five miles per hour in Pierce County within 200 feet of any shore, dock, public swimming area or log boom.
- Please obey no–wake zones.
- Natural and cultural resources are protected on our lands. Please leave all rocks, minerals or artifacts where you find them.
- Report vandalism by talking with a park supervisor or by calling (253) 502–8824.
- The display or discharge of firearms is not permitted in the parks. Fireworks are not allowed.
- Please obey all posted speed limits.

Fees

Campground fees are included in Chapters 2 – 6 which contain specific campground information.

Contact Information

Web: *www.mytpu.org/tacomapower/parks–rec*
Mail: Tacoma Power
        PO Box 11007
        Tacoma, WA 98411
Phone: 253–502–8600

Near Taidnapam Park

Counties
Benton County

Benton County operates one campground listed in this book. It is located in south central Washington near Richland. Protected by over four miles of Yakima River frontage on one side and the public lands of the Hanford Reach National Monument, Rattlesnake Mountain Shooting Facility, and Rattlesnake Slope Wildlife Area on the other, the park offers over 800 acres of transitional river–to–upland shrub–steppe habitat. It is renowned as a sanctuary for both quantity and variety of dragonflies and birds.

Weather

Summer temperatures can be quite warm – lots of sunscreen is needed – but the river helps generate cooling breezes. Winter temperatures can be quite cold with the ever present possibility of snow; however, there are many more sun days than in the west.

Regulations

- Motorized vehicles must remain on roads.
- No ORV's.
- No discharge of firearms or fireworks in the park.
- No campfires in the park.
- Alcoholic beverages are prohibited.

Fees

Campground fees are included in Chapters 2 – 6 which contain specific campground information.

Contact Information

Web: *www.co.benton.wa.us*
Mail: Benton County Parks
        7122 West Okanogan Place
        Building A
        Kennewick, WA 99336
Phone: 509–783–3118
Fax: 509–736–2708

Chelan County

Chelan County operates one campground listed in this book. It is located in the north central part of the state along the Wenatchee River on the eastern slopes of the Cascade Range. While offering a wide range of services, there is one restriction that may impact some car campers – no tents are allowed in the park.

Weather

While on the warm and dry side of the mountains, there is still a possibility of summer showers and since it is located in the foothills, evening temperatures can cool significantly. Winter brings much colder temperatures and the possibility of snow – dress accordingly.

417

Regulations

- Parents are responsible for their children's conduct.
- Do not park vehicles on the grass.
- There is a one vehicle limit per site. Extra vehicles must park in the visitor's lot.
- No tents allowed in the campground.
- No dog runs allowed in the campground.
- Pets must be kept on a leash.
- No unburned trash allowed in the fire pits.
- No offensive, profane, threatening, or indecent conduct allowed. Intoxicated persons will be evicted.
- Visitors are not allowed without office permission and must leave the park by 10 pm.

Fees

Campground fees are included in Chapters 2 – 6 which contain specific campground information.

Contact Information

Web: *www.wenatcheeriverpark.org*
Mail: Wenatchee River County Park
　　　　 PO Box 373
　　　　 Monitor, WA 98836
Phone: 509–667–7503
Fax: 509–667–9514

Clallam County

Clallam County operates two campgrounds included in this book. They are located in the northwestern part of the state along the shore of the Strait of Juan de Fuca where the Pacific Ocean connects to the rest of Puget Sound, and offer beautiful views of Vancouver Island across the water to the north and the Olympic Mountains to the south.

Weather

The area has a maritime climate – summertime day temperatures between 60°F and 70°F and winter temperatures between 30°F and 50°F. Some of the winter rain systems are blocked by the Olympic Mountains which makes this area drier than most in western Washington. As always, it is important to anticipate unexpected conditions and bring varied clothing and equipment.

Regulations

- There is self–registration at the campgrounds.
- An extra vehicle may be allowed in sites that are large enough to safely handle it as long as it remains on the site pad. It must be registered and the proper fee paid.
- The occupancy of a single campsite is limited to 6 people. Hiker/Biker sites are limited to one individual.
- A 14–night continuous camping limit will be enforced.
- Check out time is 12 pm (noon).
- Pets must be on leashes no longer than 8 feet.
- Persons under 18 years of age must be accompanied by a parent or guardian.
- Quiet hours are enforced from 10 pm to 8 am (this includes generators).
- Camping is allowed in designated campsites only.
- All fireworks are prohibited.
- Hunting or the use of firearms, bow and arrow, air or gas weapon, or other projectile devices capable of injuring or killing any person or animal or damaging any park property is prohibited with an exception of the Dungeness hunting area. Leased to Washington State Fish & Wildlife, the area is open to hunting in accordance with general hunting regulations and special park area regulations. No persons shall hunt on or at the Park, except on Wednesdays, Saturdays, Sundays, and holidays during hunting season and in compliance with Washington State Fish & Wildlife and Clallam County regulations.
- All alcoholic beverages are prohibited by State law.

Fees

Campground fees are included in Chapters 2 – 6 which contain specific campground information.

Contact Information

Web: *www.clallam.net/CountyParks*
Mail: Clallam County Parks
　　　　 223 East 4th Street, Suite 7
　　　　 Port Angeles, WA 98362
Phone: 360–417–2291

Island County

Island County operates one campground listed in this book. It is located on Whidbey Island which is connected to the mainland by a bridge. The northern portion of Puget Sound experiences beautiful summer weather with daytime temperatures between 70°F and 80°F.

Rhododendrum Park Trees

Regulations

- There is a 7 day occupancy limit each 30 days.
- Camp in designated areas only.
- Check–out time is 11 am.
- All pets must be kept on a leash.
- Horseback riding, off road vehicles, firearms, and hunting are prohibited.
- Campfires are only to be in designated fire pits.

Fees

Campground fees are included in Chapters 2 – 6 which contain specific campground information.

Contact Information

Web: *https://www.islandcountywa.gov/PublicWorks/Parks/*
Mail: Island County Parks
          PO Box 5000
          Coupeville, WA 98239
Phone: 360–679–7335
Fax: 360–678–4550

Jefferson County

Jefferson County is located in the northeast corner of the Olympic Peninsula on the western shore of Puget Sound. It is in a rain shadow created by the Olympic Mountains which often shields it from onshore weather patterns. It has two campgrounds listed in this book.

Regulations

- One motorized vehicle per site.
- Fires allowed only in designated areas.
- Pets must be kept on a leash.
- Garbage must be placed in receptacles.
- No hunting allowed.
- No tree or firewood cutting allowed.
- Quiet time is between 10 pm and 7 am.

Fees

Campground fees are included in Chapters 2 – 6 which contain specific campground information.

Contact Information

Web: *www.countyrec.com*
Mail: Jefferson County Parks
          623 Sheridan Street
          Port Townsend, WA 98368
Phone: 360–385–9129
Fax: 360–385–9234

King County

King County has one campground included in this book. The campground is located 40 minutes from downtown Seattle on the banks of the Tolt River. Though the weather is generally quite nice in the summer, it still falls under the influence of approaching Pacific weather systems. Check the forecast for appropriate clothing and equipment.

Regulations

- Maximum stay at any one site is 7 days.
- No alcohol is allowed.

Fees

Campground fees are included in Chapters 2 – 6 which contain specific campground information.

Contact Information

Web: *www.kingcounty.gov/recreation/parks*
Mail: King County Parks and Recreation
          201 South Jackson Street
          KSC–NR–0700
          Seattle, WA 98104
Phone: 206–477–4527

Footbridge at Tolt–MacDonald Park

Klickitat County

Klickitat County has one campground included in this book. It is located on the eastern slopes of the southern Cascade Range in the foothills of Mount Adams. Even though it is located on the drier east side of the mountains, summer evening temperatures can still be cool because of its elevation and there is always the chance of a shower developing. Winter brings cold temperatures and the possibility of snow – dress accordingly.

Regulations

- Camping is limited to 15 consecutive days.
- All garbage must be disposed of properly.
- Checkout time is 1 pm.
- Quiet hours are from 10 pm to 7 am.
- Generators allowed only between 8 am and 9 pm.
- No off–road vehicles are allowed.
- There is a maximum of 8 persons per campsite.
- No discharge of weapons or fireworks is allowed.

Fees

Campground fees are included in Chapters 2 – 6 which contain specific campground information.

Contact Information

Web:　*www.klickitatcounty.org/195/Guler–Trout–Lake–Park*
Mail:　Klickitat County
　　　　228 West Main Street
　　　　MS–CH 19
　　　　Goldendale, WA 98620
Phone:　509–773–4616

Mount Adams from Guler–Trout Lake Park

Pacific County

Pacific County operates one campground listed in this book. It is located on the shore of Willapa Bay which is three–quarters of the way down the state's west coast from Canada. Since it is separated from the Pacific Ocean only by the Long Beach Peninsula, there is no protection from incoming weather fronts. Summer weather is very pleasant, although preparations should always be made for possible rain.

Fees

Campground fees are included in Chapters 2 – 6 which contain specific campground information.

Contact Information

Web:　*www.co.pacific.wa.us/public–works*
Mail:　Pacific County Public Works
　　　　211 North Commercial St
　　　　Raymond, WA 98577
Phone:　360–875–9368

Pend Oreille County

Pend Oreille County operates one campground listed in this book. It is located near the eastern state border about one–third of the way down from the Canadian Border. Being on the eastern side of the state, summer weather is usually warm and dry, although mountain shower activity can develop. Winters are usually cold with the possibility of snow.

Fees

Campground fees are included in Chapters 2 – 6 which contain specific campground information.

Contact Information

Web:
www.pendoreilleco.org/your–government/parks–and–recreation/
Mail:　Pend Oreille County Parks and Recreation
　　　　PO Box 5066
　　　　Newport, WA 99156
Phone:　509–447–4821

San Juan County

San Juan County operates three campgrounds listed in this book. Located on islands in the northwestern part of the state, these campgrounds are reached using the Washington State Ferry System departing from the town of Anacortes. The San Juan Islands are considered to be among the prettiest places anywhere.

Weather

Though located on the west side of the state, this area tends to have sunnier winter weather because of the rain shadow created by the Olympic Mountains to the southwest. Summer temperatures are usually quite pleasant, although it is possible to experience morning fog that has encroached from the Pacific Ocean.

Odlin County Park

Regulations

- Persons under 18 years of age must be accompanied by an adult for overnight camping privileges.
- Please clean site of all trash before departure, using dumpsters and recycling bins provided in the park.
- Checkout time is 12 noon. Campsites not paid for by noon will be considered empty.
- Quiet hours: 10 pm to 7 am. Loud noises such as vehicle horns, loud music, and loud talking will not be tolerated. Dive compressors and generators may only be operated between 11 am and 5 pm. Chainsaws and fireworks are prohibited at all times.
- RV's and trailers are not allowed in some campsites and are not advisable on Shaw Island. Check in with park staff prior to occupying a campsite. No hook–ups are available.
- Parking allowed in designated areas only (not off pavement or gravel).
- No equipment set–up outside your registered campsite including, but not limited to a tent/awning, volleyball net, croquet set, event table and chairs as this may create hazards for other park users.
- Pets must be leashed at all times! Owners are responsible for clean up. Owners of dangerous or disturbing animals (especially barking dogs) may be asked to remove pet(s) from the park.
- Chasing or harassing wildlife in any way is prohibited. Turkeys, rabbits, deer, seals and otters are best viewed from a distance. If you are concerned about a particular animal, please contact park staff.
- Fresh water is limited in the islands. Please don't run water continuously; wash items in wash pans not under a faucet. No vehicle or boat washing. No filling RV tanks. Please help us use water wisely.
- Paths are for foot traffic only. Skating, biking, skateboarding, and moped riding is allowed on park roads only and is prohibited in all other areas.

- No cliff climbing. The cliffs in the parks are not stable and climbing can create rock slides and potential hazards.
- No firewood gathering. Burning beach logs damages our fire rings, and we prefer to manage fallen limbs and trees in the park ourselves. Firewood is generally available for purchase at the park office for a modest charge.
- Fires in established fire pits only. It is illegal to leave a fire unattended. Put your fire out completely before going to bed or leaving the campground. Fires may not be permitted during certain hazardous times of the year. Beach fires are not permitted.
- San Juan County is a Marine Biological Preserve. State law prohibits the taking or destruction of any living specimen except for food use. Taking of specimens must be in accordance with State Fisheries regulations. The low Island, just offshore of San Juan County Park, is a National Wildlife Refuge Site – do not approach any Refuge Site closer than 200 yards.

Fees

Campground fees are included in Chapters 2 – 6 which contain specific campground information.

Contact Information

Web: *www.sanjuanco.com/430/Parks–Recreation–Fair*
Mail: San Juan County Parks
          350 Court Street, #8
          Friday Harbor, WA 98250
Phone: 360–378–8420
Fax: 360–378–2075

Skagit County

Skagit County operates two campgrounds listed in this book. The county is located about one quarter of the way down the state from the Canadian border on the west side of the Cascade Range. Weather can be very wet in the winter months and as you increase in elevation, you also increase the possibility of snow. Summer is drier but there is the chance of rain, so be sure to check the forecast.

Regulations

- To ensure your stay is enjoyable, please honor all park rules and respect the campsites and privacy of others.
- Quiet hours are from 10 pm to 8 am.
- Alcoholic beverages are allowed within the confines of campsites only.
- Pets are welcome. Please observe and follow rules. Keep dogs on a leash (no more than 6ft.), pick up and dispose of waste, and do not allow pets in the restrooms.
- There is a maximum of 8 people allowed per site.
- RV sites are limited to one camp vehicle per site (RV, trailer, van, truck, etc.).
- Maximum stay is 14 days.

- Please observe and follow the speed limit of 5 mph in the park to ensure the safety of all park users.
- Park in designated areas only and please do not drive on the grass.
- Clean campsite prior to departure and deposit litter in designated receptacles (not in fire pits).
- ATVs, firearms and fireworks are strictly prohibited within the park.

Fees

Campground fees are included in Chapters 2 – 6 which contain specific campground information.

Contact Information

Web: *www.skagitcounty.net*
Mail: Skagit County Parks & Recreation
        PO Box 1326
        Mount Vernon, WA 98273
Phone: 360–416–1350

Skamania County

Skamania County operates two campgrounds listed in this book. The county is located along the Columbia River about one–third of the way along the state's southern border from the west coast. The river valley makes it an easy place to cross the Cascade Mountains, not only for people but also for wind which is why the area is known for its great wind surfing.

Columbia River Fun

Weather

The farther east you go in this county, the drier and sunnier it becomes. Summer temperatures in the mountains can be quite cool though and there is an increased chance of rain – be sure to check local forecasts.

Regulations

- One camping unit allowed per site.
- Maximum stay is 14 days.
- Quiet hours are 11 pm to 8 am.
- Dogs must be kept on a leash. No noisy dogs are allowed. Owners must clean up after their pets.

- No horses allowed without a permit.
- No fires allowed outside designated areas without a permit.
- No discharge of firearms allowed.
- No alcohol allowed without a permit.
- Motorized vehicles must stay on roadway or parking areas.
- No cutting or damaging vegetation is allowed.
- Dump waste water in designated area only.

Fees

Campground fees are included in Chapters 2 – 6 which contain specific campground information.

Contact Information

Web: *www.skamaniacounty.org/facilities–rec/*
Mail: Skamania County Recreation
        PO Box 369
        Stevenson, WA 98648
Phone: 509–427–3980

Snohomish County

Snohomish County operates five campgrounds listed in this book. It is located west of the Cascade Range crest just north of Seattle. The county goes from the shores of Puget Sound into the mountains to the east. Because of this, the climate varies from maritime to mountain with wet or snowy winters and pleasant summers. Checking the forecast is always wise to make sure you have appropriate equipment and clothing.

Regulations

- Alcohol strictly prohibited.
- Maximum 8 people in a site.
- Maximum 2 cars per site (charge for 2nd car).
- Maximum 2 tents.
- Pets must be quiet and under control at all times.
- No empty trailers in campsites.
- Boat launch is closed when trailer spaces are full.

Fees

Campground fees are included in Chapters 2 – 6 which contain specific campground information.

Contact Information

Web: *www.snohomishcountywa.gov/200/Parks–Recreation*
Mail: Snohomish County Parks and Recreation
        3000 Rockefeller Avenue
        Everett, WA 98201
Phone: 425–388–6600
TTY: 425–388–3700

Whatcom County

Whatcom County operates two campgrounds listed in this book. It is located in the northwestern corner of the state where the mainland connects to Canada. Since it is on the western slopes of the Cascade Range, winter weather can be quite wet with the mountain slopes getting lots of snow. Summers are generally much drier with the temperatures very pleasant. However, it is wise to check the forecast to ensure proper equipment and clothing.

Regulations

- Pets must be on a leash.
- Each campsite is limited to one family unit. There is a maximum of 6 people per campsite.
- Quiet time begins at 10 pm.
- Generators may run between 9 am and 5 pm. Playing a sound system outside is not allowed.
- Vehicles must park in designated areas.
- Fires are only allowed in designated areas. Cutting trees – alive or dead – is not allowed.
- The discharge of firearms or fireworks is not allowed.
- Checkout time is noon.

Silver Lake Park

Fees

Campground fees are included in Chapters 2 – 6 which contain specific campground information.

Contact Information

Web: *www.co.whatcom.wa.us/parks*
Mail: Whatcom County Parks
       3373 Mount Baker Highway
       Bellingham, WA 98226
Phone: 360–778–5850

Whitman County

Palouse

Whitman County has two campgrounds included in this book. The county is located on the eastern border of the state about two–thirds of the way down from Canada. The area is known for its gently undulating hills called the Palouse. Weather in the summer can be quite warm and sunny. Winter brings much colder temperatures and snow. Be sure to get the latest weather forecast to ensure proper equipment and clothing.

Fees

Campground fees are included in Chapters 2 – 6 which contain specific campground information.

Contact Information

Web: *www.whitmancounty.org*
Mail   Whitman County Parks and Recreation
       310 North Market Street
       Colfax, WA 99111
Phone: 509–397–6238
Fax: 509–397–5647

Cities
City of Anacortes

Anacortes operates one campground included in this book. The city is located on the shore of the North Sound, in Washington's northwest corner. Because one route of the Washington State Ferries departs from here, it is often referred to as the Gateway to the San Juan Islands.

Weather

Proximity to the Pacific Ocean influences winter frontal systems – always be prepared for wet cool conditions during the winter. You can expect warm summer conditions with temperatures typically between 60°F and 70°F. Be sure to check the local forecasts.

Regulations

- Campsites are not for day–use activities. The maximum stay is 14 days.
- There is a maximum of 8 people per campsite. Check–out time is 1 pm.

- All campsite fires must be contained in the fire pit provided and extinguished by midnight. Pets must be kept on a leash.
- Firearms and fireworks may not be discharged. Quiet hours begin at 10 pm.
- Generators may be used between 8 am and 9 pm.

Fees

Campground fees are included in Chapters 2 – 6 which contain specific campground information.

Contact Information

Web: *cityofanacortes.org*
Mail: Anacortes Parks and Recreation
        PO Box 547
        Anacortes, WA 98221
Phone: 360–293–1918
Fax: 360–293–1928

City of Chelan

Chelan has one campground listed in this book. It is located on the shore of Lake Chelan on the sunny eastern side of the Cascade Mountains in central Washington. The lake area hosts a wide variety of recreational activities with something for all tastes.

Weather

While sunny in the winter, the temperatures can be cold and snow is always a possibility. During the summer, expect lots of sun and warm temperatures between 80°F and 90°F during the day.

Regulations

- Vehicles which are not licensed for street use may not be used in the park.
- Visitors must check–in at the registration booth.
- Dogs are not allowed in the park between Memorial Day and Labor Day weekends.
- All tents and mats must be removed from the grass by 10 am and not replaced until after 6 pm.
- Grass around the paved pad may be watered on Monday, Wednesday, and Friday evenings between 11 pm and 6 am.
- While barbecues and cook stoves are permitted, no campfires are allowed.
- Alcohol is only allowed in the designated campsite area.
- Quiet hours are between 11 pm and 7 am.
- No ropes may be attached to trees, fences, or utility standards.

Fees

Campground fees are included in Chapters 2 – 6 which contain specific campground information.

Contact Information

Web: *cityofchelan.us/departments/parks–recreation/*
Mail: Chelan Parks and Recreation
        PO Box 1669
        Chelan, WA 98816
Phone: 509–682–8023

Coulee City

Coulee City operates one campground listed in this book. It is located in eastern Washington on the southern shore of Banks Lake in central Washington. Winter temperatures can be cold and snowy but there is generally a lot of sun. Summer temperatures can be quite warm but with low humidity it is a great place to dry out – be sure to take sunscreen.

Dry Falls near Coulee City

Fees

Campground fees are included in Chapters 2 – 6 which contain specific campground information.

Contact Information

Mail: Coulee City
        PO Box 398
        Coulee City, WA 99115
Phone: 509–632–5331
Fax: 509–632–5125

City of Entiat

Entiat has one campground listed in this book. Located in the eastern foothills of the Cascade Range, it is along the bank of the Columbia River in central Washington. The river provides a sunny and warm place for many summer aquatic activities. Winters may be quite cool, although certainly sunnier than the western side of the mountains.

Regulations

- Only registered campers are allowed after 11 pm.
- Quiet hours are 10 pm to 8 am.
- Check out time is 1 pm.
- Alcoholic beverages are prohibited.
- No dogs are allowed between April 15 and September 15.

- Firearms are not allowed and fireworks are only allowed with a permit.
- There is a two vehicle limit per campsite.
- There is no designated swimming area and no lifeguard so swimming is at your own risk.
- Grass sprinkler systems will be on in the RV section during most nights. Because of this, tents are only allowed in RV sites on Friday and Saturday nights.

Fees

Campground fees are included in Chapters 2 – 6 which contain specific campground information.

Contact Information

Web: *www.entiatwa.us*
Mail: City of Entiat
        PO Box 228
        Entiat, WA 98822
Phone: 509–784–1500
Fax: 509–784–1112

City of Moses Lake

Moses Lake operates one campground listed in this book. It is located in east–central Washington on the shore of Moses Lake. This area has bountiful sunshine and warm summer temperatures.

Regulations

- Alcohol is prohibited.
- Any damage to park property will be the liability of the responsible party.
- Quiet time is 10 pm to 7 am.
- The City of Moses Lake has a hazardous dog ordinance.
- Do not leave pets unsupervised. Dogs must be on a leash at all times. Please clean up after your pet. Pets must have current rabies vaccinations.
- Horses are not allowed in campground or day use area.
- Firearms and fireworks of any kind are strictly prohibited.
- Usage of non–street legal motorcycles, three–wheelers and four–wheelers are prohibited in all park areas. Motorized vehicles not allowed off roadways. There is a 10 mph speed limit inside the park boundary. Improperly parked vehicles are subject to impound at owner's expense.
- All other vehicles, including boat trailers, must be parked in boat trailer storage area/overflow parking lot.
- Live trees, vegetation or firewood may not be cut or removed from the park.
- The City of Moses Lake is not responsible for theft or loss.
- Swimming and fishing is prohibited in boat launch and moorage areas.
- Fires allowed in fire rings or barbecues only.
- Only paid campers in the campground. Visitors are welcome in day use area.

Fees

Campground fees are included in Chapters 2 – 6 which contain specific campground information.

Contact Information

Web: *http://mlrec.com/*
Mail: City of Moses Lake
        411 South Balsam Street
        Moses Lake, WA 98837
Phone: 509–764–3805

City of Oak Harbor

Oak Harbor has one campground listed in this book. It is located on Whidbey Island in western Washington. The island is connected to the mainland by a bridge. Being west of the Cascade Range, winters can be wet and cool. Summers are nicely warm with generally drier days. It is always wise to check the local forecast to ensure proper clothing and equipment.

Regulations

- All animals must be kept on a leash and owners must clean up after their pets.
- Maximum speed limit in the park is 10 mph.
- There are sewer hookups. If you choose to use the dump station instead, you are required to use a discharge hose.
- Music must be kept low, so as to not disturb other campers. All amplification systems and musical instruments must be turned off by 10:00 pm.
- No campfires are allowed in the RV Park.
- Keep your site clean. Use the provided solid waste containers.
- Check out is 12 pm (noon).
- Limit your stay to 30 consecutive days.

Fees

Campground fees are included in Chapters 2 – 6 which contain specific campground information.

Contact Information

Web: *www.oakharbor.org/page.cfm?pageId=133*
Mail: Oak Harbor Parks and Recreation
        865 SE Barrington Drive
        Oak Harbor, WA 98277
Phone: 360–279–4756
Fax: 360–279–4507

City of Omak

Omak operates one campground listed in this book. It is located in eastern Washington along the Okanogan River. Winters can be cold with the chance of snow but summers are generally quite warm and sunny.

Fees

Campground fees are included in Chapters 2 – 6 which contain specific campground information.

Contact Information

Web: *www.omakcity.com/parks.html*
Mail: Omak City Parks
        2 North Ash Street
        Omak, WA 98841
Phone: 509–826–1170

City of Oroville

Oroville has one campground listed in this book which is located in eastern Washington on Lake Osooyos. Summers are sunny and quite warm during the day and cool in the evenings. Winters can be cold and snowy but you should expect more sunshine than western Washington.

Regulations

- All pets must be on a leash. No public nuisance is allowed. Cleanup after pet is required.
- Animals prohibited on swimming beaches.
- Camper check–in begins at 2:30 pm. Check–out is by 1 pm.
- The discharge of firearms and/or fireworks is strictly prohibited, except when specifically allowed.
- Generators may be used between 8 am and 9 pm.
- Cutting any park plant material is prohibited.
- Only motorized vehicles licensed to operate on the highway are permitted in the park.
- Quiet hours are 10 pm to 6 am.
- Maximum stay is ten days.
- All campfires must be in designated locations.

Fees

Campground fees are included in Chapters 2 – 6 which contain specific campground information.

Contact Information

Web: *http://oroville–wa.com*
Mail: Oroville Parks
        PO Box 2200
        Oroville, WA 98844
Phone: 509–476–3321

Port Districts
Port of Grays Harbor

The Port of Grays Harbor has a public/private partnership involving one campground listed in this book. This campground is one of the few all handicapped accessible recreation areas in the country. It is located about half way down the state on the banks of the Chehalis River about 35 miles inland from the Pacific Ocean. Because of its proximity to the coast, it is greatly influenced by arriving weather systems. While generally sunnier in the summer, always be prepared for a change in weather.

Fees

Campground fees are included in Chapters 2 – 6 which contain specific campground information.

Contact Information

Web: *friendslanding.org*
Mail: Friend's Landing
        300 Katon Rd
        Montesano, WA 98563
Phone: 360–482–1600

Too Tense?

Port of Port Townsend

The Port of Port Townsend operates one campground listed in this book. It is located in western Washington along the Strait of Juan de Fuca that comes in from the Pacific Ocean and fills Puget Sound. While on the west side of the Cascade Range, it's at the edge of the rain shadow created by the Olympic Mountains so isn't quite as wet in the winter as much of western Washington.

Summers are very nice, though there is a greater chance of fog due to the proximity of water.

Regulations

- Children must be under adult supervision at all times. Pets must be on a leash. Clean up after your pet.
- Tent camping is prohibited.
- Quiet hours are between 10 pm and 8 am.
- Check–out time is noon.
- All campfires and open flames are prohibited.

Point Hudson Breakwater

Fees

Campground fees are included in Chapters 2 – 6 which contain specific campground information.

Contact Information

Web: *portofpt.com/recreation–and–lodging/rv–facilities/*
Mail: Port of Port Townsend
           PO Box 1180
           Port Townsend, WA 98368
Phone: 360–385–2828
Fax: 360–385–7331

Port of Wahkiakum County

Port of Wahkiakum County operates two campgrounds listed in this book. They are located on the southern border of the state along the Columbia River about 25 miles from where it flows into the Pacific. Because of this close proximity, the area experiences the brunt of frontal systems as they come on shore. Be sure to check the weather forecasts – though the summer is quite a bit drier, there is always the possibility of rain.

Regulations

- Quiet time is 10 pm to 7 am.
- Checkout time is noon.

Fees

Campground fees are included in Chapters 2 – 6 which contain specific campground information.

Contact Information

Web: *www.skamokawavistapark.org/*
Mail: Skamokawa Vista Park
           13 Vista Park Rd
           Skamokawa, WA 98647
Phone: 360–795–8605

Port of Whitman County

Port of Whitman County operates one campground in this book. It is located on the Snake River in southeast Washington.

Regulations

- There is a maximum of 8 guests per site, of which no more than 4 may be adults age 12 or above. Exceeding this limit results in a fee of $4 per additional guest.
- RV sites are limited to one RV and one tent and one vehicle or a substituted number of additional tents. Tent sites are allowed one tent and one vehicle. A second tent is allowed with a $9 fee.
- No tents or RVs or vehicles are allowed on the grass.
- Fires are permitted in fire rings when there is no fire ban and weather conditions permit. Wood must fit inside the fire ring. If unused wood is left at the site, a $25 clean up fee is charged.
- ATVs, 3 or 4 wheelers, motorized scooters, or go–carts are not permitted in the park. Motorcycles are only to be used for transportation into or out of the park.
- Pets must be on a leash at all times and owners are responsible for animal clean up.
- The discharge of a firearm or use of any type of weapon is prohibited.
- Trash should be placed in appropriate containers.
- Swimming is not permitted around the dock area.
- Children under 12 must be supervised at all times.
- Quiet hours are from 10pm until 7am.
- Checkout time is 12pm.
- Reserved spaces are held until 6pm without prior request received.

Fees

Campground fees are included in Chapters 2 – 6 which contain specific campground information.

Contact Information

Mail: Boyer Park
           1753 Granite Road
           Colfax, WA 99111
Phone: 509–397–3208

Marina at Boyer Park

Park & Recreation Districts
Bainbridge Island

Bainbridge Island Metro Park & Recreation District operates one campground listed in this book. It is located on the northeast corner of Bainbridge Island in western Washington. The park offers views of Puget Sound and the Cascade Mountains.

Regulations

- Quiet time is between 10 pm and 6:30 am.
- Display your paid ticket on the post associated with your campsite.
- Maximum number of campers per site is 8.
- No fires on the beach. Do not gather driftwood or other park wood for fires.
- If no kayakers arrive to stay at the designated kayak campsite by 6 PM, that site becomes open to any camper.
- There is a 10 night camping limit in a 30 day period.
- One car per campsite is included with the overnight fee. Tickets for each extra vehicle are purchased at the pay station and clipped to the post associated with your campsite.
- Dogs are welcome, but please keep them on a leash and remember to pick up after them.
- Please stay on main trails to protect wildlife habitat and the fragile back–beach area.
- There are no fireworks allowed in any of our parks.
- Generators may be used between 8am and 9pm.
- For emergencies please call 911.
- Please respect your fellow campers. Quiet music and voices are what keep people coming back.

Fees

Campground fees are included in Chapters 2 – 6 which contain specific campground information.

Contact Information

Web: *biparks.org*
Mail: Bainbridge Island Metro Park & Recreation District
         7666 NE High School Road
         Bainbridge Island, WA 98110
Phone: 206–842–3343

Appendix B   Reservations

Many of the campgrounds listed in this book have campsites that can be reserved. In some cases, all the sites at a location are reservable while in others a portion is maintained on a first–come, first–serve basis. At popular locations, it may be difficult to find a campsite without a reservation – an unpleasant eventuality after a long drive.

Each campground listed in this book will indicate if reservations are accepted and how to make them. If there are specific variances to general procedures, they too will be listed with the individual campground. Otherwise, this section will cover general procedures for each agency. This information may change over time and it is prudent to verify all details with the controlling agency.

Federal Agencies

Those campgrounds operated by the National Park Service, National Forest Service, Bureau of Land Management, and Corps of Engineers that offer reservations are handled through one national reservation system. The web address is *www.recreation.gov* and they can be phoned at 877–444– 6777 or TTD at 877–833–6777.

Once in contact, you will be asked for information: type of site you are looking for, the specific facility or the general area, the date of arrival, and the length of stay. You will then be given your options. After deciding what is acceptable, you will be guided through the rest of the process and given your reservation.

General Policies:

- On the 15th of each month a new six–month period of individual campsite reservations go on sale.
- Reserved campsites will be held until check–out time on the day following your scheduled arrival.
- Online reservations can be made 24/7 but the telephone call center hours of operation are:
- March 1 to October 31 – 10 am EST to Midnight EST
- November 1 to February 28 – 10 am EST to 10 pm EST
- Offices are closed on Thanksgiving, Christmas, and New Years Day.

Acceptable forms of payments vary depending on if the reservation is made online, through the call center, or in person at a campground. A bank card may be used at any time for payment but certified checks, bank checks, money orders, personal checks, traveler's checks or cash, may only be used at the campground. Foreign currency is not accepted.

Changes and Cancellations

- Camping: A $10.00 service fee will apply if you change or cancel your reservation. Changes to online reservations can only be made via 877–444–6777.
- Cancellations can be made either online or via the call center.
- All Facilities: To ensure fairness, any reservation with departure dates outside the 6 or 12 month maximum window cannot be changed or canceled until 18 days after the reservation is made.

- If an individual campsite reservation is canceled the day before arrival or on the day of arrival, campers are charged the $10.00 service fee, plus, they forfeit the first night use fee. Cancellations for a single night's use will not be assessed a service fee. (Remember to consider that the call center closes at midnight EST for determining if it is the day before or the day of arrival.)

- If the campers do not arrive at the campground and do not cancel the reservation by the times listed above, they will be assessed a $20.00 service fee and forfeit the first night use fee. Remember, reserved campsites will be held until check-out time on the day following your scheduled arrival.

- Refunds must be requested no later than 14 days after your scheduled departure date.

- If a reservation fee is charged, it is non-refundable. At some facilities, this fee is $10.00 for call center reservations and $9.00 for web reservations at *www.recreation.gov*.

- A $10.00 service cancellation fee will be deducted from the refund amount given to the customer.

- Refunds for bankcard payments will be issued as a credit to the original bankcard. Please note the charge on your bankcard statement will read Recreation.gov 888-448-1474.

- Refunds for payments made by check or money order (and cash payments at selected campgrounds) will be made by check. A refund will be processed within 30 days of receipt and approval. Please note that refund requests made during or after departure can only be processed when approved by the facility management staff based upon local policy.

- In the event of an emergency closure, the reservation system will attempt to notify users and offer alternate dates and sites (as appropriate). If this is not possible, reservations will be canceled and all fees paid will be refunded.

Washington State Parks

Those campgrounds that offer reservations and are operated by Washington State Parks and Tacoma Power use the State Parks reservation system. There is one exception that will be listed at the end of the Washington State Parks section - Fort Worden State Park.

Reservations can be made either online at *www.parks.state.wa.us* or via telephone at 888-226-7688 (888 CAMPOUT). Agents are available to make reservations between 7:00 am and 8:00 pm daily, except Christmas and New Year's days. Hours are shortened on Christmas Eve and New Year's Eve. If you make, change or cancel your reservation online, you will pay lower fees than by calling (888) CAMPOUT.

Once in contact, you will be asked for the type of site you are looking for, the specific facility or the general area, the date of arrival, and the length of stay. You will then be given your options. After deciding what is acceptable, you will be guided through the rest of the process and given your reservation.

This reservation service allows you to book a specific site - so you can book your favorite, or try something new with the confidence of knowing your site is assured. Please note that reservations are made in real-time and are site specific. You will need a credit card to complete a reservation and it will be charged before you receive confirmation of your reservation. A non-refundable reservation fee of $6.50 is charged per reservation in addition to campsite fees.

Be prepared before making a reservation. Have the following ready before going online to make a reservation or calling the Reservation Center:

- Credit card number
- Park and campsite preferences (have alternative choices ready).
- Arrival and departure dates.
- Specific customer information for each site you wish to reserve - camper's name, address, phone number, e-mail address and tent/RV equipment type.

The maximum time that reservations can be made is up to nine months prior to your arrival date. The minimum time for reserving is until 8:00 pm on the day prior to arrival. (Please note: If a reservation is changed or canceled close to the arrival date, even if the reservation was made one day prior to arrival, the maximum change or cancellation fee will apply.)

A minimum two-night reservation is required for Memorial Day and Labor Day weekends. A two- night minimum is also required on the Fourth of July holiday when the holiday occurs on a Friday, Saturday or Sunday. If you cancel one of the two nights of your reservation, there will be no refund for that night.

Washington State Parks offers campsites, cabins, yurts and vacation houses with bathrooms and other features that meet the Americans with Disabilities Act (ADA) standards. To find an ADA - accessible campsite, visit online and select Include ADA Accessible under More Search Preferences. Campsites with the note, This Site is ADA Only, are restricted for use only by persons with disabilities. If you reserve one of these sites, you must provide proof of eligibility when you check in at the park. Proof of eligibility may include an ADA placard, license plate with disability symbol or a Washington State Parks Disability Pass and valid Washington picture ID. The disability permit holder must occupy the site the entire length of the reservation.

A non-refundable reservation fee is charged for each reservation - $6.50 for reservations made online and $8.50 for reservations made by calling the Reservation Center. Non-residents pay an additional $5.00, non-refundable reservation fee. The fee to change or cancel a reservation is $8.50, if done online, and $10.50, if done by calling the Reservations Center. If you change or cancel a reservation that was made less than seven days prior to your arrival date, change or cancellation fees will apply. If you change your arrival date seven or fewer days prior to arrival, you pay for one night's stay.

Payment–in–full is required to confirm all reservations. Reservations made less than 28 days prior to arrival date must be confirmed by credit card or cash card or check.

Payment by credit card allows for faster refund processing.

Payments online must use credit, check, or cash cards. Payments to the Reservation Center for reservations made by phone may be credit, check or cash cards or checks and money orders. State Parks accepts only U.S. or Canadian checks made payable in U.S. funds. Reservations must be made at least 28 days prior to arrival day, and payment must be received within seven days of the original date the reservation was processed. Late payment will result in cancellation of the reservation. The reservation number must be written on the face of the check or money order to ensure proper posting. Mail these payments to:

Washington State Parks Reservations
PO Box 94327
Seattle, WA 98124–6627

Payments accepted at the park may be made with a credit or check card – this is preferred. Other acceptable methods are:

- Checks – State Parks accepts only U.S. or Canadian checks made payable in U.S. funds.
- Money order.
- Traveler checks in U.S. dollars.
- Cash.
- Coupons.
- Gift certificates (Gift certificates and coupons cannot be used to confirm a reservation. You may redeem them at the park when you check in and register.)

When receiving a refund, if you paid with credit card, you will give your card number so the same account will be credited. If you paid with a check or money order, a refund check will be mailed to you. For faster refunds, pay by credit or check card.

Fort Worden State Park uses a separate telephone reservation system. While the procedures are similar to what has been described, the telephone contact number is 360–344–4400. The web–site for reservations at Fort Worden remains the same as other state parks.

Public Utility Districts
Lewis County PUD

For reservation information call 360–497–7175 from May 15 to September 10 during business hours. Reservations can be made up to one year in advance by downloading a form from the website *www.lcpud.org/recreation/cowlitz-falls-campground* and mailing the completed forms, along with remittance, to:

Cowlitz Falls Campground
889 Peters Road
Randle, WA 98377

All reservations must be submitted with a $7.00 non–refundable fee and payment of the first night's camping fee. Make checks payable to "Cowlitz Falls Campground."

Reservation fees are not refundable. Cancellations must be received at least 24 hours before the first day of the reservation.

PacifiCorp Power

Reservations are required for all but one of their four campgrounds listed in this book – Swift Forest Campground. For the others, reservations are required between the Friday before Memorial Day and September 30. Reservations may be made by calling 360–238–5251 or emailing *recreation@Pacificorp.com* or online at *http://www.pacificorp.com/about/or/washington.html*.

Tacoma Power

Reservations for the four Tacoma Power campgrounds listed in this book are handled through the Washington State Parks website *www.parks.state.wa.us*, or phone 888–226–7688. Individual campsites may be reserved 9 months ahead, with each passing day adding a new day to the reserve period. However, campsites may only be reserved between May 13 and September 15. At all other times, campsites are filled first–come, first–serve. For other details, see the Washington State Parks section above.

Counties
Chelan County

The one Chelan County campground listed in this book is open from April 1 through October 31. They accept reservations early in the year by phoning 509–667–7503 or use the online link on their website *www.wenatcheeriverpark.org*.

Clallam County

There are two popular campgrounds listed in this book operated by Clallam County. Reservations for the year can be made starting early in January using a link on their website at: *www.clallam.net/parks* or via email *ParksReservations@co.clallam.wa.us*.

All online reservations are paid for with a bank card and include a $10.00 non–refundable reservation fee. Half of the campsites at each campground may be reserved. The rest are first–come, first–serve. During November and December, all campsites are first–come, first–serve. The county's website lists available sites and additional reservation rules or phone 360–683–5847 for information.

King County

There is one campground listed in this book operated by King County and they take reservations. All sites can be reserved up to one year in advance with at least one week notice by calling the Camping Line at 206–477–6149 or using the link on their website *www.kingcounty.gov/recreation/parks*. RV and tent sites that have not been reserved in advance are available on a first–come, first–serve basis, using the campground's self–registration system.

San Juan County

There are three campgrounds listed in this book that are operated by San Juan County. Reservations are strongly recommended for summer camping. Reservations are accepted only between 5 and 90 days in advance of the stay. They require full campsite payment plus a $7.00 non–refundable reservation fee by bank card for each campsite reserved. A $7.00 non–refundable change fee applies to each reservation changed after it has been made. Payments and fees are not transferable and are, at most, only partially refundable.

Beginning March 1, reservations may be made online at *www.sanjuanco.com/430/Parks-Recreation-Fair* or by phone at 360–378–8420.

Skagit County

There are two Skagit County campgrounds listed in this book. One of them, Howard Miller Steelhead Park, offers reservations which may be made from 10 months to 2 days in advance of the arrival date. A $7.00 non–refundable reservation fee is required along with the first night's deposit. All unreserved sites are available first–come, first–serve. Phone 360–853–8808 for information or to make a reservation.

Snohomish County

There are five campgrounds operated by Snohomish County and they take reservations. They utilize an online system developed and maintained by a private vendor. This system enables online reservations for facilities like cabins, yurts, vacation homes and campsites. To support the cost of this system, reservations and registrations are assessed a transaction fee. This fee is non–refundable.

Anyone can check availability using this system, but you must establish an account prior to registering or reserving. Reservations cannot be made more than nine months or less than 72 hours in advance of check–in date.

Reservations may also be made by phoning the Parks Administration office at 425–388–6600. During peak season, calls are forwarded to a reservation line where you will record your request and daytime contact number. Calls are returned in the order they are received and that can take up to two days. Please note, phone reservations incur a reservation fee, and payment in–full is due at the time of reservation. For complete system information, look at the county's website, *www.snohomishcountywa.gov/200/Parks-Recreation*, or phone 425–388–6600.

Whatcom County

There are two campgrounds listed in this book operated by Whatcom County that take reservations. Each is handled by their respective park offices via a phone call. There is a $13.00 non–refundable fee per reservation which is paid for with a credit card. Whatcom Reservations can be made beginning December 1 for the following year.

For Lighthouse Marine Park reservations, call 360–945–4911 on a Saturday or Sunday only and between 1 pm and 3 pm.

For Silver Lake Park reservations, phone 360–599–2776 during summer office hours (10 am – 6 pm weekdays and 8 am – 6 pm weekends). Other seasons have reduced office hours.

Cities
City of Anacortes

Anacortes has one campground listed in this book. Reservations must be made 14 days in advance of arrival date. Cancellations received less than 24 hours before the 1:00 pm check–in time will forfeit that night's fee. All cancellations will incur a $10.00 charge. There are 39 campsites available for reservation. The other 29 sites are first–come, first–serve. Call 360–293–1927 or use the website *cityofanacortes.org* for complete information or to link to the online reservation system.

City of Chelan

Chelan operates one campground listed in this book. Reservations may be made 9 months in advance of the date requested. Phone 509–682–8023 and use a credit card to make the reservation. October to April office hours are 8:00 am to 4:30 pm Monday through Friday. May to September hours are 8:00 am to 6:00 pm seven days a week.

A deposit of the first two nights (three for Memorial Day weekend) plus a $5.00 non–refundable fee is required. Other information is available through the office phone number listed.

City of Entiat

Entiat has one campground listed in this book. It accepts reservations by telephone at 509–784–1500. Full payment is required at the time of reservation. Payments may be made by bank card or cash. There is a $15.00 fee for reservation changes with a 24 hour minimum notice. There is no refund for cancellations received less than 7 days in advance of the arrival date. Reservations are held until 7:00 pm of the arrival date and then sold on a first–come, first–serve basis.

City of Moses Lake

Moses Lake operates one campground listed in this book. Reservations are available by phoning 509–764–3805, or fax a reservation form to 509–764–3834, or mail it to:

Cascade Park
PO Box 1579
Moses Lake, WA 98837.

If mailing the form, attach full payment. The form may be downloaded from the website: *http://mlrec.com/*. Add a $5 processing fee for reservations. Cancellations must be received at least 24 hours in advance except for weekend reservations which must be canceled by Wednesday at 5:00 pm. There is a $10 cancellation fee.

City of Oroville

Oroville has one campground listed in this book. All sites may be reserved using the link on their website: *http://oroville-wa.com*. Reservations may be made 9 months in advance. There is a 2–night minimum stay on holiday weekends. There is an $8.00 non–refundable reservation fee. Cancellations made between 8 month and 8 days prior to arrival date incur a $10.00 cancellation fee. Cancellations received less than 8 days prior to arrival lose a maximum of 2 nights site fee. Further information is available at 509–476–3321 or on the website.

Port Districts
Port of Grays Harbor

There is one campground listed in this book operated by the Port of Grays Harbor. Reservations may be made for periods when open. Reservations are recommended for holiday weekends. Call 360–249–5117 between 7 am and 9 pm for information or to make a reservation.

There is a 72 hour cancellation policy with one night's deposit required at time of reservation.

There are no refunds for early departures.

Port of Port Townsend

The Port of Port Townsend operates one campground listed in this book. Reservations are available on a rolling annual basis by phoning 800–228–2803 or 360–385–2828. There is a $7 reservation fee.

Port of Wahkiakum County

The Port of Wahkiakum County has two campgrounds listed in this book. Reservations may be made by phoning 360–795–8605 Monday – Saturday between 9:00 am and 5:00 pm or on Sunday from 10:00 am to 3:00 pm. There is a $10 charge for all cancellations. If the cancellation occurs less than seven days prior to the arrival date, there is a charge equivalent to one night's stay.

Port of Whitman County

The Port of Whitman County operates one campground in this book. Reservations may be made by phoning 509–397–3208. You will be contacted within 5 working–days to confirm the reservation. There is a $25 reservation fee (plus first night's stay for holidays and events) that will be applied to the first night's camping or forfeited in the case of a no–show. Holiday reservations require a 2–week advance cancellation or the full amount will be charged. Weekend reservations require a 4–day advance cancellation or the full amount will be charged. Cancellation fees will apply to all reservations with less than 24–hours notification. There will be no refunds except under special circumstances.

Park & Recreation Districts
Bainbridge Island

There is one campground listed in this book operated by Bainbridge Island Metro Park & Recreation District.

Reservations may be made online at the website: *biparks.org*, or by telephone at 206–842–2306 x118.

There is a $3.00 online or $10.00 telephone non–refundable reservation fee.

There is a two night minimum stay required for reservations on weekends (Fri.–Sat.)

There are no refunds for cancellations made ten days, or less, from the first day of the reservation.

To cancel a reservation, telephone 206–842–2306 x118 before 4:30 pm.

Reservations may not be made within ten days of arrival. After that day, all sites become first–come, first–served.

View from Scenic Beach Park

Appendix C   Discounts

Several agencies listed in this book offer discounts for various reasons. While the discount is valid through each agency's entire system, in cases where a private vendor has been contracted to operate a campground, the discount may not be honored.

Federal Agencies

Those campgrounds operated by the National Park Service, National Forest Service, Bureau of Land Management, and Corps of Engineers offer the following discount programs:

The former Golden Age, Golden Eagle and Golden Access Passes were replaced in January 2007 with a new series of interagency passes called the America the Beautiful – National Parks and Federal Recreational Lands Pass. All these passes will continue to be honored according to the provisions of the pass.

Annual Pass – America the Beautiful – National Parks and Federal Recreational Lands Pass – Cost: $80.

This pass is available to the general public and provides access to, and use of, Federal recreation sites that charge an Entrance or Standard Amenity Fee for a year, beginning from the date of sale. The pass admits the pass holder/s and passengers in a non–commercial vehicle (at per vehicle fee areas) and pass holder + 3 adults, not to exceed 4 adults (at per person fee areas). Children under 16 are admitted free. The pass can be obtained in person at the park, or by calling 1–888–ASK USGS, Ext.1, or via the Internet at *http://store.usgs.gov/pass.*

Senior Pass (Lifetime) – America the Beautiful – National Parks and Federal Recreational Lands Pass – Cost: $80.

This is a lifetime pass for U.S. citizens or permanent residents age 62 or over. The pass provides access to, and use of, Federal recreation sites that charge an Entrance or Standard Amenity Fee. The pass admits the pass holder and passengers in a non–commercial vehicle (at per vehicle fee areas) and pass holder +3 adults, not to exceed 4 adults (at per person fee areas).

Children under 16 are admitted free. The pass can only be obtained in person at the park. The Senior Pass provides a 50 percent discount on some Expanded Amenity Fees charged for facilities and services such as camping, swimming, boat launch and specialized interpretive services. In some cases where Expanded Amenity Fees are charged, only the pass holder will be given the 50 percent price reduction. The pass is non–transferable and generally does not cover or reduce special recreation permit fees charged by concessionaires.

Senior Pass (Annual) – America the Beautiful – National Parks and Federal Recreational Lands Pass – Cost: $20.

This is an annual pass for U.S. citizens or permanent residents age 62 or over. The pass provides access to, and use of, Federal recreation sites that charge an Entrance or Standard Amenity Fee. The pass admits the pass holder and passengers in a non–commercial vehicle (at per vehicle fee areas) and pass holder +3 adults, not to exceed 4 adults (at per person fee areas). Children under 16 are admitted free. The pass can only be obtained in person at the park. The Senior Pass provides a

50 percent discount on some Expanded Amenity Fees charged for facilities and services such as camping, swimming, boat launch and specialized interpretive services. In some cases where Expanded Amenity Fees are charged, only the pass holder will be given the 50 percent price reduction. The pass is non–transferable and generally does not cover or reduce special recreation permit fees charged by concessionaires.

Access Pass – America the Beautiful – National Parks and Federal Recreational Lands Pass – Cost: Free.

This is a lifetime pass for U.S. citizens or permanent residents with permanent disabilities. Documentation is required to obtain the pass. Acceptable documentation includes: statement by a licensed physician, document issued by Federal agency such as the Veteran's Administration, Social Security Disability Income or Supplemental Security Income, or document issued by a State agency such as a vocational rehabilitation agency. The pass admits the pass holder and passengers in a non–commercial vehicle (at per vehicle fee areas) and pass holder +3 adults, not to exceed 4 adults (at per person fee areas). Children under 16 are admitted free. The pass can only be obtained in person at the park. The Access Pass provides a 50 percent discount on some Expanded Amenity Fees charged for facilities and services such as camping, swimming, boat launching, and specialized interpretive services. In some cases where the Expanded Amenity Fees are charged, only the pass holder will be given the 50 per–cent price reduction. The pass is non–transferable and generally does not cover or reduce special recreation permit fees or fees charged by concessionaires.

Volunteer Pass – America the Beautiful – National Parks and Federal Recreational Lands Pass – Cost: Free.

This pass is for volunteers acquiring 250 service hours on a cumulative basis. It provides access to, and use of, Federal recreation sites that charge an Entrance or Standard Amenity Fee for a year, beginning from the date of award. The pass admits the pass holder and passengers in a non–commercial vehicle (at per vehicle fee areas) and pass holder +3 adults, not to exceed 4 adults (at per person fee areas). Children under 16 are admitted free.

Current US Military Pass – Cost: Free.

This annual pass covers current active duty US military members and their dependents as well as many members of the Reserves and National Guard. It covers the pass owner and three accompanying adults age 16 and older at sites where per person entrance fees are charged. The pass does not cover or provide discount on expanded amenity fees such as camping, boat launch, or interpretive fees.

4th Grade Pass – Cost: Free.

The pass allows free admission at sites that charge entrance or standard amenity fees for a 4th Grade student (if home schooled, a 10 year old child). The pass is honored for one year between September and August. It covers the pass owner and three accompanying adults where per person fees are charged.

For more information regarding the America the Beautiful Pass series, please visit: *http://www.nps.gov/fees_passes.htm.*

In general, owners of the Interagency Senior and Access Passes (and the Golden Age and Access Passes) may receive a 50 percent discount on the basic recreation use fee for individual campsites. This discount does not apply to fees for cabins, lookouts, or group facilities and it may not apply for specific facility amenities such as electricity, water, sewer, or extra fees charged for prime or premium sites. The discount number must be provided at the time the reservation is made. If more than one reservation for the same location and date(s) is made, the discount will only apply to the site the discount owner occupies. The pass and one form of identification must be presented upon arrival prior to using the facility to confirm the discount, or the full recreational use fee will be charged.

Washington State Parks

Washington State offers passes to state residents that reduce or waive camping and moorage/watercraft fees for limited income senior citizens, disabled veterans, foster parents and people with disabilities. Qualified individuals may apply for more than one type of pass, although only one pass may be used at a time. These passes are valid only at Washington state parks.

Please note: Washington State Parks pass discounts do not apply to yurts, cabins, vacation houses or other shelters providing overnight accommodations. Pass discounts also do not apply to the extra vehicle fee. The extra vehicle fee is not part of the camping fee and must be paid when checking in at the park.

Washington State Resident is defined as a resident of Washington State for at least the past 3 consecutive months. Dual-state residency will not be considered.

Foster Home Camping Pass – Cost: No Charge

Washington resident foster parents and registered relative foster caregivers who camp with the children in their care are entitled to free campsites in Washington state parks. Participants in the program may camp at first-come, first-serve parks or make a telephone reservation to camp in a reservation park (call 1-888-CAMPOUT). Eligible participants making reservations do not pay for camping but are charged the reservation fee to hold sites in the reservation system. To get free camping when making a reservation, tell the operator you are a foster care provider. Then, when you arrive at the park to register, show a Washington State Driver's License, along with a Foster Care ID card or your Foster Home License. Walk-in campers need to show these same documents at the park to receive a free campsite. Foster parents and registered relative caregivers may also use State Parks boat launches and pumpouts for free when they camp. Please note: The foster child must arrive and camp with the caregiver the entire length of stay.

Off-Season Senior Citizen Pass – Cost: $75.00

Free nightly camping or moorage from October 1 to March 31, and Sunday through Thursday in April. There is a $10 per-night fee for utility sites. Passes are available for $75 and are offered to Washington State residents 62 years and older.

Senior Citizen Limited Income Pass – Cost: No Charge

Good for 50 percent discount on nightly camping/moorage. Free watercraft launching and trailer dump. They are valid year-round and offered to Washington State residents 62 years and older with an annual household income of $40,000 or less. Applicants must also meet the requirements for a property tax exemption under the Revised Code of Washington 84.36.381.

Disability Pass – Cost: No Charge

Good for 50 percent discount on nightly camping/moorage. Free watercraft launching and trailer dump. They are valid all year round and available for one-year (short-term disability) or five-year (permanent disability) periods. Offered to Washington State residents who are legally blind, profoundly deaf, developmentally disabled or who meet the disability definition used by the U.S. Social Security Administration. Note: A Permanent Disability Parking Permit, issued by the Washington State Department of Licensing, also entitles you to the 50 percent disability discount on camping and moorage and waives the trailer dump and boat launch fee. Simply show your placard or license plate along with the issued wallet card and matching I.D. directly to the park ranger.

Disabled Veteran Lifetime Pass – Cost: No Charge

Good for free camping/moorage, campsite reservations (through State Parks central reservations system), watercraft launching, and trailer dump. They are valid year-round and offered to Washington State residents with a documented service-connected disability of at least 30 percent. Proof of identification will be required at check-in.

To Apply for a State Parks Pass

Print and complete the appropriate application from the website: *www.parks.state.wa.us.* (Also, check this web-site for further program details.) If you have trouble printing the application, you may pick one up at your nearest state park or regional State Parks headquarters. To have an application mailed to you, please call 360-902-8500, 360-902-8844 or the Washington Telecommunication Relay Service at 800-833-6388, or send an e-mail to *infocent@parks.wa.gov.* Completed applications should be delivered to:

Washington State Parks
Attn: Pass Program Manager
1111 Israel Road SW
PO Box 42650
Olympia, WA 98504

Rules for Pass Holders

- Pass must be current and with you at all times.
- Pass holder must be camping at the discounted site.
- Guests of pass holder camping at a separate site must pay the full regular fee.

Bay View Park Balancer

- Campers are limited to a 10–day stay in one park from May 1 through September 30, and a 20–day stay during the rest of the year.
- Moorage is limited to three consecutive nights at any single park area unless otherwise posted.
- Pass does not provide discounts on annual permits, reservation fees or other services (i.e., pressed fuel, shower meters, gas stoves, etc.), except as noted.
- Passes are valid only at Washington State Parks. They are not accepted at campgrounds operated by other government agencies or private businesses.
- A pass cannot be used in conjunction with any other pass or discount. Pass only valid for person issued.

Public Utility Districts
Chelan County PUD

Disabled veterans with a Washington State Parks Pass receive a $10.00 per night discount on camping fees. During the off-season after Labor Day but before Memorial Day, senior citizens over 62 also receive a $10.00 per night discount.

Tacoma Power

A $5 per night discount is available to people who are 62 years old or more, have a disability parking placard, or have a Washington State Parks disability or disabled veteran pass. The campsite must be occupied and proof of eligibility shown to receive the discount.

Counties
Clallam County

County residents receive a $3.00 per night discount on camping fees.

Klickitat County

A senior discount is available for persons over age 55 that reduces camping fees by $2.00 per night and $12.00 per week.

Skamania County

County residents receive a $5.00 per night discount on camping fees.

Snohomish County

Holders of the Washington State Parks Veterans Disability Pass camp for free unless they make a reservation; they must pay the $7.00 reservation fee.

Holders of the Washington State Senior Citizen Limited Income or Disability Pass receive a 50% discount on nightly camping.

Whatcom County

Silver Lake and Lighthouse Park offer a 50% discount for holders of the Washington State Parks Disability Pass or Disabled Veteran's Lifetime Pass. Both campgrounds also offer a $7.00 discount to county residents.

Cities

City of Anacortes

City residents receive a $4.00 per night site discount.

City of Chelan

Various off–season discounts are available depending on the time of year and length of stay.

City of Entiat

Seniors and Veterans receive a $10.00 discount per night with proof of age 62 or service identification.

City of Omak

Winter rates are reduced by $5.00.

City of Oroville

Holders of a Washington State Parks Veterans Disability Pass receive a 50% discount. There is also a $9.00 discount available for off–season.

Port Districts

Port of Grays Harbor

A $5 per night discount is available to people who are 62 years old or more, have a disability parking placard, or have a Washington State Parks disability or disabled veteran pass.

Port of Port Townsend

Various off–season discounts are available.

Index

Campground by Name

Campground by Region

Made in the USA
Monee, IL
16 July 2020